Denis Couch

Keith Baker

Denis Godfrey

Brian Chalkley

John Skinner.

J N Rees.

Graham Sander

Robert Ulman.

Ken Hall

THE FIRST ROTARIAN

Best Wishes —
Charles C. Keller

John E P Edwards.

David Wren

Bob Bacon

David Gillard

Nick Taylor

Gary Davies

[illegible]

Colin Michael

Richard [illegible]

[illegible]

[illegible]

[illegible]

[illegible]

Mike Potter

[illegible]

Michael L. [illegible]

John Reid.

Dave Oates.

Alan Coleman

J. Emrys Owen.

Dedicated to all Rotarians Past – Present – Future
and to the memory of Violet A Walsh
(1926–74)

THE FIRST ROTARIAN
The Life and Times of Paul Percy Harris
Founder of Rotary

James P Walsh

Edited by

HARRY TREADWELL

SCAN
BOOKS

ISBN 0 906360 02 1

This first edition, published May, 1979.

Photoset, printed and bound in Great
Britain by Redwood Burn Limited, Trow-
bridge & Esher for Scan Books, Scan
House, 4–8 Church Street, Shoreham by
Sea, West Sussex, Great Britain.

Published on the occasion of the seventy-
fifth anniversary of the founding of Rotary

THE FOUR WAY TEST

In compiling this account of the life and times of Paul Percy Harris, the author has adhered to the principles of Rotary's Four Way Test of the things we think, say or do; a self-analysis and test of one's motives and actions.

1   Is it the *truth*?
2   Is it *fair* to all concerned?
3   Will it build *goodwill* and *better friendships*?
4   Will it be *beneficial* to all concerned?

To these questions there is only one answer—an unequivocal affirmative. This account of the life of Paul Percy Harris is true insofar as the truth is known: it is fair to all concerned: it will, by the subject's own example of selflessness and unstinting service, build goodwill and better friendships: it will be beneficial to all concerned.

Contents

Illustrations

Foreword

Ever since I was privileged to become the seventh Editor of Rotary International in Great Britain and Ireland, I have found no one person's name more often invoked than that of Paul Harris (no one mentioned the 'Percy'). Yet few Rotarians have been able to tell me anything about him. That is, until now, with the publication of this first-ever biography of the man who founded Rotary, by James Walsh, a Member of the Rotary Club of Croydon South. Such previous lack of information has always appeared to me entirely consistent with the apparent nature of this shy, paradoxical Chicago lawyer, for no individual ever seemed less typical of the popular image of Rotarians as fulsomely gregarious fellows. The man who believed that extension and development of friendship was Rotary's basic ingredient—'the foundation rock'—was himself conspicuous by his absence at most of Rotary's large gatherings as the Movement expanded, and he cited with obvious relish Carlyle's pleasure in 'the joy of silent communion' with a friend. Silent communion has never, at least in my experience, been observed a significant feature of Rotary intercourse.

The paradox extends to the Movement itself. On the surface Rotary—the fore-runners of many service organizations which copied its pattern, some more, some less deliberately—is as intrinsically American as blueberry pie and as unexportable as Thanksgiving Day. The elements of organized 'mateyness', ritual pronouncements, compulsory singing and so forth, would have logically made Paul Harris's brainchild unacceptable to the jaded societies and sceptical sophisticates of the Old World. Yet, within six years of its birth in Chicago, Rotary was putting down solid roots abroad, first in the United Kingdom and Ireland, then afterwards in Europe and beyond. These roots have not just survived and endured, but flourished.

In his book *My Road to Rotary*, Paul Harris tried to explain that his Movement's traditions sprang from the straighforward chapel faiths of his Vermont upbringing, the neighbourly town, 'the friendliness of its folks, their religious and political tolerance', a rural way of life whose simple habits he never forgot or ceased to venerate as an ideal. Yet what could the Japanese businessman, the Indian lawyer, the German tycoon, the Kenyan teacher, find in common with this New England pastorale? In trying, at least in part, to solve the fascinating paradox, this biography opens a door on the life, and thus a window on the mind and fervent heart, of a remarkable personality.

Even as Paul Harris drew the springs of Rotary from his boyhood memories, so he admitted that, having no children of their own, he and his wife 'adopted' Rotary International. The metaphor is important, for it accepts the implication that brainchildren, like any other, grow and change and live their own new lives. Thus the future of this great world Movement, now nearly one million strong, thriving all round the globe, may be better realized from a fuller understanding of the life of this gentle, lonely man who asked his friends to lunch, and found men of every nation, creed and colour flocking to his table.

All this means that Mr Walsh has researched and written a most important book. Paul Harris said himself that his own father's writings 'took most naturally to humour . . . of an iconoclastic order'. To those who met and knew Paul Harris, such as Vivian Carter, my third predecessor as Editor of *Rotary*, 'his philosophy was that of a sceptic'. The brilliant success of Rotary proves therefore that nothing is more formidable than a sceptic with a dream. Illustration of that fact lies in the pages that follow, which will, I have no doubt, win yet more respect, admiration and understanding for the great World Fellowship that shortly celebrates its seventy-fifth birthday, to the amazement of many perhaps, but to none more, I am sure, than the watching spirit of Paul Percy Harris, that first Rotarian—the man who, on an immortal impulse, put out with charming diffidence the hand that a million hands now grasp.

David Shelley Nicholl, B.A. (Harv)
Publications and Communications
Officer, R.I.B.I.
Editor, *Rotary*

12

Prologue

'UNKNOWN, YET, WELL KNOWN'

On Tuesday, 11 February 1947, two weeks after the death of Paul Percy Harris, a memorial service was held in that magnificent place of worship, St Paul's Cathedral, London, where Harris himself worshipped whenever he was in the city. The address was given by the Dean of St Paul's, who took as his text these words from the Second Epistle of Paul to the Corinthians, chapter VI, verse 9, 'Unknown, yet, well known'.

The Dean's choice of text could not have been more appropriate, for although the hundreds of thousands of Rotarians represented at the service were familiar with the name of the man who created the world's first service club in 1905, to the world at large he remains obscure.

In view of his significant contribution to international understanding and co-operation, his relative anonymity is astonishing. Beyond all question Harris was one of the great social architects of this or any other century; yet information about him is difficult to unearth. For example, there is no separate entry for him in any major general encyclopedia, although several of these symposia of general knowledge, including the largest in the English language, come from Harris's home city of Chicago!

Yet some of these sources of reference do contain excellent articles about Rotary itself and about other service club organizations, with a fleeting reference to the fact that Rotary was founded by a young Chicago attorney named Paul P. Harris.

Compare this lack of vital data with the prolific personal details about sports personalities, film stars and others whose fame is ephemeral, and the fact that he merits no mention becomes even more difficult to understand.

Equally surprising is that even from Rotary International's own publications and communications department, little knowledge of the Founder of Rotary has been disseminated. From time to time, it is true, articles have been published in *The Rotarian* and a number of regional Rotary periodicals.

This paucity of information is certainly partly attributable to Harris's own retiring nature and his intense dislike of personal publicity, although there are, of course, his own autobiographical writings. The first of these, *The Founder of Rotary*, was published in 1928 after appearing serially in *The Rotarian* in 1926 under the title of *Rotary and its Founder*. Seven years later, in 1935, he wrote *This Rotarian Age* and, shortly before his death in 1947, Harris wrote a much more comprehensive account of his life. Entitled *My Road to Rotary*, it was published posthumously in 1948 and is largely a reminiscence of his early life in Vermont. This, as is the case with his earlier works, has long been out of print, and all three titles are now exceptionally difficult to find.

In his memoirs, Harris once remarked that he experienced a natural reluctance to tell his own story, and for a long time entertained the hope that someone else would undertake the task.

What follows is the story of an ordinary yet extraordinary man. It is an account of misfortune and adversity, of hardship and hunger, of courage and heroism, and of a great and moving romance. But above all, as any Rotarian will testify, it is the record of an incredible accomplishment by one man in his realization of a dream of international understanding, fellowship and goodwill among men everywhere.

It is told against the backdrop of the second half of the nineteenth century and the first half of the twentieth century. It is the lifetime record of a quiet, talented and compassionate human-being, endowed with a vision of a better world and an unshakeable belief in the inherent goodness of his fellows, dedicated to Christian ideals and the application of the Golden Rule, and with an unbounded capacity for friendship and fellowship. It is a rendering also of the times in which he lived and is partly the story of the Rotary movement, for from 1905 to 1947, the history of the man and the movement is inextricably interwoven.

The inexorable passage of time must not be allowed to dim the memory of Paul Percy Harris. For here we have a man who, in founding Rotary, gave a whole new meaning and purpose to the concept of man's service to his fellow man. In establishing the concept of the service club he blazed a trail, not just for Rotary, but for all those kindred and equally worthy organizations which, in working for the betterment of this troubled world, emulated the astonishing success of Rotary.

People constantly ask, 'What is Rotary? What is a Rotarian?' These are not questions that can be easily answered, for Rotary is at once simple to comprehend but difficult to define. It is a way of life which circumvents all the barriers that have for so long hindered international understanding, by transcending and scorning the negation of opposing political philosophies, differing creeds, superior technicological skills and different cultural values. It does not enter into conflict with these things, but enhances their value. It is a way of life that dignifies the human-being, for it is through service to others that men find complete satisfaction.

Harris was Rotary personified. He gave of himself gladly and wholeheartedly. He organized the good intentions of good men and directed them into the life of the community which each Rotary club serves. He brought men together and enriched their lives by demanding of them an extension of the humanitarian ideal. He welded them into an influential social force for the common good and for the progress of mankind.

These are the basic ingredients of Rotary, but fully to appreciate their value they must be experienced. Rotary is, inevitably, hard work, although there is also plenty of fun. In 1919, an American newspaper, the *Houston Chronicle*, said this of Harris and the Rotary movement: 'He organized a strange kind of club, from which men get nothing, but actually pay for the privilege of doing good.'

That expresses the philosophy of Rotary succinctly, although no Rotarian worthy of his membership will agree that he gets nothing out of it. Ask him what is the greatest single thing about Rotary and he will probably answer in one word, 'Fellowship'.

Such is the contribution and achievement of Harris. At this moment there are, in Rotary alone, more than 800,000 men in over 17,000 clubs in more than 150 countries and geographical regions of the world. In the United States alone more than five million men, women and young people, ranging from their early teens to those who are long past retirement age, are engaged in service club work. Add to these the millions more in other organizations, and one still sees only the tip of the iceberg that is due in part to the contribution

15

of Harris to a genuine international understanding.

This then is the story of one of mankind's benefactors. It is the life and times of the first Rotarian, who so fully lived up to the Rotary slogan 'Service above self', yet remained always a modest, sincere human-being, who was pleased to be regarded as 'just one of the boys'. He did not wish for a monument and indeed no monument is needed, for Rotary itself is his memorial and if those who follow him continue his work for world peace and understanding they will enrich their own lives and ennoble his memory.

CHAPTER 1

Ancestry

Harris once wrote that his ancestry is traceable to the Pilgrim Fathers; unfortunately this is the only clue he provided, and the evidence available is scanty, nebulous and inconclusive. It may well be, therefore, that there are some errors in this genealogical account as there are areas in which our knowledge of his ancestors cannot be corroborated. Here and there the author has drawn conclusions from the evidence available that may not coincide with the interpretations of others. But these are the author's own conclusions, for which no other is responsible and, if they prove to be in error, he can only assure the reader that every effort was made to verify their authenticity.

If the curtain of history is drawn back some six generations before the birth of Paul Harris, we arrive at approximately that point in time where the world marched, albeit with some trepidation, into the eighteenth century. William III, a German by birth, had ascended to the throne of England several years earlier in 1689. Although an able ruler, his reign has been recorded for posterity as one of the most controversial in English history.

One of his first acts was to reconquer Ireland, in 1690, for the English Crown, but he sullied this victory by subjecting the Irish people to a harsh regime, which included, among other injustices, the suppression of Catholicism. The inevitable result of this policy was that Ireland became wretchedly impoverished and the numbers seeking to flee the country soared rapidly. Most of the desperate population strove to reach the New World, there to gain a measure of freedom and the opportunity of a new life.

One such immigrant was a young Irishman named O'Brien. Somehow he made his way across the three thousand miles of the Atlantic Ocean to the then British-ruled colonies in North America, probably landing in Massachusetts where there was already a sizable Irish community. O'Brien is the oldest known ancestor on the maternal side of Harris's family tree. O'Brien's son was born and brought up in New England, in the area of Boston, and it was probably at this time, that the name was changed to Bryan.

Next in line was Harris's great grandfather, Reuben Bryan, who was one of the earliest settlers of the western part of the state of New York. Reuben married a Huguenot named Olive Chapelle and one of their children was named Henry. In the course of time, Henry became Harris's maternal grandfather.

The first mention of Henry Bryan places him in the new mid-western state of Wisconsin. He was one of those early Americans who pioneered the westward expansion of the burgeoning United States. Harris held his grandfather, Henry Bryan, to be a man of initiative, character and enterprise. Bryan is known to have been one of the first citizens of the new city of Racine, and became its second mayor. A lawyer by profession, he married well, his wife, the former Clarissa Forbes, having once been a schoolteacher.

Henry and Clarissa Bryan had eight children, the youngest of whom was Cornelia, Harris's mother, but little is known of the others. Harris mentions only two—his Aunt Sue (Mrs Wesley Cavelle) and his uncle, Charles Bryan, whose funeral Harris attended in Racine in 1911.

In 1849, Henry Bryan, a wealthy and astute businessman organized, financed and led a gold mining expedition to the west-coast during the feverish days of the California gold rush. It proved a foolhardy, abortive and exceedingly expensive venture. The ensuing financial problems gravely affected Bryan's family, and when he died he left nothing to his widow but a large family.

As Harris was very young when he left Wisconsin, he rarely made contact with his maternal relatives in the years that followed. He mentions them seldom and his comments in *My Road to Rotary*, are illuminating. Here he reflects somewhat dryly, yet without rancour:

> While some of the Bryans were disposed to view grandfather Harris's family from what they were pleased to consider a higher plane, they would, I fancy, have freely admitted that there was not the slightest danger that grandfather Harris would ever convert his possessions into cash, leave his family to shift for itself, and fly away to parts unknown in search of

gold, pearls, diamonds or other so called valuables as my maternal grandfather had done. It may also be stated that it was my frugal, hard-working New England grandfather Harris who made the last days of my more brilliant but less provident grandfather Bryan and his self-sacrificing wife comfortable . . .

We cannot be certain that the paternal ancestors of Harris came to the New World from the British Isles. The name Harris is a clue: it is an Anglo-Saxon derivation of Harry's son and in England is usually encountered as Harrison. In Wales it is usually shortened to Harries, but the still shorter form of Harris is essentially, although not exclusively Scottish. It is, for example, the name of an island in the Outer Hebrides off the north-west coast of Scotland and the product of the island, Harris tweed, is of international renown.

Another indication, although this is admittedly tenuous is that Harris displayed a strong affinity for Scotland and things Scottish. Robert Burns, for example, was his favourite poet. However, it must not be forgotten that Harris married into a Scottish family, and this may be the reason for his affinity.

Howard Harris, Paul's paternal grandfather, was not a native of the small New England town, Wallingford, Vermont, where he lived for most of his life. However, Harris frequently referred to him as his 'New England grandfather' and it is probable that he came either from Vermont or one of the neighbouring states. From the few photographs available, and from the vivid word portraits of Howard Harris painted by his grandson, there emerges a personality that bears a striking resemblance to men from the highlands of Scotland. 'In appearance,' said Harris, 'my paternal grandfather was an exceptionally tall and upright man of stern demeanour.' He also described his grandfather as frugal, dour, hard-working, God-fearing, sparing of words, honest and upright.

Howard Harris soon established himself as one of the leading and most respected members of the small Vermont town. He married Pamela Rustin, the daughter of Wallingford businessman, James Rustin. (It was James Rustin, incidentally, who in 1818, erected the building that has been used as a school, teahouse, technical college and church. It is known now as the Paul P. Harris Memorial Building, and the Rotary Club of Wallingford meets there every Monday evening.)

Harris's maternal grandmother was born in Wallingford and lived there all her life. Unlike her tall husband, she was diminutive, weighing precisely eighty-nine pounds, never more, never less. Harris's respect for her cannot be expressed more eloquently than in his own words: 'It is said that fine goods come wrapped in small packages, and grandmother was certainly fine goods.'

Five children were born to Howard and Pamela Harris, four daughters and a son, George, Harris's father. Two of the four girls died as children. Both were named Frances and were known as Frances I and Frances II. A third daughter, Mary, married a man named Reed before she too died at an early age. The only surviving daughter, Pamela (Aunt Mellie) married a West Rutland doctor named George Fox, and they had three children, Eddie, John and Mattie. In later life Harris came to know his cousins well, and for a while lived with them in their West Rutland home.

More distant relatives included a man named Charles Harris, although his exact relationship has never been determined. Charles Harris lived in Brattleboro, Vermont, and often visited the Howard Harris home in Wallingford when he invariably addressed Harris's grandfather as 'Uncle Howard'. Other relatives include a distant cousin, Herman Vaughan, and Dr William Fox, brother of Dr George Fox. William Fox once owned a local beauty spot named 'Fox Pond', where Harris learned to swim as a boy. Next door to the Harris home lived Ed and Lib Martindale, to whom Harris referred as 'Uncle Ed' and 'Aunt Lib', although the blood relationship was to the Fox family.

Exactly when George Harris of Wallingford, Vermont, met and married Cornelia Bryan of Racine, Wisconsin, is not known. It may have been at college, as George Harris was given the finest possible education by his father, and Cornelia Bryan came from a once wealthy family who also placed great emphasis on education. After their marriage they settled in Racine, where the generous Howard Harris purchased a drug store and a house for the newly weds.

The city of Racine stands on the western shore of gigantic Lake Michigan. It is the third-ranking city of the 'Dairy State' of Wisconsin, and is today a bustling centre of commerce with a city population of more than 95,000 and a metropolitan population of over 170,000. But more than a century ago it was a very different place. The population was little more than ten thousand having been founded only thirty-four years earlier, in 1834, by an enterprising lake captain, Gilbert Knapp.

Straddling both banks of the Root River, Racine occupies a particularly favourable site. This was one of its greatest attractions for the early settlers, the intrepid pioneers who came with the great population movement into South Eastern Wisconsin in the late 1830s. Originally it was called Port Gilbert after its founder, but three years later, in 1837, it became Racine.

In 1848, the year in which Wisconsin became a state, Racine was incorporated as a city and quickly developed as a major industrial centre for the manufacture of farm machinery and equipment. An article about Racine in an encyclopedia published in the mid-nineteenth century provides interesting reading:

The capital of Racine County, situated on Lake Michigan and on both sides of the Root River, which is crossed by five swing bridges, and whose mouth here forms an excellent harbour. By rail the city is sixty-two miles north of Chicago and twenty-three miles south of Milwaukee. In summer there are daily steamers to Chicago and the north. Racine contains a handsome Post Office and City Hall, a hospital, the Taylor Orphan Asylum, and the University of the North West (Episcopalian, founded in 1852 and formerly called Racine College). A large trade is carried on in lumber, and besides flax, flour and woollen mills, boiler works and linseed oil works, there are manufactures of ploughs, pumps, wagons, fanning mills, hardware, wire work, cordage, furniture, refrigerators, boots and shoes, rubber clothing, etc.

Within Paul Harris's lifetime Racine grew beyond recognition. Its industrial development received a considerable impetus in World War II and today there are more than two hundred different industries. Tractors and farm machinery are still among its most important products, but added to these are the manufacture of automobile accessories, power tools, iron and steel castings, electrical products, floor waxes, luggage, malted milk, house appliances and printing products.

Racine has an extensive parks system, including fine recreational areas and a zoological park of no mean repute. The city serves as an extension division of the University of Wisconsin, an educational facility that provides two years of accredited college work, while at Parkside, between Racine and Kenosha, a four-year campus of the university was opened in 1969.

But all this is a century after the birth of Harris. This is what he had to say of his birthplace in 1926, when he described it in his first short memoir, *Rotary and its Founder*:

> On the shores of Lake Michigan, the second largest of North America's great inland seas, sixty miles north of Chicago and twenty-five miles south of Milwaukee, lies a small city called Racine. It is known throughout the United States because it is the home of several nationally important manufacturing industries. The people of Racine, however, are not entirely devoted to manufacture; there are cultural interests of which Racine College (sic) is the centre.

At another point in his memoirs Harris mentions straying from the family home and down the steep river bank to the railway. And he found the middle of the road the best of all playgrounds, from which his elder brother Cecil sometimes found it necessary to snatch him from beneath the hooves of passing horses and carriages. Such memories of his earliest years, however, are probably recalled from hearsay, as Paul was only three years old when he left the city of his birth.

He was born in a large, detached frame house located at 316 Fifth Street in downtown Racine, between Wisconsin and College Avenues. Almost a century afterwards, on 4 November 1956, it was razed to make way for a new hotel. In 1952, before it was demolished, the Rotarians of Racine made a determined but unavailing attempt to purchase and preserve the Harris birthplace as a Rotary memorial. However, in the mid-1950s the Racine Rotarians salvaged much of the hardwood, which they subsequently made into more than a hundred gavels and lecterns, which have been presented to clubs and individual Rotarians throughout the world.

The Rotarians of Racine are proud, and rightly so, that although Paul Harris was raised in Wallingford and spent most of his life in Chicago, the city of Racine was his birthplace.

CHAPTER 2

The Time

What the weather was like in Racine on Sunday, 19 April 1868, we do not know. But let us suppose it was a day which dawned bright and clear. For most of the neighbouring families it was just another Sunday, but for George Howard Harris, a pharmacist, and his wife Cornelia, who lived with their two-year-old son, Cecil, in the large white-frame house, it was a special day. They were expecting the arrival of their second child.

A tall, dark, bearded man in his mid-twenties may have stepped out on to the porch of his home and looked anxiously up the street. Perhaps, as he did so, he may have heard the quick clip-clop of approaching hooves and around the corner he may have seen the horse and buggy of the doctor hastening towards him. They would have hurried into the house together, the one in a state of anxiety, the other calmly professional. A little later the neighbours may have heard the wail of a new-born child and they would have smiled, sharing the happy moment with the proud parents.

Of course it may have been entirely different. It may have been raining, and the confinement may have taken place in the Racine hospital. But all that is academic.

Thirty-seven years elapsed before the man carved his own place in history by bringing into being, in a city not far from his birthplace, the Rotary movement, and created what the great English writer, Gilbert Keith Chesterton, subsequently called 'This Rotarian Age'.

The long and eventful life of Paul Percy Harris began at a time when many American families, both in the North and the South, were mourning their dead in the grim aftermath of the Civil War of 1861–5; a war between Americans, between families; a war in which brother was sometimes pitted against brother in a tragic and horrendous conflict. In terms of casualties it was the most costly war in which the United States has ever been engaged, exceeding even the casualties of World War II and the conflict in Viet Nam. The War between the States, which ended only three years before the birth of Harris, left the nation stunned. More than one million Americans had been killed or maimed. Among them was a Union soldier named Wesley Cavelle, who left Harris's maternal aunt a childless widow.

It is hard for us, living in the last quarter of the twentieth century, to appreciate that in 1868, no one had ever seen an electric light bulb, spoken on a telephone, listened to a phonograph, seen a motion picture, ridden in an automobile, heard the news over a radio, flown in an airplane or watched television!

There are those who will assert that mankind has progressed beyond all expectations since the birth of Paul Harris in 1868, and there are those who have reservations about the so called benefits of technological and scientific progress.

The young Paul Harris gazed up at clear blue skies, unsullied yet by the smoke and atmospheric debris belching from factory chimneys or the poisonous vapour trails of high flying aircraft. The streets of Racine were still free from the fumes of automobile exhausts. The waters of Lake Michigan were pure. Yet before Harris's death the streets and the skies reeked with noxious fumes, and the water from the lake was so polluted with toxic wastes and industrial effluents, that it was unsafe to bathe in, let alone drink.

Throughout the world the markers of history were being erected at an increasing pace. In Britain, which Harris came to know so well in his later years, Queen Victoria reigned supreme over the largest and richest empire the world had ever known. In Italy Victor Emmanuel II had been king for seven years, and in Germany (or Prussia as it then was), the powerful Otto von Bismarck, Chancellor of Prussia, was uniting the Germanic states, under a rule of blood and iron, into one great nation under the hegemony of Prussia.

In a lesser known part of Europe, Christian IX reigned over the joint kingdom of Denmark and Norway, while, in nearby Belgium, the monarch was Leopold II. Leopold subsequently carved his own niche in history by financing Henry Morton Stanley's expedition to the Congo in 1879–84 and the establishment of the Congo Free State in 1885. In the Far East in 1867, the Mikado was restored to power in Japan.

Nearer home, also in 1867, the British North America Act became law, establishing the Dominion of Canada by uniting the provinces of Ontario, Quebec, New Brunswick and Nova Scotia.

The United States of America, destined within Harris's lifetime to become the richest and most powerful nation in the history of man, was still a fledgling, but already flexing its muscles. Only a century had passed since the Declaration of Independence had shrugged aside the rule of England, following the historic American Revolutionary War, and barely fifty years had passed since she again defeated British forces in the War of 1812.

Less than five years before Harris's birth, on 19 November 1863, President Abraham Lincoln delivered his immortal speech on the bloodied battlefield of Gettysburg, an address that rang around the world and became forever written in the hearts of men. But less than two years after that memorable speech, as Lincoln sat watching a play in Ford's Theater, Washington, on 14 April 1865, he was assassinated by an obscure young actor, John Wilkes Booth.

Just a year earlier, on 30 March 1867, the United States purchased Alaska from Russia for the unbelievable sum, even for those distant days, of a mere $7,200,000. The transaction has been known ever since as 'Seward's Folly'.

Such was the march of history in the years immediately preceding the birth of Harris, but of even greater interest were the events of 1868 itself. A few months before he was born, the civilized world was stunned by the impeachment and trial of President Andrew Johnson on charges alleging violation of the Tenure-of-Office Act. The proceedings took place over a period of three turbulent months until, in May, the accused President was acquitted by one vote of the charges against him. The word 'acquitted' was but a technicality: the President received nineteen votes for acquittal, but thirty-five votes were cast for his conviction—only one short of the required two-thirds majority that would have removed him from office.

In 1868 the infamous Ku Klux Klan was founded, in the aftermath of the abolition of slavery. But this was also the year in which Louisa May Alcott wrote *Little Women*, that wonderful story of Jo March and her three sisters, as popular now as it was then.

Harris had many famous contemporaries, and indeed it may well transpire that more men and women born in his lifetime were destined to achieve immortality than during any other period of recorded history. In the decade before 1868 were born such giants in the field of human endeavour as: David Lloyd George (1863), the great European statesman who, as Prime Minister, led Britain to victory in World War I; Henry Ford (1863), the automobile manufacturer; Warren G. Harding (1865), the twenty-ninth President of the United States; John Galsworthy (1867), famous for his great work of fiction, *The Forsyte Saga*, Wilbur Wright (1867), the elder of the two famous brothers who invented the airplane (his brother, Orville, was born in 1871 and, incidentally, became a member of the Rotary Club of Dayton, Ohio); Frank Lloyd Wright (1867), America's foremost architect; and John Pierpoint Morgan (1867), one of the world's greatest financiers. In 1868 itself were born Czar Nicholas II of Russia and the famous American industrialist, Harvey Firestone.

These were the years when the history of the United States was being forged by the early pioneers, explorers, trail-blazers and builders. West of the Mississippi River, not far from Harris's birthplace, Indians still roamed the great plains of central America and Canada, and violent battles were fought as the pioneers rolled westward in their Conestoga wagons.

Such were the times into which Harris was born. The tapestry of history which has unfolded since is as significant as it is fascinating. By his unique achievement, Harris has woven himself a place in that tapestry, although historians have yet to evaluate the full significance of his contribution.

Meanwhile, all was not well in the Harris household. Stormclouds of economic difficulty were building.

'Of all the charges which might have been made against my parents, parsimony would have stood the least chance.' So said Harris of his father and mother many years later, when he succinctly summed up the unhappy situation of his parents during their years in Racine.

Of all his family, of all the many close friends Harris made during his life, he must surely have viewed his parents as the most enigmatic of all. Their history of economic and marital difficulties is not in itself as traumatic as Harris may have supposed, but this did nothing to alleviate his perplexity and dismay. The sadness at the eventual turn of the events in Racine remained with him to the end of his life.

His father, George Harris, an only son, had been well educated. He was a gifted man with a good scientific background, who could and did write well on a wide variety of subjects. His efforts to derive an income from his talents were not successful, however, and he was given to vivid flights of imagination, his agile mind dreaming up all sorts of schemes for making money quickly.

Unfortunately he was not equally endowed with the determination and physical vigour needed to implement the ideas. He simply did not have the strength of character to be a good businessman. 'In the end,' said Harris, 'my father found that the ways of the world were too much for him.'

Harris's mother, Cornelia, was possessed of some of the qualities he found lacking in his father. She was determined and vigorous, but she had, of course, been brought up in a family that had known prosperity, and she took as her right the employment of hired help to assist in the everyday chores, even when finances dictated otherwise.

How objective Harris's judgement of his parents really was is debatable. Harris was a realist, a trained lawyer, not a man given to making snap judgements. He appreciated only too well the frailties of the human character. His opinion of his parents was not shared, for example, by his paternal grandmother, Pamela Rustin Harris. But her views of her son and daughter-in-law have to be regarded as equally suspect in objectivity.

Talented though George and Cornelia Harris were, both demonstrated a marked degree of irresponsibility in matters of fiscal management. They were both royal spenders, and the idea of a well regulated family budget would have been met with prompt and emphatic disapproval. 'The most approved plan, apparently, was to spend the money first and then, if possible, earn it,' said Harris. But, enjoyable though the system may have been while it lasted, it lasted longer than it should. In this direction Harris tended to be mildly critical of his grandfather, Howard Harris, who indulged his son's lack of business acumen to a fault.

Harris contended that a principal reason for his father's failure in business affairs was that he was given too easy a start with the gift of the drug store and house in Racine. Whenever he ran into financial difficulties, which was all too often, he was able to turn to his father for help. Harris summed it up nicely: 'It is more understandable if it is appreciated that having received too vigorous a boost at the beginning, my father may well have assumed that additional boosts would follow as a matter of course, which, for a time at least, was certainly true.'

His parents were kept solvent, for longer than was desirable, through the simple expedient of a series of cheques, endorsed by George Harris, but actually signed by Howard Harris. 'The officers of the Manufacturers' National Bank of Racine,' said Harris, 'early learned to admire the signature of the silent partner.'

Both Paul's parents must have realized they were courting financial disaster. Perhaps they simply pushed the problem into their subconscious and blithely continued to ignore the laws of income and expenditure, confident that somehow things would work out. It is more probable, as Harris has surmised, that they took the continuing aid from Howard Harris as a matter of course.

In 1869 the Harris family increased with the birth of a third child, Nina May, whose arrival inevitably compounded the financial problems. There had to come a time when even the patience and the resources of Howard Harris could no longer cope with the needs and demands of his son and his son's family. Warnings were issued, but to no avail, and early in 1871 George Harris suddenly found that his father's financial prop was no longer forthcoming. The crisis was upon him.

The first unpalatable fact to be faced was the sale of the business and the family home. These were purchased by a citizen of Racine by the name of Harbridge. The plan was that George Harris, again with help from his father, should re-establish himself in a new business in or near to Wallingford, where the books could be audited more frequently and a stricter control exercised over the finances of his business. For George Harris who was clearly regarded as incompetent, this was a distressing and humiliating time.

And so after only a few years together the Harris family broke up, destined never to be the same again. Harsh decisions were made for the immediate present, and plans formulated for the future.

The two small boys went with their father to his parental home in Wallingford, Vermont, where they were left in the care of their grandparents until such time as the distraught George Harris could re-unite his family. Paul was three years old. His mother, a proud woman, refused to go to Vermont with them, remaining in

Racine with the infant Nina May, taking temporary lodgings while she gave music lessons to augment the desperately depleted family resources.

For the children the family separation was less harrowing, but it left its mark. The prospect of a long trip to see their grandparents in faraway Vermont took on, for the two boys, the excitement of a great adventure; a holiday from which they would eventually return to their own comforting home. In fact, for both of them, but for Paul especially, it was the beginning of a new life.

CHAPTER 3

Early Days in Wallingford

On a warm summer evening in July 1871, two excited but some-what bewildered boys, one aged five the other only three, accompanied their father to the great Wisconsin city of Milwaukee, some twenty-five miles north of their home in Racine. There they embarked on one of the steamers plying the Great Lakes of North America. It was named the *Oneida* and was bound for Buffalo, a city and port at the Eastern end of Lake Erie, a journey of almost eight hundred miles. From there George Harris and his sons disembarked to take a train going first more than three hundred miles to Rutland, before changing for the last short leg of ten miles to Wallingford, the home of his parents. This was no mean journey for two small boys, a journey that must have taken three or four days, perhaps more.

When the train from Rutland finally ground to a halt in Wallingford, it was late at night, about eleven o'clock. The station master had long since retired and they were the only passengers to alight. The station was in total darkness, except for a small circle of flickering illumination further down the track. As they drew nearer, Paul Harris saw that in the centre of the glow stood a tall man; it was his grandfather, Howard Harris, there to meet his son and grandsons.

Through the stillness of that dark summer night the solemn little procession marched. First up Depot Street, then along Main Street to the south side of the Howard Harris home. Paul's tiny fist was held securely in what he later described as 'the biggest, firmest, warmest hand I have ever known, with enormous thumbs which made wonderful handles for a little boy to hang on to'. The tall, silent and erect Howard Harris strode purposefully along, the lantern in his other hand throwing dancing shadows on the white picket fences as they passed.

There followed a scene that was forever etched on Paul's

memory. Standing in the doorway of the house they approached, peering anxiously into the night with a kerosene lantern held above her head, was a tiny dark haired woman—Grandmother Pamela Rustin Harris, who was destined now to raise a second family as she became both mother and grandmother to the two little boys. She greeted her son affectionately but anxiously. She sensed the bewilderment of Cecil and Paul after their long journey away from their mother and home, and she knew that her son was sorely troubled at his business failure, and with the family problems they had created.

But, practical woman as she was, it was a case of first things first. On the table in the centre of the dining-room was placed a huge pan of fresh milk from their old cow, Buttercup. Alongside was another dish, filled with blueberries freshly picked from the nearby mountainside. And then something else very special, her own wonderful home-made bread.

And finally, to the fattest and most comfortable bed Cecil and Paul had ever slept in, stuffed specially for them with fresh clean straw. But first they had to say their prayers for, as they soon learned, this was a most Christian household. Like children the world over, they quickly fell asleep although, just before he nodded off, Paul wondered which had been stuffed the most—the bed with fresh clean straw, or himself with home-made bread, blueberries and milk!

In his memoirs years later, Harris wrote that as long as he lived there would remain in his mind the hallowed memories of the night he arrived in the lovely New England valley.

As thousands of fathers before and since have done George Harris had brought his children to his parental home for refuge in a time of financial extremity. He and his parents talked long and anxiously into the night of what had to be done and how the family was to be re-united.

For Paul it was the beginning of a new life. He was, in the long term, fortunate to be placed in the loving care of his grandparents. But nothing can replace completely the loss of parents, no matter what the reason, and it is easy to discern from his comments in later life, that he always regretted that he was separated from them at so early an age.

On that July evening in 1871 he had, albeit unknowingly, disturbed the serenity of the home life of his early-to-bed grandparents. Many years passed before he came to understand and appreciate the sacrifices they made on his behalf. But for the present he and for a shorter period, Cecil became the beneficiaries of a well regulated and permanent home, where everything was properly done, where Christian ideals prevailed, where no words were ever spoken in anger or prejudice and where the virtues of life were instilled into them. Harris said it was there, in that peaceful New England village of Wallingford, that his grandparents sowed the seeds from which, half a lifetime later, a great humanitarian movement would spring.

But in Wallingford, Vermont, the future held no meaning or interest for the two little boys who woke up the morning after their arrival. An understanding of their parents' problems was beyond them. They had no reason to bow to drooping spirits and no defeatism tortured their hearts. As long as they were fed, clothed and kept comfortable, all was well. To them, life was an exciting adventure. Promptly and industriously, they proceeded to explore the delights and wonders of their new abode.

The lovely Vermont village of Wallingford lies nine miles to the south of Rutland. It nestles comfortably, between Elfin Lake and Black Mountain, in a peaceful valley between two parallel ranges of the famed Green Mountains from which the state takes its name. When Cecil and Paul Harris arrived there it boasted a population of barely one thousand. More than a century later it remains a village, with a population of a little over 1,600.

There have, naturally, been changes, but many of the buildings and all the places Paul came to know so well are still there. The Main Street is now the Ethan Allen Highway (U.S. Highway 7), and visitors can still see, fronting the highway, his boyhood home, as neat and as well kept as it was all those years ago. Of particular interest are the letters H.H. standing out clearly on the roof. The old Harris home is a large, frame house, even by modern standards. Built sometime betweeen 1840 and 1850, it has fourteen rooms, although only seven were in regular use during Harris's years in Wallingford.

Still in use is the lovely First Congregational Church (now the United Church of Christ), which Paul attended regularly with his grandparents. The little red schoolhouse where he and, for a while, Cecil began their formal education, is now a Rotary memorial, and it is one of the first places visiting Rotarians go to see. District Governors especially, on their way to international assemblies and

Paul Harris, aged twenty-eight, in his first year in Chicago

Howard Harris, Paul's grandfather

conventions, are invited by the Rotarians of Wallingford and Rutland to stay over with them for a few days, and those able to accept are accorded a tremendous welcome.

One of Paul's favourite haunts was Bear Mountain, but perhaps he liked best Child's Brook, where he often went to fish. The source of Child's Brook is a spring located in the hills at the foot of White Rocks, a prominent landmark near the village. Another much visited beauty spot is Elfin Lake, known to Paul as Fox Pond. As a boy, he swam there often, and more than half a century later, on a special occasion, did so again.

There was Green Hill, noted for the abundance of low-bush blueberries; Little Pond, a small body of water which was a pond in the spring, dried up completely in the summer, became a pond again in the autumn, and was used as an ice rink in the winter; then there was the Cascades, a beauty spot less than two miles from where Paul's grandmother was born, although she never visited it; Roaring Brook, an aptly named nearby stream; West Hill, a landmark visible from the Harris orchard; Sabe's (or Sabin's) Hill, described as one of the sportiest hills in the area, marvellous for sledding in the winter and for what Paul called 'Thank you marms', big bumps in the road; and finally, the lovely Otter Creek Valley. Paul often climbed the mountainside overlooking the valley and watched the old steam locomotives crawling along 'like tiny worms'. Most are visited by enthusiastic Rotarians who congregate in the area during the summer months in convention time.

Killington Peak, a few miles further north towards Rutland, is less well known, but Paul twice climbed the 4,241 feet of this somewhat formidable mountain. He often roamed the Green Mountains for miles, not infrequently alone, and this bred in him an abiding love for the peace and beauty of the countryside. Whenever he suffered bouts of illness in later life, he invariably retreated to the outlying areas of Wisconsin and Michigan to rest and recuperate.

In his memoirs Harris has described his Wallingford home, and the lovely valleys around, in graphic detail. He also mentions all the people of his boyhood he came to know so well, and paints a picture of the lives of those New England people of the valley more than a century ago—the closeness of the villagers, the warmth, the companionship and the respect, which were so special.

Harris often revisited Wallingford, especially during the latter years of his life when he and his wife made an annual pilgrimage, usually in the autumn.

How long Paul and Cecil remained together in Wallingford is not known. Their stay was several months at least, as Paul recalls many explorations and adventures. Both he and Cecil attended the village school in the autumn of 1871. The first day remained embedded in their minds. At recess time the older boys formed a circle around three-year-old Paul and, dancing in glee, shouted, 'Oh, see the little girl boy', apparently referring of the long hair style he brought with him from Racine. Miss Sherman, the primary school teacher, rescued Paul from his tormentors and that evening his grandmother tearfully clipped off the offending curls. On Sundays the boys attended the school at the Congregational Church, where they first met Miss Lottie Townsend, the teacher.

They quickly came to know the 'unofficial' Harris family. There was Margaret McConnell, the family seamstress, who either made or altered the clothes they wore; Asa Webster, their grandfather's aged clerk, a real Wallingford character considered to be the most distinguished liar in the village; and Mr Wynne, the gardener, who told the boys marvellous stories in a broad Irish brogue. Wynne's daughter, Delia, was a 'hired girl' who helped out with the household chores. She was followed in the course of time by Mary Foley, and whenever Paul visited Wallingford in later years, he never failed to visit Mary. Howard and Pamela Harris always treated their 'hired help' with unfailing courtesy and kindness. All were considered part of the family rather than employees, and it was not in the least unusual for everyone to sit down to a meal together.

On one clearly remembered day, the boys 'Aunt Sue' (Mrs Wesley Cavelle) arrived unexpectedly from Wisconsin. She suggested that she take Cecil back to live with her. The proposal generated considerable excitement and a long discussion among the adults, which Paul recalled as 'rather animated'. The upshot was that Cecil did indeed go to live with his Aunt Sue, not far from where his mother was caring for Nina May. It seemed a logical move until such time as George and Cornelia Harris could re-unite their family.

So Paul was left with his grandparents in Wallingford while Cecil returned to Wisconsin. Except for two short periods later, they never again lived under the same roof, but they remained in touch and were clearly devoted to each other. Paul later described their separation at so early an age as 'a tragedy'.

Paul's earliest memory of his father was of a sadly worried and silent man. George Harris used to pace up and down the garden walk at Wallingford, seldom speaking, deep in thought, desperately seeking ways and means to restore his self-respect. How long he remained in Wallingford with his two small sons is not known. To the end of his days Paul retained fleeting recollections of rare occasions when he and his father went for long walks, sometimes in the company of a friend, Cal Higgins, or Mr Pincus, the Jewish clothier in the village. At other times they went to the nearby mountains to pick raspberries, blueberries and blackberries. One vividly remembered incident was when Paul, now a growing boy, asked his father to teach him to swim. He was taken to Fox Pond and, when he hesitated, was thrown headlong into the water. A kinder memory was of a glorious adventure when they went trout fishing, at which Paul became quite adept. When he brought home a particularly fine catch, his grandmother cooked the fish in a special way, and then distributed most of the succulent dishes to needy neighbours, Paul and his father being the willing distributors.

Paul's earliest recollection of his mother was one fine day in Wallingford. He saw, coming towards him down Main Street from the railroad station, a beautiful, well dressed lady. With her was an equally well dressed and pretty little girl. 'I suddenly experienced a sensation I had never known before,' said Paul. All at once he felt ashamed of his torn hat, his bare feet, and his soiled and patched trousers. The beautiful lady stopped, looked searchingly at him, and then enquired: 'Are you little Paul Harris?' 'Yes, Mam,' replied Paul, and was immediately swept into his mother's arms, and kissed passionately by a face streaming with tears.

This was the first time he had seen his mother since his departure from Racine. How long she stayed with him that summer in Wallingford, Paul did not remember, but he did recall her giving him a bouquet of lilies-of-the-valley. 'From that moment on,' he said, 'lilies-of-the-valley seemed to me the purest of flowers, a fitting symbol of motherly love.'

As Paul grew up, the world outside Vermont changed at an ever increasing tempo, but life in Wallingford proceeded at a more pedestrian pace. To the boy, day followed day with only minor variations in his life style. The long hot days of summer, the milder beautiful days of autumn, the long snow bound months of winter, and the promise of spring followed in a natural progression.

35

The naturally gregarious Paul found a friend with whom to pass the time, a red-headed boy named Fay Stafford. Years later Paul said that Fay was not only his first but his greatest boyhood chum. They met at an early age as Paul, when he called at the Stafford home for his friend, could not pronounce Fay. It was always 'Pay!'

Fay had the reddest hair anyone in Wallingford had ever seen. 'It was like a fiery flame,' said Paul, 'and it was a source of considerable embarrassment to Fay.' For many years the boys, who were the same age, shared each other's adventures, joys and sorrows. The most memorable was one winter's day, when they decided to become daring mountaineers and climb the nearby Bear Mountain.

Not long after they started out it began to snow, lightly at first, but by the time they were halfway up the mountainside, a blizzard was raging. Alarmed, they turned back, but soon lost their bearings. At first they sought shelter in an isolated barn, hoping that the storm would abate, but instead it increased in severity. In desperation they fought their way down the mountain, looking for familiar places, but no landmarks were visible beneath the blanket of snow. As darkness descended their plight became serious. Suddenly, by sheer chance, they stumbled upon the old Gulf Road, which, if they were able to keep to the track, would lead them down the route of Roaring Brook past the familiar White Rocks and into the haven of the village.

When, half frozen and desperately tired, they finally reached the Howard Harris home, they were quickly divested of their soaked clothing, given a hot mustard bath and packed off to bed. Grandfather Harris, in the meanwhile, trudged through the deepening snow to inform Fay's distraught parents of their son's safe return. Paul was none the worse for the adventure, but Fay developed a fever and was ill for several days.

Fay Stafford was the first among thousands of friends Harris made during his long life and, as with all first, he made an indelible impression. Harris never forgot his red-headed boyhood friend, and suffered deep sadness some years later when he heard of Fay's lonely death.

'One day, several years after our adventure,' said Paul, 'Fay confided to another of our friends, John Miller, that it seemed at times he was losing his mind. It was all too true. Within two days of telling John Miller how he felt, Fay became mentally unbalanced and was taken to the insane asylum at Brattleboro where, after several hopeless years, he died.'

Lacking parental discipline, Paul got up to all sorts of mischief. More often than not he was the ringleader, so much so that whenever the villagers were riled by some boyish prank, he was the first to be accused. He was frequently referred to in scathing terms as 'that Paul Harris!' Paul admitted in his memoirs that he was of a wilder disposition than most of his friends, describing himself and his boyhood companions as the 'rapscallions' of the village. One incident in particular demonstrated their mischievous, sometimes dangerous ways. Paul was challenged by another school chum, Willie Strong, to 'hobo-ride' the train from Wallingford to Manchester, twenty-five miles away. This had to be done by perching on the cow-catcher equipment on the front of the locomotive. Paul was never loath to accept a challenge. After everyone had retired for the night, he stole from his bedroom window to meet Willie Strong. After evading the guard and the locomotive engineer, they took up positions on the cow-catcher. The train sped through the night, sometimes at a speed which threatened to blow the boys off their precarious lodging. At Manchester they got off, more than a little shaken, faced now with the problem of getting back to Wallingford before their absence was discovered.

There was only one way, the same way! Back through the darkness they sped again, grimly hanging on, hoping and praying that the equipment they held on to would not be called upon to do the job for which it was designed. At Wallingford it was now early morning, and they faced the risk of being caught. But they were fortunate. Paul's early-to-bed grandparents slept the sleep of the just, blissfully unaware of the whereabouts of their daring grandson. Willie, the equally daring son of Harlan Strong, the Sunday school superintendent, also managed to return to his bed undiscovered.

Many years later, when relating this boyhood escapade, Harris dryly commented: 'It was the longest twenty-five miles I have ever travelled!'

Such were Paul's young years. He swam and fished, he played and fought, he enjoyed his adventures and indulged in the fantasies of youth. He attended school and went to church. He suffered the usual childhood maladies, he delighted in the pleasures of growing up, and bawled when life was not too kind.

These were the important years when his character was being

formed, and what better place for this to happen than in the New England village where he knew such loving care. At an early age he demonstrated his natural ability as a leader, his spirit of adventure and the indomitable courage which, time and again, saw him through hardships and the critical periods of his life.

CHAPTER 4

Two Brief Re-unions

George and Cornelia Harris made two attempts to re-unite their family. The first was in Cambridge, a village in the eastern part of the State of New York. Paul's father was employed in a toy factory in Mechanicsville, a few miles away. Harris has described this period of his life quite vividly: 'I was left alone much of the time, mother being away giving music lessons.' He was clearly unhappy and spoke of heavy clouds hanging over him, seeming at times to engulf him. 'Sometimes,' he recalled, 'they parted for an instant and permitted the lovelight to shine through. Mother put up a courageous fight, but conditions must have seemed hopeless to both my parents.'

Paul's unhappiness lasted for only a short time, however. One dark winter night, an elderly bearded man he had never seen before drew up to the house on a sleigh. His mother and the driver, a Mr Hitchcock, then took him to the railroad station, where he was put on a train in the care of the conductor and taken to Rutland where, once again, his grandfather waited to meet him.

The next attempt to unite the family was not until some time later. Once again Howard Harris subsidized his son, purchasing another drug store and home for Paul's parents. This was in the small town of Fairhaven, in western Vermont, some twenty-five miles from Wallingford.

This time all seemed favourable and the optimism of his parents, especially his father, knew no bounds. The family was accepted by the 'best' people in the town. The three children enrolled in the village school and went to church and Sunday school.

Paul's father worked hard and spent what leisure time he had with his family. On Sunday afternoons the family assembled around the piano which the ever generous Howard Harris had purchased for his daughter-in-law. Paul's father enjoyed singing, and often extemporized . . .

> The mistakes of my life have been many,
> The sins of my life have been more,
> But thank God I'm no knocker . . .

It was this last line that was improvised. Paul elaborated on this many years later, when he commented: 'Quite right, my father, you were never a knocker. Your list of friends included all sorts and conditions of men, and you were as free from religous and political prejudices as any man I have ever known.'

How long the Harris family remained together in Fairhaven is not known, but Paul must have been with them for two or three years. During this time George Harris worked in his garden during the growing season, raising abundant supplies of potatoes, strawberries, grapes and other crops. He devoted himself to the drug store, his wife and home. Gradually, however, he reverted to his weakness for a quick fortune by way of his inventions, and Cornelia again turned the housekeeping over to hired help, while she gave her time to piano lessons and organizing choirs and Welsh choral groups. The pattern was repeating itself. Sometimes, there was plenty of good food to eat, and sometimes the cupboard was almost bare. It was either feast or famine.

As Paul reflected sadly: 'It was as if neither of my parents had learned anything whatever from the unhappy events of former years. In business and domestic affairs the tragedy of Racine was being enacted all over again.'

Grandfather Howard Harris, fearfully aware of the drift, attempted to intervene with timely advice, but his son carried on spending recklessly on useless experiments and inventions. Once again the Harris children were separated. For the third and last time, Paul returned to the home and care of his grandparents.

During his time in Fairhaven, Paul attended the public school there. The principal was a man by the unusual name of Ichabod Spencer: 'A tall, angular, raw boned man with deep and severe eyes. I don't ever recall having seen the vestige of a smile on his face,' said Paul.

Spencer was a man who administered severe floggings, and brutal punishment was meted out in the presence of the youngest and tiniest of children with a fearsome rawhide whip. Harris cited one instance in particular: 'There was a little Welsh boy in our department by the name of Harry Parry, and he was incorrigible. In his case Professor Spencer wasted no words. He used but two sentences: "Harry Parry, come forward," and "Take off your coat, sir." Then, amid the boy's shrieks, Professor Spencer rained the cruel blows on, while the pallid faced children trembled in their seats.'

On one occasion, related Harris, a child was so shocked it screamed in agony, and had to be removed from the room. On yet another occasion, a boy was so frightened and stunned, he could not eat for a week.

Harris's experiences in the school dominated by the sadistic Ichabod Spencer was the last straw: 'I could put up with mismanagement in the home and in father's business affairs, but the incubus of Professor Ichabod Spencer was too much to bear.'

It is astonishing that such a brutal regime and abuse of power should have been allowed to go unchallenged, even a century ago, especially in the light of Harris's summing up of the situation: 'If Charles Dickens, before writing his *Nicholas Nickleby*, could have seen Professor Ichabod Spencer, it would not have been necessary for him to create the character of Mr Wackford Squeers. Professor Spencer was the incarnation of the immortal headmaster of the Dotheboys School, and Harry Parry an American equivalent of poor Smike.'

Although Paul returned to Wallingford, his family continued to live in Fairhaven, during which time he, Cecil and Nina May were joined by three more brothers, Guy, Claude and Reginald.

Paul maintained close contact with his family and often walked the twenty-five miles from Wallingford to Fairhaven. They in turn, especially on occasions like Thanksgiving, would congregate with other members of the family in the Howard Harris home.

Cecil, Paul's elder brother, was closer to him than any of his other brothers or his only sister. They were together for the first three or four years of their lives in Racine and, briefly, at Wallingford. Afterwards, except for the short reunion in Cambridge and the longer reunion in Fairhaven, they led separate lives.

Their paths crossed from time to time, such as when Cecil was a salesman for the Sheldon Marble Company, where Paul worked in 1888–9. In the 1920s they again worked together in the Rotary International secretariat in Chicago, where Cecil was Assistant

Secretary in Charge of Extension Work in North America.

Paul greatly admired his older brother. When Cecil died, Paul had this to say of him: 'If I were asked to name the most outstanding characteristic of my brother Cecil, I would unhesitatingly answer, courage. His courage never failed him. If he knew what fear was, he never admitted it. He took life as it came, extracting from each day's experiences the maximum of sweetness and never quailing in the face of danger or disaster.'

At the time of Cecil's death, Paul said that his brother was suffering from bodily ailments painfully manifest to relatives and friends, yet he invariably insisted all was well. As he lay dying, Cecil's last words to Paul were: 'Whatever else may be said of me, no one will ever be able to say truthfully that I didn't enjoy life while it lasted.'

When Paul's parents retired to Denver around the turn of the century, his sister Nina May went with them. There she met and married a citizen of Denver, Lucien Abbott. Of Harris's three younger brothers, all born in Fairhaven, Guy died in 1889 aged eleven and Claude was killed in the Philippines in 1898 in the brief war against Spain.

The remaining brother, Reginald, lived a long and active life and was the only member of the family to outlive Paul. In 1917 he volunteered for service in the armed forces at the time the United States entered the war against Germany. Because of an infirmity he was rejected as unfit. He immediately went into hospital and had the infirmity corrected by minor surgery. He volunteered again, was accepted and left his wife and family to serve his country.

After the war he entered the University of Wyoming, despite the fact that he was then in his thirties. Rex, as he was known, was slightly disabled during the war and, with the help of a government subsidy, gained admission as a war veteran. After four years he graduated in 1926 with a degree in business, and was offered a place on the university faculty in his subject field. He served in that position from 1926 to 1929, during which time he became a Vice President of the Rotary Club of Laramie.

In 1929 Rex accepted a position in the Rotary International secretariat in Chicago, but in 1933 he transferred his service club allegiance to take up a travelling, or field, position with another service organization, the rapidly expanding Lions International.

Reg Harris died in 1958, probably in Santa Barbara, California, where, in the mid 1970s, his widow was still living.

CHAPTER 5

The Education of a Rotarian

Harris was no exception to the rule that, to the majority of us, the discipline of school life is something to be endured, not enjoyed. He frankly admitted that he disliked school intensely, especially during his trying time under the diabolical Ichabod Spencer, and he took every opportunity to play truant. On one occasion he was unfortunate enough to encounter his father, and the summarily meted out punishment was long remembered.

But if school itself was something to be abhorred, there was the compensation of school friendships. Friends such as George Marsh, 'who could make his ears wag', Albert Mandigo, George Hitt, John Gainey, Hiram Fales, Will Coleman, George Wilder, George Sabin (who often accompanied Paul on long walks), Caleb Pennypacker, who was renowned for his perpetual grin and his trick of turning his eyelids inside out, 'Inky' Ballou, who could make his knuckles crack like a pistol shot, and, of course, Willie Strong and Fay Stafford. Here too was Paul's first 'girlfriend' Josie Lilly, on whom he had a 'crush'.

Several of these names are still familiar in Wallingford. The President of the Wallingford Club in 1976–7, for example, was Rotarian David L. Ballou.

For all his dislike of school, however, Harris was endowed with an intellect well above average, and showed promise and natural leadership at an early age. His grandfather helped. On many occasions the elderly Howard Harris sat with Paul for hours, asking him to spell words from the textbooks of the time, trying to instil into his grandson the value of a sound education. And it was Howard Harris who ensured, once Paul's elementary schooling was completed, that the way ahead was prepared for further education in high school and college.

The first year of Paul's preparatory work was spent at the

Wallingford High School under the tutelage of the headmaster, Professor William Shaw. Despite the problems generated by Paul's behaviour, Professor Shaw had great faith in his young pupil, and when Harris went on to Rutland High School, he paid high tribute to the brilliant but errant student.

While at Rutland High School, Paul lived for a while with his Aunt Mellie, Dr George Fox and their children at their West Rutland home. At weekends and during vacations he often walked the nine miles to Wallingford to see his grandparents.

Paul's college career began at an institution known as the Black River Academy, at Ludlow, Vermont, but his stay was relatively brief. For the first time in his life he was free from any form of parental control and it led to his undoing. His wild disposition and lack of discipline at the academy resulted in all manner of undesirable mischief and his so-called pranks, rather kindly referred to by the college authorities as 'an excess of spirits', were viewed with considerable disfavour. They resulted, after only one year, in his ignominious expulsion from the college—he was simply not invited back. Had Harris remained at the Black River Academy for just a little longer, it is interesting to note, he would have had as a fellow student a boy named Calvin Coolidge, the thirtieth President of the United States.

Paul's grandfather was nothing if not persevering. Despite the setback, he was intent upon ensuring that his grandson had every educational opportunity. Paul was next enrolled in the Vermont Academy, a military institution, at Saxton's River. It was a shrewd move. As a cadet officer, Paul had to knuckle down to military discipline. It worked wonders. Here, under the direction of a Major Spooner, who left a profound impression on Paul, his natural talents and qualities of leadership came to the fore, and he acquitted himself with distinction. So well did he apply himself to his work, he matriculated as a freshman at the University of Vermont in the autumn of 1885.

He liked the university, set as it was in Burlington on the heights overlooking the beautiful Lake Champlain to the west, and his beloved Green Mountains to the east. He retained happy memories of his time there, brief though it proved to be. In 1887, after only eighteen months, Paul, who was regarded as the ringleader, and three other students were expelled for allegedly transgressing the rules of the university. All the students knew the real culprit, but were honour bound not to divulge his name. Paul was yet again sent home in ignominy, although he steadfastly maintained that the expulsion in this instance was an injustice. The President of the University of Vermont at that time was Professor Matthew Henry Buckham, about whom Harris later expressed mixed feelings: 'A worthy and upright man and a great scholar, but . . .', a restrained observation that spoke volumes. Many years later the university authorities admitted the injustice, and it is to their credit that Harris and his fellow students were invited back by Dr Guy Bailey to have degrees conferred upon them.

Meanwhile, however, Paul had to endure the humiliation of expulsion. He heard once again the derisory phrase 'that Paul Harris', and this time it stung. In the military academy he had done well, his wilder tendencies brought under control. There were lessons to be learned and he learnt them the hard way. But this last incident was not without benefit. He understood only too well that his record of indiscipline, even though unwarranted on this occasion, was a cause of anguish to his grandparents, and he determined that henceforth he would justify their faith in him. He was maturing rapidly from a high spirited boy into a responsible adult, and he acted accordingly.

He prevailed upon his grandparents to give him one more chance, and they were not slow to respond. They saw the change and knew, instinctively, that Harris was destined to make his mark in the world. They knew also that they would not live to see their trust fulfilled. Aiming now for an even higher academic education, Howard Harris engaged a private tutor to prepare his grandson for entry to the prestigious Princeton University. It proved to be another shrewd move.

Harris applied himself diligently and in the spring of 1887, aged nineteen, he successfully took the entrance examinations of the university and entered its famous precincts in the autumn of the same year.

On his first day he met a Professor Huss, who took him to meet Princeton's President, Dr James McCosh. Jimmi, as the venerable Dr McCosh was affectionately known, was a famous educator who came to Princeton after an outstanding academic career in the universities of Edinburgh, Glasgow and Belfast. It was Dr McCosh, more than any other educator, who made the deepest impression on Harris, who later stated that he felt privileged to have taken logic and psychology under the fine Scottish professor with the patriarchal and scholarly appearance.

Dr McCosh retired as President a year later and was succeeded by Dr Francis L. Patton until 1902. Patton, in turn, was followed by Woodrow Wilson, the twenty-eighth President of the United States.

Harris studied only briefly under Dr Patton but, many years later, when Dr Patton had retired to Bermuda, he and Harris, by then President Emeritus of Rotary International, met again. Thirty-seven years had elapsed since their brief encounter at Princeton but Dr Patton, then eighty-four years old, remembered his former student well.

At Princeton, Paul settled down to serious study, allowing nothing to distract him. All seemed right at last but, such are the vagaries of fate, a tragedy was in the offing.

CHAPTER 6

The Death of Howard Harris

In March 1888, while Harris was at Princeton, he received a telegram from his uncle, Dr George Fox, advising him that his grandfather was seriously ill. He was urged to return to Wallingford at once. It had been a long and exceptionally hard winter, and snow was piled up to record heights. Nonetheless, Harris hurried back to Wallingford. When the train pulled into his home town it was late at night. The first person he saw as he alighted, was an old school friend, Bert Preston. Anxiously Harris asked him if he knew how his grandfather was. The stammered reply stunned Harris: 'I'm afraid your grandfather is dead, Paul.'

It was 17 March 1888, St Patrick's Day. Throughout America, Irishmen were celebrating the feast of their patron saint. But in Wallingford there were no festivities; a respected citizen was dead, and it was a time for grieving.

Sadly, Harris made his way to his home in Main Street, along the same route his tiny feet had trod seventeen years earlier with the grandparent he had come to love and respect, and whose voice he would now never hear again.

With the exception of indulging his son, Howard Harris was a shrewd man who took great care of his business affairs. 'My grandfather,' said Harris in 1946, 'spread his mantle of helpfulness over the needy of all his descendants. Even to this day, the estate of grandfather still stands open in the records of Rutland County's Probate Court, one of our family still being a beneficiary of the small remaining income.'

All Harris's family and relatives arrived for the funeral. Aunt Mellie and her three children had come the short distance from West Rutland, as also had Dr George Fox, although he had been back and forth for the several preceding days, attending to the last hours of Howard Harris. Paul's parents, his brothers and sister,

47

encountered real difficulty in travelling the twenty-five miles from Fairhaven, as also did Charles Harris from Brattleboro. At the funeral to pay their last respects were Ed and Lib Martindale from next door, Mrs Hudson Shaw, who frequently borrowed a cup of yeast from Paul's grandparents, Judge Button and his daughter Ellen, frequent visitors to the Harris home, Joel Ainsworth, a distant relative by marriage, his brother Seward, and many more. Included among them were Harlan Strong, the Sunday school superintendent, Cal Hilliard and her widowed sister, Mellie Cleghorn, who sang at the funeral service. These and many other friends demonstrated to Harris the respect and affection in which his grandfather was held.

But it was not to her son George or her daughter Mellie whom Pamela Rustin Harris turned for comfort. It was to her nineteen-year-old grandson. It was Paul who, with his Uncle George, took charge of the funeral arrangements and, after the funeral, it was Paul who was asked by his grandmother to read the last will and testament of her husband of sixty years.

Paul learned directly from his grandmother how his grandfather had gone out in the bitterly cold morning hours, after a particularly heavy fall of snow, to clear the pathway. And how, in doing so, he had contracted pneumonia, which finally quenched the flame which had burned so brightly for eighty-nine years.

A few days later Harris returned to Princeton to complete his year of study. He had been left no legacy in his grandfather's will, although one-third of the estate had been left to his grandmother. This she was to do with as she desired, including the provision of Paul's further education if that was her decision. But Howard Harris knew that his grandson would become a better man if he had to make his own way in the world. He had given his own son the best possible education and a great start in life, only to see it come to naught.

Howard Harris would not make the same mistake with his grandson. The wherewithal was there if needed, but the decision was left in the capable hands of Pamela Harris. The message to Paul was unmistakable. His future was in his own hands and he had to make it on his own. Paul would honour the memory of his grandfather by doing just that.

Pamela Rustin Harris, Paul's grandmother

The house in Racine, Wisconsin, where Paul Harris was born on 19 April 1868

CHAPTER 7

The Passing of Grandmother

After finishing his studies at Princeton, Harris applied for and obtained a position, if such it could be called, with the Sheldon Marble Company in West Rutland. Here he teamed up with his elder brother, Cecil, who was then working for the same company as a travelling salesman. Harris was employed by the company for a little over a year. To make it easier to get to and from his place of work, he again lived in West Rutland with his closest relatives, the Foxes. His grandmother was now living alone in the large house in Wallingford, but Harris went to see her frequently, often walking the nine miles in both directions.

His job with the marble company was that of office boy. Each morning he rose at 5.30 and, after breakfast, walked a mile in all weathers to the company offices. He attended to the stoves and swept and cleaned in readiness for the incoming office staff. During the day he carried out his regular chores as office boy, for the princely sum of $1.00 a day.

The company officials had been warned of his multitudinous misdemeanours in school and college, and were expecting a firebrand. But the new and responsible Paul Harris worked hard, so hard that before the year was out, he had graduated to much more important tasks. Both Captain Morse, the company manager, and W.K. Sheldon, its president, came to hold Harris in high esteem. Sheldon, asked by the President of the University of Vermont if he was aware of Harris's poor scholastic record and his expulsion from university, replied in no uncertain terms, that not only was he well aware of the allegations but that he considered Harris to have been grossly misjudged. Sheldon went on to say that he found Harris to be one of the best men he had ever employed, no mean tribute when it is appreciated that the Sheldon Marble Company then had more than six hundred employees. There was a vast disparity in

49

age between Harris and his employer, but in the course of time they became good friends. Whenever Sheldon visited Chicago in later years, he never failed to call on his one time office boy.

During this year, Harris and his grandmother spent hours discussing his future. She told him his grandfather had always treasured the hope that he would choose the law as his profession. More than that, she said, it was her husband's wish that Paul bring to that honourable profession the ideals that the two old people had tried to teach their grandson.

And so the die was cast. It was decided that Harris should enroll for a degree in law at the University of Iowa, but that first he had to spend some time in the law offices of an established firm in the nearby city of Des Moines.

It was also decided that Pamela Harris, alone now, would sell the old home and move to West Rutland to spend her remaining years with her daughter Mellie and her family. Pamela Harris would vacate her home on the day her grandson left for Iowa. That was her wish, and everyone respected it, including the purchaser of the Harris house, R.C. Taft.

Paul and his grandmother spent those last few days in September 1889 together. They talked over the past and speculated about the future. They paid their last lingering farewells to the home they loved so much. On the morning of the last day, Paul listened intently to his grandmother's last words. 'I shall be back to see you soon,' he said, but Pamela Harris shook her head sadly and made no reply. She was now seventy-eight years old and nearing the end of life's road. For her twenty-one-year-old grandson it was but the beginning.

Harris took the 11.15 morning train to Rutland. His grandmother remained behind a little longer, until her daughter Mellie came from West Rutland to collect her. As the train drew away from Wallingford, Paul gazed out of the window towards Bear Mountain, White Rocks, the cemetery on Green Hill, and all the other familiar and beloved places in his New England valley. He was not destined to see them again for quite a long time.

On his way to Iowa, Harris made arrangements to stay in Chicago for a few days with an old college friend, Robert M. Johnson, now a newspaper reporter, who was working his way around the United States.

Harris was fascinated by Chicago, which was then one of the fastest growing cities in the United States, a melting pot for men and women of all races, creeds and cultures. The city was a cauldron of crime, corruption and violence, a veritable maelstrom of social upheaval; but good things were also happening. Frances Willard started the Women's Christian Temperance Union there in 1879 and in the year that Harris first visited the city, Jane Addams established the famous Hull House for the settlement of immigrants. Harris knew instinctively that Chicago had a great future and would play an important role in the development of America. He sensed that from Chicago great ideas and great deeds would emerge, and he resolved that when the time came to settle down, he would make his home there.

From Chicago he went to the city of Des Moines, Iowa, where it had been arranged that he would read law in the offices of the well known firm of St John, Stevenson and Whisenand. Here, the once incorrigible youth again rendered an excellent account of himself and, after the mandatory year, he entered the Law Department of the University of Iowa in the autumn of 1890. Only a few weeks later, before he had settled down to his studies, he received a telegram from his uncle, Dr George Fox, informing him that his grandmother was dead.

In a letter that reached him shortly afterwards, he learned that Pamela Harris had not been ill, and there had been no warning. His grandmother simply went to sleep peacefully one autumn night, and never awoke.

Harris did not return to Wallingford for the funeral. By the time he received the news it was impossible to get back in time and there was little point in his doing so. All the arrangements were seen to by his dependable Uncle George. Sadly he carried on with his studies, now more determined than ever to justify the faith his grandparents had reposed in him.

No trace remained of the unruly, undisciplined youth who had so sorely tried the patience of Howard and Pamela Harris. His grandfather was seventy-two and his grandmother sixty when he was brought to them, but they had done their work well. In place of the child, a mature and thoughtful young man parents' Christian ideals and respect for fellow human-beings. He had learned from them the values of tolerance, compassion, kindness and respect for others.

To all intents and purposes, Harris was alone. True, he still had links with Wallingford. There was still his Aunt Mellie and her family, and, not far away in Fairhaven, his parents and younger brothers, but over the years the family connection had become ever more tenuous. With the death of Pamela Harris, the closest link of all was broken.

Harris's grandparents had moulded his character and instilled in him all those qualities that he later brought into his unique concept of a new fellowship of men which valued the dignity of the human-being and generated a new era of service to others. Howard and Pamela Harris should never be forgotten. From them came the foundation stones on which Rotary is built.

CHAPTER 8
Hardship and Hunger

When his grandmother died, Harris was short of money, and experiencing hardship and hunger he had never before known. But he was determined to succeed. Even during vacations, most of which he spent fishing in Lake Okaboja, he would take his books with him.

At the university he made a new friend, one who greatly influenced his reading interests. Will Mullin, two or three years Harris's senior, was a young man of brilliant mind who had acquired, through working in his father's bookstore, a fine knowledge of English literature.

Mullin became Harris's literary mentor and introduced him to the wonderful prose of such great Victorian writers as Dickens, Thackeray and Scott. Dickens in particular, with his masterly exposes of the apalling social conditions in Victorian England, captivated him. Harris conceived an ambition to visit the land from which such fine literature came. In his later years, as he sat at the fireside of his home, Harris would read aloud passages from the works of the former journalist.

In the summer of 1891, aged twenty-three, Harris fulfilled the ambitions of his grandparents when he graduated from the University of Iowa with a degree in law. Most of his classmates had already made arrangements to begin practising in various cities and towns. Harris, however, was not ready to settle down. Perhaps some of the 'excess of spirits' of which he was once accused still burned within him. It was in character.

A remark by one of the lecturers made a deep impression. The speaker, a practising lawyer who had himself graduated from the university ten years earlier, opined that it might be a good thing for each graduate to go first to some small town and, for a period of say five years, enjoy himself, before beginning to practise law. Harris pondered this chance remark and decided that he would not settle in any one place, or set up a shingle proclaiming that his law office was open. Instead of practising, he decided to devote about five years to seeing as much of the United States as he could and, if possible, other countries as well.

He would work his passage, lodge wherever he could, and earn whatever was offered. He wanted to meet people, to find out why men did what they did, to understand what life was like in other places and other cultures. For five years he would be a vagabond. Some of his contemporaries considered he was being totally irresponsible. Others envied him.

Almost a century later we can look objectively at his decision. Was it foolhardy? Or was he years ahead of his time? The young graduates of today think nothing of making their way to remote parts of the world before they are prepared to settle down. Indeed, they are encouraged to do so by both government and quasi-government agencies. Transportation is far easier now, but the principle is the same—to gain some experience of life before making a permanent home. Viewed from this distance in time, Harris's decision was not only far sighted, it was almost inspirational.

His decision was the prelude to a story of adventure, courage, endurance, heroism, exploration and achievement breathtaking in its scope. The picture so many Rotarians have of the founder of the Movement is of an austere, introverted and unadventurous man. The extraordinary account of his years between the ages of twenty-three and twenty-eight will require them to make a dramatic reappraisal.

Harris accepted work of all descriptions and walked hundreds of miles through mountains and wild country. He slept rough and tramped the streets of great cities during the hardest times. There were days when he went hungry and suffered considerable privation.

His experiences reinforced the values of human dignity taught him by his grandparents. He learned the underlying motives that influenced the lives of men—why some were good, and others mostly bad. He learned anew why some made sacrifices in their concern for others. He also found the incurably selfish. He wondered why some wasted their physical, mental and moral resources, while others channelled them into service to their fellow men.

To the end of his days Harris had an inquiring mind. Life and all its complications held a great fascination for him, and he was forever seeking to know more. To find out, he sometimes resorted to unconventional methods and his years as a vagabond enriched his knowledge of life more than any study of books. Through experience he gained insight into people, places, the ways in which men strive to improve their lot, and life itself in its highest and lowest aspects.

He took a calculated risk, maybe a gamble in the eyes of the more prudent, but it was one that reaped rich rewards.

Harris's incredible adventures began in the summer of 1891. Immediately after graduation he headed west for the wild mountain ranges of Idaho. Here he relaxed, fishing for trout and hunting game. During his brief vacation he brought down a black bear, no mean achievement even for an experienced hunter.

The vacation over, he headed for the golden city of San Francisco, then the mecca of all travellers to the west, on the way visiting the Yellowstone National Park, at that time still relatively unknown and free from the spoliations of tourists. When he reached San Francisco, he was penniless. As he succinctly expressed it, 'I was on my own at last'.

Harris looked up his old college chum Robert M. Johnson who, by that time, was covering the city's hotels as a reporter for the *San Francisco Examiner*. With his help, Harris obtained a similar position as a freelance on a rival newspaper, the *Chronicle*. The position was no sinecure. Reporters were paid by the column for any material considered to be of news value, plus $3.00 for any ordered assignment. The city was full of experienced newspaper men and they were invariably on first call assignments. Only rarely were there enough to go around. Harris, however, found that he had an instinctive 'nose for news', and he developed a fine style of writing and fared better than some of the experienced men.

One night, when discussing the freelance situation with colleagues at the old Palace Hotel, Harris chanced to hear Harry C. Pulliam, himself occupying a low position on the *Chronicle*'s staff, comment that he had come west not to work as a reporter, but to see California. (Pulliam hailed from Louisville, Kentucky, and later made his mark as the president of the United States National Baseball League.)

The two young men quickly struck up a friendship and soon afterwards set off for the Vaca Valley where they found employment as labourers on a fruit ranch owned by a man named Frank Buck. As soon as they had earned a stake for further travels, they criss-crossed the state in a series of hikes, including three hundred miles through the Sierra Nevada Mountains and an exploration of the now famous, but then little known, Yosemite Valley.

Shortly after starting, however, Harris became ill with malaria, and had to rest for a few days in Stockton, soon recovering his strength. When crossing the divide which separates the valleys of the various branches of the Tuolumne, Merced and Stanislaus rivers, the travellers lost their way and wandered in circles for several days. In fact they ran out of provisions before they again found human habitation. Undaunted, they carried on, but much time had been lost, and they were unable to visit the Hetch Hetchy and King's River Canyon, two of the places included in their plans.

The raisin-packing industry in Fresno in the beautiful San Joaquim Valley provided Harris and Pulliam with their next stake. Then it was on to Los Angeles, a fast developing city. Harris obtained a position as a teacher in the Los Angeles Business College, and it is interesting to note that this institution was one of the first to be represented in the Rotary Club of Los Angeles in 1909.

In all, Harris spent about eight months travelling in California, then it was time to move on, and he and Harry Pulliam parted company. Both were heading back to the East, but by different routes, although they made arrangements to meet again. In March 1892, therefore, Harris set off alone to work his way across the southern states.

His first stop was in Denver, Colorado, a city which, unknown to him then, would play an important role in later life. He demonstrated again his astonishing versatility by acting in a stock company at the old Fifteenth Street Theater (sometimes referred to as the 'People's Theater'). As far as Harris was concerned, this was merely a manner of earning a living, but it attracted the wrong sort of publicity. Concerned friends wrote, expressing their dismay that he had apparently 'gone wrong', and newsboys shouted derisory names and taunted him as he walked the city's streets.

Harris, however, had no more intention of becoming an actor

than he had of any occupation other than law. It was simply a convenient way of earning a living, and he soon found himself back in the newspaper business, this time as a reporter on the staff of the *Rocky Mountain News*.

Then followed a move to Platteville, a small community some thirty miles north of Denver, and one of the most unusual and interesting of his many jobs. At a ranch near the township he became a cowboy. When and where he learned to ride a horse has not been explained, but at the age of twenty-four he rode the range alone for days at a time, rounding up stray cattle.

Returning to Denver he again worked as a newspaperman, but this time with the *Denver Republican*. An opportunity arose for Harris to buy, at a bargain price, a railway ticket terminating in the bustling Florida city of Jacksonville, where he promptly became a night clerk at the St James Hotel. According to Harris, it was the best tourist hotel in the city at that time. However, he found the work prosaic and was soon looking around for something more suitable.

George W. Clark, a dealer in marble and granite, walked into the hotel one day, discovered that Harris had worked for the Sheldon Marble Company in Rutland, and promptly offered him a post as travelling salesman. The offer, quickly accepted, provided Harris with a marvellous opportunity to see even more of his own country.

For several months he travelled extensively through Florida and into some of the neighbouring states. He and Clark developed a firm friendship and respect for each other, and enjoyed a relationship above that of employer and employee.

By this time Harris had completed almost two of the five years he had allocated to his 'vagabondage', and the time again arrived for him to move on. He resigned on 1 March 1893, and departed for Washington, D.C., to witness the ceremonies of the second inauguration of Grover Cleveland as President of the United States.

While in the nation's capital, Harris obtained temporary employment with the *Washington Star*, but following the inauguration, moved to Louisville, Kentucky, to visit his old friend and partner in the California adventure, Harry Pulliam, now the telegraph editor of the *Louisville Commercial*.

After an unsuccessful attempt to find newspaper work, Harris obtained employment as a travelling salesman for yet another marble and granite company. By strange coincidence, his new employer was also named Clark, but this was James A. Clark, who was neither related to nor in any way connected with George W. Clark of Jacksonville. Harris was thus able to see more of the southern area of the United States. His territory covered Kentucky, Tennessee, Georgia and Virginia, and he travelled extensively through these states, visiting Cincinnati, Memphis, Knoxville, Nashville, Atlanta, Chattanooga, Savannah, Norfolk, Richmond, Roanoke and many other cities.

One day, while still working for James A. Clark, Harris found himself in Norfolk, Virginia. Here he suddenly resigned and took a boat to Philadelphia. His action was prompted by stories that men were often hired for cargo boats plying to and fro across the Atlantic, and 'help wanted' advertisements would be found in the Philadelphia and Baltimore newspapers.

As soon as he arrived in the 'City of Brotherly Love', Harris eagerly scanned the newspapers' 'wanted' columns, concentrating on those advertisements asking for seamen for ships destined for Britain. He soon found one that fitted the bill. It asked for cattlemen for a boat of British registry, the *Baltimore*. Harris signed on without further ado. Had he paused to ask a few questions of the more experienced men in the port, he may well have hesitated. But he didn't. His enthusiasm to visit Britain overcame his innate caution. It led to one of the most traumatic experiences of his life.

By dawn the following day, Harris found himself on the high seas, on his way to Britain. He had said often enough that he aspired to learn as much as he could of the practicalities of life, including its seamier aspects. His aspiration was about to be fulfilled.

The *Baltimore* had the unenviable reputation of being the worst boat of the worst line on the trans-Atlantic service. The crew and the cattlemen included some of the most depraved and vicious characters imaginable. The food was unbelievably bad, the so-called living quarters abominable, the stench of the confined animals almost intolerable. And if these burdens were not enough, Harris's misery was completed by seas just about as rough as they could be. Hunger and discomfort were not new to Harris, for in his travels across the United States he had already experienced the less salubrious aspects of life, but these were as nothing compared with the hardships, privations, physical and mental suffering which were accepted as the norm aboard the *Baltimore*.

Harris's inherent modesty made him play down what must have been one of the most horrifying experiences of his life. All he said later was that it was 'a trying experience'. It affected his own life significantly and the philosophy upon which, a little more than a decade later, the Rotary movement was founded and developed. 'Without this experience,' he wrote more than thirty years afterwards, 'I would never have believed that human beings could sink so low.'

It took the *Baltimore* fourteen stormy days to cross the Atlantic, but finally Harris set foot in Britain at the port of Liverpool on a summer's day in 1893. After a short rest to recuperate from the exhausting voyage, Harris and a friend had the satisfaction of sampling the sights of Liverpool. 'We went in all directions,' said Harris, 'but our stay was all too brief and within a few days we once again had to sign on before the mast, as was then the custom with returning cattlemen.'

For the return voyage to the United States, he and the others sailed on the *Parkmore*, a sister ship of the detested *Baltimore*. Although the return passage was not as bad, the vessel did not provide, for example, mattresses, blankets or even the simplest of eating utensils. Food, served three times each day, was known to British seamen as 'scouse' (an abbreviation of 'lobscouse'), a concoction of potatoes and water with, occasionally, small fragments of meat of questionable quality. Sometimes the diet was augmented by sea biscuits, called 'hard tack', and these were often covered with mould.

Cattlemen were considered the lowest form of life aboard ship. The crew fared a little better, but even they were infested with vermin and sores, and both parties engaged in running battles with the rats that scurried and foraged throughout the ship. In rougher weather, vast quantities of water were washed aboard, deluging everyone at all times of the day and night. There were no facilities for drying soaked clothing, and with the rest of the crew, Harris worked and slept, as best he could, in sodden clothes.

His subsequent comment—'the hardships of that first journey were anything but attractive'—must rank as one of the understatements of the century.

Most men would not have sought to repeat the experience, but Harris was sorely disappointed at not getting to see the London of Charles Dickens, and the other fabled sights of what was then the world's largest city. It speaks volumes for his character that, despite the horrors of the *Baltimore* and the *Parkmore*, he was determined to make another attempt to cross the Atlantic even, as he said, 'if it meant the cost of again enduring such debasing hardships'.

As soon as the *Parkmore* docked at Baltimore, Harris began looking for another ship. Meanwhile, the word had come down that Harris was the best man with whom the cattlemen's foreman had ever crossed the Atlantic. High praise indeed for an undertaking which would have taxed the resources of men of much greater physical strength than Harris.

Wiser now, he searched for a steamship line with a better reputation. Meantime he had to earn his keep. As it was haymaking time, he walked out to a small rural community, Ellicott City, a few miles west of Baltimore, and soon found employment but, to his chagrin, discovered that haymaking was heavier and harder work than he had expected. As always, he gave of his best, but even Harris had to admit defeat on this occasion, and he soon shifted to carrying out chores around the farmhouse in exchange for his board and lodging. It amazed him that he was unable to cope with the relatively simple work of haymaking after the rigorous and exhausting labours on the two ships.

Harris, however, needed money to replenish his meagre financial resources, and he found a position in a corn-canning factory, which paid $1.50 a day. Meanwhile, he scanned the newspapers for reports of sailings. One day his heart jumped. The *Michigan*, a ship favourably mentioned in a conversation with a former ship-mate, was about to leave for Britain. He rushed back to Baltimore and anxiously applied to the captain for employment as a cattle-man. He was immediately offered a berth as a sub-foreman in charge of a gang. The word had indeed come down that he was a good worker. Pleased though he was with his new appointment and the opportunity to visit Britain again, Harris's delight knew no bounds when he discovered that the *Michigan* was destined for the port of Tilbury on the River Thames and a mere thirty miles from London.

The *Michigan*'s living and working conditions were far superior to those of the *Baltimore* and *Parkmore*. Harris said the voyage was delightful and exhilarating. It was high summer 1893 and at long last he was on his way to London.

Harris described his visit with rare lucidity. In the years to come, he would be as familiar with London as with his home city of Chicago, but the memory of that first visit was never erased. With a young friend from the *Michigan*, he tramped the highways and byways of the sprawling metropolis from early morning until darkness. They covered great distances, cramming all they could into the time at their disposal. To save time and travelling costs, they took lodgings in London, although the best they could afford was an inexpensive boarding house in Whitechapel's Commercial Road, run by a Mr A. Leslie.

The two friends took in all the historic sights of London—the Houses of Parliament, Buckingham Palace, Trafalgar Square and Nelson's Column, Westminster Abbey, the Tower of London, Piccadilly, Hyde Park and much more. They punted on the Thames and Harris set his watch by 'Big Ben'. But it was not all sightseeing. Harris, the embryonic sociologist, was just as interested in the seamier side of London as he was in the more salubrious areas.

On returning to the *Michigan* for the homeward journey, Harris was greeted with the news that the ship had been directed to South Wales, to the port of Swansea, there to take on coal and a cargo of Wedgwood pottery destined for Philadelphia. When the ship arrived at the busy Swansea docks, the coalminers were on strike, and their departure was delayed for a few days. Harris jumped at this opportunity to visit many places of interest in the Swansea area. He walked to Mumbles and admired the great sweep of Swansea Bay, and visited nearby towns such as Llanelli, Neath and Port Talbot.

His conversations with the people of Wales reminded him of his mother's involvement with Welsh choirs in Vermont and brought to mind his unfortunate school chum, the Welsh born Harry Parry. Those few days in South Wales provided a fitting climax to his first visit to Britain.

In late August or early September 1893, Harris arrived back in Philadelphia. Within the space of a few weeks he had crossed the Atlantic four times, and had learned greatly from his experiences and ordeals.

Almost half the allotted five years to see the world had passed. There was plenty still to see, but he decided first to go to Chicago to see the superb Exposition there. Chicago kept drawing Harris like a magnet. It held a special fascination for him and he wanted to see it once more. Then he would decide what other worlds to conquer.

CHAPTER 9

A Life is Saved

Harris was almost penniless when he arrived in the great mid-western city. He sought out an old college friend who was selling tickets at the Columbian Exposition then being staged, and became his guest for a week. For a second time he covered the sights of Chicago. If there were any doubts about making Chicago his future home, they were quickly dispelled.

Towards the end of his stay, while visiting the Vermont building, he saw two people, a man and a woman, inspecting the exhibits. From a distance they looked familiar. As they turned he recognized them as his cousins from West Rutland, Eddie and Mattie Fox, whom he had not seen since leaving Wallingford four years earlier. Instead of approaching them, Harris turned on his heel and left quickly before they sighted him. He had no wish to reveal himself in his impecunious state.

Among other cities, Harris had yet to visit—New Orleans, made unique by its strong French influence. Sieur de Bienville had founded it in 1718 as the capital of the French colony of Louisiana, but it was ceded to Spain in 1764. In 1803, under the terms of the famous Louisiana Purchase, it became an American city, and was incorporated in 1805. Ten years later it was the scene of a great battle between General Andrew Jackson and the British forces, and in 1862 it was captured by a Union naval force in the American Civil War.

Harris had only one problem—how to get there? He did not have enough for the train fare, and it was a matter of principle that he never, throughout all his travels, stole a ride. Either he paid his way or he worked his passage. Moreover, wherever he went, wherever he worked, he always gave full value and a full measure of service.

He could, of course, borrow the fare. He had done so on one or two occasions in the past, but the loan was always promptly repaid.

Never short on ingenuity, Harris borrowed $15.00 from his college friend, $10.00 of which was invested with a ticket broker for the return portion of a round trip ticket from Crowley (Louisiana) to Chicago via New Orleans. Even in those days this was extraordinarily cheap, but the ticket was due to expire within 24 hours and had to be used immediately. On arriving in New Orleans, the shrewd Harris recouped $1.00 by selling the remaining part of the ticket to Crowley to another broker. With this $1.00, plus the $5.00 he still had from the loan, he obtained board and lodging with a respectable New Orleans family. The loan was repaid as soon as he saved $15.00 from his earnings.

In the 'wanted' section of a New Orleans daily paper, he read that a dozen men were wanted to pick and pack oranges in a grove in Plaquemine Parish, a small community on the exposed Mississippi Delta, about fifty miles south of New Orleans. True to his principle that no work was too humble where an honest dollar could be earned, the next day found Harris in a gang of men, on a train on a narrow-gauge railroad, heading for Buras, a township located on the delta not far from where the 'Father of Waters' empties into the Gulf of Mexico. A mile and a half from Buras was the orange grove of a man named Pizatti, the senior member of the then well known Pizatti-Oteri Steamship Company, whose boats plied between New Orleans and Bluefields, Nicaragua.

The gang immediately began work. Sleeping quarters were arranged for them in the warehouse but their meals were prepared by Pizatti's own cook, and came from the old Italian's substantial stone house. Pizatti, whose wealth derived from importing bananas, was present most of the time, helping out when necessary and working conditions were good.

This seemed just another job along the way for Harris, and the business of picking and packing the oranges (still green for fear of an early frost) went smoothly for several days. The men were not required to work on Sundays, however. This was their mandatory rest day, and 1 October 1893 seemed no different from all other Sundays.

Harris and several other members of the gang rowed across the wide Mississippi to dredge for oysters in a bayou. The morning passed pleasantly, but as they started back in the afternoon, the weather showed signs of deteriorating and by the time they were halfway across the river a gale was blowing. This rapidly increased

63

in severity as they strove to reach the safety of the land.

It was clear to those who had experienced such weather before that a hurricane was imminent. The men feared that the warehouse, which was built on a high foundation above ground level, would not withstand the fury of the elements and they, along with many frightened families whose homes were nearby, sought refuge in the only solid structure in the vicinity, the staunch Pizatti home. All were admitted without question.

The storm continued to rage during the late afternoon and evening, and the house was filled with anxious, shouting men, crying women and frightened children. Suddenly, water started pouring into the house under the doorways. When the men looked out, they were astounded to find that the house was completely surrounded by water. The hurricane had generated a tidal wave threatening all those who could not reach higher ground. The wind itself was feared, but the rapidly rising water triggered off a near panic as it became apparent to all that salvation lay in reaching shelter on higher ground and that the only such shelter was the warehouse, the building already rejected as unsafe.

They had no choice. There were several hundred yards of water between the house and the warehouse, and no one could be certain, in the darkness, how deep the water might be.

Each man seized a child and rushed out towards the warehouse. Harris caught hold of a screaming, struggling girl of eight or nine and plunged out into the darkness. The women followed, clinging to the men when they could. As they left the house, the water was little more than knee deep but it rapidly got deeper. The men raised the children higher and higher, at the same time fighting the hurricane that threatened to blow them off balance. By the time they reached rising ground the waters were tearing at their aching armpits. Finally they all made it safely. Thanks to Harris and his fellow workers, not one life was lost.

It was bedlam inside the warehouse, barely illuminated by the light of a single lantern, as more than fifty men, women and children shouted, screamed and cried in their panic. They were still in mortal danger. The hurricane was blowing towards the river and it became necessary to breach a dike, so that flood waters could be let through into the river. Like demons with whatever tools they could find—axes, crowbars, picks, shovels—Harris and his companions worked desperately to cut the dike, from the exposed side in the

George H. Harris, Paul's father

Cornelia E. Harris, Paul's mother

unrelenting wind.

When daylight came, the storm subsided, but a terrible sight greeted the survivors. The only land in view was the top of the levee and this was covered with drowned horses, cows, hogs, hens and birds, and numerous other walking, creeping and crawling things, the most repulsive of which were hundreds of squirming, writhing, deadly moccasin snakes.

Only two buildings remained standing, the half submerged Pizatti house and the warehouse. The waters all around were strewn with the wreckage of houses and, the strangest sight of all, a three-masted schooner on what, the day before, had been dry land. Hundreds of square miles were devastated and there was great loss of life, particularly in Buras, only a mile and a half away. At Bayou Creek eight hundred people died, and one island in the delta was swept clear of every living thing. Property losses ran into millions of dollars during the storm, the most violent ever to strike the Mississippi Delta.

Many years later when describing the incident, Harris said: 'The horror and the suffering of that episode still remain in my memory.'

Despite the strenuous work he undertook as a young man, Harris was of frail physique, and subject to bouts of serious illness as he grew older. This serves to emphasize the courage and indomitable spirit of the man in carrying that little girl at arms length in such frightening circumstances.

After his experience in the delta, Harris returned to New Orleans. He again failed to obtain employment on a newspaper but to his surprise discovered that his old position was still open in Clark's marble and granite company in Jacksonville, and in October 1893 he returned to Florida to renew his association with George Clark. Only seven months had passed since he last worked for his friend, but he had packed into them experiences and adventures others would not see in a lifetime.

With half his 'vagabondage' over, however, it was time to begin saving for his future. By arrangement with Clark, Harris was given new territory to travel, both in the United States and elsewhere, such as the Bahamas and Cuba.

Harris agreed to work for Clark for twelve months only and, as this time drew to a close, he notified his friend of his intention to move on. Clark, naturally, was reluctant to see him go, and asked if there was anything else he could do to help, or if there was anywhere else Harris would like to go on his behalf.

'Yes,' replied Harris, 'but I doubt your willingness to send me.' Clark quickly discovered what his salesman had in mind: it was Europe. The astute businessman was more than willing to accede to the suggestion for he saw the advantage of complying with Harris's wishes and, at the same time, helping his friend to see more of the world.

Within two weeks Harris was once more crossing the Atlantic. This time he travelled as a passenger, armed with instructions from his employer to visit the granite regions of Scotland and the marble producing areas of Ireland, Belgium and Italy. He was authorized to negotiate the purchase of the products of the various quarries and Harris, with his legal background and his knowledge of marble and granite, was the ideal man for the job.

He now had the opportunity to see more of the countries he visited. For the third time in eighteen months he set foot in Britain, but this time with a mandate and the wherewithal to travel far and wide. He visited Scotland for the first time, and spent a day or two in Edinburgh. There, unknown to him, lived a fourteen-year-old-girl in a street known as Comely Bank Avenue. Her name was Jean Thomson. More than a decade later they met in Chicago.

Harris travelled extensively, visiting England, Scotland, Ireland, France, Switzerland, Italy, Austria, Germany, Belgium and Holland. During these travels he made many new friends. Two are worthy of special mention—Frank Watts, who subsequently became a member of the Rotary Club of London, and S. A. McFarland of Carrara, Italy. Harris remembered the McFarlands with special affection. As a visitor to their home he received courtesies seldom accorded to strangers. Through their kindness, he enjoyed many tours of the northern Italian countryside.

At the end of his visit, the McFarlands, perceiving that their guest was a little short of money to continue his travels, prevailed upon him to accept a small loan. This, they argued, would enable him to visit such historic places as Piza, Leghorn (Livorno), Rome, Florence, Venice and Vienna. Harris recognized the genuine thought behind the offer and, with a deep sense of gratitude, accepted. The loan was quickly repaid. Harris never forgot the thoughtfulness of the McFarlands. Their generous gesture had given him an even broader perspective, and reinforced still further his growing belief in the ultimate brotherhood of man.

With three and a half years of his 'vagabondage' now expired, Harris gave serious thought to his plans for settling in Chicago. This brought home to him the realization of the necessity of security, and upon his return to the United States, he and Clark joined forces on a building project near Jacksonville. Six enjoyable and rewarding months were spent on this undertaking, but Harris had one more year left in which he wished to see still more of the United States. Clark, however, pleaded with Harris to remain in Jacksonville.

'Whatever the advantages of settling in Chicago may be,' said Clark, 'I am satisfied you will make more money if you remain with me.' Harris gave his classic and often quoted reply: 'I am sure you are right, but I am not going to Chicago for the purpose of making money, I am going for the purpose of living a life.'

Clark was well aware, of course, that his young partner's intention of practising law in Chicago was in accordance with the wishes of his grandfather. However, there was still one year left, and Clark made a further offer to Harris.

For preference, Clark lived in Florida, but his business interests extended through every state of the Union and he maintained an office in New York. He now prevailed upon Harris to take charge of the New York office. Harris, who was keen to know more about the largest city in the United States, accepted the offer, but on the clear understanding that it was a temporary arrangement. Harris left his friend under no illusion. He would be moving to Chicago to take up his chosen profession in 1896 and would not change his mind.

Finally, four months before the end of the five years he had allowed himself to see the world, Harris bade goodbye to his friend and turned his steps westwards. He was now almost twenty-eight years old. His boyhood was behind him, as were his recently completed travels and adventures. A wonderful foundation had been laid. He had seen life in some of its worst as well as its best aspects. He had found good in the midst of evil, and friendliness in places that appeared bereft of goodwill. He had travelled far from the tranquillity of his grandparents' comfortable home in the Green Mountains. He had suffered the hardships of the Atlantic, and had seen the squalid turbulence of slum areas in the world's largest cities. He had come through unscathed in body from the horrors of an awesome natural disaster. His travels had taken him from one side of the United States to the other, and he had visited almost all the countries of western Europe.

These experiences and the friendships he had found in unexpected places influenced the thoughts of Harris as he matured. As his years of 'vagabondage' came to an end on a cold day early in 1896, he reflected on the years since 1891 and wondered what the future held.

Would he achieve success in Chicago? Of one thing he was certain. His decision to spend five years of his life in 'knock-about' experiences had been immensely beneficial. It was an action which was right for him if not for others. Because of his experiences his vision had been broadened and he understood his fellow human-beings better.

'As the train thundered westwards from New York,' said Harris, 'I mused back over the twenty-eight years of my life, and how the vagaries of fate had dictated my upbringing. It could all have been so very different. Had my father not been compelled to sell his business and break up our home, I would not, at the impressionable age of three, have been deprived of what should have been the controlling influence of my natural guardian, my father.'

Although his grandparents lavished loving care on him, Harris never fully experienced what he called 'the priceless boon of companionship between father and son'. At a critical period in his upbringing, when he needed firm and kindly guidance, he became more or less his own master. At a time when he needed discipline, it was not forthcoming from the one source that mattered most, his parents.

Splendid educational opportunities were provided for him by his grandfather but, youth being what it is, he had placed little value on these opportunities at the time, 'for it is only natural,' he observed, 'to appreciate least those advantages and benefits most easily gained'. Instead he acquired knowledge by experience, without the help of a father's guiding hand. 'It is true,' said Harris, 'that experience is a fine and certain teacher, but it is also a slow and sometimes painful process of learning.'

He acquired, mainly by his own efforts, a unique awareness of what his attitude towards his fellow men should be. After the hardships he endured, Harris felt the task facing him as he settled down in Chicago was trifling in comparison.

The new task began on 27 February 1896. Nine years later, almost to the very day, he would bring into being a movement that, in his own lifetime, extended to every corner of the world, and made his name synonymous with 'service'.

CHAPTER 10
First Days in Chicago

Chicago, the city in which Harris chose to settle, developed around the site of Fort Dearborn, which was established in 1803 but abandoned during the War of 1812. It is located at the southern end of Lake Michigan and is ideally situated almost in the centre of a straight line across the continent. Chicago expanded rapidly, especially after the city received its charter in 1837, and became the unrivalled metropolis of the west. It was also, and this is what fascinated Harris, a social whirlpool where racial, political and religious extremes met, ultimately merging into a semblance of homogeneity.

Three years before Harris arrived to make his home in the city, a famous English journalist, William T. Stead, wrote a highly controversial book, *If Christ Came to Chicago*. Stead's outspoken criticism of the conditions at the time aroused such interest, a mass meeting for reform was called, and out of this was created the Civic Federation of Chicago. By the time Harris arrived in 1896, the Federation had already implemented some improvements, but their massive programme required unceasing effort.

With his academic qualifications and talents, Harris could have made his home anywhere in the United States. One is bound to wonder why he chose Chicago. Although it was then, and still is, an intriguing city, it.can hardly be described as the most attractive in America. Harris gave no special reason for his choice, merely commenting that he was fascinated by the city when he first visited it in 1889. Chicago's reputation for social unrest may, however, have provided the incentive.

Throughout the United States in 1896 there was a great financial depression, and Chicago was experiencing an exceptionally difficult time. The city had been hard hit by irresponsible over-building during the Columbian Exposition in 1893 and unemployment was rife. Half the stores and many of the apartments in the city were vacant, and dishonesty and corruption were the order of the day.

Under such conditions it was no easy matter for an honest aspiring lawyer to make a living. Harris first obtained a licence to practise law. He then rented, for a short period, a modest desk and some rooms in a shared office. Soon afterwards he displayed his acumen by renting a small suite of offices on the seventh floor of the Wolff Building, and sub-let the remaining offices at a rent that made his own quarters virtually rent free.

But Harris quickly learned that hanging up a shingle was one thing; obtaining clients was another. He anticipated that business would be slow initially but he had not allowed that he would be almost completely ignored. Harris, at the time, was one of two thousand unemployed lawyers in the city. He soon discovered the necessity of looking for clients.

His natural gregariousness soon won him friends and early in his legal career he became acquainted with another struggling young lawyer, Lewis Dalton. Dalton was able to provide many valuable pointers to economy. He introduced Harris, for example, to an inexpensive eating place on Fifth Avenue (which Dalton had nicknamed 'Hell's Half Kitchen') where, for a nickel, it was possible to buy a 'stack of wheats' with syrup.

In an attempt to attract clients, Harris spent much of his time about the Law Courts, familiarizing himself with their procedures. He frequently read law cases and precedents into the small hours, but it took him a long time to build up even a small practice. Had it not been for the passing of the Bankruptcy Act in 1898 he would have been faced with an even longer struggle. This Act sparked off an extraordinary epidemic of fraud which continued for several years afterwards, as clever lawyers found loopholes to the advantage of their clients. The way in which these frauds were perpetrated and the ingenious methods developed to cheat creditors is a fascinating study in itself. Suddenly the Courts were inundated, working overtime issuing attachment and repletion writs, all of which, of course, made excellent business for lawyers, and Harris's practice gathered momentum.

During these early years, Harris was the senior member of a co-partnership which consisted of himself, Elroy N. Clarke, a graduate of the University of Vermont and Georgetown University, and Lewis Dalton. The partnership, however, was dissolved within a few years, first by the departure of Clarke, who accepted an opening with United States Senator Wilcott's law firm in Denver, where he subsequently became one of the partners; and then, a year or two later, by the death of Lewis Dalton, in a mysterious accident in a blizzard while on an expedition in the Rocky Mountains in Colorado.

Harris later entered into other partnerships. One was the firm of Harris and Dodds formed in 1898. But in any such arrangement, Harris was always the senior partner, and he enhanced his growing reputation by becoming a member of the American and Chicago Bar Associations, the Chicago Press Club, the Bohemian Club and the Association of Commerce. All were prestigious organizations, which materially helped Harris to establish further his now thriving practice. He had arrived in Chicago with little capital but with a wealth of experience in the ways of men.

By 1900 the financial, economic and business conditions of the United States showed signs of improvement, and a dramatic change was wrought in Chicago's social and moral conditions. The work of the Civic Federation was now evident. A massive clean-up was under way, and the closure of wine rooms and assignation houses, especially those operating in the downtown districts, resulted in the segregation of vice into clearly defined and restricted areas. All the infamous big name gambling houses vanished and, by the turn of the century, there were few reminders of the city's dissolute past. Surreptitious vice continued, but on a greatly diminished scale, and the notorious redlight districts were strictly supervised.

With the return of prosperity came a general improvement in the physical condition of the city. Streets in the downtown area, which, had at times been impassable because of mud were repaved. The squalor of the ghetto and South Halstead Street seemed less pronounced. All in all, by 1900 Chicago was becoming more law abiding, its citizens were becoming more affluent and the days of the 'full dinner pail' were back.

Harris, however, had not yet adjusted fully to the Chicago way of life, and still found himself lonely at times, especially on Sundays and public holidays. He tried to interest himself in all manner of pursuits. He even attempted to become involved in the political scene but, as he put it, 'I found that I liked neither the game nor the people I found there'.

Harris retained his deep interest in people, and the way in which they lived held a particular fascination for him. He made a special study of the social conditions in the slum areas, and seriously considered taking up residence in them for further observation at close range. Growing within him, albeit perhaps unconsciously, was a conviction that such conditions not only could, but should, be improved.

A lover of the open spaces, Harris had no liking for the grimy, cobblestoned streets of the downtown business area, nor for its confining influence. On his free days he would, weather permitting, stroll on the green swards of the suburban parks, or along the dunes on the shore of Lake Michigan. All the while, however, a longing was growing within him to see again the green mountains, sparkling lakes and singing brooks of Vermont. This impulse to renew again the experiences and intimate friendships of his boyhood days became too pressing to ignore.

As soon as his practice allowed, he set himself a date for his departure. It proved to be an intensely nostalgic journey, but more than that, it marked the moment when a great idea was born.

Harris caught a train for Vermont with keen anticipation. Dr George Fox, his uncle, met him at the new station in Rutland and drove him to the Fox home in a phaeton. When Harris left Rutland in September 1889, he remembered an impressive enclosed station, but this had burned down. There were other changes. Where once, in front of the city's three leading hotels—the Bates House, the Berwick and the Bardwell—stentorian voiced porters had extolled the merits of their respective hostelries, silence now reigned. And the once bustling Merchants Row and Centre Street seemed to him, 'akin to the streets of Goldsmith's deserted village'.

However when the phaeton finally drew up in front of his uncle's three-storeyed house in Cottage Street, Harris received the warmest of welcomes from Aunt Mellie and her daughter Mattie, the cousin he had so studiously avoided at the Columbian Exposition in Chicago in 1893. The house was much the same as he remembered it, but gone were the peals of youthful laughter he recalled so well.

Dr George Fox was still in practice, but the years had exacted their toll and the aging physician was taking things easier at last. He spent most of his days on the side veranda away from the street, apparently meditating. He was as kind as ever, but seldom spoke, except in response to the remarks of others. But when Harris asked

73

him about his old bay horse, 'Billy', he became animated and showed much more interest. He told his nephew: 'I have owned many a horse in my day, Paul, but I can't ever recall having a bad one. The nearest thing to a human being I have ever seen in horse-flesh was Billy. He had as much affection as any child and much more obedience.' He told Harris how, in the severe snowstorm that occurred at the time of the death of Howard Harris, Billy had plodded unerringly through the deep snow from West Rutland to Wallingford, when Dr George could scarcely see the road.

Harris, his Aunt Mellie and Uncle George had a long and nostalgic talk that first evening back in Rutland. Harris heard for the first time all the details of his grandmother's death in 1890, and all that had happened during the years he had been away. He learned with regret of the deaths of some of his friends, and of those who had left Wallingford, their whereabouts no longer known.

The next morning Harris and Mattie drove the nine miles down the valley to Wallingford. They took the old Creek Road, every turn of which reminded Harris of his boyhood days. Down that very road, Harris realized with a pang of grief, the family funeral party had borne the remains of his grandmother on a beautiful October day in 1890, while he continued sadly with his law studies in Iowa.

As they approached Wallingford the landmarks became more frequent and poignant. They passed the Jay Newton, Robert Marsh and Hudson farms, the fair grounds, the Catholic church, the Hull farm, and the Stafford house, the home of Fay, Harris's ill-fated red-haired friend.

Then came the moment for which Paul had waited so long. They drew up before his old home. He savoured the memory for the rest of his life.

From the old Howard Harris home, now occupied by R.C. Taft and his family, the cousins went to the cemetery on Green Hill. Here they spent reverential moments at the graveside of their grandparents. Their ideals had become Harris's ideals, but the process had been so gentle and so gradual, neither grandparents nor grandchild were aware of it. Yet, they were crystal clear— integrity, tolerance, unselfishness, frugality and kindness, principles that, in the course of time, became the cornerstones of Harris's vision of a new brotherhood of men.

After spending a few more days with the Fox family, Harris took up quarters at the inn in Wallingford, and he was soon busy renewing acquaintance with old friends and familiar places. One person who helped him bridge the gulf between the pulsating present and the still well remembered past, was his old Sunday school teacher, Anna Laurie Cole. When Harris penned the final words of *My Road to Rotary* in 1946, Anna Laurie Cole was still alive, by then well into her nineties. Another such to bridge the gap was Mary Foley, once his grandmother's domestic help.

One after another, Harris visited the favourite places of his boyhood: Otter Creek, the swimming hole near the covered bridge where he and other naked youngsters had once disported themselves within plain view of passing vehicles and shocked neighbours; Fox Pond, renamed Elfin Lake since his departure; and Child's Brook. These, and the mountains and the hillsides, were all visited in turn. And as he gazed once more at the valley where he had known such happy days, he was astonished to discover that few changes had in fact taken place.

Fundamentally, he was the same boy out of whom the man had grown, and as he dreamed of the incidents of his boyhood while looking down the mountainside, he drank in the peace and tranquillity and stored it in his private gallery of happy memories. He recalled how some of his fantasies had come true. He had visited the land of Tom Brown of Rugby, Shakespeare and Dickens. He had seen for himself the rugged beauty of the land of Robert Burns and Walter Scott, and had been bewitched by the sombre beauty of the Lakes of Killarney in Ireland, from whence had come his maternal ancestors. He had climbed the Eiffel Tower in Paris, viewed the glory of a sunset over the Alps, seen the Leaning Tower of Pisa, the brilliant shading of Italian skies, and so much more.

He had been privileged to see these and other wonders of the world during those five vagabond years. The dreams of his early days had largely come true. Now there stirred within his mind another dream. Would it not be wonderful, he mused, if by some wave of a magic wand, he could take back to Chicago the friendly, well-knit life of a village community? He recalled how delightful and stimulating were the evenings when the men of the village would gather together in one place to discuss their problems. In such a community there would be the doctor, the lawyer, the blacksmith, the grocer, the hardware store owner, the veterinary surgeon and so on. Each would be a specialist in his own field. Each helped the other with his own blend of skill, knowledge or experience and

75

thereby contributed something to the benefit of his fellow villagers. Each would trade with the other, for there were no others with whom to trade. And underlying all the discussion, all the banter, was a marvellous spirit of friendship between the villagers, whether they were transacting business or just discussing generalities. It was surely here, on this green Wallingford hillside, that the concept of Rotary came to Paul Harris, although even he could not have realized the significance of his musings.

Soon his vacation came to an end, but Harris was content now that he had once again seen his boyhood home. The urge to return would repeat itself time and again in the years to come, but he was still a young man, with more than half his life still in front of him.

Harris returned to Chicago refreshed in mind and body, ready once more to take on the task of making a living. He carried within him also the glimmering of an idea, hazy as yet and still years away from fulfilment.

As he turned to take a last lingering look at the scene of his youth, life must indeed have seemed good to Harris.

There is in America an incredible city named Chicago; a rain coloured city of topless marble towers that stand among waste plots knee-high with tawny grasses beside a lake that has grey waves like the sea. It has a shopping and office district that for miles around is a darkness laid on the eyes, so high are the buildings, so cluttered up the narrow streets with a gauntly striding elevated railway, and a stockyards district that for miles around is a stench in the nostrils. . .

So wrote the British journalist and author, Rebecca West, in the 1920s, and it is an accurate picture of the Chicago Harris knew so well. The energetic pace of life in its major thoroughfares was created by quick footed pedestrians, horsedrawn carriages, streetcars, and—a new fangled mode of transport—the automobile.

Back in the 'incredible' city, Harris settled down once more to his practice. His income steadily increased and so did his ways of spending money. His circle of acquaintances grew and his membership of the Press Club provided an opportunity to indulge in the writing of short stories, several of which were good enough to be published by a newspaper syndicate. In the Press Club he met many men of literary attainment and lunched with such celebrities of the time as Opie Read, Bolling Johnson, Colonel Visscher, Press Woodruff and Forrest Crissey. The names of these men are unfamiliar now, but at the turn of the century they were known in every household.

Still a confirmed bachelor, Harris developed a remarkable knowledge of the Bohemian life of the city. Nothing delighted him more than to guide his out-of-town friends to the lesser known parts of Chicago, where he had an intimate knowledge of practically every Italian, Greek, German, Scandinavian and Hungarian restaurant. He loved to study life in all its aspects, and getting to know people from all levels of society held a special fascination for him. To facilitate his studies of the different localities, he changed his place of residence with astonishing frequency. Over a period of fifteen years from the time he arrived in Chicago, he lived in no fewer than thirty different parts of the city and its neighbouring suburbs, such as Beverley Hills, Hinsdale, Evanston and Morgan Park. Only business considerations prevented him from adopting similar migratory habits for his office locations.

On Sundays he attended the services of all the religious denominations he could find. Although he most frequently attended the Central Church during the famous pastorates of Newell Dwight Hillis and Frank Gunsaulus, he could also be found at the services of such diverse faiths as Ethical Culture, Christian Science, Quaker, Theosophical, Roman Catholic, Bahite, Jewish, Methodist, Presbyterian, Baptist and Congregational.

But Harris remained lonely. The fact was he had many acquaintances, but few close friends. He took long solitary walks in the parks of Chicago. It was so different from the well known faces and voices of the village. The vision that had formed on the hillside above Wallingford stirred again, and began to take on more tangible form. It was probably at about this time that the concept of a new club for men first occurred to him. Others say the idea came to him one summer evening when he was walking in Rogers Park, a suburb of Chicago, with a business friend who had invited him to dinner. As they strolled, Harris noticed his friend addressed most of the people they met by their Christian names. The greetings were cordially reciprocated, the smiles of welcome genuine.

Harris continued his solitary excursions. He ventured further into the country, but even there the tranquillity and friendships he sought remained elusive. Occasionally he took an all-day boat excursion on Lake Michigan. This offered a temporary and enjoyable diversion but no escape from the faceless crowds. Wherever he went, to the beaches, the parks or the boats, he found swarming holidaymakers. Everywhere there were people, but nowhere a familiar face. What he sought, although perhaps not fully aware of it, was the neighbourliness and familiarity of a small community.

Harris sought true friends, the sort who double life's joys and halve its griefs. One of his favourite quotations, always to hang on the wall behind his desk, were the words of Emerson: 'He who has a thousand friends has not a friend to spare.' In those early days in his adopted city, Harris had neither the thousand nor the one.

He grew to understand more and more that men needed the companionship of those of their own kind. He already knew, from his own experiences, that betterment in human affairs comes through travel and communication, and that this could be accomplished by first visualizing the need, and then experiencing the suffering.

Harris was one of those rare people with the priceless gift of understanding the needs of others, and he began also to think of ways and means to meet those needs. He realized that his experience in Chicago was also that of hundreds of other young men who had come from villages and small communities to make a life in the great mid-western metropolis.

Could he, wondered Harris, find some way of bringing other lonely people together? The memory of the walk in Rogers Park recurred frequently. He recalled how deeply impressed he had been by the easy friendliness and banter that had been evinced in the casual encounters, where everyone seemed to know everyone else. They were not only friends, he realized, they also traded with each other. Was this the elusive link for which he was searching?

There was no good reason why he should not, even in the midst of the city, bring some of his business friends together as a group which could meet socially on an arranged and regular basis. To a limited extent, such groups already existed in Chicago and other American cities, but there was no cohesion about such groups, no organization, no discernible pattern. There were also, of course, clubs and societies composed of men of a particular profession, trade or business. Harris was himself a member of the Chicago Bar Association, the Chicago Press Club and other similar organizations.

Gradually, Harris's dream came into sharper focus. He thought again of Vermont, where all the proprietors of the different businesses, the tradesmen and the professional men talked to and patronized each other. If a club were formed on a similar basis, reasoned Harris, there would be an especial advantage to its members in that each could have the exclusive representation of his particular calling.

In effect, it would be a mutual help club or, as one critic later described it, a 'back-scratching club', but there was one vitally important difference, the members must be friendly men, for fellowship and friendship would be the keynote of the group. This was the foundation from which the concept would progress to goodwill, understanding and service.

Harris reflected on the lessons in tolerance his grandparents had taught him, and he decided at an early stage that tolerance was also an essential ingredient. There must never be, he decided, any restrictions on the political leanings or religious allegiances of the members, and all must have a broad tolerance of each other's beliefs and opinions. Harris knew that if men were unable to accept their fellow men for what they were, there could be no fellowship, no friendship.

What Harris desired, in essence, was the transfer of the simple, uncluttered life, informal friendships and mutual helpfulness of village life, to the vaster social milieu of the city. And so the stage was set. Harris was at last ready to put his idea to the test.

He cautiously approached some of the men he knew best to ascertain their reactions. In nearly every instance the response was favourable. Harris's new club had no name then, but what he conceived we know today as the service club movement, and the time was ripe for it to be presented to a world whose social conscience was astir. In Wales, for example, at almost the same moment, a great religious revival was in the offing, and similar thoughts were being expressed elsewhere in the world.

Even Harris, however, with his almost uncanny vision of the future, could not have perceived, early in 1905, just how successful his concept was to prove.

CHAPTER 11

The Genesis of Rotary

According to meteorological records, the evening of Thursday, 23 February 1905, was bitterly cold. The skies were clear enough, but the ground was iron hard and there was thick ice on the river and the lake. The twentieth century was only five years old, and the ills that afflicted the world were as prevalent in America and in Chicago as elsewhere. Business was in a bad way, corruption and crime were rife, and the spirit of people everywhere was at a low ebb.

It has been said that nothing good comes out of Chicago. Unjust. This is the city from which Frances Willard chose to launch her Women's Christian Temperance Union in 1879 and where Jane Addams established Hull House in 1889. There are many other instances of much good coming out of Chicago. Perhaps there was no better place to found the service club movement and perhaps there was no time more opportune than the beginning of the twentieth century. It was certainly a time of change.

That evening of Thursday, 23 February Harris, now a well established lawyer, arranged to dine with one of his friends, who was also a client. His name was Sylvester Schiele, and he was in business as a coal merchant. Their choice of restaurant, Madame Galli's, was well known, and one of Harris's favourite eating places. It was frequented also by many celebrities of the day, including an up and coming young Italian tenor, Enrico Caruso. Visitors to Chicago today, however, can no longer visit this famous restaurant; it was demolished years ago and on the site, 18 Illinois Street, there now stands a huge, windowless building.

Over their leisurely meal, Harris outlined to his friend his idea for a new club for business and professional men. They would not only band together for social purposes but they would also be of material help to each other. Harris had mentioned the idea to Schiele on a previous occasion but now expanded his thoughts.

The Harris home in Wallingford, Vermont

Elfin Lake, Wallingford, a favourite childhood haunt
of Paul, across which he swam in 1935, then aged
sixty-seven

Another favourite boyhood haunt, the 'Old Swimming
Hole' at Otter Creek, Wallingford

There would be a unique advantage, said Harris, in each member having the exclusive representation of his particular trade or profession. In such a club, all memebers would be obliged to bring all their legal business to Harris's law firm; all would order their coal from Sylvester Schiele; all would get their printing requirements from another member, and so on. On this reciprocal basis, each member would enjoy the benefit of each other's custom. Harris emphasized also that those admitted to membership would naturally become friends as well as business acquaintances and would, as a result, deal fairly with and have trust in each other. Indeed they had to if they were to survive in membership. Those with a lesser standard of business ethics would soon be found out and excluded from the benefits of mutual trading. Harris remembered these principles from his Wallingford days, and he could see the advantages that would accrue from the establishment of a similar trading group in a large city.

Schiele grasped the concept immediately, and became enthusiastic about it. He agreed to go with Harris to meet two other businessmen to whom Harris had spoken, and who were now waiting for them in a nearby office. They were also clients of Harris and they already had some inkling of what he had in mind. The two men were Gustavus Loehr, a mining engineer, and his friend Hiram E. Shorey, a merchant tailor, whose shop was located in the Loop.

It is not without significance that all four men came from villages or small communities. Harris from Wallingford, Schiele from Clay City, Indiana, Loehr from Carlinville, Illinois, and Shorey from Litchfield, Maine. All admitted to being lonely in the city and to missing the close-knit life of the villages they had left behind.

And so the scene was set. Harris and Schiele crossed the river from Madame Galli's and made their way the short distance to the Unity Building. There they ascended to the seventh floor and knocked on the door of Room 711. Loehr and Shorey were waiting for them.

It was a small office, sparsely furnished with little more than a desk and a chair, but from that humble room a great social movement was ready to spring.

Still there for all to see is the Unity Building, although it is now known simply as 127 North Dearborn Street. A fine sixteen-storey block, it was built in 1893, the year of Harris's greatest adventures, by John Peter Altgeld, a former Governor of Illinois, who named it after his dream of ethnic unity in Chicago. Today its tiers of bay windows look down on Picasso's famous five-storey high sculpture, *Woman of Steel*. And along a brightly carpeted corridor on the seventh floor is an oak and frosted glass door, upon which is stencilled the notation that in this very room the first meeting of the world's first Rotary club was held by Paul Harris and three friends on Thursday, 23 February 1905.

A unique feature of the Unity Building is that it leans 86cm (almost three feet) to the north from the perpendicular but this, alarming though it may appear, is perfectly safe. Harris once occupied office space here, and another great name associated with the building is that of Clarence Darrow, the famed American lawyer.

The official date of the founding of Rotary has long been accepted, and Harris has confirmed this in his writings, but there is nonetheless an element of doubt about it. An early heading of the Chicago Club's stationery, for example, carries the notation that Rotary was founded on 26 February 1904! Harry Ruggles, one of the first five members of the club, maintained to the end of his life that he discussed the idea with Harris in 1904, and that he did four jobs of printing for the club in 1904, of which the item quoted above may have been one. So when did Rotary start? Was it in 1905 or was it in 1904? The answer may be that an attempt to launch the club was made in 1904, and indeed the evidence points to this, but that it was not successfully started until 1905. This is supported by the extant records of the subsequent meetings.

However, on that Thursday in February, Loehr and Shorey listened intently to Harris's explanation of his plan for the new club, and they became as enthusiastic as Schiele. By the end of that historic first meeting, considerable progress had been made. All perceived clearly the business advantages to be gained from membership, and all promised to try and bring a friend along to the second meeting. This was scheduled for two weeks later, 9 March, at Harris's law office in the Wolff Building.

That was how it all started. Four successful but lonely men who needed the companionship of their own kind. Harris offered them that and something more besides, a group in which each member would be of immense benefit to the others through the simple expedient of mutual trading. Harris did not at the time broach anything beyond companionship and the mutual profit motive.

What about the three men whom, with Harris, brought into being one of the most significant social organizations of the twentieth century? Harry Ruggles was undoubtedly right when he claimed that he and Harris discussed the idea in 1904. Harris would have sounded his ideas out on several friends. Rotary did not just happen. Harris was much too methodical a man for an impulsive gesture. In his judgement Schiele, Loehr and Shorey were the right men to form the first group. Let us see them as Harris saw them, three-quarters of a century ago.

Sylvester Schiele was a particularly friendly and approachable man. He was of German parentage and came from Clay City, Indiana, where he had suffered considerable hardship as a child. He had lived in a log cabin, when snow filtered through gaps in the roof and formed drifts on the floor. Unaided, he established a profitable business in Chicago, but he was also the natural guardian of his younger brothers and sisters, as well as some nieces and nephews. Schiele volunteered to serve with the United States armed forces in the brief Spanish-American skirmish in 1898, and also fought in the Santiago de Cuba campaign. He took a great interest in the welfare of others, became a key figure in charitable undertakings, and was forever at the centre of community activities and church work. Harris held him in high regard as a great humanitarian. They became the closest of friends and lived next to each other for many years. They visited each other frequently and even had adjacent holiday homes in northern Michigan. In death they are still not far apart. Harris, at his own request, was buried in a grave only one place removed from that of his lifelong friend.

Gus Loehr, although also of German parentage, was by contrast temperamental and volatile. One moment he could be heard talking vehemently and gesticulating wildly. Within seconds the mood would pass and he would become as gentle as a lamb. Loehr was generous almost to a fault. He would cheerfully give his last cent to help a friend, and no one was too lowly to be the recipient of his sympathy. Elevator operators, janitors, cleaners, all mourned the loss of a true and compassionate friend when Loehr died, a few years after he shared in the founding of Rotary. He was, without doubt, a man of character. Harris described him as a stormy petrel, with a personality that challenged everyone he met. Loehr's business affairs were as volatile as his personality, and the financial instability of his profession as a mining engineer resulted first in his

83

resignation from Rotary and eventually, only a few years later, in his untimely death. How long Loehr remained active in Rotary has not been recorded. He was certainly present at the third meeting on 23 March, but there is no mention of him thereafter. He nonetheless occupies an honoured place in the annals of Rotary, for it was in his small office that the first official meeting of the first Rotary club took place.

Hiram Shorey was also a congenial man, with a kind and agreeable disposition. A merchant tailor by profession, he constantly extolled the virtues of Maine, from whence he hailed. He was devoted to his native state and never a summer passed without a visit. Shorey sought to inculcate this same love of Maine in the heart of his son, who was to be educated there. It was Shorey's deepest wish that, when the time came, he would spend his declining years there, and in due course his wish was fulfilled. Like his friend, Loehr, Shorey attended most of the early meetings of Harris's new club, and he was in fact elected the first Recording Secretary, and the fourth meeting of the club was held in his tailor's shop in the Loop. In the long term, however, due to circumstances beyond his control, he felt compelled to relinquish his membership. He nonetheless maintained his interest in Rotary and cherished the memory of the movement's founding days.

Thus, of the original four men, only Harris and Schiele remained in membership of their creation up to the time of their deaths. Loehr and Shorey, however, earned their own places in the history of Rotary by being there when they were needed, on 23 February 1905.

The second meeting of the new club (still to be given a title) in Harris's law office was attended by seven men. The original four were joined by Harry Ruggles, who was recruited by Harris the day after the first meeting, William Jensen and Albert L. White. All were destined to play a significant role in the development of Rotary.

Ruggles, like the others, came from a small community. His birthplace was in northern Michigan, where he had been raised under considerable hardship. In 1887, when he was about sixteen, he and his Methodist family moved to Chicago, where he attended the Northwestern University, working part time as a salesman for a printing firm. He subsequently purchased a one-third interest in the firm and eventually bought out the remaining partners. A naturally friendly man, he was exactly the type the club needed. It was Ruggles who introduced singing to Rotary, now traditional in the United States, although not quite as popular in other parts of the Rotary world. Ruggles was the fifth member of the new club, so he is not usually referred to as a founding member, although his contribution exceeded by far the short memberships of Loehr and Shorey. Ruggles printed the first issue of *The National Rotarian* in 1911, and handled all the Chicago club's printing needs for many years. He is remembered also as the club's champion recruiter of new members, and is credited with the introduction of two-thirds of the first two hundred Rotarians in Chicago. When Ruggles retired he made his home in Los Angeles. On 23 October 1959, while en route to a meeting of the Rotary Clubs of Cathedral City and Palm Springs, he died of a heart attack. His son, Kenneth, became President of the Rotary Club of Chicago in 1956–7, a rare distinction in Rotary, as Ruggles himself was the fourth president from October 1908 to January 1910. The Ruggles family lived in Hinsdale, a suburb of Chicago, where Harris was a frequent visitor. The measure of respect in which Ruggles was held by his fellow members is best expressed in Harris's own words: 'As I look back over the field of early events, the work of Harry Ruggles so completely overshadows all others in connection with the founding of the Chicago club that it shocks my sense of justice to see him excluded from pictures of those times.'

William (Bill) Jensen, a real estate dealer, was introduced by Ruggles, and is considered to be the sixth Rotarian. Two weeks later, at the club's third meeting, he was elected Corresponding Secretary. The fifth meeting was held in his office at Regelin, Jensen and Company, 105 Washington Street, Chicago.

The seventh Rotarian, Albert L. (Al) White, was a manufacturer of pianos and organs. It was intended that the seventh meeting of the new club should be held at his establishment in the Chicago suburb of Englewood but, as this was a long way out, the members decided on a convenient hotel instead. This set the pattern for future meetings. Al White went on to become the second President of the Chicago club, succeeding Schiele in 1906.

The third meeting of the new club took place on Thursday, 23 March. The venue on this occasion was Schiele's office at 12th and State Streets. Although he was the leading figure of the group, Harris was averse to taking office at this stage, always preferring to work behind the scenes, and he nominated Schiele as President, Shorey as Recording Secretary, Jensen as Corresponding Secretary and Ruggles as Treasurer. Thus, although Harris was the founder of Rotary, Schiele was the first President.

It was at this third meeting that a title was sought for the new club, and it is one of the most fascinating and amusing chapters in the history of Rotary. A number of suggestions had already been made, and some of them were seriously considered; the Chicago Civic Club, the Conspirators Club, the Blue Boys, the Lake Club, Friends in Business, Windy City Roundup, the Booster Club, the Chicago Fellowship, the Chicago Circle, Men With Friends, Trade and Talk Club, and the FFF (Food-Fun-Fellowship) Club. This last suggestion prompted an unknown wit to remark that it could also stand for Free From Females!

One suggestion considered seriously was the Round Table Club. It was eventually rejected, but it is interesting to note that many years later, within the Chicago club, an officially approved 'club within a club' developed, which is called the Round Table Group. Later still, in 1927, in Norwich, England, a service organization entitled Round Table was launched for men up to the age of forty. It is now one of the strongest service organizations in the world for this age group.

Up to the third meeting, none of the titles offered had touched off a spark of enthusiasm. Harris has been credited with the suggestion of 'Rotary'. It was he who observed that they were all meeting in each other's offices in turn, on a sort of rotating arrangement; why not call it the Rotary Club? And so the title came into being.

No one thought much of it at the time, but years later it was described as a divinely inspired suggestion, for this, among all the titles offered, was by far the most unusual and the most distinctive. It proved to be a title that was not easily translated into other languages and, as the movement surged around the world, the name of Rotary, or even a slight variation of it, like 'Rotaria', came to be recognized as meaning only one thing—Rotary International.

The club's fourth meeting was held on 6 April at Hiram Shorey's tailor's shop, and the fifth at Bill Jensen's real estate office. The sixth and what eventually transpired to be the last meeting held in a member's office took place on 6 May in Ruggles' printing shop at 142 Monroe Street. Thereafter the members met at hotels and restaurants in different parts of the city. The first of these was at the old Palmer House, the second at the Breevort Hotel and the third at the Sherman House. In those early days the club adhered to the principle of rotation, and in turn came such diverse venues as the Chicago Beach Hotel, the Columbia Yacht Club, the Hyde Park Hotel, Madame Galli's, the New Southern Hotel, the Stratford Hotel, Vogelsgang's Restaurant and many more. Some of these establishments have long since disappeared to make way for new office and apartment buildings. But one that hasn't and is today's regular meeting place of the Rotary Club of Chicago is the Sherman House.

The membership of the Chicago club grew rapidly, and the 1905 group included such giants of Rotary as Charles A. Newton, who attended the third meeting. An insurance executive, he organized, unaided, the New Orleans club in 1910, became President of the Chicago club in 1923–4, and eventually retired to California. Arthur Irwin, the proprietor of a laundry, was another who attended the third meeting. Rufus F. Chapin (known to his fellow members as 'Rough-house') was Rotary International's first treasurer, and became President of 'Old No. 1' in 1918–19. Montague 'Monty' Bear was the proprietor of an engraving firm located at 57 Washington Street. He is credited with designing the first Rotary wheel in 1906. Bernard E. 'Barney' Arntzen was also known to his friends as 'Cupid'. An undertaker, he became the club secretary in 1908. Max Wolff, like Harris, was a lawyer, and he, Harris and Newton formed a three-man committee to frame the first constitution and by-laws. Charles Schneider was the club character. A florist, he brought a carnation for every member to the early meetings, but had to cease when the membership passed the fifty mark.

With men such as these and others too numerous to mention, the success of Harris's club was assured. Unlike other social movements, it was evolutionary rather than revolutionary in character and therein lies its strength. It has been able to adapt itself to the changing needs of society and to different cultures, customs, and the ways of life of the people of all nations. Harris was always aware of this and observed, on more than one occasion, that Rotary a generation hence would be different from the Rotary of today, and that Rotary the generation after that would be different yet again.

In those early days Rotary was described as a selfish movement, and to some extent the criticism was justified. The Chicago club's literature in the first few years emphasized the business advantages of membership. In fact, prospective members were often directly approached on the basis of business gain. In those first euphoric years of fellowship and friendship, allied to business advantages, Rotary did indeed look inward to the benefits of internal and mutual reciprocity of trade. Records extant in Chicago show that all the transactions between members were carefully recorded—first between members of the Chicago club, and then between members of other clubs.

But Harris's agile mind was already looking ahead. Now that the first club was successfully launched, others would follow in the course of time. But first he had to persuade his fellow members that his ideas were viable, that Rotary could become a powerful and influential movement for the common good not just for that of its members. The time had arrived to look outward rather than inward. Members had to understand the value of helping their fellow citizens as well as themselves. Harris had set himself a long and arduous road. It would tax his reserves to the utmost.

CHAPTER 12

The Wheel Begins to Turn

With increasing momentum, the Rotary Club of Chicago grew in stature. Its concept was unique and it captured the interest of the city's business and professional men. The club had no precedent, although single, isolated clubs on similar lines had been formed in Europe many years previously. One of these actually used the name 'Rotary', but Harris said he knew nothing of this at the time. Such clubs were not service clubs, nor were they clubs for business men, however, but tended to be more in the nature of literary circles or discussion groups, and they were often hidebound by rules, regulations and rituals.

Harris's new club was composed almost entirely of men who had already achieved a measure of success in business. Only later would salaried and non-profit making professional men be admitted to membership. Most of the early members had come to Chicago from small towns or villages, and the club's organization held instant appeal.

One attraction was freedom from petty restrictions. Men were attracted to a club where there were no absolutely rigid rules and no rituals. It was a club which was fun to belong to, where a member could be on first name terms with fellow members, irrespective of station, a tradition which holds true in Rotary to the present day.

Rotary offered a splendid opportunity for fellowship and the development of new friendships, as well as new business contacts. Another attraction was its exclusivity: membership quickly became a status symbol. For those fortunate enough to be admitted to membership, the club was like an oasis in the desert of their big-city loneliness. It filled a great need and wrought great transformations in the lives of some members.

Harris was elated. He was now confident that within his own lifetime, the movement he had generated in Chicago would spread throughout the United States, perhaps even further. He still had his law practice to attend to, but almost all his spare time was now directed towards developing Rotary. He took time off from his practice to contact men he thought could help. He bombarded friends with letters, old school friends, friends he had made during his travels, anyone he considered would be interested.

He drove himself hard and drove others just as hard. More and more helpers became available, men such as Adolph Jahn, B.O. 'Sunshine' Jones, Max Stienz, Will Neff (the first official 'greeter' in Rotary), and Fred Tweed, an enthusiast of community service. In 1906 the tradition of ladies' nights was introduced, and the membership grew even more rapidly as wives perceived the nature of the club their husbands had joined.

Rotarians, and others, have often wondered why Harris, although acknowledged as the founder of Rotary, was not elected to any sort of office until the third year of the club's existence. The truth was he refused to take office in those formative years. He was the architect rather than the builder, and he left the day-to-day administration to others. But his judgement in the direction of club affairs was followed and it was Harris who usually nominated the officers.

In the first two years, as the membership steadily increased, Harris ensured that club activities were almost entirely social. In this way he established a contagious spirit of fun and fellowship in an informal, easy, carefree atmosphere, and the formula was eminently successful.

Thus far, Harris had remained in the background, coaxing, cajoling, pushing the club forward. Now, with over eighty members it was time to pull rather than push, and when Albert White stepped down from his presidential term in February 1907, Harris allowed his name to go forward as President.

Immediately there was a perceptible shift in purpose. Harris wrote to his old friend in Jacksonville, George Clark, urging him to establish the first club in Florida. He travelled to New York and attempted to start a club there, but found his ambitions baulked as being too premature. He told his fellow members of his dream to see Rotary clubs established in every important city in the United States, and urged them to do everything they could to spread the movement.

Until Harris became President, the emphasis was on the business and social advantages of membership. Some members reaped substantial business advantages, others did not, but all were aware of the power and value of fellowship. What Harris now did was direct that power towards those in need. Under his inspired guidance there began a move from self-interest to an increasing concern for others. Despite opposition from some members he would not be swayed, and he now bent his indefatigable efforts to the achievement of his purpose.

Harris divided his plans for the immediate future into three avenues of activity. First, he advanced the growth of the Chicago club; second, he endeavoured to extend the service club concept to cities such as New York, San Francisco and New Orleans; third, he strove to introduce the concept of community service into the objectives of the movement.

His first ambition presented no real problem. Indeed, such was the popularity of the new club, applications for membership were pouring in. The second objective proved more difficult, but the problems were not insoluble, and he knew that time would take care of the opposition. It was his third objective that presented the greatest enigma.

The idea of service to the community was far removed from the original concept of the club. The members were not only wary of what they considered to be sheer vagary, they were also not prepared to jeopardize a good thing. Harris's first urgings fell on many deaf ears.

Nothing daunted, Harris reasoned that the most practical way of introducing community service would be to find a worthwhile cause and then induce members to work for it. This is what eventually happened, with the help of Donald M. Carter, a member who strongly supported Harris and vociferously advocated a policy of civic service.

An accident can change the course of a life or history itself. It so happened that the civic leaders of Chicago were giving some thought at that time to the provision of public conveniences in the city, but no one seemed prepared to take the lead.

Harris saw his opportunity. As President of the Rotary Club of Chicago (although the club was still unknown to most of the citizens), he called a meeting to consider this question, sending invitations to all the recognized civic leaders.

It was a bold and masterful tactic. Harris's strategy was successful and when the meeting took place more than twenty organizations were represented, among them the Chicago Association of Commerce, the Commercial Club, the Industrial Club, the City Club and the Y.M.C.A. In addition, the Mayor sent along representatives of the city administration.

As a result of the meeting, an executive committee of three, including Harris as the representative of Rotary, was formed. In Chicago at that time, only saloons and department stores provided public conveniences, and as these could be used only by patrons of the saloons and stores, vested interests were at stake. Powerful influences were brought to bear on the committee and Harris and his fellow civic minded workers operated under great difficulty.

Their eventual success is a chapter in itself. Let it suffice to record that the first public conveniences in Chicago were eventually built outside the City Hall. They are still there, a reminder of Rotary's first participation in public affairs, its first example of community service. The cast-iron entrances, next to the imposing pillars of the City Hall, look old fashioned now, but the facilities are just as serviceable today as they were more than seventy years ago.

In itself, the achievement was neither an earth-shattering nor historic event. What was important is that it marked a significant turning point in Rotary policy. The club was now looking outwards rather than inwards.

Harris was satisfied for the moment. He had proved to his fellow members the idea that an organization dedicated to service to others was a workable concept. In all probability he had little idea what the nature of that service would be in the future, but he was confident that time and social needs would determine its direction.

With his community service concept now established, Harris turned his thoughts to his second objective, the creation of other Rotary clubs throughout the United States. Early in 1907, during the first year of his Presidency, he made a second attempt on New York. The friends he had contacted on the previous occasion were Dr Vernon O. Whitcomb, an old University of Vermont classmate, then practising osteopathy in New York, and Daniel L. Cady, another classmate, who was now a lawyer. Now Harris turned to a close friend in the Chicago club, Fred Tweed, a manufacturer of glass signs, who was an enthusiastic supporter of the concept of community service.

On Harris's behalf, Tweed went to New York and brought Whitcomb, Cady and some of their friends together. But progress was slow and it was not until 1909, much to Harris's disappointment, that the Rotary Club of New York was founded.

He always wanted New York to be the second club in Rotary but by 1909, it was the sixth. In 1908 and early in 1909, four cities in the 'Golden West' had seen the value of Rotary, and in quick succession had established the second, third, fourth and fifth clubs making 1908 a year which stilled some of the vociferous opposition to Rotary extension.

The honour of becoming the second club fell to San Francisco, and again it was one of the Chicago club's members who was instrumental in bringing it into existence.

During the spring of 1908 Harris, still flitting from one residence to another, was staying at the Hyde Park Hotel in Chicago. It was at about this time he met an old university roommate, Manuel Munoz, an American of Spanish descent. To escape from the hot summer months in Chicago, the two men rented rooms in Elmhurst, a suburban town just outside the city, but in the autumn they moved back into Chicago and rented a suite of rooms in the Del Prado Hotel. By now, Harris had interested Munoz in Rotary and submitted his friend's name for membership. Munoz was duly admitted, a step that proved significant for the Movement.

Munoz was a salesman for the Sperry and Hutchinson group, and from time to time travelled to the West Coast on business. On one such trip he was in San Francisco, and had occasion to do business with a man named Homer Wood, who became interested in what Munoz told him about the Rotary Club of Chicago.

A lawyer by profession, Wood immediately contacted Harris and began to correspond with him about the possibility of forming a club in San Francisco. The result is now Rotary history. In November 1908, Wood was the prime organizer of the world's second Rotary club, thereby earning himself an honoured place in the annals of Rotary. The importance of the occasion was highlighted by the engagement of a well known American industrialist, Charles M. Schwab, as the principal speaker.

Wood went on to found the third Rotary club in nearby Oakland in 1909; assisted, with the aid of Arthur Holman and Roy Denny, in the formation of the fourth club in Seattle; and, with his brother

Walton Wood and Jerry Muma, formed the fifth club in Los Angeles.

Wood was one of the grand old men of Rotary. He became President of his own beloved San Francisco club in 1910, and in that year served on a commission to call the First Rotary Convention in Chicago. Wood lived on to serve the Movement for sixty eight more years, and when he died in July 1976 at the age of ninety-five, he had contributed immeasurably to Rotary's development.

There were other highlights for Harris in 1908. On the same evening as his inauguration as President of the Chicago Club, he inducted into membership two men whose names became an indelible part of Rotary history—Chesley R. Perry (see Appendix) and Arthur Frederick Sheldon. A remarkable man, Sheldon was the head of a highly successful school of salesmanship after previously running a book selling outfit. Sheldon coined the slogan 'He profits most who serves best'.

Harris had cause to remember 1908 in other ways, one of which caused a great furore in the Chicago club. At a meeting, it was arranged that one member, George P. Foster, an Illinois Congressman, should launch a mock attack and denunciation of Harris, who was himself a great practical joker. At the appropriate time Foster made his move and attacked the shocked Harris with a scathing criticism of the way in which Rotary affairs were being conducted. It was so convincing that Harris resigned on the spot and the club was in an uproar. It took a long time to erase the damage and thereafter all such jokes were banned.

In October 1908, Harris, realizing that his organizational abilities were needed for the expansion of Rotary, resigned as President to devote all his spare-time to extension work. By now he envisaged a worldwide fellowship of men in Rotary, all striving to serve their local communities. Chesley Perry had by this time been converted to the policy of extension, and the two men began to bombard the larger cities in the United States and elsewhere with letters, offering to visit and speak where necessary.

Their campaign bore fruit. In 1909 the seventh club was formed in Boston and Rotary stretched from coast to coast. It was not only Harris who was elated now, but most of the 'doubting Thomases' who had opposed extension. Rotary had caught on and there was no knowing where it would stop. The work of Harris and Perry took on a new dimension as they travelled to city after city, making fine speeches and encouraging the formation of clubs. The membership of the Chicago club continued to grow. Inducted into membership in 1909 was Herbert C. Angster, who became its President in 1914, and District Governor of the then 8th District in the following year. He remained a powerful voice in Rotary affairs until his death in January 1965.

The most extraordinary happening of 1909, was the formation of a 'second' Rotary club in Los Angeles. This was not an official club but one started by an entrepreneur named Herbert C. Quick. Quick was unemployed at the time and saw a golden opportunity to make money by selling memberships in an organization that he brazenly called the 'National Rotary Club of Los Angeles'. This caused great consternation in Chicago and there was a flood of angry letters to and from the promoters. The recriminations continued for some time. Indeed, it was not until 1912 that two level-headed men, one from each club, thrashed out their differences and consolidated the rival clubs into one organization.

As 1909 drew to a close, Harris and Perry worked hard at their self-appointed task of extension. One attempt to start a club in Canada had failed, but the groundwork was not wasted and within a year a second attempt succeeded. Meanwhile, Harris and Perry formulated a plan to bring together all the existing clubs at a national conference. Only seven clubs existed as they drew up the blueprint, but it was clear there would be double that number within a year. It was hard work, however. 'There were times,' said Harris, 'when I was weary and discouraged.' But this did not prevent him from aspiring to new horizons in Rotary.

Perry headed a specially appointed commission from the seven clubs of San Francisco, Oakland, Seattle, Los Angeles, New York, Boston and Portland and it was finally arranged that the conference should be held in Chicago, at the Congress Hotel, from 15–17 August 1910.

Meanwhile, Harris found time to travel to Minneapolis and St Paul where, despite vigorous opposition, he inaugurated two more clubs.

The basis of the first conference was that each club was entitled to one delegate for each fifty members, and as there were then approximately 1,800 Rotarians in the sixteen existing clubs, most clubs were able to send at least two delegates. No fewer than fourteen clubs were represented at the roll call: Boston, Chicago,

Kansas City, Lincoln (Nebraska), Los Angeles, Minneapolis, New Orleans, New York, Portland (Oregon), St Louis, St Paul, San Francisco, Seattle and Tacoma. Among the delegates were such dedicated Rotarians as Werner Hencke, who became the first Sergeant at Arms; Irwin 'Jerry' Muma, President of the Los Angeles club; Homer Wood of San Francisco; and Frank Thresher of Minneapolis, who it was, in 1911, suggested the publication of an official magazine.

Although only twenty-nine in number, the enthusiastic delegates bent to their appointed task with a will, hammering out a formula for the formation of a National Association of Rotary Clubs. It did not take them long. In just a day or two these pioneers brought into being the forerunner of Rotary International. Harris was unanimously elected the first President of the Association, and the equally dedicated Perry, who chaired the convention, was elected Secretary.

Immediately afterwards offices were rented in the First National Bank Building. These served as headquarters for both the National Association and the Chicago club. Some years later Harris moved his law office into the same building.

Plans were immediately made for the formation and admission of still more clubs. In retrospect, it seems strange that such a significant movement should have started with only twenty-nine delegates present. Today, Rotary conventions number delegates in their thousands.

No sooner had the National Association of Rotary Clubs come into being, however, than it became necessary to retitle it the International Association!

A Chicago club member, William Lauder, brought his Canadian cousin, P.A.C. McIntyre, to one of the club meetings. McIntyre was so impressed that he asked to meet Harris and Perry, and on his return to Winnipeg, he set about the task of organizing the first Canadian club. Although this did not come about as quickly as he had hoped, he eventually succeeded and before the end of 1910, 3 November to be precise, the Rotary Club of Winnipeg was formed, becoming the first club outside the United States, and making Rotary an international movement.

The year 1910 represented a pinnacle of achievement for Harris, Perry and their supporters. Life had been breathed into a movement which was destined to encircle the world and become one of the great social achievements of recorded history. Harris knew there was still a lot to be accomplished, but he now knew that the foundations were well and truly laid. Around him he had gathered a dedicated band of Rotarians to whom he would eventually hand over the reins of administration. He had toiled long and hard in the five years since 'the miracle of Dearborn Street', and it had taxed his reserves almost to the limit. He still had a law practice to see to and had to pay heed to the economic necessities of everyday existence. Moreover, shortly before his forty-second birthday in the balmy days of spring 1910, he had met his future wife.

CHAPTER 13
A Bonnie Scottish Lassie

Between 1905 and 1910 Harris had little time for leisure, but nevertheless in 1907 he became a charter member of the Chicago Prairie Club, an organization which arranged walks through the wooded areas and pleasant countryside in the hinterland. Harris, an inveterate walker, took great pleasure in the long rambles and easy companionship of his fellow members. On those weekends when he was free he would be found exploring anew the open areas of suburban Chicago.

On a Saturday afternoon in the spring of 1910 he was with a group that had been allocated a wooded area to the south-west of the city, an area known generally as the Beverley Hills-Morgan Park district. As rambling was an inexpensive and popular form of recreation, the Prairie Club had grown quickly and in under three years had more than two thousand members.

Also on the ramble through Morgan Park was a Mr H.B. Davidson who, as it happened, was a member both of the Prairie Club and the Rotary Club. Davidson had invited two young ladies to join the group for the day, Miss Jean Thomson and her sister Mary. Whether Davidson actually introduced the sisters to Harris is not known. Nor did it matter. Fate or destiny made its own arrangements!

In climbing through a fence Harris tore the sleeve of his fine tweed jacket. Jean Thomson noticed his dismay and offered to repair the rip for him. Many years later Jean said: 'It is strange, but I cannot recall whether I ever mended that tear or not.' Harris, however, was adamant that she did, and he is almost certainly right. He had that sort of memory and she was that sort of woman—forever busy with needle and thread.

Just three months after that meeting, on 2 July 1910, Jean Thomson from Edinburgh, Scotland, became Mrs Paul P. Harris.

It was a curious coincidence that in the same year that Rotary became an international movement, Harris married a lady born many thousands of miles from Chicago in a city Harris had, in fact, visited and admired sixteen years earlier.

Rotarians the world over know Harris as the founder of Rotary, but few of them know much about the woman who was his wife for almost thirty-seven years and his widow for sixteen more.

Jean Thomson's parents were John Thomson, once of a tiny village called Auchenblae in Kincardineshire, Scotland, not far from Aberdeen, and Ann Youngson, from the city itself. They were married in 1873 and quite soon afterwards moved to Edinburgh.

Jean was their fifth child but their second daughter of an eventual family of four sons and four daughters, although one of the boys died in childhood.

She was born on 8 November, 1881, at 9 Cumbernauld Street, Edinburgh, where her parents first set up home after leaving Aberdeen. Not long afterwards, however, they moved to 41 Comely Bank Avenue, and it was here that the young Jean Thomson spent her childhood.

The Thomson household was a happy and deeply Christian one, and all the children followed in the spiritual pathway paved for them by their parents. One son, the Rev John Youngson Thomson, who received his ministerial training at the McCormack Theological Seminary, acted as Chaplain to the Lord High Commissioner at the General Assembly of the Church of Scotland in 1931.

Jean Thomson was strikingly attractive. She was also pleasant in manner and speech, with gracious ways which endeared her to all she met. Rotarians in many countries recall the visits of Harris and his wife, and how charming they both were.

In her early youth, Jean Thomson served for a time as a lady's maid with several well known families, including that of Admiral Sir Charles Beresford, a friend of the then Prince of Wales (afterwards Edward VII). These experiences provided invaluable training for the years ahead, enabling her to mix easily and well, and to feel at ease with people of high rank and station.

In the course of time the Thomson family grew up and dispersed. Two brothers, Alexander and James, left for Canada about the turn of the century, taking with them their sister Annie, who married a man named Peter Walker, once a teacher in Tarbert, Scotland, and they settled down to a life of farming in Alberta.

In 1907 or 1908 Alexander and James moved on to Chicago, where they both obtained employment in the famous Marshall Field department store. Soon after settling in the city they asked their sister Jean to come and keep house for them, and eventually the entire Thomson family was reunited when the parents, John and Annie Thomson, the remaining son John, and the two remaining sisters, Mary and Joey, also came to live in Chicago.

Mary Thomson found work with the First National Bank, and Joey Thomson obtained a similar position with the Union Trust and Savings Bank. John Thomson, Jr, after he had completed his ministerial training at the Seminary, eventually returned to Scotland as an ordained minister, and took up positions at Leith, Leadhills, Greenock and, finally, Annbank in Ayrshire. Several years later Miss Joey Thomson, on a visit to her native Scotland, met the Rev John Howe, whom she had known since childhood, and they were married in Edinburgh in 1925. Her brother, the Rev John Youngson Thomson, officiated at the wedding. In the course of time the Howes had two sons, John and Andrew. The latter followed his father into the ministry and became minister first at Bettyhill and afterwards at Alness, Ross-shire.

Mary also returned to Scotland to live with her brother John at his various ministries. She never married. The last of the Thomson children to die, she was buried in the Newington Cemetery, Edinburgh, in April 1977, close to other members of the family.

Mrs Harris's parents settled in Chicago and remained there until 1935 when, well into their senior years, they decided to return to their native land to, as they put it, 'be buried in the old soil'. There they lived with their son and daughter at Annbank. When they died they were buried, according to their wishes, at the Newington Cemetery.

But, on her wedding day in July 1910, Jean's parents and all her sisters and brothers were present to see her become Mrs Paul P. Harris.

CHAPTER 14

Rotary Reaches Out

With the establishment of a permanent secretariat in 1910, much of the work Harris had borne for five years was transferred to other shoulders. It had been a long, arduous and sometimes painful grind, as Harris had to contend with heartaches as well as headaches. Overall, however, Rotary was making steady progress. The pendulum was gaining momentum.

Harris said more than once there were times when he felt desperately weary. All through the founding and growth of Rotary he had to keep up with his expanding law practice, and now he had a wife and the making of a home to see to. He knew that the time was near when he must hand over administrative responsibility to men such as Perry. He knew also, however, there were important objectives that only he could achieve.

He had, for instance, to win over the remaining 'doubting Thomases' in his own club. Harris's conception of Rotary and its future was far ahead of theirs, and they still opposed expansion despite the establishment of clubs in San Francisco, New York, Los Angeles and elsewhere. Harris predicted that Rotary would in time become established in other countries, but they were still sceptical. True, Rotary had become an international movement with the creation of the first Canadian club in 1910, but this was almost by chance. In any event, the Movement was still confined to the North American continent.

He was now ready to propose an even more radical advance: the establishment of Rotary overseas. This, he was certain would be met with strenuous opposition.

Together, beginning in 1910 and throughout 1911, he and Perry planned the extension of Rotary abroad. To Harris, Great Britain was the obvious target and London the automatic choice. Then another of those strokes of fortune that can change the course of history happened. Arthur Sheldon, that 'super salesman' member of the Chicago club, had a representative in London, and was soon going to Britain to see him. Another Rotarian, Harvey C. Wheeler of Boston, also had a business contact in England and his help was promised.

Sheldon arrived in London early in 1911 and met no difficulty in enthusing his representative, E. Sayer Smith, to co-operate with Harvey Wheeler, now also in London, in the formation of a club there. The first meeting was held on 3 August 1911 and Wheeler was elected the first President. However, he had to return to the United States by the end of the year, and on 1 January 1912, a Canadian, Arthur Bigelow, succeeded Wheeler as President.

Harris and Perry were, understandably, elated. They immediately asked Sheldon and Smith to go to Manchester and duplicate their London success. But before they could do so, Harris received the electrifying news that a club had been formed in Dublin, Ireland.

Unknown to Harris and Perry, an immigrant from Dublin arrived in California in 1885, and became a member of the San Francisco club in 1908. His name was Stuart Morrow, and when he returned to Dublin in 1910, he brought the idea of Rotary with him—and the opportunity to benefit himself!

On 22 February 1911 the Rotary Club of Dublin was formed by formal resolution, with Morrow himself as the organizing secretary. A month later, when elections were held for the offices of president, secretary and treasurer, Morrow retained his special position.

By July 1911 Morrow had moved to Belfast, where he organized the inaugural meeting of the Rotary Club of Belfast, with William Wallace as President. This meeting was held on 24 July, just ten days before the inaugural meeting of the Rotary Club of London. If Harris was disappointed that London was not the first overseas Rotary club, it certainly never showed. On the contrary, he and Perry saw immediately the value of Morrow's work and at once contacted and authorized him to continue. By the spring of 1912 Morrow was in Glasgow, where he quickly organized a club. A few months later, he turned up in Edinburgh, Mrs Harris's native city, and in September, with R.W. Pentland as the founder President, established the Rotary Club of Edinburgh. In 1913 he established clubs in Liverpool and Birmingham.

Thus, of the first eight Rotary clubs in Britain, Morrow was responsible for six, while Smith and Sheldon were mainly responsible for the London and Manchester clubs.

Morrow was without doubt one of the most extraordinary characters of Rotary's early years. His motives were open to doubt, yet he did a great deal to introduce Britain to Rotary. He was in effect a paid organizer. His job was either to start up a new club (where he retained part of the entrance or membership fee), or to recruit new members for the clubs he had established. In 1914, for example, he came to London and set himself up as a paid organizer, and in the case of the London club he received £1.00 for each new member he recruited. For this service he became known, somewhat facetiously, as 'Old Pound a Nob'.

Soon afterwards, however, he fell foul of the Council of the Rotary Club of London and his recruiting activities were stopped. By then World War I had broken out but, somehow or other, Morrow inveigled his way aboard a ship bound for the United States. Ten years later he turned up in London again, not as a Rotarian, but as the founder of the Soroptimist Clubs of America! Just how this incredible man came to found the female equivalent of a men's service club has not been explained but there he was, in 1924, presenting the charter of the Soroptimist Club of Greater London. A remarkable and irrepressible character to the end, Morrow died in California in 1942 at the age of eighty-seven.

Back in Chicago, with the doubters now vanquished, Harris and Perry directed their attention to another of their objectives—the publication of a journal for the rapidly increasing Rotary membership. This they named *The National Rotarian*, and Harris charged Perry with the responsibility of the editorial administration. It has been published regularly ever since, although it is now known simply as *The Rotarian*.

The two men were also busily occupied in making arrangements for the second Rotary convention, which was to be held at Portland, Oregon, from 21–23 August 1911. It was at this convention that Frank Collins introduced the famous Rotary slogan of 'Service above self' (although it was not officially adopted until 1950). At the same time Arthur Frederick Sheldon coined his immortal phrase, 'He profits most who serves best'. The second convention was attended by 149 delegates, and there were some great Rotarians among them: James Pinkham and Ernest Skeel of Seattle, for example, introduced the platform that year. In the elections which were an integral part of the proceedings, Harris was unanimously re-elected President of the National Association, and Perry was returned as General Secretary. Harris is the only man ever to have served two terms as President, Rotary's highest office.

Before the close of 1911 Harris made a sad journey to Racine, the city of his birth. This was probably the first time he had returned since leaving forty years earlier. He returned now to attend the funeral of his last surviving uncle on his mother's side of the family, Charles Bryan of Kentucky.

By 1912 Harris was tired. He was forty-four and for the past seven years he had worked tirelessly on behalf of Rotary. He had seen the movement extend to more than fifty clubs in the United States, Canada and Britain, with a total of about five thousand members. It had become large enough to be divided into eight administrative divisions (later called districts), of which five dealt with the United States, two with Canada, and one with the whole of the British Isles. But the nervous energy that had been his driving force during the formative years and his two presidential terms, had taken its toll.

At the third Rotary convention, held at Duluth, Minnesota, from 6–9 August 1912, Harris presided over a gathering of 598 delegates. Only two years had passed since the first constitution had been drawn up at the first convention in Chicago, but it was already in need of revision. Although Rotary had become international with the establishment of a club in Canada, and still more so with the formation of clubs in the British Isles, the movement was still known as the National Association of Rotary Clubs. This was rectified at Duluth when the title was changed to the International Association of Rotary Clubs.

But by far the most important event at the Duluth Convention was Harris's decision to step down from the Presidency. Beset with health problems he was ready to retire, although he would, of course, continue to follow the affairs of Rotary, study and suggest ways of improvement, contribute articles to *The National Rotarian*, and generally render service in an inconspicuous and unobtrusive manner.

The Rotarians of 1912, however, were in no mood to allow Harris to go as quietly as he wished. Immediately upon his resignation as President, they elected him President Emeritus for life. They did so as a tribute to the man who had written a new chapter in the history of mankind by bringing into being, not just Rotary itself but the whole concept of the service club movement. In 1912 it was still just Rotary, although a similar organization known as Sertoma was in the process of formation. Within a decade there would be several kindred organizations, all emulating Rotary with the same dedicated goal of placing service to others before themselves.

And so Harris was allowed to retire. Even before he met Jean Thomson, he had promised himself that if ever he had a home of his own, it would be in the Morgan Park area, the site of the only hill in Chicago. In 1912 he fulfilled that promise. He built a fine new house on the hill overlooking the woods where he first met his wife. Officially the address was 10856 Longwood Drive, but all Rotarians in the years that followed came to know it by another name, 'Comely Bank'. Paul and Jean Harris had named their lovely new home after Mrs Harris's childhood home in Edinburgh, Comely Bank Avenue. They spent the whole of their married life there, and in his writings Harris described the home they loved as 'a comfortable little American house fashioned after the dictates of our own hearts'. On another occasion he fondly referred to it as 'a rendezvous for Rotarians from all parts of the world'. To delight the Harrises even more as they moved into their new home, came the news that a Rotary club had been established in Mrs Harris's home city of Edinburgh!

Glenn Mead of Philadelphia succeeded Harris as President. He and Harris remained close friends for the next thirty-five years and the Meads were frequent visitors to Comely Bank. One of the great pioneers of Rotary, Mead died on 24 May 1954. Such was his prestige in his native city, a street is named after him.

Harris noted with interest the new Rotary clubs that were formed in 1912, including Toronto, Edinburgh, Manchester and Glasgow, but one that afforded him particular pleasure was the Rotary Club of Jacksonville, Florida. To assist in the club formation he sent one of the Chicago members, Elmer Murphy, to help his old friend and employer, George W. Clark. Harris was thrilled when Clark was elected the Founder President.

But it was not all Rotary in 1912. This was the year when another man entered Harris's life and greatly influenced his love of literature. He was Joseph J. 'Little Joe' Parker, a well known lawyer from Canton, Ohio, who became a member of Harris's law firm. Well into his sixties then and old enough to be Harris's father, he was a former partner of Judge Day, who subsequently became a Justice of the United States Supreme Court. Parker was a colleague of William McKinley, the twenty-fifth President of the United States, and when McKinley won the Presidency in 1896, he asked Parker to try all the cases remaining on his calendar. A student of French and Russian literature, Parker helped Harris to appreciate the works of foreign authors but, said Harris, 'he had no time for the works of Dickens'. Parker remained with Harris for ten years and was greatly missed when illness compelled him to retire in 1922.

Compared with the previous frenetic decades, the years from 1913 to 1919 were quiet for Harris, especially as shortly after his resignation as President, he suffered a serious physical breakdown from which he took a long time to recover. He was, moreover, a married man with domestic responsibilities. No longer could he hare off to faraway places at the drop of a hat to organize new clubs.

Perry, his stalwart lieutenant, was now the full-time General Secretary of the International Association, and had taken the reins of administrative responsibility. Harris was pleased: 'I am neither happy nor successful in the playing of a central role,' he said. He preferred and was content to take a back seat. He remained available for consultation as and when the need arose, and his interest in Rotary in no way abated. When his health improved, an office was established for him in the secretariat in Chicago, and from there he worked quietly and unobtrusively.

Harris's withdrawal from direct involvement in Rotary affairs, however, led to an unfortunate misunderstanding. Members began to wonder if there really was such a person as Paul P. Harris. He seldom attended the international conventions, and only rarely accepted invitations to speak at Rotary meetings, assemblies and conferences. Some thought he was dead, others that he was physically incapacitated, and were amazed when they met him to find that he was as mobile as anyone else.

Perhaps even more disturbing was the speculation that something was amiss between Harris and the administrative leaders of Rotary. An uneasy ground swell began to spread through the movement. Rotarians throughout the world had been told the great movement they had joined was founded by a young Chicago

106

attorney named Paul Harris but few knew anything more. Little wonder then that, as convention succeeded convention and he was never seen, speculation became rife.

Yet there was nothing wrong. Harris disliked the blaze of publicity. He was a fine speaker, but abhorred appearing on a public platform. As more and more doubt was cast on his existence, Harris's attitude changed, but that was several years later.

Meanwhile, from his less involved role, Harris watched the progress of Rotary. In 1913 he followed closely the proceedings of the fourth Rotary convention, held in a city he remembered well, Buffalo, New York. Among the 930 delegates were representatives from Britain and Ireland for the first time. Russell F. Greiner of Kansas City succeeded Mead as President. More and more clubs came into existence including those in the British cities of Birmingham and Liverpool, both started by the enterprising Stuart Morrow. A strange development in England was the formation of a more or less unofficial club at the seaside resort of Brighton, about which no one knew for some time. The eight clubs already formed by Morrow and Smith had organized into a loose association and, on 4 May 1914, formed themselves into the British Association of Rotary Clubs. Brighton, however, pursued an independent existence until 1917.

In 1914 Harris followed just as closely the proceedings of the fifth Rotary convention in Houston, Texas, when the number of delegates swelled to 1,288. With pride he noted the establishment of the one hundredth Rotary club in Phoenix, Arizona, which city boasted a population of only 10,000 at the time. He was pleased also when an old friend, Frank L. Mulholland of Toledo, Ohio, was inaugurated as the fourth Rotarian to hold the office of President, and heard with interest that a study of the philosophy of Rotary had been commenced. But his pleasure was tempered by the outbreak in August of World War I. The conflict involved the nine clubs in the British Isles in several kinds of war relief work, including the housing of Belgian refugees. They were led by R.W. Pentland, the Founder President of the Edinburgh club and the first President of the British Association of Rotary Clubs.

In 1914 Harris met Harry Lauder and Walter Drummond. Lauder, one of the great stage comedians and singers of all time, was a member of the Rotary Club of Glasgow. He spoke and sang to the members of the Chicago club and in 1916 wrote the words and music of a song entitled 'In the Rotary'. Drummond was a Melbourne businessman who visited Harris at Comely Bank with a view to introducing Rotary to Australia. The outbreak of war, however, prevented any development of this idea and nothing further was heard from him until 1921.

In 1915 the number of clubs in Rotary doubled! Barely twelve months after the formation of the one hundredth club, Charter No. 200 was granted to the Rotary Club of Columbus, Georgia. The 1915 convention was held in San Francisco, a city which held many memories for Harris, and Allen D. Albert of Minneapolis became the fifth President of the International Association. The rapid expansion of Rotary called for further reorganization and the first districts (formerly divisions) were created. Fifteen districts were allocated to the United States, three to Canada and one to Great Britain and Ireland.

In Britain, Newcastle upon Tyne joined the existing nine clubs, who intensified their efforts in war relief work, adding a new lustre to the ideal of Rotary service. Of special interest to Harris in 1915 was the creation of a third service organization for men, the Kiwanis, which not only emulated Rotary as Sertoma had done in 1912, but added a new dimension to the service club concept. Rotary was still by far the major service organization, but it was no longer blazing the trail. Its great work was being augmented and supplemented by kindred organizations. Imitation, Harris knew, was a sincere form of flattery.

By 1916, with his practice prospering, Harris moved his office from the old Unity Building to the more prestigious First National Bank Building. In this year Harris saw another of his ambitions realized when two members of the Rotary Club of Tampa, Florida, Angel Cuesta and John Turner, with the help of Ernest Berger, established a club in Havana, Cuba. This was the first Rotary club to be formed in a non-English speaking country. Only a short time earlier Elmer Murphy, a Chicago Rotarian, had investigated the possibility of a club in Cuba, but reported that Rotary was a peculiarly Anglo-Saxon institution that would never catch on in other countries. Yet again Harris had predicted that it would, and yet again he was proved right.

Perhaps with some astonishment, certainly with pride, he observed that 3,591 delegates attended the seventh Rotary convention at Cincinnati, Ohio, in 1916. They inaugurated as their

President, Arch C. Klumph of Cleveland, Ohio, who was later to be immortalized in the annals of Rotary as the creator of the Rotary Foundation. In 1916 there were 257 clubs in existence—230 in the United States, thirteen in Great Britain (Leeds, Aberdeen and Leicester were formed in 1916 despite war time restrictions), thirteen in Canada and, of course, one in Cuba. In round figures the membership totalled 27,000. Also of interest to Harris in 1916 was the publication of *A Talking Knowledge of Rotary*. Written by Guy Gundaker, a close friend of Harris, it was the first comprehensive statement of Rotary ideals and activities.

The war in Europe had been raging for almost three years when the eighth Rotary convention was held in Atlanta, Georgia, in 1917, and the United States had just become embroiled in the conflict. The eighth convention has since been referred to as 'The Great Patriotic Convention', and the 2,588 delegates heard reports of American Rotary clubs taking on war service of all kinds—Liberty Bond drives and campaigns for food, clothing, tobacco, books and magazines for army training camps.

Yet the convention still found time to establish the first Endowment Fund (the forerunner of the Rotary Foundation), and an interest in crippled children was aroused. E. Leslie Pidgeon of Winnipeg became President of the International Association, the first to come from a country other than the United States. Yet another landmark arrived with the formation of the three hundredth Rotary club in Huntington, Indiana. Of greater personal interest to Harris, however, was the chartering of a club in Racine, Wisconsin, the city of his birth. From Britain came the news that in addition to the establishment of clubs at Portsmouth, Bristol and Perth, two clubs had been formed in Wales at Cardiff and Llanelli, adding yet another country to Rotary's growing family of nations.

In Harris's own Chicago club the patriotism of Joseph M. Hahn and James Anderson resulted in the composition of 'The Rotary March'. The success of the movement was further endorsed when two more service organizations were created—Lions International for men, and the world's first service organization for women, Altrusa International.

As World War I drew to its close in 1918, a record 4,145 Rotarians gathered in Kansas City for the ninth convention—a special 'Win the War' convention. John Poole, of Washington, D.C., was elected President and gave the news that the four hundredth club had been established in Fort Scott, Kansas, and total membership had passed the 40,000 mark. In far-off South America another man was carving himself a niche in Rotary history. Born Herbert Coates in Britain, he was by 1918 a South American businessman who went by the Latinized name of Herbierto Coates. On a business trip to the United States he was greatly impressed with Rotary, and on returning to Uruguay he organized the Rotary Club of Montevideo, the first club to be established in the southern hemisphere.

With the cessation of hostilities Rotary advanced more rapidly, and a significant leap forward was made in 1919 as the concept spread to the Philippines, China, India, Panama and Argentina, bringing the number of countries in which Rotary was represented to fifteen. The tenth Rotary convention, held in Salt Lake City in 1919, was attended by 3,038 delegates, and in that year another milestone was achieved when the five hundredth club was chartered at Fremont, Nebraska.

Yet another men's service organization came into being when a group of Optimist clubs joined together to found Optimist International, and women's service clubs really came into their own with the founding of Zonta International and the National Federation of Business and Professional Women.

Harry Lauder (now Sir Harry) returned to visit his old friends in the Chicago club, but it was not an occasion for singing and dancing. He had lost a son just before the end of the war, and he delivered a moving and eloquent address in which he condemned war. It was at this meeting that he coined the phrase 'Rotary is the golden strand in the cable of international friendship'. The members of the Chicago club had cause to mourn three of their own members who did not return from Europe. Harris knew them well—Andrew Lowndes, D.E. Whipple and Douglas Wray.

Not far away, in Seymour, Indiana, a Dutch businessman named Anton Verkade attended a Rotary meeting, and was greatly impressed. Three years later he established Rotary in Holland and is fondly remembered as the Father of Dutch Rotary.

Harris recalled other memorable moments in 1919. On 20 November the Rotarians of the Chicago club and their wives, at separate meetings, were addressed by Dr Charles E. Barker, a member of the Rotary Club of Grand Rapids, Michigan. His subjects were, respectively, 'A Father's Responsibility to His Son' and 'A Mother's Responsibility to Her Daughter'. Dr Barker was way ahead of his time—people simply did not openly speak about sex education in those days. But Barker was an important man—President Taft's personal physician—and commanded the respect of his audiences. Over a period of thirty years Dr Barker spoke to more than nine million students and adults in more than four thousand communities!

Earlier in 1919 Harris had some space to let in his office in the First National Bank Building. A young attorney named Reinhardt acquired the vacant rooms. He and Harris took an instant liking to each other and two years later the young man became a partner in the new law firm of Harris, Reinhardt and Vanier. Reinhardt also joined Harris as a member of the Rotary Club of Chicago, became a director in 1927–8 and a Vice President in 1933–4.

CHAPTER 15

The Death of Cornelia Bryan Harris

In the summer of 1919 Harris was called to his parents' home in Denver, Colorado. His mother was greviously ill after many years of poor health, and Harris was at her bedside as she died. 'By this time,' he said, 'my mother was badly broken in health, and was totally blind and helpless.'

Harris entertained mixed feelings about his parents. He clearly deeply regretted, and may have resented, their inability to provide him with a normal home life. Although, as he sadly observed, no one could have wished for a finer upbringing than was given him by his grandparents, he had seen little of his parents when, as a little boy, he most needed them.

He made frequent references to his father's lack of courage, while at the same time extolling this quality in his mother. He observed, as an example, that the extravagances of his father were less conspicuous than those of his mother but, conversely, were certainly far more personal. Cigar bills and kindred expenses could hardly be considered among the necessities of life, said Harris, but then neither could the employment of a maid when none was needed. The truth, painful though it must have been to Harris, was that no one could describe either of his parents as good providers for their family.

Harris was fifty-one when his mother died and she was into her seventies. They had in effect been separated for forty-eight years, the only reunions being the two abortive attempts to set up homes in Cambridge and Fairhaven. His mother was perhaps handicapped by being the baby of a large family, and she obviously came to regard as her right the luxuries and conveniences of a high standard of living.

Grandmother Harris and Paul, as he grew older, sometimes had quite heated arguments about who was the most to blame for the

The 'little red schoolhouse' in Wallingford, Vermont

Paul Harris in the uniform of the Vermont Military Academy

unhappy circumstances of his parents. One comment by Pamela Harris, revealing though it was, greatly angered Harris at the time: 'Your mother is very wasteful, Paul; some women can throw more food out of the back door with a spoon than their husbands can put in the front door with a shovel. Your mother seems to me to be that kind of a woman, I am sorry to say. The idea of her keeping a servant and sometimes two of them was ridiculous when your father was having all that he could do to supply necessary food for her and the children.'

It was easier for Pamela Harris to see the faults of her daughter-in-law while, conversely, she seemed oblivious of her own son's faults. In his hurt, Harris answered with some asperity: 'Mother kept help in the kitchen so that she could go out and give music lessons. We would have starved to death if she hadn't.'

'Oh no, it has never been that bad, Paul,' replied his grandmother, 'and the first duty of a mother with six children is to stay at home with them. Whatever else may happen, that's where her place should be. If she will attend to her family, things will come out right somehow. I have seen many cases where it has worked. Providence seems to take care of widows with children. Pa would never have let them suffer if things were going right in the home and, more than that, your father would have done much better in his work if he could have had the inspiration of a good well regulated home. That would have been much better than gee-gaws, or anything else money can buy.'

Harris knew, deep in his heart, that there was logic in what his grandmother, who never spoke ill of anyone, had said. It brought him to the realization that happiness, contentment and peace depend far more on orderliness, thoughtfulness and kindliness than upon impractical genius, spasmodic effort and keeping up appearances. To the end of his life, however, Harris insisted that his mother was wonderfully courageous while his father, he said, could hardly lay claim to that virtue.

Harris never turned to his parents for aid, no matter how troubled the times. Indeed, over the years, he had learned not to depend on them. 'On the contrary,' he said, 'it had always remained for me to help them in their times of trouble, which were regrettably frequent.'

CHAPTER 16

Rotary in the Post-War Years

In creating the Rotary movement Harris had, as someone later commented, 'builded better than he thought'. Harris always had a clear vision of the future of Rotary, and the remark is a little less than generous. However, even Harris did not foresee the speed with which his great concept would be accepted.

He blazed the service club trail, and others were quick to follow the course he had set. In 1920 came the establishment of Civitan International (the first club had been organized in 1917), yet another service organization for men. Rotary played no small part in assisting the formation of these new clubs. Where Rotary clubs were already in existence, and where the classifications were filled, Rotarians unhesitatingly recommended eligible men for membership in the new organizations—Kiwanis, Lions, Civitan, Sertoma, etc.

Rotary itself was still expanding and there seemed no limit to its boundaries. History was made yet again in 1920 when the first Japanese club was organized in Tokyo, and the 7,213 delegates attending the eleventh Rotary convention at Atlantic City had even more to cheer about. They heard that Angel Cuesta, the Tampa Rotarian who founded the first non-English speaking club in Cuba, had duplicated his feat in Spain, his native country, where he established the Rotary Club of Madrid, the first Rotary club in continental Europe. Cuesta had, moreover, financed his own trip and left a substantial sum of money for the furtherance of community service in his native city.

Two other great friends of Harris were in the news in 1920. Estes Snedecor of Portland, Oregon, was inaugurated as the International President at the convention, and George Treadwell, who only the year before was a Charter Member and Secretary of the Rotary Club of Shanghai, was appointed full time secretary of the Chicago club. Treadwell continued as secretary for twenty-seven years until 1947.

The twelfth Rotary convention in 1921 was historic in that it was the first to be held outside the United States. Where more fitting than the city where Mrs Jean Harris was born—Edinburgh? Harris, however, was still in indifferent health and pre-occupied with the demands of his law practice, and was not able to join the 2,523 delegates at the convention. Nonetheless he played no small part in the convention's organization, and it was at his suggestion that Arthur Sheldon delivered an inspired address to the delegates.

The year 1921 was outstanding for Rotary and for Harris. Two special commissioners, both great friends of Harris, were appointed to spread Rotary's objective of 'International goodwill and peace'. Their names are inscribed indelibly in the annals of Rotary history. They were James W. Davidson of Calgary, Alberta, and Colonel J. Layton Ralston of Halifax, Nova Scotia. They gave of their time freely in the establishment of clubs in Melbourne, Australia, and Wellington, New Zealand, and brought into Rotary such great future members as Sir Henry Braddon and William Osborne in Australia, and Sir George Fowldes in New Zealand. Jim Davidson went on to further the cause of Rotary in the Far and Middle East some years later, while Jim Ralston became a great Canadian statesman. From 1926 to 1930 he was the Canadian Minister of National Defence, the Minister of Finance from 1939 to 1940 and, for a second term, the Minister of National Defence during World War II, from 1940 to 1944.

Elsewhere in the world, clubs were established for the first time in South Africa, Mexico, Peru, Denmark and France, where the Rotary Club of Paris grew out of the Allied Rotary Club of Paris, which had been in existence since 1918.

The second Canadian to be President was inaugurated at Edinburgh and although Crawford McCullough came from Fort William, Ontario, his name lent itself well to the historic venue of the 1921 convention. Appropriately, as the convention was held in Britain, the one thousandth Rotary club was formed in the ancient city of York.

In 1922 Harris attended a meeting of the Rotary Club of Washington, D.C., and while in the capital, laid a wreath at the Tomb of the Unknown Soldier. Curiously, the name of the Rotary Sergeant at Arms of the Washington club in those days was George Harris, a name identical to that of Paul's father.

Raymond Havens of Kansas City became the President of Rotary International in 1922, when at the thirteenth Rotary convention at Los Angeles, attended by 6,096 delegates, the Constitution and By-laws were thoroughly revised. The title, International Association of Rotary Clubs, was shortened to its present title of Rotary International. Similarly, the title of the British Association of Rotary Clubs was changed to Rotary International in Great Britain and Ireland. Certain other points of procedure were also clarified and a standard club constitution was made mandatory for all clubs organized thereafter.

With new clubs organized in Brazil, Norway and Holland, the time had long since passed when the sceptics wondered whether Rotary would succeed. The question now being asked was how far the movement was destined to go? Harris's reply was the same; 'The best is yet to be.'

There was an element of danger at one time that the movement would split into different factions, especially at national levels. But in the capable hands of the brilliant administrator, Perry, and a now highly efficient secretariat, the danger was averted.

Harris frequently paid tribute to those who did so much to help in the advance of Rotary, and in 1922 he singled out one remarkable instance of 'service above self'. Fred Teele was at that time employed as a civil engineer and was President of the Rotary Club of Mexico City. So impressed was Teele with the ideals and objectives of Rotary, he resigned his $18,000 a year position to take up a $5,000 a year post spreading the cause of Rotary in Europe. As a result of Teele's hard work and self-sacrifice, a branch office of Rotary International was opened in Zürich, Switzerland, in 1925.

The fourteenth Rotary convention in 1923 was held in St Louis, Missouri, the home of one of the earliest clubs. It was a notable convention in that the 6,779 attending delegates were addressed by Warren G. Harding, President of the United States, who said: 'If I could plant Rotary in every community throughout the world, I would do it, and then I would guarantee the tranquillity and forward march of the world.'

Delegates heard reports of the tremendous response from clubs all over the world to alleviate the distress caused by the great earthquake which had devastated Japan. They were told that Rotary had spread its umbrella yet again by admitting new clubs from Belgium, Italy and Chile. And before they left St Louis, the

116

delegates installed as their President, Guy Gundaker of Philadelphia, one of Harris's greatest friends.

In little more than a decade Harris saw his dream spread to all the continents. It had jumped the Atlantic to Britain and Europe, crossed the Pacific to China, Japan, Australia and New Zealand, and back across the Indian Ocean to India and South Africa. South America had also been conquered.

During this time Harris remained in the background. He contented himself with his membership and some minor activity in his own Chicago club and visits to a number of clubs in the United States. His law practice was now thriving and Reinhardt, a fellow club member, was a wonderful partner and associate. Even so Harris, now fifty-five, declined an invitation to attend the unveiling of a plaque in his honour at Racine. In so doing he revealed a particularly instructive side of his character.

The Rotarians of Racine are proud, and rightly so, that Harris was born in their city and they have honoured his memory in a number of ways. But they were deeply disappointed when Harris declined to attend the unveiling of his plaque in Island Park in 1923. Throughout his life Harris fought shy of personal publicity, submitting only when it was inevitable. He always placed the interests of Rotary above himself and in the following letter, dated 29 October 1923, he explained why he declined to attend the ceremony at Racine.

My dear Harold

Friday of last week my friend Jack Hollowell was taken sick and has been confined to bed ever since. His secretary called me up on Friday morning and asked me if I would go to his home on Saturday, as he had a matter concerning which he desired to talk with me. I gladly responded and Saturday morning Jack laid before me, in eloquent terms, your generous intentions towards the writer.

Rotary has many different aspects to me. Sometimes its progress seems like a succession of fine impulses. It was certainly a fine impulse which prompted you and your club members to tender me the honor which you have in mind. Though I was but little more than three years old when our family moved to Vermont, I have very vivid memories of my childhood days in Racine. My grandfather, Henry Bryan, was the second

Mayor, I believe, and my father was in business there for some years. Cornelia Bryan, my mother, was the youngest child of a large family, most of whom lived and died in Racine. I attended the funeral of my last surviving uncle, Charles Bryan of Kentucky, in Racine twelve years ago.

The names of Northrup, Blake and Case were associated with my childhood days in Racine. I have visited on two or three occasions the old nurse who piloted my steps in the very early days. I believe she died a few years ago and that her husband died about the same time.

I think that Harbridge is the name of the man who bought my father out and that he still lives in Racine.

From the above you will gather some impression of what Racine has meant to me. The memories are, of course, a bit shadowy but nevertheless distinct enough so that they are indeed memories. Mr. Northrup, Sr., on the occasion of one of my visits, took me to see the humble home in which I first saw the light of day. I was born on the shores of old Lake Michigan and shall presumably spend all my remaining days there. More than half my life has been spent not far from the lake shore.

I cannot be otherwise than deeply appreciative and seriously impressed with the sentiment that you and yours have manifested and it is therefore with the deepest possible regret that I have to inform you that it would be entirely inconsistent with all of the past precedents established by me were I now at this time to play a part in the ceremonies you have planned. I suppose that my position may impress you as strange and I must admit that I feel that explanations are quite as likely to deepen the misunderstanding as they are to clear things up. Perhaps I can not advantageously go further than to state that I seem by nature best adapted to serve Rotary in my own quiet way. There are many others whose service naturally inclines in another direction. I have at times, in recognition of more or less insistent demand, endeavoured to mould myself to fit the popular conception but my efforts have thus far failed. I am afraid that I must always remain just myself and as the Creator fashioned me.

I am neither happy nor successful in the playing of a central part. My visits to clubs are therefore confined to instances where there is work to be done and where I seem to be the one upon whose shoulders the responsibility particularly falls.

Believe me most sincerely and gratefully yours,

Paul Harris

The ceremony of dedicating the plaque at Island Park thus went ahead without Harris, but his absence in no way affected his relationship with the Rotary Club of Racine. Members had their just reward a year later when, on 14 October 1924, Harris was the distinguished guest of the club. At this meeting he told the story of his life 'and a most interesting one it was indeed', reported the *Racine Journal News* the following day. Strangely, however, there is apparently no record of this visit in the files of Rotary International.

It was a memorable year in other ways for Harris and the Rotary movement. At the great fifteenth convention held at Toronto, a record total of 9,173 delegates heard that the total membership had passed the 100,000 mark and that Switzerland and Bermuda had joined Rotary's ranks. Everett W. Hill of Oklahoma City was inaugurated as President of Rotary International for 1924–5, while in Britain another great friend of Harris, the Rev Canon W. Thompson Elliott of Liverpool, began his year as President of Rotary International in Great Britain and Ireland.

In Chicago in 1924, Rotary made news of a different sort. One member, Almer Coe, an optician, was approached by the police to see if he could identify a pair of spectacles in their possession. He could and did and that solved the memorable Bobby Franks murder. Coe had made the spectacles for the son of a prominent Chicago family, a boy named Nathan Leopold. Leopold and a school friend, Richard Loeb, planned and committed what they thought was the 'perfect crime'. Both were imprisoned. Loeb died behind bars many years later but Leopold, rehabilitated, was released in 1963.

Harris had not been back to Wallingford since his visit there in 1900, and he had never taken his wife to see his boyhood home. Now, a quarter of a century later, he decided to revisit the scenes of his youth. In the spring of 1925 they made the long journey from Chicago to the still vividly remembered places of his early years. Together they visited the spots he knew so well. Despite the passage of time little had changed. In his mind, as he showed Wallingford to his wife, Harris lived again the halcyon days of the 1870s and '80s.

The old house his grandfather built some eighty years earlier was as staunch and proud as ever. The couple visited the old swimming hole at Otter Creek and Fox Pond, now called Elfin Lake. They lunched at the modern True Temper Inn, which now occupied the site of the old town tavern of the stage coach days. They called in to see Anna Laurie Cole, Harris's old Sunday school teacher, and Mary Foley. In turn they visited the little red schoolhouse, the fine old church and the home of Fay Stafford. And, of course, they spent some time at the hillside cemetery where his grandparents and other relatives lay buried.

Harris thought back to the time when he and his brother Cecil, now working as an extension officer in Rotary International, had arrived in Wallingford, to be welcomed by their anxious grandparents. Harris's thoughts turned also to his parents. Of his father, now living alone in Denver, and of his mother, who had died six years earlier. 'But it was my grandparents,' he said, 'who early in life instilled in me the ideals I later brought to Rotary.'

The sixteenth Rotary convention was held in Cleveland, Ohio, from 15–19 June 1925, and all attendance records were again broken when 10,216 delegates were present to welcome in as their new President, Donald A. Adams of New Haven. Once, in Hartford, Connecticut, in the company of Adams, Harris was suddenly taken ill at a meeting and rushed to the Yale hospital. Fortunately he quickly recovered and the following evening addressed a large gathering at New Haven. Harris and Adams recalled this episode whenever they met, which was often.

It was in this same year that Joey, Mrs Harris's sister, who had come to the United States with her seventeen years earlier, returned to Scotland to marry her childhood sweetheart, the Rev John Howe. The couple eventually settled at Dundee and Harris and his wife visited the Howes there on several occasions in the years that followed.

Rotary continued to grow. Clubs were established in five more countries in 1925—Guatemala, Austria, Portugal, Czechoslovakia and Hungary. Another landmark was passed when Club No. 2,000 was chartered at Ketchikan, Alaska.

In 1926 Harris first departed from his policy of remaining in the background, when, for the first time since the inception of Rotary twenty-one years before, he visited a Rotary club on foreign soil.

It was with a deep sense of pride that the Rotary Club of Bermuda welcomed and entertained Paul and Mrs Harris on the evening of 17 March, on the occasion of the second anniversary of their charter night. Included among the guests on that historic occasion were a number of local celebrities, one of whom was Dr Francis L. Patton. Dr Patton, an honorary member of the Bermuda club was, it will be recalled, President of Princeton University during part of Harris's time there in 1888. In his address that evening Dr Patton paid eloquent tribute to his former pupil and to the movement Harris had created. During the days that followed Paul and Mrs Harris were entertained to tea by the venerable eighty-four-year-old educator and his wife.

A few months later the seventeenth Rotary convention was held at Denver, Colorado. The 8,888 delegates who attended heard of the further advance of Rotary into Sweden, Finland, Venezuela and Colombia, and of the creation of yet another service organization, the Round Table, in Great Britain, founded by Louis Marchesi, a member of the Rotary Club of Norwich.

Harry H. Rogers of San Antonio, Texas, was Rotary International's President in 1926–7 and he was as enthusiastic as everyone else when Round Table was founded. Rotary was now well established in Britain, but there was nothing similar for the next generation of businessmen and young executives. In the United States there were at least two such organizations, Active and the club called 20–30, and others were springing up in Canada and Australia.

CHAPTER 17

The Passing of George Harris

Paul's father, George Howard Harris, died in his Denver home in December 1926, aged eighty-four. Like his father before him, George Harris retired in his forties after inheriting the family fortunes on the death of Pamela Rustin Harris in 1890.

There is no doubt that Harris's father, despite his shortcomings, was an intelligent and well educated man; nor is there any doubt that he made a number of determined attempts to re-establish himself after his series of business failures. Unfortunately these efforts were of an impractical nature. He dreamt up a series of inventions which would bring him instant wealth including such oddities as a newspaper holder to hang on the wall, a lamp-chimney cleaner, and a device intended to protect railway companies against the misappropriation of cash fares, which were then paid by passengers to the fare-collecting conductors on trains.

None of these inventions brought him the success and the fortune he pursued. George Harris also considered himself to be a good writer, and indeed had flair. He wrote articles for newspapers and periodicals, and several were published and paid for, but nowhere did he find the fame and fortune he so earnestly sought. He had acquired a quite astonishing range of knowledge and his contributions roved over a surprisingly wide field with nothing, apparently, beyond his reach or, perhaps, his imagination. History, politics, religion, philosophy, geology, science—all were within his sphere and he was never backward in expressing his opinions.

Even in the midst of his tribulations George Harris retained a sense of humour. When an unspecified newspaper published one of his longer and better articles without tendering compensation George Harris sarcastically remarked: 'Thank God I wasn't charged for advertising space!'

Harris recalled another instance of his father's humour with this little piece of philosophy: 'Son, the cheapest commodity there is in the world is advice. Everyone is willing to give it. No one wants it. You might as well keep it to yourself.'

Harris was at times severe in criticism of his father, but it was perhaps the venerable Howard Harris himself who rendered the final verdict. When the old man died in 1888, he willed that one-third of his not inconsiderable estate should go to his daughter, Mrs George Fox, another third to his widow to dispose of as she pleased, but the remaining third, he directed, was to be held in trust by Dr George Fox for his only son, George, who would have the income from this throughout his lifetime.

George Harris objected strongly and vehemently to the trustee-ship, and in his rage against what he considered a rank injustice he subsequently brought charges against his brother-in-law for malad-ministration of the trust. 'Uncle George', as Harris referred to his uncle-in-law, attempted to explain the trusteeship to Harris, but Paul would have none of it. 'No explanations were needed,' said Harris. He regarded his Uncle George as one of the most honour-able men he had ever known.

One suspects that Harris aided his parents on more than one oc-casion, especially in the later years when his law practice prospered, but he admits to only one instance of direct financial assistance. When he came of age in 1889 Harris had saved $1,500, a substan-tial sum of money almost a century ago. The moment this became available, Harris paid the obligations of his father's family, 'of which there were many and of a pressing nature'.

But whatever reservations Harris retained about his father's weaknesses, he cherished one fond memory. At the time of his mother's death in 1919 he wrote: 'My father waited tenderly on my mother for those latter years, lifting her from her bed and placing her on her wheel chair, patiently feeding her with a spoon, hanging on to her every word.'

'It was,' averred Harris, 'the great transformation of my father's life, compensating for and expiating the shortcomings of the earlier years.'

CHAPTER 18

In the Steps of Rotary

Harris, often accompanied by his wife, began to appear in public. He was seen at Rotary conventions and assemblies, and toured many parts of the United States, Canada and Mexico, visiting clubs whenever the opportunity offered.

In 1927, the year in which Lindbergh completed the first solo flight across the Atlantic, Harris returned to Racine again, but this time in his official capacity as President Emeritus of Rotary International. He was there to attend the second annual conference of what was then the 13th District. The conference was held on 28–29 April and it was on this occasion that he delivered a major address to 639 Rotarians and 'Rotaryannes' in which he reviewed the first twenty-two years of Rotary. It was received with tumultuous applause and the President-elect of Rotary International, I.B. (Tom) Sutton of Tampico, Mexico, who was also at the conference, had reported: 'Paul Harris made a splendid speech, very comprehensive, and by far the best I have heard him make.' The following day the *Racine Journal News* carried Harris's speech and the main proceedings of the conference in exceptional detail.

Throughout 1927 Harris was the recipient of publicity of a quite different nature when a silent motion picture film was made of 'A Visit to the Home of Paul Percy Harris'. The film was made under the direction of a member of the Chicago club, 'Chic' Sale. Still in the archives of Rotary International, the fifty-year-old film would probably evoke some amusement today for its quaint early motion picture technique, but it remains invaluable as a record of Comely Bank, the Harris home for thirty-five years.

Arthur H. Sapp of Huntington, Indiana, was inaugurated as the President of Rotary International at the eighteenth convention. For only the second time the convention was held overseas, at Ostend in Belgium. The proceedings were opened by King Albert, himself a

Rotarian, who observed in his address to the 6,413 delegates that he thought he might be the only one in his classification! The King said a great deal more than that, however, re-affirming the concept of Rotary in these words: 'The great Rotarian ideal, essentially a humanitarian ideal of brotherhood, may have an efficient application in the broad sphere of international relationship. Friendliness in international relations can be fostered by friendliness in international trade.'

Frank Lamb, a member of the faculty of the University of California, published in 1927, *Rotary—A Business Man's Interpretation*. Lamb, one of the great Rotarians of the era, visited Australia and greatly influenced the development of Rotary there.

Harris was himself busily engaged in compiling his first book in 1927. The year previously he had written *Rotary and Its Founder*, his first autobiographical work, and this had been published serially in *The Rotarian* between June and November 1926. He was now engaged on a revised edition, which was scheduled for publication in book form in 1928 under the title of *The Founder of Rotary*.

It had been a good year for Rotary. Seven more countries had been brought within the sphere of influence—Paraguay, Costa Rica, El Salvador, Ecuador, Bolivia, Java (Indonesia) and, to everyone's delight, the last of the major European nations, Germany. Few had the foresight, however, to visualize that Rotary in Germany would be extinguished within a decade.

It was an interesting year also for Harris's own Chicago club, although the incident was not relevant to Rotary per se. Four of the club's members, George Lytton, Virgil Brown, Sheldon Clark and Herman Fabry, officiated at the famous second Dempsey-Tunney heavyweight championship fight. This was the controversial 'long count' contest in which Tunney was knocked down but then went on to win.

As 1927 drew to a close plans were formulated for Harris to visit Rotary clubs overseas, and soon he was to embark on a decade of intensive travel on behalf of Rotary. During these ambassadorial journeys he and his wife were scheduled to visit every continent and meet thousands of Rotarians in almost every country where Rotary had become established.

But, as he worked on the manuscript of his first volume of memoirs, Harris reflected on the accomplishments of less than a quarter of a century. The concept of Rotary had captured the interests of sincere and dedicated men everywhere. Many of these men were of high rank or had risen to positions of fame and prestige through meritorious achievements. But of perhaps even greater significance was that where men were unable to gain admission to Rotary because their classification was occupied, they had initiated alternative service clubs, following in the steps of Rotary.

When Harris brought the Rotary Club of Chicago into being in 1905 he introduced the concept of the civilian service club in a new and organized form, and although businessmen's luncheon clubs in a less tangible form had been in existence for several years prior to 1905, it is now acknowledged that the Rotary Club of Chicago was the first of its kind—the true service club, the first organization to incorporate community service in practical terms.

The luncheon clubs which preceded it were quite different. They were, in the main, loosely organized gatherings with no discernible pattern of administration. As such it is doubtful whether they would ever have amounted to anything more than small localized meal-time get-togethers.

Harris had a far more viable plan when he met with Schiele, Loehr and Shorey in the Unity Building. His method of organization was unique, almost radical, and included even then were all the essential features of service clubs as we know them today. The vital ingredient was the principle of classification. This restricted membership in any club to a specified quota (in Rotary's case it was to be, with certain limited exceptions, one member from each business or profession). With some modifications here and there, all the service organizations that followed Rotary have been based on the original plan, as was the constitution of the Rotary Club of Chicago and, subsequently, Rotary International itself.

The fact is, when Harris conceived the idea of the civilian service club, he generated a highly significant social phenomenon, one that succeeded beyond the wildest dreams of the first Rotarians. From a single club in 1905 Rotary alone has grown to almost 18,000 clubs in 1978. This is a tribute to Harris and to those who had the vision and the faith to believe that man's inherent goodness will be irresistably drawn to a way of life that is, in itself, a powerful force for peace and understanding among men of all races, creeds and cultures. Of even greater import than the success of Rotary itself is that it triggered off the whole service club movement. Men are always ready to jump on the bandwagon of success and Rotary was certainly that.

There were those, such as the organizers of the 'National Rotary Club of Los Angeles', who saw a commercial opportunity, and there were those who applied for Rotary membership in the early days for business gain rather than from humanitarian motives. But these were the exceptions, not the rule, and when the value of Rotary was understood it brought in its wake a multiplicity of similar organizations based, for the most part, on the service principle as enunciated by Harris.

Harris's club was to all intents and purposes another club for businessmen, albeit with differences, in which it was intended that members traded with each other on an exclusive and reciprocal basis. In those days Rotary's critics (and they were plentiful) alleged that the arrangement was a purely selfish one, a criticism that was not altogether without justification. The early members were not, it is true, concerned with helping any but themselves in the field of commerce. But, along with this basic policy of developing mutual business interests, Harris from the outset instilled into the membership a new and significant element, the spirit of fellowship and friendship. The members quickly became aware that they could be of assistance to each other outside their business interests, and from there it was but a short step to the realization that this same principle of service could be applied to others not directly connected with the membership.

This is the principle on which all service clubs have been organized and operate. It matters little whether the club is Rotary, Lions, Kiwanis, Civitan or any of the many others. What matters is that each provides community service where there has been none before. Harris, with Rotary, provided the impetus.

The service club movement of modern times is both gigantic and influential. It is a movement which has brought nothing but good in its train and in this sense it is unique. Over more than seventy years Harris's creation, in either its original or modified forms, has developed and adapted itself through experience to meet the changing needs of society, the fluctuating requirements of each generation, and the needs and customs of changing cultural values. It is this adaptability that is one of the keys to the success of Rotary and its kindred organizations. Perry, the first General Secretary of Rotary

127

International, expressed it admirably and succinctly when he observed that Rotary (and by analogy the entire service club movement) is an evolutionary rather than a revolutionary movement.

Rotary's membership rules have been subjected to fierce criticism from time to time. This is inevitable and due primarily to the unique rule of admitting only one member from each classification in each club. This has made membership both privileged and exclusive, and therein lies both a strength and a weakness. It means, for example, that if there are ten equally good medical practitioners in a small community with only one Rotary club, nine must be excluded from membership. Inevitably this aroused resentment. It meant that men who could make excellent Rotarians were excluded. Such men, anxious to make their own useful contributions to the community seek alternatives, and the result is the creation of parallel organizations. And so an impetus, unintentionally, was given to the whole service club movement. The total number of men involved in service to their communities grew rapidly from hundreds to thousands and eventually to millions.

That the new organizations followed in the wake of Rotary in no way detracts from their great service work, and the value of such organizations to the communities they serve is inestimable. They provide service where Rotary, with its numerical limitations, cannot meet all the diverse needs of a community. The various service organizations do not compete with each other but work in close harmony, frequently co-operating directly in major projects. 'Fellowship and friendship,' said Harris, 'are the foundation rocks on which Rotary was built.' This same spirit of fellowship, friendship, goodwill and service is inherent in every service organization.

In general terms Rotary and its sibling clubs can be described as 'associations of business and professional men (or women) devoted to the principle of service to society'. The typical service club exemplifies this by combining fellowship and friendship among its members with voluntary community service in a wide variety of forms. Each organization, without exception, stresses the essentials of good citizenship irrespective of country, and the highest ideals of service. Each has its own high principled motto and carefully thought-out creed. In the instance of Rotary the motto is 'Service above self'. Sertoma International has as its motto 'Service to Mankind'. The Kiwanis say simply 'We build', and the Lions, 'We Serve'.

128

The Green Hill Cemetery in Wallingford, Vermont, where
Paul's grandparents and other members of the Harris family
are buried

Rotary's 'First Four' – Silvester Schiele, Paul Harris, Hiram Shorey and
Gus Loehr

The Unity Building in Chicago, where, on 23 February 1905, Paul Harris
brought three friends together

The majority of service clubs are in or near cities and usually have between thirty and fifty members, but there are some notable exceptions, especially in Rotary. In Chicago for instance there is only one Rotary club, Harris's 'Old No. 1', and this has a membership of almost seven hundred. Houston, Texas, is even bigger, with over eight hundred members and there are sufficient classifications to make clubs of this size possible. But against this reluctance to divide and sub-divide there are those who maintain that single clubs with large memberships are unwieldy and prevents members from getting to know each other individually.

Most Rotary and other service clubs meet on a given day each week for lunch, although some others prefer to meet every two weeks. Another variation is that some clubs meet during the evenings; some even meet for breakfast! Rotary is traditionally a luncheon club, more so than the other service organizations, but there is an increasing tendency to form evening clubs.

The value of the work of the service club organizations cannot be overemphasized. Several hundred thousand community projects are implemented each year. These range in size and complexity from such simple projects as sponsored walks and Easter egg hunts, to major long-term projects such as the building and equipping of hospitals and homes for senior citizens.

All are deeply concerned with and strongly support youth activities and all have formed junior service organizations for younger people, an example of which is Rotary's Interact and Rotaract clubs for high school, college students, and other young men and women up to the age of twenty-eight. These are, of course, further extensions of the original concept, which have come into being since the death of Harris.

Let us look now in more detail at the service club organizations which sprang into being during Harris's lifetime.

129

CHAPTER 19

Rotarians, Kiwanis, Lions *et al*

By far the largest organizations are Lions International, Rotary International and Kiwanis International. Rotary is the oldest of the three major service clubs and the most international. It has more clubs outside the United States than either the Lions or the Kiwanis although both, especially Lions International, are extending their territories.

The International Association of Lions Clubs, better known by its shorter title, Lions International, currently ranks as the world's largest service club organization. It has adopted more lenient rules than Rotary in that it does not follow the classification principle as rigidly. As a result it has recruited from a wider field than both Rotary and Kiwanis. At the time of writing Lions International has more than 26,000 clubs and more than one million members in 150 countries or territories, giving an average club membership of about forty. Club activities are well planned and fall into eleven distinct groups: work with boys and girls; citizenship and patriotism; civic improvement; community betterment; education; health and welfare; international youth exchange; safety; sight conservation and aid to the blind; agricultural needs; and United Nations and international affairs. The Lions were founded by an insurance executive named Mervyn Jones and came into existence in 1917. By 1920 the membership had doubled and clubs had been established in Canada. Since then clubs have been founded in all parts of the free world. Lions headquarters are in Oakbrook, Illinois.

Kiwanis International, founded in Detroit in 1915, is the third largest organization. The latest information available gives it a total membership of more than 300,000 in more than six thousand clubs (an average of fifty per club). Most of the clubs are in the United States and Canada, although Kiwanis are now represented in forty other countries. The title, an unusual one, is derived from an old Indian word meaning 'We make ourselves welcome'. Its rules for membership are more rigid than the Lions but more lenient than Rotary; they may, for example, recruit two members from each business or profession. As with Rotary and Lions, the Kiwanis are well organized and have well planned activities similar in most respects to the community and international projects of its two kindred organizations. Kiwanis have greatly expanded their influence by sponsoring two boys' service organizations—Key Club International for high school students, and Circle K International for college students. These correspond approximately to Rotary's Interact and Rotaract clubs, although Interact and Rotaract admit both sexes to membership. There are about 3,700 Key Clubs with a membership of more than 90,000, and eight hundred Circle K Clubs with some ten thousand members. (Rotary's Interact is composed of about 3,500 clubs with a membership of almost 80,000; Rotaract has about three thousand clubs with a membership of 60,000.) Although founded in Detroit, the headquarters of Kiwanis International is now in Chicago.

In addition to the three principal organizations there are a number of smaller associations. The first of these was the Exchange Club. This was founded in Detroit in 1911 when a group of businessmen who for some years had been meeting informally at lunches decided to emulate the success of Rotary. In 1917 the title was changed to its present one of the National Exchange Club. Very much smaller than the 'Big Three', it has never captured the interest of a sizable membership. By 1960 this was quoted as 85,000 in 1,500 clubs, but a more recent source quotes only 45,000 members. All the clubs are in North America and the association's headquarters are in Toledo, Ohio.

In 1912, in Kansas City, Missouri, a physician, George W. Smith, finding his classification in the Rotary club already filled, founded Sertoma International, a clever title which comes from the slogan 'Service to mankind'. Although an active organization with sound objectives and well planned activities, it has only 32,000 members in 850 clubs in the United States, Canada, Mexico and Puerto Rico. The headquarters of Sertoma International are in the city where it was created, Kansas City, Missouri.

Optimist International came into being in 1919 when eleven hitherto independent Optimist clubs convened in Louisville, Kentucky, to found a new organization. The most unusual feature of

Optimist International is that it attempts to develop optimism as a philosophy of life. But it is also an active service club and promotes good government, civic affairs, respect for the law, patriotism, service to youth and friendship among all people. As with the major organizations it promotes and sponsors a wide range of community service projects, laying special emphasis on work with young people. The organisation has a membership of more than 100,000 in more than 3,000 clubs. Its headquarters are now in St Louis, Missouri.

Civitan International was founded in 1920 in Birmingham, Alabama (where it still has its headquarters) by a physician named Courtney W. Shropshire. It dedicates itself to displaying the Golden Rule in action and to the task of developing better citizenship. Its motto, 'Builders of good citizenship', spells out its policy. Although small in numbers, with only 35,000 members in 1,100 clubs, Civitan's activities include the care of orphaned and crippled children, aid to mentally retarded children, aid to veterans, the control of crime and city improvements. It has expanded internationally and there are now Civitan clubs in Europe. It has also sponsored Civitan clubs in some four hundred high schools and colleges in the United States.

While the foregoing are the principal service club organizations service clubs have also been created specifically for men in the twenty to forty age group. Five of these organizations banded together on 8 April 1945, to form the World Council of Young Men's Service Clubs (better known to its members as Wo-Co). These were the Kinsmen clubs of Canada, the Apex clubs of Australia, the Active and 20–30 clubs in the United States, and the Round Table clubs of Britain and other parts of the world. In 1960 the Active and 20–30 clubs amalgamated into one organization, Active 20–30 International.

The Kinsmen clubs, which were founded in Hamilton, Ontario, in 1920, are confined to Canada and are the only all-Canadian service clubs. They were founded by Hal Rogers, the son of a Rotarian who greatly encouraged his son's enterprise.

Apex clubs are found only in Australia, South East Asia, Papua, New Guinea and Sri Lanka. The first Apex club was formed on 10 March 1931, after developing from a more nebulous group formed in 1930, the Geelong Young Business Men's Club. When the Apex clubs held a conference in Geelong in 1932, Harris sent them a long message of encouragement.

The Active 20–30 clubs are confined to the United States and Central America. Both clubs were founded in 1922, Active in Aberdeen, Washington, and 20–30 in Sacramento, California, by a young businessman, Paul Claiburne.

Round Table, as previously mentioned, was founded in Norwich, England, in 1927, by a young member of the Rotary Club of Norwich, Louis Marchesi. The title, incidentally, was one of those proposed for Harris's new club in 1905. Round Table has been particularly successful, and although by far the greater proportion of its members come from the British Isles, the movement has developed internationally and there are 'Tables' in fifty-three countries—wherever the four other young men's service organizations have no representation.

One of the drawbacks to membership in a young man's service club is that membership is automatically terminated at a given age, usually forty. Many of those leaving graduate to membership of Rotary, Lions, Kiwanis or one of the other clubs with no age limit. Unfortunately, however, many are lost to service clubs because their classifications are filled or they are ineligible on other grounds such as residence or place of business.

One attempt to overcome the disappointment experienced by those forced to resign their membership occurred in 1936 when a '41' club was started in Britain. There are now many such clubs but they are not, despite the fine work frequently carried out by them, recognized as true service clubs.

Thus far we have looked at organizations designed only for men, but the service club movement initiated by Harris has also been applied to women, and there are now several women's service organizations.

Among them is the pioneer Altrusa International. This was organized in Nashville, Tennessee, in 1917 'to help solve community and world problems and promote international understanding'. It followed Rotary's example in that it admitted to membership in each club only one member of a specific business or profession. Clubs have been established in the United States, Canada, the British Isles, Mexico, Bermuda, Guatemala, Puerto Rico, India, Australia, New Zealand and the Philippines. The latest statistics give Altrusa a membership of 18,000 in 550 clubs. The movement's headquarters are in Chicago.

In 1919 the Quota club was organized in Buffalo, New York, by the Kiwanis club of that city. It has been described briefly as a civic service club for women holding executive positions or owning their own businesses, but it follows generally the principle of service to the community. Its motto is, 'We share'. Quota has established over four hundred clubs in the United States, Canada, Mexico and Australia, and claims more than 12,000 members. Its headquarters are now in Washington, D.C.

Also in 1919, in St Louis, Missouri, came the much better known National Federation of Business and Professional Women's Clubs, which is now represented in almost every country. It grew out of the work women performed during World War I. With 178,000 members it is by far the largest of the women's service organizations and publishes a well known periodical, the *National Business Woman*. The movement's international headquarters are in Washington, D.C.

Zonta is another service organization for women. Like the preceding two it was founded in 1919 and, like Quota, originated in Buffalo, New York. It describes itself as a classified civic service organization of women in the business world and in the professions. With headquarters in Chicago there are 630 clubs in forty-five countries with approximately 15,000 members.

Although not the largest, Soroptimist International is perhaps the best known of the women's organizations. It was founded in Oakland, California, in 1921 by, it will be recalled, the astonishing Stuart Morrow who, ten years earlier, established Rotary in the British Isles. Membership is confined to professional and executive businesswomen and, like Rotary, each member must represent a different business or profession. The stated purpose of Soroptimist International is to advance world peace and the status of women. The association is divided into three federations—the Americas, Great Britain and Ireland, and Europe. The international headquarters are in Philadelphia. In the mid-1970s the movement claimed a membership of more than 45,000 women in thirty countries. The title is compounded from the Latin words *soror* (sister) and *optima* (best).

In 1921 the Rotary Club of Macon, Georgia, aided and counselled in the formation of yet another women's organization, Pilot Club International. Pilot promotes international peace, cultural relations, high standards in business and community improvement. It has about 17,000 members in the United States, Canada and other countries. Its headquarters are still at Macon.

In Great Britain, in addition to the Soroptimists and the other international women's organizations, there are two major service organizations—the Inner Wheel, membership of which is confined to the wives of Rotarians, and the Ladies' Circle, which similarly confines membership to the wives of members of Round Table clubs. The first meeting of Inner Wheel was held at Manchester on 10 January 1924. The ladies wanted to use the name of Rotary in the title of their new club but permission for this was refused by Rotary International. The first Ladies' Circle club met in June 1930. Both have expanded internationally and have well organized co-ordinating secretariats for similar clubs in the United States, Canada, Australia, New Zealand and elsewhere. A name often applied to the wives of Rotarians, especially in the United States, is 'Rotaryannes', but it has no official standing.

All of these service organizations, whether they be for men, women or young people, have the same basic objective of community service. Each is treading its own road in its own way, but all have one aim in common—understanding and co-operation between men and women of every race, every creed and every culture, and the realization of the ultimate dream of permanent peace and goodwill.

Significantly, no service clubs are permitted to exist behind the Iron and Bamboo curtains, or anywhere else where there is a totalitarian regime. There were once Rotary clubs in such countries as Czechoslovakia (the ill-fated Jan Masaryk was a Rotarian), Latvia, Estonia, Rumania, Poland, Bulgaria, China and Cuba. There are none in these countries now, nor were there any in Germany, Italy or Spain during most of the years they were governed by Hitler, Mussolini and Franco.

Harris witnessed some of these disappointments during his lifetime but his faith in Rotary never wavered.

CHAPTER 20

Outward Bound to Europe

Both Harris and his wife had long wanted to return to Britain—he to see again the places he had visited more than thirty years earlier, she to see the homeland and the family she left behind twenty years before. The opportunity came in 1928. For Mrs Harris especially, who was suffering from a nervous disorder, the benefit of her native air and a reunion with her brothers and sisters seemed a quick way to recovery. For both of them it was a journey to be remembered for the rest of their lives.

Harris looked forward to the voyage. He was returning to Britain, not as a deckhand on a cattleboat, nor as a salesman for a marble and granite company, but as the founder and President Emeritus of Rotary International. As such he was assured of a tremendous welcome by many of the almost three hundred clubs that had by now been chartered in the British Isles.

The couple sailed from Montreal in May after Harris attended a meeting of the Rotary club of that city. The Rotarians of Montreal accompanied the couple to the docks and gave them a great send off as the *Laurentic* steamed down the St Lawrence River to the open Atlantic. At that time the ship was one of the largest and best of the famed passenger liners plying the North Atlantic and it was an ideal crossing. They landed in Glasgow to a warm welcome from Mrs Harris's brother, sister, cousins and friends, and for the next few days were feted in Greenock, where the Rev. John Youngson Thomson then had a ministry.

Then Harris took off alone to travel through Britain and Europe on a goodwill Rotary tour, while Mrs Harris remained in Greenock in the kind and capable hands of relatives. Travel in those days was arduous and time consuming and for sixty-year-old Harris, exacting. In ten weeks he visited more than fifty clubs and spoke at most of them. When time allowed, he visited traditional beauty spots.

From Greenock, birthplace of James Watt, he travelled to the Burns country around Ayr where, as he put it, 'I worshipped at the shrine of the immortal bard of Ayr, Robert Burns, and sat at the same table where Robbie, Johnnie, Tam and their companions were wont to sit all those years ago'. Robert Burns also had a wife named Jean and had written a poem specially for her. It was a great Harris favourite:

> Of a' the airts the wind can blaw
> I dearly like the west
> For there the bonnie lassie lives
> The lassie I lo'e best:
> There wild woods grow and rivers row
> And monie a hill between;
> By day and night my fancy's flight
> Is ever wi' my Jean.
>
>   *   *   *
>
> There's not a bonnie flower that springs
> By fountain, shaw or green;
> There's not a bonnie bird that sings
> And minds me o' my Jean.

After Ayr, Harris paid a long anticipated visit to the Lake District and the Lakeland town of Keswick. Next he travelled south to the Shakespeare country and made a lightning visit to Oxford, where he met William Morris (afterwards Lord Nuffield) whom he described as the 'British Henry Ford'. While in the midlands he also visited Warwick and Kenilworth Castle. The Rotary Club of Warwick had been disbanded the year before Harris's visit and was not re-chartered until 1965.

From the midlands Harris went directly to London, where he was met by two well known British Rotarians, Tom Stephenson, the President of Rotary International in Great Britain and Ireland, and Vivian Carter. Carter, recently resigned as the Secretary of the British association, had, only a few months previously, published *The Meaning of Rotary*, but without identifying himself as the author.

Two hectic days of enjoyable British hospitality followed, including a visit to the London home of Harris's favourite author, Charles Dickens, who lived at 48 Doughty Street from 1837 to 1839. A visit was also paid to the original 'Old Curiosity Shoppe' and other places of interest, but what pleased Harris above all else was the welcome he received at Waterloo Station where he went to wish 'Godspeed' to 275 British and Continental Rotarians on their way to the International Convention at Minneapolis.

Harris made his first ever speech to a British Rotary club in Birmingham in May 1928. He chose as his subject, 'The Genesis of Rotary', and in his dry way he later described his talk as a dismal effort. That, however, was not the opinion of the many Rotarians who came to Birmingham to hear him.

From Birmingham he crossed the Irish Sea to Belfast where he spoke again. After the meeting he was driven by enthusiastic Belfast Rotarians to see the famous Giant's Causeway. Wherever he went, a sight-seeing trip was invariably a part of the programme.

Harris travelled the length of Ulster and over the disputed border into Eire to a meeting with the Rotary Club of Dublin. While in the city he visited the President of Eire, William Thomas Cosgrave. Dublin, naturally, held a special fascination for Harris for it was here that the resourceful Stuart Morrow established, in a somewhat unorthodox but nonetheless effective way, the first Rotary club in the British Isles in 1911.

Harris recrossed the Irish Sea to Liverpool, the first city in Britain he visited when he landed there from a cattle boat in 1893. Here he gave a memorable speech on 'Rotary and Its Critics'. Even he admitted the speech was one of the best he had ever delivered. During his short stay he was taken to see the magnificent Liverpool Cathedral in the course of construction and, something more diversionary, the famous soap works at nearby Port Sunlight, a model industrial town founded by the firm of Lever Brothers.

A zig-zag journey across the waist of England followed, beginning with two days at Leeds. His itinerary from there included short visits to Harrogate, where he dedicated a boys' camp, York (the one thousandth club in Rotary), and several cathedrals, castles and abbeys in the vicinity. It was but a short journey from Leeds to Nottingham, the home of Robin Hood and the city where Charles I had raised his standard to begin the Civil War in 1642. But of greater interest to Harris was a visit to the university established by Jesse Boot Trent, a pioneer of workers' welfare in Britain and the founder of a nation-wide chain store.

Harris's first speech in London was at a luncheon meeting of the

Rotary Club of London in the Hotel Cecil. Several countries as well as many cities were represented at the large gathering. The same evening he addressed a second meeting of London Rotarians and their wives, held especially for the outlying clubs of the London area such as Croydon, Streatham, Hammersmith and Watford. The next day he visited the Houses of Parliament, remembered so vividly from his first visit in 1893, and the other traditional sights in London. Before leaving for the West Country that evening, he lunched with and addressed the Rotary Club of Kensington.

By the time darkness fell over London, Harris was in the historic city of Plymouth, the port from which his ancestors may have sailed generations earlier. He spent three wonderful days in Devon and Cornwall. He took tea with Lord and Lady Seaton at their country home, was driven up and down and across the beautiful south-west coast area of England, and spent an hour in the delightful village of Clovelly, 'where the main street is like a staircase, too steep for wheeled vehicles'. These and such pleasant interludes as rambles across the moors made famous in *Lorna Doone*, and fleeting visits to fascinating villages took up a great deal of time. Yet Harris, to the delight of the Rotarians of Plymouth, Torquay, Bideford and Kingsbridge, attended meetings of those clubs. Kingsbridge, Harris noted two years later, was compelled to disband because of the economic depression and was not re-chartered until 1957.

From Devon, Harris travelled north to Bristol. 'I went there to deliver a message about Rotary. The Rotarians of Bristol in turn delivered a message to me, a message of enthusiasm and dedication it would be hard to better,' he said.

His remarkable itinerary continued into Wales. He had been in Wales once before, it will be recalled, but that was in 1893 and far to the west in Swansea. Now he arrived at Newport, to be met at the railway station by a splendid gathering of Welsh Rotarians. His first stop was at the house of Walter Meacock, whose home on a hilltop commanded magnificent views of the Welsh landscape. After an excellent tea with the Meacocks he was driven to Cardiff, and taken on a tour around the fine castle, which is situated in the city centre. That evening Harris addressed a great inter-city meeting. Not only all the Welsh but many English clubs were represented.

The next day Harris made a journey which, even by today's standards, was quite incredible. He breakfasted in Cardiff, took the

139

train for London, transacted some business there, raced a further fifty miles into Kent to address a noon meeting of the Rotary Club of Canterbury, made a pilgrimage to the famous cathedral, was driven to Dover, crossed the English Channel to Calais and, despite a delay through an irregularity with his passport, caught the train to Paris.

And it all went according to schedule. He got out of bed in Cardiff and that same evening went to bed in Paris. According to Harris the Rotarians of Canterbury had actually begun to serve lunch before he left London!

Harris's first European tour as the Founder of Rotary began with a great meeting of the Rotary Club of Paris. He delivered an address which, because of the need to translate it, was somewhat abbreviated. Nonetheless it received tumultuous applause from the Rotarians who had come from all over France to hear him. A nostalgic visit to the Palace of Versailles and then to the American Cemetery followed.

On a sultry June evening, after two days in the French capital, Harris embarked on a sleeper railcar for Switzerland and the city of Zürich, the European headquarters of Rotary International. He was met at Zürich by a fellow Chicagoan, Russell Williams, Rotary International's Assistant Manager. Williams was his guide for the rest of the stay in Switzerland and saw to his every requirement.

The first Swiss function was a splendid meeting in Zürich itself, followed by a truly memorable drive through the beautiful Swiss mountains, along the shores of the gemlike lakes to Lucerne and Interlaken and on to the lovely city of Berne. By the time they reached Berne Harris and his escort were two hours behind schedule, but still waiting was a great gathering of Berne Rotarians and their ladies, who could scarcely contain their excitement. Harris was accorded a welcome he never forgot.

Another delegation, this time headed by T.C. Thomsen, the Rotary Commissioner for Europe, met him in Basle. Before another spirited meeting Harris was shown the sights of the city, including a visit to the first Swiss university, founded by Pope Pius II in the fifteenth century.

From Basle, Harris travelled by train to the historic city of Strasbourg where the French national anthem, *La Marseillaise* was written during the French Revolution in 1792. A dinner with the

Rotarians of the newly chartered club was followed by another sight-seeing tour, including a visit to the famous cathedral.

Before leaving for Cologne, Harris spent a day in Mayence (Mainz) and the next day took a relaxing cruise down the Rhine. He arrived in Cologne about 6.30pm, earlier than had been anticipated and made use of the spare time writing some urgent letters before the dinner at 8pm. He became so engrossed in his work that he failed to notice the arrival of the anxious German Rotarians who stood around, politely waiting for him to finish his letters. The evening meeting, said Harris, was a memorable one. The Rotary Club of Cologne had only been in existence for a few weeks and newly chartered members from all the cities around were keen to mark the occasion. Among them were the President of the prestigious University of Cologne and its Professor of Sociology. After the meeting the Cologne Rotarians took Harris to the top of an observation tower from which he had a magnificent view of the city, brilliantly lit up for an exhibition then in progress. Etched forever in Harris's memory was the splendid panorama, with Cologne's superb cathedral as a magnificent backcloth.

From Cologne Harris crossed the Dutch border to spend three days with Anton Verkade, who, it will be remembered, went to a Rotary meeting in Seymour, Indiana, in 1919, and on his return to Holland set to work establishing clubs in his own country. In Verkade's company Harris attended meetings at The Hague on one day and Amsterdam the next. Of his host, Harris said this distinguished Rotarian gave him a practical demonstration of Rotary in action, 'a demonstration which gladdened my heart'.

Harris's last meeting in Europe was across the border in the great German port of Hamburg. Here he rejoined T.C. Thomsen and they spent the day discussing the progress of Rotary in Europe, which had forged ahead in the 1920s, despite the economic recession. That last evening in Germany saw Harris at yet another splendid gathering of Rotarians from many parts of Germany. Rotary had been established in Germany the previous year, but had already made great strides and its future seemed assured. Harris did not speak at either Cologne or Hamburg, partly because of the problems of translation, partly because of Germany's different customs.

However, he was disappointed that he did not meet the President of the Hamburg club, Dr Wilhelm Cuno, who was attending the

Rotary convention in Minneapolis. Dr Cuno was a man of some prominence. From November 1922 to August 1923 he was the Chancellor of Germany and remained a powerful voice in the German government until his death. He helped greatly in the establishment of Rotary in Germany, and he was reported to have said that he would rather promote the ideals of Rotary than be Chancellor of Germany again. When Dr Cuno died in 1933, Rotary lost one of its greatest champions.

Next day Harris boarded a tiny steamer which sailed down the Elbe and crossed the North Sea back to Britain. But his hectic peregrinations were far from over.

There was no Rotary club in Grimsby when Harris landed there in 1928, and arrangements were made for him to make the comparatively short journey by rail and ferry to the city of Kingston upon Hull. He arrived ahead of schedule and was missed by the eager reception committee, much to its perplexity and chagrin. All was quickly set to rights, however, and the Hull Rotarians took Harris to see their city hall. He was much more interested in another sight on the tour, the birthplace of William Wilberforce, the great emancipator and anti-slavery crusader. The sight-seeing was the prelude to another great inter-city meeting and just the first session in another whirlwind day.

Doncaster Rotarians who had come to Hull for the lunch-time meeting whisked him almost one hundred miles to Clumber Park, near Newark, Nottinghamshire, the seat of the late Duke of Newcastle. More than 1,300 Rotarians from the midland and northern counties of England were assembled there for an outdoor meeting. Harris needed to use an amplifier but even with this aid it is doubtful whether everyone present heard him. It mattered little. They were able to see him and those fortunate enough to have met him previously had a wonderful time renewing his acquaintance. Harris on his part, made new friends from Leeds, Nottingham, Harrogate, York and other cities he had visited only a few weeks before.

Later that day Harris was driven to Doncaster where yet another huge gathering of Rotarians and their wives had assembled to meet him. So tight was the schedule the meeting was not timed to start until 9.30pm, but 'by the time I started speaking,' said Harris, 'the hour hand was pointing to eleven.'

That day far outdid any other day in Harris's itinerary. The total numbers attending the gatherings at Hull, Clumber Park and Doncaster set new highs. In timing and mileage covered it was at least the equal of the dash from Cardiff to Paris.

In Newcastle upon Tyne Harris was given another tremendous reception, followed by the greatest of the inter-city meetings held during his tour. To Harris, this was Rotary fellowship at its best— the rounds of handshaking, the warm personal greetings and, as had been the case everywhere, the signing of autographs.

After the Newcastle meeting Harris was taken for the now traditional sight-seeing drive, this time along the historic Hadrian's Wall. His Newcastle friends gave him another unexpected treat the next day by driving him over the hills and through the dales of northern England and southern Scotland, taking in on the way the breathtaking scenery of the Sir Walter Scott countryside. But in making this diversion Harris arrived in Edinburgh too late to connect with a train for Glasgow, where he had arranged to meet his wife. 'But that,' he commented, 'was but a pleasure deferred, and the next day saw us together again.'

There was time still for visits to some of the Scottish clubs but before this Harris and his wife did some personal sight-seeing alone. At least one day was spent in the Trossachs, that beautiful wooded gorge in Scotland's central region, made famous in Scott's poem, *The Lady of the Lake*.

The privilege of being the first Rotary club in Scotland to be addressed by Harris fell to Glasgow. It was in all truth a memorable meeting, one which Harris himself described as a feast of fellowship. It was also the first time since the meeting in Birmingham in May that Harris spoke about 'The Genesis of Rotary', which he had edited and polished to his satisfaction. And, as Harris was speaking, who should walk in but the immortal Sir Harry Lauder, a long-time member of the Glasgow club. Harris stopped to shake hands with his old friend before continuing his speech. The most moving moment for Harris, however, came at the end of the meeting, when the Rotarians of Glasgow, led by Lauder, rose spontaneously to sing two of Scotland's sweetest songs—'Should Auld Acquaintance be Forgot' and 'Will You No Come Back Again?'

Following the meeting, Harris and his 'bonnie Scottish lassie' attended a happy gathering at the home of one of the club members. A day or so later they journeyed to Dundee, there to stay and rest awhile with Mrs Harris's sister, Joey. During their visit, Harris attended a meeting of the city's Rotary club. Yet again many Scottish clubs were represented to hear his speech.

But the highlight of their tour of the Scottish clubs came a day or two later, when Mrs Harris at last returned to Edinburgh, the city of her birth. Harris had heard his wife say often that her love for her native city was so deep she would have crawled there on her hands and knees.

Harris attended the Edinburgh club's noonday meeting alone, as this was for men only. Mrs Harris attended a special evening reception, and the rapturous welcome accorded them was for her as much as for him. It was an impressive reception and the couple were greeted with prolonged applause when they entered the room. The Rotarians of Edinburgh are naturally proud that the First Lady of Rotary was born in their fine city.

Scottish though the occasion was, the gathering included more than a sprinkling of English Rotarians. Among them was George Mitchell who, with his wife, had travelled four hundred miles from Somerset on the off-chance that Harris would sit for a sculpture. It was a request Harris could not possibly deny.

Reluctant to let their distinguished visitors go, the Edinburgh Rotarians suggested a late night drive around the city. It was already past midnight, but the party drove out to the great Forth Bridge and then around the city, viewing, as best they could in the darkness, all the places of interest.

Especially memorable, however, was the visit to a cemetery in a run-down part of the Scottish capital which, for more than ten years, was the home of the 'greatest little dog ever to draw the breath of life'. The story of 'Greyfriars Bobby', immortalized in Eleanor Atkinson's heart-stirring tale of the ultimate in canine love and devotion, is the story of the little Skye terrier who accompanied his master to Edinburgh every market day. When the dog's master died in 1858 he was buried in Greyfriars Cemetery. For the next ten years, until his own death at the age of fourteen, the little terrier slept on the grave of his master, defying all attempts to move him. It was Mrs Harris who suggested to her husband that he might like to see the statue erected to 'Bobby'. The time? 1.30 in the morning!

Finally, on 14 July 1928, the triumphant tour was concluded and Harris sailed from Glasgow to the United States. Mrs Harris stayed on for another two weeks to attend the Keswick Religious Convention with her brother, but she was there to see him off and so, to

Jean Thomson – later Mrs Paul Harris

Comely Bank, the Harris home in Chicago

Harris's surprise and pleasure, were the President and other members of the Glasgow club. Another surprise was an invitation from a representative of the White Star Line for the party to dine before the ship sailed.

During his tour of Britain and Europe Harris experienced several moving moments, but the most poignant came on that last evening. While talking with the Glasgow club's President during dinner he remarked that it would be nice if all visiting Rotarians were accorded the honour of having sung to them 'Should Auld Acquaintance be Forgot' and 'Will You No Come Back Again?'

Harris was suddenly aware of the Scotsman's reproving look. The terse reply could not have been more eloquent: 'We dinna sing songs like that for everyone.'

CHAPTER 21

Wallingford: Harris Becomes Ill

Shortly after Mrs Harris's return from Britain, the couple were off on their travels again. On this occasion they did not have quite as far to go. Their destination was Wallingford for the chartering of a club in Harris's boyhood home.

The eagerness of Rotarians for miles around was reflected in the number of applications to be present. It soon became apparent that there was no public building in Wallingford that could possibly accommodate everyone. Not to be denied, the sponsoring club, Rutland, turned to one of its charter members, past President R.C. Taft. This was the same R.C. Taft who purchased Harris's boyhood home after the death of Howard Harris forty years previously. In the intervening years he and Harris maintained contact and became firm friends. Taft was also the manager of the American Fork and Hoe Company, which had taken over the old Batchellor Fork Company of Harris's younger day. It was appropriate that Taft was the person chosen to make arrangements to hold the charter meeting in the old factory.

By the day of the meeting scores of willing employees had dismantled a substantial portion of the plant, moving heavy machinery into other parts of the building and bringing in more than four hundred seats.

As the evening approached the miracle was accomplished and Wallingford suddenly found itself with an improvised assembly hall capable of accommodating an unprecedented audience—almost half the population of the small Vermont township.

From over the hills of New England, from over the Green Mountains and from all the neighbouring states, Rotarians came to welcome and pay tribute to Harris and to cheer into Rotary International the new Rotary Club of Wallingford.

As a prelude to the charter meeting, six Rutland Rotarians, all boyhood friends of Harris, purchased what is frequently referred to as the 'little red schoolhouse', the primary school where the three-year-old Harris began his formal education. They then established Paul P. Harris Testimonial, Inc. Twenty years later, a year after Harris's death, the Wallingford club was given the stewardship of the building. Ever since it has been known as the Paul P. Harris Memorial Building and to this day the Wallingford Rotarians operate and maintain it as a memorial to the boy who grew up in their village and became the founder of Rotary. The continuity of the stewardship is assured. On 1 July each year the officers and directors of the club automatically become the trustees and officers of the corporation. In 1962 the Rotarians of Wallingford gained clear title to the building and immediately constructed a new modern kitchen at a cost of $6,500.

The one-time school (it has had many other uses) is now the weekly meeting place of the Wallingford club and each year Wallingford Rotarians, together with members of the Rutland club, invite District Governor nominees, en route to the International Assembly, to stop off for a few days and enjoy the traditional New England hospitality of their splendid 'Homestay' programme. The moment the guests arrive they are greeted by warm hearted, open handed small town Americans, whose sole object in life is their guests' personal comfort. The visiting Rotarians are not merely entertained, but thoroughly spoiled. Included in their itinerary, of course, are meetings of the Rotary Clubs of Wallingford and Rutland and conducted tours of the childhood haunts of Harris.

It is just as Harris has affirmed in his memoirs: 'The genealogy of my contributions to the movement goes back to my valley, the friendliness of its folks, their religious and political tolerance. In a way, the movement came out of the valley.'

The 'Homestay' programme is an introduction to real American hospitality as Harris knew it in his boyhood. More than that, the guests come away understanding better the warmth, the spirit of fellowship and neighbourly concern that motivated Harris to found the Rotary movement.

Harris was touring Europe when the nineteenth Rotary convention was held in Minneapolis in 1928. The 9,428 delegates heard that Rotary had spread yet again, into Malaya and Greece, thanks to the indefatigible Jim Davidson. During the 1920s Davidson and his wife travelled extensively on behalf of Rotary, carrying Harris's

147

concept to the countries of the Orient, the Middle East, India and southern Europe. So dedicated was Davidson in the cause of Rotary he took no compensation whatsoever except for travelling expenses. For three years he journeyed by plane, train, bus and even caravan. He established clubs in Siam, China, Japan, Egypt, India, the Straits Settlements and several countries in southern Europe. Yet when he left America Davidson knew that he did not have long to live, and died soon after his return. Davidson's last words about Rotary were 'I was deeply impressed by Rotary's unique genius for uniting divergent elements for a common community good.'

The travels of 1928 did much for Harris. He had discovered that his popularity, far from diminishing the contributions of others, as he had feared it might, enhanced the standing of both Rotary and all the great pioneers who had helped build it into an international movement. He had long avoided the spotlight of public appearances because he worried this might make him a cult figure. He had stayed away from international conventions for the same reason. That fear was now gone. Rotary was established in its own right, and while there would always be respect and admiration for Harris, he perceived there was no longer any danger that the man would appear more important than the movement.

Memorable though 1928 had been, it was also a tiring year for Harris. The physical strain which his travels imposed were not without penalty, and 1929 was not far advanced when he suffered a severe setback. While vacationing in northern Michigan during the summer he had a massive coronary from which it took him almost two years to recover. His plans for further travel and visits to clubs in the United States were cancelled immediately. Deep concern was expressed throughout the Rotary world, a concern tinged with disappointment in many places, especially where arrangements for visits were already well advanced.

Harris was also unable to continue with the law practice, but his kindness and humanitarian qualities reaped their reward. Help was offered from all directions and he was deeply moved. The most valuable of all came from his partner and close friend, Fred Reinhardt, who immediately took charge of Harris's personal and business affairs.

From his sickbed Harris followed the proceedings of the twentieth Rotary convention of 1929 held in Dallas, Texas attended by 9,508 delegates who heard of the continuing work of Davidson and the establishment of new clubs in Egypt, Palestine, Ceylon, Burma, Nicaragua, Luxembourg, Yugoslavia and Romania. Rotary however, ceased to exist in the latter two countries with the outbreak of World War II ten years later, and both are now behind the Iron Curtain.

In 1929 Admiral Richard E. Byrd, a member of the Rotary Club of Winchester, Virginia, flew over the South Pole, carrying with him a Rotary flag presented by the Rotary Club of Wellington, New Zealand. In 1933 the flag was presented to Rotary International by District Governor Thomas List in the name of the Rotarians of New Zealand. This was the second occasion on which Admiral Byrd had taken a Rotary flag on an epoch-making flight. In 1926, on a flight from Spitzbergen to the North Pole, he carried with him a small silk Rotary banner given to him by U.S. Senator Tasker L. Oddie of Nevada. On the Admiral's return, the autographed banner was presented to the Rotary Club of Reno.

But 1929 was mostly a dismal year for Harris. And for the world generally it was a black year. In October the New York Stock Exchange crashed, bringing in its wake worldwide depression, bankruptcies and suicides. However, by early 1930 Harris was on the road to recovery, and although he still had some way to go, he was well enough to make a trip to California and the cities of Los Angeles and Bakersfield.

Despite the world trade recession Rotary held firm in 1930 and the convention that year celebrated the twenty-fifth anniversary of the founding of the movement. It was fitting that this Silver Anniversary celebration should be held in Chicago, where it all began. It was fitting also that a new record total of 11,008 delegates assembled in the 'windy city'. Within only a quarter of a century Rotary had become established in fifty-three countries, and the movement was still gathering momentum. Because of his health Harris was unable to be present, but his usual message to the delegates was a highnote of the convention.

Yet again the magnificent work of Davidson was the main talking point. His ambassadorial work had resulted in the chartering of new clubs in Algeria, Morocco, Rhodesia, Singapore, Kenya, Siam, Hong Kong and India. Another new country was added to Rotary's 'League of Nations' when the first club was chartered in Estonia, a country now almost forgotten. The little Baltic nation, was integrated into the Soviet Union in 1941 and was thus sadly lost to

Rotary. Rotary's total membership, it was reported, had passed the 150,000 mark, and the First European Regional Conference was held at The Hague, Holland, attended by more than eight hundred Rotarians from twenty-three European countries.

In Britain Sir Charles Mander became President of Rotary International in Great Britain and Ireland. At the R.I.B.I. Conference in Edinburgh he extended an invitation to the famous playwright, George Bernard Shaw, to address the delegates. In declining the invitation Shaw is reported to have said: 'I can tell where Rotary is going without travelling to Edinburgh to find out. It is going to lunch: and that is as far as it will ever get in this country.'

By 1931 Harris was almost fully recovered but he was still unable to make the long journey to Vienna, Austria, for the twenty-second convention.

There were a number of notable features about the Vienna Convention. For the first time in Rotary's twenty-six years, the President of the movement came from a country outside North America. Sydney Pascall of London, a great personal friend of Harris, became the first British and the first European Rotarian to hold the highest elected office. Other notable features were the magnificence of the musical entertainment, and the issue, by the Austrian government, of six commemorative stamps. These have since become collector's items.

News about Rotary was mixed in 1931. New clubs were established in Poland, Danzig and the Lebanon but, because of the serious effects of the world economic depression (Great Britain was compelled to abandon the gold standard), eighteen clubs were lost. News from the far side of the world, however, was more encouraging and interested Harris deeply. Australian Rotarians who were involved advised him of the formation of a new service organization for young businessmen. Known as Apex, it was formed at Geelong, a small but important seaport fifty miles south east of Melbourne, on 10 March, 1931. The new club quickly gained in popularity, and similar clubs were formed in other Australian cities and towns.

The mixed fortunes of 1929, 1930 and 1931 can hardly have been happy years for Harris personally but, as 1931 drew to a close, he prepared for another journey to Europe, this time as the official delegate of the prestigious Chicago Bar Association, to attend the International Congress on Comparative Law at The

Hague. It was also, he perceived, another great opportunity of extending his travels on behalf of Rotary, especially in the countries of northern Europe.

CHAPTER 22

A Tour of Scandinavia

The twenty-third Rotary convention was held in Seattle, Washington, from 20–24 June 1932, but the continuing world depression resulted in a decreased attendance of 5,182 delegates and the loss of a further twenty-seven clubs. There was also a drop in the total membership of about two thousand but, even so, a new club was chartered in the remote Baltic province of Latvia, and authorization was given for the opening of a branch office of Rotary International in the Far East. This was sited in Singapore in 1935 but in 1939 it was relocated in Bombay.

Fully recovered now from his near fatal attack of 1929, Harris was able to undertake his journey to Europe. In the thirty-six years he had practised law in Chicago, Harris had earned a reputation as an attorney of high standing. He was an influential member of the American Bar Association, the Illinois State Bar Association, and the Chicago Bar Association. He served for two years as the Chairman of the Committee on Professional Ethics for the Chicago Association, during which time, as he put it, 'I saw several members walk the plank.' Among his legal colleagues were friends such as Edgar Bancroft, who was appointed the United States Ambassador to Japan in the 1930s, and Dean John H. Wigmore, considered to be America's greatest legal scholar of the time. Harris also served on a number of important committees, particularly the International Committee of the American Bar Association. It is indicative of his standing that he was one of only three delegates from the nine thousand strong Chicago Bar Association. The American Bar Association was represented by Wigmore and a number of other great legal minds of the era.

On Tuesday, 9 August 1932, Harris was in the English university town of Cambridge to attend the luncheon meeting of the Rotary Club of Cambridge. With him was an old friend, Hugh

Galloway, then the President of R.I.B.I. Others present included the Deputy Mayor, the Chairman of the Cambridgeshire County Council and the Master of Sidney Sussex College. There were, of course, many Rotarians present. Represented at the meeting were places as far distant as Aylesbury, Bangor (North Wales), Croydon, Düsseldorf (Germany), Hitchin, Kingston upon Thames, London, St Andrews (Scotland), Welwyn Garden City and Harris's own club, Chicago.

Next day, en route to Holland, Harris visited the Rotary Club of London to celebrate the twenty-first anniversary of the club's charter. More than three hundred people sat down to lunch at the opulent Great Central Hotel in the Marylebone Road. This magnificent hotel, which lost money from the day it opened is now a block of offices, but it remains one of the city's most famous edifices.

At the lunch, Harris spoke about the history of Rotary, with particular reference to London's part in its growth. He reminded everyone present that Rotary had not brought anything new into the world. Centuries before his own concept of Rotary, a club on the so-called classification principle was in operation in the city of London. This was typical of Harris. He was forever crediting others with contributions to the humanitarian ideal of Rotary. It was he, nonetheless, who put them into practice.

Following the legal congress at The Hague, Harris began his tour of northern Europe. At Copenhagen in Denmark his sense of humour was demonstrated when he willingly accepted a role as a long-tressed beauty in a play, and the Rotarians of Denmark cheered him long and loud for his acting. Harris, it will be recalled, was an actor for a short time in 1892 in Denver, Colorado.

Then, for the first time as far as is known, he initiated the splendid tradition of planting trees of friendship in all the countries he visited. Bergen in Norway appears to have been the first city. This was followed by the planting of similar trees in Goteberg and Stockholm in Sweden, Helsingfors in Finland, Tallinn in Latvia (now lost behind the Iron Curtain), and Berlin. In the course of the next four years trees were planted in every continent, but the idea appears to have originated in Europe.

In 1933 Harris was accorded one of the many honours bestowed upon him, one which afforded him particular satisfaction. At Burlington his own alma mater, the University of Vermont, conferred upon him an Honorary Doctor of Law Degree. It was an honour that, in view of the indignity of the expulsion more than forty years before, was especially pleasing.

At Boston, in the neighbouring state of Massachusetts, the twenty-fourth Rotary convention was held from 26–30 June. Rotary suffered another net loss in membership although no fewer than 107 new clubs were chartered, including the first in Bulgaria. The 8,430 delegates heard of an unusual Rotary first when Auguste Picard, the famous Swiss physicist, ascended 55,577 feet into the stratosphere by balloon, carrying with him a flag presented by the Rotary Club of Zürich. Within a decade Rotary flags had been flown over the North and South Poles and into the stratosphere!

Harris was instrumental in the launching of a Spanish language edition of *The Rotarian* (*Revista Rotaria*) in 1933. Of even greater interest, was the increasing use by clubs everywhere of the short business creed, *The Four Way Test*. This was compiled in 1931 by Herbert J. Taylor, a member of the Chicago club. In due course Taylor, a great friend of Harris, became President of the Chicago club (1939–40), District Governor of the old District 147 (1941–2), and eventually President of Rotary International in 1954–5, when about half a million copies of *The Four Way Test* were distributed.

As he prepared himself for three years of intensive ambassadorial work on behalf of Rotary, Harris reflected on the phenomenon of Rotary. To the end of his life he disclaimed that he was a visionary, although he saw before anyone else the role of Rotary as a force in community service. Long before Rotary became an international movement his speeches predicted the spread of the Movement's ideal of service to every corner of the world. He had seen the movement not only survive but grow stronger during a world war. He had battled with the sceptics and won. His faith was justified by the fact that even in the midst of the great depression of the 1930s Rotary proved itself to be a stabilizing influence of inestimable value, living proof of its invisible power for good.

CHAPTER 23

Idyll in the Cotswolds

On 22 February 1934, curiously only one day short of Rotary's official anniversary, Paul and Mrs Harris left Chicago for a tour of Britain and South Africa. It was an exacting itinerary, including a stay of six weeks in Britain, during which Harris was to attend a crucial meeting between R.I. and R.I.B.I. officials in London.

On their way to New York, where they embarked on the *Majestic*, the couple stopped at Elyria, Ohio to visit Rotarian Edgar Allen, the founder of the International Society for Crippled Children. Harris and his wife had taken a special interest in the society, both having held high office in the organization and had served on several of its committees.

In New York they were met by the President of Rotary International, John Nelson, the Movement's indispensable General Secretary, Ches Perry, and several other highranking Rotarians, all of whom were in the party travelling to London. The purpose of their visit was a discussion with officers of Rotary International in Great Britain and Ireland about difficulties that had arisen from the special relationship between R.I. and R.I.B.I. 'It was,' said Harris, 'a task fraught with danger, as all present recognized.' (This is not a subject relevant to this account of Harris's life and those who are interested in knowing more about the delicate situation, now happily resolved, should read the excellent account of the protracted negotiations in Levy's *Rotary International in Great Britain and Ireland*.)

To save time, Harris and the official party disembarked at Plymouth instead of Southampton. There was no time to visit the Rotary Club of Plymouth, but local Rotarians were out to greet them in force and amid a salvo of hellos and good-byes the party took a sleeper to London, bound for the Mayfair Hotel near Berkeley Square, where they were greeted by concerned officers of

R.I.B.I.

The ensuing discussions continued for several days but at the end little in the nature of tangible results could be claimed by either party. However, Harris commented later: 'I venture to say that there could have been no more fortunate outcome than that attained. Suspicions had been dispelled, the atmosphere had been cleared, and future friendly relations assured.' In fact the two sides agreed to differ, and a solution to the problems was not arrived at until the mid-1960s.

It was Mrs Harris's intention to leave for Scotland immediately after the London conference, but she felt in need of a rest after the ocean crossing and she decided to travel north after the planned District Conferences at Worcester, Watford and Newport. This meant an eight-day break for the couple and an unexpected opportunity to spend a week resting and recuperating in a part of England neither had before visited. On the advice of W.W. Blair Fish, General Secretary of R.I.B.I., they selected the Cotswolds, because of the area's tranquil beauty and its, as yet, unspoilt countryside.

On the Sunday afternoon before their departure they visited some old friends. These included Fred Burley, an Australian Rotarian who now lived in the suburbs, and Wilfred Andrews, the Sittingbourne Rotarian who was President of R.I.B.I. in 1930–1. Among the guests at a dinner that night was Wickham Steed, a famous English journalist, and a well known authority on international affairs, who was at one time editor of *The Times*.

The Harrises had intended to go to the tiny village of Bibury in Gloucestershire, but fate decreed otherwise. On arriving in Oxford they took a side-line (long since discontinued) to the village of Fairford, where they planned to stay for one night before continuing to Bibury. But, upon disembarking at Fairford, they found that the village was two miles from the railway station, and they had to summon a taxi to take them to the local hotel. When they finally arrived at the Bull they caused considerable excitement: Americans arriving during the season were rare enough, but in March they were unheard of.

The couple's initial reaction to the eighteenth century inn was one of dismay; they had long become accustomed to the warmth of centrally heated American hotels, and they found the old Bull depressingly cold and damp. As Harris remarked: 'We would have said good-bye to the Bull had there been any warmer hotel available, but there was none, and there was naught to do but make the best of it.' But British hospitality is traditional, and a well prepared dinner and roaring fire did much to restore their drooping spirits.

Assistant Manager at the time was a Miss Cornish, and she had a keen eye for business. It was, of course, hardly the time of year when paying guests were plentiful, and she was not of a mind to lose two clearly affluent Americans. Little by little Miss Cornish indicated that the hotel in Bibury was no better heated than the Bull, before playing her ace card—the triumphant announcement that Mr Walters, the proprietor, owned a fine American car and would be delighted to take his guests for drives through the beautiful Cotswolds.

Harris may well have had his doubts, but the couple opted to stay in Fairford. It turned out to be a wise choice. Mr Walters, true to his word, took them to all sorts of places they might otherwise have missed—lovely villages such as Quenington and Colne St Aldwyns, and the long sloping hills and gentle rolling valleys that made the scenery so exquisite. The couple also took long hikes alone, and attended services at the local chuch, where they admired the unique painted windows. They went to a church bazaar and also enjoyed an itinerant Punch and Judy show in the company of children as delighted and entertained as they. In the dark cold evenings Harris was welcomed by the local tradesmen, laughing and chatting intimately over their mugs of ale before the warming fire. 'It was as though,' said Harris, 'everything was done to order for us.' They could not have enjoyed themselves more.

Harris, of course, had not announced his presence in the area, and as there was no Rotary club in the village, he felt sure he would remain undiscovered. But he had forgotten the efficiency of the Rotary grapevine, especially in a rural area such as the Cotswolds. One morning, to his astonishment, a party of Rotarians from Cirencester, the nearest town of any size, descended upon the couple, eager to do all they could to make their visit a memorable one. Harris had been to the village bank to cash some traveller's checks and was instantly recognized by the manager.

The Cirencester Rotarian who 'won' the privilege of being the couple's guide during their remaining days in the area was a man named Leach. One never to be forgotten day he took them to a small town on the Thames, which Harris particularly wished to visit—Wallingford. Harris later wrote: 'I was interested in Wallingford because I was brought up in Wallingford, Vermont, a beautiful little village in the Green Mountains. It was a long but interesting drive. On arrival at the quaint little city we went at once to the church which occupied a position in the public square. While walking about we met an English gentleman of about my age. He volunteered some information and being thereby encouraged, I asked him what other places of special interest had best be visited. He answered, "The home of William Blackstone stands on the bank of the Thames. I suppose you know who he was?" With high enthusiasm I replied I certainly did; that his commentaries occupied an honoured position in all law libraries in America.'

Harris's informant, who turned out to be something of an eccentric, showed the party other interesting sights in Wallingford, and invited them home to tea in a fine old house named Cromwell Lodge, pointing out the Blackstone home on the way. The view of the countryside from the host's home was in itself worth the journey, said Harris, which, incidentally, was made in pouring rain.

Before they left Wallingford, their guide, Mr Ponking, took the Harrises to a local book store and presented them with a small volume about the town. 'An extraordinary character was Mr Ponking,' said Harris, 'who apparently disliked all things American, or professed to.' Their last sight of Mr Ponking was his disappearance into a department store, the façade of which bore the legend, 'Ponking and Co'. To his dying day, Harris was never sure whether Mr Ponking was the greatest spoofer he had ever met or just an extraordinary character who blew hot or cold as the mood struck him.

It was a memorable day and a fitting conclusion to their visit to the Cotswolds. 'If we had to do it again,' said Harris, 'we would go about it the same way. We would go to the Bull and we would manage to be there in the off-season, in order that we might better enjoy the comfort of hot-water bottles, grate fires and the cosiness of ingle nooks and the special attentions of Mr and Mrs Walters, and be taken in hand by the managing Miss Cornish. We shall never forget the Cotswolds.'

The Bull is still there fronting the Market Place in Fairford. Externally it remains much as the Harrises saw it in 1934, as do the surrounding buildings. Internally the inn has been modernized, and the lounge and the 'Stable Restaurant' refitted, yet it retains its original atmosphere with many beamed ceilings, exposed stone walls and old open stone fireplaces. The Walters and Miss Cornish are long since gone, of course, and no record remains of the visit of Paul and Mrs Harris.

The day after their visit to Wallingford, the genial Mr Walters drove the grateful couple to Worcester, taking in en route brief visits to two of the most beautiful of the Cotswold villages, Broadway and Chipping Camden.

At Worcester Harris was reunited with John Crabtree, the President of R.I.B.I., and W.W. Blair Fish. The Conference provided a first-class programme and Harris was greatly impressed by the dedication of the Rotarians who were present. He noted with particular interest the group meetings on Vocational Service and International Service which he chose to attend. After business was completed the couple were taken on a tour of the Malvern Hills, which they found disappointing after the Cotswolds: 'More rugged and more patronized by pleasure seekers.'

The Harrises moved on to the Watford Conference of the London District, making their headquarters at the Russell Hotel (then the Rotary Hotel) in London, where Harris had direct contact with the board members of R.I.B.I. On Sunday the Harrises attended services at St Paul's in the morning and The Temple in the evening, experiences that brought back to Harris vivid memories of the migratory and venturesome days of his first visit to London in 1893, and the more leisurely sight-seeing of 1928.

At Watford, Harris met such distinguished British Rotarians as Herbert Schofield, the President of R.I.B.I. in 1931–2, Canon W. Thomson Elliott, the President in 1924–5, and Stanley Leverton, already prominent in British Rotary circles although, surprisingly, he did not become President of R.I.B.I. until 1952–3. Harris again enjoyed the speeches at the Conference, but the words that warmed him deeply as he walked into the hall was the simple salutation extended by District Governor Ted Spicer: 'Welcome, Paul.' Two papers delivered at the conference particularly impressed Harris. The first, by Canon Elliott, dealt with the need for Rotary clubs in small communities. The second, by Stanley Leverton, described his experience of Rotary in Egypt and the success of the Cairo club.

During Tuesday evening, 20 March, Paul and Mrs Harris attended a comedy play, *Ambrose Applejohn's Adventure*, staged by the London Rotary Players under the able direction of Leverton.

It was a fine evening's entertainment, played to a packed house in a well known London theatre. Salvos of applause followed each act and there were curtain calls without number, but the highlight of the evening came at the end of the performance. Harris was visibly moved when a specially composed song of welcome was sung to him and his wife by Leverton, the actors and the audience. 'It was, I am sure,' said Harris, 'far beyond my deserts.'

With two days to spare before the Newport Conference, the Harrises visited the famed Wye Valley. On their arrival at Newport they were met by the inevitable reception committee, led by an old friend, Walter Meacock, the immediate past District Chairman. With Meacock was Godfrey Phillips, the President of the Newport club, and several other Rotarians. Meacock and Phillips drove the Harrises to the Beaufort Arms, a popular hotel in the Wye Valley, situated directly opposite the ruins of Tintern Abbey. It was an idyllic spot. The scenery, and the welcome and comfort they were accorded at the Beaufort was more than they had dared hope.

Newport held special memories for Harris. Six years earlier he had visited Newport briefly and Cardiff at greater length. He renewed his acquaintanceship with the gifted and humorous T.J. Rees of Swansea (who went on to become President of R.I.B.I. in 1942–4) and met, perhaps for the first time, such well known Welsh Rotarians as District Chairman J. Winterbotham of Llanelli, the District Chairman elect, Charlie Burn of Cardiff, and the District Secretary, Ernest Ablett of Swansea. He met many others, of course, and Harris took particular pleasure in presenting the District 15 Golf Cup to the winner, another Llanelli Rotarian, A.E. Morgan.

On the afternoon of the first day of the conference Mrs Harris spoke to the ladies of the Inner Wheel on the subject of clubs comprised of the wives, mothers and even sisters of Rotarians in the United Kingdom and the United States. She suggested the Crippled Children movement as a suitable project for the ladies' clubs. The following morning Harris took the platform and delivered what the District Governor (then called District Chairman) described as a forceful and vigorous address.

After the morning session Mrs Harris left for Scotland. Harris, however, remained behind to the end of the conference and throughout the following weekend. The luncheon and dinner functions of the last day were gala events, conducted with

Paul Harris photographed with Chesley Perry in 1923

Mrs Paul Harris

an informality which gladdened the heart of the fun-loving Harris. He made particular mention of his friend, Meacock, whose *pièce de résistance* was a rendition of 'Cockles and Mussels' in a voice that Harris described as 'anything one might call it'.

On the Sunday after the conference, Harris, Meacock and Phillips drove into Cardiff and along the coast to the pleasant seaside resort of Porthcawl on the eastern side of the great sweep of Swansea Bay. As Harris gazed across to Mumbles Head in the far distance, the memory of his first visit to Wales in 1893 flooded back. Before returning to Newport the three friends took tea in a hospitable seaside cottage. Harris spent his last night in Wales in Meacock's home, and the next morning took the train for the long journey to Glasgow to rejoin his wife.

'I did not leave Newport without sadness,' said Harris. 'It had been delightful to meet Godfrey Phillips and his charming family of little ones, who so adore their father; it had been delightful to make many other new friends and also to meet good old Walter again.'

That District 15 Conference at Newport is still remembered as one of the best ever held in Wales. Everyone enjoyed the great civic reception and ball provided by the Mayor and Mayoress who, incidentally, returned specially from a business trip to London to welcome the Harrises. Still recalled are the fine speeches by Harris, Mrs Harris and John Crabtree, and the good time the ladies had on a coach tour to the Wye Valley and tea at Tintern Abbey.

But above all, the Rotarians who attended the conferences at Worcester, Watford and Newport treasure the memory of the time when the Founder of Rotary and his wife came to see them.

On his arrival in Glasgow, Harris was met by his wife, her brother John, and delegates from the Rotary Clubs of Edinburgh and Dunfermline. Arrangements were already in hand for Paul and Mrs Harris to attend an important function in Edinburgh, but the Dunfermline Rotarians had come to press for attendance at their club also.

The meeting of the Glasgow club was open to the ladies as well as a large gathering of Rotarians from the adjoining cities, and Mrs Harris accompanied her husband. Harris had often told his wife about his visit to Glasgow six years earlier. The welcome now was just as warm.

Following the meeting came a typical Harris gesture. On his

previous visit he had heard of a Glasgow Rotarian, George
Walker, who was stricken with a paralysis that had confined him to
his bed for many years. Harris was not able to visit Walker at that
time, but wrote to him and kept in touch during the six years that
elapsed. Now he was in Glasgow again, Harris's first request was
that he and Mrs Harris be taken to see the dying Scotsman. The
club's Vice President immediately offered to drive the couple to
Walker's home. Harris's own words eloquently describe their meeting with George Walker: 'He greeted us with hearty good cheer,
though blindness had recently been added to his list of afflictions.
Night and day he lies on the flat of his back, unable to turn either
right or left, and yet his spirit is triumphant. For George, a condition seemingly far worse than death had lost its sting. If there ever
was a case of spirit conquering flesh, it is George's case. It is difficult to conceive of any further affliction being visited upon him, but
if it comes, George will, I am sure, rise to meet it in the same old
dauntless way. As I saw him lying there, it seemed to me that no one
could have the experience that I was having without being influenced by it. One could hardly be the same man again after having
looked upon George Walker. Jean felt quite as deeply moved as I—
probably more so.'

After tea with the President of the Glasgow club, Matthew and
Mrs Lindsay, Paul and Mrs Harris and the Rev John Thomson
drove to Annbank in Ayrshire, where Mrs Harris's brother than
had his ministry, having moved from Greenock a few years earlier. They stayed for almost a week, taking a well earned rest,
although they forayed forth to nearby places on several occasions.
The day following their arrival at the Old Manse, for example,
they visited the Rotary Club of Paisley where, to her astonishment
and delight, Mrs Harris was presented with a beautiful Paisley
shawl more than one hundred years old.

They visited other cities in the area, although the only mention
of a club meeting was at Ayr, where they were given a tremendous
greeting in Robbie Burns style. The Rotary Club of Ayr had come
into being in 1931, in between Harris's first visit in 1928 and his
present sortie into the Burns country.

On a particularly memorable occasion they dined with the Hon
James Brown, a Labour Member of Parliament who was once the
Lord High Commissioner to the Assembly at Edinburgh. He en-
tertained them at what Harris described as 'his humble miner's

cottage near Ayr'.

After their week at Annbank the couple set off for Dundee, where they were met by Mrs Harris's younger sister, Joey, her husband, the Rev John Howe and their two small children. Mrs Howe was ten years younger than Mrs Harris, and the youngest of the Thomson family.

Harris was scheduled to meet the Rotarians of Dundee for what they euphemistically described as a tea meeting. It turned out to be an inter-city meeting of no mean size, with many Scottish clubs represented, including a strong delegation from St Andrews. Harris would have loved to visit every Scottish club, but he was compelled by the shortness of his tour to forgo the pleasure of a visit to St Andrews on this occasion. He did, however, assure the contingent that he would come to see them as soon as possible and, in the fullness of time, kept his promise. Another pleasant surprise lay in store for Mrs Harris when, during the course of the meeting, she was presented with a handbag made of flax, woven with the colours of the old Prince Charlie tartan.

On 4 April 1934, the day following the meeting at Dundee, Mrs Harris and Paul made a memorable return to her native city of Edinburgh. They were received in the City Chambers by the Lord Provost, William J. Thomson (a happy and appropriate coincidence of name) and the Lady Provost. Flanking the entrance as they walked up the steps were Highland pipers, resplendent in Ross tartans, who played them in to the stirring tune of 'The Road to the Isles'. That evening the Lord Provost presided at a special banquet given in the couple's honour. For Mrs Harris, then fifty-two, it was one of the most emotional experiences of her life.

Next day they attended the weekly meeting of the Rotary Club of Edinburgh, which was held then, as it still is today, in the North British Station Hotel. Yet again they were accorded a tremendous welcome from a gathering of more than two hundred Rotarians and their wives. In his address, Harris paid high tribute to his wife for her help and devotion, not only to him but to the Rotary movement. He received a standing ovation which continued until the President finally had to call for order. There was another pleasant ceremony for Mrs Harris. On behalf of the club the President, Robert E. Douglas, presented her with an inscribed silver salver as a memento of the occasion. It was thereafter one of her most treasured possessions.

During the various ceremonies attending their visit, several photographs were taken of Paul and Mrs Harris, and a motion picture film was made for the archives of Rotary International. It so happened that their visit coincided with an annual Scottish event of great importance, the Assembly in Edinburgh of the Lord's Provosts (mayors or chief magistrates) of every municipality in Scotland, and the Harrises were invited to attend the closing banquet. Harris was asked to speak and did so briefly, choosing Chicago as his subject.

The last visit to a Scottish Rotary club, at least for the time being, was at Dunfermline, the birthplace of Andrew Carnegie, the renowned Scottish-American industrialist and philanthropist. At the lunch meeting Harris spoke at some length, giving thumbnail sketches of the lives of some distinguished American industrial tycoons including, naturally, Andrew Carnegie.

After the meeting a large party of Rotarians accompanied Harris and his party to nearby Gleneagles, where they all took tea at what is probably one of the best located hotels in the world and, of course, known internationally as the home of one of the world's great golf courses.

Mrs Harris and her sister returned to Dundee but, after an evening meeting at Dunfermline and a night's rest in Edinburgh, Harris travelled to Newcastle upon Tyne, to be met by his old friend Hugh Galloway and Deans Forster, the immediate past President of the Newcastle club. After lunch with his friends and their wives, Harris was taken for a drive into the spectacular Cheviot Hills which separate England from Scotland. There he took dinner in the magnificent country home of Hugh Galloway's brother before the long drive back to Newcastle. Galloway, a keen amateur photographer, took several pictures of Harris on this occasion.

Harris did not attend a meeting of the Newcastle club in April 1934, but the next day he more than made up for that. His schedule included an address to a luncheon meeting of the Leicester Rotary Club followed, in the evening, by attendance at a big inter-city meeting at Nottingham. And it all went according to schedule. Some twenty miles north of Leicester Harris was met by Percy Groves, President of the Leicester club who, with Mrs Groves, drove him to their city through the charming town of Melton Mowbray, described by Harris as 'a gem of an English village set in charming hills'.

A surprise awaited Harris at the Leicester meeting. When he met someone he had, until then, known only by correspondence. Ebenezer Hancock was the author of a small publication, *Keeping Young Past Eighty*, and Harris averred that he had been the best American customer of the eighty-four-year-old author, and that he had presented many copies of Hancock's book to friends 'in need of a boost'.

At the meeting, by request, Harris spoke on 'The American Experiment', although his own preference was the subject of 'Tolerance and its bearing on our Sixth Object'. This he now reserved for the evening meeting at Nottingham, but as many Leicester Rotarians accompanied him to that meeting, they had the bonus of both.

At Nottingham, Harris met again several friends from his 1928 visit, including Fred Gray, the Nottingham Rotarian who was a candidate for the Presidency of R.I.B.I. in 1934, Percival 'Pa' Almy of Torquay (who became the R.I.B.I. President in 1938–9), Harry Bennett and Harry Dodgson. As arranged, Harris spoke on the Sixth Object of Rotary at the well-attended inter-city meeting and banquet. Afterwards a large party repaired to Fred Gray's home for an informal chat and the sort of fellowship Harris relished so much.

On the morning of 10 April Harris, accompanied by Harry Bennett and a member of the Rotary Club of Rugby, set off for the well known Midlands town, made famous by Thomas Hughes's book, *Tom Brown's Schooldays*. Harris had a special reason for visiting Rugby. Rotary there, as in several other cities in Britain, suffered severely from the depression of world trade in the 1930s and his visit was opportune. No fewer than eight British clubs were disbanded between 1927 and 1933, and three more were closed in 1934, but Rugby was not one of them. At the impromptu meeting hurriedly called, Harris explained why the movement in Rugby should not be abandoned. There is no doubt that his forceful address greatly influenced the members in favour of continuing.

The meeting over, Harris went to see the famous old school, but the most interesting moment was a visit to the chapel, where the illustrious Dr Thomas Arnold lies buried beneath the chapel floor. A voracious reader, Harris was fully informed of the pioneering educational work of the famed English scholar.

Following a night's rest in Rugby, Harris returned to London, arriving in time for a meeting of the London club at the Russell Hotel. The next day he visited the Rotary Club of Streatham, the

165

first of the small clubs in the London district. With him was Ted Unwin, the Rotarian who successfully advocated over a period of several years the extension of clubs in London. Harris had particular reason to remember this visit. A member of an adjoining club (not identified) was the speaker. His speciality, apparently, was invective, which he brought to bear with devastating effect on such subjects as war debts and tariffs. He wound up with the statement that: 'It is therefore clear that America would not persist in her irrational, obdurate way much longer.' As this was a speech with strong political overtones, it caused considerable embarrassment to the host club and, on the drive back to London, the Streatham club's vice-president voiced his concern. Harris, however, was much too wise and experienced an attorney to take umbrage although, he did subsequently warn of the dangers of political controversy within Rotary.

That evening Mrs Harris returned from Scotland to rejoin her husband to prepare for their voyage to South Africa the following day. At 10.30 next morning, at Waterloo Station, a party of forty Rotarians, several of whom had journeyed from distant places, were there to see the couple off to Southampton and the *Armidale Castle*, the ship that would take them to Cape Town. Even as Harris was leaving London, an inter-city meeting was assembling in Southampton, where Harris delivered yet another of his 'friendship chats'. The send off at the pier was a moment for the couple to treasure, the Southampton Rotarians cheering their guests away and watching and waving until the ship disappeared down the Solent and out of sight.

CHAPTER 24

Visit to South Africa

The voyage proved to be all the Harrises had hoped, although Mrs Harris had a few queasy days crossing the Bay of Biscay. Their first port of call, four days out of Southampton, was Madeira, where they spent a few hours ashore, in the flower scented island festooned with roses and bougainvillaea, where wine, lace, fruits and vegetables were the chief items of commerce.

A day or so later they passed Teneriffe, and from there it was empty ocean for six thousand miles to Cape Town. The days slipped by agreeably, and the daily routine was breakfast, quoits, writing, reading, lunch, a nap, and more writing, reading and walking until dinner. The gregarious Harris, of course, soon made friends with several fellow travellers.

When they were about a thousand miles out from Cape Town, the couple were delighted to receive a welcoming cablegram from Rotarians eagerly waiting for them at the great South African port.

The couple were prepared to see a beautiful city. Friends and fellow passengers told them of the charms of Cape Town but, as Harris commented: 'No words can describe the majesty of the city's background as one enters the harbour. Towering above the port is the magnificent Table Mountain, raising its head three thousand five hundred feet above South Africa's gateway city.'

The welcome they received at the dockside literally overwhelmed them. As well as great numbers of Rotarians and their ladies, there were photographers, newspaper reporters and radio interviewers. They were in Cape Town only a few hours, but they were received by the Mayor and other civic dignitaries. Then they were placed in the hands of the Thomas Cook representative, who had the task of arranging their week's tour through South Africa—no easy matter. Everything had to be timed exactly so that the Harrises would be back in Cape Town seven days later for the important South African Conference. Had they been able to travel by air, it would have been a simple matter, but Mrs Harris was adamant that she would not fly, and the entire journey was made by train and boat, a somewhat arduous one given the immense distances to be covered.

On the afternoon of their arrival in South Africa, the Harrises took a train for Johannesburg by way of Kimberley, a journey entailing two nights and a day of constant travel on a narrow-gauge railroad. Although they broke their journey in Kimberley (there was no club there then), it was an exhausting trip. By the time they arrived in Johannesburg, in the early hours of the morning, they were, said Harris, 'two rather mussed up Americans'.

The reception accorded them in Johannesburg followed the now traditional pattern. No club could have expressed a welcome more spontaneous than that of the Rotarians of the golden city of the Transvaal. The welcoming committee rose at an unconscionable hour to meet the couple, and no effort was spared to ensure their brief stay was as pleasant as possible. Early in the morning they were shown the sights of the city, and then driven to Pretoria, the administrative capital of South Africa, where a special meeting of Rotarians from the city and outlying areas had assembled. Tea was served, followed by brief speeches and the ever warming rounds of Rotary fellowship before, all too soon, they were driven the thirty-five miles back to Johannesburg for a splendid club meeting attended by many representatives from every neighbouring club.

A large party, led by the Mayor and Mayoress, escorted the Harrises to the railway station immediately after the meeting. The Mayor extracted from the couple a promise to send him information concerning the role of Rotary in the Crippled Children Movement. This was the subject of Harris's speech at the meeting and it generated considerable interest. Before he left South Africa, Harris received five packages of literature from the International Society for Crippled Children. Some was immediately forwarded to Johannesburg, and the rest distributed to other interested clubs. Harris heard shortly afterwards that the Mayor and Mayoress had taken immediate steps to establish an organization in the interests of handicapped children.

That same day, barely twelve hours after arriving in Johannesburg, the couple took a train for Durban by way of Pieter-maritzburg, where they stopped briefly. They found Durban, an important coastal city, different from the rugged industrial region of the Transvaal. Harris described it as a colourful city, distinctly English in character. The British influence, he noted, was manifest by a fine race track and polo grounds. The seafront, with its façade of luxury hotels, especially impressed them. Harris addressed another large meeting in Durban, and again stressed his interest in crippled children, whereupon the Durban members took the Harrises to visit the club's home for delinquent boys. Although this was not exactly what Harris had in mind, he was nonetheless impressed by this demonstration of community service by the Rotary Club of Durban.

The remainder of the tour was made by boat. 'It was far more restful,' said Harris thankfully. From Durban they sailed on the *New Winchester Castle* back to Cape Town, with calls at East London and Port Elizabeth.

At East London Paul and Mrs Harris were present at a splendidly attended meeting where Harris, found himself, on the receiving end of a practical joke. For the first time in his Rotary life, he was 'fined' for an alleged violation of Rotary law! What the law was he never did discover—not that the Rotarians of East London cared. Their object was achieved when Harris was fined half-a-crown. This was promptly withdrawn from circulation and framed along with his signed photograph, probably the only one of its kind. The Harrises were ashore at East London for only a few hours, but there was time enough to learn about a successful vocational and manual training club for underprivileged boys which the East London Rotarians were operating.

Another day's sailing brought the ship to Port Elizabeth, and the couple were driven on another sight-seeing tour before Harris attended a lunch-time club meeting for men only) and a reception at which ladies were also present. Both the Harrises spoke to a big gathering, which included a number of South African Rotarians on their way to the Cape Town Conference. They also met the South African District Governor nominee, Cecil Buchanan. (He accompanied them to the conference and afterwards sailed with them to Southampton before connecting with another ship which took him to the International Convention at Detroit.)

Yet another day's sailing brought the party full circle to Cape

Town. In less than a week the Harrises had travelled more than three thousand miles! Directly upon arrival they went to the Mount Nelson Hotel, the conference headquarters, and Harris soon found himself busily engaged with both business and social affairs relating to the conference. Here the couple at last caught up with District Governor Hugh Bryan, the eminent South African Rotarian they missed during their brief stop in Pietermaritzburg. Bryan was a graduate of Cambridge and he delivered a great speech in reply to an address by General Jan Christian Smuts, the famed South African soldier-statesman.

In addition to General Smuts several important men attended the conference. Including the Governor General of South Africa, the Earl of Clarendon (George Herbert Hyde Villiers).

The main conference speaker was, of course, General Smuts. His speech included, some thrusts at the United States generally and Chicago specifically, to which Harris could not respond at the time. Later, however, he did have the opportunity to reply to further unfavourable comments by the General on conditions in the United States. Harris retaliated good naturedly in kind and more than held his own. To the General's credit, he frankly acknowledged the merits of the reply.

Paul and Mrs Harris lunched twice with General Smuts, whom Harris described as 'a once confirmed Afrikaaner, but by now an imperialist'. The General was educated in an English university and was, at that time, the Lord Chancellor of St Andrews University. The Harrises also lunched with the Premier of South Africa, General J.B.M. Hertzog, an 'irreconcilable Afrikaaner', according to Harris.

On the last day of the conference Harris was escorted to one of Cape Town's beautiful parks to plant a tree of remembrance and friendship. After the ceremony, Hugh Bryan presented him with a miniature silver spade as a memento of the occasion. However, the memento of their visit most treasured by the Harrises was an album of photographs. This was arranged chronologically and covered the entire period of the tour. The first pictures showed the *Armidale Castle* steaming into Cape Town Harbour; the last showed the *New Winchester Castle* as it steamed out into the South Atlantic.

Harris, who was somewhat susceptible to weather changes, contracted a severe chill as they crossed the equator. He was still unwell when they arrived in London, and it was deemed sensible to cancel his engagements to attend inter-city meetings in England, much to the disappointment of the organizing clubs. Instead, Harris went directly to Scotland, where he thought he might be able to visit some of the smaller clubs which, because of their remoteness, seldom saw officers of Rotary International, much less the Founder himself.

CHAPTER 25

The Remote Clubs of Scotland

With the exception of a club council meeting in Edinburgh, Harris's first official function in Scotland was a visit to the Rotary Club of Perth. This was scheduled on the day of the club's regular meeting but, because of the uncertainty of Harris's condition, no commitment was made until the last moment. This did not deter the Rotarians of Perth. When he did appear, Harris was given a rousing welcome. The visit was brief but there was sufficient time for the couple to visit two magnificent recreational parks where, said Harris, 'every form of athletic activity for young and old was catered for'.

From Perth the Harrises proceeded north to Inverness for another fine reception and meeting. It was 31 May 1934, and the visit is recalled for us by Hugh Miller, a surgeon still active in the Inverness club:

> I arrived late for the lunch and sat down at the only vacant place, which was at the 'top table', quite unaware that I was attaching myself to such distinguished company. I was to be married two days later, and when I was leaving the Infirmary I was given a send-off by a group of nurses who had thrown confetti over me. I suppose I gave a little bow as I was introduced to Mrs Harris, and some confetti fell into my soup. You can well imagine, I'm sure, that this was greatly enjoyed by Paul Harris and his lady, who showed great interest in my marriage, which was to be to the daughter of a founder member of our club, Alex Grant, who was also present. I remember the happy, friendly way in which they were concerned in a personal and family event.

While at Inverness the Harrises were taken to see Culloden

Moor, the battlefield where Bonnie Prince Charlie was defeated in 1746 by the Duke of Cumberland after a bitter and controversial conflict. They also attended a meeting at the small burgh of Elgin, about forty miles east of Inverness. Afterwards they visited Lossiemouth, a small Scottish port where the British Prime Minister, Ramsay MacDonald, had his home.

While Harris was touring the smaller clubs of Scotland he received a telegram from Rotary headquarters in London saying it was too late to cancel all the meetings scheduled in England. It queried whether he was sufficiently recovered to attend the big intercity meetings at Cheltenham, Shrewsbury and Manchester. Harris, now fully recovered, replied that he could and would keep these engagements.

Paul and Mrs Harris took an instant liking to Aberdeen, the granite city, and Harris, especially, retained fond memories of his first visit there. The couple were given a fine sight-seeing tour of the area, of particular interest because of Mrs Harris's connections there. Auchenblae was almost certainly included in the itinerary. The couple went out as far as Balmoral and returned through Ballater and Banchory. On the return journey they called in unannounced at the home of the Aberdeen club's past President, whose name was Baker. In a letter printed in the February 1956 issue of *The Rotarian* twenty-two years after the visit, Joseph J. Baker, the son of the past President, recalled his meeting with the Harrises:

When I was a youth, an incident occurred which I look back on as the highlight of my Rotary life. We were at our country home in Torphins one Sunday in May when, about six o'clock, a car drew up and out got Willie Webster, President of the Rotary Club of Aberdeen, and his wife, and another lady and gentleman. When my father, a past president of the club, went to greet them, Willie Webster calmly said, 'I have brought Paul Harris to see you'. You should have seen my father's face! Paul and his wife were touring Scotland and had come to Aberdeen for the week-end. Such were their charm and simplicity that within five minutes Paul was in the kitchen discussing squab pie with my mother, while Mrs Harris was helping to weed the garden.

When they were going away, I asked the great man if I might take his photograph. He readily assented, but pointed out that as the light was rather bad, it might not come out; and he produced from his pocket a photograph of himself and told me to tell my friends that this was the one I took.

Paul Harris visited Aberdeen three years later—again without notice. When I shook hands with him, he gave me a sharp look and then said, quite casually, 'Hello there! How did that snapshot turn out?'

A truly great man who never let his fame or success make him forget the simple things in life.

Harris and his wife travelled to Edinburgh the next day where, for a time, they parted company. Mrs Harris went to Annbank to spend some time with her brother and sister while Harris continued south to Cheltenham. Here he met many old friends, including a Rotarian named Scott Langley, who went with Harris on another brief run through the fondly remembered Cotswolds. At the big inter-city meeting that followed, Harris met many Rotarians from the nearby (and not so nearby) cities.

Another inter-city meeting followed in the historic county town of Shrewsbury, strategically located on the River Severn on the border between England and Wales. It was a splendid assembly and, said Harris, 'I could not have been shown greater courtesy'. He made special mention of the Mayor, 'who gave himself to my service for the entire day'.

Harris's last official function in England in 1934 was a third great inter-city meeting at Manchester where, yet again, there was a capacity attendance, with many clubs represented. 'In fact,' he recalled, 'it was the biggest meeting the club had ever had.' His visit, after a second evening meeting, was concluded with a tour of the offices of the *Manchester Guardian* and the magnificent new public library.

From Manchester he made the short journey to Liverpool for lunch with officers and past officers of the Liverpool club, before embarking on the *Laurentic* which, after calling at Glasgow, where Mrs Harris joined him, sailed for Montreal. After a quiet and uneventful crossing the couple enjoyed a brief tour of the French-Canadian city. A visit to Quebec was followed by a brief stop in Toronto to see some friends. Then it was off to Mackinac Island for a week at the International Assembly before returning to Detroit for the twenty-fifth Rotary Convention.

CHAPTER 26

The Award of the Silver Buffalo

Having no children of their own, the Harrises took a particular interest in the International Society for Crippled Children. Wherever they went they encouraged others to take up Edgar Allen's valuable work, and as a direct result of their efforts, branches of the society were established throughout the United States and in other parts of the world.

Harris was also closely associated with the Boy Scouts of America movement, as indeed were many members of his Chicago club who, with Rotarians from other clubs, became Scout executives and leaders.

At the Detroit Convention in 1934 Harris, tried to conceal his involvement under a cloak of anonymity but was almost forcibly escorted to the platform by sixteen Boy Scouts. There, to the thunderous acclaim of the thousands of Rotarians present, Walter W. Head, President of the Boy Scouts of America, invested Harris with the significant and seldom awarded Silver Buffalo Citation. Turning to the cheering Rotarians, Head said: 'No man has accomplished more distinguished service to boyhood than Paul Harris. He has set a new standard in professional attitudes and ethics, which translates into selfless service for anyone, however humble, who is in need. Truly, this is Christianity in action.'

In the years that followed Harris was the recipient of many other awards and decorations, but the Silver Buffalo award of the Boy Scouts of America was one that held a special place in his affections.

Of the 7,377 delegates at the Convention, Harris singled out two for special mention, John Ilott and William Lyon 'Billy' Phelps. John Ilott was a New Zealand Rotarian who was to become the Governor of District 53 in 1935. During the Convention he suffered a severe heart attack, but his robust constitution eventually pulled him through. 'Billy' Phelps was a Rotarian from New Haven whom Harris held in high regard. A Professor of English at Yale University, Phelps was an internationally known author of a considerable number of scholarly literary criticisms. He spoke to the Chicago club several times, but at Detroit he simply appeared suddenly from a crowd, said, 'Paul—Billy Phelps', and promptly disappeared back into the throng. On the occasion of Harris's visit to the New Haven club, Professor Phelps wrote a brilliant editorial about the founder of Rotary. Harris himself acknowledged it as one of the two best he had ever seen.

The news about Rotary in 1934 was encouraging. New clubs were established in Iceland and Lithuania, but of even greater importance was the assembling of the first Council on Legislation and the emergence of the Institute of International Relations. The latter was sponsored by the Rotary Club of Nashville, Tennessee and became the forerunner of similar clubs everywhere.

After the Convention the Harrises returned to their home in Chicago, more than a little weary after their astonishing series of voyages, civic receptions, assemblies, speeches and sight-seeing tours. Yet within six months they were scheduled to commence an even more exacting tour on the other side of the world.

On 22 January 1935, Chicago was bitterly cold. That evening the Harrises left from the city's Northwestern Station at 9.30pm to tour the Far East and Chesley Perry, inevitably, was there to see them off.

The first stop was at Council Bluffs, Iowa, where they were greeted by an unexpectedly large delegation led by an old friend, 'Jake' Perkins, the Rotarian chiefly responsible for the first draft of the Rotary Code of Ethics in 1914. 'Jake', a well known journalist, later wrote for the *Chicago Tribune* under the pseudonym of 'Aborigine'.

At Omaha, Nebraska, the delegation was led by another old friend, Hugh Butler, then a director of Rotary International. It was the same story all along the route of the couple's journey across the western United States. Wherever they stopped Rotary club delegates were waiting to greet them, even if the stop was for a few minutes only. The journey acquired something of the appearance of a Presidential whistle-stop tour.

One delegation, at Cheyenne, Wyoming, was doomed to disappointment. The train arrived after the Harrises, unaware that a delegation of Rotarians had made a special effort to meet and greet them, had retired. Next morning, to their amazement, they received a bouquet 'From the Rotarians of Cheyenne', a gesture that expressed more eloquently than mere words not only the respect of the Cheyenne delegation but their disappointment as the train pulled away without a sight of Harris. He cabled them his sincere regrets and his and his wife's gratitude for the thoughtful gesture.

At Ogden, Utah, the Harrises saw for the first time (on this trip) the majestic Rocky Mountains. And, of course, the inevitable delegation of enthusiastic, energetic, business-like Rotarians descended upon them. It was the same at Eldo, Nevada, where they were joined by two members of the Eldo club. A little further on two other travellers joined the train, one of whom proved to be the Attorney General of the State of Nevada, the other a judge of the Supreme Court. Harris was in his element in such company, and was sorry to bid goodbye to his legal colleagues when they left at Reno to attend a meeting of the Nevada State Bar Association. As compensation, however, their places were taken by a party of Nevada Rotarians also headed for San Francisco and the big District Conference there.

Five days out from Chicago, Paul and Mrs Harris were met at Oakland by a large and happy group of District officers, and they proceeded to San Francisco by way of the Oakland ferry. As they crossed the great bay they could see in the distance the infamous island of Alcatraz where, at that time, Al Capone was incarcerated.

At the Conference, on 28 January, Harris joined Rotary International President Robert E. (Bob) Hill, Past President Almon Roth and several other local and national dignitaries. Harris sat next to the Mayor of San Francisco, His Excellency Angelo Rossi, whom he discovered was the son of Italian immigrants from Genoa. Nearby sat the city's Chief of Police, 'Bill' Quinn, the son of Irish immigrants. 'Where else but in the great melting pot of America would one find a Mayor of Italian descent, and a chief of police of Irish descent?' mused Harris as he rose to speak to more than one thousand Rotarians representing seventy-two clubs from California, Hawaii and Nevada.

After the meeting Harris, at his own request, met the surviving members of the original San Francisco club. 'Each and every member seemed near to me,' he said later, 'their enthusiastic acceptance of Rotary in 1908, and the splendid missionary work they did in Oakland, Los Angeles, Seattle and elsewhere, constituted high spots in the history of the movement, and at the same time afforded us much needed encouragement.'

Paul and Mrs Harris also met the other members of the official party who were to accompany them as far as the great conference of Asian clubs in the Philippines. Among them were Tsunejiro Miyaoka, a director of Rotary International, Mr and Mrs George Olinger of Denver, and Mr and Mrs George Fitch of Shanghai.

The party's departure must rank as one of the most extraordinary even in the extraordinary annals of that city. Police Chief Quinn, rushed the party to the quay—escorted by an imposing motor cycle squad with sirens shrieking. As Harris dryly commented: 'It terrified the unsuspecting citizens along the route, who sought shelter wherever it could be found. They must have thought a revolution had broken out in their fair city.'

On board the S.S. *President Coolidge* it was time for the party to get down to the Rotary business ahead. However, the ship ran into exceptionally heavy weather, an unexpected encounter which struck down all but two of the party—Harris, the seasoned ocean traveller, and Miyaoka.

Miyaoka was an extraordinarily gifted man. He had an outstanding record in diplomatic circles, having served Japan as Minister Plenipotentiary in Washington, its Chargé d'Affaires in Berlin, and as a counsel for the Japanese Department of Defence. He was, like Harris, an attorney by profession, and a member of both the American and Canadian Bar Associations, and the Japanese attorney for several important American corporations, including the gigantic United States Steel Corporation. He was selected by President Calvin Coolidge as the non-American representative of the United States to serve in all matters pertaining to the construction of the William Jennings Bryan Treaty with Uruguay. With such a background, the seventy-year-old Japanese Rotarian was obviously of inestimable value as a member of the Board of Directors of Rotary International.

When the inclement conditions permitted, President Bob Hill held delightfully intimate mini-conferences during the five-day voyage to Hawaii. Among those participating were George Olinger and George Fitch. Olinger was the incumbent Governor of District 7 of Rotary International, and had a record of long and distinguished service in the movement. He was particularly conspicuous in the cause of youth. He had twice been Chairman of

Rotary's Boys Work Committee, and also found time to lend his creative ability and dedication to a youth organization known as the 'Highlanders', which, at that time, boasted more than ten thousand members.

Fitch had also rendered distinguished service to youth. Most of his life had been lived in China, and for several years he was in charge of the extensive and valuable work of the Young Men's Christian Association in that country. Fitch was a close friend of an eminent Chinese Rotarian, Dr Fong Foo Sec, who, shortly before, had served on Rotary International's Board of Directors.

Other fellow passengers, but not of the official party, included Rotarians F.A. Kehl of St Louis, R.F. Walker of Chicago and J.E.E. Markley. Yet another of interest to Harris was J.P. Bailey, an ex-member of the San Francisco club. He was one of those unfortunate Rotarians who lost their classification when moving to another city. Another former Rotarian was a Dr Weigle, the Dean of the Divinity School of Yale University. He was once a member of the New Haven club and a close friend of Don Adams and William Lyon Phelps. He and Harris, sometimes with their wives, had long and animated talks during the voyage.

As the S.S. *President Coolidge* neared Hawaii the rough weather suddenly worsened. The gale at times exceeded one hundred miles an hour. It was, said the captain, the worst weather he had experienced in sixteen years plying the Pacific. When the fury was at its height the ship made no headway at all and when she finally hove into sight of Hawaii, the Rotary party was six hours behind schedule.

CHAPTER 27

Journey into the Sun

As the ship was nudged into its berth by fussy little tugs, a municipal band sounded a fanfare of trumpets, and bursts of multicoloured confetti filled the air. Long streamers of every hue were hurled aboard and joined the ship to the shore. But above it all rose the unique welcome of the Hawaiians, the lovely lilting *Aloha, Aloha*. Suddenly the band ceased playing, and a double quartette of singers burst into a thrilling song of welcome. Accustomed though they were by now to tumultuous receptions, the Harrises found this spontaneous outpouring of affection beyond their powers of description.

As soon as the gangplank was lowered the Rotarians of Hawaii sprang aboard and festooned them with beautifully coloured leis, the floral expressions of *Aloha*, meaning 'Welcome' to those arriving and 'Godspeed' to those departing. All visitors are greeted in a similar fashion, of course, but a special form of lei, known as the 'Ilima wreath', is reserved for distinguished visitors, and the Harrises had these draped around their shoulders. The last occasion on which the 'Ilima wreath' had been used was a year before, when the islanders welcomed Franklin D. Roosevelt, the first American President to visit Hawaii.

The moment the Harrises stepped ashore, more Rotarians arrived from all directions. Paul and his wife were 'captured' by the President of the Honolulu club and borne away in triumph. President and Mrs Hill were similarly 'captured' by the Chairman of the Reception Committee, while others made for the Olingers, the Fitches, Miyaoka and the rest of the party. A fantastic drive through the streets of Honolulu followed. One moment the cavalcade was hurtling through a well kept avenue lined with buildings of impressive architecture, the next through narrower streets of a less salubrious nature. In open country the Harrises viewed for the first time the exotic and luxurious Hawaiian flora—the ancient and gigantic banyan trees, monkey pods, sausage trees and other strange plants.

Their destination was a country club in the hinterland, where a large assembly of Rotarians had been waiting for hours. In view of the ship's delayed arrival, some of the ceremonies were curtailed, but both Paul Harris and President Bob Hill spoke to the gathering. Hill, who was an excellent speaker, enthralled the audience with his witty sallies, but it was Harris who held their attention with his story of Rotary.

After the reception came the usual round of autographs and photographs and a word or two with as many as could be accommodated. Another scenic drive followed. The *pièce de résistance* was a view from the famous Nuuanu Pali, a mountain top at the upper end of the Nuuanu Valley, a long, deep valley surrounded by distant mountains with, far beyond, the now lazy looking Pacific Ocean.

Back in Honolulu, at what was once the Iolani Palace, the Harris party met the island's governor and were shown the state's legislative chamber with its imposing portraits of the eccentric Queen Liliuokalani, who had visited Washington frequently in a quest for government aid, Queen Emma, and that idiosyncratic old monarch, King Kalakaua.

The Rotarians of Hawaii certainly accorded the party one of the warmest welcomes they had experienced in all their travels—and an equally rousing send off. With the party went two members of the Honolulu club, Charles Frazier and John Erdman.

The storm that had plagued Harris's party most of the way from San Francisco to Hawaii had still not abated when they left Honolulu, and the eight-day voyage to Japan was again tempestuous, with more howling gales and raging seas. All bad things come to an end eventually, however, and although the ship lost another twenty hours battling against the unrelenting elements, the majestic cone of Mount Fujiyama at long last appeared over the horizon.

The Harrises, and the fifteen other Rotarians and ladies who now comprised the party, were welcomed ashore at Yokohama, Japan's chief port, by a large and dignified party of Japanese Rotarians. Leading the delegation were E.W. Frazar, a tall stately man of American parentage, Shunichiro 'Shun' Mizushima, and 'Sam'

Namura. Accompanying them were more reporters and cameramen than Harris had ever seen together in one place. The enthusiasm of the welcoming Rotarians was visibly demonstrated by their inspired display of a flag bearing the Rotary emblem.

Harris was well aware that only twelve years previously Yokohama had been utterly devastated by an earthquake. In the interval the industrious Japanese had completely rebuilt the city and not a sign of the ravages remained.

The visitors were driven to Tokyo, eighteen miles away which took in a sight-seeing tour of the Japanese capital, along the boulevards and past the Emperor's Palace to the great Shrine of Buddha.

The two Presidents, Harris and Hill, planted a tree of friendship in the grounds of the Imperial Hotel, which prompted Harris to relate an anecdote about the famous hotel, which was designed by a fellow Chicagoan, Frank Lloyd Wright. The three hundred room hotel was not only architecturally significant, it was also designed to endure. After the 1923 earthquake, someone excitedly cabled the eccentric architect: 'The Imperial still stands.' Back came Wright's laconic reply: 'Of course!'

Lunch was taken in true Japanese style, served by geisha girls at the celebrated Maple Club. It was here that Harris met a Rotarian he greatly respected, Umekichi Yoneyama, the founder of Rotary in Japan and a distinguished businessman. It was Yoneyama who now took charge of the Harrises, showing them how to use chopsticks, and explaining Japanese customs and beliefs. He explained how reverence was implanted in the minds of Japanese children at an early age and how they were taught that their lives did not belong to them, but to their Emperor. Life must be freely and gladly given whenever the occasion demanded. During the afternoon Yoneyama took the couple to the most interesting parts of Tokyo, including a visit to the main office and retail store of the famous Kokichi Mikimoto, where they saw a film about the pearl industry.

At an evening banquet presided over by Yoneyama, Harris met two great Japanese statesmen—Prince Iyesato Tokugawa and Viscount Makoto Saito. The Prince was a member of a Japanese noble family, and his father was the last of the Shoguns, the real rulers up to the time of the dynasty's dissolution in 1867. Prince Tokugawa had visited the United States on a number of occasions. In 1921, when he was the President of the Japanese House of Peers, he was a delegate to the Washington Conference on the Limitation of Armaments. And in 1930 he addressed the Rotary Convention in Chicago on the occasion of the movement's twenty-fifth anniversary.

Viscount Saito, an admiral of the Japanese Navy, was the Keeper of the Privy Seal. Only a year previously he had relinquished the office of Prime Minister, to which he was appointed in 1932. Sadly, only a few months after he and Harris sat together at the memorable Rotary banquet, the seventy-seven-year-old Admiral was, on 26 February 1936, assassinated by terrorists.

Following the banquet Harris and his party took an overnight train west to Kyoto, the centre of the silk industry and, until 1869, the classic capital of the country. A goodly party of Japanese Rotarians accompanied them, including Baron and Baroness Togo, the Baroness making herself responsible for Mrs Harris's welfare. Harris's last sight of Tokyo was of the many smiling and waving Japanese Rotarians, led by Yoneyama. (A life size bust of the great Japanese Rotarian was on Harris's desk as he wrote his memoirs in the last year of his life.)

At Kyoto the following morning the party enjoyed a Japanese style breakfast at the city's principal hotel before being taken for a drive around the city, which included a visit to a beautiful country estate with superb rock gardens and lagoons. The tour also took in the Hijo Detached Palace and, as there were intermittent showers, frequent calls were made at conveniently located pagodas, where refreshments were served, these unexpected diversions delighting the Harrises.

During the afternoon the party was driven to Osaka, sometimes described as the 'Chicago of Japan', where Harris met Shozo Murata, Governor of Rotary's 70th District which, at that time, encompassed all of Japan, with its twenty-two vigorous clubs. Today that single district comprises twenty-one regions with more than 1,200 clubs and 70,000 members, making Japan the second largest country in Rotary, despite the virtual cessation of activity during World War II.

Representatives from almost every Japanese Rotary club attended the reception and luncheon. They cheered Harris as he came into the dining room, but he was nonplussed when confronted with another Paul Harris at the head table—a bust in bronze, cast by a Japanese artist at the request of Yoneyama. This was ceremoniously presented to Harris, and District Governor Murata, also the president of the Osaka Steamship Company, made immediate arrangements to ship it to Chicago on his own line.

Murata drove Paul and Mrs Harris the short distance to Kobe, where they embarked once again on the *President Coolidge*, which had sailed from Yokohama during the two days they were visiting five Japanese cities. Frazar, 'Shun' and 'Sam' who, with Miyaoka, had become virtually indispensable, came with them as additions to the official party for the voyage to Manila.

A delegation of Chinese Rotarians, headed by the President of the Shanghai club, was present to greet the Harrises when the ship docked. Shanghai was then one of the most talked about cities in the world. In 1927 it was captured by rebel Chinese troops and when the party of Rotarians arrived there on a February evening in 1935 they could still see in the heavily bombarded city the scars of the bloody carnage.

The party was immediately whisked away to a banquet at the Metropole Hotel, the most luxurious in the city at that time. Waiting to welcome them was the Mayor of Shanghai, an important Chinese businessman. It fell to President Hill to reply to the Mayor's welcome and he did so eloquently. Harris also spoke as, to his intense satisfaction, did Mrs Harris.

After a night's rest aboard the *President Coolidge* the party arose refreshed. If they were expecting a rather unkempt city, one with extremes of poverty and affluence, they had an agreeable surprise. They were confronted with a fine, modern city built on western lines with skyscrapers, hotels and office blocks, which would not have been out of place in Europe or America. One of the buildings they went to see, or rather what was left of it after the bombardment, was the Commercial Press, a great institution, which had done so much for the education of the Chinese people. Harris had a particular interest in this project, as one of his many friends, and a great Rotarian, Dr Fong Sec, was long associated with it.

They also visited the city's hinterland, where the Chinese residents were building a new city. 'It was,' said Harris, 'a magnificent undertaking. The new city was beautifully laid out, with broad open spaces, and decoratively landscaped according to Chinese standards. The municipal building was an adaptation of Chinese art to modern utilitarianism, decidedly ornate, and worthy of more study than we were able to give it in the time available.'

Back in Shanghai Harris performed the now traditional ceremony of planting a tree of friendship, which he did in Gordon Park in the presence of several city officials and the usual gathering of Rotarians. A visit to the American Consul was followed by the Shanghai club's luncheon, at which both Harris and Hill spoke. Harris and his wife were later taken by a club member, Hugo Sandor, to see the American Club and other places of interest. Sandor, a Hungarian by birth, was the immediate past President of the Shanghai club. He was a true cosmopolitan and a keen student of international affairs, holding that Shanghai was the most exciting city in the world and China the most fascinating country.

Within three years Sandor's dreams ended in sadness. In 1937 Shanghai fell to the Japanese army and it remained occupied until 1946, when it was surrendered to the Chinese Nationalists. The Rotary Club of Shanghai was immediately reformed, but its life was all too short. In 1949 the city fell again, this time to the Communist forces of Red China. There is no Rotary club in Shanghai today, and one cannot help but wonder what became of Hugo Sandor, Percy Chu (the club President at the time of Harris's visit), and all those other Rotarians who welcomed and fêted Paul and Mrs Harris, President Bob and Mrs Hill and the other members of the touring party. And the tree of friendship Harris planted in Gordon Park? Is it still there? If so, is it still identified? Perhaps, in time, some enterprising Rotarian will find the answers.

From Shanghai the *President Coolidge* steamed down the east China coast to Hong Kong, where a club was established in 1930. The party grew yet again with the addition of several Chinese Rotarians, including the quaintly named Percy Chu. When asked how he came by the name of 'Percy', Rotarian Chu replied that this was not the name given to him by his parents. He just happened to like it, and helped himself!

About the brief visit to Hong Kong Harris had this to say: 'We were amazed at the beauty of the harbour and of the city itself. The harbour is almost surrounded by lofty hills upon which English homes have been erected. We drove over the nearby hills and our motorcade wound its way around other hills in the back country. Grand scenery spread before us in all directions, and we were not long out of sight of the placid Pacific Ocean. We have heard enthusiasts designate Hong Kong as the most beautiful city in the world, and it is certainly entitled to the distinction of being designated one of them.'

Part of the drive included a trip through a peaceful valley which led them to the Repulse Bay Hotel, where they took tea with their hosts and had numerous photographs taken in the spacious gardens. Then it was back to the city, to the island capital of Victoria and an afternoon banquet. On this occasion Harris delivered a major address on the problems with which some of the Rotary clubs in China were coping.

One last official duty remained, a visit to the palatial residence of the British Governor. With them was Ted Hall, the Chairman of the Manila Conference Committee. He and Mrs Hall came to Hong Kong to escort the party on the last leg of the voyage. Swelling the ranks were numerous recruits to the already sizable Chinese and Japanese contingents, and included among them were two Rotarians from the Manchurian city of Mukden, Mr Scheinhutte and Mr Hjeng, the latter being the Czechoslovakian Consul. Mukden, now under Communist rule, is yet another city to have disappeared from the world of Rotary.

As the *President Coolidge* moved majestically out of the harbour: 'The lights of Hong Kong dotted the hillsides like jewels. It was indeed a beautiful scene. Hong Kong was appropriately named. In English the words mean "Fragrant Harbour".'

It was a happy international group that voyaged from Hong Kong to Manila. By this time there were representatives on board from all the countries of the Pacific littoral. There was a gratifying atmosphere of the friendship invariably present at Rotary gatherings; informal meetings, tea parties and the exchange of seats at tables were commonplace. Members of the party mixed with different racial groups, and on one occasion the wife of a Japanese Rotarian, a Mrs Kodama, invited all the ladies to tea, a ceremony which was conducted in the customary Japanese manner.

Of some significance was a meeting between Japanese and Chinese Rotarians. Three Japanese were sitting in the ship's lounge, conversing with Harris and other Americans. Harris noticed a Chinese Rotarian, Dr C.T. Wang of Shanghai, crossing the room and beckoned him to join the group. Relations between China and Japan at that time were, in diplomatic parlance, strained. Dr Wang came to the table and was warmly welcomed. He then wrote a note: 'We Chinese Rotarians are desirous of the friendship of Japanese

Rotarians.' This was handed to one of the Japanese who, after reading it, passed it on to the next and so on around the group. Rotary friendship transcended the uneasy relations between the two most important nations in the Pacific.

When the delegates arrived in Manila, the climate was oppressive, almost prostrating. Harris was affected and, despite the comfortable quarters he and Mrs Harris were assigned at the palatial Manila Hotel, he contracted a cold on the second day of the Conference. This necessitated his staying in bed for a while, thereby depriving him of the opportunity to attend several sessions and some of the evening entertainments.

Harris soon recovered, however, and spent much of his time listening to the excellent papers bearing upon Rotary problems and activities in the Pacific area. In between sessions he and Mrs Harris explored Manila. Once an unkempt and unsanitary community, Manila had been transformed into a healthy and beautiful city by someone Harris knew well, Daniel Burnham, the American architect who also mastermined the 'Chicago Beautiful' plan in 1908. Burnham's philosophy appealed to Harris: 'Make no little plans . . . make big plans.'

When the Conference ended the Harrises had five days to spare before leaving for Australia. They decided to rest and recuperate high in the cool air of the mountains, in a small city named Baguio (also planned by Daniel Burnham). There was no Rotary club in the city at that time, but it is interesting to note that one was established there only two years later.

Before the party left Manila, farewells had to be said. President Hill and his wife Gertrude were bound in a different direction, as were George Olinger and his wife. Off back to Japan were Everett Frazar, 'Shun' and 'Sam'.

At Baguio, Paul and Mrs Harris were joined by a New Zealand Rotarian, Harry Guthrie, who orginally joined their party in Japan and was later to be their host in New Zealand. The couple's days in Baguio were spent in resting after the strenuous weeks of travel, but they nonetheless found time to visit the gold mines a few miles away and to explore other points of interest. During their stay they rested at a comfortable country club, used, a few years later, by the Japanese Army during their occupation of the Philippines.

On the Sunday of their departure there was a flurry of excitement among the officers of the quaint but staunch Japanese ship, the *Kitano Maru*, when the Harrises embarked for Australia. With great ceremony they were shown to the two tiny cabins and bath quarters that had been engaged for them. Harris subsequently discovered he was being accorded VIP treatment. 'The courtesy and attention we were shown,' said Harris, 'could not have been bettered on the largest and most luxurious of liners.'

The *Kitano Maru* cast anchor three times en route to Australia, and the couple seized the opportunity on each occasion to see more of the Pacific lands. The first stop was at Davao, on the island of Luzon, the centre of the hemp industry in that part of the world. There was no Rotary club to be visited but, because of the enthusiasm Harris generated in his talks to local businessmen, a club was established there in 1938.

The second port of call was Manado, in what was then the Dutch East Indies, and it was in this unlikely place that Paul and Mrs Harris met one of the great Christians of the twentieth century, Kagawa. The town was in a state of excitement over the visit of the famed Japanese evangelist and the congregation at a meeting at the town hall overflowed the hall's capacity. The Harrises found room, however, and heard Kagawa speak in English, with his remarks translated into both Dutch and the native tongue.

They discovered to their delight that Kagawa was also a passenger aboard the *Kitano Maru*, and was booked to speak to several Rotary clubs in Australia. They quickly made a friend of the Japanese Christian and heard much from his own lips about his doctrines and beliefs. At his Sunday morning services on board ship, Mrs Harris sang hymns while Harris sat in the congregation.

As the ship wound its way through the many islands of the South Pacific, Harris had plenty of time to read and write. There was entertainment in plenty—Japanese parties, dinners, dances, films and other events—but the Harrises preferred the quieter life of discussions with fellow passengers such as Kagawa, and the five New Zealanders and one Australian who were travelling with them.

The last stop before arrival in Australia was Thursday Island off the north coast of Queensland. This they found of little interest and merely spent a few hours ashore in Port Kennedy, 'a dejected, hot and muggy town', remarked Harris.

A pleasant surprise was in store for Paul and Mrs Harris before they disembarked at Brisbane. The ship's officers presented them with two tokens of their esteem: a living evergreen tree, dwarfed after the Japanese custom, and, in Harris's words, 'a titanic master-piece of art in confectionery', which according to Captain Idena, was prepared by the ship's cook, who worked on it for two weeks. It was fashioned like a Japanese garden and was so heavy two men were required to lift it. Harris arranged for the splendid work of culinary art to be transported to the all-Australia Conference at Melbourne, where it was placed on exhibit. After the Conference it was presented to the city's hospital for crippled children.

It spoke volumes for the popularity of the Harrises that they should be singled out for such tokens of respect by those not connected with Rotary.

CHAPTER 28

'Down Under'

Harris's first scheduled meeting was in Brisbane, where he was met by Fred Birks, a former Second Vice President of Rotary International and often referred to, especially by Harris, as 'The Grand Old Man of Rotary in Australia'. He had travelled more than six hundred miles to meet the Harrises and placed his automobile and chaffeur at their disposal. In the event they were used for more than one thousand miles of travelling.

After delivery to their hotel by Walter Darker, the immediate past District Governor of Rotary's 76th District (all of Northern Australia), the Harrises attended the almost mandatory Civic reception. It was a ceremony to be repeated in almost every city and town they visited in Australia and New Zealand. Although the sixty-seven-year-old Founder of Rotary was sometimes weary, he appreciated the honour. At the ceremony in Brisbane Harris met the Lord Mayor and the American Consul and it is an indication of the respect he commanded as President Emeritus of Rotary that civic dignitaries were almost always the first to greet him.

After the ceremony the Reception Committee of the Brisbane club noted Harris's wan appearance (he was not feeling well when he landed), and decided that a drive into the countryside and a breath of fresh air was what was needed. Finally, 'and it was a stroke of genius', commented Harris wryly, the committee took the couple to see their magnificent new crematorium!

Harris's sense of humour was contagious. He asked if the institution was proving a success, and was told that the 'chief cook' had yet to receive a complaint!

At a packed inter-city meeting Harris made one of his finest speeches. Many of the Rotarians in the audience, who would never have another opportunity of meeting Harris, travelled hundreds of miles for the occasion. Newspaper interviews, radio broadcasts, more receptions, a visit to a crippled children's home, and a drive up a nearby mountain followed in quick succession before the exhausted couple were able to retire.

Next morning Paul and Mrs Harris, accompanied by Birks, took a train for Sydney in New South Wales, a journey that took more than twenty-four hours. When they at last drew into a well kept and clearly affluent suburban district of Sydney another day had begun.

First to greet them was an old friend, Tom Armstrong, Governor of the then 76th District of Rotary, whom they had not seen since the Convention in Detroit the previous year. Another old friend was Sir Henry Braddon, who had become the Resident Commissioner for Rotary in Australia. Harris once remarked about him that 'he had a unique awareness of the concept of Rotary'.

As they were due back in Sydney at the end of their tour of Australia, the Harrises spent only two days in the city on this first visit. There was time enough, however, to attend a luncheon meeting of the Rotary Club of North Sydney, where Harris spoke briefly, and to plant a tree of friendship in a public park. The tree chosen was an Australian wheel tree, the flower of which bears a striking resemblance to the Rotary wheel. They also paid a visit to the offices of the Sydney Society for Crippled Children, and Mrs Harris addressed a meeting of the Inner Wheel.

During their short visit the Harrises stayed at the Wentworth Hotel, selected by Birks because the proprietor, 'Daddy' Burch, was not only a Rotarian but a native of the United States. Harris renewed many friendships in Sydney, meeting again such respected leaders of Rotary as Professor William Osborne, another Resident Commissioner, and Ben Gelling. Gelling was first the Secretary, and later the President, of the Sydney club, and managed the Sydney Society for Crippled Children. All were travelling on to Melbourne for the combined Conference of the 65th and 76th Districts of Rotary which, at that time, encompassed the whole of Australia.

The welcome the Harrises received at Melbourne could not have been more emotional. Waiting for them at the station was one of their dearest friends, Angus (later Sir Angus) Mitchell, the then Governor of the 65th District. Mitchell and his wife Teeny were to be their hosts for the duration of their stay in Melbourne. After the usual round of greetings the couple were driven to the Mitchell's

191

beautiful home at Mindanao, a plush residential part of the city. And how they were hosted! On the afternoon of their first day a grand reception was given by the Mitchells for more than 450 Rotarians and their wives. This was held in the spacious gardens at Mindanao, and a huge marquee was erected to provide everyone with protection from the intermittent rain. Each person was greeted by Harris, Mrs Harris, Mitchell and Mrs Mitchell as they arrived. When the afternoon drew to a close the procedure was reversed, and there were individual good-byes.

During their stay Paul and Mrs Harris made a special and personal visit to the home of the parents of one of their dearest friends, the late Walter Drummond. Drummond, it will be recalled, visited Harris at Comely Bank in 1914 with a view to introducing Rotary to Australia. World War I prevented any further development, but when Ralston and Davidson came to Australia in 1921, Drummond was instrumental in organizing the Rotary Club of Melbourne and became the club's second secretary. An architect by profession, Drummond was twice a guest at Comely Bank, and his untimely death grieved the Harrises deeply. The first tree planted in their Garden of Friendship was dedicated to his memory. Appropriately, it was a splendid blue spruce, and they found a photograph of it hanging on the wall of the home of Drummond's aged parents.

Before the opening of the first Conference session the Harrises were received at the executive mansion of the Governor of Victoria, Lord Huntington. The deliberations of the Conference, and the excellent papers presented, are on record elsewhere. Harris was equally impressed with another feature, the singing. 'I was unable to recall ever having heard any Rotary singing worthy of special mention in any British club, except those in Wales and some Canadian clubs. In Australia they not only sang, but sang as well if not better than in the United States, where club singing has always been an integral feature of Rotary meetings,' he said.

The Melbourne Conference was a success. The spirit was good, the papers excellent, the entertainment of the highest order.

Mrs Harris made a name for herself at the Conference. At one gathering she addressed three hundred ladies and Harris slipped into the meeting unnoticed (or so he thought). He took pride in his wife's activities. As he put it, 'I experienced a peculiar sense of gratification in realization of the fact that Jean was sharing my responsibilities'.

Paul and Jean Harris being welcomed by the Lord Provost of
Edinburgh during their tour of Scotland in 1934

Paul and Jean Harris relaxing at Comely Bank

Jean Harris's grave, Newington Cemetery, Edinburgh

Former General Secretary of Rotary International, George Means, at
Paul Harris's graveside in Mount Hope Cemetery

Angus and Mrs Mitchell were tireless in their out-of-Conference-time activities. Almost every evening they gave dinner parties at their home to large parties of distinguished Rotarians. They provided Harris with an exceptional opportunity to spend five minutes with each Rotarian in a special room set aside for the purpose, which enabled Harris to make personal contact with a much greater number of Rotarians than he could have done at a large assembly. Whenever he was in a group, everyone wanted to speak to him, only to be interrupted immediately by someone equally eager. It was a cause of embarrassment to him to have to turn from one to another as they clamoured for his attention. The Mitchell's arrangement was at least a part solution to the problem, and he appreciated the gesture.

Harris delivered at least three speeches during the Conference, one to a combined meeting of the delegates of the two Australian districts, the others to each group separately. Between sessions he was able to take time out for a variety of other activities. He laid a wreath at the magnificent war memorial which dominates the city, and planted trees of friendship in a public park. These, incidentally, were near to a similar tree planted by Past International President Sydney Pascall during his goodwill tour of Australia. Another pleasant diversion was a visit with Mitchell to the nearby city of Essendon, a north-western suburb of Melbourne. There he attended one of the first meetings of the newly chartered club and, typically, visited some invalided Rotarians.

On the Sunday after the close of the conference, Harris was the guest speaker at an all-Australia broadcast from one of the principal churches in Melbourne. This enabled him to deliver the message of Rotary to thousands outside the Movement's ranks. It was a fitting climax to the impressive week-long conference.

Shortly before the assembly dispersed, the Rotarians of Australia demonstrated their abiding respect and admiration for Harris. As they gathered for the last messages, Harris was called to the platform to be presented with a highly artistic office desk made of Australian black wood.

The next day the Harrises and the Mitchells set sail for Tasmania—and a confrontation with 'bandits'.

Once known as Van Dieman's Land, Tasmania is a beautiful island about 250 miles south of Australia. The capital, Hobart, is on the south side of the island; Launceston, where the party landed, is in the north. The crossing was choppy but Harris, impervious to the unsettling effects of stormy seas, discussed Rotary affairs with Mitchell and Sinclair McGibbon, a Rotarian who travelled all the way from Perth in Western Australia to attend the Melbourne Conference and to accompany them to Tasmania.

At Launceston the party was met by Charles Mounds, a Rotarian house guest at the Mitchell's home during the Conference. Aware of the rigours of the voyage, Mounds whisked the group to his home, beautifully situated on a hill overlooking Launceston and a sublime valley. However, soon after they lunched, the party returned to the city for an inter-club meeting which Harris addressed. After the meeting the party toured some of the spectacularly beautiful scenery of northern Tasmania.

Harry Cummings, a past District Governor of the 65th District, joined the party at this stage and accompanied it on a one hundred mile drive to the capital, Hobart. Here the schedule was more ambitious—a civic reception, planting a tree of friendship in a public park, group photographs, a luncheon meeting (which was broadcast), and an evening meeting to which the ladies were invited.

While quite casually discussing the crime situation in Chicago, Harris said that although he had lived in the city for forty years, and had walked the streets at all times of the night, he had never been accosted or robbed.

The Hobart Rotarians were not slow to appreciate the opportunity presented. Having said good-byes, the party was being driven comfortably along the highway north to Launceston when, suddenly, it was confronted by a gang of 'desperados', armed with sawn-off shotguns, revolvers, masks and all the requisite paraphernalia of the bandit. Harris and other members of the party were ordered out of the car and divested of their Rotary insignia. True, other badges were substituted but somewhere in Tasmania today there is a Rotary lapel emblem that was once the property of Paul Harris.

That afternoon the party steamed down the river from Launceston on its way back to Melbourne. This time it was a pleasant crossing. It had been a short visit to Tasmania but a delightful one. Harris visited only two clubs but in both he received the same enthusiastic welcome he was accorded wherever he went. Because of the broadcast at Hobart the ladies at the evening reception were able to discuss Rotary matters in far greater detail, and Harris commented on how valuable the mass media could be. While in Hobart he received several letters from unknown people, not Rotarians, who heard the broadcast. One of these was from a man living alone on a distant island who wrote that although he was not a Rotarian, the broadcast meetings were pleasures he looked forward to throughout the week. More than that, the writer felt identified with the objectives and ideals of Rotary.

The incident on the highway from Hobart was one that brought a smile to Harris's face. Once again, the practical joker himself, had been upstaged. He was more amused when, after relating the story to an Australian friend, he was told: 'Well, of course, you did know that Hobart was founded as a penal colony in 1804?'

When Harris visited Tasmania in 1935 there were only three clubs on the island—Hobart, Launceston and Devonport. The last named is not far from Launceston and was undoubtedly well represented at the inter-club meeting. Today there are thirty-three active Rotary clubs on this still quite thinly populated island. What greater tribute can Tasmania pay to the memory of the man who began it all so many years ago?

Back in Melbourne the Harrises were again the guests of the hospitable Mitchells, and on the day of their arrival Harris attended meetings of two of the smaller clubs in the Melbourne area, Geelong and Dandenong. At the inevitable civic reception at Geelong the Mayor was unusually gracious, and his speech was highly complimentary—except in one detail. He kept referring to Harris as 'that great American, the Honourable Paul Jones'. On the first occasion the audience let this pass, thinking it to be just a slip, but when it happened again someone interposed and whispered, 'You mean Paul Harris, your Worship', to which the Mayor replied, 'Yes, quite so, I mean Paul Harris', and forthwith proceeded again to refer to Harris as 'Paul Jones'.

When Harris responded he skillfully turned the situation to his advantage by saying that he could not have been paid a higher compliment than to be mistaken for the illustrious Paul Jones. As Harris sat down the Mayor leaned over and handed him a book, whispering apologetically as he did so, 'Darned if I didn't make the same mistake in the inscription'.

At Geelong Harris renewed his acquaintance with John Buchan, a prominent member of the Young Australia League. Buchan was also prominently identified with the Apex clubs movement, an organization of young businessmen similar to the Round Table clubs of Britain, the Active 20–30 clubs of the United States, and the Kinsmen clubs of Canada.

That evening the Rotary Club of nearby Dandenong received its charter from no less a person than the Founder of Rotary himself. Few clubs can claim that distinction, certainly no other in Australia. Today the Dandenong club has more than one hundred members. Are there still any among them who were present on that historic evening in 1935?

It was not easy to leave Melbourne, said Harris, as they bade fond farewells to their many friends. They could not have been more warmly received, nor more regally entertained. The long drive north to Sydney was made up of a party of eight. With the Harrises were the Mitchells, Dan Hellings and George Shaw (two Melbourne Rotarians) and their wives. On the outskirts of Melbourne the party was met by a huge delegation of Rotarians from all the clubs in and around Melbourne. Farewells were not new to Paul and Mrs Harris, but, as Harris observed, 'the last is just as emotional as the first'.

The party's first stop, after a halt along the way for the traditional cup of 'Billy Tea', was at Albury, New South Wales, where a civic reception was once again tendered. The Mayor, Alfred Waugh, was also a Rotarian whom the Harrises had met at the Melbourne Conference. Waugh, a cripple, had already served as Mayor for ten years. Shortly before the visit he was the recipient of an unusual honour, the Order of the Orange, bestowed upon him by the Queen of Holland to mark a unique service which Waugh and the townspeople of Albury rendered two Dutch fliers in the Centenary Air Race from Croydon, England, to Melbourne. The aviators apparently lost their way and, with night falling, were desperately searching for a landing field. Waugh and his Town Clerk ordered the city lights to be extinguished and summoned all automobile owners to assemble their vehicles around a race track, with headlights blazing a safe landing path. Waugh's quick thinking may well have saved the lives of the two flyers. The Queen of Holland certainly thought so.

In the curiously named city of Wagga Wagga, 320 miles southwest of Sydney, the party attended an afternoon reception and club meeting, after which Harris made another nationwide broadcast from the Methodist Church. After a night's rest at the home of the club's President, a Rotarian named Castles, the party drove on to the Australian capital.

Canberra was of special interest to Harris. An entirely new city, it was built to circumvent the rivalry between Sydney and Melbourne to be designated the nation's capital. When the city was first mooted, a number of world renowned architects were invited to submit plans. The successful design was the inspired work of Walter Burleigh Griffin of Chicago, a man well known to Harris. It was remarkable that during his tour of the Far East and Australasia, Harris viewed the work of three Chicago architects—Wright's Imperial Hotel in Tokyo, Burnham's cities of Manila and Baguio in the Philippines, and Griffin's Canberra. Harris said of the city:

It was indeed a dreamland plan. Evergreen trees predominate and the plantings are so arranged that there are brilliant colours at all seasons of the year. Twenty thousand rose bushes have been planted along one avenue. On the hills surrounding a broad level valley in which flows a meandering river and also in the valley itself at strategic points, groups of buildings have been erected. Here they are residential, here educational, governmental, commercial, civic, etc. Wide stretches upon which sheep are feeding separate them, and eighty miles of splendid roads lined with three million trees, shrubs and flowers connect them. Among the trees are avenues of the famous black and silver wattles which bloom in September in grand pageantry. There are also avenues of flowering plum, peach, cherry and almond trees and endless lines of the more common elms, poplars and cypresses.

The party's first function was at an evening meeting at a hotel built along the lines of a sublimated California bungalow. Attending were a number of government officials, members of the legislature and several titled personalities, including Sir Robert Garran, President of the Rotary Club of Canberra, whom Harris had met at the Melbourne Conference; when correctly addressing his fellow Rotarian as 'Sir Robert', Harris was immediately instructed to 'Cut the Sir'. Thereafter they were Robert and Paul.

Under Garran's guidance the entire party, enlarged by the

presence of Tom Armstrong, into whose territory (the 76th District) they had now passed, visited all the places of interest in Canberra. In the House of Representatives Harris had an opportunity to chat with the war-time Prime Minister of Australia, William Morris Jones, a Welshman by birth. Through the courtesy of another member of the Canberra club, Colonel White, Harris and his party were invited to take tea with the leaders of the three political parties of the day.

An even more memorable visit was made during the afternoon of the party's second day in the city, when they were received by Sir Isaac Isaacs Governor General of Australia and Lady Isaacs at the Executive Mansion. Although already eighty years old (he lived to ninety-three) Sir Isaacs's intellect was unimpaired and his intimate knowledge of the decisions of the Supreme Court of the United States astonished Harris. The Governor General and Lady Isaacs received the party most cordially and personally escorted them through the superb mansion. To the end of his life Harris remembered his animated discussions about points of law with the elderly jurist, and marvelled anew at a mind that was 'fairly scintillating with energy'.

After three glorious days in the 'dream city' it was time for the Harrises to continue their journey and for their companions from Melbourne to go their different ways. As they said their farewells Harris expressed the hope that their friendship would not be likened to 'ships that pass in the night'. His hope was realized. He and Mrs Harris met the Mitchells time and again in the years that followed and they became the closest of friends. Mitchell went on to become President of Rotary International in 1948–9 and wrote the moving foreword to Harris's last work, *My Road to Rotary*.

Fred Birks sent his car and chauffeur to Canberra for the journey to Sydney and made arrangements for the Harrises and Armstrong to visit some of the clubs along the route.

The first was at Goulburn, where the party again met George Smith, the club's Vice President. It so happened that Smith was the warden of the penitentiary in Goulburn, and the Harrises were offered the choice of visiting this or an important manufacturing plant. Needless to say, the couple were more interested in people than machines. Smith ran his prison on humanitarian lines, and Harris noted that when Smith approached any of the prisoners they smiled rather than scowled, an eloquent reaction. Harris also noted the sparkling eyes of the prisoner who gathered a bouquet and presented it to Mrs Harris.

Prompted by his visit to the penitentiary, Harris mentioned to Smith that he had just finished reading a book entitled *Sing Sing Doctor*. This was written by Dr Amos Squires, a former Director of Rotary International, and it related the author's experiences and observations over a period of more than thirty years as the chief medical officer at one of America's most famous prisons. Squires was in contact with tens of thousands of prisoners and as part of his duties had participated in 138 executions. In *Sing Sing Doctor* Squires expressed his revulsion against all methods predicated on the theory of punishment, a philosophy akin to the humane methods adopted by Smith. Both these Rotarians were practical men, not theorizers or dreamers, and the almost complete abolition of capital punishment in the second half of the twentieth century confirmed Harris's contention that both men were years ahead of their time in their approach to the treatment of prison inmates.

With Armstrong, Harris visited a new club in the pastoral village of Nowra, a community usually referred to nowadays as Nowra-Bomaderry. It lies about one hundred miles south of Sydney on the east coast of New South Wales. Even today the population is barely 13,000, yet the Rotary club there (chartered in 1934) boasts a membership of almost seventy.

The last call before Sydney was the important manufacturing city and seaport of Wollongong, about forty miles south of the party's destination. A thoroughly representative Rotary meeting was held, with the Mayor, an immigrant Irishman, gracing the occasion with his presence. Harris noted that 'big business' was unusually well represented in Wollongong so it surprised him to note that one club member, Dr Kirkwood, was a strong advocate of social reform. At the same time he was unquestionably a popular club member. Harris pondered the apparent anomaly and produced one of his significant observations: 'The writer's natural inclinations have been to adhere to the old doctrine of avoidance of controversial issues in Rotary, but he is not dogmatic in that regard. It might even be possible, if the members of all clubs would be as tolerant as the members of the Wollongong club seem to be, and if care be taken always to have both sides of controversial issues ably represented, that great good would come of it.'

The route from Wollongong to Sydney was mainly along the

lovely coast road of New South Wales. At times this rose to about one thousand feet above sea level, providing one of the most magnificent scenic panoramas in the world. On Harris's journey the party stopped at Sublime Point for a view of the coastal scenery below, and then drove along Lady Carrington Drive and through a National Park system of 33,000 acres. At one point they encountered an aborigine who instructed Harris on how to throw a boomerang and allowed him to get in some practice.

Finally the Harrises arrived back in Sydney. This time they approached the city from the south and their route lay through less salubrious areas. They were rejoined by Birks and by his daughter, Mrs Somerville. After a brief rest the couple were driven to visit Birks' son and family in Wamberal. They were also taken by Armstrong to visit his home in Newcastle, one hundred miles north of Sydney. Once a penal colony, Newcastle had become the centre of the Australian steel industry. Primarily an industrial city, Harris noted that it also had fine bathing beaches and was near a beautiful lake where the recreational facilities were second to none.

There were drives around the city and the surrounding countryside, the usual round of receptions, a civic welcome, dinners and the planting of a tree of friendship. Mrs Harris spoke to a group of ladies who, said Harris, were reluctant to let her depart and clung to her to the last moment of their stay.

There was time for only one more club visit. This was at Parramatta, a small municipality fifteen miles west of Sydney. Here, after his penultimate Rotary meeting in Australia, Harris planted yet another of his trees of friendship, now rapidly encircling the globe. En route they visited Koala Park, a well known sight-seeing spot.

The couple's last functions in Australia included a cruise around the superb Sydney Harbour on a yacht belonging to the Premier of New South Wales, a farewell meeting with the members of the Rotary Club of Sydney and a visit to the university, where they were the guests of the University's President, Wallace. He was born in Scotland and naturally he and Mrs Harris had much in common. They chattered away enthusiastically about their native country and it transpired that not only had they known each other in childhood, but they were, in fact, distantly related! It need hardly be added that the dinner lasted well into the small hours during which Wallace and the Harrises went back over their lives and the people they had known.

After four eventful weeks, the time came to leave Australia.
Angus Mitchell came six hundred miles from Melbourne to see
them on their way. He, Armstrong and an army of Rotary friends
escorted the couple to their boat for New Zealand. Everyone present knew that for most of them this was the last goodbye and there
was more than the usual sadness in the parting. The Harrises had
been showered with kindly attentions and tendered the most
generous hospitality. The Australian Rotarians, from the newest
members at Dandenong to those who had long occupied high office
in Rotary could not have done more to make their visit such a
joyous and memorable one.

CHAPTER 29

The Land of the Maoris

The voyage from Sydney to Wellington took three days, which surprised Harris. He, like many people, did not realize that Australia and New Zealand, although close neighbours, are in fact almost 1,500 miles apart.

The ship docked at Wellington and the Harrises were still breakfasting when they were suddenly confronted by a brisk, businesslike, middle aged man who said, 'Don't get up, finish your breakfast' and then, almost as an afterthought, added his name, 'John Ilott'.

Ilott had suffered a serious heart attack at the Detroit Convention the previous year. Doctors gave him one chance in a hundred of surviving, yet there he was, a picture of health. The Governor of Rotary's 53rd District, Ilott had inveigled his way aboard the ship before the regular landing to take his guests by surprise. Waiting on the dockside was Mrs Ilott and, after the usual round of greetings from those who had come to welcome them, the couple were driven to Ilott's beautiful home high above the city. During their stay in New Zealand the Harrises used it as a base from which to visit all parts of North and South Islands.

The civic reception which preceded the noon meeting of the Wellington club was unusually impressive but, as Mrs Harris felt unwell, she was unable to attend. This greatly disappointed the Lord Mayor and his lady, 'which fact they made no attempt to conceal'.

In addition to the assembly of Rotarians, civic dignitaries and businessmen, members of the Dickens Fellowship, an international organization to which both the Harrises subscribed, were present, The Fellowship's president entreated Harris to remain just one more day in Wellington so that he could summon all the local members for a special meeting, even promising that they would all come dressed up as Dickensian characters—David Copperfield, Oliver Twist, Micawber, Scrooge and so on. Harris regretfully declined the invitation, explaining that the schedule was already made up for every day of their visit. However, he found time to remedy the disappointment by attending a meeting in Auckland a week or so later, to which the Wellington members were invited.

'The noonday meeting in Wellington was a great success', said Harris, 'and the attendance was as large as could be accommodated. The Wellington club's roster contained an unusually distinguished array of names. No less than six New Zealand Rotarians had been knighted by King George V, some of them after they became Rotarians. Generally speaking, the social standing of the Rotary clubs of the Antipodes was higher in 1935 than anywhere else in the British Commonwealth, including Great Britain herself.'

At dinner at the Ilott's home the Harrises met John Ilott, Jr, a promising light-heavyweight boxer who was in training for an important contest in Dunedin. Dinner over, the Ilotts drove the Harrises to the harbour, where they took a boat for an overnight sail to Christchurch, the main city of South Island.

Christchurch, not to be outdone by any other city, accorded the Harrises a magnificent civic reception, a nationwide broadcast, newspaper interviews, rounds of sight-seeing and a variety of social functions and entertainments. During the afternoon of their first day they visited an excellent art gallery (the gift of a Christchurch Rotarian), a boys school and the university.

Dunedin was the next major city on the itinerary, but they did not go there directly, but halted at strategic points along the lovely east coast. The first stop was at Timaru, where the train's conductor obligingly held the signals long enough for Paul and Mrs Harris to be given a chorus of hellos and goodbyes by local Rotarians. Another unscheduled stop was made at Oamaru where club members, headed by Frank Milner, a well known New Zealand Rotarian, expressed their appreciation by entertaining the couple to luncheon at the station café!

First to greet them as the train pulled into Dunedin was their travelling companion on the *Kitano Maru*, Harry Guthrie, who, Harris was delighted to learn, had been successfully nominated for membership of the Board of Directors of Rotary International for the coming year. Guthrie was their host during the visit to Dunedin, a city that Harris described as the most 'Scottish' of all the New

Zealand cities. At the great inter-city meeting that evening Harris delivered the 'guest of honour' speech, to which Milner responded.

The Easter holiday began the next day. It was intended that the Harrises should use the holiday as a rest period before their return to Wellington, but Harris had other ideas. What Rotarian so far away from home could be content to rest when there is still work to be done?' he asked. At his request, impromptu club meetings were hurriedly arranged at Gore, a small town between Dunedin and the south coast, and at Invercargill, a small but important seaport 110 miles south of Dunedin. It was typical of Harris. He loved to drop in unannounced at a club meeting, sometimes to the consternation of the unsuspecting company.

Because of the holiday exodus the meeting at Invercargill was sparsely attended, and the chagrin of those who missed Harris's surprise visit maybe easily imagined. Although not a large city, indeed its population is less than 40,000, there are four clubs in the Invercargill area with a total membership well in excess of two hundred. At the meeting Harris reminded members that it was from their city Admiral Richard Byrd carrying with him a Rotary flag set off on his Antarctic expedition.

The meeting at Gore was so hastily called and so small in attendance, that it was held in the home of Bert Smith, one of the delegates to the Manila Conference. The club in Gore, chartered in 1927, had already done sterling work in the community. The extraordinary success of Rotary in the Antipodes can be gauged from the fact that clubs are frequently established in very small communities, of which Gore is an excellent example. Forty years after Harris's visit its population is still less than five thousand, yet its membership of sixty-plus is far higher than in many larger towns and cities.

The Easter vacation over, the Harrises bade their Dunedin friends farewell, and took the boat back to Wellington. First came a formal call on the new Governor General of New Zealand, Viscount Galway. The Harrises were his first official callers. 'John tried to impress him with a sense of my importance, but His Lordship had better judgement of values and refused to be impressed,' said Harris.

In the company of the Ilotts the couple began their northward journey to Auckland. First stop along the way was at Palmerston North, where a capacity inter-city meeting of seven clubs was held.

From as early as five o'clock in the morning Rotarians converged on the city for the assembly. Some came hundreds of miles and among the clubs represented were Hamilton, Gisborne and New Plymouth. After the meeting there was the customary civic reception and a splendidly organized social evening.

Next morning the party left for Tongariro National Park for a few days rest before the last visits to clubs in the north island. There was a stop for a 'Billy Tea' near Taihape, and then it was on through forests and mountains to a superbly located chateau for the night. Harris, prepared for the visit by reading as much about New Zealand as he could, but the realization far exceeded the expectations. He found the country 'quite breathtaking—a sportsman's paradise'.

John Ilott, Jr. arrived at breakfast having fought and vanquished his two remaining rivals for the National Amateur Championship at Dunedin. Harris did not recognize him. His arm was in a sling, his eyes were black and swollen, and his face quite badly cut.

A few days sojourn in the fabulous National Park brought the party to a series of mountain tops, beautiful lakes, winding rivers, extinct volcanic craters, thermal springs, spouting geysers, 'Billy Teas' (which the Harrises now looked forward to immensely) and an unexpected and fascinating meeting with a group of Maoris. 'Several of them spoke English with a pronounced Oxford accent,' said Harris, 'and one of them had even been knighted!'

In the little town of Rotorua, a lovely community at the southern end of Rotorua Lake, another inter-city meeting was held, with Rotarians again travelling considerable distances to be with the Harrises. It was at this point that the Ilotts said their goodbyes and handed their charges over to Harry Valder, the immediate past District Governor.

Valder and his wife took their guests to the famed Waitomo Caves near Te-Kuiti to spend the night before the next day viewing the glow-worm caves, one of the most remarkable natural wonders in the Antipodes. There was no Rotary club in Te-Kuiti at that time, although one was formed in 1947, the year of Harris's death.

At Hamilton, the Valders home town, the Harrises parted company with their hospitable guides. For the last leg of their New Zealand tour they were driven by two members of the Auckland club who had come to meet them.

Viewed from a Rotary standpoint, the visit to Auckland was probably the most significant of the tour. It was in this city that Sir George Fowldes and Charlie Rhodes (both deceased at the time of Harris's visit) introduced Rotary to New Zealand. The success of the movement throughout the country was due to their influence and hard work. When Davidson and Ralston came to New Zealand in 1921 to further the cause, Sir George (he always insisted that his fellow Rotarians called him 'George') was President of Auckland University. He became Rotary's first Resident Commissioner in New Zealand. After his death his widow maintained her interest in Rotary and the Harrises not only visited her, but had the pleasure of her company at a number of Rotary functions in Auckland.

Charlie Rhodes was almost equally responsible for the phenomenal growth of Rotary friends in his home on one evening each week. They were informal gatherings but immensely successful and after his death his widow, with the assistance of her son and daughters, resumed the meetings and the Harrises were delighted to be invited. Also present one evening were Lady Fowldes, Sir George Wilson and Sir Clutha Mackenzie, two of the Auckland club's four knighted members at that time.

The Harrises had already spent an afternoon with Sir George and Lady Wilson, viewing their marvellous collection of paintings and prints, painstakingly gathered from the art centres of Europe. Sir Clutha Mackenzie was a remarkable man. He was blinded during World War I, but claimed that the loss of his hearing would have been a far more serious matter. He was a fine Rotarian and the President of the New Zealand Institute for the Blind.

At the inter-city meeting at Auckland, Harris made another of his telling speeches. Seated next to him was a Rotarian he greatly admired, 'Dear Old Hutch'. 'Hutch' was for many years secretary of the Auckland club and his absorbing interests were Rotary and the Institute for the Blind. Although he was in poor health when the Harrises arrived, he insisted on attending the meeting, but it was not without cost. Twenty minutes after the meeting he lay prostrate in a small room at the rear of the dining-room under the care of a hastily summoned physician. Later that night Harris and his wife called to see the seriously ill seventy-three-year-old Rotarian, and they learned from others that when 'Hutch' heard of their visit to New Zealand he said, 'Good, then I shall remain here that long'. He did but died shortly afterwards.

At the civic reception Harris, at the request of the President of the Noise Abatement Society of Auckland, made reference to the Society in his remarks and as a result the Society received unprecedented newspaper publicity.

Harris also spoke at a meeting of the Travel Club, attended by over three hundred members, and Mrs. Harris addressed a meeting of the ladies of Rotary and other civic minded friends. Her theme was again the International Society for Crippled Children, urging this as a worthwhile project.

The couple's last function in New Zealand was a gathering of the Dickens Fellowship. When Harris arrived at the Assembly Hall, every seat was taken, and as he looked out over the huge audience, a great feeling of fellowship possessed him. The gathering was a mixed one of both sexes, young and old. They had in common the love of the literature of Dickens and his ideals.

Next day the Harrises embarked on the *Mariposa* to return home. In his memoirs Harris posed this question: 'We had been on a long journey at great expense to Rotary. Had it paid?' The Rotarians of Australia, New Zealand, Japan, China and other Pacific countries, by their enthusiastic greetings everywhere, provided the answer. Harris planted trees of friendship in Japan, China, Australia, Tasmania and New Zealand. His journey was worthwhile.

It took sixteen days, including stopovers along the way, for the *Mariposa* to cover the journey from Auckland to San Francisco. The ship was one of the newest of the Matson Line, speedy and air conditioned. The Harrises were accompanied on the long voyage by twenty-two Rotarians and their ladies, some of whom embarked at Sydney, others at Auckland. All were travelling to the International Convention at Mexico City. Included in the party were Fred Birks and his daughter, Garnet Buss and his wife from Bundaberg, Queensland (they were the Harrises' table companions for the voyage), and the two District Governor nominees for Australia—John Duncan of Sydney, who was succeeding Tom Armstrong, and Ernest Short of Adelaide, succeeding Angus Mitchell.

The ship's first stop was at Suva in the Fiji Islands. Here the Rotary party wandered somewhat aimlessly at first, before lunching at a tourist hotel on the shore adjacent the city. An interesting visit to a Fijian village followed a meeting with the village chief.

Previous efforts to establish a Rotary club in Fiji, had met with no success, but Harris now added his personal prestige to the efforts and, as a result, the Rotary Club of Suva was established a year later.

The Harrises caught their first homeward sight of the 'Stars and Stripes' at Pago Pago, in the Samoan Islands. As the ship set sail, a band made up of Samoan boys under the leadership of an enthusiastic American Marine played them out of harbour.

At Honolulu two bands were playing the passengers ashore. One played for Harris, the other for the Salvation Army General, Evangeline Cory Booth, with whom Paul and Mrs Harris made friends during the voyage. The seventh child of General William Booth, the founder of the Salvation Army, she was a fine orator, poet, musician and author. The Hawaian air was alive with music that day, and everyone festooned with the fragrant leis.

At the Honolulu club's luncheon Harris regaled members with an account of his Far Eastern travels. As the *Mariposa* rounded the famed Diamond Head, outward bound, the leis were cast into the sea so that the waves could bear them back to their donors, laden with the love and gratitude of the departing guests.

In San Francisco the Harrises took their leave of Fred Birks. He and his daughter were off to Mexico City but Harris had first to attend a Conference at Edmonton, Canada. Travelling with them as far as Vancouver were Archie Campbell and his wife from Melbourne. Thereafter the Harrises travelled unescorted for the first time in months. They took what is known as the Shasta Route, Vancouver by way of Seattle.

The stop in Vancouver was brief, but long enough for the Harrises to visit a dear friend, Lillian Dow Davidson, the widow of Jim Davidson. They were able to give her first hand impressions of the work accomplished by her husband on behalf of Rotary in the countries they had visited.

A few days rest before the Edmonton conference was spent at the home of Mrs Harris's sister, Annie, in Calgary.

At the large Canadian assembly Harris was particularly impressed by the speech of the President of the University of Alberta whose name, coincidentally, was Wallace. Like his namesake, the President of the University of Sydney, he was a Scotsman by birth. Harris again related his experiences of the Far Eastern tour and made his own inimitable impact upon the conference. Mrs

The Paul P. Harris Room at the secretariat of Rotary International

Paul Harris with artist John Doctoroff

Harris also spoke to a large gathering of the ladies.

The conference over, the Harrises at last returned to Chicago. They had completed an arduous journey on behalf of Rotary at an age when most are content to take a back seat. A month in Australia, three weeks in New Zealand, and seven weeks in Japan, China and the Philippines constituted a major tour even by today's standards. Other Rotarians holding high office had been to Australia before Harris—Bill McConnell of Britain, Frank Lamb of California and Past Rotary International President Sydney Pascall. All were great ambassadors, as were the pioneering Davidson and Ralston, but none made the impact of the founder of Rotary in person.

The weary couple were met at Chicago by a small but distinguished gathering—Donato Gaminara, the First Vice-President of Rotary International, two well known British Rotarians, Tom Young and Herbert Schofield and, of course, Chesley Perry. 'It was good to be home again', said Mrs Harris. But for Paul it was a fleeting visit. He remained at Comely Bank just long enough to take a bath, change his clothes and pack his suitcases before he set off again on another long trip to Mexico for the twenty-sixth Rotary Convention.

CHAPTER 30

Silver Anniversaries

Rotary became an international movement when a club was formed in Winnipeg in 1910. It was appropriate that the twenty-sixth Convention, twenty-five years later, was not held in the United States. Mexico City was chosen and 5,330 delegates from all over the world attended. It was at this Convention that an important change was made in Rotary policy, when the 'Objects of Rotary' were revised from six to four.

It had been a good year for Rotary, despite the continuing world depression. And although Hitler was now in power in Germany, the clubs there had not yet been subjected to Nazi pressure. Delegates heard that yet another country had joined the fold, Tunisia. They heard also about the efforts of Bolivian and Paraguayan Rotarians in organized relief work for prisoners of war in their countries. Rotary succeeded where the politicians and diplomats failed. Before he left Mexico, Harris planted a tree of friendship in the city. It was an appropriate time to do so.

On his return to Chicago, the Harrises entertained Ernest and Mrs Short of Adelaide at Comely Bank, and a few days later welcomed Harry Guthrie. When Fred Birks and his daughter Elma (Mrs Somerville) returned from a vacation in England they were also guests.

Some of these guests were still at Comely Bank on 2 July, when Paul and Jean Harris celebrated their silver wedding anniversary. As they looked back over their quarter of a century together the Harrises marvelled anew at what had been accomplished. They had seen Harris's brainchild spread to every continent and almost every country of the world, and they had themselves visited all but one of the continents.

The Harrises marked the occasion by visiting Wallingford, to dedicate the 'little red schoolhouse' as the Paul P. Harris Memorial

Building. The story has been told many times but here again, in the words of Bill Wedwalt, a member of the Wallingford club, and a past District Governor of Rotary's 787th District, is an account of the occasion:

> During that visit, Paul decided that he wanted to visit his boy-hood haunts. Charter Member Harry Townsend accompanied him on his trek. Finally they arrived at Fox's Pond, which had once been owned by a relative of Paul's. We know it as Elfin Lake. Paul said, 'It was from this point that as a boy I used to swim across the pond. I think I will do it once more.' The more remonstrances that were made, the faster Paul divested him-self of his clothes. Finally, Harry said, 'By God, you're not going alone.' They both swam the half mile across the lake, and while they rested on the rocks Paul spoke of his boyhood in Wallingford. Paul was sixty-seven years old at the time.

Another club to celebrate its silver anniversary in 1935 was Cleveland. Harris was guest of honour. He travelled there in a private railroad car furnished by the old Nickel Plate Railroad which, on its arrival, was met by a delegation which took breakfast aboard. A photograph of the occasion shows Harris in the company of the then President of Rotary International, Ed. R. Johnson, Past International President Arch C. Klumph, International Director James Card, and Fred Sowers, secretary of the Cleveland club. Harris reminded them of the time he and Chesley Perry visited Cleveland in 1909 while trying to found clubs in all the major American cities, and the great Convention in 1925 when, for the first time, the number of delegates exceeded 10,000. The charter members of the club in turn recalled the stirring speeches made by Harris and Perry on both occasions.

One other incident in 1935 is worth recalling, unrelated though it may appear. A teenaged typist, Marlin Tabb, came to work in Rotary International's secretariat. It was intended to be temporary employment for two weeks, but Tabb remained for forty-two years until his retirement in 1977, by which time he had worked in all the main departments—incoming mail, central files, service to clubs, programme division, Rotary Foundation, and the finance division. In those forty-two years Tabb participated in thirty-nine international meetings, travelled to fifty countries on Rotary's behalf, managed twenty-one international conventions and four regional conferences, and was three times international assembly manager. Yet, in 1935, he was too shy to accept a Thanksgiving Day dinner invitation from Paul and Mrs Harris! He always regretted it.

Towards the end of the year the Harrises began preparing themselves for another rigorous tour, due to start in January 1936. But first, in October 1935, Mrs Harris took leave of her parents. No one could tell of the parting better than Harris himself:

One cold day in the autumn of 1935, a party consisting of a score, or thereabouts, of people assembled at a tiny and somewhat dilapidated railway station in the outskirts of Chicago waiting for the coming of what ordinarily was a through train. On this occasion special arrangements had been made with the railroad company to have the train stop to take aboard four people, an old couple and two younger. The old couple were my Jean's father and mother, the younger, her brother and sister.

The others were members of the one and only Church of the Original Secession located in the Chicago district. They were assembled to see their fellow members off. It was not expected that they would ever see the old folks again, the father having passed his ninetieth birthday, and the mother not being much younger. Even Jean, at the time, had little expectation of seeing her parents again. For many years, it had been her custom to be with them a part of every day, and the break was momentous. Father and mother were returning to their native land for the express purpose of being buried in the 'old soil'. Though they had lived in the United States more than a quarter of a century they had never become Americans. In a cemetery lot in Edinburgh lay all that remained of Jean's revered maternal grandfather, and his aged daughter entertained no fonder hope than to be laid at his side.

Under the circumstances, one might have expected something in the nature of a demonstration that dreary October morning, but his expectations would not have been realized. No tears were shed, there were no lingering embraces, no final admonitions. In fact there were none of the customary outlets of emotion, nothing to mark the occasion as unusual or significant in the eyes of a passing stranger. It might have been a most ordinary, commonplace event, a parting for a week or even a day, as neighbours might part from each other at a garden gate.

But beneath the surface, carefully concealed from inquisitive eyes, there were emotions in abundance; they had been painfully disciplined and subjugated lest they dare to creep to the surface. The parting at the station that dreary October day was nothing new; over and over again it had been rehearsed by day and through sleepless nights, and a thousand times, it had been gone over in their prayers; even the grief of it had been liquidated through spreading it over a long period of time. To the participants there was nothing new or familiar about the parting at the railway station, and to observers, nothing.

(The brother referred to in Harris's account of the parting was James Hay Thomson. The sister was Mary Thomson.)

CHAPTER 31

The Last Continent

The Harrises left Chicago on 16 January 1936 on the first leg of a carefully planned tour of South America. They had read just about everything they could obtain from their public library, from steamship companies, Pan American Union and the embassies of the various South American countries. Two books they found particularly helpful were, *South American Observations and Impressions*, by James (Lord) Bryce, a former British ambassador to the United States, and *Understanding South America*, by Clayton Sedgwick Cooper. Harris was surprised and delighted to discover that Cooper was a member of the Rotary Club of Miami.

A bizarre aspect of their preparations was the need to obtain from the Chicago Police Department no fewer than twenty-five authenticated certificates to the effect that neither of them had been under arrest during the preceding five years or, for that matter, at any other time.

They set off from Chicago by overnight train to Washington, where they were met by the Secretary to the Chilean Legation. The arrangements had been made by Manuel Gaete Fagaldo of Santiago, Chile, a Director of Rotary International. They lunched with the Chilean Ambassador and visited the headquarters of the Pan American Union. The Harrises also took the opportunity of visiting the new home of the United States Supreme Court, of particular interest to Harris, the attorney.

The couple travelled alone to New York to catch their ship. They relaxed as the train sped northwards through territory familiar to Harris—Baltimore, the scene of his first departure to Britain, and Princeton Junction, where the couple caught glimpses of buildings on the university campus, causing Harris to remark: 'Momentarily the weight of nearly half a century fell from my shoulders, and I was a student once again.' Shortly afterwards they passed through

Newark, New Jersey, the scene of a visit only a few months earlier. Minutes later they were in the familiar confines of New York.

The following day, the Harrises arrived at Pier 31 on the North River—and ran into problems. Because of Mrs Harris's susceptibility to sea-sickness, a spacious cabin and bath was reserved for them on the *Santa Elena*, a vessel of the Grace Line. But, due to some oversight, the cabin had been sold from under them. They were obliged to accept quarters in a small cubby hole in the bow of the ship from which the usual occupants, the purser and chief steward, were summarily removed.

This was bad enough, but when Harris learned that another Grace Line ship, the *Santa Monica*, on which they had booked a state room and bath for the journey from Buenaventure (Colombia) to Callao (Peru), had been taken out of service, the usually imperturbable Harris had plenty to say.

The mistakes posed serious problems for the schedule as it was not possible to travel by road or rail for much of the journey down the west coast of South America. However, they were already aboard and on their way, and there was nothing to do but await developments.

As in the Pacific the year before, they soon ran into rough weather, and after rounding Cape Hatteras on the coast of North Carolina the storm increased in severity. It compelled all bad sailors, including Mrs Harris, to take refuge below, but she soon found the small cabin in the bow of a ship was not the best place to be in turbulent seas. The storm was of such force the captain turned the *Santa Elena* into the wind and idled along slowly in the interests of safety. The ship arrived twelve hours late at Puerto Colombia.

This first leg of the voyage was little short of disastrous. Accommodation was over-subscribed by 100 per cent and the whole affair badly managed. Harris was forever ready to see the other side of a situation but even he, under these circumstances, was irate. Mrs Harris found the voyage a very trying experience, but they had to remain on the *Santa Elena* until they reached Colon at the Atlantic end of the Panama Canal. It was small comfort to know that whatever awaited them on the Pacific side could not be worse.

Puerto Colombia is a small seaport on the Atlantic coast of northern Colombia, about twelve miles north-west of Barranquilla. It was here that the Harrises first set foot, thankfully, in South

America. Barranquilla was the nearest city with a Rotary club and a delegation was waiting to greet them, although some of the plans to entertain the Harrises had been frustrated by their delayed arrival.

However, in the company of Hubert Baker, Rotary's Commissioner for South America, and a host of other friends, the Harrises visited the historic city of Cartagena, second only in importance to Mexico City during the Spanish conquests. They went to see the ancient cathedral and drove through the lush hinterland before returning to the city for a meeting of the Cartagena club. This was held in the magnificent home of the young club President. 'It was so palatial', said Harris, 'the *Santa Elena* could have been accommodated with room to spare!' It was an interesting meeting, as was a meeting with the Barranquilla club at that city's Del Prado Hotel. When Harris returned to the ship for the short journey to Colon, he felt more content than at any time since leaving New York.

At Colon the Harrises were glad to quit their unhappy accommodation aboard the *Santa Elena* and attend a joint meeting of the Rotary Clubs of Cristobal-Colon and Panama City. Several distinguished guests attended the assembly, including Harmodio Arias, President of the Republic of Panama, members of his cabinet and a number of leading educators. Before the meeting Harris planted another of his trees of friendship in a public park overlooking the sea.

At Panama City the couple were greatly relieved to find that their new ship, the *Santa Maria*, although smaller, was quite different from the *Santa Elena*. The service was excellent and the accommodation far superior. Moreover there was no overcrowding. Harris said they could happily have prolonged their voyage on the *Santa Maria* but unfortunately, the ship carried them only as far as Buenaventura on Colombia's Pacific seaboard.

They found Buenaventura, despite its grandiloquent name, hot and humid. Its location near the equator had once made it one of the worst places in the world for plagues of yellow fever, typhoid and other miseries.

Arrangements were made for a long and difficult journey across three ranges of the Andes to the capital city of Bogota, two hundred miles to the east. However, the Rotarians of Cali, a city 105 miles inland, anticipating the problem, came to meet the Harrises, and engaged a private railroad car for their use. The railroad to Cali entailed an ascent into the mountains, and as the heat and humidity of the coast receded, a magnificent panorama of mountain peaks and valley scenery began to unfold. The view gave the party so much pleasure that their anxieties about transport down the western seaboard soon abated.

At the sixteenth-century city of Cali, an attractive community high up in the mountains (at about the same altitude as Denver), the Rotarians of Cali and nearby cities were waiting and the party was quickly spirited away to a hotel where an enthusiastic reception had been arranged.

A truly sumptuous suite of rooms was awaiting the Harrises. Dinner that evening, held in the home of the club's President, was not so much a meeting as a restful social gathering, at which the couple were able to conduct animated discussions with their fellow guests. Much was learned about the South American attitudes to Rotary.

The party stayed in Cali for three days. Drives about the city and its suburbs, visits to places of interest, and dinners and parties filled every moment. The highlight of the stay was a district and inter-club meeting, which enabled Rotarians from much further afield to meet their Founder President. Everyone of importance attended—the Mayor, who spoke in glowing terms of the friendly relations between Colombia and the United States, distinguished civic leaders and other dignitaries.

Early on the fourth day a huge delegation saw the party off on the train to Armenia, a small city about one hundred miles to the north. Here the railroad terminated and the rest of the journey to Bogota was made by car. It was a drive which wound through some of the most magnificent mountain scenery in the world. At Ibaque, sixty miles west of Bogota, the Harrises were delighted to be joined by their old friend, Cesar Andrade of Guayaquil, Ecuador. Not only had he come a long way to meet them, but he accompanied them and Baker to Bogota and the two hundred miles back to Buenaventura.

During the evening of their second day out from Cali the Harrises arrived in Colombia's capital city. Its full title at one time was Santa Fe de Bogota, and it is so full of beautifully designed buildings it is frequently referred to as the 'Athens of South America'. During their stay the couple were the guests of the American

217

Minister, William Dawson, who it should be added, had the signal honour of being the first President of the first Rotary Club in South America, at Montevideo, and he and Harris were soon engrossed in a discussion about the progress of Rotary in the various South American countries.

Through the Dawsons, the Harrises were able to meet representatives of other countries. And on one occasion, during a luncheon at the Dawson's home, the President of Colombia, Alfonso Lopez Pumarejo, was present with his Minister of Foreign Affairs.

The entire stay in Bogota was full of incident. An immigration official called to investigate formally the right of the Harrises to remain in Colombia, and it was only after a gruelling cross-examination that permission was granted. Harris later discovered that in fact a special dispensation had been made in their case—but only after both he and Mrs Harris were fingerprinted. They had travelled to almost every country in the world, but Colombia remains the only country to have in its 'criminal' files the fingerprints of Paul Percy Harris, Founder of Rotary!

Harris twice met the Bogota club secretary, Miguel Antonio Atuesta who, on each occasion, brought his entire family of twelve children to meet Mrs Harris. Another interesting diversion was a visit to the former home of the great South American soldier, statesman and revolutionary leader, Simon Bolivar, the 'George Washington of South America'.

Finally, the party prepared to drive back over the formidable mountains. For Harris the journey was a painful one. He was suffering from a virus of unknown origin which caused him to comment: 'I could neither stand up nor sit down. It could not have been in a more awkward place!'

From Armenia, which had no Rotary club at that time, the party attended special meetings of the clubs in Pereira and Manizales, both of which had been chartered two years earlier in 1934.

By the time they reached Cali considerable anxiety was being expressed about their next ship. Ever since they left Buenaventura Baker had bombarded the Grace Line officials with cablegrams demanding information about the reservations that had been cancelled on the *Santa Monica*. He was eventually advised that accommodation was reserved for the Harrises on a sister ship, the *Santa Lucia*, which would take them from Buenaventura to Callao, Peru. But when Harris discovered the accommodation comprised an inside cabin (an unbearable prospect in the tropics), he promptly refused. The impasse was resolved when the captain offered the use of part of his quarters, an offer which Harris, albeit reluctantly, accepted.

At Cali, Baker left the Harrises to return to Barranquilla. Andrade, however, accompanied them as far as Buenaventura, before he too flew home to Guayaquil to prepare his District for their visit. Both were scheduled to join the Harrises again at the South American Regional Conference at Valparaiso.

CHAPTER 32

The Land of the Incas

Guayaquil, in Ecuador, lies just to the south of the equator. The Harrises had already crossed that imaginary line four times—twice off the west coast of Africa, twice in the Pacific. This time, to their surprise, they found the climate off South America's Pacific Coast far more equable. Off Guayaquil at least the annual temperature range was from 65° to 90° Fahrenheit, while in such American cities as Chicago and New York, the temperature could range from 20° below to over 100°.

The *Santa Lucia* arrived early in the morning in the Gulf of Guayaquil, and the forty miles run up the Guayas River to the city provided a pleasant change from the open Pacific. As planned, Cesar Andrade accompanied by a large delegation of Ecuadorian Rotarians and civic dignitaries, was there to meet the couple. Andrade, whom the Harrises had entertained at 'Comely Bank', was the incumbent District Governor. He organized the splendid reception and luncheon meeting, and the huge assembly burst into tumultuous applause when, during the reception, Harris was ceremoniously awarded the Order of the Sun, one of the Ecuadorian government's highest civil awards. Harris accepted the honour with modesty; he was moved, naturally, but steadfastly maintained that the decoration was as much a tribute to the Rotary movement as it was to him.

The next call was in Peru. The couple landed at Callao, the chief seaport of the small but historically significant republic. Although it lies only eight miles to the west of Lima, Callao is a city in its own right. Almost two hundred years before, in 1746, Callao was destroyed by an earthquake and tidal wave, and suffered further damage during the War of the Pacific, waged between Chile, Bolivia and Peru from 1879 to 1884.

As soon as they disembarked the Harrises were warmly greeted by members and wives of the Callao and Lima clubs. As they were driven to Lima along a splendid highway, Harris described an amusing incident:

> At the intersection of the boulevard on which we were travelling, and another thoroughfare, we beheld an interesting sight. It was a monument crowned with a wrecked automobile. On the base of the monument a phrase in Spanish had been inscribed. At our request our friends translated it. It read: 'He who walks one step at a time travels far.' Nothing more; in fact nothing more was needed. Our friends stated that at first a Ford car was given the high position, but that the Ford agency in Lima, not wishing to monopolize the honour, had supplied the city authorities with a wrecked car of one of their competitors in exchange for what remained of the Ford—a delicate compliment for the discerning Mr Ford to pay a rival!

Paul and Mrs Harris were impressed with Lima. The wide boulevards were lined with noble trees and every few blocks these widened out into lovely flower filled parks, adorned with historical monuments of great artistry and originality. Lima is well named 'The City of the Kings'.

The couple were reunited with an old friend, Fernando Carbajal, the Governor of Rotary's 71st District, who was their host during their stay in Lima. However, it was back to Callao for the first club meeting. After the luncheon, the party visited a restaurant, partially supported by the government, which fed thousands daily with excellent meals at low cost. The building was spotlessly clean and architecturally beautiful, and Harris expressed keen interest in this practical demonstration of Latin American concern for the welfare of the poor.

The stay in Lima was not surpassed anywhere during the tour. The Grand Hotel Bolivar saw to their every need, and there were many meetings with old friends. A number of distinguished Rotarians were members of the Lima club. Several served as District Governors and at least one, up to the time of the visit, as a member of Rotary International's Board of Directors. Another old friend they were delighted to meet was Federico Puzet, once the Peruvian Ambassador to the United States. He had been a guest at Comely Bank more than once and had assisted greatly in the extension of

Rotary in South America.

The Harrises were in the Peruvian capital only a few hours when they were joined by Manuel Gaete Fagaldo who, with his daughter, had flown from Washington to be with them. (It was Fagaldo who made the preliminary arrangements for Harris to meet Sr Trucco, the Chilean Ambassador, in Washington immediately before their voyage.) Fagaldo and his daughter accompanied the official party part of the way to Valparaiso, and joined them again in Buenos Aires a few weeks later.

There was much for the Harrises to do in Lima and Callao. Trees of goodwill were planted in both cities. The tree in Lima was planted near a public playground which had been financed by the Rotarians of the city, and to Harris fell the honour of officially opening the playground to hundreds of children eagerly waiting to sample its delights.

Included in the itinerary in Peru was a reception by the faculty of St Marco, the oldest university in the western hemisphere, and visits to several of the exclusive American and British public schools. The Harrises also took tea with the American Ambassador, lunched with the American Consul, and visited the famous cathedral and the tomb of Pizarro. They visited hospitals, were interviewed by newspaper reporters, lunched with past and present officers of the Lima Rotary Club, and attended a game of soccer between the national teams of Argentina and Peru.

There were more honours for Harris. At a special ceremony he was decorated with Peru's Order of the Sun by Dr Carlos Concho, the Minister of Public Works. At another ceremony honorary membership of the Peruvian Bar Association was conferred upon him. The Harrises visited and talked at length with the President of the Republic, Oscar Alfredo Benavides, not formally at his palace in Lima, but informally at his seaside home. There were also two splendid meetings of the Lima club, both of which were attended by members of the Peruvian government and civil dignitaries.

Callao provided the farewell dinner, and the Harrises were given another tremendous send-off. Although members of several smaller clubs were waiting for the *Santa Inez* the Harrises new ship, to call briefly as she worked her way down the Pacific seaboard it was, for all practical purposes, the official end of the Peruvian visit. But contact was maintained with the Lima club, one of their members, Jaime Linares, travelling with the Harrises as far as Valparaiso.

Linares was fat, jolly and handsome. His command of English was limited, which gave rise to much laughter on occasion, and no one enjoyed the laughter more than the irrepressible Peruvian. When, for example, Linares ordered duck at mealtimes, he would express himself emphatically with a 'quack, quack'. When he wanted chicken it was 'cheep, cheep'. Linares also attempted to act as Harris's interpreter at the stops they made along the way. The results were sometimes hilarious. Harris suspected that at times he and Linares were talking about entirely different subjects. But it did not matter. More important was the sincerity and the fellowship generated at the receptions, and Linares contributed handsomely to these.

Whenever and wherever possible, the Harrises went ashore to attend the dinners and receptions arranged at the various ports of call. At other times the stops were so brief that the Harrises had only minutes for receptions in the ship's lounge. Fleeting though such meetings were, Rotarians came long distances just to see the Harrises and, if possible, shake their hands. It was a moving demonstration of their devotion to Rotary and an expression of their gratitude to Harris.

The exact ports of call made by the *Santa Inez* after leaving Callao are not recorded. Harris said later that it was a joy to meet Rotarians from Arequippa, Mollendo and Tacna. Of these three, however, only the club at Arequippa was in existence in 1936. Tacna was not established until 1938 and Mollendo did not receive its charter until 1949.

CHAPTER 33

Into the Mountains

The *Santa Inez* was the fourth of the Grace Line ships in which the Harrises had sailed since leaving the United States, and at last they were provided with the accommodation they had reserved. This made the voyage from Callao to Valparaiso pleasant and enjoyable.

By the time they arrived in Arica, Chile, where a Rotary club was established in 1927, their earlier disappointments were far behind, and they received a rapturous welcome. Arica is a small but important seaport at the extreme north of the three thousand miles of Chilean coastline. It is also the terminus of the railway from La Paz in Bolivia. For many years the port was claimed by both Peru and Chile and was the cause of the bitter War of the Pacific. The dispute was not properly resolved until 1929 when the League of Nations awarded the port to Chile but, at the same time guaranteed it as a free port for Peru, and an outlet for Bolivia via the railroad.

Antofagasta, situated approximately halfway between Arica and Valparaiso, was the next port of call. This brought the Harrises to within six hundred miles of their destination—the First Regional Conference of Rotary Clubs in South America at Valparaiso and Vina del Mar. They were able to spend some hours ashore at Antofagasta and a luncheon meeting was held at a golf club overlooking the sea. Before the luncheon the couple were shown the sights of the city and visited a vacation school sponsored by the local Rotarians for poor and ailing children from the arid districts of the interior. A group photograph recorded the visit.

The voyage down the long Chilean coast to Valparaiso took sixteen days. Two short stops were made at Chanaral and Coquimbo, enabling the Rotarians from those areas to visit the Harrises. The couple disembarked early one morning at Valparaiso to a vociferous welcome. In Vina del Mar, Valparaiso's beautiful sister city, they stayed at the Hotel O'Higgins, one of the finest hotels in South

America and named after the Irish-born soldier-statesman, Ambrose O'Higgins, who rendered such conspicuous service to Chile in her struggle for independence.

Valparaiso itself is often referred to as the 'City of Bouquets' because of the delightful practice of planting flowers in every crack and crevice in the rocks rising above the drive skirting the Pacific. Throughout their tour the Harrises found this same charm of expression in all the Latin American countries. Harris cites instances of this in his memoirs. One in particular is worthy of mention. One day, while driving around the city, he noticed an inscription in Spanish on the gateway of an imposing estate. Translated into English the inscription read 'Evening Peace'. In fact, the establishment was what we would less considerately term an old people's home.

As the Harrises arrived in Valparaiso several days before the start of the conference they were able to relax and sightsee in Valparaiso, Vina del Mar and Santiago, the Chilean capital, in a far more leisurely manner than had been possible at Colombia, Panama, Ecuador and Peru. Among the well known Chilean Rotarians to greet them were Dr Eduardo Moore and Dr Luis Calvo Mackenna. Moore, a past Vice President of Rotary International, was largely responsible for the success of Rotary in Chile which, at that time, stood fifth in the number of clubs in one country. He was chosen as the most suitable delegate to introduce Harris at the banquet of the Ibero American Conference.

It was Dr and Mrs Mackenna, however, who took charge of the Harrises during most of their stay. Mackenna, a resident of Santiago, was the area's District Governor. The Harrises and the Mackennas soon became firm friends. Harris especially, found the story of Mackenna's ancestry fascinating.

Calvo, as Harris referred to Mackenna, was the grandson of an Irish immigrant and one-quarter Irish. The name Mackenna was held in the highest respect in Santiago and had been given to one of the city's famous boulevards. The original Mackenna built this boulevard in what was once the bed of a meandering river. But the most conspicuous of the first Mackennas accomplishments was the transformation of a blemish in the landscape into a thing of beauty. There was a formidable rock and the city, being unable to grow over the mountain, grew around it. 'No one ever thought of it as a thing of beauty any more than a man would think of a wart on the end of his nose as a thing of beauty, until along came Mackenna,' said Harris. For a generation and more, under Mackenna's eye, regiments of mules slowly plodded up the mountain, carrying loads of precious black earth to cover the rock. The resultant mountain was then planted with flowering plants and Santiago's blemish was turned into beautiful 'Santa Lucia'.

Harris's first official call was on the President of Chile, Arturo Alessandri, at his summer residence. The Harrises in fact arrived three minutes late—to find that the President had been called away on an important engagement! Not to be denied, they returned the next day, on time, and had a long and interesting talk. They found that he held the work of Rotary in high respect and was an admirer of Franklin D. Roosevelt. They also visited the Governor of the Province and the Mayors of Valparaiso and Vina del Mar.

As soon as the local Rotarians had shown the couple most of Valparaiso, the Mackennas drove them over the mountains to their home city of Santiago. En route they called in at the *estancia* of Mrs Mackenna's sister, where no fewer than four hundred employees rendered every form of service necessary to the successful operation of the cattle and sheep ranch. Mrs Harris was delighted when Mrs Mackenna told her that the father of all the sheep grazing on the hills came from Scotland.

Four days were spent in Santiago before the party returned for the conference at Valparaiso. They were days crammed with the wonderful fellowship of the Santiago Rotarians—meetings, dinners, receptions, a great inter-city meeting, a picnic and a delightfully informal excursion to a vineyard a few miles away.

Harris fell foul of an intestinal disorder in Santiago and at a banquet shortly after his return to Valparaiso he feasted, unwisely as it transpired, on shellfish, which aggravated the disorder. The attack which followed was so severe that it prevented Harris from participating in the opening sessions of the conference. At one point his medical advisers actually demanded that he abandon his immediate arrangements and cancel the scheduled tour of the east coast, recommending that he catch the first available ship back to the United States.

Although he was now sixty-eight, Harris's determination to see things through was as strong as ever. Within two days he was back on his feet, and soon making speeches and attending the usual rounds of luncheons, dinners and receptions. He took good care, however, not to over-indulge again.

At the great conference, which was attended by delegates from all the South American countries (together with one from Cuba), Harris was decorated with the Chilean Order of Merit by the country's Minister of Foreign Affairs. The Minister also delivered an address in which he pleaded for the development of better understanding between the countries of South and Central America. 'It was a timely speech,' said Harris, 'indicative of the Minister's regard for Rotary, which he clearly envisaged as a force which could do so much for international understanding and goodwill.'

Other noteworthy features of the conference were the receptions given by the Mayor and City Council of Valparaiso, and the luncheon by the Mayor and his council of Vina del Mar, although it should be pointed out that there was no club in Vina del Mar at that time. There was no doubt in anyone's mind that the First South American Regional Conference was a great success. So also were the many banquets, dinners, luncheons, receptions, balls and other social functions that the Rotarians of Latin America so much enjoy. The traditional fellowship of Rotary was very much in evidence.

Harris related one anecdote from the conference. On the border between Chile and Argentina, high up in the mountains, there is a titanic statue known as 'The Christ of the Andes'. As the result of a resolution passed unanimously by the delegates a bronze plaque was affixed to the pedestal of the monument, bearing this inscription: 'These mountains will crumble to dust before Chile and Argentina violate their oath made at the feet of Christ.' Harris's subsequent comment was: 'It causes one to speculate on what the effect of such statues erected on other borderlines between Christian countries would be. Would the psychological effect be better or worse than that of huge, grim fortresses bristling with ponderous guns?' An interesting speculation indeed, especially in view of World War II which was waged with such bitterness only three years later.

One last official function remained to be carried out in Valparaiso: the planting of a tree of friendship. Of all the trees he planted, Harris maintained that no similar ceremony was so well attended as that at Valparaiso. 'It seemed to me that every delegate from the various countries represented, everyone, from the Mayor of the city and members of his council down to the scores of humble onlookers who were attracted by the music of the band and the serious faces of the participants, sensed what was going on and found inward satisfaction in the proceedings.'

It was a notable tree-planting ceremony in another sense. Each of the delegates brought with him a sack of soil from his own country and this was solemnly emptied into the hole dug for the tree. The idea was typical of the emotional nature of the Latin Americans and a splendid demonstration of friendship, fellowship and international understanding, the cornerstones of Harris's concept of Rotary.

The morning after the close of the conference, the Harrises were driven to the railway station for a journey, after a brief halt at Santiago, to Osorno and the panoramic lakes region between Chile and Argentina. A large group gathered at the station to shake their hands, exchange last words and wish them Godspeed. As at Sydney, Cape Town, Auckland and other cities, everyone understood that it was a last opportunity to be with the Founder of Rotary. The couple always found farewells harrowing and this was no exception. There were few dry eyes as the train drew away from Valparaiso,' said Harris.

At Santiago there were more farewells. It was here they said au revoir to Hubert Baker, whom they fondly expected to meet in the United States at the International Assembly at Buck Hills Falls. Alas, it was not to be. Before they could be reunited, Baker died suddenly, and Harris more than anyone appreciated what a devoted friend he had lost. From Baker's own lips he and Mrs Harris had heard of his efforts on behalf of Rotary in South America.

Taking over from Baker was another Rotary field representative, James Roth. He was to accompany them for the remainder of their time in South America except for the last few weeks in Brazil. The Harrises and Roth had a five-day train journey in front of them as they crossed the South American continent, but it represented a well earned respite for the weary couple.

The route selected avoided the high altitudes of almost 20,000 feet encountered on a more direct route. The journey took longer, of course, but provided an opportunity of spending a few days in the magnificent lake district on the Chilean-Argentinian border, the 'Switzerland of South America'.

First the party travelled five hundred miles south to the city of Osorno. Although essentially Chilean, Osorno has a strong German element. At the time of Harris's visit it was reputed to be the country's fastest growing city. The Harrises and Roth spent two days there and attended two meetings of the Osorno club, whose members also took them to see the famed Swallow Falls, aptly named after the swallows that hover over the tumbling waters and make their homes in the greenery flourishing on the islands of rocks that divide the falls into numerous cascades. In Harris's opinion the Swallow Falls were more beautiful than Niagara Falls, 'being far less torrential and with a much more inspiring setting'.

From Osorno the party journeyed to the lake district set high in the Andes and spent two nights in the mountain resort of Peulla. Harris had this to say of the idyllic setting: 'To me the Chilean-Argentinian lakes seemed more like the fjords of Norway than the lakes of Switzerland. The mountains rise precipitously out of the water in true Norwegian manner. Many of them were snow capped and the highest were snow clad half the distance down. The most inspiring of all is glorious Osorno, rival of Fujiyama, Popocateptl and Rainier.'

The first day at Peulla was spent pacing the verandah. Torrential rain fell and all that could be seen were fleeting glimpses of the towering Andes. The rain abated a little during the afternoon of the second day, and the Harrises immediately went for a brisk walk through the surrounding forest.

Despite the inclement weather they enjoyed the rest and felt greatly refreshed. Harris especially, after his debilitating illness in Valparaiso, benefited from the respite. The hotel's menu was fairly good, except for the absence of fresh fruit, but during their stroll the Harrises noticed that the woods were literally festooned with blackberry bushes and ripe berries. Mrs Harris asked if they could be served some of them. The waiter was astonished. He did not think anyone would want to eat so common a thing as blackberries! However, he despatched a boy to gather some and the Harrises were soon enjoying an abundant dish of the wild fruit smothered with thick cream. They wondered afterwards if they had not inadvertently provided the proprietor with the recipe for a rare dessert!

The last leg of the long journey across the continent took thirty-six hours on a non-stop train from San Carlos de Bariloche to Buenos Aires. A small resort town on the southern shore of Lake Nahuel Huapi, Bariloche is the rail terminus on the eastern slope of the Andes. A Rotary club was established there in 1938: had it been chartered two years earlier it might well have been honoured with a visit from the Founder of Rotary.

The journey across the wind-swept desert of the Rio Negro region of Argentina was uninteresting. Harris wrote: One travels the first twenty-four hours over a desert which keeps the atmosphere supplied with dust, fine enough to blast its way through small cracks about the casements of the windows, and abundant enough to make miniature piles upon the floors and bed covers. North America has no monopoly of dust storms. About the time good agricultural country is reached, it is time to go to bed again and little of it is seen until the train approaches Buenos Aires, the metropolis of all South America.

The train would certainly have passed through the city of Bahia Blanca, where a club was established in 1927, but there is no record of a stop or meeting there. But Rotarians from Bahia Blanca and other cities not too distant from the Argentinian capital travelled to Buenos Aires to greet the Harrises, who spent eighteen glorious days there.

CHAPTER 34

Eighteen Days in Argentina

For their stay in Argentina Harris chose the Continental Hotel of Buenos Aires, which was comfortable but not over luxurious. On their own initiative, the city's Rotarians made arrangements for the couple to transfer to a more palatial hotel. This was under-standable: they felt that nothing short of the best was compatible with the dignity of Rotary and the importance of their guests. But Harris would have none of it. He expressed it admirably: 'We thought, however, that the prestige of the movement would not suffer materially in the estimation of our South American friends if we followed our own naturally simple tastes and at the same time conserved the resources of the organization in which we are all so deeply interested. In a movement of unlimited possibilities of worthy accomplishments, we think that lavish expenditures are not in the best taste.'

David Spinetto, President of the Rotary Club of Buenos Aires, was responsible for the couple during their stay in Argentina. Nor-mally this would have been the responsibility of the Governor of the 63rd District, Victor Abente Haedo of Paraguay, but un-fortunately, political disturbances in Paraguay prevented Haedo from attending Harris, a duty he would have loved. These same dis-turbances prevented Harris from visiting Paraguay and Bolivia, which greatly disappointed him. The two countries had been en-gaged in border warfare from 1932 to 1935 and the situation was still unstable. Harris was aware of the great part played by the Rotary clubs of Paraguay and Bolivia in relieving the distress of prisoners of war, and paid high tribute to them in his memoirs.

A luncheon at the famed Jockey Club of Buenos Aires opened their visit. This is more than a club of racing enthusiasts, being also an art gallery, library, athletic club and social club, all combined in one magnificently appointed edifice.

The luncheon party consisted of the élite of the Rotary Club of Buenos Aires—judges, lawyers, doctors, engineers, publishers and editors. Among the several Americans present were the managers of the National City Bank of New York, General Motors, General Electric and other important corporations. After the lunch came the traditional sight-seeing trip, which Harris described in his inimitable style:

> Of all cities in the world, which does Buenos Aires most resemble? To me there can be no question. Buenos Aires most resembles the city to which it most frequently turns for its inspirations in art and culture. To the citizens of Buenos Aires, the one city which stands far above all others in the things which they most admire is Paris. As one drives up the Avenida de Mayo, he can well imagine himself in Paris. The buildings are of uniform height, and throughout its entire length the broad sidewalks are shaded by high trees. This seems astonishing to visitors from countries where shade trees are sacrificed in the interests of traffic. Imagine New York's Fifth Avenue and Chicago's State Street widened to one hundred and twenty feet, and lined on both sides with majestic trees, giving comfort to shoppers and affording ample space for sidewalk cafés, and you will have some conception of B.A., the largest city south of the equator and the second largest Latin city in the world, Paris, of course, standing first.

The Harrises attended many functions, luncheons, dinners and receptions following in almost uninterrupted succession. A reception was given in Harris's honour by the United States Ambassador, Mr Weddell which was attended by many of the business and social leaders of the American colony. Ambassador Weddell was well aware of the prestige and value of Rotary, and his interest was expressed in the serious discussions he had with Harris about the movement in South America. He personally conducted the Harrises about the palatial house and grounds, which, at that time, was the most costly of all American embassies.

On another day Harris planted a tree of friendship in the lovely suburb of Palermo, in the Parque Tres de Febrero. He also, at an unusually well attended ceremony, placed a wreath on the tomb of San Martin, Argentina's revered soldier-statesman.

An important organization initiated by the Rotary Club of Buenos Aires, was the Instituto Cultural Argentino Norteamericano. It was the brainchild of a past President of the club, Dr Cupertino del Campo, a talented Rotarian who also served Rotary as the Governor of his District. Dr Campo extended an invitation to Harris to address the students. Accompanied by Ambassador Weddell, Harris afterwards toured the Institute, visiting several classrooms. More than three thousand Argentinians were studying English there at the time, and Harris was impressed by the earnest application of the young people to their studies. The influence of Rotary was apparent in the statement printed on the Institute's stationery: 'The Instituto Cultural Argentino Norteamericano; organized by Argentine citizens, is a private association and, as indicated by its name, exclusively for promoting cultural understanding, with entire avoidance of commercial or political matters . . . It believes finally that this loyal and friendly collaboration must be beneficial to both democracies, whose ideals, which are parallel notwithstanding racial differences, may together work for a still higher level of civilization.'

The statement bears a striking resemblance to the Fourth Object of Rotary, and was certainly akin to Harris's own philosophy.

At one of the meetings of the Buenos Aires club, when both the Harrises were present, prizes were presented to pupils of the city's public schools. The winners were seated at tables immediately in front of and below the speaker's table, at which were seated several distinguished guests, including the ranking general of the Argentinian Army. Harris tells the story:

The contestant sitting next to Jean and me was a boy of ten or twelve years of age. We were both taken with the youth's respectful yet absorbing interest in the events of the meeting. Nothing seemed to escape him and he was what might be termed a handsome little man. We learned that he was an orphan. The general also manifested interest in the boy and soon called the sergeant-at-arms to him, whispered a few words, after which the sergeant-at-arms walked to the table below, placed his hands on the chair of the boy, and looked up at the general inquiringly. The general nodded his head, and the matter was, for the time being, closed. Later, the Chairman announced that an unexpected but happy incident had arisen, of which he would like to make an announcement. The general had decided to adopt the boy and to give him every advantage within his means. When called upon to say a word, the general, a veteran of many wars, arose and modestly and somewhat hesitatingly said that the facts were as had been related; that while his conclusion had been reached quickly, it had not been reached thoughtlessly, and the boy would be given every advantage which would have been given him if he were of his own flesh and blood. The child fixed his eyes upon his future father as two hundred Rotarians burst into applause. To us, it was an incident truly magnificent, and we will never forget that army general standing there with the plaudits of his fellow Rotarians ringing in his ears.

During their stay in Argentina the Harrises paid brief visits to three other cities—La Plata, Rosario and Tigre. At La Plata the party visited the enormous Swift meat packing plant, said in 1936, to be the country's largest and most modern. At one point Harris found himself in the company of the secretary of the La Plata club, and discovered that he was an American astronomer who taught in the university at La Plata. He had come there from the University of Wisconsin and had been selected because he possessed an enquiring mind. That enquiring mind subsequently turned to Rotary and Harris suddenly found himself discussing and resolving Rotary problems the club secretary was not even supposed to know anything about. Harris was greatly puzzled until the secretary, whose name was Dawson, explained that he was the son of one of Harris's old friends, Charlie Dawson of Oklahoma. 'You're a man after my own heart,' chuckled Harris when he found out that he had been foxed.

Rosario, where Rotary was established in 1922, lies almost two hundred miles north-west of Buenos Aires. Harris makes no mention of a meeting here, observing only that the city of 600,000 inhabitants is in the centre of a wheat producing area, in a province populated principally by Italian immigrants.

Tigre, where a club was formed in 1931, is a beautiful seaside suburb, twenty miles north of Buenos Aires. The Harrises visited it on a Sunday afternoon. Again, Harris makes no mention of a meeting, but said that there was no shortage of Rotarians from Tigre and elsewhere there to greet them.

234

Before leaving Argentina the official party made a special visit to the Uruguayan city of Montevideo. In terms of actual distance it was not far, only 135 miles to the east, but as it was on the other side of the Rio de la Plata, it entailed a night's sail. (The story of this special visit is described in chapter 35.)

Back in Buenos Aires, the Harrises attended a farewell luncheon. This was held on the roof garden of the only other hotel in the city to rival the famous Plaza, where the Rotary Club of Buenos Aires meets. Invitations to the luncheon were sent to all leading Rotarians in the district and to the chief executives of the principal North American business houses. The meeting, being the last for the Harrises, affected the Argentinians. There were no speeches, only brief and warm expressions of goodwill. The Harrises also said goodbye to Jim Roth, who had been their guide and adviser all the way across South America and whose duty was now done. They had breakfasted and dined together for several weeks, and had discussed all manner of subjects at all times of the day and night.

But Roth's greatest contribution were his interpretations of Harris's speeches before the South American clubs. According to Harris, Roth invariably won the plaudits of the assembled Rotarians by his skill in translating English into instant Spanish. In Brazil, where they were now headed, the official language was Portuguese, and Roth's duties were taken over by Armando Pereira.

235

CHAPTER 35

Montevideo and on to Brazil

In about the mid-1880s a young rail engineer came from Britain to South America to carve out a career in the developing continent. His name was Herbert Coates but he soon became known as 'Don Herbierto'. Coates, a deeply Christian man and a lay delegate, played an important part in promoting the interests of the Methodist Church and the Young Men's Christian Association in Latin America.

Sometime after the turn of the century he came to the United States for a conference of the Methodist Church, and realized that there was tremendous scope in South America for the products of the United States. He gave up his position with the railway and established agencies in Uruguay, Argentina and Brazil for the products of a number of principal manufacturers in America. The agencies prospered and Coates soon became an influential figure in South American affairs.

On one of his business trips to the United States he was invited to a Rotary meeting. He was intrigued and took the concept back to Uruguay. At that time feelings against the United States were running high in the Latin American countries, and the first question asked of him when he broached the subject of Rotary was, 'What are the Yanks getting out of it? Where do their profits come in?' It says much for Coates that despite the scepticism and suspicion, he not only established the necessary confidence but fanned the flame which swept Rotary through South America like a bush fire.

It was Coates who established, in 1918, the first Rotary club in South America, in his adopted city of Montevideo. This accomplished, Coates travelled thousands of miles, at his own expense, organizing more clubs. He became Rotary's High Commissioner for the whole of South America, the 'Father of Rotary in South America', just as Yoneyama was in Japan, Sir George Fowldes in

New Zealand, Sir Henry Braddon in Australia and Anton Verkade in Holland. They were all great ambassadors for Rotary. Small wonder that Harris held Coates in high esteem.

Who then more appropriate to greet the Harrises as they stepped ashore? With Coates was another great Rotarian, Donato Gaminara, the First Vice President of Rotary International in 1935. Earlier still, when he was Governor of the 63rd District, Gaminara had based a campaign of extension on the premise that Chicago was not as evil as its reputation. Meeting little success he reversed his tactics and stated categorically that Chicago was the worst of all cities. He reaped unprecedented success!

Two trees of friendship were planted in Montevideo, one in a public park alongside an artistic and expressive piece of sculpture, the other in the grounds of Crandon School, founded by an old friend of the Harrises, Mrs Frank Crandon of Evanston.

While in the city the couple met the President of Uruguay, Gabriel Terra, and had a long talk with him. There was a happy sequel to the meeting. When Harris returned to Chicago he was presented with a signed portrait of President Terra at a meeting of the Chicago club by a representative of the Uruguayan government. The portrait was framed and hung in Harris's office.

From one South American club in 1918 to 119 clubs by 1977 is a page of Rotary history that can be credited mainly to Herbert Coates. Although when the Harrises visited Uruguay in 1936 there were Rotary clubs in other Uruguayan cities such as Paysandu and Merceded, there is no record of visits to any cities other than the capital.

Two and a half days sailing from Buenos Aires brought the Harrises to Santos, reputed to be the greatest coffee exporting port in the world. It is also a city of considerable beauty, with miles of superb beaches washed by the South Atlantic.

One of their oldest friends, Armando de Arrudo Pereira, who had travelled from his home in Sao Paulo, welcomed the couple. Pereira was well known in Rotary circles through his translation into Portuguese of Harris's *This Rotarian Age*. In 1940 he became the first South American President of Rotary International.

Following a tour of the city the Harrises attended an impressive meeting of the Santos club at a palatial hotel fronting the beach. After the meeting Harris planted a tree of friendship in a public park. 'A feature of the simple ceremony was the intense interest shown by the onlookers,' said Harris.

It was then on forty-five miles up the mountains to the inland city of Sao Paulo, Pereira's home town. One of the features of the entire South American tour was that all the major American automobile manufacturers vied with each other for the honour of providing the Harrises with suitable transport. In Argentina, for example, they had been the guests of General Motors, and an executive of that corporation provided a car, as well as a chauffeur, during their eighteen days in Buenos Aires. In Brazil it was the turn of the Ford Motor Company, whose manager at Sao Paulo met them with a brand new Zephyr to drive them back up the mountains to the city. Appreciative though they were, the Harrises expressed a wish to travel by train in the company of the many Sao Paulo Rotarians who were at Santos to meet them. Thus, as they enjoyed the scenery from the train and participated in the fellowship of the accompanying Rotarians, the Zephyr raced up the winding mountain roads to be at the railway station to meet them.

The couple were scheduled to remain in Sao Paulo for a few days. Another elaborate hotel had been engaged for them, despite Harris's protests that somewhere less ostentatious was preferred.

During the visit the Harrises attended dinners, receptions and social affairs until their heads swam. The enthusiasm of the Sao Paulo club knew no bounds, and a huge party participated in the planting of a tree of friendship in the Praca de Republica. But the nicest touch of all came at the club's luncheon meeting. Someone had an inspired idea—to present Mrs Harris with a bouquet of Scottish heather as a reminder of her native land. But the presentation was more than that. It was a truly eloquent expression of the respect of the Sao Paulo Rotarians for their leader and his 'Bonnie Scottish Lassie'.

A group of Rotarians from both the Santos and Sao Paulo clubs accompanied the couple on an all-day trip to the city of Campinas, the centre of Brazil's coffee producing district, where they were entertained at two huge coffee plantations. Harris made no mention of attending a meeting of the Campinas club, which was chartered in 1931, although he mentions meeting some of the club members. On another day the Harrises visited Armando and Mrs Pereira at their home, and Harris planted a personal tree of friendship next to one planted by Pereira's father.

On another occasion a visit was made to a unique enterprise, Sao Paulo's world renowned snake farm, where research into snake venom has gained international recognition. The Harrises were shown how venom was extracted from the deadly reptiles, and how horses were innoculated to obtain the serum that would save lives, not only in Brazil, but throughout the world. What fascinated Harris most was a species of poisonous frog and he gave a vivid and amusing description of these rare creatures: 'They neither move nor give other signs of life until the mouth of their enemy opens. When that event takes place, the frogs, with the deadly aim of veteran tobacco chewers, shoot a mouthful of their special brand of poisonous saliva into the mouth of their enemy, and if their enemy happens to be a poisonous snake, there is nothing he can do but die; if on the other hand, the marauder happens to be a non-poisonous reptile, he simply spits the dose out and proceeds to his banquet. Why nature has arranged things this way is quite beyond me, but I have started out to tell the story of the Instituto Serum Therapico and I have related it just as it was given to me.'

The days in Sao Paulo were eventful and enjoyable but all too short. The Harrises took a train for Rio de Janeiro, the *ne plus ultra* of beautiful cities and the last stop of the South American tour. They left behind one of the most rapidly growing cities in the world. During their visit in 1936 Sao Paulo boasted a population of one million; by 1960 its population was more than five million.

Rio de Janeiro (the River of January), so named because the explorer Alfonso de Sousa discovered it on 1 January 1532, gave the Harrises a tremendous reception, although it was much more formal than usual. The large Reception Committee ceremoniously escorted them to an imposing hotel, the Gloria. There, in a spacious and ornate hall, a carefully prepared address of welcome was read by a former President of the Rio de Janeiro club. Harris, who consistently protested that he and Mrs Harris were simple ordinary people, felt they were being honoured beyond their deserts. The Rotarians of Rio de Janeiro did not agree. They were honoured by the visit of the Founder of Rotary, and for them there was no question of the importance of the occasion.

They provided Harris with a secretary who also filled the role of guide and interpreter. The couple were invited to meet the President of Brazil, Getulio Vargas. They travelled to his summer home in Petropolis, a lovely city in the mountains twenty-seven miles north of Rio. The President, a short and rather stout middle-aged gentleman with a great knowledge of the world, received the Harrises hospitably and with far less formality than would have been the case had the invitation been extended to the more sumptuous presidential palace in the city.

There were the inevitable luncheons, dinners and receptions, and, in addition, regular and special club meetings in and around Rio. Harris addressed the Chamber of Commerce, made a radio broadcast (which was translated into Portuguese), gave newspaper interviews, met the judges of the Brazilian Supreme Court, and planted a tree of friendship in the horticultural gardens. As in Chile and Argentina the couple were invited to more Brazilian homes than they could possibly manage. Some invitations they were able to accept and on one occasion spent a night in a mountain resort.

Harris described as 'unique and magnificent' the occasion when more than three thousand schoolchildren assembled for a special Rotary Day in one of the city's largest cinemas. Special films were shown to the children and prizes were awarded to those who had distinguished themselves during the year. The assembly was not held for the purpose of making Rotary known to the children, but rather to impress upon them the importance of the principles of Rotary. 'If the shouts and frequently the screams of three thousand youngsters were any indication, the presentation registered on their impressionable minds. I venture to say that few, if any, left the meeting without a clearer conception of that which is good. I venture to say that they left with the feeling that the big, grownup men who came into their lives during the course of that meeting were all right human beings, of the type which they would like to be sometime,' said Harris.

At the last function of the tour Harris, in civic recognition of his and Rotary's contribution to welfare in Brazil, was decorated with the Brazilian Order of the Southern Cross.

From their hotel, the Harrises were ceremoniously escorted to the dockside by a small but distinguished group of their most intimate friends. It was drizzling with rain and there was a delay before the ship finally cast anchor, but those who assembled to see them on their way remained until the gangplanks were drawn in and stayed waving their farewells until the ship faded into the enveloping darkness.

Harris's last sight of South America was, appropriately, the dominating outline of the famed Sugar Loaf and Corvocado with its imposing figure of Christ pronouncing a benediction on the ship as it steamed out of the magnificent harbour.

CHAPTER 36

Dash to Buffalo

The journey home took fourteen days, including a stop of a few hours at Trinidad. If the voyage was tranquil, the arrival in New York was not. Before their departure for South America the Harisses agreed to visit Buffalo, New York, to attend the Buffalo club's twenty-fifth anniversary meeting. Not only was the assembly expecting to welcome the Harrises, but Chesley Perry was also on his way as the ship approached New York.

But 'the best laid plans of mice and men . . .' and the couple were anxiously speculating whether they would arrive in time to get through immigration and customs and still catch the train to Buffalo. The President and members of the Buffalo club watched the ship's progress with equal anxiety.

By the time the ship docked all hope of arriving in New York in time had vanished—or so it seemed! Suddenly the influence of Rotary was brought to bear on the problem. Radio messages poured in with instructions and pleas. As it was now too late to travel by rail, arrangements were hastily made to expedite the couple's passage through the rows of officials on the wharf, and seats were reserved on the first airplane to Buffalo.

Mrs Harris, however, was adamant that she would not make a journey by air, so it was agreed that while Harris flew to Buffalo, she would come on by train. They would be reunited at the rail station in Buffalo following the meeting. The problems appeared to be resolved, but there was more trouble in the offing. Immediately on arrival at Newark airport, Harris was informed that on account of heavy cloud over Buffalo, it was impossible for the aircraft to land safely.

Harris cancelled his reservation which was instantly snapped up by a passenger bound for Detroit. Then the weather suddenly cleared and only a series of agonized entreaties from the official party resulted in someone giving up his seat. To that unknown sympathizer, the Rotarians of Buffalo must have rendered heartfelt thanks. A turbulent flight in the teeth of a thunderstorm followed. Mrs Harris, meantime, was on a fast train heading for Chicago via Buffalo.

At Buffalo airport the enterprising local Rotarians were waiting with a police escort to bring Harris to the meeting. With sirens wailing he was rushed to the banquet hall in time to make an eagerly awaited speech about his visit to South America. Chesley Perry made his inimitable contribution, and all was well in the end. How Rotarians who came to Buffalo that evening to see and hear Harris cheered him when he made his dramatic entry.

An hour later Harris and Perry were escorted to the rail station to rejoin Mrs Harris, who had left New York two hours before Harris's plane rose from the field at Newark. He had done more 'hustling' in the ten hours since landing in New York than in the entire three months in South America.

A few weeks later the twenty-seventh Convention of Rotary International was held at Atlantic City and, despite the continuing gloom of world economic depression, was attended by 9,907 delegates. Another milestone announced was the formation of the four thousandth club at Hanover, Pennsylvania. New clubs were also started in the Fiji Islands and Sarawak.

In three remarkable years the Harrises had visited every continent—Europe, Africa, Asia, Australasia, North and South America—and many countries where Rotary had been embraced—Japan, China, The Philippines, Australia, New Zealand, South Africa, Colombia, Panama, Peru, Ecuador, Chile, Argentina and Brazil.

The year 1936 had been memorable in other ways. In Britain, Edward VIII became King, then abdicated because of his unswerving devotion to the woman he loved; Italy annexed Ethiopia and fomented the troubles that led to World War II; and the Spanish Civil War began, bringing with it the end of Rotary in that country for almost forty years. In Europe the Rotary movement was experiencing problems as the Fascist and Nazi regimes of Mussolini and Hitler compelled clubs to disband. The menacing clouds of war were beginning to form, and within five years all the great nations were to be involved in a global conflict. But there was still time for the Harrises to make one more journey to Britain and Europe.

CHAPTER 37

The Legion of Honour

When Mrs Harris's aged parents left Chicago in October 1935 she did not expect to see them again. Happily, however, the Board of Directors of Rotary International, early in 1937, extended an invitation to Harris to attend the International Assembly at Montreux, Switzerland, and the International Convention in Nice in Southern France. The time was propitious. Mrs Harris missed her parents, who had lived only a few blocks from Comely Bank and it was her practice to call on them as frequently as she could. The daily calls were replaced by long fond letters. She knew that this was almost certainly the last opportunity to be with them.

Harris arranged to leave his wife with her parents and family in Scotland while he went on to attend the assembly and convention. He also intended to proceed from Nice to visit Rotary clubs in the eight or nine countries in south-east Europe not included in his previous itineraries. That was the plan but in the event the unstable situation in Europe dictated otherwise.

The International Assembly at Montreux was never forgotten by those who attended. The setting was superb, with the towering Alps rising majestically above Lake Geneva. The official party, including Harris, were accommodated at the Palace Hotel. Harris was delighted with Switzerland. On one occasion he and a friend took a stroll into the foothills surrounding Montreux and into a quarter of the city rarely frequented by visitors. On another day he and several members of the party were driven completely around the lake and paid a brief visit to the impressive but strangely silent buildings of the wilting League of Nations.

Before leaving Switzerland, Harris recounted the incident of his 'lost' passport, inadvertently left in luggage consigned ahead of the party. 'In the forlorn hope that I could retrieve the indispensable document, I rushed to the railroad station, and there poured out my story to an astonished Swiss official. The look of agony I received in return was imprinted on my memory to my dying day. The official gestured mutely to a mountain of luggage in the car. No words were needed. It was packed solid from floor to roof. There then occurred what I can only describe as a minor miracle. Right on top of the colossal pile of valises, suitcases and other paraphernalia was my own unique and easily recognizable suitcase, and the day was saved.'

The Convention at Nice was of a special nature. The host to the delegates was Charles Jourdain-Gassin. Throughout the war, despite the ban by the occupying German forces, he served as Rotary's District Governor, and immediately after the Liberation was instrumental in re-establishing the disbanded clubs. The incoming President of Rotary International was Maurice Duperrey, a member of the Rotary Club of Paris. He was the first Frenchman to be elected to Rotary's highest office and, with the exception of Sydney Pascall, the first European. Adding lustre to the Convention was Albert Lebrun, the President of France. President Lebrun manifested his appreciation of the value of Rotary by travelling through the night to Nice. He twice addressed delegates and deeply impressed them with his awareness of the Movement's concept.

Harris, naturally, was one of the delegates appointed to greet the French President on his arrival, and it was mandatory that the Reception Committee wear morning coat and high hat. Harris religiously carried this formal attire throughout all his travels, but never had occasion to use it. Thinking that such formal dress would not be needed in France, he decided to leave it behind.

Obtaining a morning coat was not difficult, Harris borrowed one from George Hagar, a fellow member of the Chicago club. The hat, however, posed a problem. He was able to borrow one from another friend, Howard Feighner, but it was far too small and 'perched on my bald pate like a peanut' said Harris. He was compelled to creep back to his hotel and the reception committee which greeted the French President was short of its most distinguished member.

During the stay in Nice, Harris took every opportunity to see all the sights. He was sixty-nine years old but had lost none of his vigour; he walked everywhere, and when the places he wanted to see were too far, took a car part of the way and walked the rest. He visited the lovely little winter resort of Grasse, seventeen miles west of Nice, where small bottles of concentrated essence of perfume are extracted from tons of flowers. There was no Rotary club in Grasse then (one was established in 1956), but the accompanying Rotarians presented him with a $5.00 bottle of the extract which, when diluted, made enough perfume to last Mrs Harris for many a year.

On another day he went to Monte Carlo and visited the famous casino. He was fascinated to see so many people from so many different walks of life gambling their fortunes away. Harris makes no mention of a visit to the Rotary Club of Monte Carlo, although it is interesting to note that one was established there that same year.

In the company of some of the most intimate of his many friends, Harris spent a few days on the Cap d'Antibes, where a joint meeting of the new and old Boards of Directors of Rotary International was in session. During the deliberations the Rotary Club of Antibes entertained the entire party, and one evening took it to view the splendid city and harbour of Cannes.

Perhaps the most interesting of all these diversionary excursions was an unexpected visit to a little cemetery on the Riviera. Harris wrote: 'One of the sights which escapes the view of most visitors to the Riviera is a gentle cross of white marble marking the spot where the Rev Henry Francis Lyte was buried in the month of November 1847. Who was Henry Francis Lyte? Few know—I must admit that I did not—but we all know the child of his imagination. Are these words familiar? "Fast falls the eventide, the darkness deepens, Lord with me abide. When other helpers fail and comforts flee, help of the helpless, O, abide with me." These words raised an English country preacher to the ranks of the immortal.'

Harris planned to visit Italy, Yugoslavia, Bulgaria, Rumania, Czechoslovakia, Austria and Hungary after the Convention, but the worsening situation in Europe made this inadvisable. He drew up a new schedule. He decided he would, on the return journey, visit those parts of the British Isles he had not been able to include in his previous tours—the Channel Islands, the Isle of Wight, the Isle of Man, some places on the mainland and the Hebrides.

Accompanied by several of his closest friends, including Angus Mitchell, Percy Scurragh (a Canadian Rotarian) and Armando Pereira, Harris left for Paris. En route the party spent a night at the great seaport of Marseilles. In Paris the party split up. Mitchell and Scurragh went on to London; Harris and Pereira, with Will Manier and others stayed in the French capital for several more days, attending the trade exposition and the celebrations of the homecoming of Rotary International's new President, Maurice Duperrey.

Harris and Pereira spent several happy and interesting days touring the sights of Paris, so many of them familiar to Paul from his previous visits. He climbed the Eiffel Tower on his first visit forty years earlier and now, at the age of sixty-nine, he did so again.

The reception accorded to Duperrey by the Rotary Club of Paris was an historic event, especially as Albert Lebrun, the President of France, was there in his official capacity to honour four Rotarians, including Harris and Manier, by investing them with the Légion d'Honneur.

President Lebrun afterwards entertained Harris and the other decorated Rotarians at his palace. He impressed Harris as a man of extraordinary vigour. 'Of medium size and middle age, he seemed fairly bristling with energy; his hand was warm, his grip firm, and his pink cheeks, which any young lady might have envied, contrasted with his black hair and indicated good digestion and circulation. He should be good for many years of service if he remains that long in popular favour,' wrote Harris. Harris's words were prophetic. In 1939 President Lebrun was re-elected President and remained France's titular head until 1944, when he recognized Charles de Gaulle as the head of the Provisional Government. The last President of the Third French Republic, Lebrun is regarded as one of the best Presidents of France.

The morning after the investiture Harris bade goodbye to Pereira, Manier and the others, and set off for the small seaport of St Malo in Brittany, from whence he would embark on the short sea journey to the Channel Islands.

He arrived in St Malo late in the afternoon after the long train journey. It was colder than usual for the time of year and raining rather heavily, but the Rotarians of St Malo (who had not been given much notice) were equal to the occasion, and were soon showing their distinguished guest the sights of their small but ancient city. After an evening meeting and dinner Harris was escorted, somewhat ceremoniously, to his ship. Thanks to the long hours of daylight at that latitude he reached Jersey before darkness fell.

CHAPTER 38

"The Islands of the British Seas"

Although the Channel Islands are close to the French coast they are, of course, British possessions and have been so since the time of William the Conqueror. To all intents and purposes, therefore, the continent of Europe was now behind Harris forever.

On previous tours Harris knew his schedule well in advance. On this occasion, however, because of the abrupt change in plans, it was different. Rotarians in Jersey knew that Harris was on his way but did not know when to expect him. Thus, when he arrived there was no reception committee. Not that Harris minded. Indeed, his penchant for visiting clubs unannounced was well known. When signing the visitor's book he would simply write Paul P. Harris, Chicago. On occasions he was not immediately recognized and this caused great consternation in some places. Harris, of course, revelled in such situations.

After docking at St Helier, Harris made his way to the Hôtel de France then, as now, the meeting place of the Rotary Club of Jersey. It was quite late and he left a note for the hotel's proprietor, who was a club member. Early the following morning the proprietor introduced himself, and shortly after breakfast the club President arrived. After a series of hurried telephone calls a special club meeting was arranged for that day.

Harris was taken to see everything of note on the island. Jersey, although the largest of the chain of islands lying off the south-west coastline of the Cherbourg peninsula, measures only twelve miles from east to west and about four miles from north to south, but into its forty-five square miles is packed some of the finest coastal scenery in the world.

A wealth of beautiful flowers grows on the island, and Harris was delighted to see the colourful sub-tropical gardens of mimosa, camellias, hydrangeas and a wide variety of ferns. He was there at the end of June. Had he been present on the last Thursday in July, Harris would have enjoyed the famous 'Battle of the Flowers', held annually in the streets of St Helier.

Harris visited the recently appointed Lieutenant-Governor of the island, an English nobleman. The Channel Islands are, of course, self governing. The main islands of Jersey, Guernsey, Alderney and Sark make their own local ordinances, although major laws must receive the sanction of the British government. In theory the Lieutenant-Governor can veto any legislative measures not considered in the best interests of Britain. In practice he never does so. The Channel Islands have far less rigid income tax laws than the mainland, and they have long been tax havens for the affluent. Another curious feature is the recognition of two official languages: on Jersey it is French but on Guernsey it is English.

Of particular interest to Harris was a visit to Mont Orgueil Castle, a fine example of a medieval fortified castle. Dating from about 1200, it was once the home of Sir Walter Raleigh, and it was here also that Charles II sought refuge from the militant Oliver Cromwell, who had beheaded his father, Charles I.

Before Harris's departure for Guernsey the President of the Jersey club entertained him at his home and took the opportunity to present his guest with a rare original signature of Victor Hugo, a writer much admired by Harris.

The Rotarians of Guernsey were forewarned of Harris's arrival and a delegation turned out to meet him. Included in the welcoming group were the President of the Guernsey club, whose name was Fella, and the immediate past President, a Rotarian named Stonelake. Harris met Stonelake in Chicago some time before and it was the Guernsey Rotarian's description of his home that fired Harris's ambition to include the Channel Islands in his travels.

During the afternoon Harris was taken out in a private yacht and, to his delight, was allowed to take the helm for a while. This expedition took the party on an offshore tour of the smaller neighbouring islands of Sark and Alderney. Harris was interested in the many grottos that are a feature of the islands. He recalled that it was reputed that in one of the grottos the hero of Hugo's *Toilers of the Sea* did battle with an octopus. Although Jersey and Guernsey are only a few miles apart, Guernsey is several degrees cooler and, as a result, fruits and vegetables are normally grown under glass. In Jersey, on the other hand, they grow in the open.

249

A visit of particular pleasure was to the manor home and eight-hundred-year-old estates of a distinguished resident of the island, Sir Havilland de Sausmarez, an honorary member of the Guernsey club.

Harris was delighted to walk up a steep street in the centre of St Peter Port to Hauteville House, the once splendid four-storey home of Victor Hugo. The great French writer lived there during the entire period of his fourteen years exile from France and wrote his immortal *Les Misérables*.

A special club meeting was held in St Peter Port on 30 June attended by both Sir Havilland de Sausmarez and the Lieutenant-Governor of the island, Major General Sir Edward Broadbent. In his speech to the fifty-five Rotarians present (a record at that time), Harris jocularly referred to the fact that he had not been offered a single glass of the famed Guernsey milk during his five days stay.

As he was about to embark on the boat to Southampton the following morning, a delegation marched on to the quay in solemn ceremonial, bearing a bottle of rich, yellow Guernsey milk, to which were fastened two cups tied with green and white ribbons. 'I was somewhat in doubt what to do with it,' said Harris. 'An incipient headache was warning me to abstain from food. I remembered, however, that someone said that milk, if taken without other food, is easily digested. Enough. When lunch time came I drained that bottle of Guernsey milk to the last drop. What happened? My headache soon disappeared and I enjoyed a peaceful sleep on the couch in my stateroom which my thoughtful friends had provided me, all the way to Southampton.'

Three years later the Channel Islands were occupied by German troops and by the time the Rotarians of Jersey, Guernsey, Alderney and Sark were liberated in May 1945, the opportunity for Harris to return had passed.

The Isle of Wight, England's largest offshore island, lies in the English Channel about halfway along the South Coast. It is twenty-three miles long (from east to west) and eleven miles wide (from north to south), and into its 145 square miles is packed some of the finest scenery and historic treasures of Britain.

Harris arrived on Thursday, 1 July 1937, and almost left the following day! Having disembarked at the major mainland seaport of Southampton he immediately transferred to the ferry which took him across the four miles of the Solent to the world renowned yachting centre of Cowes on the Island. He went straight to the 'Rotary' hotel, had an early dinner, and called on the President of the Cowes club, a nearby stationer. The club's bi-weekly meeting had been held the previous day, and it was doubtful if another could be called at such short notice. Harris wondered if he should press on to London but he telephoned the immediate past President of the Rotary Club of Shanklin and explained his dilemma. No one on the island, of course, had any idea that Harris was coming to see them. Years later, in 1975, in conversation with a member of the Ventnor club, I was told that the news of Harris's arrival 'came like a bolt of lightning, but when we recovered, the scenes of enthusiasm were like nothing I have experienced in Rotary before or since'.

The reaction to Harris's telephone call was immediate. In his own words: 'The telephone wire seemed to turn hot, all in a second. When I hung up my receiver, I realized that London was not to see me for some days to come.'

Early next morning Harris was heartily greeted by Bertram Hill, President of the Rotary Club of Ryde and by the club's President-elect, During the morning the threesome explored Cowes on foot and visited the world famous club of the Royal Yacht Squadron (one of the party was a member). After lunch they crossed the Medina River and set off by car to see some of the most interesting places on the island. Almost immediately they passed Osborne House, the favourite residence of Queen Victoria. The House, designed for her by Albert, the Prince Consort, and Thomas Cubitt, was built in 1846. Here the Queen spent many of her regnal years, especially after the death of the Prince Consort, and died there on 22 January 1901.

On the outskirts of Newport, the island's capital, the party came to Carisbrooke Castle, where Princess Beatrice, the aged daughter of Queen Victoria, was still living. Harris was intrigued to discover that donkeys were still being used to draw water from the well-house, which dates from the 1500s and is in use today.

The tour continued over what Harris described as exquisitely beautiful hills, along peaceful pastoral valleys, along the edge of cliffs high above the sea and finally into one of the loveliest hamlets he had ever seen. 'It was truly Old England at its best,' he remarked.

During the late afternoon the party passed through the charming seaside villages of Ventnor, Shanklin and Sandown, eventually arriving in Ryde, where Harris stayed in one of the several residential hotels on the broad avenue of the seafront.

In the days that followed, Hill took his guest to many other beauty spots on the island. These included the wild grandeur of the southern coastline and the magnificent cliffs that look down on the Needles and Alum Bay with its famous coloured sands. Harris had never seen such natural wonders. 'The beaches and the cliffs were of every imaginable hue—red, blue, yellow, purple, white, black and grey—it was truly a magnificent sight,' he said.

Other visits were made to Tennyson's Down, the Roman Villa at Brading, discovered in 1880, Appuldurcombe House, near Wroxall, built in 1710, where Capability Brown designed the gardens, Arreton Manor, which has an interesting collection of furniture, toys and relics of Charles I (at one time imprisoned in Carisbrooke Castle), the windmill at Bembridge and, a real beauty spot, Winkle Street at Calbourne, with its fine old watermill.

One historic house not mentioned by Harris is Winterbourne, in the lovely village of Bonchurch, just outside Ventnor. Now a well known hotel, Winterbourne was once the home of Charles Dickens, Harris's favourite author, and it was here that Dickens wrote *David Copperfield*. Harris, however, did visit the home of Lord Tennyson, the son of the great poet. Lord Tennyson was not at home at the time, but the party drove through the grounds where the first Lord Tennyson had lived and written his unforgettable poems.

At his own request Harris was driven over the hills in the centre of the island (Arreton Down) from where there are unsurpassed views over the entire island. Another afternoon he visited the home of J.B. Priestley, the famed author and lecturer. Two or three years earlier Priestley's home was chosen to illustrate an article about the island in the *National Geographic* magazine.

Of all the places he visited on the Isle of Wight, Harris treasured one above all others. He described it as 'a tiny village in the back hills'. It was given the delightful name of Godshill and legend has it that the lovely church, dominating the village, was at first built on low ground, but supernatural forces moved it to the hilltop on which it now stands, hence Godshill.

For the farewell the members of the four Rotary clubs on the island—Ryde, Newport, Cowes and Shanklin—made an almost 100 per cent attendance at the inter-club meeting at Ryde. There was also a contingent from Portsmouth, the great naval depot clearly visible a few miles across the Solent. After the assembly a large party accompanied Harris to the end of the long pier where he took the ferry to Portsmouth to catch a train to London.

Three years after his visit Harris learned that the Rotary Club of Cowes (which had been chartered in 1925) disbanded, and it was not revived until 1965. But all the other clubs on the island remained intact and rendered splendid service during World War II.

But that summer evening in 1935, as the island receded into the darkness, Harris recalled that the Romans knew the Isle of Wight by another name, Vectis. He likened it to a gem, the most precious of them all, a diamond.

On his way north to the Isle of Man, Harris made his first stop at the Buckinghamshire town of High Wycombe, thirty miles north-west of London, where he was the guest of the Vicar the Rev Wilfred Float. They had previously, met in Mexico City in 1935 and in Chicago in 1936, when they lunched at Harris's favourite restaurant. The Vicar, was a member of the High Wycombe club, the Governor of the 109th District, and a member of the General Council of Rotary International in Great Britain and Ireland.

Mr Float now resides at Rottingdean, near Brighton, Sussex. When interviewed in November 1976 he did not look a day over sixty (he was actually ninety-five). His handshake was still firm and he was as alert as a man half his age. His memory of Harris was remarkably vivid, and he described him as 'one of nature's gentlemen', adding: 'He was shy, especially in the company of ladies, but he had a marvellous facility of being able to make friends easily. He was the same with everyone, and all who met him took an instant liking to this kindly man. There was nothing of the snob about him, and he was never affected by his success in life. He was a very sincere yet a very humble man, although he had no great personality and did not stand out as someone exceptional in a gathering.'

The cleric questioned whether Harris's devotion to Rotary affected his career as a lawyer. In his memoirs Harris makes light of any such possibility, and it would appear that he was in fact eminently successful in his practice.

On that first day in High Wycombe the schedule included a large inter-city meeting, at which Harris was the principal speaker. Mr Float chuckled as he recalled the story Harris told them of the bird that flew backwards, 'as it preferred to see where it had been rather than where it was going'. 'Paul Harris', added Mr Float, 'always talked sense, although he sometimes used analogies to make his point.'

After the meeting, the friends went for a long drive through the British countryside, calling at Eton to see the famous boys' school and at Windsor to view the castle. Next day, Harris, the Vicar and his assistant went on a coach excursion to Arundel and Chichester on the Sussex coast. The other occupants of the coach were elderly ladies, members of Mr Float's church. Harris recalled that these ladies enjoyed their annual excursion: 'It did seem at times as if the Vicar, his assistant and I ought to do something about it, but there were only three of us and I, not being over robust, trembled to think what might happen in the event things got out of hand, so to speak,' said Harris.

The party visited Arundel Castle, the chapel and a nearby Catholic Cathedral. During the afternoon they visited the cathedral in nearby Chichester. On view was an extraordinarily fine stained-glass windows and a collection of relics, among which were a bishop's staff and signet ring, exhumed from the tomb in which they had rested for more than six hundred years.

There were many places in and around High Wycombe which Harris wished to visit, but time pressed. He was unable to see the homes of such celebrities as Benjamin Disraeli, William Penn, the founder of Pennsylvania, and Edmund Burke. He did, however, visit the historic park and village of West Wycombe and the Hell-Fire Caves, scene of some wild meetings in the 1700s. The day following his visit to Arundel and Chichester, Harris took his leave of Mr Float and his kind and hospitable mother.

His next stop was at Loughborough, where he attended the Assembly of the old 7th District. For the one night's stay he was the guest of the District Chairman-elect, Emerson Huston. That evening Harris took the greatest pleasure in investing his host with the Chairman's chain of office. In an address to two hundred Rotarians from many neighbouring clubs, Harris said that if Rotary did not change a man for the better, then Rotary had done nothing for that individual. He sometimes felt, he continued, that it would be a good thing if there was a period of probation for prospective members, with the spirit of the movement ever before them, to see if they really wanted to be Rotarians and fulfill their obligations.

'After seventy years of life,' said Harris, 'I believe that the doctrine of acquisition is false. I don't think that any happiness can be gained except by an unselfish life, and the nearer we approximate to that goal, the happier our lives will be. Even in times of depression in America, when suicides were daily occurrences, Rotary held together those men who were not worshipping the false god of acquisition. They were upheld by the philosophy of Rotary until the arrival of better times.'

The following morning, having been joined by an old friend, Fred Gray (President of R.I.B.I. in 1934–5), Harris and a party of local Rotarians visited the unique school of Dr Herbert Schofield, a former President of R.I.B.I. (1931–2).

Then to Manchester, where Harris addressed another large inter-city meeting. Immediately afterwards, in the company of another old friend, Will Nixon, he journeyed to Liverpool, where they spent the night before taking the morning boat to the Isle of Man.

Lying almost exactly in the middle of the Irish Sea, thirty miles west of England and twenty-seven miles east of Ireland, the Isle of Man, like the Channel Islands, has its own legislative and judicial body, the Tynwald. This passes laws on domestic affairs although the final decision remains the prerogative of the British Parliament. Larger than any of the Channel Islands, it measures about thirty-three miles from north to south and about thirteen miles from east to west.

The clubs on Jersey and the Isle of Wight were taken almost completely unaware by Harris's visit, but Fred Gray and Will Nixon were given sufficient time to make arrangements for the remainder of the tour. The visit to the Isle of Man, and the timetable for Harris's four day stay, was mapped out with meticulous care.

Accommodation was reserved at the Castle Mona Hotel, once the residence of the Duke of Atholl, and it was here that Harris and the delegation of welcoming Rotarians repaired for lunch. Harris visited the grave of the famous Manx novelist, Hall Caine, and later visited Grebo Castle, Caine's strange, brooding home, where he wrote such works as *The Deemster, Manxman* and *The Woman Thou Gavest Me.* Caine wrote his novels in bed, whereas Victor Hugo did all his standing up! Harris commented: 'What a pity that they did not compromise and both write sitting down.'

Harris found Grebo Castle depressing. It seemed to him to be far too much shut in and lonely. 'If the tall trees lining the roadway had been cut down and topped, a beautiful view of the hills would have been revealed, but manifestly he was not partial to views.'

One Sunday, Harris and several of the members of the Douglas Rotary Club went to a hillside near Kirk Bradden to attend an outdoor religious service. Harris was astounded. It was the biggest congregation he had ever seen. The lowest estimate of the number was ten thousand; other estimates were much higher. All were young people and the preacher was the fiancé of the daughter of the President of the Douglas club, Commander Parkes. The young man delivered a ringing sermon with the aid of a loudspeaker. He was the president of a local theological seminary.

On another evening Harris attended a dance, and yet again was astonished by the crowd. On an acre of hardwood floor, thousands of young dancers swayed to and fro to the music. Harris later discovered that the crowds he saw everywhere were mostly formed of holidaymakers from the Lancashire cotton mills, all of which closed down at the same time for what is known as 'wakes week'. As many as 25,000 would arrive in a single day.

One afternoon, in misty rain which made visibility poor, the party visited Castleton and Rushen Castle.

The Seventh Earl of Derby initiated at Castleton, the horse race now known the world over as the Derby. Rushen Castle, once the home of the Kings and Lords of Man, was also interesting, with its unusual tower clock with only one hand which Elizabeth I presented to the island in 1597.

Another feature of Rushen Castle is the legend of the giants who are reputed to exist in great numbers in the caves beneath. 'I didn't see any of these,' chuckled Harris, 'but what's the good of living in a land of giants, witches and fairies unless one believes what is said of them?'

The Rotarians of the Isle of Man went out of their way to entertain Harris in their homes, one such being the home of Deemster (Judge) Cowley. A visit was made to a municipal housing project for working people, known in Britain as 'council housing', and to

August 1942, A reunion of some of the surviving members of the Chicago club in 1905. Harris is shown standing. Seated around the table are Robert C. ('Bob') Fletcher; Montague ('Monty') Bear; Harry Ruggles; Sylvester Schiele; Bernard ('Barney') Arntzen; and Rufus ('Rough-House') Chapin

Chesley R. Perry, 'The Builder of Rotary'

Harris at work in his office in the R.I. Secretariat in downtown Chicago.
The office has been preserved in R.I's new headquarters at Evanston

The famous statue of Christ ('Cristo de los Andes') on the international
boundary between Chile and Argentina

the Douglas Rotary Club's own special project, a 'crêche' or day nursery for the babies of working mothers. Harris, however, expressed reservations about this project. He wrote: 'All was well with one exception: the children neither laughed nor smiled. Perhaps the absence of happiness was due to the home influences which, in the case of day nurseries, remain elements to be considered.'

Harris's last evening on the Isle of Man was devoted to a special meeting of the Douglas club, where he spoke for about fifty minutes about his travels to all corners of the world.

Before sailing on the afternoon boat Harris attended the regular lunchtime meeting of the club, where he heard Sir Gordon Campbell speak. Then, escorted by the many friends and Rotarians who had been so diligent in ensuring that his stay was full of interest, Harris made his way to the ship which was to take him back to Liverpool. As he stood at the rail waving goodbye to the Manx Rotarians he smiled at the answer he received to his query as to why Manx cats were without tails? 'It was a romance. Once upon a time a gentleman cat fell in love with a lady rabbit. Their children never knew what they were, nor cared. Aft of their mid scuppers they were rabbit, for'ard, just cat!'

In Liverpool, Harris was met by several members of nearby clubs, a privileged few of whom motored with him to Kendal. The party arrived early enough to view the waters of Lake Windermere and its superb backdrop of mountain ranges. It was actually 11pm, but at that time of the year and at that latitude, the twilight lingered.

Next morning Harris revisited the lovely Lakeland villages of Grasmere, Derwent and Keswick, and other delightful spots in the Lake District that he had not seen on previous visits. Then it was back to Kendal for a noon inter-city meeting. Immediately afterwards he was driven part of the way to the border city of Carlisle. Somewhere along the way, probably near Penrith, Harris was met by the President of the Carlisle club, his host for the night.

Next day Harris caught a cross-country train to Newcastle upon Tyne, where he was greeted by many old friends at an inter-city meeting. His last function in Newcastle was to attend an evening dinner, and his last night in England was spent at the home of one of his oldest friends, Tom Armstrong.

257

Next morning he took a train back to Carlisle, changed to a northbound express and crossed the border into Scotland where, at Kilmarnock, he was reunited with his wife. He found her much improved in health. The long daily walks in the open air had returned the colour to her cheeks, although her stay was marred when her sister Mary suffered severe injuries in an automobile accident.

In the normal course of events Harris would have stayed with his brother in law, the Rev John Youngson Thomson, but the Old Manse at Annbank was filled to capacity and he took a room at a hotel in Ayr. Each day he drove the few miles to and fro. After a week or so of this arrangement, which included attending a meeting of the Ayr club, the Harrises set out across Scotland to the tiny seaside resort of East Haven, a few miles north of Carnoustie. The Rev John Howe, his wife Joey (Mrs Harris's sister) and their two sons, John junior and Andrew were vacationing there.

On the way Harris attended a meeting of the Glasgow club and then kept his promise to the Rotarians of St Andrews by visiting them. A report of his address to the St Andrews club appeared in the *Edinburgh Evening Dispatch*. Harris paid high tribute to the Scotsmen who played such an important part in the development of Rotary in India and South America. 'It was a worldwide organization,' concluded Harris, 'and all the elements seemed to be working together in harmony.'

The Harrises stayed with the Howes for a week. Again, because of accommodation problems, Mrs Harris stayed with her sister at East Haven and Harris took a room at the Bruce Hotel in nearby Carnoustie. There was no club in the town at that time (they waited until 1956 for a charter), but he visited the Rotary Club of Arbroath, a visit later recalled by Mrs Harris's nephew, the Rev Andrew Howe as his first Rotary meeting when, as a young boy, he was carefully drilled on how to behave on such an occasion.

Harris had one more island to visit, the historic Isle of Skye. It was a long train journey from Dundee up the east coast of Scotland to Aberdeen and Inverness before crossing over to the west coast to the Kyle of Lochalsh. Breaks in the journey for meetings at the two cities provided welcome relief.

Harris had his interest in the Isle of Skye whetted, many years previously, by a book written by Alexander Wilkie, a prominent member of the Edinburgh club and a respected friend. Wilkie was President of the British Association of Rotary Clubs in 1920–1. It was he who issued the invitation to the International Association to hold the 1921 Convention in Edinburgh, the first outside North America. Harris and Wilkie frequently discussed the possibility of rambling the island together but, unfortunately, their ambition was never realized.

He and Mrs Harris would have liked to stay longer on the romantic isle, with its wild and beautiful scenery. First they stayed at a hotel in Lochalsh but later moved to another at Kyleakin, and were delighted with both. From the latter especially they made long sorties into the surrounding hills and along the rugged coastline with its many unspoilt bays, framed by the 3,000 feet high Cuillin Hills. Because time was limited, the couple were not able to visit the nearby islands of Lewis and Harris, and had to content themselves with views of the distant hills rising from the sea. Harris wanted to visit Harris, the island which bore his name, but it was not to be.

The couple went to see Flora Macdonald's grave at Kilmuir, where she died in 1790, and the imposing Iona cross which marks the spot. On the cross are inscribed the words of Dr Samuel Johnson: 'Her name will be mentioned in history and, if courage and fidelity be virtues, mentioned with honour.'

There never has been a Rotary club on Skye, and with a population of less than eight thousand spread over its 1,200 square miles, the problems of transport were clearly apparent. For those few days, however, the Harrises devoted themselves to an uninterrupted enjoyment of whatever took their fancy. They loved every minute and Harris (a great fisherman) said he would have dearly loved to fish the sparkling brooks for the speckled and brown trout he saw in the clear, ice cold waters.

Harris said of Skye: 'It would be impossible to compare it with the other islands of which I have written. Skye is so unsophisticated and primitive. None of the other islands mentioned has more of romantic interest. The story of the wanderings of Bonnie Prince Charlie can hardly be exceeded in romantic interest by any story of any prince in history. One can certainly picture the worn and weary prince, bedraggled and footsore, decisively defeated by the Duke of Cumberland, seeking refuge on the island, and of his meeting with Flora Macdonald, and of his wanderings in her company, disguised as her Irish maidservant, "Betty Burke".'

Early one morning Harris and his wife bade the Hebrides a fond farewell and took a small boat through several beautiful lochs, and along the Sound of Sleat, to the small port of Mallaig. Here they caught the train which winds its way through the superb scenery of the western Highlands, passing through Fort William and along the foot of towering Ben Nevis to Spean Bridge. At this spot, a few years later, American Rangers and British Commandos were welded into the world's finest fighting force at the Commando Training Centre at Achnacarry. It was on then through the glens and along the familiar shores of Loch Lomond to Glasgow. Here they changed trains for the journey to Edinburgh. That night they were safely ensconced in their customary hotel, the North British.

The following day, Thursday, 15 July 1937, Harris attended his last Rotary meeting in Britain when he sat down to lunch with the members of the Edinburgh club. Harris spoke only briefly, then settled down to listen to W.B. Hislop, a director of R.I.B.I., describe the International Convention at Nice. He heard again, with satisfaction, that 5,790 delegates from sixty-five countries had been there to be addressed by President Lebrun. The Edinburgh members were told that new clubs had been started in The Netherlands, the West Indies, Mexico, Syria, Monaco and Venezuela, although this encouraging news was offset by the sad reports of clubs disbanding in Germany. As a result of Nazi pressure, forty-two clubs in Germany (and the Danzig club) had closed their doors, although some continued meeting in secret.

That afternoon Harris joined a large Rotary outing to Newbattle Abbey, an ancient castle a few miles from Edinburgh, which had recently been remodelled into a school for adult education. The walls were still adorned with priceless paintings by some of the old masters.

Harris returned to the United States alone. (Mrs Harris and her brother, Alexander, followed in mid-September.) In his heart Harris knew that time was fast running out, and as the *Transylvania* pulled away from the dock, the sadness of the departure was more poignant than ever before. As the shores of Scotland receded, Harris knew it was 'Farewell, Britain' for the last time.

He wrote an account of his last tour of Britain and Europe as the ship plowed its way across the Atlantic to Boston:

Viewing my journey in its entirety, it seems to me that it has been fairly successful. The first part was, of course, cut out for me in advance, the Assembly at Montreux, the Convention at Nice and the board meeting at Antibes. The adventurous part came afterwards. The cancellation of my plans to visit south-eastern Europe seemed necessary; there remained the question: What now? The exploration of the islands of the British seas seemed to be a wise substitute, and I am convinced that it was. Now that it is all past, I have a thousand happy memories tucked away in the inner recesses of my brain. They will not, I trust, grow dim; at present they are vivid. All expense, inconvenience and labour seem to me to have been justified. I am sure that Jean's mind will now be at rest. She knows that all is well in the Old Manse in Ayrshire. Father and mother are in good health—rejuvenated, I might say. The plan of 'lying in the old soil' seems to have been indefinitely postponed.

CHAPTER 39

The Last Years of Peace

After the hurry and scurry of the years between 1934 and 1937, the events of 1938 must have seemed mundane to the Harrises. True the clouds of war over Europe became more threatening, especially when Germany marched into Austria, and shortly afterwards began prohibiting Rotary club meetings. But such turns in history were a long way from the United States, and with more time on his hands, Harris began to look for new interests. At the age of seventy he found one. He decided to learn to paint, an activity at which he became quite proficient. A photograph of the times shows an exhibition of his work, which may have been at Palm Springs, California, where he and Mrs Harris took a vacation in 1938.

The Convention of Rotary International in that year was held at San Francisco from 19–24 June. There was an attendance of 10,432 delegates but, despite the movement's total membership passing the 200,000 mark, news about Rotary throughout the world carried an air of gloom. Eleven clubs were disbanded in Austria, and in Italy, where Rotary had been under pressure for some time, Mussolini imitated Hitler and banned thirty-four clubs from holding further meetings. These were but the grim prelude to what would happen during the next five years when, in the thirty-three countries that were either invaded or controlled by the Axis powers, no fewer than 484 clubs and 16,700 members were lost to Rotary. Many clubs were re-chartered when liberation came but some, in Communist controlled countries, were lost for all time. However, it was reported at the Convention that clubs in Cyprus and the Anglo-Egyptian Sudan were added to Rotary's growing family of nations.

The Rotary Convention in 1939 was the thirtieth in the series, and 9,241 delegates attended a great assembly at Cleveland, where Harris made one of his rare addresses to delegates. For Rotary it was a year of mixed fortunes. The loss of clubs and members in the

Axis dominated countries continued, yet progress was made with the admission of new clubs in other countries. In overall terms the gains offset the losses, and new countries and regions were opened up with the chartering of clubs in French West Africa (Senegal), and the island of Guam in the Pacific. And another milestone was passed when the Rotary Club of Rockmart, Georgia, became the five thousandth to receive its charter.

The outbreak of war in September stunned the entire civilized world. The United States remained at peace as a non-belligerent, but in Britain and France the Rotary clubs prepared themselves for new avenues of service to refugees, prisoners of war, and maimed men, women and children.

In the United States, Harris and Rotary established a unique first. On the evening of 8 December 1939, the Rotary Clubs of Albany, Troy and Schenectady met simultaneously in their respective cities in eastern New York State. Dinner was served early. As the dishes were cleared away and cigars lit, the air of expectancy increased. At each of the three meeting places television receivers were installed. Suddenly, these flickered into life and Rotarians of three cities, miles apart, cheered as they recognized Paul Harris, Walter D. Head, the President of Rotary International that year, and Chesley Perry. It was television history in the making. For the first time anywhere the audience was able to see and be seen in three cities simultaneously on a 'network' television programme.

Not long afterwards, in February 1940, Harris was again on the air when he delivered a nationwide radio broadcast.

In the Spring of 1940, German forces invaded Denmark, Norway, Belgium, Holland and Luxembourg wiping out, for the duration, Rotary in those countries. Shortly afterwards France capitulated to the advancing German armies and more Rotary clubs closed.

The war badly affected the thirty-first Rotary Convention in 1940. Only 3,713 Rotarians attended the assembly at Havana, Cuba and only three European Rotarians were present—two from Britain and one from Hungary. Those who were there heard that authorization had been granted to contribute $50,000 from Rotary funds for direct war relief through the Red Cross. Unanimous approval was given to the establishment of a Rotary Relief Fund, designed to alleviate the suffering of Rotarians and their families caught up in the hostilities. Delegates further approved a statement of policy in *Rotary and the World Conflict*, which contained these significant words: 'Rotary is based on the ideal of service and where freedom, justice, truth, sanctity of the pledged word, and respect for human rights do not exist, Rotary cannot live nor its ideals prevail.'

Sometime during 1940 Harris participated in another event, the significance of which will not be known until 2040. In that year, the Chicago Museum of Science and Industry will deliver to the Rotary Club of Chicago an hermetically sealed capsule. It contains a wire recording, on which will be heard the voices of Paul Harris, Harry Ruggles, Charles Newton and other famous early Rotarians.

'What struck me then,' said Leland D. Case, Chairman at the time of the club's Information Committee, 'was that all levity disappeared as the men recorded sentiments to be exposed to human ears a century hence. Some were so emotionally charged they even wept as they groped for words.'

CHAPTER 40

America at War

In 1941 Harris reached the age of seventy-three, and photographs of the time show clearly that the weight of years was beginning to tell. His spirit, however, remained undiminished and he continued his unflagging work in the cause of Rotary.

On 11 and 12 May he returned to Racine, his birthplace, for the last known time. He went as guest of honour to attend the Fourth Annual Conference of the 144th District, which, by then, had expanded to forty-four clubs and more than two thousand members. The Rotarians of Racine, in their Golden Anniversary publication, faithfully recorded the visit for posterity.

The District Governor was Delbert J. Kenny, the President of the Racine club was Russ Zahn, and the Conference Chairman, R.J. Ritz. Also invited with Harris was his lifelong friend and neighbour, Sylvester Schiele, at that time the First Vice President of the Chicago club.

The Conference was attended by 950 Rotarians and their wives. Also present was the Mayor of Racine, Gleason Morris. There was an address by Julius Heil, a Madison Rotarian, an afternoon reception for Harris and a magnificent evening banquet. The *Racine Journal-Times* reported next day: 'No sooner did Paul P. Harris, Founder of Rotary, who was born in Racine, enter the banquet room than Rotarians and Rotaryannes rose in unison as a tribute.' Harris was profoundly moved by this token of esteem in his native city.

A month later Harris addressed the thirty-second Rotary Convention in Denver, Colorado (his last visit to the city he had come to know so well). Despite the war, no fewer than 8,942 delegates attended. Only one, however, came from war-torn Britain—Ted Spicer, a Past President of the Rotary Club of London, and one of Harris's oldest friends. In addition to Harris's own speech, the

Convention heard two other great addresses. The first, 'The State and Its Citizens', was delivered by one of the giants of Rotary, past R.I. President Will R. Manier.

The second was unusual in that the speaker was not present. It was broadcast directly from England by R.I. Vice President Thomas A. Warren, and was heard with perfect clarity by the huge audience. 'Whilst he was speaking,' said Ted Spicer, 'you could have heard a pin drop, and when he had finished, I do not think there were many dry eyes in the place. When the President (Armando Pereira) stood up, he quite unashamedly had tears running down his face, and said that the only answer one could give just now was for the whole audience to stand and say as one man: 'We are with you, Tom . . .' The whole immense audience rose and said those words as though they very definitely meant them.'

Delegates again heard that more clubs had been disbanded in countries overrun by the German and Italian armies, but the organization of clubs elsewhere once more offset the losses. The reports of Rotary service were most impressive. As a result of the contributions to the Relief Fund, food parcels were sent to Rotarians held captive in European prisoner-of-war camps and, in neutral Switzerland, clubs were organizing relief measures for Belgian and French refugees, especially women and children. In China seven of the eighteen clubs established there were carrying on, contributing to war relief, assisting American and British airmen, and maintaining refugee camps—even as they were being bombed out of their meeting places. The Chinese clubs were also trying to cope with an inflation rate which raised the cost of living by an unimaginable 7,000 per cent!

In the United States, clubs rendered assistance to over-burdened draft boards, sponsored increased food production drives, and gave effective aid in organizing civilian defense measures. But perhaps the most significant contribution was the inauguration of 'The Americas Speak' weekly radio broadcasts.

In beleagured Britain the Rotary clubs organized many mobile canteen units to aid those made homeless by the devastating air bombardment. Clubs also promoted other civilian relief measures, despite meeting under the most difficult conditions. But five clubs—Cowes, Canvey Island, Leatherhead, Tiverton and Spalding—were forced to disband.

Two days after the Denver Convention the war took a dramatic turn when Germany invaded Russia. In August, Roosevelt and Churchill met in great secrecy in mid-Atlantic and then made public their historic Atlantic Charter, forging new links between the two major English-speaking nations, and laying the foundations for the United Nations Charter.

On 17 October, Hideki Tojo, one time head of the Japanese secret police, and Minister of War in the Konoye cabinet, became the Prime Minister of Japan. Seven weeks later a carrier-borne force of Japanese planes attacked Pearl Harbor, bringing the United States into the war. Three days later the United States formally declared war on the other Axis powers and the conflagration encircled the world.

For Harris, as for countless others, it was a sad ending to the year. Only six years previously he had been fêted by his many Japanese friends. What had happened, he wondered, to such fine Japanese Rotarians as Tsunejiro Miyaoka, so recently a member of the Board of Directors of Rotary International? And to those unforgettable characters, 'Shun' Mizushima and 'Sam' Namura? And what of Anton Verkade in Holland, Maurice Duperrey in France, and the hundreds of other Rotarians he met during his world travels of 1934–7?

Japanese armed forces swept all before them in the Pacific and south-east Asia in the early months of 1942. Hong Kong fell quickly, as also did the Philippines, except for a pocket of resistance at Bataan. This finally fell in April, but United States forces continued to hold out on the little island of Corregidor in Manila Bay.

In a dark, maladorous tunnel, shortly before the fall of Corregidor on 6 May, seven Rotarians, the handful left of the Rotary Club of Manila, held a meeting. Among them was their club President, Hugo Miller, who had escaped in a small boat from Manila, and Carlos P. Romulo, a former Director and past Vice President of Rotary International. Everywhere around the small group, wounded men were writhing in agony, with more casualties arriving all the time. With the butt of an army pistol, President Miller called for order and put before the other six Rotarians the first item of business, which was to confer honorary membership on General Douglas MacArthur.

A few days later the United States showed that it was far from defeated when General 'Jimmy' Doolittle led a fleet of carrier-based planes in the first air raid on Tokyo. And in May and

June respectively, the United States Navy, despite its awesome losses at Pearl Harbor, inflicted heavy and significant defeats on the Japanese Navy in the great naval engagements of the Battle of the Coral Sea and the Battle of Midway.

Despite the difficulties of travel, 6,599 delegates attended the thirty-third Rotary Convention in Toronto, where Harris spoke to the assembly on what was to prove one of his last appearances at a major Rotary function. It was at this Convention that his staunchest ally, Chesley R. Perry, retired from the office of General Secretary after thirty-two years of inestimable service. Perry was immediately offered the title of Secretary Emeritus, but he declined the honour. 'I want to remain one of the boys,' he said.

Perry was succeeded as General Secretary by the Rotarian who had been his assistant since 1930, Philip Lovejoy. A native of Maine and graduate of the University of Michigan, Lovejoy came to the Secretariat in Chicago after serving as President of the Rotary Club of Hamtramck. He continued in office until 1952, when he retired to Florida, where he died in 1966.

The Toronto Convention, held as it was in a country which had close ties with Britain, had deep emotional overtones. Only two British Rotarians were present, R.I. Vice President Tom Warren, and the immediate past President of R.I.B.I., T.D. Young. Their journey across the Atlantic took six weeks! The Convention closed with the entire assembly rising to sing the rousing march from Elgar's *Pomp and Circumstance*, more familiarly known as 'Land of Hope and Glory'. It was an emotional moment.

During 1942 the fortunes of war swung decisively in favour of the Allies. In August, United States troops landed in Guadalcanal, the first of the steps taken in the long advance towards Japan. In September the Battle of Stalingrad began. In October came the Battle of El Alamein in North Africa and a resounding defeat for Germany. Suddenly the Axis powers were retreating from the countries they had so ruthlessly conquered. In November an armada from the United States landed troops in North Africa, and the retreating German and Italian armies found themselves threatened from the west as well as the east.

By February 1943 the Battle of Stalingrad was over, and thousands of demoralized German troops surrendered to the Russians. Almost simultaneously, Japanese resistance ended at Guadalcanal. Shortly afterwards every German soldier was cleared from North

Africa and the Allies prepared to liberate Europe.

Earlier in the year Harris held a nostalgic reunion at his home, Comely Bank, with six of the surviving members of the Rotary Club of Chicago who were enrolled during 1905. At that meeting were Sylvester Schiele, the first club President; Montague 'Monty' Bear, designer of the first Rotary emblem; Bernard E. 'Barney' Arntzen, affectionately known as 'Cupid'; Rufus F. 'Rough-house' Chapin, Rotary International's first Treasurer; Harry Ruggles, the 'Fifth' Rotarian; and Robert 'Bob' Fletcher, who held the classification of 'architect'. The seven long-serving Rotarians chatted, joked, indulged in some light-hearted horseplay, and reminisced about the good old days. Photographs taken of the occasion show that some of the men put on the gloves for a bit of boxing. Harris, however, looked noticeably frail in these photographs, and it was evident that he was entering the twilight of his life.

There were, it appears, twenty-three members of the club of 1905 alive at the time of the reunion, but no explanation has been given of why only seven gathered together for the celebration, although those named were certainly the very earliest members of the Chicago club. The historic get-together was concluded when the seven men sat down to dinner in a rustic inn not far from Comely Bank.

The thirty-fourth Rotary Convention was held in 1943 at St Louis, Missouri, but with the United States now at war, the number of delegates was much reduced to 3,851. Those present were gratified to hear that the United States War Production Board, in recognition of the meritorious salvage work by clubs throughout the United States, had presented Rotary International with a special citation. Rotary itself was already looking ahead to the end of the war, giving careful consideration to the problems of the post-war period. Amazingly, for the first time since 1939, Rotary was extended abroad when a club was organized in Trujillo in the Dominican Republic. And, despite the restrictions of war, clubs in Finland, Sweden and Switzerland continued to engage in service to war victims. Although only 112 delegates came from twenty-two countries outside the United States, the Convention was held on a wave of optimism.

By mid-1943 the tide of war definitely turned. In July Sicily fell to United States and British forces, and before the month was out the

Fascist regime in Italy collapsed, and Mussolini was imprisoned. Italy surrendered in September, but the German troops continued to fight. In October, Americans advanced up Italy and captured Naples. On the other side of the world, in the far from peaceful Pacific, other United States forces landed on Tarawa and Makin in the Gilbert Islands. As the year drew to its close, Roosevelt, Churchill, Stalin and Chiang Kai-Shek held a series of conferences in Teheran and Cairo, in which they reiterated their terms of unconditional surrender to the German and Japanese leaders.

On 4 June 1944, the United States Fifth Army occupied Rome. The excitement had hardly died when the world was electrified by the news that American, British, Canadian and French forces had established a bridgehead in Normandy for the final assault on Hitler's 'Fortress Europe'. Hitler hit back. On 17 June the first of the V-weapons, the 'flying bomb', was hurled against Britain. It was a new form of warfare which, for a while, threatened to reverse the advance of the Allies. On the other great war front in the Pacific, the Battle of the Philippine Sea ended in another defeat for the Japanese.

In July an attempt was made to assassinate Hitler and end the war before Germany sank beneath the ruins of unconditional surrender. The attempt failed, and the blood bath that followed discouraged further attempts.

August brought more good news. Rumania, once Germany's ally, declared war on its former colleague in arms. Paris was liberated by United States and Free French forces, and the United States 7th Army landed in the South of France. A month later Brussels fell to the advancing British 2nd Army, and the threat of the V-weapons receded. But an attempt to end the war in 1944 with an airborne landing at Arnhem was doomed to failure, and a heavy loss of crack airborne troops. In October, General Douglas MacArthur began his invasion of the Philippines, holding true to his promise to return. A few days later the Battle of the Leyte Gulf was fought, putting the Japanese Navy out of the conflict.

Yet the year ended in near disaster when the Wehrmacht launched a surprise offensive in the Ardennes and threatened to isolate the Allied Armies in a second Dunkirk. Known as the Battle of the Bulge, it was in effect the dying spasm of the German Army.

The thirty-fifth Convention of Rotary International in 1944 was held in Chicago. Only 403 delegates attended, and the gathering was forever afterwards known as the first of the 'streamlined' conventions. Despite the small attendance, there was plenty to discuss. The 'work pile' idea which was expounded at the 1943 Convention was shown to be successful. Designed to gauge and stimulate postwar work, it had gained widespread acceptance and application not only by Rotary clubs, but by other organizations. In March a number of American clubs set aside one meeting for a 'China Day' programme, which directed attention to the problems of China and her long-suffering peoples. The President's Award was another innovation. This is presented to the club in each Rotary district judged to have the best record of outstanding achievement in the four principal avenues of Rotary service.

Only officers of Rotary International were permitted to attend the thirty-fifth Convention, because of the restrictions on transportation. But the news quickly spread through the movement that a new club had been started at Pindicherry in French India. This was only one of 169 new clubs admitted to membership in 1943. The delegates heard also of 32,000 Finnish children who were being cared for in Swedish homes, a great humanitarian work in which the Rotary clubs of Sweden played a prominent part.

And throughout the world, some parts of which were free again, Rotary clubs staged programmes on the Monetary and Financial Conference at Bretton Woods. Later in 1944, after the Dumbarton Oaks Conference at Washington, D.C., further programmes were staged on post-war peace and security.

The end of the most costly war in history came in 1945 when first Germany, and then Japan, bowed to the Allied terms of unconditional surrender. But first, in January, Franklin Delano Roosevelt was inaugurated President of the United States for a fourth successive term, although he was already in poor health. In February, United States forces captured Manila, and on the same day Roosevelt, Churchill and Stalin began their talks at Yalta. Eight days after the talks ended, United States Marines stormed ashore on the Japanese island of Iwo Jima. On 23 February (Rotary's official birthday), the 'Stars and Stripes' was raised above the island. On 1 April more American troops began the assault on Okinawa and Japan prepared for the invasion of their mainland. But eleven days later, on April 12, came the stunning news of the death of President Roosevelt. Had he lived nine more days he would have seen Russian forces reach the outskirts of

Berlin, trapping Hitler in his Chancellory.

On 28 April Mussolini and his mistress, Clara Petacci, were captured and executed by Italian partisans. The war in Europe was almost over, and on 29 April all the German armies in Italy laid down their arms. Finally, Hitler committed suicide in his Berlin bunker. The city surrendered to the forces of the Soviet Union followed, on 7 May, by the capitulation of all German forces.

The thirty-sixth Convention of Rotary International, in 1945, was the second of the 'streamlined' war-time conferences, again in Chicago. Attendance was again restricted to officers of Rotary International, and only 141 were registered. Only the first Convention in 1910 had a smaller attendance. The convention opened on 31 May, and the delegates reconvened on 5, 12 and 19 June. Meanwhile representatives from fifty nations assembled in San Francisco formally to establish the United Nations. They were called together to consider the pattern for post-war peace and prosperity, along the formulae hammered out at Dumbarton Oaks in 1944.

Rotary International was invited to send representatives to make suggestions for a new era of international goodwill and understanding. No fewer than forty-nine Rotarians served as delegates, advisers or consultants. In thirty-three of the fifty participating nations Rotary clubs made positive contributions. This recognition of the prestige and value of Rotary was as much a tribute to Harris as it was to the movement.

In July, scientists who in December 1942 achieved the first controlled atomic chain reaction in Chicago, exploded the first atomic bomb at Alamogordo, New Mexico. But the advent of the Atomic Age was viewed with grave misgivings by many. Twenty days later a Flying Fortress bomber, *Enola Gay*, took off from a Pacific atoll. A few hours later the first atomic bomb used in warfare was dropped on the Japanese city of Hiroshima. Three days later a second bomb was exploded over Nagasaki, and the war in the Pacific was over.

It was also a historic year for Rotary. In March the Rotary Club of Guam was re-admitted to membership, the first club to be re-organized in Axis held territories. Two new commissions were formed, one for the re-organization of clubs in Europe, the other for the re-establishment of clubs in the Far East. Soon afterwards sixty-eight clubs were re-admitted—sixty-six from France, Belgium, Norway and the Netherlands, and two from the Philippines.

A gathering of Rotarians at Schenectady, New York in 1939, watching
Harris, Perry and other officers of Rotary on television

A gathering of the first fourteen Presidents of the Chicago club on the
occasion of their fifteenth anniversary in 1920

The Unity Building as it appeared during 1905, the year in which Harris brought Rotary into being. A bronze plaque commemorating the genesis of Rotary was placed near the entrance in 1955

In April, at the request of the United Nations Relief and Rehabilitation Authority, Rotary clubs in the United States spearheaded local committees in a nationwide, used-clothing drive. As a result, more than 150 million pounds of used (and sometimes nearly new) clothing was collected. On 28 May the first shipment was made to Greece, Yugoslavia and Italy.

Not to be outdone, Rotary clubs throughout Canada engaged in a similar drive from 1–20 October. Sponsored by Canadian Allied Relief, on behalf of UNRRA, the Rotarians of Canada responded magnificently and collected eleven million pounds of used clothing—far in excess of their target of five million.

In November 1945 Rotary clubs throughout the world observed United Nations Charter Week and took the opportunity to spread understanding of the United Nations Charter, in which Rotary had played so prominent a role. A booklet was published by Rotary International, *From Here On*, containing not only the full text of the charter, but interpretative comments and discussion questions. The first printing and distribution was so successful, two more printings were required for an eventual total of 100,000 copies. Another edition was produced in Spanish for distribution to Ibero-America.

From almost every club in America, Britain and the other Allied nations, members had served in every sphere of the global conflict. Among the twenty-two members of the Chicago club to serve in the United States Armed Forces, was Colonel Frank Knox, a newspaper publisher, who became the Secretary of the Navy under Roosevelt.

And, despite the setbacks of war, Rotary clubs grew from 5,112 in 1942 to 5,472 in 1945.

CHAPTER 41

The Last Award

In 1928 the Rotary Club of Chicago granted official status to a committee that had been under consideration for several months. Its purpose was to accord public recognition to any citizen of Chicago who had rendered distinguished service locally, nationally or internationally. It became known as the Chicago Merit Awards Commission and for more than forty years has remained one of the Chicago club's most important bodies. The Commission has eighteen members, all of whom are Rotarians, appointed each year by the President of the Chicago club. Having recommended candidates for the Merit Award—the Commission does not make the final choice. This is the prerogative of a special Jury of Awards, the members of which are chosen by the Commission from the heads of the leading Chicago business firms, civic organizations, educational institutions and other bodies.

To avoid any possible charge of prejudice, the Jury is deliberately kept non-Rotarian in its composition. The Commission keeps a meticulous record of the achievements of possible candidates (who must be citizens of Chicago), and then recommends to the Jury of Awards.

The first award was made in 1931. This and the subsequent awards up to 1939 were in the form of plaques or engrossed testimonials. Since then a gold medallion, $4\frac{1}{2}$ inches in diameter, has been awarded. One side shows a design symbolic of the award, the other carries the text of the recipient's citation. Over the years the Chicago Merit Award has become one of the highest honours of its kind ever conferred by an American organization.

The first recipient was Julius Rosenwald, one of America's greatest philanthropists. As a businessman he was known throughout the United States as the president of the gigantic Sears Roebuck and Company organization from 1910 to 1925. In 1917 he created the Julius Rosenwald Fund for the 'well-being of Mankind' but his best known and most valuable act of service was, undoubtedly, his gift to Chicago of its world renowned Museum of Science and Industry in 1929.

It was with a deep sense of pride that the Merit Award Commission in 1946 put forward for consideration by the Jury of Awards, the name of Paul Percy Harris, the Founder of Rotary. It was the highest tribute the Rotary Club of Chicago could have paid him, and no one deserved it more. It came during the last year of Harris's life, and it was the last award he received.

Earlier in the year, from 24 January to 14 February, the United Nations General Assembly was held in London, and it was a source of deep satisfaction to Harris that Rotary International was again invited to send representatives. Three observers attended, thus maintaining close contact with the United Nations organization. Another three Rotarians were present to observe the Second Session of the Security Council in New York on 25 March.

It was an active year for Rotary. Further funds, totalling $10,000, were allocated for the relief of Rotarians and their families affected by the war. The worldwide plan of Rotary Foundation Fellowships was announced, with awards for one year's study in a country other than that of the student's residence. The purpose was to give practical aid to potential leaders with qualifications that would equip them to make outstanding contributions to 'the advancement of international understanding, goodwill and peace'.

The thirty-seventh Convention of Rotary International was held in Atlantic City, New Jersey, from 2–6 June 1946. No fewer than 10,958 delegates were present and they had plenty of decisions to make. A crucial issue was the future location of Rotary International headquarters. The choice lay between Denver and Chicago. The Council on Legislation had decided in favour of Denver, but this was hotly challenged from the floor of the Convention. A debate was arranged, with three speakers (all Americans) favouring Denver, and another three (two Americans, one Briton) supporting Chicago. Chicago carried the day, and the decision of the Convention in rejecting the Council's recommendation meant that the whole subject had to be debated again at San Franciso in 1947. After another impassioned debate Chicago won again, but Harris never knew the final decision.

As the mid-year point approached, the organization of new clubs and members promised to reach record-breaking proportions. Even more heart-warming was the welcome extended to clubs that had been disbanded or discontinued in the Axis dominated countries.

These were the last reports Harris received about Rotary. Nearly all of them were encouraging, but he received one sad item of personal news from Glasgow. An old friend and a founder member of the Glasgow club, William Park Laidlaw, died just eight days before his 102nd birthday. He was late coming into Rotary at sixty-eight, yet put in thirty-four years of meritorious service.

As 1946 drew to a close Harris was ailing. Frail though he had become, his spirit remained unquenchable. To the very end his life was Rotary. His pen was still in use (all his letters were written by hand) as he completed the manuscript of his last book, *My Road to Rotary*.

CHAPTER 42

'Never Send to Know for Whom the Bell Tolls'

Paul Percy Harris died on Monday, 27 January 1947 at the age of seventy-eight. He died peacefully in his home, Comely Bank, Longwood Drive, in the Morgan Park district of Chicago, the home where he and his 'Bonnie Scottish Lassie', had spent thirty-five happy years.

The previous week the Board of Directors of Rotary International assembled in Chicago under President Richard C. Hedke for a routine meeting. On Saturday, 25 January the business was concluded and all but a few of the directors were en route to their respective countries.

Although all knew Harris was ill, the news of his death came as a shock which reverberated throughout the Rotary world. A deluge of telegrams, cablegrams and letters flooded Rotary headquarters in Chicago and Comely Bank.

On the day he died, a Church Conference began its deliberations at the Stevens Hotel, Chicago. Among the delegates was a Rotarian, Lee Tuttle, from Asheville, North Carolina. Tuttle became a well known author and General Secretary of the World Methodist Council. In his book *Name Dropping by an Expert*, Tuttle recalled that on 29 January the city was in the grip of a typical Chicago blizzard, but he was determined to attend the last rites for Paul Harris the following day.

Early that day, recalled Tuttle, it stopped snowing, although it resumed later as the mourners left the church, 'softening the harsh winter scene with a gentle blanket of fresh white snow'. Tuttle made his way to Morgan Park, twelve miles south-west of the city, first by commuter train, then on foot through the partially cleared streets to the little Morgan Park Congregational Church where the simple funeral service was held.

He joined many Rotarians and friends of Harris from the Chicago area who had come, despite the difficult conditions, to pay their last tributes to the Founder of Rotary. Present were Richard C. Hedke, the incumbent President of Rotary International, and past Presidents Arch Klumph, George C. Hager and Tom Warren. There also, inevitably, was the ever faithful Chesley Perry.

To Harris's own Rotary Club of Chicago fell the honour of providing the pallbearers and the ushers. They had all been close friends of Harris for many years. The ushers, drawn from the earliest members of the club, were Max Goldenberg, Charles H. Eckel, Max C.O. Stienz, George Landis Wilson, B.O Jones and George A. Stephen. The eight pallbearers were all Presidents of the Rotary Club of Chicago—the then President, Alex G. Shennan, and past Presidents Herbert C. Angster, Charles J. Becker, Charles E. Hedrick, Howard K. Jackson, Herbert J. Taylor, Richard E. Vernor and Paul A. Westburg.

The service was conducted by Harris's own pastor, the Rev Hugh S. Mackenzie. The eulogies were voiced by three Rotary leaders, expressing what was in the hearts of more than 300,000 Rotarians in seventy lands.

Chesley Perry spoke for the Rotary Club of Chicago, past International President Tom Warren spoke for Rotarians in the eastern hemisphere, and President Richard C. Hedke spoke for Rotarians everywhere.

The service over, the body of Paul Percy Harris was reverently placed in a grave next but one to that of his lifelong friend, neighbour, and co-founder of Rotary, Sylvester Schiele, the first President of the world's first Rotary club. The last resting place of Paul Harris can be seen in the Mount Hope Cemetery in Chicago. It is marked by a simple headstone, crowned by his immortal emblem, the distinctive Rotary Wheel.

On the day Harris died a wave of grief swept through the world of Rotary and beyond into the lives of countless millions. He left behind a host of friends who experienced an emptiness they had never known before. From them, and from thousands more who never met Paul Harris, expressions of grief and sympathy arrived in Chicago, 'as a tidal wave would crash on a beach' said one heartbroken Rotarian.

CHAPTER 43

The Last Accolades

In March 1947 the editors of *The Rotarian* asked four Rotary leaders to record their tributes to the modest man who founded Rotary. The Board of Directors unhesitatingly granted my request to reprint these in full:

Richard C. Hedke, Detroit, Michigan. President of Rotary International and long-time friend of Harris.

'The story of the life of Paul Harris is the story of man at his best.

'Conquering obstacles which rose before him, Paul Harris attained the heights of worthwhile living. Woven into the very warp and woof of his character was his devotion to high ideals. There burned within the man the spirit of friendliness and kindliness.

'Many have been warmed and cheered by this great man. The example which he has given us for noble living reached its climax in his love and devotion to his "Scottish lassie", Jean. Never has there been an example of finer companionship and more successful marriage than that which they gave to the world.

'We are grateful to Paul Harris for conceiving and for organizing Rotary International. It is the finest flowering of the great ideas and ideals that activated his life. Rotary has its worldwide importance today because of what Paul gave to it. Rotary came from his compelling conviction that men in business and profession could be and should be friends. He needs no monument of marble or stone to mark his life, for he has given to the world an organization whose members shall cherish his memory in love undying. Our day needs desperately to learn again the lessons of friendship. To answer this need and to honour its Founder, we shall do all in our power to carry the Rotary spirit of friendliness and the high principles of service and helpfulness to all the world.

'The passing of Paul Harris leaves a void in our midst which never can be filled. Edwin Markham, the American poet, speaks of the passing of Abraham Lincoln as the falling of a mighty tree which leaves an empty place against the sky. There is an empty place within our hearts because of the passing of this dear friend. The utter simplicity, the gallant purpose, and the complete consecration which he gave to life shall ever be an example for us to ascend the steep pathways of more noble living. Henry Wadsworth Longfellow, in *The Builders*, expressed well the challenge that comes to us from the life of Paul Harris:'

> Let us do our work well,
>   Both the unseen and the seen;
> Make the house where gods may dwell
>   Beautiful, entire, and clean.
>
> Else our lives are incomplete,
>   Standing in these walls of time,
> Broken stairways, where the feet
>   Stumble, as they seek to climb.
>
> Build today, then, strong and sure,
>   With a firm and ample base;
> And ascending and secure
>   Shall tomorrow find its place.
>
> Thus alone can we attain
>   To those turrets, where the eye
> Sees the world as one vast plain,
>   And one boundless reach of sky.

Thomas A. Warren, Wolverhampton, England. Immediate past President of Rotary International.

'I, a son of England, stand in a privileged place. By the accident of circumstances, I represent tens of thousands of men from all the way across the great eastern hemisphere.

'We for whom I speak come from China, from India, from the islands of the Pacific, from Australia, from New Zealand, Africa, the countries of the Middle East, Europe, Great Britain and Ireland, and many other countries. We differ in colour, creed and culture; but we stand united as the faithful followers of the leader who has now set out on the greatest of all his journeys in search of the Peace. This time he will find it. He will find it eternally—so well and so nobly has he served.

'Few there are—few there ever could be—who might so translate inspired vision into courageous action as to recruit men from almost every nation for a mission demanding absolute selflessness and sacrifice. Yet that is what Paul Harris did. He prayed, "Thy kingdom come, Thy will be done on earth as it is in Heaven," and away into the uttermost parts of the earth he strove—and strove successfully—to bring that prayer into better and wider effect. And all of us from the north and the south, the east and the west, are bettered for having come within the shining influence of that fine American citizen.

'We sorrow for our dear Jean. We wish for her the peaceful contentment of happy retrospect when once the first sharp pangs of temporary parting are assuaged.

'For our leader we cannot really mourn. We sorely feel his loss, and pay him homage and give thanks for the immense influence that he has had upon us.

'But Paul Harris is not dead. His spirit lives on. It abides everywhere. It is woven into the very fibre of other men's lives. As we take leave of his mortal self, we re-dedicate ourselves to the never-ending task he has inspired and bequeathed to those who will assuredly follow his paths down the years to come.

'May God, in His all-providing mercy, grant eternal peace to this great soul.'

Glenn C. Mead, Philadelphia, Pennsylvania. Second President of Rotary International, 1912–13.

'I first met Paul Harris in Chicago in the summer of 1911 when I joined the Chicago delegation to attend the second Annual Convention of Rotary Clubs to be held in Portland, Oregon. We were joined in Minneapolis by delegates from that city and travelled overland on the "Soo Pacific" via the Soo Line and Canadian Pacific Railway. Paul was a good traveller and good company all the way; his duties and responsibilities as the first President of the newly formed Association in no way interfered with his sociability and good humour, and that was characteristic of him throughout his life.

'Paul was re-elected President and with others I accompanied him back directly to the starting point in Chicago. We were a small group and because of that and the Convention excitement over, the fortunate few of us had a better chance of getting acquainted with our leader and the Founder of Rotary. A year later we made the trip to Duluth, Minnesota, by boat from Chicago. The delegations were larger and filled the ship. It was a trip long to be remembered and a happy time for Paul. At the close of the Convention he was elected President Emeritus by the grateful and appreciative delegates. From that time to the end of his life his zeal, interest and devotion to the cause of Rotary never slackened.

'I think Paul felt relieved after his two years in office and was glad to get back to his active law practice. He was an able, alert and studious lawyer, deeply interested in his profession and the activities of the Chicago Bar Association. At Rotary Conventions he took the greatest interest in the lawyers' group meetings, and impressed his fellow barristers with his broad knowledge of the law and his earnest and sincere interest in their welfare. His legal training and experience well fitted him for grappling with the varied and difficult problems arising from the growth and expansion of Rotary.

'Paul was a clear and profound thinker, as his numerous books and writings reveal. He was always genial and never too serious, so that it was a joy to meet him and converse with him no matter what the subject might be. He was well read, well informed, kept himself abreast of the times, and knew what was going on everywhere.

'In personal intercourse Paul seemed always to be at his ease; he never set himself up as an oracle above and beyond his friends and fellow Rotarians—he was just one of us. We not only prized his friendship, but wanted to see him and talk and laugh with him whenever the opportunity offered. It would be a great oversight not to realize and appreciate what a fund of good humour Paul Harris possessed; and there was never any barb in his fun and joking—it was simply the privilege and relaxation of friendly intercourse.

'Many Rotarians think that the best thing about Rotary is its fine fellowship, of which Paul was a splendid type and example. But the Rotary that he founded is far more than a mere association of men and clubs; it has become a worldwide movement based on service and goodwill among men.

'Paul Harris never claimed to have founded a new philosophy; he referred to the spirit of Rotary as an ancient principle of ethics. What he did was to teach men of all nations and of all races to join together in practising and applying it.'

Chesley R. Perry, Chicago, Illinois. General Secretary of Rotary International, 1910–42.

'Not far from Comely Bank, the home and garden he loved so well, many Rotarians and other friends gathered in a suburban Chicago church to do honour to Paul Harris, the inspired and far visioned Founder of Rotary. But we who were there realized that the deep sorrow we felt was shared by hundreds of thousands of men and women around the world whose lives had been touched by forces for good loosed by this man's ideas and ideals.

'If he had consciously planned it so, he could hardly have equipped himself better for the role he was to play as the founder of a worldwide movement. Paul was a great traveller and started early. Born in Racine, Wisconsin, he spent his boyhood in a New England valley with his grandparents in Vermont. Then he went to an academy and to the University of Vermont, to Princeton University, to the University of Iowa.

'Stirred by a desire to see the world and to know its peoples, he moved on into the Rocky Mountains, to the Pacific Coast, to Louisiana and Florida, then across the ocean to England and Scotland, to France, Italy, Germany—always paying his own way by such employment as he could find. Paul always travelled under his own steam.

'A few weeks ago I sat talking to him in the dining-room of his home. He was rather shaky, but still fighting the good fight. Finally he said that we must go into the other room where the ladies were. He had me give him my arm with a stiff elbow, and with the help of his cane in the other hand we went through the hallway. As we approached the doorway to the other room, he said: "Now, drop your arm, Ches, and I'll go in under my own steam." And he did so.

'As Paul travelled, he not only made his pathways on the face of the earth, but he kept opening new pathways in his brain by his thinking. What he saw and what he heard he turned over and over in his mind. He realized that people lacked understanding and goodwill, that people were strangers to one another, and he wanted to do something about it.

'Finally in the gay and turbulent '90s he settled in Chicago, which for more than fifty years was to be his home. Here he began to practise law, but the mere acquisition of money was not his inspiration. He was lonesome for fellowship, for friends, for mutual helpfulness. In his office hangs a large plaque: "He who has a thousand friends has not a friend to spare."

'So Paul founded a club of young men who wanted to be friends, who wanted to be helpful to each other, men of different businesses and professions who except for the Chicago Rotary Club would never have known each other. He promoted rollicking good fellowship among them and a personal interest in each other's ambitions and problems. He encouraged their minds to travel in unfrequented channels of thought. He taught them to be thoughtful of and helpful to not only each other, but other people as well. He insisted that all participate in making the club succeed, for he had the inspiration, perhaps subconsciously, that in a democratic society nothing will be truly successful without participation, active personal participation by the people. That lesson our city, our state, our nation, and the United Nations have not yet fully grasped, but Rotary continues to point the way to education, participation, understanding, goodwill, fellowship.

'As the years went by, illness came upon Paul Harris and his activity in the Chicago Rotary Club had to be lessened, but his interest in it never waned. When he had recovered sufficiently to resume an active participation in Rotary, he found that his child had grown into a great international movement. In fact, before he was stricken he had started his child on the road to national and international greatness. Rotarians of many lands demanded that he give something of himself to them and he did generously. His travels for Rotary took him to all the continents, and everywhere he spoke for understanding and friendship.

'Fortunately for Paul and for the Rotary movement he took unto himself a wife many years ago—Jean Thomson, his bonnie Scottish lassie. All through the years she has been his constant, faithful companion and we pay grateful tribute to her for her gracious and immeasurable contribution to the Rotary career of our distinguished leader. We hope that her sorrow and loneliness will be softened by our sympathy and by a mutual realization with us that we all should be happy that Paul at last is at rest in a peacefulness that we all hope to attain. We pray that her years on this earth may yet be many, sweetened by the memory of Paul's glorious life of service to mankind.'

He was a friend whose heart was good,
Who walked with men and understood.
His was a voice that spoke to cheer
And fell like music on the ear.
His was a smile men loved to see,
His was a hand that asked no fee
For friendliness or kindness done.
And now that he has journeyed on
His is a fame that never ends.
He leaves behind uncounted friends.

CHAPTER 44

As Jean Remembered Paul

In *The Rotarian* of February 1950, Mrs Harris wrote of 'Those Years with Paul'. No comment is necessary; her words are eloquent enough:

'It was on a Saturday afternoon in the early spring of 1910 that I first met Paul. Quite unknown to each other, we had both joined in one of the weekly hikes of the Chicago Prairie Club, and it was this that brought us together. Perhaps I should add that a rip in Paul's jacket had a wee bit to do with it.

'Paul, as you know, was a lawyer in Chicago at the time. Five years before, he and some of his young business friends had formed the first Rotary club. A bit later he had helped to found the Prairie Club, which for him was a way of getting back to the out-of-doors he had learned to love so deeply in his Vermont boyhood.

'When a thoughtful acquaintance, Mr H.B. Davidson (who was a member of both of the new clubs) asked my sister and me to go along on the Saturday hike, we leaped at the chance. It would be something like the long walks to the seashore we often made in our bonnie Scotland which we had left three years before.

'So, as our happy company of hikers met and started into the woods in the southwestern part of Chicago, there were introductions of the new hikers, to be sure. However, it was not until Paul tore the sleeve of his fine Harris-tweed jacket on a barbed-wire fence that he and I spoke. The sight of that rip seemed to call up my Scottish instincts—how many garments I had repaired for brothers and sisters in our home in Edinburgh!—and I offered to mend the tear for the dismayed young man in the tweed cap and flowing stock.

'It is strange, but I cannot recall whether I ever mended the tear or not. It did not seem to matter, for three months later, on a lovely noon in July, we were married. Two years later we returned to those same woods to move into our own home on the hill—the only hill in Chicago. Shut off from the drive by tall old oaks, surrounded by all manner of wild fruit trees, and a block from the nearest street light, the house was just what Paul loved. Sometimes it seems that it was all foreordained. Paul had always said that he wanted to marry a Scottish lass. He had also said his home must be on a hill.

'When I was asked to recall for you some of my memories of the thirty-seven wonderful years Paul and I had together, I hesitated. I was not sure I could do it. Then I remembered something that happened long ago in Melbourne.

'During our Rotary visit to that great Australian city, Paul was to address four hundred women of a Crippled Children's Society, but many previous speeches and much travel had tired him so greatly that at the last moment he proved unequal to the task. "Jean," he said, "you must make this talk for me."

'"Why, I can't do it," I protested. Never had I ever addressed any large gathering. "What if I can't think and seem foolish? What if I fail?"

'"You won't fail," Paul answered. "You *can* do it, Jean."

'So, offering a little prayer, I went ahead. Somehow, as I thought of the things of the heart that bind all women and little children the world over together, words came somewhat easily. Well, an hour after the meeting began, I saw Paul slip in at the back of the room. He was smiling his wide smile at me. His wife who could not make a speech was talking on and on. So once again perhaps I can find words enough.

'As I look back on our years, filled as they were with wonderful travel, visits with famous persons, and great gatherings of people here and there, I think the one thing we sought most was simple contentment. And we found it in simple easy friendships, in good neighbours gathered at our hearth, in good books, in the woods, and in things in tune with nature. Often, when we were young, we walked twenty-eight miles to the church and back on the Sabbath, enjoying each step of the way. Sometimes, putting on old clothes, we would hike to a little clump of wild crabapple trees, and the next day we would have fresh tart jelly for breakfast. Perhaps there would be some for the neighbours, too. We could not waste an apple, Paul always insisted, being a New Englander. He quite forgot the sugar needed to save them, however.

'One of the first purchases after we had moved into our own

house—which Paul named Comely Bank after the street on which I had lived in Edinburgh—was a set of Dickens. Night upon night Paul read to me the wonderful true-to-life stories of that master mind as he exposed bad conditions of society. Who does not love Scrooge and Tiny Tim, Micawber and Little Dorritt? Sometimes Paul's dear old Aunt Parker would listen. If Paul suspected that she were dozing, as she sometimes did, he would inject amusing remarks about her into his reading.

'"Paul," she would cry, as she awakened, "that wasn't Dickens!" Then Paul would slap his knee and laugh. How he loved his little pranks and jokes. They never hurt, however, for he never let them.

'If Paul blessed the lives of men with Rotary, as many, many Rotarians have thoughtfully written to me, how greatly Rotarians and Rotary blessed our own lives. They gave us so many priceless experiences that I could never enumerate them all.

'We had been married but a month, I remember, when the first few clubs that had sprung up here and there in the United States met in Chicago to form a national organization and elected Paul their President and Chesley Perry their Secretary. We wives played a very small part at conventions in those days; our young men were struggling to find themselves.

'Soon Paul had two questions to answer. One was: could he take time from his law practice to travel on Rotary matters? The second was: if he started to travel, could he ever stop? Time answered both questions and over the years he was able to do both in moderation. Our first Rotary trip together took us to California, and perhaps I was a bit self-conscious. How would the ladies of these Rotarians receive me? When one of them, seeing my lace-collar or hair-do, exclaimed, "Why it's Jo from Little Women," I still was not certain. But when such wonderful hosts as Harvey and Edna Johnson, of Los Angeles, took us to clubs up and down the coast and on all manner of sight-seeing excursions and when we found ourselves talking with wholly new acquaintances as if they were lifelong friends, I was seeing in a new way what a wonderfully friendly thing this was our men had started. It is odd how little, unimportant things come to mind when one looks back on a thrilling experience of that kind. I recall how at the time Paul was temporarily on a diet of tomatoes only. Everywhere, good-humoured Rotarians plied him with tomatoes, often by the case. Then one day our new friends took us on what was to us a hair-raising ride through the mountains which were shrouded with fog. As we safely reached the end of the ride and stopped for supper, we were greatly relieved. Picking up his menu Paul declared, "No tomatoes! I want a large stack of buckwheat cakes and syrup!"

'There came in time our first sea voyage together, which took us back to my native heather, and then other trips, with the constant wonder of meeting people of other ways. There was the fine Japanese Rotarian, for example, who told us it was his custom to sit at the feet of Buddha for four hours each morning. To his Christian wife he gave funds for the building of a YWCA. I remember too the great Japanese Christian leader Kagawa, whom we met on a ship bound for Australia. He wanted to conduct Sunday worship services on board and needed someone to sing hymns. Perhaps you can guess whom my Paul suggested! It was most interesting to hear Kagawa's life story, how he lost almost all his eyesight by living in conditions so awful that he had contracted a terrible eye disease. While aboard ship he was completing his one hundredth book before his sight failed.

'In Australia our dear friend Angus Mitchell and his lovely wife, who is now gone, entertained us in their beautiful home, with as many as sixteen guests for dinner and many nights of enriching fellowship. Later we were able to have them at Comely Bank and at Onekama in Michigan where we spent our summers.

'In South Africa we talked long at a luncheon with General Smuts and General Hertzog. The former gave me a remedy for seasickness. And so it went, our travels to every continent showing us over and over that people are so alike the world around, that the heart beats just as tenderly under whatever skin.

'Then to our joy many friends we had met in far places and near came to us at Comely Bank. There was Angus, as I have said, and there were Fernando Carbajal, of Peru, and Armando Pereira, of Brazil, and Cesar Andrade, of Ecuador, and Sir Charles Mander (it was to him that Paul wrote his last letter), and scores and scores of others. Sometimes men and women from eight or ten different lands would be with us for tea. One afternoon only weeks before Paul passed away, J.C. Penney called upon us, coming in the company of Colonel Abells of the Chicago club. Mr Penney wanted to meet Paul, feeling, he said, that the principles on which he operated his famous stores were quite like those of Rotary. And over a cup of tea, of course.

'The quiet of our woods seemed to delight Glenn Mead, of Philadelphia, when he first visited us. He was the first President of Rotary after Paul, you may remember. Sitting for a long while on our front porch, he came in to claim that he had counted thirty-five species of birds in the trees. Then there was the fine Hindu gentleman in his turban and all. For two days he and I good-naturedly argued the merits of our respective religions.

'Sometimes it would be some of Paul's dear friends of the Chicago Rotary Club—our lifelong neighbour, Sylvester Schiele; the ever faithful Chesley Perry; Harry Ruggles; Rufus Chapin; and the others. Sometimes it would be the night for a discussion club Paul had organized in our basement. What a rich exchange of ideas took place around that long table there, especially when Rotarians from distant countries were among the guests.

'Yes, Paul's real forte was meeting people, learning how they looked on life, drawing them out. Through all our years together, he loved to go around the neighbourhood talking with people—the station master, the monument maker, the farmer who knew all about chicken raising. Every man interested him. Perhaps this will illustrate:

'One day soon after we had acquired our home, a man knocked at our door and offered to cut down any tree in our woods for 25 cents. Paul accepted his offer and soon had the man doing little jobs here and there. Mac, which was his name, had no fixed address anywhere, so for years all his mail came to our home. Paul had arranged it. When Mac became too old to work, Paul obtained a pension for him. Not long ago I saw old Mac and he said, "Mrs Harris, there are no days like those when Paul was there. He was my best friend."

'One thought which Paul and I often discussed in his last years was that, while the world grows more and more complex, we all need to simplify our lives somehow. We need to calm our fevers. We need more reading, more talking in our homes, more simple hospitality. More neighbourliness. Paul has written of the well-beaten path twixt our house and that of Sylvester and Jessie Schiele. He wished that there might be more such paths between all the homes on every street. Rotary, he saw, was helping to mark them out.

'If I were to say anything to the wives of Rotarians, it would be this: Encourage your husbands in their Rotary work. They are better men when they return from their meetings. Rotary stands for high ideals, with its men always attaining to the better. In the home mothers and wives have a very special part to play in bringing up children in the ways of righteousness. I for my part should like to see a return of the old-fashioned custom of all the family going to church and the children to Sunday school. It warms my heart to see my old Sunday-school scholars grown up with homes and families of their own. This, too, makes for a wholesome community and joy in later years.

'Paul sometimes said that though he was at the beginning of the stream, it was the tributary efforts of all the thousands of men who have poured in their strength and knowledge and love which have made Rotary the great organization that it is.

'And above this, Paul felt deeply that for the things that are true and real and inmost about any human movement we acknowledge the Eternal Power.'

CHAPTER 45

'What Sort of Man Was He?'

In the foregoing eulogies, all of which were written at the time of Harris's death or soon afterwards, there can be no doubting the high esteem in which he was held. But does this tell us all we would like to know about this man of so many talents? In the following pages we see him again through the eyes of those who viewed him from other platforms.

The Rev Andrew Youngson Howe, who is presently a minister of the Church of Scotland at Alness, Ross-shire, a nephew of Harris by marriage, vividly recalls the occasions on which Paul and Mrs Harris came to visit his family in Dundee, Scotland, and particularly their last visit in 1937:

> I was a small boy at the time, but I remember how thrilled I was to have an uncle who would play horses on the front lawn, and allow me to act as a cowboy riding on his shoulders. It was during that time that I attended my first Rotary meeting when, along with my parents, we were guests at a Rotary function in Soutar's Rooms in Arbroath, held in honour of my uncle's visit to Scotland. It was for me an awesome occasion, and I well remember the way in which I was drilled on how to behave. It was there that my uncle acquired a lifelong liking for 'Arbroath Smokies'.
>
> My Uncle Paul was a tall sparse figure, rather like what one would imagine Abraham Lincoln to have looked like. He was full of fun, and interested in children.

On a visit to Chicago some years ago, Mr Howe had the privilege and pleasure of speaking at the Number One Rotary Club and afterwards, in the company of one of Harris's oldest friends, visited the grave in Mount Hope Cemetery. In April 1977 Mr Howe was a special guest at the Annual Conference of Rotary International in Great Britain and Ireland, and presented an oil painting of Harris to an appreciative audience of more than five thousand delegates.

Oren Arnold, a professional author who wrote a splendid history of the Rotary Club of Chicago, *The Golden Strand*, tells us quite a lot about the activities of Harris within the club and briefly surveys his life:

> The truth is, he rode no white charger, he carried no flaming sword. He was, rather, a very average young man much too busy to take on outside obligations, much too harrassed by the demands of earning a living. They say he was good-hearted but prone to procrastination. However, he had one saving grace—he recognized his own shortcomings.

Arnold, it should be added, apparently never met Harris.

Dorothea Kahn Jaffe was a reporter with the *Christian Science Monitor* in 1935, when she was assigned to interview Harris on the occasion of the thirtieth anniversay of the founding of Rotary. She had never met him previously and did not know quite what to expect. 'It was,' she said later, 'an assignment I shall never forget.'

> The man who received me at the door exhibited the manners and features of a New England aristocrat . . . he struck me as friendly and reserved, you might even say shy. Mr Harris had been received and honoured by kings, presidents and premiers, and other notables and organizations in a number of countries where Rotary was established, but there wasn't a hint of pretentious pride in his manner. He spoke simply, his spare Yankee face lighting up with a smile now and then.

During the course of the interview the writer also discovered that Harris was fond of the outdoor and wild life, and noted that he did not care much about attending international conventions and sometimes missed them. The main reason, apart from poor health, was that so much was made of his position as the founder of Rotary when he did attend. This embarrassed him, but when he heard word going around that he stayed away from lack of interest, he came back to let himself be seen and to show his support.

Justus C. Johnson first met Harris in July 1896. He was then a high school student who had answered an advertisement in the *Chicago Tribune* asking for 'a young man to read law and tend office while lawyers are in court'. Johnson said he was interviewed by Harris in a tiny room on the seventh floor of the Wolff Building at 91 Dearborn Street. With them at the interview was Harris's partner, believed to be Lewis Dalton, although Johnson said his name was Bedford.

Johnson got the job and read much of Blackstone, and recalled with what patience and clarity Harris would explain weighty words and ideas. He felt that Harris was more like an older brother than an employer, someone to whom he instinctively felt he could turn for advice and help. Harris's humanitarian outlook and compassion for people made a deep impression even on his young mind.

Eventually Johnson decided that the practice of law was not for him and chose to take up a position with a railway company. He saw little of Harris for several years. Some time later Johnson became the 'information man' at the old Chicago Union Station, and there encountered his former employer quite often. Harris spent weekends at Hinsdale, Johnson's home town, where Harry and Mrs Ruggles also lived. Sometimes, said Johnson, the former high school student and the founder of Rotary would ride to Hinsdale together.

Johnson would also occasionally drop into Harris's law office, by then at the First National Bank Building. 'No matter how busy he was,' said Johnson, 'his cordial greeting and friendly handshake gave assurance that I was welcome.' One day, over lunch, he and Harris talked about the old days and the office at the Wolff Building, of how they met, and of Lewis Dalton's mysterious disappearance in Colorado. And he recalled the sadness on Harris's face as his friend related the story of the fruitless search and the discovery of a skeleton wedged between two boulders, and how identification was made through fragments of clothing and a watch found at the bottom of a crevice. Johnson, as did so many others, counted it a great experience to have known Harris as a friend for so many years.

Fred W. Reinhardt was not only one of Harris's closest friends and a fellow member of the Rotary Club of Chicago, but his partner from 1921 to 1947 in the law firm of Harris, Reinhardt and Vanier (afterwards Harris, Reinhardt and Bebb).

In an article written for *The Rotarian* in 1955, Reinhardt

recalled how, while looking for new office accommodation, he first met Harris in April 1919.

He called on Harris, on the tenth floor of the First National Bank Building, inspected the premises, and immediately signed a lease. 'It began as a business arrangement, developed into a friendship, and soon afterwards became a partnership.'

Reinhardt knew Harris professionally, a side of the founder of Rotary about which we know little. His recollections of Harris as a lawyer confirm what others have said of him—he was thorough, painstaking and conscientious. 'He was,' said Reinhardt, 'a lawyer who held that the practice of law is a trust relationship of the highest order, and while he freely acknowledged that no profession has been more dishonoured by its members, it is also true that no profession has been more honoured.'

Reinhardt saw Harris as a quiet, exacting, scrupulously honest lawyer who, as the head of the firm, conducted a serene and happy office.

In the twenty-eight years of their association Reinhardt never heard a word spoken in anger by anyone to anyone within the office.

Paul Harris set high standards and everyone abided by them. He was proud of his profession and took a deep interest in upholding and improving it. He was at all times very patient with the young men who came to the firm directly from law school, and he insisted that no person had the right to practise law unless he was prepared to give every legal matter submitted to him the most conscientious attention and preparation. Sincere and kind though he was, Paul would not countenance the slightest neglect.

But it was in his choice of cases that Harris's character showed through. He accepted no criminal cases, no domestic quarrels, no trial work. He chose instead the fields of corporate, real estate and probate law, and had a better than fair reputation in Chicago. Harris's classification in the Rotary Club of Chicago was: 'Lawyer: Corporation, Real Estate and Probate' and Reinhardt, as an Associate or Additional Active member, held exactly the same classification.

'Paul Harris was held in high esteem by his Chicago colleagues,'

295

wrote Reinhardt. 'In 1906 he became a member of the Chicago Bar Association and served on several of its committees, and in 1932 represented the Association at the International Congress on Comparative Law at The Hague. From 1911 onwards, through craft assemblies of lawyers at Rotary conventions, he worked unceasingly for higher standards.'

In conclusion, Reinhardt said of Harris that although he was a voluminous writer, nothing indicated Paul the lawyer quite as clearly as a scholarly, yet human, paper he wrote for the Chicago Bar Association's *Record* in 1927. Entitled 'The Evolution of Professional Ethics', the entire paper is worth everyone's reading.

Angus (later Sir Angus) Mitchell and his wife were particularly close friends of the Harrises and the sadness expressed in Mitchell's tribute to his departed friend needs no amplification. It was written on the day that the great Australian Rotarian took office as the President of Rotary International in 1948, and was printed as the foreword to Harris's posthumous *My Road to Rotary*:

As I was leaving Sydney on a flying boat for my home in Melbourne, Australia, in January 1947, I learned that Paul Harris was dead and realized that a great man and a dear personal friend had been taken. Though our homes were geographically on opposite sides of the world we had been for a quarter of a century, close personal friends. Paul was a great man. His devotion and dedication to Christian ideals, his unbounded capacity for friendship, his keenness of perception and his uncanny ability to visualize the future, coupled with his genuine appreciation of current problems, made him great. Whenever privileged to be with him I was inspired by the burning enthusiasm which, despite his ill-health and frail body, carried him on in his work.

On the flying boat my thoughts kept reverting to my friend and the many personal incidents which stressed his life. I recalled a wonderful week which my wife, my daughter and I spent with Paul and Jean Harris one summer in Onekama in Northern Michigan. Paul knew all the folks of the village, called most of them by their first names, and had a cheery word for all.

And there came vividly to my mind one of the last occasions when I saw him—at his home in Chicago, winter time with a heavy fall of snow. As I came down fairly early that morning to their little breakfast room I saw Paul tramping through the snow to little platforms in the trees. On these he was placing nuts and biscuits for the birds and squirrels. This was a regular job for this frail man whose big heart responded to the needs of all living things. Yes, the founder of Rotary was a simple man but one with a great vision—peace and a truly neighbourly world. To aid in its implementation he travelled extensively, meeting and appreciating men and making friends everywhere he went. He was a normal, lovable human being, balanced, competent, friendly, with a supreme confidence that just such ordinary human qualities would work wonders among men and nations.

Roger Levy, who joined the staff of Rotary International in Great Britain and Ireland in 1931, says of Harris in his fine history of the Rotary movement in the British Isles:

Everywhere he impressed those who met him, and heard him, with his simplicity and sincerity, and his refusal to be seen as a visionary. He had happened to found a club which turned into an international movement, but he remained a gentle, humourous and friendly man until his death in 1947—a quiet American who was unforgotten by those who had the privilege of meeting him.

For the last tribute let us look at the words of Sir Winston Churchill. They were not said about Harris, but they apply to him in even greater measure:

Solitary trees, if they grow at all, grow strong; and a boy deprived of a father's care often develops, if he escapes the perils of youth, an independence and vigor of thought which may restore in after life the heavy loss of early days.

Paul Percy Harris was such a tree.

CHAPTER 46
Mrs Harris Goes on Alone

Paul's death dealt Mrs Harris a grievous blow. She and her husband had not been blessed with children, a great disappointment to them, and there was no immediate family to assuage her grief.

With deep regret and the greatest reluctance she decided that she could not live alone in the house that held so many wonderful memories, and Comely Bank was put up for sale. The fortunate purchasers were Mr and Mrs John W. Huck who, although not connected with Rotary, were more than mindful of the great esteem in which their predecessors were held all over the world.

Mrs Harris, had no desire to live a life of inactivity and after taking up residence at one of Chicago's many hotels, gave her services voluntarily to the religious and philanthropic work being carried out in the city by the little known Pacific Garden Mission. For several years she did wonderful work in caring for and helping unfortunates such as 'Skid Row' derelicts, deprived children and housebound cripples. These were ennobling activities of great benefit to those she comforted. They were helpful to herself also in filling the void which had opened with the death of her husband.

But as time passed Mrs Harris felt an increasing urge to return home to Scotland to be near the surviving members of her family.

Before she left America, the officers of Rotary International invited her to attend, once more, their International Convention. The occasion was a special one, the Golden Jubilee Anniversary Convention. Where else could that be but in the birthplace of Rotary, Chicago itself ? The proceedings of the 1955 Convention movingly record Rotary's tribute to the widow of its founder:

The widow of Sylvester Schiele, first President of the No 1 Rotary Club, Mrs Jessie Schiele, was presented at this point on the programme and then, as the session was drawing to a

298

dramatic climax, the Chairman announced a very special guest. The audience, anticipating what was to follow, quietly rose, as Ches Perry escorted to the stage Mrs Jean Harris, the widow of the Founder of Rotary—the 'bonnie Scottish lassie' whom Paul had married in 1910 and who, by his side for nearly four decades, had watched the Rotary movement grow and flourish until his death in 1947. The introduction was brief but impressive and as Ches concluded, the draperies at the back of the stage slowly parted, revealing a large life-like portrait of the Founder. Mrs Harris responded briefly, expressing her gratitude for the welcome. And as she concluded, a small girl crossed the stage and handed her a beautiful bouquet of yellow roses.

The day before the convention opened Mrs Harris now seventy-four years old, paid the last farewell to her husband. She and Mrs Schiele took part in memorable ceremonies at Mount Hope Cemetery, where Harris and and Schiele lay buried.

Sometime during 1955 Mrs Harris returned to Scotland. Like her parents twenty years before she went back 'to be buried in the old soil' when the time came. For a while she stayed with her brother, the Rev John Youngson Thomson, at Annbank where her other brother James and her youngest sister Mary were also living. She also spent some time with her other sister Joey (Mrs John Howe) at Dundee, before finally obtaining furnished apartments in Edinburgh, the city where she was born and where she wished to spend her remaining years. Shortly afterwards the Edinburgh club learned of Mrs Harris's presence, and on behalf of the club the President sent her a floral tribute and a special letter of welcome. The Rotarians of Edinburgh kept in close touch with her until her death.

By this time, Mrs Harris no longer felt able to take any active part in public life but in August 1962, on the occasion of the Edinburgh club's Golden Jubilee celebrations, she agreed to attend a small private reception to meet the principal guests, among whom was Carl P. Miller, the President-elect of Rotary International.

A little over a year later on 9 November 1963, the day after her eighty-second birthday, following a severe illness which had necessitated her removal to a nursing home, Jean Thomson Harris died. She wished a private funeral. Her brother-in-law, the Rev John

Howe, conducted a service at a funeral parlour. Her nephew, the Rev Andrew Youngson Howe, conducted a private service at the graveside.

In Newington Cemetery, Dalkeith Road, Edinburgh, just inside the main entrance, a simple headstone marks the grave of Jean Thomson, widow of Paul. P. Harris, 'a lady who was steadfast in faith and rich in service'. Lying in the same grave is her brother James Hay Thomson, who died in June 1970. Nearby are the last resting places of her parents and grandparents, and the last member of the family, Miss Mary Thomson, who died in April 1977.

Harris, the founder of Rotary, and his wife Jean lie buried thousands of miles apart, he in the great city of Chicago in the American midwest, she in Scotland's most historic city. But though their mortal remains are far apart, they are together now, as Mrs Harris said, 'in the Eternal Power in which we both had such faith'.

Jean Thomson Harris shared with her husband the glory that is Rotary, for she did far more for the movement than is generally realized. Rotary was Harris's brainchild, certainly, but it is a living memorial to them both.

The home on the hill in Chicago they so lovingly built, furnished and tended with care is still there, separated from Longwood Drive by tall old oak trees and all manner of wild fruit trees. And in Harris's famous 'Friendship Garden' can still be seen the trees of friendship and goodwill planted by loving hands. The exterior of Comely Bank remains as it was in 1947. Still standing near the front door is one of the Harris's favourite souvenirs, a large stone temple lantern presented to him by Japanese Rotarians during the couple's tour of the Far East in 1935. Inside the house no trace remains of the cream and tan dark stained woodwork of the Harris years. The current scheme is predominantly red, blue and grey.

Mrs Harris paid her last visit to Comely Bank in 1955, shortly before she returned to Scotland. It was a poignant moment. The Hucks have raised a family of three sons in the fine old house. Paul and Jean Harris, would have delighted in the knowledge that after their departure, it became a home brimming with the play and laughter of children.

No plaque marks Comely Bank as the home of the Founder of Rotary. According to Mr and Mrs Huck, many Rotarians visited them in the first years following the death of Harris, but callers are now few and far between. They are unaware, however, that Rotarians from all over the world still come quietly to gaze at Comely Bank, although they may only stand at the foot of the upward curving drive and remember.

Mrs Harris has not been forgotten. In April 1978 a plaque was erected on the house where she was born, 9 Cumbernauld Street, Edinburgh. This was donated by the Rotary Club of St Louis following a suggestion by Alex C. West, a past President of the Rotary Club of Edinburgh.

West also suggested the cultivation of a rose in memory of Mrs Harris. This was developed by an Aberdeen Rotarian, Alex Cocker, and it became available during 1976. It is described in the grower's catalogue as:

Jean Thomson Harris (Cocker, 1976) Approx. height 2–2½ ft. Sweet fragrance.

This lovely rose is named after the wife of the founder of Rotary International. It is a short growing plant, and a very effective one, with double flowers of bright orange salmon shaded peach yellow. A really attractive short bedding rose excellent for cutting in between Hybrid Tea and Floribunda. A great provider of new shoots and blooms from its neat, compact bush.

Parentage: (Heidelberg × Fragrant Cloud) × (Heidelberg × Kingcup).

CHAPTER 47

'For His Memorial, Look About You'

Before his death Harris expressed a wish that no funds of Rotary International be used to perpetuate material memorials to him, but used instead for the purpose of advancing international understanding. The Boards of Directors throughout the years have respected his wish. In 1953, for example, they declined a proposal made by the Rotary Club of Racine that Harris's birthplace, then scheduled for demolition, be purchased and preserved as a Rotary shrine. This is not to say that the Board were unsympathetic. On the contrary. They understood and appreciated the interest which motivated the Racine Rotarians to make a determined but unavailing effort, between September 1952 and February 1953, to acquire Harris's birthplace as a permanent memorial.

Despite this setback the Rotary Club of Racine has ensured in other ways that Harris's memory will be preserved in their city. On 22 April 1951, at precisely 11.30am, Charles Krause, the then President of the Racine club, dedicated a plaque at the south-west corner of the Hotel Racine, which now occupies the site of Harris's first home. On 19 April 1961, the ninety-third anniversary of the birth of the founder of Rotary, the Rotary Room of the Racine Y.M.C.A. was also dedicated to his memory. In that same room there is a fine portrait of Harris, framed in wood salvaged from the house in which he was born.

In their Golden Anniversary booklet, published in 1967, the Racine Rotarians carefully documented all they have accomplished to commemorate the memory of Harris. Included in the booklet are the names of the four Rotarians who salvaged the wood from Harris's birthplace—Paul Heestand, Glenn Patrick, William Peterson and Ralph Webber.

In Chicago there are many memories but few memorials of Harris. The Unity Building where he, Schiele, Loehr and Shorey brought Rotary into being, still stands, although dwarfed now by far higher modern buildings. Comely Bank is still there, of course. As far as is known, no proposal was ever made to preserve this as a Rotary monument, but had one been made the decision of the Board of Directors of Rotary International would have been the same as for the proposal to preserve the Harris birthplace. At Evanston, in Rotary International headquarters, there is much memorabilia of Harris, including an exact replica of the office he used in the earlier headquarters in downtown Chicago.

Several portraits have been painted. The two best known are those by Trebilcock and Doctoroff. There are an equal number of sculptures, the best known being that by Isoa Morioka of Japan in 1932. None of these, however, in accord with Harris's expressed wish, have been marketed commercially.

Harris's own choice of a memorial, would undoubtedly have been in the form of the Rotary Foundation which provides funds for worldwide exchange of mainly young people in the interests of better international understanding on a personal level. He had, on many occasions, expressed his deep interest in the Foundation and its far reaching possibilities. It was Harris's opinion that a large Foundation fund offered a practical means of actively promoting Rotary's objective of international service and understanding.

The Rotary Foundation developed from an idea presented by Arch Klumph when President of the International Association of Rotary Clubs at Atlanta, Georgia, in 1917. It was just the germ of an idea then, but it took root and grew and, a decade later, at the International Convention in Minneapolis in 1928, approval was given to amend Rotary International's by-laws to provide for the Foundation under the supervision of a Board of five trustees.

Three years later the Board of Directors of Rotary International, together with the Trustees of the Rotary Foundation, organized the Foundation as a trust in the state of Illinois.

Progress was delayed, however, by the economic recession of the 1930s, and it was not until 1938, at the San Francisco convention, that approval was given to a plan presented by the Board to raise two million dollars. A start was made immediately, but before the campaign made any real impact, it was interrupted by the outbreak of World War II.

When Harris died in 1947 his passing became the unwitting instrument that created the Rotary Foundation as we know it today. Long before his death Harris intimated that no flowers were to be sent to his funeral. He expressed the hope that those who did feel moved to honour him in death would meet his wishes best by making a donation to Rotary funds to promote international understanding.

The fund was re-named the Paul Harris Memorial of the Rotary Foundation. No finer tribute could have been devised. Here indeed was the memorial worthy of the Founder of Rotary, providing for a new generation of leaders, young men and women to be imbued with Rotary's principles of international goodwill and understanding.

Within months of his death, plans were formulated, and the first eighteen Rotary Graduate (Paul Harris) Fellowships were awarded. They were made possible by the flood of generous contributions which poured in immediately after Harris's death, almost reaching the target of two million dollars which had been set at San Francisco in 1938. By mid-1948, the contributions amounted to $1,775,000.

We do not need plaques or monuments, paintings or sculptures to remind us of Paul Percy Harris. Rotary itself is his memorial, and whenever or wherever Rotarians gather, he is remembered. The movement he created in 1905 has grown into a gigantic and influential force for the betterment of mankind, irrespective of religious tenets, political creeds or national cultures, and the Paul Harris Memorial of the Rotary Foundation is its outward manifestation.

Had it not been for the genius of Harris, millions of people the world over would never have experienced the wonderful friendship, fellowship and concept of service which is so uniquely Rotary's. His was a life that touched the lives of countless millions and left them better for it. Yet he remained to the end of his days, in his own words, 'just a simple Chicago lawyer'.

This account of the life and times of Paul Percy Harris began in St Paul's Cathedral, London. We can appropriately end there, for it can truly be said of Paul Harris, as is written of Sir Christopher Wren and St Paul's Cathedral:

'For his memorial, look about you.'

Chesley R. Perry – Builder of Rotary

In his memoirs, written forty years after the founding of Rotary, Harris said of Chesley Perry: 'If I can in truth be called the architect, Ches Perry can with equal truth be called the builder of Rotary International.' It is a well deserved tribute, for no man, apart from Harris himself, gave so much to Rotary and its ideals. For thirty-two years, Chesley R. Perry served as the General Secretary of Rotary International, from the organization of the National Association of Rotary Clubs in 1910 to his retirement in 1942. And even after handing over the reins of administration, he remained active in his own Chicago club, including service as President in 1944–5. For fifty-two years he served the Rotary cause with absolute dedication. The story of Harris would not be complete without reference to the life of his staunchest ally.

Oddly, although they had the greatest respect and admiration for each other, Harris and Perry were never really close friends. Harris noted this in *My Road to Rotary* when he remarks, somewhat wistfully: 'No one could by the widest stretch of the imagination say that Ches and I were chums in the usual acceptance of the word.' When they met in the Rotary International Secretariat, they would greet each other with cheerful 'good mornings', but they seldom went to lunch together. Perry, was a dedicated executive who preferred to take a light lunch in his office and continue to work without a break.

'Ches had his idiosyncrasies,' said Harris, 'and I had mine. Some things were natural to Ches, others were natural to me, but something more important than mere chumminess was growing up steadily throughout the years; a genuine affection born of respect for each other.'

Only four years younger than Harris, Perry was born in Chicago on 12 September 1872, the son of a merchant who owned a chain of stationery stores. As a boy he worked in his father's store as a janitor, and simultaneously had a newspaper route. Later, he found employment as an assistant in the Chicago Public Library, an experience that stood him in good stead in later life. In 1898, aged twenty-six, he went to Cuba as a soldier and as a correspondent for the *Chicago Times Herald*. When he was eventually discharged, he had attained commissioned rank as Lieutenant.

Although an intelligent, articulate and remarkably knowledgeable man, Perry received little in the way of formal education, his parents being of the opinion that knowledge acquired through experience is more useful than that acquired academically. Be that as it may, he was an insatiable seeker after knowledge and was voracious in his reading, which ranged over an astonishing array of subjects. By his own admission he had a good knowledge of such diverse subjects as theology, pedagogy, literature, city planning, mathematics, civics, sociology, geology, biology, zoology, anthropology, chemistry, accountancy, history, journalism and library science. As if this were not enough, he admitted also to knowing a little about mining, printing, insurance and retailing, fields in which he had some practical experience. He could also read well in French and Spanish.

In appearance Perry, although not in fact a big man, gave the impression that he was, due to his upright military bearing and immaculate grooming. Even more introverted than Harris, he was not one of the back-slapping, glad-handed, hail-fellow-well-met boys. He tended to be reserved and modest, almost shy, but when he did shake hands his grip was firm and positive, and one knew intuitively that behind the modest exterior there dwelt a strong personality with very definite views and attitudes. Someone who knew exactly what he had to do and how he had to do it. His most striking feature were his eyes. They were large, luminous and penetrating, and he looked directly at people without wavering. Some of Perry's contemporaries considered him to be too serious, almost cold, but Harris and others knew otherwise. They were aware that he felt uncomfortable if the spotlight of publicity was focused on him. In reality, he loved the fellowship and jollity of Rotary.

What distinguished Perry was his total commitment to Rotary. From the day he was inducted into membership he was an active participant in all the Chicago club's projects and business. Like Harris, he soon perceived that Rotary had a future, and strongly supported the expansion of the movement and the furtherance of Rotary's ideals of service.

From the time he was appointed General Secretary in 1910, he worked almost continuously, weekends and holidays alike. His goal, with Harris, was that all mankind adopt the ideal of Rotary, and the ordinary working hours of every day were simply not enough for him. It is reported that he took only one vacation in twenty-five years. Perry was not only efficient, he was a practical and far-seeing man. He knew that Harris, in creating Rotary, had brought into being a new concept of community service, of thoughtfulness and helpfulness to others, a modern day restatement of the ancient Golden Rule, the one common law that has sustained all the world's major religions and philosophies. He perceived clearly that the world, at the beginning of the twentieth century, was ready for the concept of Rotary, and he bent all his considerable talents and energies to the task of extending it beyond national boundaries. Harris had, as it were, provided Perry with the blueprint. Perry, in turn, had the ability and know-how to get the job done.

He was not one of the original members of the world's first Rotary club, and did not become a member until 1908, when he was introduced by Ruggles, the 'Fifth Rotarian'. He was immediately impressed by the new club and its aims, and it astonished him to see the fine spirit of fellowship that prevailed among the members, and the way in which Rotarians helped not only each other but also their competitors.

Perry instantly grasped the meaning of and embraced the philosophy of Rotary, so much so he was soon interpreting it for others in the clearest and most succinct terms. A striking example of this is the statement of Rotary service he made quite early in his association with the movement:

The solution of our problems of human relationships depends upon each individual accepting and implementing the ideal of service in all contact with others. That is the great objective of the Rotary movement. The word 'Rotarian' in business must be equivalent to the word 'Sterling' on a piece of silver. Rotarians must develop their full potential not in collective action but in persistent, persuasive action as individuals.

Perry, as his record demonstrates, was a brilliant administrator.

His talents are evinced by the way in which he systematized the whole legal processes of Rotary, and the manner in which he organized the diverse services and reach of the Rotary International secretariat. This he saw as the heart of the movement, pumping life to every corner of the world of Rotary, a service centre for all Rotarians, and the one essential source for the storing and dissemination of Rotary information. It was Perry who brought *The National Rotarian* (now *The Rotarian*) into being, and he remained its editor until 1929, when the pressure of work compelled him to relinquish the editorial helm to others.

Like Harris, Perry was an idealist and a dreamer, but a dreamer with a practical mind. Both he and Harris knew there were enough good men in the world to change the course of history—if only they would. In their own Chicago club they had experienced the invisible power for good that is inherent in Rotary, and that Rotarians can and do sometimes accomplish more for international understanding and goodwill than statesmen and warriors. But they knew also that Rotary had to progress slowly, 'for human nature', said Perry, 'cannot be changed in the twinkling of an eye'.

Perry's first assignment in the Chicago club was as Chairman of a committee appointed to revise the club's constitution. But his first major achievement in Rotary was his efficient organization of the first Rotary Convention in 1910, when he brought to Chicago delegates from fourteen of the sixteen clubs then in existence, to form the National Association of Rotary Clubs. Perry himself chaired that historic first convention and, when it ended, he found himself elected the movement's first General Secretary. Thereafter, year after year until 1942, he was re-elected to office. Initially the position was not a full-time appointment, and Perry continued to run his cement brick machinery business at the same time. But as Rotary grew, he found the work load increasing to an extent where it interfered more and more with his business. Finally, the newly formed Association asked him to serve as its full-time Secretary. Perry replied that he would accept the appointment if he was paid an annual salary of $5,000. The Board of Directors did not hesitate.

Perry was one of those natural leaders who led by example. He never asked others to do what he could not do himself. He was an orderly man with a penchant for punctuality. He was always on time, and he was a stickler for accuracy. His dictum was 'Check and double check', and he paid meticulous attention to detail. At the same time he was no martinet. Respected and admired by all those who worked with him, he was never Mr Perry but simply Ches, and his door was always open. Like the Rotary movement, which was both his life and his hobby, he recruited by example and his secretariat was built up with care by staff who were devoted to him.

Perry saw the Rotary movement not as an evangelistic call, trying to convert men to its ideals, but as one which would draw members only by attracting those who could recognize the value of its achievements in practice. 'If the ideal of service does not appeal,' he counselled, 'a man will not become a Rotarian.' To Perry the individual Rotarian was more important than the individual club. 'The best way to reform the world,' he said, 'is to reform oneself.' And again: 'All Rotarians should preserve their opportunities to participate in control of the Association, as delegates, as officers.' Otherwise, he warned, an officer caste could develop within the movement, and its essential democratic character would be destroyed.

Harris was right to describe Perry as the 'Builder of Rotary'. Together they made a great partnership, and from 1910 to 1942 they consulted long and frequently. Sometimes things would go as Harris planned. At other times Perry's pragmatic approach convinced the 'architect' that the 'builder's' way was best. In his memoirs Harris recalled how, in 1910, he encountered opposition within the Chicago club to his plans for the expansion of Rotary. Perry was in the opposition's camp initially but Harris, in appealing for his support, convinced him that the dream was viable. From that moment on, no one did more for the internationalization of Rotary than Perry.

If a portrait has emerged of an efficient, cool, almost ruthless administrator, nothing could be further from the truth. It was Perry's unbounded energy, his total dedication and his natural modesty which, at times, made Perry seem remote. He was in fact a friendly man.

In his younger days he was an exceptional athlete. He played football, baseball and basketball. He was a golfer of no mean ability, a bowler, a hunter, a swimmer and a tennis player. He was adept with rifle and pistol. He could ice skate and ride a horse. He was just as proficient at indoor pastimes, and knew such games as pinochle, bridge, billiards, snooker and cribbage. And in the social graces he could waltz, two step, fox trot and dance the virginia reel!

At the age of seventy, Perry retired as General Secretary of Rotary International. His service had been long, valuable and distinguished. He was offered the honorary title of 'General Secretary Emeritus', but politely declined. Upon his retirement he married his secretary, the former Emma C. 'Peggy' Schafer, and they made their home in an apartment on Chicago's famed Lake Shore Drive. There they enjoyed eighteen years of happy retirement, although Perry remained active in the Chicago club.

On 21 February 1960 (just two days short of Rotary's fifty-fifth anniversary), when he was eighty-eight years old, Chesley Perry died soon after taking a brisk walk on a bitterly cold and snowy afternoon. At his own request, his ashes were scattered over Lake Michigan, just off the Chicago shoreline, the city where he had spent his entire life and where, with Paul Harris, he built his own memorial, the Rotary movement as we know it today.

Bibliography of Books
and Sources Consulted

Allen, Ivan *Rotary in Atlanta* Rotary Club of Atlanta, 1938

Arnold, Oren *The Golden Strand; an informal history of the Rotary Club of Chicago* Quadrangle Books, Chicago, 1966

——"The Widening Path; an interpretative history of Kiwanis" Kiwanis International, Chicago, 1957

Barty-King, Hugh *Round Table; the search for fellowship 1927–1977* Heinemann, London, 1977

Carter, Vivian ('A Rotarian') *The Meaning of Rotary* (with an introduction by John Galsworthy) Percy Lund Humphries, London, 1927

Casey, Robert J. and Douglas, W.A.S. *The World's Biggest Doers; the story of the Lions* Wilcox and Follett, Chicago, 1949

Chicago, Rotary Club of: Survey Committee *Rotary?* University of Chicago Press, Chicago, 1934

Cook, Frederick Francis *Bygone days in Chicago* A.C. McClurg and Co., Chicago, 1910

Creasey, John *Round Table; the first twenty-five years* National Association of Round Tables, London, 1953

Davidson, Lillian Dow *Making new friends* (with an introduction by Paul P. Harris) Rotary International, Evanston, 1934

Dedman, Emmett *Fabulous Chicago* Random House, New York, 1953

Ferguson, Charles W. *Fifty million brothers* Farrar and Rinehart, New York, 1937

Grant, Bruce *Fight for a city* (with a preface by Joseph A. Matter) Rand McNally, Chicago, 1955

Harris, Paul Percy *My Road to Rotary* (with a preface by Sir Angus Mitchell) A. Kroch and Son, Chicago, 1948

——*Peregrinations* Rotary International, Evanston, 1935–7

v.1 (never published) was to have included two smaller publications, *Visit to Great Britain and South Africa*, and *Sidelights on the 1937 Convention* (see below)

v.2 An account of five months travel in the Far East and Australasia (1935)

v.3 An account of four months travel in South America (1937)

—— *Sidelights on the 1937 Convention and a Post-Convention Tour of the Islands of the British Seas* Rotary International, Evanston, 1937

—— *The Founder of Rotary* (with a foreword by Chesley R. Perry) Rotary International, Evanston, 1928

—— *This Rotarian Age* (with an introduction by Chesley R. Perry) Rotary International, Evanston, 1935

—— *A visit to Great Britain and South Africa* Rotary International, Evanston, 1934

Hewitt, C.R. *Towards my neighbour; the social influence of the Rotary club movement in Great Britain and Ireland* Longmans, London, 1950

Lamb, Frank H. *Rotary; a businessman's interpretation* Rotary Club of Hoquiam, Hoquiam, 1927

Leonhart, James Chancellor *The fabulous octogenarian; Courtney W. Shropshire, MD, Founder and First President of Civitan International* Redwood House, Baltimore, 1962

Levy, Roger *Rotary International in Great Britain and Ireland* Continua Productions, London, 1978

Lewis, Lloyd and Smith, Henry Justin *Chicago; the history of its reputation* Harcourt Brace, New York, 1929

Lichauco, M.F. *1001 questions and answers on Rotary* Philippines, Backman Inc., Quezon City, 1961

Los Angeles, Rotary Club of *History of the Rotary Club of Los Angeles* Rotary Club, Los Angeles, 1955

Love, R.S. and Branson, V.M. *Apex; the first twenty-five years* Apex, Adelaide, 1955

Lynd, Robert S. and Lynd, Helen Merrell *Middletown; a study in American culture* Harcourt Brace, New York, 1929

Marden, C.F. *Rotary and its brothers* 1935

Minneapolis, Rotary Club of *The story of Minneapolis Rotary* (foreword by Paul P. Harris) Rotary Club, Minneapolis, 1935

Mountain, William J. *History of the Rotary Club of San Francisco*

Rotary Club, San Francisco, 1940

Mulholland, Frank L. *Rotating in the Orient* (foreword by Frank D. Waterman) privately printed, Toledo, 1930

Racine, Rotary Club of *Golden Anniversary 1917–67* Racine Rotary Foundation, Inc., Racine, 1967

Rotary International *Adventure in Service* Rotary International, Chicago, 1946

—— *Official Directory* (annually) Rotary International, Evanston

—— Proceedings of the Annual Conventions of Rotary International. Published continuously since 1916. Before 1916 the Convention Reports were published in *The Rotarian*, except 1910 and 1911, which were published in booklet form. Rotary International, Evanston

—— *Rotary: Fifty years of service* Rotary International, Evanston, 1955

—— *Service is my business* Rotary International, Chicago, 1948

—— *Seven paths to peace* Rotary International, Evanston, 1959

Stare, Fred A. *Some Wisconsin Rotary history* Rotary International Districts 625 and 627, Wisconsin, 1962

Sutherland, Douglas *Fifty years on the civic front* Civic Federation, Chicago, 1943

Thompson, Gordon S. *Of dreams and deeds; the story of Optimist International* Optimist International, 3rd ed., St Louis, 1973

Tyre, Robert *The Cross and the Square; the Kinsmen story 1920–70* Association of Kinsmen Clubs, 1970

Zapffe, Carl A. *Rotary!* The Rotary Club of Baltimore, Baltimore, 1963

Sources

Biography Index H.W. Wilson Co., New York, 1946 to date

Collier's Encyclopedia Crowell-Collier-Macmillan, New York

Current Biography H.W. Wilson Co., New York, 1940 to date

Dictionary of American Biography Scribner, New York

Encyclopedia Americana Grolier, Inc., New York

Encyclopaedia Britannica Encyclopaedia Britannica, Chicago

Reader's Guide to Periodical Literature H.W. Wilson Co., New York, 1905 to date

Who Was Who in America 1897–1968 Marquis, Chicago

World Book Encyclopedia World Book-Childcraft International Inc., Chicago.

Periodicals

The Civitan Official publication of Civitan International

Gyrator Official weekly publication of the Rotary Club of Chicago

The Kiwanis Magazine Official publication of Kiwanis International

The Lion Official publication of Lions International

The Optimist Magazine Official publication of Optimist International

The Rotarian Official publication of Rotary International

Rotary Down Under Official publication of Rotary International in Australia

Rotary Official publication of Rotary International in Great Britain and Ireland.

Acknowledgements

In writing this, the first full account of the life and times of the Founder of Rotary, the author has striven to make Paul Harris come alive, to portray from the factual information the warmth of a life being lived.

It could not have been accomplished without the unstinting assistance of others. Some, whose lives touched upon those of Paul and Jean Harris, provided invaluable first-hand impressions and source material of inestimable worth. Others helped by researching sources that, because of distance, were difficult of access. Yet others aided by simply expressing a deep interest in the project, thereby encouraging me when I found the task daunting or when I was hyper-critical of my efforts.

So many people were involved, Rotarians and non-Rotarians alike, the naming of all individually would make a book in itself. In the following roll-call, which remains an inadequate expression of gratitude for so much help, I have doubtless omitted, and thereby wounded, some whose help was beyond measure. To them and to all who threw me a lifeline when I floundered in maelstroms of conflicting facts, I am especially indebted. At the risk of invidiousness, however, I must in all sincerity and gratitude, single out the following for special mention:

Rotarian Harry A. Stewart, the General Secretary of Rotary International during the four years of the book's preparation, who not only took an intense interest in the project from the outset but went to great lengths to provide basic information including, for example, photostat copies of the series of articles by Paul Harris, printed in *The Rotarian* in 1926, and many of the illustrations which appear in this volume. His advice and guidance was readily forthcoming whenever it was requested and this is greatly appreciated.

Dr William H. Nault, Executive Vice-President and Editorial Director of World Book—Childcraft International, Inc., Chicago, is deserving of special mention. He and his editorial staff researched not only their own vast archives but also source material in the Chicago Public Library.

Rotarian Alex Anderson, a past President of the Rotary Club of Edinburgh, Scotland, researched the life of Mrs Jean Harris and provided almost all there is to know about the gracious first lady of Rotary. His brief but brilliant biography of Mrs Harris in the April 1974 issue of the *Edinburgh Rotary Bulletin* needed little amplification.

Rotarian the Reverend Richard P. Armstrong, Secretary of the Memorial Rotary Club of Wallingford, Vermont, and Pastor of the First Congregational Church there, supplied splendid photographs of Harris's boyhood haunts and other material pertinent to his early years.

From the beginning, Rotarian James C. Thornton of the Rotary Club of Racine, Wisconsin, went to exceptional lengths to meet my requests for information about the Harris family in Racine. He provided photographs of Harris's birthplace and a photostat copy of the Racine club's invaluable *Golden Anniversary Handbook*.

Rotarian Dan C. Paxton is the Executive Director of the Rotary Club of Denver, Colorado, a city which featured prominently in the life of Harris and his parents. Rotarian Paxton rendered great service by verifying data from the Bureau of Vital Statistics. He was instrumental in putting me in touch with: Rotarian R.E. McWhinnie, who has been a member of the Rotary Club of Laramie, Wyoming, for some fifty years and, in 1942–3, was the District Governor of the 113th District (now the 545th District). Past District Governor McWhinnie knew Paul Harris well and met him on several occasions. Of greater import, however, was Rotarian McWhinnie's personal knowledge of Reginald Clayton Harris, Paul's younger brother.

Rotarian John H. Edwards of the Rotary Club of Merthyr Tydfil, Wales, is a past President of Rotary International in Great Britain and Ireland, and a former Director and Treasurer of Rotary International. Throughout the years of research, writing and rewriting, Rotarian Edwards was a source of advice and encouragement.

Rotarian Peter T.B. Lawrence, a past District Governor of my own 114th District, also took great interest in the project and aided inestimably by introducing me to: the Rev. Wilfred L. Float, a former member of the General Council of Rotary International in Great Britain and Ireland. Wilfred Float met Harris on three occasions, and in July 1937 was host to him in High Wycombe, England. When I interviewed the ninety-four-year-old Rotarian at Brighton in 1976, I found his vivid memories and impressions of Harris remarkably lucid.

Rotarian J.L. Hunter Scott, a member of the Rotary Club of St Andrews, Scotland, was President of Rotary International in Great Britain and Ireland in 1976–7, when I mentioned the project to him. 'If it is not done soon it will be too late', opined President Hunter, and promptly directed me to: the Rev. Andrew Youngson Howe—and a treasure trove of information. The Rev. Howe is the nephew of Mrs Jean Harris and is Harris's nearest surviving relative. He provided a mass of invaluable source material, much of which has never been published before. This, together with his intimate family knowledge of both Paul and Mrs Harris, has greatly enhanced our knowledge of the two central personalities of this work.

Rotarian Roger Levy, former editor of *Rotary* for many years, has been most helpful in a number of ways, and his study of the history of Rotary in the British Isles provided several fascinating nuggets of information about Harris and many of the giants of Rotary in the Movement's formative years.

His successor in office, Rotarian David Shelley Nicholl, has given freely of his expertise and advice in assembling and presenting the factual material. I am grateful also for his enthusiasm and encouragement, including the publication of excerpts from this book in *Rotary* during 1978 and 1979.

My thanks are due also to my fellow members and their ladies of the Rotary Club of Croydon South. Their friendship and fellowship has uplifted me through the sometimes arduous years of research, and they lightened my burden whenever they could.

I am profoundly grateful to Mrs Dorothy Speaight and her husband John. They read the manuscript in its entirety, corrected errors of fact, brought some grievous discrepancies to my attention, offered cogent critiques and clarified my perceptions.

To my sons Robert and Peter I must express my gratitude and appreciation. Not only did they help with constructive suggestions but

317

bore with infinite patience the domestic chaos of half-finished manuscripts, reference books and ancillary items which they found in places which should have been occupied by objects of greater utility.

Last but by no means least I must record my appreciation of the incredible amount of work put in on the manuscript by my publisher and editor, Harry Treadwell. A member of the Shoreham and Southwick club, Harry meticulously scrutinized every word in the original manuscript and came back with suggestions which not only saved me from over-writing and an embarrassment of errors but improved the work enormously. In a number of ways the work has been accomplished only because of his direct participation. I am especially grateful.

James P. Walsh
Croydon, England   1979

Index

Included in the index are brief descriptions of persons, not mentioned in the text, who were known to Paul and Mrs Harris. Where pertinent, the date of charter of each Rotary club is given after the entry.

319

The Torah

Collected from the pages of
The Jewish Observer
by

Rabbi Nisson Wolpin,
Editor

Profile

A Treasury of Biographical Sketches

Published by

Mesorah Publications, ltd

in conjunction with
Agudath Israel of America

FIRST EDITION
First Impression . . . March, 1988

Published and Distributed by
MESORAH PUBLICATIONS, Ltd.
Brooklyn, New York 11223

Distributed in Israel by
MESORAH MAFITZIM / J. GROSSMAN
Rechov Harav Uziel 117
Jerusalem, Israel

Distributed in Europe by
J. LEHMANN HEBREW BOOKSELLERS
20 Cambridge Terrace
Gateshead
TYNE AND WEAR
England NE8 1RP

ISBN
0-89906-860-X (hard cover)
0-89906-861-8 (paperback)

Typography by CompuScribe at ArtScroll Studios, Ltd.
1969 Coney Island Avenue / Brooklyn, N.Y. 11223 / (718) 339-1700

Printed in the United States of America by Moriah Offset
Bound by Sefercraft, Inc., Brooklyn, NY

Table of Contents

◄§ Great Women

The following biographical sketches appear in *The Torah Personality* of the ArtScroll Judaiscope Series (in order of appearance): Rabbi Chaim Brisker (Soloveitchik); Rabbi Yisrael Meir HaKohen (*Chofetz Chaim*); Rabbi Avraham Yeshaya Karelitz (*Chazon Ish*); Moreinu Yaakov Rosenheim; Rabbi Yechiel Yaakov Weinberg (*Seride Esh*); Rabbi Meir Simcha HaKohen (*Or Same'ach*); Rabbi Yoseif Rosen (Rogatchover *Gaon*); Rabbi Chaim Ozer Grodzensky; Rabbi Aaron Yoseif (Reb Archik) Baksht; Rabbi Yoseif Kahaneman (Ponevezher *Rav*); Rabbi Michael Ber Weissmandl; Rabbi Chaim Meir Hager (Vizhnitzer *Rebbe*); Rabbi Yisroel Alter (Gerer *Rebbe*); Rabbi Nochum Mordechai Perlow (Novominsker *Rebbe*); Rabbi Yoel Teitelbaum (Satmar *Rav*); Rabbi Moshe Yitzchok (Reb Itzikel) Gewirczman; Chacham Yoseif Chaim (*Ben Ish Chai*); Rabbi Yaakov Culi (*MeAm Loez*); Rabbi Raphael Chaim Yizchak Karigal; Chazan Gershom Mendes Seixas; Rabbi Abraham Joseph Rice; Rabbi Yissachar Dov Illowy; Chazan Samuel Myer Isaacs; Rabbi Jacob Joseph; Rabbi Dr. Hillel Klein; Reb Elimelech Gavriel (Mike) Tress; Rabbi Yoseif Eliyahu Henkin; Rabbi and Mrs. Baruch Shapiro.

The following biographical sketches appear in *The Torah World* of the ArtScroll Judaiscope Series (in order of appearance): Rabbi Jacob Ettlinger (*Aroch LeNeir*); Reb Shraga and Golda Frank; Rabbi Pesach Pruskin (Kobrin); Rabbi Boruch Ber Lebowitz (Kaminetz); Rabbi Elchonon Wasserman (Baranovich); Rabbi Meir Shapiro (Lublin); Rabbi Menachem Ziemba (Warsaw); Rabbi Yosef Yitzchak Schneerson (Lubavitch); Rabbi Dov Ber Weidenfeld (Tshebin); Rabbi Yerucham Levovitz (Mir); Rabbi Yisrael Yaakov Lubchansky (Baranovich); Rabbi Dovid Kronglas (Baltimore); Rabbi Moshe Schwab (Gateshead); Sarah Schenirer; Dr. Leo Deutschlander (Bais Yaakov Movement); Rabbi Aharon Kotler (Kletzk — Lakewood); Rabbi Reuvain Grozovsky (Kaminetz — Monsey); Rabbi Joseph Breuer (Frankfort — Washington Heights); Rabbi Avraham Kalmanowitz (Mir — Brooklyn); Rabbi Chaim Leib Shmulevitz (Mir — Jerusalem); Rabbi Eliyahu Meir Bloch (Telshe — Cleveland); Rabbi Raphael Baruch Sorotzkin (Telshe — Cleveland); Rabbi Gedalia Schorr (Yeshivah Torah Vodaas — Brooklyn); Rabbi Yitzchok Hutner (Yeshivah Rabbi Chaim Berlin — Brooklyn).

Contributors to this volume:

Mrs. Chaya Baumwolspiner lives in Lakewood, New Jersey, where her husband is a member of the Kollel of Bais Medrash Govoha. She is a regular contributor to London's *Jewish Tribune* as well as other publications.

Rabbi Yitzchak Chinn, a talmid of Reb Shraga Feivel Mendlowitz, is the rabbi of the Gemilas Chessed Congregation of McKeesport, Pennsylvania.

Rabbi Yaakov Feitman, a well-known author, lecturer, and educator, is rabbi of Young Israel of Cleveland, and wrote biographies on the Or Some'ach and the Rogatchover Gaon that appear in Judaiscope's *The Torah Personality.*

Rabbi Lipa Geldwerth, a member of the faculty and administration of Yeshiva Torah Temimah in Brooklyn, wrote a biography of the Tshebiner Rav that was published in Judaiscope's *The Torah World.*

Mrs. Devora Kitevits, a graduate of Bais Yaakov Seminary, is principle of the evening department of the Seminary. She expresses gratitude to (Rabbi) Avrohom and Rivke Kaplan, who are the source of much of the material for her chapter on Rebbetzin V. Kaplan, which is part of a larger work in preparation.

Rabbi Eliyahu Meir Klugman, who studies in the Kollel of Mirrer Yeshiva in Jerusalem, wrote the biography of Rabbi Chaim Leib Shmulevitz that was featured in *The Torah World.*

Rabbi Chaim Uri Lipshitz, currently a resident of Jerusalem, is a pioneer in Jewish journalism in America, and author of numerous *seforim* as well as books on Jewish themes.

Mrs. Nehama Consuelo Nahmoud, who resides in Jerusalem, is a well-known author of articles on Sephardi themes. In deference to the subject matter of her chapters, transliteration of Hebrew words and names are rendered in accordance with Sephardi pronunciation.

Mrs. Shoshana (Nekritz) Perr, a frequent contributor to *The Jewish Observer,* is Program Director of Camp Bnos in Liberty, New York, a counselor and therapist with Torah Umesorah Counterforce Program, and is currently in private practice. She is a granddaughter of Rebbetzin Yaffen, subject of her chapter in this book.

Rabbi Yaakov Yosef Reinman, a long-time *talmid* of Bais Medrash Govoha in Lakewood, is the author of *Shufra Dishtara,* a comprehensive analysis of Talmudic contractual law, and the translator of the English language edition of the inspirational classic *Menoras Hamaor.*

L. M. Reisman is an accountant by profession and writer by avocation. In deference to the subject matter of his chapter, the transliteration of Hebrew words is presented in Sephardi pronunciation.

Rabbi Nosson Scherman, noted author and lecturer, is general editor of ArtScroll, edits *Olomeinu* (Torah Umesorah's magazine for children) and is a member of the Editorial Board of *The Jewish Observer.* Rabbi Scherman expresses gratitude to the Feinstein and Tendler families — especially Rabbi Mordechai Tendler — who reviewed the manuscript of the chapter on Rabbi Moshe Feinstein and offered valuable information and insights.

Chaim Shapiro, a Baltimore resident, has written a number of articles for *The Jewish Observer* that evoke the Pre-War Europe of his childhood; many of these have been published in the Judaiscope anthologies, *The Torah Personality* and *The Torah World.*

Mrs. Ruth Steinberg, born in America, lives in Jerusalem with her husband who studies in a Kollel there.

Rabbi Hanoch Teller is a noted author, whose most recently published book is *Courtrooms of the Mind.* He studies and teaches in Jerusalem.

The biographical sketches in this book first appeared
as articles in The Jewish Observer,
a monthly journal of thought and opinion
published by Agudath Israel of America.
The Editorial Board of the The Jewish Observer is chaired
by Dr. Ernst L. Bodenheimer.

The Torah Profile

"HE MAY LOOK LIKE a mortal being, just another man of flesh and blood," said the Chazon Ish regarding a *ben Torah* he passed on the street, "but in truth he is not. He's actually a *malach* — an angel of G-d."

The Chazon Ish, the much revered sage of Bnei Brak, was not given to exaggeration, and indeed he was describing a *ben Torah* — every *ben Torah* — as he saw him: A person immersed in Torah is not just another man responding to his environment or reacting to events, as others do. He is a totally different creature, as different in kind from his fellow man as a human is from the beast, as any animal is from vegetation. He encompasses all that lower forms of creation possess, but on a different level — on a Torah level.

Generally, we know an individual by his or her way of viewing things, by the way he understands and interprets events, by his un-thinking responses as well as by his well-thought-out goals, by his deliberate acts as by his inadvertent gestures. How are we to view the Torah scholar, the *talmid chacham?*

A *talmid chacham*, literally, is a wise student. A truly diligent student absorbs more than the master's lesson; he also learns to duplicate his thought processes and anticipate his conclusions, as well. So, too, does the consummate *talmid chacham* fashion his thinking so that in its way, it reflects *daas elyon* — Divine thought.

He does this when relating contemporary problems to obscure passages of *Chazal*. And he does so when his instinctive assessment — his "*nireh li*, it appears to me" — draws upon no specific folio in Talmud, but (as was said by Rabbi Yisroel Salanter) instead flows from a reservoir of sensitivities and reactions that embraces all of *Shas*, the full scope of the Written and Oral Law.

"When two people are attracted to each other in a forbidden relationship," said the Chazon Ish, "the masses call it 'romantic love.' A Torah perspective, however, views it as an *issur kareis* — a transgression that destroys a person physically and spiritually."

The opinions of the Torah personality, then, express *daas Torah* and his actions are crowned with *Kesser Torah*. His perspective highlights his very life as a profile in Torah.

The year was 1939, and only a limited number of visas were available for the burgeoning refugee population. Who should get priority, young yeshiva families, or the senior *Roshei Yeshiva?* The problem was brought to Rabbi Chaim Ozer Grodzenski, undisputed head of European Torah Jewry, who advised, "Give them to the senior scholars."

This caught those who posed the question by surprise. Wouldn't humanitarian concerns — saving young families — dictate otherwise?

Explained Reb Chaim Ozer: "The young heads of families will be caught up in all the pressures of adjusting to a new life in America — getting a position, finding suitable housing, and so on. *Hatzolah* will hardly appear on their agenda. The older *Roshei Yeshiva*, however, will be able to put personal concerns aside and throw themselves into rescue activity. My suggestion *is* the humanitarian one."

And so it was.

The *Maharal* of Prague (*Chiddushei Aggados, Chelek*) explains the comparison of the consummate man to "the tree of the field" (*Devarim* 20:19), to denote his rootedness: just as a tree sinks roots into the ground, stays fixed to its place, and absorbs its nourishment from the soil — affecting the growth and flavor of its fruit — so, too, does the Torah personality strike its roots upward, into the Heavens. As an inverted tree of sorts, the Torah man absorbs nourishment from the Divine wisdom of the Torah, and stays fixed, unperturbed by the winds of change — be they breezes of fashion or the stormy furies of turmoil and war. He is shaped by his source of guidance, and develops as a man of Torah, as the Torah Profiles in this volume will illustrate:

• Torah minds think Torah thoughts. And make Torah decisions. People who have so absorbed Torah into their veins, so to speak, tend to honor Torah directives in the most inadvertent gesture ... as did an ailing *Rosh Yeshiva*, when he instinctively reached for a cup of water with his tube-encumbered right hand instead of his free left hand, because the dignity of the *bracha* he was about to recite called for using the right.

• The man of Torah may search the skies for inspiration for his *tefilla*, because all the heavens are his *siddur*, and he sees vivid lessons in *chinuch* in every inch of the earth, because the entire world reflects the Torah that serves as its blueprint. Thus it is no surprise when the master Torah teacher imparts an unexpected lesson to his students when he lifts a stone in a garden and "teaches" the insects nestled beneath it the glory of the expanded horizons of a sun-lit world, and charges his disciples: "Thus will you also enlighten your own students."

• Women, too, can lead glorious Torah lives. Such as the brilliant, yet self-effacing young lady, who had begged and then insisted her way into Sarah Schenirer's famous seminary in Cracow — and eventually brought higher standards of Torah living to the hostile shores of America, complementing and reinforcing the Torah revolution of the American yeshivas, from the 1940's to the present ... Or the devoted nurse who could not brush aside her tears when treating a maimed yeshiva student, injured in the pogrom in Chevron in 1929, for fear of compromising the sterility of surgery.

• Great Chassidic masters, whose very lives were given to succor, sustain, and strengthen others ... a towering Sephardic *chacham*, who, as the mentor of a promising Sephardic youth, took his student's place behind the grocery counter to free the young man to pursue his Talmudic studies.

The biographical articles in this book comprise little touches and master strokes, which together draw awe-inspiring profiles of men and women who achieved extraordinary measures of greatness, by virtue of leading Torah lives. These lives were on an exalted level by virtue of being guided and enriched by Torah, making these individuals the contemporary counterparts to the Tribe of Levi, who, according to the *Rambam:*

> ... did not gain a portion in the Land ... because they were set apart to serve G-d, to teach His righteous ways and just statutes to the multitudes ... They are G-d's army ... and He [in turn] bequeathes His riches to them.
>
> Not only the Tribe of Levi, but every single person whose spirit so directs him and helps him understand on his own to separate himself and to serve and worship Him, to know Him, and to go upright as G-d fashioned him ... Such a person is holy of holies. G-d is his portion for eternity ... like the *Kohanim* and *Levites* (*Hilchos Shemita V'Yoveil* 13:12, 13).

Such are the men and women whose lifestories are gathered in this book to form a composite of "The Torah Profile."

Nisson Wolpin

❧ European Gedolim

Profiles of men whose greatness
reflected 3,300 years of
Jewry's role as a Torah people,
as it was shaped by a millennium of
Jewish life in Eastern Europe.

Lipa Geldwerth

The Torah-Mentsch

An examination of the life and accomplishments of Reb Yisroel Salanter

5570/1809—5643/1883

ঙ "He Looked into the Torah and Fashioned Man"

U PON BECOMING ENGAGED TO Reb Yisroel Salanter's granddaughter, the prospective groom, Reb Chaim Ozer Grodzenski, wrote a lengthy, involved *shtickel Torah* (discourse) to his future father-in-law — which he, in turn, sent to Reb Yisroel.[1] Reb Yisroel responded to his own son-in-law:[2] "I am convinced that you have selected an outstanding Torah scholar as a *chassan* for my granddaughter. But it is written, (*Devarim*, 22:10) '... את בתי נתתי לאיש הזה', 'My daughter I have given to this (*Ish*) man ...' First let us establish that he is worthy of the title '*Ish*' (*Mentsch*). "

This incident capsulizes Reb Yisroel's goal in planting the *Mussar* Movement. For as G-d had created Man, Man in turn must create the *Mentsch* within himself. Reb Yisroel sought this *Mentsch* in every man, and he taught the world how to find the *Mentsch* even when it was eclipsed by layers of sin. G-d used the Torah as his blueprint for creation,[3] Reb Yisroel saw the Torah as the prescription for the *Mentsch*-ideal. His genius equipped him to be מסתכל באורייתא ובורא איש, to delve into the most hidden recesses of Torah literature to rediscover the once obvious, to forge the Torah-*Mentsch*.

Dozens of books and articles have been written about Reb Yisroel. Storybooks tend to depict him as the kindly saint, not comprehending that his בין אדם לחברו, his *tzidkus* (righteousness) in dealing with others, was but another aspect of his בין אדם למקום, his service of G-d[4]... Others condensed a multifaceted *gaon hador* (outstanding scholar of his generation) into just a pioneering *baal mussar* (teacher of ethics) — seeing all his colors through a monochromatic lens, doing a disservice to his name as well as to their own cause ... And, of course, modern literary psychoanalysts presume too much and end up seeing too little.

Today, a century after his passing, let us look back at Reb Yisroel, whom Rabbi Chaim Soloveitchik of Brisk regarded as מעין הראשונים, "akin to a *Rishon*" (the great Early Commentators of the eleventh-fifteenth centuries).[4a] Let us catch a glimpse of his unrivaled stature in Torah and *Yiras Shomayim* (Fear of Heaven), his greatness of mind, his sensitivity of spirit and his genius of heart, his keenness of insight, his creativity of thought and his daring in action. But above all, let us acquaint ourselves with the forest, instead of being overwhelmed by its own trees.

◆§ The Early Years: A Thunderbolt

The facts have all been recorded. Reb Yisroel was born in the fall of 5570 (1809)[5] in Zager,[6] a provincial town near Kovno, Lithuania, to a prestigious rabbinic family ... Recognized as a prodigy, he was sent, at the age of twelve, to study under the celebrated *Gaon* of Salant, Reb Hirsh Braude, who came to refer to him as *"Alfasi Kattan."*[7] Rabbi Akiva Eiger lauded the *chiddushim* (novellae) he produced in his teens as *"gaonus she'b'gaonus"* — absolutely ingenius. Reb Yisroel married at fifteen years of age. While his young wife cared for their livelihood he developed into a rare *talmid chacham* with a widely admired approach in *pilpul*.

During the eighteen years that Salant was his home, one moment in particular was to galvanize his life and eventually revolutionize the Torah world:

> *Reb Yosef Zundel (1788-1868), a disciple of Reb Chaim Volozhiner, was a man whose saintliness remained hidden from the average eye. Yet young Yisroel took notice of him and developed close contact with him. Yisroel realized, however, that he would see only what Reb Zundel would allow him to see. So he tried to observe him undetected, from afar, following him out to the fields while Reb Zundel would retreat there for contemplation. Once Reb Zundel noticed and exhorted him: "Yisroel, study mussar and become a yerei Shomayim!"*[8]

Reb Yisroel would relate years later that this precise moment left an everlasting impact on his life. His close disciple, Reb Itzel Peterburger (Blazer), would later describe the incident: "When he heard his master's command to learn *mussar*, it entered his innermost heart like a fire; he then began this study of *mussar*." From that day on he cleaved to Reb Zundel, until his mentor moved to Jerusalem.

◦§ Nistar — After All

At first, Reb Yisroel planned to emulate his master, to be a *nistar* (a hidden saint), moving to a community where he was not known and to assume a humble position, such as a water carrier. The first requirement he set for himself was the mastery of the entire *Shas* (Talmud) by heart. When halfway through, he abandoned his plan, realizing that his generation had greater need for an active leader who could exert his influence amongst the broadest of circles than for a saintly recluse.[9]

Reb Naftoli Amsterdam, one of his leading disciples, would later comment. "The Rebbe at first wished to be a *nistar*, and then reconsidered. In the long run, however, he succeeded, and the true measure of his greatness has always remained hidden from others."[10]

◦§ Consistency — In Change

While tracing the various stages in Reb Yisroel's life, a striking feature emerges. He had a willingness to make radical changes, whenever he found such necessary — by virtue of a shift in circumstances or because of a reassessment of his personal goals. For example, during his early years, Reb Yisroel decided to veer totally away from *pilpul*, in which he had gained expertise and widespread admiration. He had felt that he was sacrificing truth for the personal gratification gained from the intellectual stimulation of the *pilpul* approach. Eventually he returned to *pilpul* because he feared a tendency toward arrogance and complacency in expecting to determine the *Gemara's* meaning by concentrating only on the page before him ... Other striking examples of change will follow.

One is also struck by the multiplicity of activities he undertook over the years and in so many different locales. Yet all were unified by one underlying commitment — to help people probe beneath the surface, to bring out their own inner greatness. The chronological account that follows traces the variety of activities he pursued toward this one goal.

‎ⴺ The Vilna Years: Taking Vilna by Storm

Reb Yisroel and his close friend Reb Shmuel Salant (Reb Zundel's son-in-law, later famous as *Rav* of Yerushalayim) had together resolved not to accept any rabbinic posts during this period; for example, they both rejected separate bids from the prestigious community of Brisk. Yet when invited to give *shiurim* as a *Rosh HaYeshivah* in Rameillas Yeshivah in Vilna, Reb Yisrael accepted, replacing Rabbi Eliezer Teitz, famed disciple of Rabbi Akiva Eiger. Thus, in 1840 he entered the lives of the Jews of Vilna, to leave an unforgettable impact on the "Jerusalem of Lithuania."

Reb Yisroel took the people of Vilna by storm — especially its yeshivah *bachurim* — through his brilliant lectures — reverting to *pilpul* again, as he saw fit — and with his *mussar* discourses. But Reb Yisroel feared that his success was creating envy among fellow faculty members; so he left Rameillas Yeshivah to lecture in another *beis midrash*.[11]

During this period, he attracted the attention of his peers and won the deference of such outstanding scholars as Reb Izek'el Charif and Rabbi Yoseif Dov Soloveitchik, author of *Beis Halevi*.[12] He also re-published a number of lesser-known *mussar* works. Reb Yisroel then began lecturing for *baalei battim* (laymen) — shoemakers, porters and wagon-drivers flocked to his talks, as he considered each audience and addressed them according to their own level.

At that time *Maggidus* (preaching) no longer played the commanding role it once did a century earlier; *rabbonim* left it to wandering, lesser luminaries. Reb Yisroel, coupling a magnificent gift of speech with a heartening simplicity, raised the standard of *Maggidus* to its former glory.

Like a bird, man can reach undreamed-of heights as long as he works his wings. Should he relax them for but one minute, however, he plummets downward.

A person lives with himself for seventy years, and after it is all over, he still does not know himself.

With the word "Echod" in the Sh'ma, the Jew crowns G-d as King over the entire cosmos and all four corners of the world, but sometimes he forgets to include himself.

Man is a drop of intellect drowning in a sea of instincts.

Spirituality is like a bird: if you tighten your grip on it, it chokes; slacken your grip, and it flies away.

He organized more knowledgeable *baalei battim* into groups to study the *mussar* classics *Mesillas Yeshorim* and *Chovos Halevavos* with greater depth, and established his first *Beis Hamussar*, a room set aside to serve as a retreat from worldly turmoil, dedicated to the study and absorption of *yiras Shomayim* (fear of G-d). Not meant to replace a *Beis Haknesses* or *Beis Hamidrash*, but to supplement them, this *mussar* retreat was close enough to the *Beis Hamidrash* to avoid loss of time spent in study.

Reb Yisroel viewed the *Beis Hamussar* as both a "clinic" — following the Rambam's approach to human frailty in character or *yiras Shomayim* as a disease-condition[13] — and as a haven from the swirling winds of contemporary corruption. In his words: "Enter this fortress, draw the bridge up behind you, and leave the world beyond the moat!"[14]

◆§ Courage and Controversy

Two unforeseen developments rocked Reb Yisroel's stay in Vilna. The first was related to Reb Yisroel's attitude toward matters of health. He accepted doctor's orders as *halachah* (Torah law), implicit in the command of "ונשמרתם מאד לנפשותיכם", "And you shall guard your lives" (*Devarim* 4:15). When health concerns conflicted with other *halachos*, he usually decided with a consistent leniency as far as the latter was concerned. He seemed to share Reb Chaim Brisker's view: "I am not lenient in regard to *Shabbos* or Yom

Kippur; rather I am stringent in the laws of preservation of life!"[15]

Since Reb Yisroel never rendered any halachic decisions in Vilna, not even for his own household,[16] he must have experienced enormous personal conflict during the peak of a cholera epidemic that devastated Vilna in late summer 1848. Reb Yisroel had committed himself to the city's welfare — renting hospital quarters with five hundred beds, while his own *talmidim* nursed the stricken around the clock, seven days a week, with patient care on *Shabbos* no different than on the other days of the week. As Yom Kippur approached, he feared that the fast would weaken the people and make them dangerously susceptible to the often-fatal disease. Reb Yisroel hung placards throughout Vilna urging all who felt weak to eat on the fast day, to stave off any threat. He did this without consulting others because he apparently realized that he would not gain a consensus for such a radical, yet — in his view — essential move. Immediately after *Shacharis* on Yom Kippur, he himself rose to the *bimah*, and according to some accounts, publicly made *Kiddush* and ate some cakes to encourage all those in need to follow suit. Needless to say, there were great protests, but Reb Yisroel ignored them and reportedly made his way to other *shuls* as well, to urge others to join him.[17]

This daring episode provoked strong and mixed reactions in different circles, and was long debated.[18] For all the esteem he commanded, the *Beis Din* of Vilna summoned Reb Yisroel for an uncomfortable exchange, [19] with Reb Yisroel demonstrating clearly that his command of Torah knowledge put him beyond their ability to challenge him.

⊷§ Hashlamah vs. Haskallah

At that time, the impact of the German *Haskallah* (the Enlightenment Movement, which was enamored with secular culture) was beginning to make its mark on Russian Jewry, especially in Vilna. The *Maskillim* prevailed on the Russian government to help them revamp the traditional *chinuch* by demanding changes in curriculum, and they succeeded in opening several of their own elementary schools, as well as a Rabbinical Seminary in Vilna. They promoted an education that synthesized Jewish and secular knowledge for motives that went beyond a "broader education"; they were aiming at reshaping the minds and hearts of the youth, distorting the true face of Judaism.

The *Maskillim* were attracted to Reb Yisroel by his all-encompassing knowledge and were fascinated by his independence and originality, but they had totally misunderstood him and his reactionary attitudes toward *halachah*. The *Maskillim* brought considerable pressures upon him to serve as head of their Seminary. Russian Minister of Education Avaroff even interrupted one of his *shiurim* hoping to influence him[20] with magnificent offers.

Some *Rabbonim* argued that Reb Yisroel, with his rare gifts, was the only one who could save the situation and redirect the course of this ill-conceived Rabbinical Seminary, but Reb Yisroel adamantly refused. On the one hand, he was confident that the Seminary did not have staying power, and was not worthy of all the efforts required in attempting to lead it properly. Moreover, in a letter to Rabbi Yaakov Lipschitz (later secretary to Kovno Rav, Rabbi Yitzchok Elchonon Spector), he outlined his philosophy of unadulterated *rabbanus:* "... knowledge of *Shulchan Aruch* and piety is not sufficient ... For *psak* we require *gedolei Torah!*"[21] —

and these would not emerge from a *Haskallah*-oriented seminary.

The pressures brought to bear upon Reb Yisroel to head this institution made his continued stay in Vilna unbearable, so he left for Kovno in the winter of 1848 ... Reb Yisroel's approach was eventually vindicated, for the government later deemed the Vilna Seminary and its counterparts in other cities ineffective, and shut them all down in 1873.[22]

The Kovno Years: The Maggid

Upon his arrival in Kovno, Reb Yisroel was engaged by the elders of the city[23] to supervise "all matters relating to piety," a position he soon left[24] to become Kovno's "official *Maggid*."[25] The *Rav*, Rabbi Leib Shapiro,[26] had insisted that Reb Yisroel only come to Kovno if he assumed some official capacity there.[27] Reb Yisroel obviously found this position a fitting forum from which to disseminate his *mussar* approach. Yet, this too came to a quick end, presumably due to the anti-*mussar* sentiments, which in Vilna he had hardly experienced.[28]

The Rebbe

Despite setbacks, Reb Yisroel maintained his vision and resolve. He once wrote: "Give me ten great disciples, and I will alter the face of our time and revolutionize the Jewish world!"[29] This call did not go unheeded. A well-known philanthropist, Tzvi Neveizer,[30] supplied the necessary means for Reb Yisroel to open a new *Beis Hamidrash*. Some one hundred and fifty students flocked to this new Torah center, including a number of future Torah leaders — Rabbi Eliezer Gordon (later *Rav* and *Rosh Hayeshivah* of Telshe), Rabbi Yaakov Yoseph (*Maggid* of Vilna and Chief Rabbi of New York City), Rabbi Yitzchok Blazer (*Rav* of Petersburg), Rabbi Yerucham Leib Perelman (the "Minsker *Gadol*"), Rabbi Naftoli Amsterdam (*Rav* of Helsingfors, Finland), Rabbi Simcha Zissel Ziv ("*Alter* of Kelem"), Rabbi Shlomo Dovid Grodzenski (*Rav* of Ivye, father of Reb Chaim Ozer of Vilna), to mention some of the better-known disciples.

Reb Yisroel was, indeed, a unique *Rebbe*. His concern for his *talmidim* encompassed all aspects of their lives. In his yeshivah, he did away with the belittling system of *essen kest*,[31] in which the *bachurim* were dependent on the generosity of the local townsfolk, eating paltry meals in different homes daily. He insisted that *kavod haTorah* required that the hosts bring the meals to the yeshivah,

Tales of Reb Yisroel

The hundreds of stories about Reb Yisroel that have been preserved portray unusual intellectual gifts, a multifaceted genius with keen sensitivity to other people's needs as well as a willingness to meet their needs, and an overwhelming sense of mission. Many are well known: Reb Yisroel, absent from *shul* for *Kol Nidrei* because he was comforting an infant and its frightened babysitter, and this was of greater importance ... sensing the disappointment of a youngster who (he understood) was shifted from *Maftir* to a regular *aliyah* to make room for Reb Yisroel, and inviting the boy to recite the *Haftorah* for him after *davening*, while others were kept waiting ... advising disciples that the greatest *hidur* (enhancement) in baking *shmurah matzos* is to deal gently with the widows and other poor women working the dough ... taking a young man to task for being so involved in *Selichos* preparation that he did not reply to someone else's greeting: "Must your *teshuvah* be at the expense of his 'Good Morning'?"

Other tales, not so widely circulated, are the following, taken from *Meoras Hagedolim:*

● When disciples in Lithuania pleaded with him to return from Germany to fight *Haskallah,* he replied with a parable: A farmer was chasing a team of runaway horses down a hill. He shouted to a man sitting under a tree further down the slope to stop them. The fellow did not respond. Reaching him, the farmer asked him why he made no effort to stop the horses. "Wait here until they reach bottom and I'll bring them back for you. If I'd have grabbed them on their headlong charge, they'd have dragged me down with them. At the bottom of the hill, their energy is all spent and they can be led back."

Said Reb Yisroel: "Lithuanian Jewry is plunging headlong into *Haskallah.* I cannot grapple with them without being dragged down. The Jews of Germany have reached bottom."

without anyone knowing who was whose specific guest.[32] Even sons of wealthy families ate from these meals, to put an end to social differences amongst the students.

He was deeply concerned about the manners and general

Appearance of the *talmidim* so as to inspire proper respect in the eyes of the local *baalei battim*,[33] and thus enhance the young man's self-image. This effort bore results. Soon many respectable families, which earlier had shied away from a son-in-law "a *batlan*," were vying for *chassanim* who excelled in Torah.

⋅§ Battei Mussar

The main thrust of Reb Yisroel's energies, however, was to produce *gedolei Torah*, great Torah personalities, guiding his students to *shleimus* — completeness and integrity. When he recognized potential in a young man, he dedicated himself totally to his development.[34]

With his remarkable insight he realized the aptitudes and talents of each student, directing him along his individual path, though the yeshivah curriculum was always uniform. He organized special *chaburos* (study groups) to transmit his ideas. Should an uninvited individual enter, Reb Yisroel would cease speaking immediately.[35]

This was also a time of great personal growth for Reb Yisroel. He secluded himself for days on end, hammering out his ideas, perfecting his own character, later relaying what he saw fit to his ten select *talmidim*.[36] Disciples of this era later recalled the profound insights they had gained in those sessions.[37] Eventually Reb Yisroel began to withdraw from offering regular *shiurim* in *Gemara*, which he delegated to Rabbi Eliezer Gordon.[38]

In Kovno, as in Vilna, Reb Yisroel organized individual *battei mussar* for different strata of society, including one in the "Woodcutters' *Kloiz*," a structure which stood in testimony next to the sawmill until 1921, when it was destroyed by fire.[39]

⋅§ The World At Large: A New Focus

The great opponents of the now-blossoming *mussar* Movement — motivated by sincere misgivings — felt obligated to react despite their reverence for Reb Yisroel as an individual. They shared many of the fears of earlier *Misnagdim* in their opposition to *Chassidus* — that *mussar* would create a new sect, veering off the mainstream of *Yiddishkeit*. This opposition, coupled with the fact that Kovno did not match the challenges and opportunities of Vilna (among other factors), brought about a shift in Reb Yisroel's area of activity. Even though Reb Yisroel had won fame and a following in Lithuania, he spent most of the next twenty-five years of his life

Tales of Reb Yisroel

● Reb Yisroel's powers of concentration were so intense that he was often oblivious of where he was. One evening he was strolling in Koenigsberg, and did not return. Failing to respond to the questions of a gendarme, he was jailed as a suspicious alien ... After his disciples arranged for his release, the authorities wrote on his passport: *"Immer in philosofish gedanken versunken.* (Always immersed in philosophical thought)."

● He once failed to show up in *shul* for the first *minyan* — his regular time. After several hours passed, a search party was launched, and several children found him sitting on a large stone outside the city, *tallis* bag in hand, lost in thought. The shouts of the children brought him back to reality, and he became aware that the townspeople were concerned over his absence. Reb Yisroel was so anxious to assure them of his safety that he outran the children to return to town.

crisscrossing Europe on various projects aimed at bringing estranged Jews back to *Yiddishkeit*, raising the level of commitment of observant Jews, working behind the scenes to protect Jews from all sorts of threatening decrees, only to return to Kovno during his final years.

This new phase began when Reb Yisroel visited Halberstadt, Germany, in 1857 for medical treatment. He stayed on in Germany to begin a major battle against the *Haskallah*, which Reb Yisroel saw as the single greatest threat to authentic *Yahadus* at that time. Its distortions of Judaism, its misleading humanism, and its assumption of non-Jewish values were the roots of the Reform Movement, which Rabbi Samson Raphael Hirsch was battling in Germany[40] and the *Ksav Sofer* was contending with in Hungary.[41] Yet, unlike the Reform *kehillos* and rabbinates, the *Haskallah* posed a subtle and pervasive menace. In those places where Reform had not yet taken root, the *Haskallah* was an enemy not easily recognized by the naked eye, and the battleground was not clearly defined. For sure, the *Maskillim* did not lack organizational skills, nor were they short of forums from which to spew forth their propaganda, but their approach was to subvert, not convert. Leaders of both *Chassidim* and *Misnagdim* recognized the threat of

Haskallah, and joined forces in strengthening their positions and in repelling the threat.

Reb Yisroel, ever the original activist, concluded that the best defense was a forceful, fresh counter-offensive. He saw a place of secular knowledge in the overall makeup of the individual,[42] but such knowledge was only acceptable for the proper reasons, for the proper people, in the proper time and in the proper place. What he abhorred was the absence of the perceptible *lehavdil* — the recognizable distinction between Torah wisdom and secular knowledge.[43] The two could not be uttered in the same breath, pronounced with the same gravity, articulated in the same halls. *Chazal* (the rabbis of the Talmud) teach that "G-d has naught in this world but only the four cubits of *halachah*." Secular studies, then, must be excluded from the rabbinical seminary by the "only" of the *Chazal*.

Germany was the source of the plague, and it was there that he hoped to save what he could.[44] He settled in Koenigsberg and was soon deeply involved with the Jewish youth enrolled in the local university. He scheduled regular *shiurim* in *Navi* (Prophets) for them, and was generally aided by the *Rav* of Koenigsberg, Rabbi Yaakov Mecklenberg, author of *Ha'Ksav V'Hakaballah*.[45] While there, he published his *Iggeres Hamussar* (Letter on the Study of Ethics)[46] — a work that has been reprinted scores of times.

◄§ The Memel Approach

In 1860, he was in the border city of Memel. An important port city and mercantile center, it attracted hundreds of Lithuanian Jews to its commercial opportunities, which continued nonstop, seven days a week. *Shabbos* was not even a nostalgic memory in Memel's bustling main streets.

Realizing that Berlin exerted a stronger pull on Memel than did Vilna, Reb Yisroel did not take a harsh, uncompromising stance against Sabbath desecration in that setting. Instead, he resorted to a soft, graduated approach. In his first sermon he explained the concept of *Shabbos* to the people on their level, concluding that *chillul Shabbos* at the port was intolerable because of the writing involved — the major Sabbath desecration of running a business. He did not discuss the actual portering of goods. Many agreed that they could postpone their writing until the weekdays, while the loading and unloading continued.

Some weeks later he suggested that without too much sacrifice, it should be possible not to send shipments, even if goods did arrive.

Tales of Reb Yisroel

● In advance of a public Talmudic address, Reb Yisroel posted a list of a hundred references. Upon entering the auditorium to present his discourse, Reb Yisroel checked the list and found that a prankster had replaced his sheet with another list of a hundred references picked at random. He turned pale, and took his seat for the ten minutes that the introductions were made. He then stepped up to the *bimah* and delivered a brilliant discourse, tying together all hundred random citations.

His disciple Reb Naftoli Amsterdam later commented, "It did not take Reb Yisroel ten minutes to draw upon his knowledge of *Shas* to weave together a new *pilpul*. He turned pale because on the one hand he was reluctant to display his phenomenal intellectual abilities by presenting an 'instant' Torah discourse. Instead, he planned to rise to the *bimah*, declare his inability to give the posted lecture, and take his seat. On the other hand, this would prove to be a grave set back to his campaign to spread *mussar*. After much analysis and inner conflict — which was why he had turned pale — he decided to present the spontaneous speech, much against his nature."

Slowly this approach too became acceptable to the merchants. After a period of time, he convinced them that even the unloading was not vital — and the Jewish merchants of the city ceased all their port activities on the *Shabbos*. A revolutionized Memel emerged.[47]

While there, he lectured in Talmud and *mussar* for young men studying there, caring for all their needs. He also lectured for Jewish university students in Memel.[48]

►§ "So Much More That I Could Achieve"

As he continued to travel, Reb Yisroel's influence over the hundreds of *talmidim* and thousands of local *baalei battim* kept driving him to persevere. "There is so much more that I could achieve," was a comment that frequently fell from his lips, a dream that never ceased to haunt him, as many anecdotes testify.

Even a remote hint at the passage of time suggested undeveloped opportunities for growth and accomplishment. For instance, when he was sitting in a *shul* during the auctioning of *kibbudim* (synagogue honors), for "100 groschen ... 200 groschen," he began to weep. When asked why, he pointed to his gray beard: *"Ich bin 'grau shon'* (I am gray already) and I've accomplished so little!" — a reflection prompted by the "groschen" of the bidding.[49]

It was during this time (1860-61) that he launched the publication of the celebrated Torah journal *Tevunah* (Wisdom). His purpose: the enhancement of Torah prestige and the promotion of discussion on human personality and character refinement.[50] It enjoyed the participation of the *Gedolei Torah*,[51] and though only twelve issues appeared, it was greatly respected and most popular.

◆§ "Amongst My People"

Reb Yisroel mastered the German language and adopted the German manner of dress, to advance his work in Tilsit, Berlin, Frankfurt, Halberstadt, and other cities.[52] As always, he was impeccable in appearance — shining shoes, sparkling buttons on his frock — dressed in the manner of a dignified layman. His impact on the lives of German Jewry appears in retrospect to have been profound. This was strengthened by his close ties with Germany's Torah leadership: Rabbi Ezriel Hildesheimer, Rabbi Meir Lehmann, and Rabbi Samson Raphael Hirsch. He encouraged the founding of various institutions of learning in Germany, and applauded organized *halachah shiurim* for girls.[53] Throughout this period, Reb Yisroel's correspondence with his *talmidim* in Russia[54] demonstrated that his passionate concern for them was unaffected by time and distance. He was even active in establishing two *battei midrash* for workers and tradesmen in far-away Russia between 1865 and 1869.

Eventually — sometime between 1869 and 1871 — Reb Yisroel returned to Vilna, when a devastating plague struck the area, claiming his wife. Now with her passing, Reb Yisroel concentrated even more on his German activities, while mourning her for the rest of his days.[55]

◆§ Return To Kovno

All at once back again in Kovno at age 67, Reb Yisroel planted a seed: the Kollel Knesses Bais Yitzchok in Kovno. Its purpose — the furtherance of *Hora'ah and mussar*, Rabbinics and Ethics — by supporting and guiding exceptional Torah scholars in their development as authorities. The project received the blessings, and eventually the name, of the Kovno *Rav* and *poseik hador* (the generation's outstanding authority in *halachah*), Rabbi Yitzchok Elchonon Spector. It was joined by such *chavrei hakollel* (fellows) as Reb Naftoli Herz (later *Rav* of Jaffa), Rabbi Naftoli Amsterdam, Rabbi Chaim (Telsher) Rabinowitz, and Rabbi Yitzchok Meltzan, among others.[56] Reb Yitzchok Elchonon's son accepted the administrative responsibilities, while Rabbi Avrohom Shenker and Rabbi Nosson Zvi Finkel (later revered as the *"Alter* of Slobodka") conducted the internal affairs of this great institution. Under the latter's guidance, publication of the *Eitz Pri*[57] inspired the world of Torah and *mussar*, featuring essays by both Reb Yisroel and Reb Yitzchok Elchonon — including a foreword by the then lesser-known Reb Yisroel Meir *HaKohein*, author of *Sefer Chofetz Chaim*. The fruit of Reb Yisroel's seed nourished generations of yeshivos and sustains ours today.

The true glory of the *Kollel* was realized under Rabbi Yitzchok Blazer (Peterburger), whose rousing *sichos* (lectures) were the *Kollel's* life-force. Reb Yisroel would, upon occasion, visit Kovno, and, of course, again address the *Kollel*.

Several "second-generation" institutions were then formed: Reb Simcha Zissel founded the Talmud Torah in Kelem. In Vilna a *mussar* yeshivah was established by Reb Yaakov Yoseph, while Reb Nosson Zvi Finkel started the yeshivah in Telshe, and eventually raised the banner of *mussar* in Slobodka with "Knesses Yisroel," named for the great mentor of them all, Reb Yisroel Salanter.

The impact of these individuals and their institutions on the future great citadels of learning — Telshe, Mir, Kamenitz, Grodno, Kletzk, Chevron, Ponoviez, Ner Israel, R' Chaim Berlin, Lakewood, and all their branches and seedlings — is now part of the vital history of Torah in Europe, Eretz Yisroel, and America.

Vilna, Kovno, Koenigsberg, Memel, Berlin — Reb Yisroel's map stared back at him: *There is so much more to achieve.* He reportedly considered coming to America to establish a proper Jewish community and formal *kehillah*, but decided against attempting to build a spiritual life in a country where the atmosphere is set by a constitution that guarantees separating Church and State, religious principle and day-to-day life.[57a]

⇜§ Mission in Paris

Yet, Reb Yisroel did move on to Paris at the age of seventy, despite illness and chronic severe headaches (which at times made it agonizing for him to give public addresses). *Why Paris?*[58] The generally accepted view is, to help organize a *kehillah* under a qualified *Rav*. Rabbi Yehoshua Heschel Levin of Vilna did, in fact, become *Rav* there due to Reb Yisroel's influence. Others claim his purpose there was to arrange a French translation of the Talmud. (Reb Yisroel's goal was to have *Shas* translated into Russian and German as well.)

His Paris agenda also included offering spiritual direction for the Russian-Polish elements of the Jewish community — all incredible undertakings for an aged, ailing foreigner.[59] His living conditions, however, were miserable, and after two near-fatal mishaps, he finally left.

Returning to Koenigsberg, he filled a spiritual vacuum left by the departure of the *Malbim* from that city's rabbinate. He made one more trip to Russia to recharge his disciples with the fire of *mussar*, visiting Kovno, Minsk and Vilna (where he yet found time to study some of the Vilna Gaon's manuscripts). Before returning to Koenigsburg, he instructed Rabbi Yaakov Lipschitz to take up his talented pen and to give expression to Reb Yisroel's opposition to a newly proposed Rabbinical Seminary sponsored by Baron Ginsburg.[60]

⋙ The Will of the Devout . . .

Reb Yisroel, seventy-three years of age, having achieved what scores of others may only dream of accomplishing, took ill in Koenigsberg, in his attic apartment in the home of his friend and patron, Reb Eliyahu Ber. Reb Yisroel instructed the household that come what may, no one was to desecrate the *Shabbos* on his behalf. This curious demand was in total opposition to *halachah*, which Reb Yisroel himself had so valiantly championed.

Nonetheless, he was not to be dissuaded. He explained that this was not misplaced *frumkeit* (piety) or *tzidkus*, but *halachah*: the *Gemara* rules that shepherds are not to be saved from disaster since their livelihood is by theft. (Their animals would regularly graze in neighboring fields.) "Since," Reb Yisroel continued, "people provide me with assistance believing that I'm a *tzaddik*, I too must not be saved since I'm living by false pretenses!"

That week, Reb Eliyahu Ber's son, Binyomin, visited his sister, wife of Reb Yitzchok Elchonon's son, in Kovno. When Reb Yitzchok Elchonon inquired after Reb Yisroel's welfare, he related Reb Yisroel's strange demand. Reb Yitzchok Elchonon replied that he should relay to Reb Yisroel: "The Kovno Rav says that you must allow yourself to be saved even if *chillul Shabbos* is involved."[61]

"The will of the devout shall be fulfilled" — Reb Yisroel's final illness had begun on *Motza'ei Shabbos*, 20 *Shevat*, and his passing was shortly before sundown, *Erev Shabbos*, on 25 *Shevat*, 5643/ 1883.

Notes and Sources

1. See *Sheilos U'Tshuvos Achiezer*, III, No. 53.

2. Rabbi Eliyahu Eliezer Grodnanski, *Rav* in Vilna, and disciple of Reb Yisroel.

3. *Midrash Rabba* to *Bereishis* I, and see R"Dal ad loc.

4. *Ohr Hamussar* I, pp. 77-78, quoting his great disciple Reb Naftoli Amsterdam.

4a. Rabbi Yaakov Kamenetzky quoting Rabbi J. B. Soloveitchik of Boston in an interview granted for preparing this article.

5. As evident from the text of his tombstone in Koenigsberg, reprinted in *Ir Vilna*, p. 128.

6. *Tnuas Hamussar*, Vol. I p. 138, gloss. 4.

7. A reference to Rabbi Yitzchok Alfasi, towering Talmudic scholar of 11th-century Fez, in North Africa.

8. *Nesivos Ohr*, p. 124.

9. See *Nesivos Ohr*, p. 111.

10. Rabbi Yaakov Kamenetzky.

11. R. Dovid Luria, see *Nesivos Ohr*, p. 109.

12. *Tnuas Hamussar*, p. 150, gl. 5.

13. *Shemonah Perakim*.

14. *Ohr Yisroel*, letters no. 5, 6, etc.

15. *Ishim Veshitos*, R. S.Y. Zevin, pp. 64-65.

16. *Sridei Aish*, R. F.F. Weinberg, IV, 289. Some have attributed Reb Yisroel's reluctance to serve as a *Rav* to his having arrived at halachic conclusions different from many established local *minhagim, Tnuas Hamussar* p. 377.

17. *Tnuas Hamussar* I, pp. 160-161, no. 8 for sources.

18. Rabbi Boruch Ber Lebowitz, many years later, said a *shiur* to analyze the *halachah* in question.

19. R' Yaakov Kamenetzky related details to the writer, as transmitted to him by Rabbi Dovid Lebowitz, who had heard a report from the Chofetz Chaim, who had been in Vilna at the time.

20. See *Tnuas Hamussar* I, p. 164.

21. *Zichron Yaakov* III, p. 132. See *Tnuas Hamussar*, pp. 165-169 in detail.

22. *Reb Yisroel Salanter*, Emanuel Atkes, ibid., p. 191, cites a contemporaneous letter written in Vilna from the Ginsburg Archives referring to the appointment of a dean to the Seminary "in place of the Salanter who fled to Kovno."

23. See *Shvil HaZahav* of R. Mordechai Eliasberg, introductory chapters by his son Yonassan, p. XII (Warsaw: 1897).

24. *Nesivos Ohr*, p. 113.

25. Reb Naftoli Amsterdam in *Ohr Hamussar*, I, p. 78.

26. Father of Rabbi Raphael Volozhiner, *Rosh Yeshivah* of Volozhin, and author of *Toras Rafoel* and son-in-law of the Nitziv. His daughter became R' Chaim Brisker's wife.

27. *Tnuas Hamussar* I, pp. 179-180.

28. See *L'Toldos HaYehudim B'Kovno* by Lipmann (Kaidon: 1931), p. 228. *Shvil HaZahav* XVI. For full perspective of the *mussar* conflicts of that time, see *Pulmus Hamussar*, by Rabbi Dov Katz (e.g., p. 21).

29. *Tnuas Hamussar*, I, p. 171.

30. Ibid., I, p. 170.

31. *Zichron Yaakov*, II, pg. 8.

32. *Zichron Yaakov*, op. cit.

33. *Tnuas Hamussar*, I, p. 172.

34. *Sridei Aish*, IV, p. 291.

35. *Ohr Yisroel*, p. 121.

36. *Tnuas Hamussar*, I, p. 174.

37. *Ohr Yisroel*, ibid.

38. *Tnuas Hamussar* I, p. 175.

39. *Tnuas Hamussar*, I, p. 176, no. 20.

40. See *The History of Orthodox Jewry in Germany*, by Herman Schwab, London: 1950.

41. See *L'Toldos HaRiformatzion HaDatis B'Germania V'Ungaria*, by Y.Y. Greenwald, 1948.

42. *Tnuas Hamussar* I, pp. 218-221, 226.

43. *Eitz Pri*.

44. As related by Rav Yaakov Kamenetzky.

45. This unique gaon shared an unusual interest in the *Gra* of Vilna with those — such as Reb Yisroel — of the *Gra's* "Cheder," as evident from his fruitful collaboration in the fascinating work *Eliyas Eliyahu* by Rabbi Yehoshua Heshel Levin dealing with the ways and works of the *Gra's*.

46. Originally printed together with the *Tomer Dvora*, under the title *Even Yisroel*.

47. *Tnuas Hamussar*, I, p. 184.

48. *Tnuas Hamussar*, I, p. 185.

49. *Me'oros Hagedolim*.

50. See introduction to *Tevunah*, no. 1.

51. Rabbi Yoshe Ber Soloveitchik, Rabbi Yosef Shaul Natanzohn, Rabbi Yitzckok Elchonon Spector, Rabbi Shlomo Kluger, among others.

52. *Tnuas Hamussar*, I, p. 186.

53. Ibid., p. 192.

54. *Ohr Yisroel*, pp. 48-68.

55. *Tnuas Hamussar*, I, p. 192.

56. Ibid., p. 193.

57. Vilna 1881.

57a. Rabbi Yitzchak Hutner quoting R' Itzel Peterburg's wife.

58. Rabbi Yaakov Kamenetzky, as a disciple of Rabbi Naftoli Amsterdam and the *Alter* of Slobodka, possessed a wealth of detailed information regarding Reb Yisroel's Paris stay. He offered the following:

Under Alexander II, many reforms in the Russian regime were realized, ameliorating some of the barbarous policies of Nicholas I. The appearance of Jews on the economic and cultural scene, however, provoked dormant anti-Semitic feelings, even among intellectuals (such as the novelist Dostoyevski). Early in 1881, the Czar was assassinated by revolutionaries, and the Jews served as a convenient scapegoat. Terrifying pogroms erupted in southern Russia, and continued sporadically for several years.

Reb Yisroel, weary but tireless, utilized connections in France to persuade the Parisian Rothschild to influence his cousin in London to lend his considerable prestige to pressure *The London Times* into dispatching correspondents to the scene of these atrocities and to report them to the Western world.

The Russian regime protested the bad press to the British Foreign Office, which politely explained that freedom of the press was an accepted feature of life in Britain. While Russian Jewry's problems were far from solved, Reb Yisroel's clandestine activities were effective in mitigating some of their more open manifestations.

59. *Tnuas Hamussar*, I, pp. 230-236.

60. *Tnuas Hamussar*, I, p. 238.

61. Rabbi Yaakov Kamenetzky, who heard it from Binyomin Ber himself. See also *Ir Vilna*, p. 128, transcript of Reb Yisroel's tombstone.

The "Aruch HaShulchan"

Rabbi Yechiel Michel Epstein

5589/1829—5667/1907

I F THE WORDS of Torah are our sustenance, the *seforim* which
elucidate, illuminate, and explain the intricacies of Torah learning
and thought can surely be likened to the table that stands set before
us, arranged for sequential service, beckoning, awaiting our
partaking of its food. Thus, Rabbi Yoseif Caro gave us the "set
table" — the *Shulchan Aruch* — enabling Jews to nourish
themselves with a Torah life for generations. And, following in this
noble tradition, some three centuries later Jews were once again
invited to partake at the table: this time, the table of the *Aruch
HaShulchan*[1] of Rabbi Yechiel Michel HaLevi Epstein.

Rabbi Yechiel Michel was born in the White Russian town of
Bobroysk, near Minsk, in the year 1829 (20 Shevat 5589). According
to his son Reb Baruch, the family had its roots in Spain, where their
name was Benvenisti. With the expulsion of the Jews from Spain in
1492, the family made their new home in the Hessen (Germany)
township of Epstein, and soon adopted that as their name.

When Rabbi Chaim of Volozhin opened the first yeshivah
(before, boys would study Torah in *batei midrash*, and every *Rav*
was also a Rosh Yeshivah), he issued a call in 1802 "to all who are
capable of opening a yeshivah and teaching as I am doing" to follow
suit and establish yeshivos. In response to that letter a yeshivah was
founded in Bobroysk by Rabbi Akiva Altshull.

Rabbi Altshull's wife ran a successful business, and he devoted
himself solely to his yeshivah and his learning. Rabbi Chaim
Volozhin used to call him "the servant of *Hashem* without pay," for
he took no salary for his efforts. Hence little Yechiel Michel did not
have to wander to a far-off town to learn Torah. He stayed home
and attended Rabbi Akiva Altshull's yeshivah, astounding his
teachers with his quick wit and sharp mind.

❧ The Podryachick in Bobroysk

The huge Russian Army was always in need of clothing, footwear, and food. Roads and railways had to be built to accommodate mass troop movements. To help fill these needs, many Jews became *podryachicks* — contractors to the army. Reb Aharon Yitzchok Epstein, Yechiel Michel's father, was one such contractor, a wealthy resident of Bobroysk. Like many a father, he hoped that one day his son would join him in business, another *podryachick*.

The *Rav* in Bobroysk at that time was the *gaon* Rabbi Eliyahu Goldberg, who had studied in Volozhin in the days of Reb Chaim. The young and talented Yechiel Michel was unknown to him, for he was a modest and retiring child. When they finally met at a *simcha* of one of the townspeople, the *Rav* was amazed by the youngster's breadth of knowledge and his deep understanding of Torah. He convinced the boy's parents that such a son must dedicate his life to Torah. He also impressed upon the youngster himself the firm conviction that Torah, and Torah alone, should be his calling.

❧ The Podryachick in Mir

In Mir (home, of course, to the famed Mirrer Yeshivah) there lived a well-to-do contractor by the name of Reb Yaakov Berlin. His son had married the granddaughter of Reb Chaim Volozhiner, and would later succeed his father-in-law Reb Itzel to become Rosh Yeshivah in Volozhin, world famous as the *Netziv* — Rabbi Naftoli Zvi Yehuda Berlin.

The *podryachik* of Bobroysk met the *podryachik* of Mir, and a *shidduch* took place. Yechiel Michel Epstein married Michla Berlin, and the future *Netziv* became a brother-in-law to the future *Aruch HaShulchan*.

Years later, when the *Netziv* had been left a widower, a *shidduch* was proposed between Bashe Mirel, daughter of the *Aruch HaShulchan*, and her cousin, the son of the *Netziv*. "Why should I marry the son of the *gadol hador*," she asked reasonably, "if I can marry the *gadol hador* himself?" Thus, brother-in-law became father-in-law, as the *Netziv* married the daughter of the *Aruch HaShulchan*. Out of this union came the famed Rabbi Meir Berlin.

How is it that a *podryachik* in Mir can boast of a son who becomes a *Netziv*, and a son-in-law who would compose the *Aruch HaShulchan*? Perhaps the following episodes will shed light on the character of Reb Yaakov Berlin, the contractor of Mir.

As a rich businessman, he often traveled abroad, bringing home antiques, precious glassware, and other items of value. One day a maid broke a most expensive vase. His wife railed at the girl for her clumsiness and carelessness.

Said Reb Yaakov to his wife: "You have no right to scream at her."

"What? She breaks my most expensive vase, and I can't scold her?"

"If you have a monetary complaint against the girl," he replied, "call her to the *Rav* for a *din Torah*. But to scream — you have no right!"

His wife was delighted. "An excellent idea," she said. She turned to the maid: "Put on your coat, we are going to the *Rav* for a *din Torah*."

The two women donned their coats, as did Reb Yaakov.

"Where are you going?" asked the wife.

"To the *Rav*."

"I don't need you to be my advocate, I can speak for myself."

"I have no intention of being your advocate. I'm going to speak for the girl. She is scared and nervous and won't be able to defend herself!"

When his daughter Michla married the future *Aruch HaShulchan*, Reb Yaakov presented a huge sum of money to the couple, to enable the *chassan* to study Torah undisturbed.

Banks were unknown in the wasteland that was Russia, and it was customary to invest large sums of money with wealthy businessmen, in some sort of "partnership," to avoid the prohibition of accepting interest. The Epsteins' *nadan* was invested with a man in Slutsk — and not long afterwards, the man went bankrupt!

The children ran to Reb Yaakov. Perhaps, they suggested, if he would travel to Slutsk he could save at least a portion of their investment. Reb Yaakov traveled to Slutsk, and returned empty handed.

"Did you not see the man?" they asked.

"No, I did not," came the reply. They looked at him astonished.

"Why are you surprised?" Reb Yaakov asked. "I went to Slutsk, and did some investigating. The man is, indeed, bankrupt. Since that is the case, I am forbidden by *halacha* to see his face, for it would put him to shame!"

With the loss of the dowry, Mrs. Epstein opened a store, which met with little success. Rabbi Yechiel Michel soon saw that he would not be able to sit and learn without financial worries, as he had hoped.

He met the *Rav* of Bobroysk, Rabbi Eliyahu Goldberg, and told him of his loss and his financial worries. The *Rav* quoted to him *Midrash* on *Shir HaShirim* (which also appears in *Tanna D'Vei Eliyahu*): "A *talmid chacham* who stops learning to pursue some other endeavor, and does not succeed, should see this as a good sign, for it proves that *HaKadosh Baruch Hu* loves his learning." In the same way, the *Rav* intimated, *Hashem* was giving direction to Rabbi Yechiel Michel to change from his previous arrangement.

Having seen this potential for greatness in Reb Yechiel Michel, Rabbi Goldberg gave him *smicha* (ordination) and encouraged him to become a *Rav* and a *poseik* (decisor of *halachic* matters).

⋰§ "The Rebbe Loves that Litvak"

In 1864, Rabbi Yechiel Michel Epstein, on the advice of the *Rav* of Bobroysk, became *Rav* in Novozivkov, a town divided between Chassidic adherents of Lubavitch and Chernobil. A strange place, perhaps, for a *misnaged* to begin a life of *rabbanus*, but a fortunate choice for the *Rav* and for the town.

Although he was the scion of a family of *misnagdim*, Bobroysk, his home town, was very much a Chassidic city. The *misnaged* Rav Eliyahu Goldberg had close relations with the Chassidic *Rav* of Bobroysk, Rabbi Hillel of Poretz, who had been the right-hand man of the Lubavitcher Rebbe, Reb Dov Ber. This Reb Hillel had had a great influence on the town, and on Rabbi Yechiel Michel himself.

Since he was now serving as *Rav* of what was primarily a Lubavitcher community, Reb Yechiel Michel decided to visit the Lubavitcher *Rebbe*, Reb Menachem Mendel, who was known by the title of his *sefer*, the *Tzemach Tzeddek*.

The venerable Reb Mendele, as he was affectionately called, received the young Litvak with open arms. The two would meet daily, sometimes twice a day, and "talk in Torah learning." They became fast friends, and after spending an entire month there, it was hard for them to part.

Before Reb Yechiel Michel's departure, the Rebbe presented him with a special, unasked-for gift — *smicha*. Then the Rebbe, in spite of his advanced age, accompanied him all the way down the road.

The news spread quickly among the Lubavitch communities

around the land: *The Rebbe loves that Litvak!* Soon a number of Chassidic cities were after him to become their *Rav.*

It was in Novozivkov that he wrote his first *sefer, Or LaYesharim,* a commentary on the *Sefer HaYashar D'Rabbeinu Tam* (published in Zytomir in 1868). It included approbations of Rabbi Yehoshua Leib Diskin, the *Rav* in Shklov (and later of Lomza, Brisk, and then Yerushalayim); the *Tzemach Tzeddek;* and Reb Aharon, the Chernobiler *Rebbe.*

In Novozivkov, too, he conceived of writing his monumental *Aruch HaShulchan,* and began to compose his work.

After nine years in Novozivkov, he was invited to take the *rabbanus* of the town of Lubch, in the Novarodok district. It happened that the city of Novarodok was searching for a *Rav* when the news came that Reb Yechiel Michel Epstein was about to take the *rabbanus* in Lubch. They rushed a delegation, and snatched Reb Yechiel Michel out of the hands of the Lubchers!

He served in Novarodok[2] for thirty-four years (1863-1907), until his *petira* on the 22nd day of Adar, 1907. Many cities appealed to him to become their *Rav,* but he refused all offers.

In Novarodok Rabbi Yechiel Michel wrote the *Aruch HaShulchan,* for which he is best remembered. It soon became a handbook for many *rabbonim* and *poskim.* Rabbi Yerucham Yehuda Leib Perlman, the *Rav* of Minsk and famed "Minsker Gadol," who was much older than the *Rav* of Novarodok, never *paskened* a *she'eila* without first checking the *Aruch HaShulchan!*

One can derive an esthetic pleasure from the exquisite presentation of the text when studying the words of the *Aruch HaShulchan.* Before stating the practical *halacha,* there is an introduction to clarify the spirit of the law. The *halacha's* background, its roots in the Torah and its interpretations by the *chachamim* and *poskim* are all presented. Only then is the final opinion offered.

◄§ His Other Writings

In addition to the sixteen-volume *Aruch HaShulchan,* which took many years to compose, Reb Yechiel Michel wrote *Mical HaMayim,* a commentary on *Yerushalmi,* and *Leil Shemurim,* a commentary on the *Pesach Haggadah.*

Once he had disposed of all city business and *she'eilos* (halachic queries), he would lock himself up in his "*Beis Din shtub*" (he would write nowhere else!) and begin. His memory was phenomenal, and he never had a need to rewrite or edit. Other than paper, ink, and pen, the table had upon it a *Gemara, Rambam,* and *Beis Yosef* — and nothing more.

Printing in those days was very primitive. Every word, every letter had to be set by the hand of the *zetzer.* At the print shop, every *zetzer* would fight to get his manuscript, because of the beauty and clarity of his handwriting.

✒ The View of the "Maikil"

Rabbi Yechiel Michel was known as a *maikil* — one who takes the lenient view — as opposed to a *machmir* — one who holds by the more stringent opinions. The concept of *maikil* versus *machmir* is a difficult one to grasp, one which has often been misunderstood, and a few explanatory words would be in order.

Throughout the generations, there have been people who have complained about the burden of Torah. The past few centuries have seen many who wished to "reform" Judaism, to thrust off the *ol haTorah,* the yoke of Torah.

A delegation of these reformers once came to Rabbi Azriel Hildesheimer of Berlin. They tried to convince the *Rav* of the need to shorten prayers and ease the burden of *mitzva* performance and restrictions. This, they insisted, conformed with the way people were leading their lives anyway, and ultimately would attract more young men to *shul.*

Rabbi Hildesheimer replied with a parable. Once a businessman declared bankruptcy. He finally settled with his creditors for fifty cents on the dollar.

When the time came to pay, the man offered them notes. The creditors laughed in his face: "We settled for fifty cents on the dollar in order to get cash. Notes? We'd rather keep the old notes, which are at least written for the full amount of what is owed!"

"You, *meine Herren,*" concluded the wise *Rav,* "don't pay cash. You want to pay with new notes, which you have no intention of honoring. I would rather keep the old notes, the ones worth full price!"[3]

What, then, is a *maikil?* It is certainly not one who tries to reform, water down, or bend the *halacha* in any way.

In the development of *halacha,* received from Moshe *Rabbeinu* at Sinai and handed down through generations, through the *Tana'im, Amora'im,* and *Geonim,* differing opinions are sometimes given. A *Rav* of stature, one with *"breite pleitzes"* (broad shoulders), may throw his weight, his Torah weight, on the side of one opinion or the other.

For instance, no *Rav* may unilaterally give a ruling that differs with that of the *Rambam*. But if *Rashi* had stated an opposing opinion, a *Rav* great in Torah learning and understanding may, under certain circumstances, choose to rule in accordance with *Rashi's* opinion, rather than *Rambam's*.

In some ways, it is easier to be a *machmir*, and generally choose the stricter view, rather than take the responsibility of a *maikil* for abiding by the more lenient opinion.

How was the *Aruch HaShulchan maikil*? A case in point illustrates his manner of making a ruling:

It was the second night of Pesach, and the *Rav* of Novarodok was preparing to begin the *seder*. The family and guests sat around the table.

Suddenly, a woman entered the room, her hand clutching at something. "Rebbi," she said in a voice full of pleading, "I was cooking a chicken and I found this in the pot."

She opened her fist and inside was a single grain of wheat. *Chometz* on Pesach, forbidden even in the smallest amount!

The *Rav* asked her to sit down, and apologized to his guests. "I must go into my *Beis Din shtub*." He locked himself in the room, and after more than an hour, he finally emerged. With his face dripping with perspiration, and his shirt collar soaking wet, he pronounced his verdict: Kosher!

After she left, he begged forgiveness of his guests, explaining: "I could not sit down to the *seder* knowing that the woman and her family would not have a piece of chicken for the holiday. More, there is a question of the dishes, and there is an entire week of Pesach ahead! I had to find a *heter* for her! And thank Heaven, I found one!"

Indeed, Reb Chaim Brisker used to say: "I'm not a *maikil*, I'm merely a *machmir* when it comes to *pikuach nefesh* (saving a life) and therefore it appears that I am lenient in the laws of *Shabbos* when *pikuach nefesh* is involved."

Sometimes, his stubbornness in being a *maikil* had some interesting results. When he first arrived in Novarodok, he immediately ordered that all *shuls daven* the *Kabbolas Shabbos* and *Ma'ariv* ushering in the Sabbath a good time before *shkiya* (sundown), while the sun was still high in the sky. He even ordered that *Kiddush* be recited, and the meal eaten, before *shkiya*.

In those days, it should be remembered, people did not own clocks or calendars. Women would light candles whenever the *shuls* began *Kabbolas Shabbos*. He would say: "By making *Shabbos* earlier, I'm ensuring that every wagon driver has stabled his horse before sundown. If we would begin to pray at sundown, we might cause the candles to be lit after *shkiya*, causing *chillul Shabbos* (desecration of the Sabbath)."

Naturally, there were those who did not accept this new ruling, and they wished to make a second *minyan* after sunset, taking a stricter approach to the time of *davening Ma'ariv*. To put a stop to this, the *Rav* began a custom of ascending the *amud* immediately after his *Ma'ariv minyan*, and "talk in learning" with the yeshiva boys for hours. Then they could not make their second *minyan*.

The *Aruch HaShulchan's* fluency in Russian proved helpful to him. In his later years, when he attended conferences of *rabbonim*, he was usually chosen to act as spokesman to the government officials in their efforts to halt anti-Semitic acts. He was one of the few *gedolim* who could address the government officials without a translator.

His son Reb Boruch married the daughter of the *Rav* of Pinsk and settled there. Reb Boruch was a bookkeeper in Pinsk, yet he found the time to write the monumental *Torah Temima* that we enjoy today.

Rabbi Yechiel Michel Epstein truly left *Klal Yisroel* a heritage which enriches us to this very day — a table beautifully set, an *Aruch HaShulchan*, which helps to sustain us.

Notes

1. Rabbi Epstein's major work, the *Aruch HaShulchan*, clearly makes reference to its halachic precursor, the *Shulchan Aruch* of Rabbi Yoseif Caro.

When the first volume of the *Aruch HaShulchan* was published, the *maskillim* ("enlightened" ones) were furious. They were very bothered by the publication of any new *seforim*, and jokingly said that they looked forward to the day when all the titles would be used up, and publishing would cease. Then came the *Aruch HaShulchan*. "*Gevalt!*" they cried. "Now they will merely reverse the old titles and publish anew!"

2. It was in this very town that Rabbi Yosef Yoizel Horowitz founded the Novarodok Mussar movement. He became known as the "*Alter* of Novarodok" (see "The World of Novarodok," in *The Torah World*).

3. It is told that a delegation of *maskillim* once came to Rabbi Yoshe Ber Soloveitchik in Brisk. "The *rabbonim* are too rigid, too strict," they said, "all their *chumros* make life unbearable and should be eliminated!"

The *Rav* of Brisk listened most seriously, and then nodded. "I have given thought to these *chumros*," he said, "and have decided to do away with some of them in my next *sefer*."

Delighted, the *maskillim* respectfully asked if the Rebbe would mind letting them in on his secret. Which of the *chumros* would he abolish?

"Certainly," Rabbi Soloveitchik replied. "I'll let you in on six of them:

"(1) Some *poskim* insist that *Ma'ariv* can be prayed only until midnight. This is too harsh on people; I say let them *daven* until daybreak.

"(2) Some claim that only a great *talmid chacham* may don *Rabbeinu Tam tefillin;* I say anyone who wishes may do so.

"(3) Some say that the *piyutim* (liturgical poetry) in the prayers are considered a *hefsek* (interruption) and I say they're part of prayers.

"(4) Some say that if one forgets to count *Sefira* for one night, he may not count with a *brachah* anymore. I say he may count with a *brachah.*

"(5) Some say that even when *Erev Tisha B'Av* falls on a *Shabbos* one may not learn Torah. I say it is permitted, *l'kovod Shabbos.*

"(6) Some say it is forbidden to fast on Rosh HaShanah, and I say one may fast, even on both days!"

The *maskillim* realized, to their chagrin, that these *chumros* to be eliminated were being given "tongue-in-cheek" (and not halachically, of course). They left, resigned.

Chaim Shapiro

Rabbi Malkiel Tenenbaum

Rav of Lomza
5607/1847—5670/1910

IT HAPPENED ON *Shabbos Shuvah*, that awesome *Shabbos* that falls between Rosh Hashanah and Yom Kippur. All of the Lomza *kehillah* had crowded into the *shul*, eager to enjoy their *Rav's drashah*, to hear his exhortations, to share in the blessings which he would bestow.

The crowd was so great that many were forced to stand outside the *Beis Medrash Hagadol*, taking their places near the open windows. Solemnly the *Rav* passed through the multitude and made his way to his place near the *Aron Kodesh*.

"Beloved Jews," he said, "my duty to you today is to speak words of *mussar*, words of reproach, to teach and to guide you. But if I cannot guide my own children, how can I possibly guide others? How can I fulfill my obligations as *Rav*? Therefore I resign my position. And may *Hashem* bless you with a *gemar chasima tovah*, a good year."

Slowly he stepped down and took, not his seat on the right side of the *Aron Kodesh*, but a place on a crowded bench.

A moment of shocked silence was followed by utter pandemonium. In the balcony, the sound of weeping could be heard, for if the men considered their *Rav* a *talmid chacham* and *poseik*, the women knew him as the *tzaddik*, the one whose prayers could intercede for them and their families.

My mother used to tell me this tale of Reb Malkiel's resignation, and the furor it caused in the town. A young girl herself at the time, she heard the story recounted endless times, in vivid detail, by her mother. She would tell of the crowd that spontaneously formed and followed the *Rav* to his home to implore, to beg him to reconsider.

Delegations of *ba'alei battim* (laymen) went in and out of the *Rav's Beis Din shtub*. My *Zeide*, Reb Chaim Velvel Szeniak, put away the *Rambam* that he was studying, got up from his sick bed, and joined one such group. Though it was against doctor's orders, for he was very ill, and though she was normally very careful of his health, his wife, my *Bobba*, remained silent. She, too, sensed the urgency of his mission, and was ready to make whatever sacrifice necessary to keep Reb Malkiel as Lomza's *Rav*.

The *kehillah* saw no reason to censure their *Rav* for his wayward children. It was well known that *Rav* Malkiel's wife had been influenced by the insidious beliefs of the *maskilim*, and her children were following in her path. No, Lomza was a *kehillah* that wanted its *Rav* back. But would it get him?

After much pleading, the word spread through the crowd surrounding the *Rav's* home: "He is staying!" Such joy! Such relief! Reb Malkiel had agreed to stay on as *Rav*.

Such were my mother's memories of the *Rav* of Lomza, Rabbi Malkiel Tenenbaum, and the universal esteem in which he was held.

~§ It Started Near Pinsk

Reb Malkiel was born in 1847 in Motele, a tiny hamlet near Pinsk. He learned in Volozhin and Eishishok and, like many a Torah scholar, married young.

When he was twenty-six he became *Rav* of Bodki, a small town in the area of Grodno. In the fourteen years spent there he pored over his *seforim*, and began work on his six-volume work "*Divrei Malkiel*."

His halcyon days as scholar, author and small-town *Rav* ended in 1887, when the city of Lomza invited him to head their *kehillah*.

The challenge of heading a city full of distinguished *talmidei chachamim*, the vastly expanded opportunities to teach, to influence, to guide, drew Reb Malkiel as to a lodestone. It was in Lomza that his fame as a *poseik* grew. *Rabbonim* from all over the globe sent their questions to him; in the last six months of his life alone, he answered several hundred *she'eilos!*

His infallible logic and penetrating insight soon became evident. The fresh clarity of his thought can be seen in his interpretation of the custom, followed in Lomza and common throughout Europe, of burying women who had died during childbirth in a special place set aside in the cemetery.

Many people felt that the source of the *minhag* lay in the verse: "Women die in childbirth for three sins: for not exercising care in family purity, *challah*, and candlelighting." Reb Malkiel, though, dismissed the notion entirely, and explained thusly:

It states, in *Mesechta Shabbos*, that Rabbi Yosi prayed for a share with those who died while performing a *mitzvah*, for to do so is to die *al kiddush Hashem*, for the sanctification of G-d. Further, in

Babba Basra, we are told that no one can stand in the *mechitzah* of martyrs.

To give birth to a child, to bring the next generation into this world, is surely one of the greatest of *mitzvos*. In those days, when obstetrical care was almost unknown and childbirth fraught with risk, a woman who chose to bear children was performing an incomparable *mitzvah*. And if she died in the process, was she not, then, to be considered as one who died *al kiddush Hashem?* If so, no others could be with her, and she was placed in an exclusive portion of the cemetery, buried next to others who had performed the same valiant deed.

As for the dictum that attributes death in childbirth to violation of three sins, that refers to death at the precise moment of childbirth. The women in Lomza succumbed minutes — or perhaps days — afterwards, not at the time of birth. They were to be revered as *kedoshim* — martyrs.

The Rav's Decisions

In 1904, during the Russo-Japanese War, thousands of Jews were drafted into the Czar's army and shipped to the Far East. Since the Russian Army's casualty reports were sketchy, incomplete and unreliable, large numbers of women faced the grim prospect of living out their lives as *agunos*. To avert this catastrophe, Reb Malkiel set up a text for a *get* that every married soldier gave to an agent, to be delivered to his wife in the event that he had not returned by a certain time. If, by some miracle, the man would return after the *get* had been accepted, he could always remarry his former wife. Because a *Kohen* was not permitted to marry a divorcee, even if she had been his own wife, Reb Malkiel also drafted a conditional *get* especially designed for *Kohanim*. In a short time, *Rabbonim* from all over Russia were using his text.

During the Second World War, when many Jews in Palestine volunteered for the British Army to fight the Nazis, it was Reb Malkiel's text that was used by all married soldiers as protection for their wives.

Interestingly enough, Reb Malkiel spent many hours studying *Kabbalah*, and he would sometimes cite the *Zohar* in his *p'sak halachah. Zohar*, he felt, could be used for *p'sak*, except in those instances when it actually contradicted the *Gemara*.

His interest in *Kabbalah* had unexpected repercussions in Lomza. For years, the town's *maskilim* had tried, in vain, to receive the permits necessary to open a school of their own. The School Superintendent, however, refused to grant permission unless the town's Rabbi approved the scheme; *Haskalah* being anathema to Reb Malkiel, approval was routinely withheld.

After a few years, though, the *maskilim* received their coveted permit from the Russian official. Everyone in town was certain that the superintendent had accepted a bribe, but the truth soon came out. It seems that one of the canny *maskilim* had shown the superintendent one of the *Rav's* Kabbalistic writings, translated into Russian. For one uninitiated into *Kabbalah*, the Hebrew and Aramaic text can sound obscure and strange; in Russian it was practically incomprehensible! The school superintendent ruled that one who wrote such "*chapookha*" (nonsense) should not be arbiter on a school's permits!

◆§ Farewell Journey

In 1910, a conference of *Rabbonim* was convened in St. Petersburg. Among those attending were Rabbi Chaim Soloveitchik of Brisk, Rabbi Dovid Friedman of Karlin, Rabbi Meir Simcha of Dvinsk, Rabbi Yitzchok Zelig Morgenstern, the *Rebbe* of Sokolov, and Rabbi Malkiel of Lomza.

As they rode the train homeward, the *Rebbe* of Sokolov was horrified to see his seatmate, Reb Malkiel of Lomza, lurch forward and fall into his arms. There on the train, on the 5th day of Nissan 5670 (1910), the *Rav* of Lomza was *niftar*. He was only sixty-three years old.

When the train pulled into the nearest station of Rezice, the *kehillah* there expressed their desire to bury the *Rav* in their town. But the townspeople of Lomza protested vehemently: Let the *Rav* be brought to his home of twenty-three years!

The train arrived in the station of Czerwony-Bor, fourteen kilometers from Lomza, in the evening. The road was lined with Jews reciting *Tehillim* and weeping. They bore their beloved *Rav* upon their shoulders that dark long night, and finally brought him to his place in the *Beis Medrash*, the place where he had learned so much Torah, *paskened* so many *she'eilos*, *davened* such fervent prayers. The weeping crowd eulogized their leader and asked his forgiveness.

The memory of Reb Malkiel illuminated the city of Lomza like a beacon for many years after his *petirah*, and those who had known him never forgot the image of their beloved *Rav*.

Rabbi Yechiel Mordechai Gordon

*The
Prince
of
Roshei
Hayeshivah*

Rabbi Yechiel Mordechai Gordon
5643/1883—5726/1966

WHEN THE DAUGHTERS of Reb Lazer Shulavitz, founder of the Lomza Yeshivah, came of age and he began his search for suitable husbands for them, he also was aware that he was searching for heirs apparent. So he wrote his old friend Reb Nosson Tzvi Finkel, the *"Alter* of Slobodka," for a recommendation. Quoting their mentor Reb Yisroel Salanter, Reb Lazer wrote: "את בתי נתתי לאיש הזה — Foremost he must be an *ish* — man enough to take over the Yeshivah."

The *Alter* immediately recommended "Mottel Troker" — Yechiel Mordechai Gordon.

When Reb Mottel's father had brought him to Slobodka at the age of twelve, his reputation preceded him as the *Iluy* of Trok (genius of Trok — a town near Vilna). In his older years he became known as the Prince of the *Roshei Yeshivos,* for reasons that will be obvious to the reader.

✒ The Wedding

The wedding took place in the Yeshivah, in 1905. The bride agreed to allow her young husband to return to Slobodka to pursue his studies. Within the year she died, and — communications as they then existed — the tragic news did not reach him until after the funeral.

Reb Lazer did not want to let this gem out of his hands, so he went to Slobodka and pleaded with the young man to consider marrying his second daughter and take over the Yeshivah. Reb Yechiel Mordechai refused: *It has not been decreed in Heaven that he be Reb Lazer's son-in-law, for he is not qualified to be a Rosh Yeshivah — why should he put the life of the second daughter in jeopardy?*

"Suppose the *Chofetz Chaim* promises you a long life together?" asked Reb Lazer. "Would you still refuse?"

Of course, he could not. So the two went to Radin to see the *Chofetz Chaim*, and after receiving his blessings the wedding took place. In 1907 he became the *Rosh Yeshivah* at the age of twenty-four.

Rabbi Nisson Waxman (later of Petach Tikvah) tells of a visit to Lomza some twenty-five years later. He called on Reb Yechiel Mordechai, but somehow the *Rosh Yeshivah* was not himself. He soon found out that the *Rebbetzin* was critically ill.

Shortly afterward, Rabbi Waxman was surprised to meet the *Rosh Yeshivah* at the railroad station. As if reading his mind, the *Rosh Yeshivah* told him, "When we married, the *Chofetz Chaim* promised me *arichas yomim* for my *Rebbetzin*. She is very sick, and I'm going to Radin to collect on the *Chofetz Chaim's* promise."

Apparently the *Chofetz Chaim's* second *berachah* and prayer helped for only a short time, for she died soon afterward.

To be a *Rosh Yeshivah* in Lomza was a demanding assignment. The same factors made the Lomza rabbinate an extremely selective one. The Lomza tradition required the *Rav* to deliver a *shiur* (Torah lecture) in the Yeshivah annually, on or before *Shavuos*, and a *mussar shmues* (lecture on an ethical topic) in *Elul*. This automatically eliminated all but the most qualified candidates for the *Rabbonus*. As an additional "test," the *talmidim* of the highest class would "talk in learning" with the *Rav* and report to him for *semichah* (ordination). These were the students for whom Reb Yechiel Mordechai said a *shiur* when only twenty-four!

✺ World War I Years

During the First World War, the Czar's generals ordered all yeshivos along the German border to evacuate their towns. Lomza, however, remained intact. The studies continued as usual, but the material situation deteriorated from day to day. The local Jewish community was in financial ruin because of the war, and contact with America, the only source of support for the Yeshivah, was cut off. Thus, the Yeshivah could not grant admission to the many refugee *bnei Torah* arriving almost daily.

Reb Yechiel Mordechai had heard that a particular young man he had turned away was unusually gifted. He immediately dispatched messengers to bring him back to the Yeshivah, but he could not be located. He then sent boys to neighboring villages, where the young man was finally found. He remained in the Yeshivah for three years, becoming one of its outstanding scholars. The young man, Reb Yaakov Kamenetzky, was subsequently well known beyond Lomza circles as *Rosh Yeshivah* of Mesifta Torah Vodaath, and a member of Agudath Israel's *Moetzes Gedolei HaTorah* (Council of Torah Sages).

Years later, when Reb Yechiel Mordechai Gordon met Rabbi Kamenetzky in New York, said *rebbi* to *talmid*: "Because of you, Reb Yaakov, I made a vow never to refuse admission to any one, no matter what!"

✺ The Post-War Years

On November 11, 1918, Poland declared its independence, and less than two years later, it was already entangled in a war with the Soviet Union. Western democracies intended to kill Communism in the bud, or at least arrest its growth within the borders of Russia. For that purpose, they instigated a war between Poland and Russia. Poland's Marshal Pilsudski had a dream of his own — a Poland from sea to sea (from the Baltic to the Black), but Poland had neither the arms nor the strategic resources for such a war. The West supplied both: A flow of ammunition began, and strategy was directed by the French Military Mission under General Weygand, drafted behind the scenes by a tall, thin, obscure French colonel named Charles DeGaulle.

Soon the Polish Army marched into Kiev, capital of the Ukraine and reached Minsk, capital of White Russia. Then the Red Army fought back. The front line seesawed until the Soviet offensive collapsed at the very gates of Warsaw on August 15, 1920. The Poles called it "Cod nad Wisla" (The Miracle on the Vistula).

In the meantime, Poland declared a general mobilization, and yeshivah students received draft notices. While Christian divinity seminaries were granted deferments, the anti-Semitic Polish Government refused to defer students of the Lomza Yeshivah, the only such yeshivah in all Poland.

Reb Yechiel Mordechai went to Warsaw to intervene. He approached the dean of the Jewish members of the Sejm (the Polish parliament), Dr. Noach Prilucki. Dr. Prilucki was an old *maskil*, and while he seemed sympathetic to the *Rosh Yeshivah's* complaint, the old *haskalah* awakened within him.

"Lomza *Rosh Yeshivah*," said he, "tomorrow I shall call on the Minister of War. Can I tell him that you train rabbis for Poland, citing that your curriculum includes Polish history, grammar, and geography? — Can you at least promise me a few hours a day for secular studies?"

"A decision such as this," replied Reb Yechiel Mordechai, "I cannot take upon myself. I must seek advice."

"Even though in the meantime your boys are being drafted and sent to the battlefield?" asked Dr. Prilucki.

"Yes, even at that price," replied the *Rosh Yeshivah*.

Actually, the *Rosh Yeshivah* could have decided on the spot, based on the Volozhiner precedent of 1893. Acting on the instigation of the *Maskilim*, the Czar's government had delivered an ultimatum to the Yeshivah in Volozhin: either introduce secular studies or close the Yeshivah. A special committee of Torah leaders convened in St. Petersburg, with the *Chofetz Chaim*, the Rogachover, and the Lubavitcher *Rebbe*, among others, participating. The Brisker *Rav*, Reb Yoseif Dov Soloveitchik, pronounced the final *psak:* "We are not the caretakers of *Hashem*. We can only perform our duty. We created a yeshivah for *Hakadosh Boruch Hu*. If it is the Divine will to close it, we have no choice but to conform. We can never agree to mix קודש וחול — the sacred with profane."

The Yeshivah was closed. Many considered the closing down of this major yeshivah a national tragedy and the action of the *gedolim* a major error. However, in a few years it proved to be a blessing. Instead of one yeshivah, in Volozhin, where admittance was limited to those in the genius category, a number of yeshivos flourished all over Lithuania and Russia, led by the former students of Volozhin — Kovno, Slobodka, Mir, Slutzk, Lomza, Brainsk, Meychet, Telshe, and Brisk, among many others.

However, Reb Yechiel Mordechai would not judge Dr. Prilucki's offer himself, for the difference between a *direct* order, such as in Volozhin, and an *indirect* one, such as in Lomza, could be a crucial factor in such a decision. And so could the alternatives — closing a yeshivah (Volozhin) or draft in the Czar's army.

Back in his hotel room, he fell asleep and dreamed of the *pasuk:* *"All leaven or honey you shall not burn as an offering to Hashem." Foreign elements — whether sour or sweet — can never be mixed before Hashem.* The message was obvious, but Reb Yechiel Mordechai would not rely on a dream to close the yeshivah. The war made communicating with the *Chofetz Chaim* or Reb Chaim Brisker or Reb Chaim Ozer Grodzenski of Vilna impossible, so he returned to Lomza to seek the advice of his *Mashgiach*, Reb Moshe Rosenstain (a disciple of Kelm).

After much consideration, the *Mashgiach* said, "It is clear that *Hakadosh Boruch Hu* requires *mesiras nefesh* from us for Torah. We are not obligated to display *mesiras nefesh* for secular studies, however. We cannot mix the two; *kodesh* and *chol* — the sacred and the profane — cannot dwell together."

"But boys are being drafted," protested the *Rosh Yeshivah.*

The *Mashgiach* was a firm believer in the Vilna *Gaon's* "*Goirel*," a lottery that indicated a decision through selection of a *pasuk.* The quotation selected — a Divine command to Moshe — read: "From twenty years old and upward, all that are able to go forth to war in Israel: you shall number them by their hosts, you and Aaron" (*Bamidbar* 1:3).

His own name was Moshe, so with a student by the name of Aaron he set out to solve their dilemma, in accordance with the command in the *pasuk.* They established contact with the chairman of the local draft board — for American dollars (he refused to accept the Polish *zloty*) he would free all *bnei Torah.* It was illegal to possess dollars, but these were his terms.

The *Mashgiach* justified this "illegal" approach, for *bnei Torah* should have been deferred as were Christian divinity students, except for the Pole's anti-Semitism that denied them their legal rights.

If Poland was anti-Semitic, the army was tenfold worse.

Honoring *Shabbos* and *Kashrus* was practically impossible. Hence, *bnei Torah* from all yeshivos threatened by military conscription arrived in Lomza finding a place to learn, with room and board, thus establishing residency there. With American currency, they were safe. For the next twenty years — as long as Poland was independent — Lomza served as a haven for such *bnei Torah*.

◄§ Expansion and Upheaval

When "Return to Zion" became a reality, Reb Yechiel Mordechai began to speak of the "Torah following the people" — of a yeshivah in *Eretz Yisroel*. His deep love for *Klal Yisroel, Toras Yisroel* and *Eretz Yisroel* all culminated in decisive action: In the summer of 1926, he took forty students from Lomza to a newly established branch in Petach Tikvah. (All forty were of draft age and lacked the necessary "*Minchah L'Eisav*" funds.) Now he had two yeshivos to care for — his love for both was unlimited, and so were the debts incurred. He would travel to America and Africa, and on the way back always stopped over in Petach Tikvah for a few months, to say *shiurim*. In September, 1939, as he was about to return from a trip to America, the Germans attacked Poland, forcing him to remain.

As one of the only European *Roshei Hayeshivah* in America during the war, he was a prime force behind the creation of the *Vaad Hatzalah*. Personally in a state of poverty, he nonetheless found money to send packages to *bnei Torah* in Russia. This act of charity became known to me in a most personal way.

As a tank officer in the Polish army stationed in the U.S.S.R., I was facing death daily. I wanted desperately to inform someone of my general whereabouts — and that I was still alive. Then, after the war, my parents who were under the Nazis could be informed! So I wrote only one line (in Russian) — that I am alive — and signed my name without a return address. (I did not dare write more to a foreign country!) I mailed it to "Rabbi Yechiel Mordechai Gordon, N.Y., Delancey Street" (I didn't remember the building number), never knowing if my post card had reached its destination — until after the war when I came to Windsheim-Bei-Nurenberg.

The *Vaad Hatzalah* had organized a yeshivah there, attracting *bnei Torah* from all corners of Europe, including Russia. The *bachurim* told me that a stream of packages had begun to arrive in my name. They did not have the slightest idea of my whereabouts, but they did realize that if the packages were not quickly claimed, they would be stolen by the postal employees. So the boys forged documents with my name and accepted all the parcels. Standard *Vaad Hatzalah* packages, they saved them from starvation.

Soon a better type of package arrived — every two weeks from my "relatives." When I protested that I had no relatives in America, they asked, "And who is Rabbi Gordon?"

I heard the same story in the other *Vaad Hatzalah* yeshivah in Bailly, near Paris. Apparently, he also suspected that I might have been with the Kamenitz Yeshivah in Siberia, for he had sent personal packages addressed to me there also.

Among the first of his *talmidim* to emerge from the concentration camps alive was Reb Moshe Mordechai Krieger (later in the Crown Heights section of Brooklyn). The *Rosh Yeshivah* immediately sent him funds to go from camp to camp to search for *bnei Torah*. When Reb Yechiel Mordechai learned that Moshe Krieger had endured five years in various concentration camps, never tasting *treife* food, he could not get over it. "Only Torah and *Mussar* can ripen a person to such *mesiras nefesh*," he declared, crediting his *Mashgiach*, Reb Moshe Rosenstain, with this achievement. In the dark days, when the full tragedy of the destruction became known, this was the only ray of light reaching the *Rosh Yeshivah*. If Reb Moshe Krieger had special *zechusim* (merit) of his own to survive Buchenwald, the *nachas* he brought his *Rosh Yeshivah* was one more major *zechus*.

⋘ "The Bone of His Tenth Son"

Reb Yechiel Mordechai's entire life seemed to be a long list of tribulations, bringing to mind Rabbi Yochanan's experiences recounted in the Talmud: *He had lost ten sons during his lifetime — the tenth one fell into a fire and his entire body was consumed, except a small bone. Rabbi Yochanan dedicated his life to comforting people in distress. When necessary, he would point to the little bone of his tenth son, proving that life must go on, citing himself as an example.*

After the war, many who had survived were broken in spirit and body. After losing one's entire family, who has the will to live? Who cares to go on? Then, one meets Reb Yechiel Mordechai, radiating *bitachon* and *emunah* — faith and trust — full of life and vigor in spite of all that happened. Life must go on, and he served as the best example! Married at twenty-two, his wife died during their first year, and he could not even be at the funeral . . . His second wife bore five children, and then became ill and passed away . . . His son Shneur had stood guard at the Yeshivah in Petach Tikvah during the Arab pogroms, and was shot, at the age of twenty! . . . His daughter, Chaych'ke, married an outstanding *lamdon* (Talmudic scholar) in the Mirrer Yeshivah, Reb Eiz'l Kostukowski (a nephew of Reb Chaim Ozer), and he could not attend the wedding for lack of fare. They had two children he had never seen . . . His youngest son, Yudele, was *Bar Mitzvah* while he was away in America . . . And, finally, they all perished at the hands of the Nazis, including his eighteen-year-old daughter, Itke (one son died in New York) . . . For sixty years he was a *Rosh Yeshivah*, for sixty years he carried two yeshivos on his shoulders, and in the end, except for his many *talmidim* and admirers, he remained alone.

In spite of all this, he was undaunted. Every letter I received from him in Germany was like a shot of adrenalin, awakening me and recalling me to life.

◁§ The Rosh Yeshivah's Secret

What was his secret? What was the source of his strength that enabled him to overcome personal tragedy? I found the answer when I arrived in America. His closest friends told me that he cried bitterly in the privacy of the night, weeping over his lost children and the terrible destruction of the war — but not a sign of it during the day, while he faced people.

His father-in-law, Reb Lazer Shulavitz, would tell of an encounter between his *Rebbi*, Reb Yisroel Salanter, and a Jew on the day before Yom Kippur. He had greeted the man and inquired after his welfare. In reply, the man began to weep — "I'm worried about the Day of Judgment we are facing tomorrow."

The man's gloomy countenance surely frightened others. Reb Yisroel told him: "Your heart is a *reshus hayochid* (private domain). You can cry within it all you wish. But your face is a *reshus horabbim* (public domain), and you have no right to burden others with your problems and fears. The rule in *Pirke Avos* (1:15), 'Receive all men with a cheerful countenance,' applies even on Yom Kippur Eve."

Such was also Reb Yechiel Mordechai's practice.

Soon afterward, I shared a personal experience with him that revealed even more of his greatness in *emunah*. He loved to hear stories about his children and grandchildren. He asked me every little detail, even though seven long years had passed since I had last seen them in Vilna. (They had escaped from Lomza to Vilna with the Yeshivah.) Apparently I was the last to see them and served as his final link with them. So I would tell him all that I remembered, time and again, until there was nothing more to tell.

Once while traveling the subway together to the Yeshivah office, I mentioned the *Kiddush Hashem* his daughter Chaych'ke had created in Lomza. (There were a number of versions of the tale, and I was not sure which was authentic, but I did my best with what I knew.)

> His daughter, Chaych'ke, was preparing herself for her marriage to Reb Eiz'l — her mother had died and her father was away in America. Her uncle, her father's brother in America, sent a personal wedding gift of five hundred dollars through the *Rosh Yeshivah* ... Chaych'ke gave away the entire five hundred dollars to an orphaned friend who was also about to marry.
>
> (In another version, Chaych'ke met that girl and asked her when she was planning to get married. The orphan girl replied, "Never, because my *naden* of five hundred dollars is loaned to the Yeshivah, and the Yeshivah cannot pay its debts." Chaych'ke then gave her her own funds.)
>
> Chaych'ke's beauty was such that she did not need the money for a tailored wardrobe, but five hundred dollars was a fortune those days, even in America, and surely in impoverished Poland! The story became widely publicized, and Isaac Remba, a non-religious journalist, expressed everyone's feeling in classical Polish: "Dawnej Gordonoweej, obecnie Kostukowskiej, ale zawse tej samej Chajczce." ("Previously Miss Gordon, presently Mrs. Kostukowski, but always the same Chaych'ke!")

Tears streamed down his cheeks into his gray beard, and I was sorry for bringing up the matter. Then, to my embarrassment, he embraced me and kissed me, right there in the crowded subway train. Holding on to my hand he repeatedly whispered to himself: "*Nachas in Olam Habo.*" I was witnessing the minting of a new phrase: "*Nachas in Olam Habo.*"

As we left the train, he held on to my hand, and we walked in silence all the way to the office. He entered with a big, cheerful "*Gut Morgen.*" Rabbi Halpern (the office manager) later remarked to me, "The *Rosh Yeshivah* seems so happy — as if he had just received a million-dollar donation."

Said I, "More than that ... something that cannot be valued in money — Have you ever heard the phrase, *Nachas in Olam Habo?*"

He had not.

Later, as I was leaving, the *Rosh Yeshivah* said, "Look up *Midrash Tanchuma* on the *pasukim* of *Orlah.*" I was puzzled, for the laws of *Orlah* concern the planting of trees in Israel; during the first three years, the fruit is forbidden. How did this relate to his personal tragedy and his strange phrase?

I dropped into one of the Hebrew bookstores that lined Delancey Street and found a *Midrash Tanchuma* (*Vayikra* 19:23-24): "... and you shall have planted all manner of trees for food, then you shall count as forbidden the fruit thereof; three years shall it be sealed unto you; it shall not be eaten. And in the fourth year, all the fruit thereof shall be holy for giving praise unto the L-rd." To which the *Midrash Tanchuma* comments: "... It refers to a child — *for three years* he does not converse; *the fourth year he is holy*, for his father dedicates him to Torah, when he begins to praise Hashem; *and in the fifth year you shall eat his fruit*, referring to the child embarking on Torah study ... In this world a man begets a son, leads him to school, works hard to teach him Torah; then he dies, and he has no *nachas* from him ... However, in the World-to-Come I shall remove the *yeitzer hora* from your sons, you shall give birth and be happy with *nachas* ..."

Such is the source of strength for a Torah Giant even in the face of a personal and national tragedy.

❀   ❀   ❀

Reb Yechiel Mordechai was invited by Rabbi Nisson Waxman, the *Rav* of Lakewood, New Jersey, to open a yeshivah there. He rejected the idea, for his heart and mind belonged to his yeshivah in Petach Tikvah. (Rabbi Waxman then invited *Hagaon* Reb Aharon Kotler, who accepted the invitation.) However, for the sake of his *talmidim* who survived concentration camps and internment in Siberia, he established a *Kollel* in Brooklyn. As soon as all had settled, he moved to Petach Tikvah.

Rabbi Gordon died in Israel in 5726/1966, at the age of eighty-three. Before he died, he published the first volume of his נתיב ים. His *talmidim* published the second volume after he died. He endured a seemingly bitter life that spanned the major epochs of recent history, but he brought joy, courage, and purpose to the lives of many. May he enjoy his *nachas* in *Olam Habo!*

Torah Leaders in Eretz Yisrael

*Men whose greatness was enhanced
by the extra dimension
of sanctity of living a life of Torah
in the Holy Land.*

Reb Hirsh Michel's
Yerushalayim Shel Ma'alah

5600/1840—5666/1906

I T WAS AN HOUR after midnight, in November 1868. The rain was pouring down so hard that night that the well-trodden streets of *Battei Machseh* were riverlets. In the midst of the storm, the door of the Sephardi *shul*, Chessed Keil, opened to a cobblestone alley.

Battei Machseh, in the heart of the old Yishuv, was fast asleep. The few who might have ventured out at this hour remained at home, for the downpour posed a double threat. In addition to the obvious health hazard, there was fear of the Turks who incarcerated in the dreaded Akishle prison anyone caught out at night without a lit candle — no matter what the weather.

The door to the *shul* closed, and a man emerged from the doorway with clothes draped over his head and shoulders. He wasn't carrying a candle — he never did. The clothes were not to protect him from the rain, but to protect his identity. Every night at one hour after midnight, he made this trip, checking each corner to see if anyone was there.

Reb Hirsh Michel was on his way to his *chavrusa*. His every step and every act was veiled in secrecy. But the little that we do know about — he was described as "The Yerushalaimer *Tzaddik*" — is a portal to *Yerushalayim shel Ma'alah*.

Yerushalayim shel Ma'alah is not a geographic location. The Midrash relates that there is a heavenly Jerusalem in congruence with the earthly Jerusalem. And the celestial angels who make up the Jerusalem above found their counterparts in Jerusalem below one hundred years ago, when amongst humble tinsmiths and cobblers were pious individuals who spent the major part of their days engaged in spiritual pursuits. The paragon of tzidkus and yira of this saintly generation was Rabbi Yehoshua Tzvi* Michel Shapiro.

---

* "*Tzvi*" translates in Yiddish as *Hirsh* ("deer"); hence Reb Hirsh Michel.

৺§ Tender "Tzidkus"

Reb Hirsh Michel's penchant for *kedushah* was apparent at an early age. When Hirsh Michel was eight years old he tasted his first apricot. He found its surprising sweetness and succulence so delectable that he considered the fruit indulgence, and abstained from eating any for the rest of his life.

At the age of seven, he completed *Babba Metzia* in just a few nights, obviously comprehending it well. The *Ravad* (head of the *Beis Din* of Chevron), Rav Shimon Menashe, and the other local Rabbinic luminaries enjoyed discussing Torah subjects with the young prodigy, but Hirsh Michel avoided such encounters. He felt that too much time was wasted in both discussion and travel, and only consented to meet with the elder scholars on fast days when his concentration was weak.

> One afternoon, a merchant outside the Chevron Synagogue heard painful wails emanating from inside the shul. He dropped his wares to try to be of help, but found the synagogue door locked. The merchant scaled the window railing but couldn't see a thing inside. He then heard another shrill cry which grew louder and longer. He summoned the shamash who unlocked the shul door and found the little feet of nine-year-old Hirsh Michel protruding from behind the paroches.
>
> Fearing discovery, he covered his face and ran outside. "Someone must be ill in the Shapiro home," the men reasoned. Yet, to their astonishment, everyone was well. Hirsh Michel had been pouring out his heart over the Temple which lay in ruin, imploring the Almighty to hasten its restoration.

When Hirsh Michel was eleven, he heard about Reb Yisroel Salanter for the first time, from a Lithuanian immigrant. Stories about Reb Yisroel and the nascent *Mussar* movement so inspired the youngster that he made his first request from his father, Reb Yaakov Koppel: a copy of the *Mussar* classic, *Mesilas Yesharim*. His father acceded to the request and had the *nachas* of seeing his son memorize and embody its each and every word.

At age seventeen, Hirsh Michel married the daughter of the famous *gaon* Rabbi Nachman Koronell. After his marriage, he returned to Jerusalem, which he had left for Chevron as a young boy, to study under Rabbi Yosef Steinhart (Rav Yosef "Charif" — the Sharp One), a nephew and disciple of Reb Chaim Volozhiner.

The Torah giants of Jerusalem flocked to greet Reb Hirsh Michel, but he tried to avoid them. Reb Hirsh Michel had moved to Jerusalem to study undisturbed, not to be a center of attention. His desire to study by himself, however, was soon to change.

◂§ The Kutna Influence

Not long after Reb Hirsh Michel returned to Jerusalem, Rabbi Moshe Yehuda Leib, the *Rav* of Kutna, Lithuania (who was succeeded by the celebrated Reb She'ala), also arrived. The Kutna *Rav* became the local focal point of Torah study — Jerusalem's *talmidei chachamim* spent a good part of their day in his home involved in Talmudic discussions; only Reb Hirsh Michel remained in the *Beis Midrash*. His daily schedule consisted of learning an entire *Mesechta* with all of the commentaries every day, in addition to his *mussar* studies. In fact, he never would have met the Kutna *Rav* had his father not insisted that he present himself to him.*

It did not take the Kutna *Rav* long to realize that the young man was superior to the other scholars and was worthy of his undivided attention. The elderly *Gaon* felt duty bound to impart all of his knowledge to this exceptional young man, and later quoted him extensively in his *seforim*, *Zayis Ra'anon* and *Tiferes Yerushalayim*.

◂§ The Extraordinary Routine

After the passing of the Kutna *Rav* in 1866, Reb Hirsh Michel returned to his old practices. Every night immediately after *Maariv*, he slipped away to the sparsely attended Sephardi synagogue, Chessed Keil, for a long night of prayer and study. He would gently place his cane on the table where people were learning and ask them to rap him on his fingers if he would doze off. He would then repair to a corner where he studied from a *Shulchan Aruch*, *Choshen Mishpat*, which he held in his hands. With his sweet voice, he rapidly read through the text with *Shach*, *Taz*, and other commentaries, occasionally repeating a phrase or two. So he studied, standing perfectly still, hour after hour, night after night, never requiring the cane to keep him awake.

---

* In 5659 (1899), when the German Kaiser visited Jerusalem, Reb Hirsh Michel was caught in a similar dilemma: should he join the rest of the town in going out to recite the rare blessing "Shenossan," which is said upon seeing a monarch, or continue learning in seclusion? His difficulty was solved when a bottle of boiling water smashed on the floor and scalded his legs. He thanked G-d for this omen and joyfully returned to his studies, absolved from any obligation to bless the king.

One night, however, Reb Hirsh Michel's eyelids began to drop ... The others in the *Beis HaMidrash* felt themselves unworthy of disturbing such a saint, and did not dare touch him. When he awoke he was so pained by his drowsing that he trembled, his eyes ablaze. He tightened his fingers around the *Shulchan Aruch* as if to say, "Who knows what spiritual heights I forfeited by just these few minutes?" He took the people to task: "Why do I need a cane if it isn't going to be used?" — then resumed his learning with fiery diligence.

Reb Hirsh Michel never slept for an extended period of time, never after midnight, nor did he lie on a bed. Every night at eleven he rested his head against the wall while still standing, and instructed those nearby not to allow him to sleep for more than ten minutes. He would awake by himself, wash his hands and return to learning as before until exactly midnight. Reb Hirsh Michel then hurried to a *mikveh*, immersed himself and returned to the *shul*. He tilted his hat over his eyes, removed his shoes, placed ashes on his forehead and sat on the cold stone floor to say *Tikun Chatzos*, bemoaning the absence of the Divine presence, the destroyed Temple, the *Sifrei Torah* that were burnt, the death of *tzaddikim*, the desecration of G-d's name, the exiles, the growth of Reform, as well as other aspects of *galus*. Reb Hirsh Michel mourned each loss as if it were his own personal tragedy, until the floor was wet from his tears. When he completed the *Tikun*, he put on his shoes and returned to the corner, remaining erect and engrossed in his studies until sunrise when he *davened* every morning.

ᴇᴥ No Breaks in the Pattern

On an Erev Shabbos in 5643 (1883), Reb Hirsh Michel appeared to be on the brink of death. The doctors of Jerusalem conferred at his bedside and decided that his only hope for recovery was an immediate operation. Reb Hirsh Michel calmly asked if that would affect "making Kiddush" in the evening. They replied that Kiddush or any other such activities would be out of the question for the next three days. "If I can't make Kiddush," he declared, "then I don't need an operation!"

The following morning the doctors examined him and to their utter amazement found that his condition had totally improved and that he no longer needed surgery.

❀   ❀   ❀

In 5663 (1903) Reb Hirsh Michel fell mortally ill and again Jerusalem's doctors visited him. Their consensus was that Reb Hirsh Michel's condition was fatal and they prohibited him to learn or exert himself in any way. When the doctors left, he began to cry and called for his student, Rabbi Yaakov Moshe Charlop. He asked Reb Yaakov Moshe to read to him the Ran at the beginning of Meseches Pesachim.

"But you are not allowed to learn," Rav Yaakov Moshe protested.

"If I am really going to die," Reb Hirsh Michel responded, "then when am I going to learn if I don't learn now?"

And so they studied all that day deep into the night, Reb Yaakov Moshe totally forgetting that his Rebbe was sick.

❈ ❈ ❈

One Succos, Reb Hirsh Michel fainted in his succah and appeared to be minutes away from death. His students struggled to revive him and then tried to carry him into his house, but Reb Hirsh Michel refused to budge. Rabbi Yehoshua Leib Diskin, Jerusalem Rav, ruled that Reb Hirsh Michel was not to be listened to, and was to be brought into the house at once ... Years later he explained, "I was afraid that I was at the very end of my life. How could I depart from the precious mitzvah of sitting in the succah with just minutes left to live?"

❈ ❈ ❈

For a time, Reb Hirsh Michel was advised to wear a pouch of hot stones to ease intestinal pain. His concentration was so intense during davening that one Shacharis a burning coal amongst the stones ignited the entire pouch. In spite of smoke emitting from his clothing, he was oblivious to what was happening. Only when he finished Pesukei DeZimrah did he realize that he had sustained a third-degree burn. On another occasion, he did not realize that a hornet had stung him while he was davening Shemoneh Esrei, even though his neck was swollen red.

◄§ Among the Few Who Succeed

Regarding the Talmudic dictum: "Whoever has enough bread . for today and questions what he will eat the next day is a small believer" (*Sotah* 48), Reb Hirsh Michel* used to comment: "*A kattan amannah*, a small believer, is an *apikorus kattan* . . .*"

The *Gemora* relates that many tried to live by Rav Shimon Bar Yochai's system of exclusively learning and forgetting about worldly pursuits, and failed. He commented, "If many tried and failed, this implies that a few succeeded. Is there anything wrong with striving to be among that minority?"

Reb Hirsh Michel fasted frequently. Otherwise his diet consisted of a piece of bread — which he measured to be exactly a *k'beitzah* (an egg-size, the minimum for a blessing over washing the hands) — dipped into oil, and a glass of unflavored hot water.

> *His students were once curious as to why he was in an exceptionally good mood. He explained that he had fasted that day because he had no food. He continued; "There are two opinions in the Gemara as to whether one who fasts is a sinner or a pious individual. I have fasted by default, and have therefore avoided this dispute."*

When his father, Reb Yaakov Koppel, died in 5652 (1892), Rabbi Yehoshua Leib Diskin asked Reb Hirsh Michel to succeed his father as the head of the Suvalk Kollel. This placed him in a dilemma. The very notion of accepting a public position that required so much social interaction was contrary to his chosen way of life. On the other hand, how could he refuse Reb Yehoshua Leib? Reb Hirsh Michel secretly engaged ten men to join him at the *Kosel Hama'aravi*. There they prayed fervently that Reb Yehoshua Leib would retract his offer.

Reb Hirsh Michel guarded even his most ordinary actions from the public eye — whether on his way to perform a *mitzvah*, or simply going to the *Kosel*. Every *Erev Rosh Chodesh* after *Maariv*, Reb Hirsh Michel walked to *Kever Rochel*, in Bethlehem. He would arrive before midnight, and at *Chatzos* he would say the entire *Tehillim*, and then return to Jerusalem in time for the sunrise *minyan*, showing no signs of exhaustion.

One *Erev Rosh Chodesh*, Reb Hirsh Michel allowed a young man to accompany him, on the condition that no one else join them. They were engaged in a deep discussion of *mussar* until they encountered another man, also going to *Kever Rochel*. Reb Hirsh

---

* Reb Hirsh Michel viewed *the Rama's* ruling (*Yoreh De'ah* 246), that one may not worry about the morrow, as the very fountain of Jewish life.

Michel dropped back, allowing the other two to continue ahead. After a ways, the young man noticed that Arabs were hurling rocks at Reb Hirsh Michel. He ran to Reb Hirsh Michel's aid, and apologized profusely for leaving him behind: "I had no choice," he pleaded. "The man who joined us is a stranger from abroad. It seemed appropriate to befriend him."

"You behaved properly," Reb Hirsh Michel responded, "but the *mitzvah* didn't require my involvement. Had I remained, I would have had to interrupt my thoughts every minute to answer his questions about, 'What is this?' and, 'What is that?' — I would have violated Rabbi Yaakov's ruling, (*Avos* 3:7) He who is walking by the way and studies, and interrupts his study and exclaims: 'How beautiful is this tree!' 'How fine that field!' — forfeits his life! Therefore, I never travel with strangers." . . . because when was Reb Hirsh Michel *not* studying on the way?

◆§ Secret Man of Letters

Reb Hirsh Michel maintained the same secrecy in his writings as he did in his private life. He was determined to publish his manuscripts, which he considered to contain genuine Torah truths. He felt supported by an omen: His entire cellar was once gutted by a fire, save a large box of his works. Yet, they had to be published anonymously. Even then, he rewrote them for publication quoting extensively from *Rishonim* and *Acharonim* to make his original appear as if it were simply an anthology.

> *Leaders of the Sephardi kehillah once approached Reb Hirsh Michel for a letter encouraging the saying of Tikun Chatzos. He produced a major treatise, outstanding in brilliance and fear of Heaven. How did he protect his identity? By writing the entire manuscript in Rashi script so that the courier would neither understand it nor be able to trace its origin.*

> *To further disguise his authorship, Reb Hirsh Michel quoted verbatim from numerous Sephardi seforim throughout the book. He also saw to it that the text of the Tikun Chatzos was printed together with his work, so he could entitle the volume "Tikun Chatzos" — and exclude the author's name.*

Several *seforim* were steered into Reb Hirsh Michel's hands before publication. He wrote detailed, lengthy addenda and corrections to them, which were published in conjunction with the original work without the author or the public ever finding out who was behind it.

Another example of his distaste for recognition was in 5659 (1899), when two brothers in Bombay sent a query to Rabbi Y. S. Alishar of Jerusalem: They were fighting over an inheritance and would only accept a ruling decided by the "Chacham Bashi," chief rabbinical authority. Rav Alishar refused to issue a decision unless Reb Hirsh Michel would attach his signature to the responsa. The overly modest Reb Hirsh Michel finally agreed to help the brothers — signing the document simply: "Tzvi ben Yaakov."

◄§ A Painful Departure — in Kedushah

The last six years of Reb Hirsh Michel's life were plagued with a painful, debilitating disease ... On Thursday, 9 Elul, 5666 (1906), after saying *Tikun Chatzos*, Reb Hirsh Michel returned home, very weak. He tried to prepare himself for the morning prayers — to no avail. In exhaustion, Reb Hirsh Michel collapsed.

He awoke just as the first streams of light diffused over *Har Habayis* — the Temple Mount. His attendants had just arrived and he motioned for them to don him in his *tallis* and *tefillin*. Reb Hirsh Michel tried to concentrate so that he could pray at sunrise as usual, but he could barely move his lips. Somehow, he mustered the strength and even stood for the *Shemoneh Esrei*.

After *davening*, an attendant brought him a drink of water, but he could not even murmur the blessing. He motioned to the attendant to say the *brachah* and he drew the cup to his lips. After numerous attempts, it was clear that he was not able to swallow.

Early that Thursday morning, every yeshivah and Talmud Torah in *Battei Machseh* was storming the gates of Heaven with their prayers and *Tehillim*, and delegations were dispatched to all of the holy places to offer prayers on Reb Hirsh Michel's behalf.

By Friday his flagging condition deteriorated even more. At *shacharis*, a *shamash* had to turn the pages of the *siddur* for him.

As evening approached, his attendants changed his clothing into the all-white apparel he customarily wore on *Shabbos*. Although literally on his deathbed, he somehow gathered the stamina to pray standing up for the first three and the last three blessings of the Friday night *Shemoneh Esrei*.

After *davening*, his students carried him to the dining table where someone made *Kiddush* for him. He made several unsuccessful attempts at tasting the wine. At *"Hamotzi,"* Reb Hirsh Michel could not even move his teeth. They tried dipping bread crumbs into the soup so that it would be easy to swallow — but this also was of no avail. Desperate to perform at least one *mitzvah* at the *Shabbos* table, Reb Hirsh Michel gestured for his *siddur.* At every Sabbath meal he sang *Askinu Seudasa:* "Prepare the feast of perfect faith ... prepare the feast of the king ... this is the feast of ... the Presence ... come feast with it ... " He glanced into the *siddur* for a few seconds, his eyes welled with tears and then hinted for them to carry him back to bed.

Shabbos morning Reb Hirsh Michel remained in bed asking for neither his *tallis* nor his *siddur.* Everyone in Jerusalem now knew how serious the situation was ... After *Shabbos* he gathered his last ounce of faltering strength and gestured, to make his last will. Those present could not understand what he wanted, and this afflicted Reb Hirsh Michel with even more pain.

Sunday morning, *Parshas Ki Savo,* a doctor examined him and summoned his students. All of Jerusalem poured into *Battei Machseh.* A *chazan* led the crowd in responsive *Tehillim* on behalf of the *Yerushalaimer Tzaddik,* while *minyanim* were dispatched to the *Kosel* and other sacred places.

After hours of *Tehillim,* the *chazan* suddenly fell silent. The sea of humanity started breaking into waves to allow an old man wearing a black silk robe to get through. Ninety-year-old Rabbi Shmuel Salant, the venerable *Rav* of Jerusalem, who no longer set foot out of his own house, had also come to participate in the prayers. Reb Shmuel instructed those present to join him in changing Reb Hirsh Michel's name to "Yehoshua Tzvi Michel Chaim." "O trustful Healer, send recovery and compassion, kindness and mercy to the poor spirit and soul of Yehoshua Tzvi Michel Chaim ben Raitzeh Golda ... Even if it has been decreed ... that he die from this illness, changing his name can alter the decree. He is no longer who he was; just as his name was changed so also may his verdict be changed ... *me'attah va'ad olam, Amen selah!"* But it was too late.

Yerushalayim's greatest scholars and *tzaddikim* had all crowded into the Shapiro home. With broken hearts and unmatched fervor they said *Shir Hama'alos* as their tears drowned out their cracked voices. With the awful realization that they were losing their master, they cried out *"Shema Yisroel!"* ... *"Hashem Hu*

HaElokim" — "Aleinu leshabei'ach" — At high noon the sun dimmed, and the great light of Israel was extinguished.

On 12 Elul, 5666 (1906), the Sephardi and Ashkenazi Rabbis issued a moratorium on work in Jerusalem, and all yeshivos and chadorim were dismissed, to attend the tzaddik's funeral.

◄§ Key to Greatness

While preparing Reb Hirsh Michel's body for burial a strange copper key was discovered in his hand. No one had ever seen it before or had any idea which door it unlocked.

One person present remembered that when Chacham Sasson Persaido, the head of Beit Kel Chassidim Yeshivah died, a similar copper key was found in his hand. "Rav Nachum Levi of Shadik," someone else recalled, "also had such a key on his body when he passed away." But then, too, its significance was a mystery.

When Rabbi Shmuel Salant later made a condolence visit to the Shapiro home, he felt obliged to reveal exactly how great a loss Jewry has suffered with Reb Hirsh Michel's passing: "When the holy Rav Nachum of Shadik came across the Midrash that says that there is a special hidden place on earth where G-d moans His exiled Kingdom, he began to cry. If the Almighty has a specific place to weep over the galus, then certainly we too should designate a secret place to pray for the restoration of the Divine Kingdom.

"Adjacent to the Spring of Shiloach, where Rabbi Yishmael the High Priest used to immerse himself, is a skeleton structure within two inner courtyards, hidden from the public eye. Reb Nachum designated this ruin to be the hiding place of Yerushlayim shel Ma'alah and had a locksmith prepare a lock that could be opened by special copper keys. These keys were entrusted to a group of men who had sanctified their bodies and purified their sight from an early age. In all of Yerushalayim shel Ma'alah, only thirteen tzaddikim were deemed worthy of possessing such keys, and Rav Yehoshua Tzvi Michel Shapiro was the most deserving of all!"

Rabbi Nosson Scherman

The Steipler Gaon

*Perspectives
and Dimensions
of Greatness
in Torah*

Rabbi Yaakov Yisroel Kanievsky
5659/1899—5745/1985

✥§ Perspectives on Greatness

I N ALL GENERATIONS *there are people of supreme holiness upon
whom Divine Inspiration (ruach hakodesh) rests, as the Sages
say, "The World has not less than thirty-six tzaddikim who accept
the Divine Presence (Shechina) every day" (Succa 45). This means
to say that they cling to Him, Blessed be His Name, so that His
Presence rests upon them. Thus we have sensed clearly that in all
generations, even in the generations not long before ours, there have
been holy and pure people who have merited Divine Inspiration
such as the Gaon Reb Yehoshua Leib Diskin of the Holy City,
Jerusalem. There were many others, but it is impossible to specify
any lest it be taken as a slight against other righteous and holy
people who were omitted. All this is part of the kindness of Hashem
Yisborach, in order to strengthen the hearts of our brethren, the
Children of Israel, toward perfect faith and toward His service.*

(The Steipler Gaon in *Chayei Olam* I ch. 30)

Had anyone suggested to Rabbi Yaakov Yisroel Kanievsky, the Steipler Gaon, that the above paragraph was an apt description of himself, he would have reacted with annoyance and derision, as he did several years ago, when an American *rosh yeshivah* consulted him concerning a matter of vital importance to his yeshivah. The Steipler protested that he was unqualified to respond. The *rosh yeshivah* pointed to the line in his letter of inquiry that said, "We have no one to whom to turn except for מעלת כבוד תורתו, his Torah eminence."

The Steipler laughed and repeated mockingly, "His Torah eminence, his Torah eminence, his Torah eminence! Have I not told you I am not qualified?"

Nevertheless, he did respond, because notwithstanding his far less than exalted opinion of himself, he could not free himself of the duty of helping people who sincerely felt that they had nowhere to turn but the humble flat on Rechov Rashbam, where there sat a man so totally immersed in the study of Torah and the service of G-d that all the world looked upon him as the living embodiment of the Sages' dictum, "Israel, the Torah and the Holy One, Blessed is He, are one."

✥ Mocking His Own Greatness

Which man alive took his own greatness less seriously? In his own eyes, he was always a student, a disciple of the *Alter* of Navarodok — Rabbi Yoseif Horowitz — Rabbi Avraham Yafen and finally, the *Chazon Ish*, his brother-in-law, mentor, and the beacon he followed from the time he arrived in Bnei Brak in 1934 until his own passing fifty-one years later. In his introduction to *Kehilas Yaakov*, the brilliant series of works on most of the Talmud, he wrote — and *meant* it — that he is hopeful that students may find an occasional provocative idea in his volumes, and if so, their publication was worthwhile. He once walked through the street with a hammer to repair his son's bookcase because, as he put it, "My Chaim is a great *talmid chacham* and it would be *bitul Torah* for him to make the repair." ... To a teen-ager who wrote him bemoaning his lack of success in Torah study, the Steipler was not above writing a warm letter filled with verbal caresses, encouragement and sound, practical advice on how best to realize his potential. When he noticed a window that was stuck in Lederman's *Shul* where he prayed regularly, he brought a can of oil and lubricated it himself.

It was always a source of wonderment to him that people wanted to buy his *seforim*. He attributed their popularity to the fact that Reb Mordeche'le, the Horon-Steipler Rebbe, had blessed Reb Chaim Peretz Kanievsky that he would have a son whose Torah would illuminate the world. Said the Steipler, "If people want to buy *seforim* because of their contents, then they would not buy my *seforim* because they contain nothing of interest. But since the Horon-Steipler *Tzaddik* gave my father a blessing — who can argue with a blessing?" And because he attributed a major part of his success in Torah to the *Rebbe's* blessing, the Steipler could never display enough gratitude to the *Rebbe's* descendants.

Indeed, no one can doubt — despite his derisive and vociferous protests — that he was one of the select holy and righteous people upon whom the *Shechina* rested daily ... especially in recent years when knowledge of his awesome greatness reached the far corners of the world. The modern ear is jarred by the term "miracle worker," and the rational mind keeps distance from *mofsim*. But how else can one explain the Steipler's unerring eye when reviewing the hundreds of *kvitlach* — slips of paper with a Hebrew name and a petition on it — that were brought to him daily, requesting help, *refuah*, advice, prompting his immediate responses: "The doctor's diagnosis is wrong" ... "They already asked me last year. They'll have a child; they just shouldn't pester me." ... And sometime no response, which had its own implications. There could be no doubt that he possessed Divine Inspiration. In a sense, this in itself was supremely inspiring, for it illustrates how high a human being can rise through pure faith, total immersion in Torah study, and unquestioning devotion to every jot and tittle of the *Shulchan Aruch*.

◆§ Can We Learn from Miracle Workers?

But in another sense, there is a problem here. For although we revere and marvel at miracle workers and possessors of *ruach hakodesh*, there is little we can learn from them. If we read the Steipler's life as page after page of miracles, blessings, and insights far beyond our ability to comprehend, much less emulate, then we deprive ourselves of the *lessons* of his life, for *we* are so far from Divine Inspiration that we do not even dream of aspiring to possess it.

To speak of the Steipler primarily in those terms is to miss the point, for his life has much to teach us, *every one of us*, in most practical terms. Instead of looking for miracles, we should look for the Jew behind the miracle, and the values that made him what he was. We find them in the stories, in his writings, and in the themes he stressed over and over and over again in his advice and counsel.

Faith in G-d and in the complete, unalterable truth of the Torah — to the Steipler this was the basis of everything. He urged constantly that all Jews eschew speculations and develop their faith in G-d and knowledge of Torah. He recognized, of course, that people could have problems of *emuna* and would have to seek answers in such classics as the writings of Rav Saadia Gaon, *Rambam*, *Kuzari*, and Rav Samson Raphael Hirsch, or in discussions with contemporary thinkers. But he saw this as akin to treatment for a disease. Good health is preferable to open-heart surgery. So is firm faith in the word of G-d infinitely preferable to heroic treatment to repair the spiritual maladies brought on by doubt.

Torah study and Torah knowledge are the prime lifelong privileges and responsibilities of every Jew. The Steipler's only love was the Torah and it was a love that he pursued endlessly, tirelessly for twenty and thirty hours without eating or sleeping. He could not countenance claims that someone had not been successful in his studies and therefore should close his *Gemora*: Someday the Heavenly Court will ask everyone what he has learned and how much he tried. Ultimately, his success will be measured not by his peers but by his Maker. If so, why despair? The goal is to do one's *own* best — and to do it constantly. He counseled study and review, not an infatuation with *chiddushim* — novellae. Let one study and review tractate after tractate, and the *chiddushim* will not only be a natural outgrowth of great knowledge, they will be true.

Torah is the source of all knowledge and cosmic power. The human being who makes himself one with the Torah simultaneously gains knowledge and understanding of breathtaking scope. Small wonder, therefore, that the Steipler, like the *Chazon Ish* before him, could advise on every manner of question. In his incredible modesty he denied any special powers, and he was right. It was not the human being named Kanievsky who was superior, it was the Torah that he had made one with himself.

He was totally unselfish. Whether in showing gratitude to the offspring of the *Rebbe* who blessed him or responding to human needs, he was a servant not only of the lofty and impersonal concept of *Klal Yisroel*, but of insignificant, ordinary Jews.

Once, during his last few years, he had been bedridden all day.

Not until nearly midnight was he able to begin seeing the people who had been waiting several hours to seek his advice and blessing. After about half an hour, the Steipler burst out in anguish, "All day I could not learn. Even now, people come and keep me from my learning." The pain of a man torn from his *Gemora* was palpable and agonizing. The waiting visitors felt uncomfortable and began to disperse. But the Steipler would not let them. They had waited for him and he must see them.

As a teen-ager he had sacrificed his health and risked his life to build Novarodok yeshivos in Communist Russia and as a venerable sage he devoted himself to his people in other ways. All his life he balanced his love for Torah with his duty to its people. Because he did both with utter devotion to the will of G-d, he succeeded in both.

The Steipler will remain with us if we permit his teachings and example to live on. Some of us can learn from the books of his Torah heritage; all of us can learn from the book of his life. "The righteous are greater in death than in life," because the shock of their loss awakens us to what they had to tell us. Let us, therefore, glean his teachings and incorporate them into our lives and those of our children.

If we do, then in the words of the Horon-Steipler *Tzaddik's* blessing, the son of Reb Chaim Peretz and Bracha Kanievsky will continue to illuminate the world with his Torah.

Rabbi Eliyahu Meir Klugman

The Steipler Gaon:
Dimensions of a Torah Personality

Rabbi Meir said: Whoever engages in Torah study for its own sake merits many things; furthermore, [the creation of] the entire world is worthwhile for his sake alone. He is called, "Friend, Beloved." He loves the Omnipresent, he loves [His] creatures, he gladdens the Omnipresent, he gladdens [His] creatures. [The Torah] clothes him in humility and fear [of G-d]; it makes him fit to be righteous, devout, fair and faithful. It moves him away from sin and draws him near to merit. From him people enjoy counsel and wisdom, I am understanding, mine is strength. [The Torah] gives him kingship and dominion and analytical judgment; the secrets of the Torah are revealed to him; he becomes like a steadily strengthening fountain and like an unceasing river. He becomes modest, patient, and forgiving of insult to himself. [The Torah] makes him great and exalts him above all things.

THE TRUE ESSENCE of the Steipler — the great *gaon* and *tzaddik* of our generation — is beyond our grasp. The best a writer can do is present some anecdotes, sayings, and incidents from his life, and show how they illustrate a few of the dimensions that Rabbi Meir, in *Avos* 6:1, attributes to him who learns Torah *lishmo* (for its own sake).

Reb Yaakov Yisroel was born on 9 Tammuz 5659 (1899) in the town of Horon-Steipel, Russia, to Reb Chaim Peretz Kanievsky, a Chernobler *chassid* and his wife Bracha. Reb Chaim Peretz died when Yaakov Yisroel was but seven years old. Food was scarce in their home, so when students of the Novarodok Yeshivah were scouting for *talmidim*, his mother sent him with them saying, "Let him go and learn ... and he'll have food to eat as well."

He celebrated his *bar mitzvah* in the yeshivah — alone; he received a pair of *tefillin*, said a Torah discourse and returned to his studies. When he was eighteen the *Alter* of Novarodok sent him to head the yeshivah in Rogatshov. A short time later he was drafted into the Red Army. After his discharge, he joined his Novarodok comrades in trying to found yeshivos under the Communists, but when that became impossible, he crossed over to Poland and studied in the main Novarodok Yeshivah in Bialystok. There, in 1925, he published his first *sefer, Shaarei Tevuna*. In his pocket he kept *haskamos* (approbations) from Rabbi Chaim Ozer Grodzensky of Vilna, Rabbi Menachem Ziemba and the Ostrovtzer; he did not include them in the *sefer* because he lacked money to cover the additional printing costs.

The *sefer* came into the hands of the *Chazon Ish* in Vilna, who upon reading it decided that Reb Yaakov Yisroel was eminently suited as a husband for his sister Miriam. Many years later the *Chazon Ish* told someone, "When my faculties were sharp I was able to read *chiddushei Torah* and deduce the level of the author's *yiras Shomayim* — his fear of Heaven. It was on this basis that I selected the *Rosh Yeshivah* (as he always referred to the Steipler) to be my brother-in-law." After his wedding he became a *maggid shiur* in the Novarodok Yeshivah in Pinsk.

In 1934, at the urging of the *Chazon Ish*, he moved to *Eretz Yisroel*, and assumed the position of *Rosh Yeshivah* of the Novarodok Yeshivah in Bnei Brak. After a number of years the Yeshivah closed and he went to learn every day in *Kollel Chazon Ish* — a post-graduate-level yeshivah. He assisted the Chazon Ish in heading the *kollel* and assumed its leadership after the *Chazon Ish* passed away. He said *shiurim* regularly, but, with advancing years, their frequency decreased until he said a *shiur* but once a year, on the *Yahrzeit* of the *Chazon Ish*.

> *Rabbi Meir said, "Whoever studies Torah*
> *for its own sake merits many things."*

The Steipler's remarkable dedication to Torah study was evident in his *hasmada*, his unceasing toil in Torah, which was *the* hallmark of his personality from early youth until his passing. His *mitzvos, kedusha, prishus* — his personal piety — all found their roots in his Torah *lishmo*. Those who studied under him in Novarodok recall that he would not eat in people's houses as would the other students because of the precious time lost from learning while walking to their houses. Instead, the meals were brought to him in the *beis midrash*. If his meal didn't arrive he would study in hunger, as he would not take the time to find a meal. In his youth, he was known for regularly going amazingly long stretches without sleep, and even in his old age he would never sleep more than three hours a night.

A public figure once wanted to discuss some community matters with him in privacy. He was told to come in the middle of the night. When he entered the room, the Steipler was engrossed in learning. Not wishing to disturb him, the visitor sat and waited. It was close to two hours before the Steipler realized that someone was in the room, so involved was he in his studies.

Indeed, the picture in the mind's eye of tens of thousands of people who came from all over the world to consult with him will always be that of the figure hunched over a *sefer* in that small, *seforim*-lined room on Rechov Rashbam 10, learning yet a bit more before receiving the next visitor — even snatching moments of Torah study between questions from the same person.

He once had difficulty understanding a *Mishna* in *Mikvaos* and as a result did not eat a meal for three days. Only when he finally understood the difficult *sugya* (topic) did he partake of food. He learned Torah in his every waking moment — and always, always, in dire poverty, often owning but one suit of clothes.

The *Rambam* in *Hilchos Talmud Torah* that he quotes in his *Birkas Peretz* perhaps describes him best: "The words of Torah do not endure with one who is feeble in his efforts nor with those who learn in comfort and indulge themselves with food and drink. They endure only with one who gives his life for them [i.e., words of Torah] and continually makes his body suffer, does not give sleep to his eyes ..." The Steipler explains *inter alia*, "Each and every pain and difficulty that a person suffers for Torah, every effort expended in learning Torah does not go to waste. As a result one will be rewarded with the acquisition of Torah and its understanding, in one area or another ... Therefore he who studies Torah in anguish and pain will merit that his Torah will endure."

"... lishmo — for its own sake ..."

In a letter to a *bachur* he writes, "The Ben Torah will not be successful unless his entire aspiration is the Torah alone, i.e., to grow in Torah and *yiras Shomayim*. If there are additional reasons for learning, even though they seem to be subordinate to your main ambition of becoming proficient in Torah, it will be impossible to be truly successful ...

"... he loves the Omnipresent ..."

His love of G-d was manifested in his fastidious devotion to His commands, the *mitzvos,* and the joy with which he performed them.

U.S.S.R. 1920: In the Russian Army, Reb Yaakov Yisroel refused to violate the *Shabbos.* After one such incident, his commander punished him by making him run the gauntlet between two rows of soldiers beating him as he ran through. No one would have ever known the story if he hadn't mentioned it years later to his Rebbetzin. "Never," he told her, "never did I experience such pleasure as when I was getting beaten for keeping *Shabbos.*"

A friend of this writer, a grandson of the *Kochav M'Yaakov* (father of the Tshebiner *Rav*), once visited the Steipler. He returned a few weeks later and again mentioned that he was a grandson of the *Kochav M'Yaakov.* The Steipler said, "Wait. Perhaps you know other grandchildren of his in Jerusalem. One of them was here a few weeks ago — he left something here."

He went to the other room and returned with a bag upon which he had written, "Left here by a grandson of the *Kochav M'Yaakov.*" My friend opened the bag and realized it was his own scarf which he had unwittingly left there a few weeks before, and said so to the Steipler. The Steipler thereupon took the bag from him and recited, "I am hereby prepared to fulfill the *mitzva* of *hashovas aveida,* returning a lost article, as is written in Your Torah ..." and proceeded to say all the relevant verses in the Torah. Then with a broad smile and a hearty *yasher koach,* he returned the bag to its owner.

A young man in Bnei Brak used to type the handwritten manuscripts of *Kehilos Yaakov* to be submitted to the printer. Late one winter night the typist heard a knock on his door, and found the Steipler standing there. The young man was taken aback — did he make some grievous typing error? "I came to pay you for today's work," said the Steipler. "You left the papers at my house when I wasn't home, so I came now."

"But I specifically told you when I accepted the job that it is not necessary for you to pay me right away."

"True," said the Steipler, "you wanted to be sure that I wouldn't transgress the prohibition against delaying payment to a worker even overnight; but what about the positive commandment I have of *'beyomo'* — paying a worker on the very same day?"

"... loves His creatures ... and gladdens them ..."

In *Birkas Peretz* the Steipler explains that *Yaakov Avinu* retained the name Yaakov even though he was subsequently called Yisroel, because each name represents different aspects of *Klal Yisroel* — each is of equal importance. These two dimensions aptly describe the two complementary facets of the Steipler's personality. He was Yaakov Yisroel: On the one hand, Yisroel who "struggled with *Elokim*" — whose entire life was involvement in the Divine. And he was Yaakov, in its meaning of *eikev* — the heel of a person, a person of simplicity with earthly dimensions (see *Nefesh Hachayim* on *Yaakov chevel nachalaso*), living with people as a person — possessing an unparalleled insight into the human condition, not hesitating to get involved in a person's lowliest and most earthly problems (see his various letters).

For many years he was *Chasan Torah* in Lederman's *Shul* on Simchas Torah, and he would give a *kiddush* in his house after *davening*. Every year when Simchas Torah was over, he would take off his *kapote*, don an apron and spend the next few hours washing every dish and cleaning every table until the house was spotless. "Just because I make a *simcha* doesn't mean that the household has to suffer." He would then study through the night to compensate for time lost from learning. This he did after every Simchas Torah until the last few years of his life, when it became physically impossible.

His was the broad shoulder upon which thousands would cry. He would console and comfort people from all walks of life, most of whom he did not even know. He took each supplicant's problem personally, and seemed to experience it with him.

Every night before he went to sleep he would say a few chapter of *Tehillim* and *daven* for the sufferings and troubles of his people, and especially for all those who had requested that he *daven* for them. Family members would find him late at night crying bitterly and praying brokenheartedly for those in need.

One of the people close to him once moved about some of the scores of *kvitlach* on the table. The Steipler told him, "Don't look at them. You won't be able to stand it. People have so many troubles, one has to be made of steel to be able to listen to all the suffering people tell me about."

He would often tell people who came to him with their worries, "You're complaining about difficulties? One *may* not take this world to heart. You should know, I had a difficult life. There were times when there was simply no food in the house. We would make *Shabbos* on black bread. In the Novarodok Yeshiva in Bnei Brak I had everything. Torah, *mussar, yiras Shomayim.* The Yeshiva gave me everything, except for one — *salary.*

"I had so much pain in raising children.* I had a son-in-law, a jewel (Reb Shaul Burzan); he was taken from me, and in addition, it was my task to support them all. From the age of seven I was orphaned. Believe me, I had so many reasons to take *Olam Hazeh* to heart and to remain a complete *am ha'aretz* — ignorant of Torah. But *Hakadosh Baruch Hu* had pity on me and helped me not to take this world too seriously. Please, please, don't take this world to heart."

He often borrowed money on his own responsibility to give to people sorely in need, incurring many debts of this nature. He would send money in ingenious and untraceable ways to people who would be embarrassed to accept their barest necessities from others.

" ... The Torah clothes him in humility ..."

"Why do people come to me? I don't know. I guess it's because they know I'm an old man and I'm always home, so why not? Someone else might not be home."

He never permitted anyone to serve him: "You probably learned *halachos* at some point in your life. One may not allow himself to be served by a *baal halacha.*"

One *Erev* Rosh Hashanah he told his family, "On Rosh Hashanah every person looks for some merit or good deed with which he can face his Creator. What can *I* say? I have accomplished nothing. I must find something. Tomorrow I will let them take me to Lederman's. When people will see an old man *davening* — admittedly, not as loudly as is proper; still, when they see a broken old man who comes to *daven* even though according to the *din* he is exempt from coming to *shul*, it is an inspiration. When I was small and saw an old man *davening*, it made a powerful impression on me. At least then I will have something with which to face *Hashem.*"

---

* Today each is outstanding in his own right. His son, Hagaon Rabbi Chaim Kanievsky, is widely recognized for his many *seforim* including the very popular *Shoneh Halachos* and, recently, *Derech Emunah*, a *Mishnah Berurah* type of work on laws of *Zeraim*, where he codifies and explains the *halachos* relating to the Laws of the Land.

"... and fear of G-d ..."

His fear of G-d was evident in his *yiras cheit* — fear of sin — which was legendary. He was once about to drink a glass of tea, when someone sitting next to him mentioned that there was a fly in the drink. He couldn't sleep the entire night, he said, because he realized that if that person hadn't been there to tell him, he could have ingested a forbidden insect.

Those who knew him from his days in Bialystok tell of the time there was a loud discussion in the *beis midrash*. Picking up his head from the *Gemora*, he was told that some thought that jacket linings might possibly contain *shaatnez* (forbidden mixture of wool and linen). Without another word he tore the lining out of his jacket and resumed learning as if nothing had happened.

One *Shabbos* in his later years he was walking home from *shul* when it started to pour. He sat down on a bench on Rechov Rashbam and called over a child and requested him to help him remove his shoes and socks. He then put on the shoes and continued home. He had a hole in his shoes and was afraid that by walking he would squeeze out water from his socks, which is forbidden.

He dozed off in the middle of his first encounter with his future wife, Miriam, sister of the *Chazon Ish*. The latter, who had arranged the match, was naturally upset and asked him why this happened. Reb Yaakov Yisroel explained that his current routine was to learn for thirty hours at a stretch and then to sleep for six. Since he was coming by train (a six-hour trip) where it would anyway be difficult to learn, he decided to study the thirty hours before the trip and sleep for the six-hour train ride. When he boarded the train, however, and saw the upholstered seats, he was afraid that they might contain *shaatnez*, so he stood for the duration of the trip, and thus had not slept the previous thirty-six hours.

He considered *mussar* vital to his spiritual well-being, and learned it every day of his life. When he sat *shiva* for his mother, he asked the *Chazon Ish* if he was permitted to learn *mussar* during the *shiva* even though it is Torah, which is normally forbidden. The *Chazon Ish* replied in the affirmative.

"... and it makes him fit to be righteous, devout, fair and faithful ..."

The Steipler once appeared at a *bar mitzvah* uninvited. He walked up to the *bar mitzvah* boy, sat down next to him and spoke to him for a minute. The family and guests were astounded. He hadn't been invited and hardly knew the family. — And what did he say to the boy? The *bar mitzva* boy later explained that several years earlier, the Steipler hasd seen him walk into Lederman's *Shul* on Yom Kippur with a large *sefer* in his hand. He had gone over to him and said, "*Yingel,* today we *daven,* not learn." The boy replied that it was not a *Gemora* but rather a large-size *machzor*. The Steipler had then made it his business to find out when the boy would be *bar mitzvah,* because as a minor he could not grant *mechilah* — forgiveness — for having been misjudged. He found out when and where the *bar mitzvah* was being celebrated so he could ask for forgiveness at the first possible opportunity.

There were times when he smoked, but never during the *shmittah* Sabbatical year, when there were halachic questions about using Israeli tobacco. Someone once asked him, "Doesn't it bother you not to smoke during *shmittah?*"

"*Shmittah* to me," he replied, "is like *Shabbos.* I simply don't need it."

When in the Russian Army, he once drew guard duty in the sub-zero Russian winter. The Army provided a special greatcoat for those on outside duty, but Reb Yaakov Yisroel was not sure that the collar did not contain *shaatnez*. While it is forbidden to wear *shaatnez,* not to wear the coat in such frigid weather was *pikuach nefesh,* a matter of life or death, which overrules the prohibition of *shaatnez.* He concluded that if he did not put on the coat for the first ten minutes his life would not be in danger. After that . . . he then said to himself. "I won't die from another ten minutes," and so he passed the entire night "just ten minutes more" until he was relieved from guard duty. As a result, however, his inner ear was irreparably damaged, and he became progressively more hard of hearing as he grew older.

Someone once quoted a thought from the *Kochav MiYaakov* to him. He commented, "I have the *sefer*. I bought it many years ago from a man selling old *seforim* on Rechov Allenby in Tel Aviv. When I came home I realized that he had undercharged me: he probably was not aware of the *sefer's* value. So I went back to find him but he wasn't there anymore, so I've never used it."

". . . it draws him away from sin . . ."

The Steipler only accepted money from a select few. One of this group once received a substantial sum for the Steipler from someone who was himself penniless. This recipient surmised that the source of the money was a relative of the donor, a notorious *apikores*. The money was put together with other sums and brought to the Steipler before *Yom Tov* with no comment as to its source. After *Yom Tov* the Steipler's daughter returned a portion of the money: "My father says he doesn't need it." The amount returned corresponded to the penny with the amount received from the questionable source.

"... From him people enjoy counsel and wisdom ..."

Thousands of people knocked at his door for advice on every question imaginable: the yeshiva *bochur* for a *derech halimud* (methodology in Talmudic study), the businessman with a financial question, the communal *askan* on a *klal* issue, the *rosh yeshiva* regarding a policy matter in his institution, the *rebbi* with a *chinuch* query, the layman with a medical question, and all for a *bracha* or a *tefilla* for success in their endeavors. Each person went away with the feeling that he had consulted this generation's *Urim V'tumim* (the *Kohein Gadol's* breast-plate, which furnished answers to queries posed by *Klal Yisroel*). Often no answer was also an answer ... Whether or not one fully understood the reasoning behind the counsel proferred, one did not question its value.

There are countless stories of a reply or a remark by the Steipler that seemed to be at variance with popular thinking or not in consonance with the petitioner's knowledge of the situation under question. But סוד השם ליראיו — "the secrets of *Hashem* and of His universe are with those who truly fear Him." Ultimately his counsel proved correct.

From where comes the ability of one individual to give advice and counsel on the vast variety of problems the world has to offer? And how does one explain the fact that when he said something that appeared to be in contradiction with the facts, he was invariably correct?

The Sages teach that an unborn infant is taught the entire Torah and has the spiritual power to "see" from one end of the universe to the other. Before birth, this Torah knowledge is taken from him. Why only the Torah knowledge? Why is he not also deprived of his *other* spiritual gift, the ability to be all-knowing? The answer is simple: All spiritual accomplishment derives from the Torah. Take away the embryo's Torah and all other knowledge disappears with it. On the other hand, the person who imbibes

Torah, absorbs Torah, and becomes unified with Torah, becomes remarkably knowledgeable of the world. With the regaining (to some extent) of the prenatal status of vast Torah wisdom comes the accompanying ability to "see" all that the universe encompasses.*

..." *Eitza*" refers to counsel in non-spiritual matters. After the passing of a Bnei Brak resident in Tammuz 5739/1979, his widow found among his papers a note that read: "Be sure to say *Yom Kippur Kattan* — the special penitential prayers." Upon seeing this, the widow became very agitated, and asked her son what he knew about the note. She added that on *Rosh Chodesh Tammuz* evening, her husband had omitted *Yaaleh Veyavo* from the *bentching*. She had stopped him in the middle and reminded him that it was *Rosh Chodesh*. He blanched and for a few moments was unable to continue. When his wife asked him what was the matter, he replied that he had forgotten to recite *Yom Kippur Katan* that day. She was puzzled. "It's an optional prayer — it's not like forgetting to *daven* or *bentch*," she said.

The husband did not reply ... That month he passed away.

The son explained that a number of years before, two brothers of the deceased has died at a young age. He had sent his son to the Steipler to ask what to do so that no harm befall him. The Steipler advised him to say the *Yom Kippur Kattan* prayers every month. For many years the husband made sure to say it regularly; this was the first time he had forgotten ...

He once proposed a match to a man who was divorced because he was incapable of having children. The woman, however, could bear children. The prospective husband protested that it was not fair to her. "Don't worry," the Steipler replied, "you will have children."

A while later the husband reported to the Steipler that this wife was suffering from various pains. "*Baruch Hashem*," the Steipler said, "she's expecting."

"But it's impossible for me to have children and the pains have no connection to pregnancy," protested the husband.

"*Baruch Hashem*, she's expecting," the Steipler persisted.

The wife underwent tests, which proved negative. "What do they know," said the Steipler. "*Baruch Hashem*, she's with child."

The following week she underwent another examination and the results were positive.

---

* Based on an explanation given by the late Satmar Rebbe to Rabbi Leib Mallin and Rabbi Moshe Shisgal.

The flashes of insight he evinced when perusing a *kvittel* were often astounding.*

On a number of occasions he was given a *kvittel* with a request to pray that someone be blessed with children. This writer is aware of cases where he refused to bless specific names on the list. "He doesn't keep family purity; I won't give him a *brachah*" " — and he was invariably right. One such person who had sent a *kvittel* with a neighbor from the United States was so shaken by the Steipler's awareness of this from merely looking at his name that he became a *baal teshuva*.

A student at a well-known Jerusalem yeshiva went to the Steipler for a blessing a few days before his upcoming nuptials. Upon reading the *kvittel*, the Steipler asked him, "Who will be officiating at your wedding — your *mesader kedushin?*"

"My *Rosh Yeshiva*," the boy replied.

"Please tell him that I must see him immediately."

When the *Rosh Yeshiva* came, the Steipler asked him, "How do you permit a Jewish girl to marry a non-Jewish boy?" The *Rosh Yeshiva* thought that perhaps he had not heard him correctly. The Steipler repeated the question. Thereupon he investigated the matter and it turned out that the boy's mother had converted to Judaism many years before, when the boy was an infant. Her conversion was not valid for the son, so he had remained a non-Jew.

There are many similar stories. An explanation? We have none ... other than the few paragraphs from *Chayei Olam* that were quoted from the introductory section.

"... toshiya — spiritual counsel ..."

Yeshivah *bachurim* and *kollel yungeleit* would often ask for advice on how to succeed in their studies or for guidance when they felt that their learning was not up to par. He would tell many *bachurim*, "You're depressed, and I'll tell you why: because you learn to gain recognition. You have to learn for one reason only: This world is like a marketplace of sixty, seventy years duration. Afterwards you will come to a world where nothing, nothing at all has value. Not money, not honors, not family nor lineage. Only *blatt*

---

* Rabbi Elchonon Wasserman remarked that the Chofetz Chaim somehow knew whatever he needed to know about each person who came to see him. The Brisker Rav explained that the Chofetz Chaim devoted his entire life to be *mezakeh es harabim* — inspire others to righteousness — which merits access to the requisite knowledge for the task. In his old age it was no longer possible for him to gather all necessary information for each person, so *Hashem* provided him with the required information to continue his work.

Gemora and hours (spent learning) have value there. It is as if you come to a country where all of your cash is worthless. You could have been wealthy in your hometown, but over there all your riches are useless. The only currency is *blatt* and hours [learned]."

He would be asked for advice on the entire gamut of problems that troubled *Bnei Torah*. In a letter he writes:

"The main remedy ... is to toil at Torah study even when one has no desire (to learn) and when worried. Also to pray to *Hashem* that He should protect you from any transgression. Everything you wrote about your depression will disappear completely if you learn diligently for five years without paying any attention, even if it seems as if you are not as happy as your friends. (In truth, every person has his own problems, even if they are not apparent to others.) Problems such as yours are common among *Bnei Torah*. They disappear completely when one becomes outstanding in Torah. The main thing is to take no notice at all of matters of prestige; ultimately you will receive recognition. You are always thinking of yourself. Your entire letter is filled with 'I, I, I,' and this is your problem. You must toil like an ox at his yoke and not think that all of life should be as you please. The present will be as it will be and the future — your standing will be assured if you will learn with *hasmada* and *daven* about what bothers you." (See *Chayei Olam*, Section II, Chapters 11 and 12 for other advice about success in learning.)

He would often tell people to learn as much *mishnayos* and *midrash* as possible with their children. "Learn it simply without any big questions, and it will enter their heads easily. As one gets older, learning becomes more difficult ... with so many questions, one hardly gets anything accomplished." He would also tell people to study *mussar* for ten minutes each day with their children.

"... wisdom ..."

A granddaughter came of age and he asked someone to find her a *shidduch*. When asked what he should look for in a *bachur*, the Steipler replied, "Look for a *seichel hayashar* (roughly, a rational mind), *hasmadah* and good character."

"What do you mean 'good character'?" that person queried. "Doesn't learning Torah make one into a *mentsch*?"

"A person who learns diligently," the Steipler replied, "has as his best friend his *shtender* — his desk, with which he sits day and night. The *shtender* is always healthy, never asks him to throw out the garbage, never needs a kind word; so why shouldn't he be nice to it? But you don't necessarily learn good *midos* from this."

"But doesn't the Torah refine a person?"

Replied the Steipler, "If a person is unrestrained in his behavior and then settles down to study Torah, the Torah will modify his conduct, but learning Torah will not force one to be good. For that one has to work on oneself and study *mussar*."

He did not hide his impatience with older bachelors who were pursuing a fantasy — the perfectly suited mate, with good looks, brains, wealth, family, idealism . . . .

"Many times," the Steipler commented, "young men in their mid-twenties and older, cry to me, 'Where's my pre-destined *shidduch*?' I tell them, 'You met her already five years ago, but passed her by in your search for the perfect wife. She has since married someone else.' "

He would stress time and again to *yeshiva bachurim*: "A *yeshiva bachur* must be aware that *Hashem* has twenty-four hours and these hours are the currency with which one can buy greatness — in Torah, *mitzvos* and in *mussar*. Eight hours sleep is the average that one must sleep. It need not be in one stretch. Six at night and two in the day, or seven and one is also fine, each person according to his needs. Two hours a day are to be spent at *davening*, another two hours for eating and taking care of other bodily needs — altogether twelve hours. So one is left with twelve undisturbed hours net. With these twelve hours one can finish the *mesechta* every *z'man* and in five or six years finish *Mo'ed*, *Nashim*, and *Nezikin*, and then become knowledgeable in *Kadoshim*, *Taharos* and *Zera'im*. In this way one can become a *gadol b'Torah* and be proficient in the entire *Shas*. The trouble is that some learn only eight hours. The Talmudic adage, 'If you leave me [Torah] for one day I shall leave you for two,' means that if you waste four hours, then the eight that you *have* studied are canceled out. You spend your entire life in income and expense. The income of eight hours is spent through the toll of the four wasted hours and your entire life you will *earn* nothing."

He would advise married men, "You must help your wife. If you help her as much as possible and in the *kollel* you truly spend your time at study, she will be understanding, and *Hashem* will spare you unnecessary distractions."

"and strength . . ."

He devoted his days to people who came to be comforted and strengthened. He would often tell them, "I envy your suffering. It is an asset that one should not sell for all the money in the world." His words constantly encouraged the depressed and the downtrodden.

A *maggid-shiur* (lecturer) in a yeshiva once came to him with a student who had spent five years in the yeshiva apparently without success. "Perhaps," said the *Rosh Yeshiva*, "it is time for him to go to work." The Steipler turned to the boy and asked him gently, "When you entered yeshiva were you able to learn *mishnayos* on your own?"

"No," replied the boy.

"Were you able to learn *Kitzur Shulchan Aruch* when you came to yeshiva?"

"No."

"And now?"

"Yes, I can," was the answer.

The Steipler said firmly to the *Rosh Yeshiva,* "For shame! Is this called lack of success in learning? Let him stay in yeshiva and he will be successful."

". . . The Torah gives him kingship and dominion . . ."

He was the undisputed leader for a large segment of the Torah community in *Eretz Yisroel.* Because so many religious issues are intertwined with community facts of life in Israel, both religious leaders and political figures sought his counsel on countless matters.

The Steipler made it clear on numerous occasions for many years, that he viewed Agudath Israel as the sole political vehicle for accomplishing Torah goals and maintained this loyalty to Agudath Israel in the practical sense for most of his life. In a letter responding to a query several years before his passing, he wrote:

"One must vote for Agudath Israel. Aside from the call of our great contemporary rabbis to do so, we have the directive of Torah giants of the previous generations, such as Rabbi Aaron Kotler and the Gaon of Tchebin, whose views are still binding, for the situation has not changed since then . . . In addition to strengthening religion, a vote for Agudath Israel represents a powerful *Kiddush Hashem*, for it is a public declaration that the voter is a loyal servant of G-d. To endeavor to increase the vote for Row *Gimmel* (Agudath Israel) is certainly a precious *mitzva* and a great source of merit."

His dominion was not only over the rank and file of Torah Jewry, but even over its undisputed halachic decisors. Several years ago a halachic question arose as to whether one was permitted to cooperate with the census takers in Israel: Is it included in the prohibition against counting Jews? Rabbi Yoseif Shalom Eliashuv, one of the leading halachic authorities of *Eretz Yisroel*, ruled in the affirmative, but when he heard that the Steipler forbade it, he reversed himself in favor of the Steipler's opinion.

"The secrets of Torah are revealed to him,
and he becomes like a steadily strengthening fountain . . ."

The Steipler was and is literally the teacher of tens of thousands of people who study his *seforim*. The volumes of *Kehilas Yaakov*, which are studied the world over by the most eminent *Rosh Yeshiva* as well as the simple beginner, are among the very few *seforim* ever written on topics in *Shas* to achieve widespread acceptance during the author's lifetime. It brings to mind the *Pri Megadim's* assertion that if a *sefer* is very widely accepted it is conclusive evidence that its author has learned Torah *lishmo* (for its own sake).

He selected what to publish with painstaking care. He would review each chapter six or seven times before publishing, removing almost half the manuscript, in making certain to publish only what he felt was correct beyond any doubt. He would often remove more chapters in a second edition.

His *seforim* were never sold in stores — only in his house. Nor would he sell complete sets to individuals. "Why do you need a set — to fill the bookcase?" And yet there is scarcely a *yeshiva bachur* the world over who does not own and use one or more of his *seforim*.

The *Sefer Shiurim Shel Torah* discusses the measurements pertaining to various *mitzvos*. He studied the entire subject in one *bein haz'manim* (intersession) after which he wrote the *sefer*.

There are hundreds of *gematrios* in the last section of his *Birkas Peretz* on *Chumash*. These demonstrate how a saying of *Chazal* on a given *pasuk* very often contains the exact numerical equivalent of a corresponding phrase in the Torah. The Steipler once remarked that these come to him effortlessly during the Torah reading on *Shabbos*. During the following week he would check them for accuracy.

The Steipler, when he had the strength, would accept any request to act as *sandek*, holding the child at his *bris*. Asked why the

Rama's statement that being *sandek* brings one wealth did not hold true in his case, he answered that the *Rama* refers to whatever is important to the individual. "For me, it means my *seforim*."

> *". . . He becomes modest, patient*
> *and forgiving of insult . . ."*

His humility was legend. As public a person he was, his true *tzidkus* will never be known. From the little he inadvertently did reveal we can appreciate how much of his essence can never even be glimpsed.

From the Diary of a Visitor
as related by Yaakov K. to the writer

Bnei Brak, Winter 5743 (1983)

I come from Jerusalem and arrive at the Steipler's house on Rechov Rashbam 10 at 11:25 p.m. A fire had recently destroyed my house and I came to ask (as thousands did) what the Hand of Providence was pointing to. At 12 midnight about twenty people remain in the courtyard, also waiting to see him. The Steipler's daughter notifies us that there will be no more audiences tonight. The others leave. At 12:30 a.m. she tells me that she must close the outer door. I ask her if she knows of a place to sleep, and she suggests Lederman's (the Steipler's *shul*, further down Rashbam) — people learning there would take me home, she said. So I go to Lederman to spend the night.

At 1:30 a.m. the door opens and the Steipler, walking laboriously and with much difficulty, enters and walks over to me. "Come," he says, "my daughter mistakenly thought there was a question of *yichud*. We will bring a bed into my apartment."

He refuses to let me assist him as he walks quickly (for him), each breath exceedingly difficult. He collapses onto the last bench before his house and tells me to sit down next to him. After five minutes he stands up and we climb the stairs to his house. When he enters his daughter says to him, "I didn't want you to go."

He replies, "I didn't allow her to go as it is not proper for a woman to walk with a man in the street so late at night."

She tells me, "I wanted to awaken the boy who sleeps

During the lifetime of the *Chazon Ish,* the Steipler kept himself totally obscured from the public eye and subordinated himself to his illustrious brother-in-law on every matter, public or private. More recently, the mutual respect, admiration and cooperation between the Steipler and the Ponevezh Rosh Yeshiva, Rabbi Elazar Shach, was most remarkable.

When signing a public proclamation together with Rav Shach, he would insist that the latter sign first.

A woman in Bnei Brak suffering extreme pain was advised by her doctor to undergo surgery. When she asked the Steipler for his

---

with him but he didn't allow me to. He just put on his hat and went." He then sits down and takes deep ragged breaths for a few minutes. I apologize for putting him to so much trouble, to which he replies, "I didn't do anything. People think that when one gets older one is free of obligations."

In the meantime his daughter sets up a bed in the small room where he learns and receives visitors, and he brings me water for *negel vasser.* I ask if I can use the alarm clock. He replies, "Of course," and sets it for me.

At 2:10 a.m. I ask the daughter what time her father goes to sleep. She replies, "Sometimes in a little while, sometimes not at all."

After talking with me for a few minutes over a glass of warm tea he returns to his *Gemora.* "I have deficits (in learning) to make up."

At 5:30 a.m. I awake and find him already up. When I return from davening he is sitting and learning. He insists that I eat breakfast — in the room where he learns. In the middle, someone comes to speak to him. He says to me, "Sometimes people don't like others to hear when they discuss private matters with me, so I will go to the other room."

I protest, "Let *me* go to the other room."

"No," he says, "you stay here and eat. I will go to the other room."

Another person enters and the same scenario repeats itself. As a parting present he insists that I accept some money and some *seforim* ... Two days before the Steipler had refused to serve as *sandek* at a *bris* because the steps into the house were too difficult to maneuver.

---

approval, he replied, "I can't advise you to proceed. Surgery is dangerous, and the doctor's medical evidence is speculative . . . Ask Rav Shach. His *muskal rishon* — first thought — on any matter is *Daas Torah*. Do you think that when he talks to you he is not thinking in learning? Whatever he tells you is, in effect, the Torah that is talking."

They went to Rabbi Shach and told him the entire story. Rabbi Shach replied, "According to Torah law you should undergo the operation — but with one condition. Reb Yaakov Kanievsky must give you his blessing. In that case the operation will surely succeed."

With Rabbi Shach's Torah judgment bolstered by the Steipler's warm blessings, the surgery was successful. There are countless similar stories.

*"The Torah elevates him and exalts him above all things" . . .
a human being like us, yet so far beyond our perception. This
is the sum total and sole description of such a life.*

On Friday night, the twenty-third day of Av, after a month-long illness he returned his pure and righteous soul to his Creator at the age of eighty-six.

In each of the notebooks-upon-notebooks of *chiddushei Torah* written over the last forty years, he always reserved the last page for keeping a record of all his debts and loans . . . "I owe: . . . 50 to *Ma'aser*, 200 to so-an-so, . . . owes me 30, . . . etc." — a full page at the end of each notebook. A member of the family related that the last entry in the last notebook of *chiddushei Torah* reads as follows:

בס"ד, כ' תמוז – איני חייב לאיש מאומה, שבח לא-ל עליון

"20 *Tammuz:* I do not owe anyone anything. Praise G-d."

Approximately 200,000 people came in the sweltering Bnei Brak heat to the most massive funeral in *Eretz Yisroel* since the *Churban*. They were all there. The *yeshiva bachur*, the manual laborer, the *Rosh Yeshiva*, the professional, the Chassidic *Rebbe*, his followers, the Bais Yaakov student . . . businessman and *kollel* fellow, housewife and *cheder yingel*, Sefardi and Ashkenazi, male and female, young and old — they all came to honor and take leave of their father, teacher and leader, to take leave of the man the Tshebiner Rav called the *tzaddik* of their generation.

How, one wonders, did the Steipler — great as he was — become so universally respected? It is beyond our meager abilities to understand this unique phenomenon. The aforementioned *mishnah* in *Avos*, in its description of one who learns Torah *lishmo*, concludes: ומגדלתו ומרוממתו על כל המעשים — [The Torah] elevates him and exalts him above all things.

Rabbi Ezra Attia: Builder of Torah

A Sephardi Torah giant, brought up in poverty, passed on a legacy of spiritual wealth through Yeshivat Porat Yosef, which he headed for forty-five years.

Rabbi Ezra Attia
5645/1885—5730/1970

QUITE LITERALLY, Rabbi Ezra Attia built the foundations of twentieth-century Sephardic Jewry. In forty-five years as *Rosh Hayeshivah* of Yeshivat Porat Yosef, he trained thousands of *talmidim*, many of whom serve Sephardi *kehillot* in Israel, the United States, Latin America, and the Orient. They and their *talmidim* constitute the bulk of today's Sephardi Torah leadership. In a culture where only the elite engaged in full-time learning past *bar mitzvah* age, Rabbi Ezra introduced, almost single-handedly, the concept of universal higher yeshivah education, and his efforts raised the stature of the yeshivah student in the Sephardi world.

Rabbi Ezra achieved all this with extraordinary efforts and by his own personal example. His life was completely devoted to Torah; he took nothing more from this world than what he needed to sustain himself. In his years at Porat Yosef, he invariably went from morning to night with nothing more than a glass of tea for breakfast and tea with a piece of matzah for lunch. Of this, he left half the matzah uneaten. Moreover, from the way he taught Torah, his *talmidim* learned a unique perspective and a way of life.

✒️ The Aleppian Way

Rabbi Ezra Attia was born on 15 *Shevat*, 5645 (1885), in Aleppo (Halab), Syria, known as a Torah center since ancient times. *Rabbeinu* Saadya Gaon lived there for several years, and the *Rambam* once wrote, "In all the Holy Land and Syria, there is one city alone — and it is Halab — in which there are those who are truly devoted to the Jewish religion and study of Torah." When Rabbi Ezra was born, the community, several thousand families strong, supported approximately fifty rabbis, many through Yissachar-Zevulun arrangements, whereby a merchant (Zevulun) shares in the Torah studies of the scholar (Yissachar) that he supports. The Alliance Israelite Universelle, a destructive force elsewhere in the Middle East, claimed only ten-fifteen percent of the city's Jewish children; the vast majority learned in the traditional *kuttabim* (*cheder*-like schools).

Rabbi Ezra's ancestors included, among others, Rabbi Shemtov Attia, a *talmid* of Rabbi Yosef Karo, who quoted him in *Avkat Rokhel*. When Rabbi Ezra's father took him as a young boy to learn under Rabbi Eliahu Dweck, one of Aleppo's renowned *melamdim*, Rabbi Dweck told the father after two weeks that he couldn't add to the boy's knowledge and understanding. When Rabbi Ezra was sixteen years old, his family moved to Jerusalem, joining a growing community of rabbis from Aleppo. Soon after, his father died.

His widowed mother, determined that her sons would be able to study without distraction, supported them by cleaning houses. Years later, Rabbi Ezra would recall, "When I was young, I studied Torah under impoverished circumstances. Through G-d's mercy, my mother and I merited to have a whole *pita*. Sometimes, we'd have a whole egg and divide between us, half for my mother and half for me. I was never bothered by hunger." Rabbi Ezra's mother had to borrow a coat for him to wear to his wedding — he could not afford one of his own.

In his youth, Rabbi Ezra would arise at midnight and go to the *Bet Midrash* Shoshanim LeDavid, learning and praying until sunset the following evening, when he would eat his only meal of the day. As a result of this demanding schedule, he mastered vast amounts of the *Gemara* with commentaries and major *poskim*.

He came to the attention of Jerusalem's *rabbonim* at an important gathering in the house of the president of the Bucharian *kehillah*. Present was the *Av Bet Din Sefardi* of Jerusalem, the

Gaon Rabbi Yedid HaLevi, author of numerous *sefarim*. He asked a question on a *Gemara*, which many attempted to answer, but Rabbi Yedid refuted them all.

Rabbi Ezra, sitting in the rear of the room, rose and said, "If the *chachamim* will allow, I believe I have an answer." He then gave an answer which Rabbi Yedid refuted. The question remained unanswered.

Seated opposite Rabbi Yedid was Rabbi Shelomo Laniado, who knew that the host of the gathering kept an excellent library with copies of every *sefer* published in the Middle East for several centuries. He asked a servant to bring him a very old and virtually forgotten *sefer, Mishmoret Kehunah*. In it, Rabbi Laniado found the question, Rabbi Ezra's explanation, and Rabbi Yedid's refutation. The *sefer* concluded that in spite of the refutation the answer was valid. Rabbi Laniado slipped the open *sefer* under the table to Rabbi Yedid. Rabbi Yedid read the page, and asked aloud, "Who gave me that last answer to my question?" Rabbi Ezra rose nervously. Rabbi Yedid then said, "*Rabbotai*, this young man has given the only valid answer to my question."

◄§ Up from Obscurity

Rabbi Ezra applied to join Rabbi Yedid's *shiur*, but Rabbi Yedid told him that he did not need a *shiur*, and instead studied *Choshen Mishpat* privately with Rabbi Ezra — as a colleague rather than as a *talmid*.

In 1907, Aleppian Rabbi Ezra Harari-Raful founded Yeshivat Ohel Moed. Rabbi Ezra — only twenty-two at the time — joined the faculty of the new institution with Rabbi Yedid, Rabbi Laniado, and Rabbi Avraham Ades. Rabbi Ezra became very close to Rabbi Ades, but continued to attend the *shiurim* of many of Jerusalem's *gedolim*.

With the outbreak of World War I, the Turks began harassing the Yeshivah's students. Rabbi Ezra with his wife and family fled to British-occupied Cairo, where he spent the war years. Far from interrupting his work, it was the beginning of his important life-accomplishment: the renaissance of Torah among the Sephardic and Eastern Jews.

Rabbi Ezra arrived in Cairo almost totally unknown. Attempting to go into business, he exhausted his limited funds in a short time, and found himself in difficult straits. On the brink of starvation, he met Nissim Nachum, a wealthy refugee who provided him with support and introduced him to community leaders.*

Rabbi Ezra opened a yeshivah, Ahaba veAchva, in the basement of the Cairo rabbinate. The yeshivah grew to over one hundred students, some of them transferees from the secular school. Many who entered barely knew how to read Hebrew; within two years, they were all studying Talmud. Classes that he had organized for workingmen grew as well, increasing the Torah consciousness of the community, and inspiring many *baalei teshuvah* in the process.

৩ A Tearful Farewell to Cairo

By the end of the war, Rabbi Ezra was one of Cairo's most respected rabbis. Besides the yeshivah, he sat on the *bet din*, and was consulted regularly by the community. He returned to Jerusalem with a tearful farewell from a grateful community, but his relationship with Cairo continued for many years thereafter. In 1947, in response to the city's request, he sent two of his finest *talmidim* to Cairo: Rabbi Shelomo Kassin, who was expelled by the Egyptian government for "Zionist" activities soon after he arrived, and Rabbi Ovadia Yosef, who stayed for three years, in spite of tremendous government pressure.

The Jews of Cairo kept Ahaba alive. A 1947 visitor saw a vibrant institution where two hundred boys, ages seventeen-twenty, learned Torah on a higher level. He met the *melamdim*, who impressed him with their learning and *yirat Shemayim*. When he asked them who taught them, they all had one answer, "Rabbi Ezra Attia." In the early 1950's, Cairo's Jewish community began to disintegrate under the pressures of emigration and Nasser's anti-Jewish regime. Nonetheless, Ahaba functioned until the 1960's.

Rabbi Ezra returned to Yeshivt Ohel Moed in 1919, to give a regular *shiur*. He studied with the dean of Sephardi *mekubalim*, Aleppian *Gaon* Rabbi Chaim Shaul Dweck, and later with the *Saba Kadisha* (Rabbi Shelomo Eliezer Alfandri: 1826-1930) when he moved to Jerusalem. This pattern was only slightly altered when, in 1923, Yeshivat Porat Yosef opened, fulfilling a fourteen-year-old dream.

---

* Rabbi Ezra met Nissim Nachum in an unusual way. After *Minchah* at a *shivah minyan*, Rabbi Ezra was asked to teach some *Mishnah*. His explanations were so clear, that the entire *minyan* requested that the short lesson continue for forty minutes and that he return the next day. One of those present then told Nissim Nachum of the new rabbi in Cairo who "made the words of the Torah as sweet as honey and clear as water."

Nachum, who knew Rabbi Ezra from Jerusalem, said, "Rabbi Ezra Attia here in Egypt? I must see him!"

From Calcutta to Baghdad, to Jerusalem

Sometime before his death in 1909, Rabbi Yosef Chaim, the Ben Ish Chai, was approached by Yosef Shalom, a wealthy Iraqi Jew living in Calcutta, who offered to build and endow a large yeshivah in Baghdad. The Ben Ish Chai's advice: Build it in Jerusalem opposite the *Kotel*. Mr. Shalom died in 1911, leaving his entire estate to establish and maintain a yeshivah — in Jerusalem, opposite the *Kotel* — a task assigned to Rabbi Ben-Tzion Chazan, a *talmid* of the Ben Ish Chai. The difficulties were many. All land around the *Kotel* was owned by the Islamic religious authorities, who only sold after protracted, delicate negotiations. The discovery of archeological artifacts, which by law called for a complete excavation, posed further problems. Finally, in 1923, Yeshivat Porat Yosef, named after its benefactor, opened. Ohel Moed merged with the new institution: Rabbi Shelomo Laniado became its *Rosh Hayeshivah*, and Rabbi Ezra Attia its *mashgiach*.*

The yeshivah was barely two years old when Rabbi Shelomo Laniado died at the age of forty-eight. Upon the invitation of the yeshivah's directors, Rabbi Ezra succeeded him as *Rosh Yeshivah*, a position he held for forty-five years, building Porat Yosef into an outstanding institution and inspiring many more *yeshivot*.

Porat Yosef was unlike any Sephardi yeshivah then in existence. Until it opened, advanced Sephardi *yeshivot* were housed in synagogues and rarely had more than thirty students. Porat Yosef had its own building, and initially had no space limitations. Yosef Shalom's estate provided an endowment which allowed it to support poor students and compensate teachers on a regular basis. These factors allowed it to grow. Starting with fifty *talmidim*, by 1930 it had two hundred *talmidim* ranging from ten-year-old boys to men in *kollel*. Ten years later, it had expanded to three hundred, and was severely straining its endowment. By 1950, several branches were opened to accommodate its continued growth.

A Sephardi Approach to Torah and Mussar

Rabbi Ezra sought to rebuild Sephardi Torah leadership from within, to train Sephardic *talmidei chachamim* to serve communities around the world. He involved himself personally with each student of the yeshivah. He examined the youngest boys every two

---

* According to one of the yeshivah's original *talmidim*, Rabbi Laniado originally refused the position, asking the directors to appoint Rabbi Ezra instead.

or three months. Older boys heard his *shiur* daily, in addition to individual sessions with him every other week or so. *Kollel* men had *shiurim* with him each evening. On Thursdays, he addressed the entire yeshivah with a *mussar* lecture, sometimes for as long as two hours. He always carried a copy of the *mussar* classic *Chovot Halevavot (Duties of the Heart)* on his person, and advised students to do the same. He once said, "Without Torah and *mussar*, we'd all be lost, G-d forbid!" In accordance with his directions, every class in the yeshivah began each day with a short *mussar* lesson.*

He once declined an invitation from an organization whose Torah observance he felt was suspect. When questioned about it, he replied, "After I've lived my one hundred and twenty years, I will stand before the heavenly court." He displayed his copy of *Chovot Halevavot* from his pocket and continued, "I do not want the author of this *sefer* to ask me, 'Why did you take me there?'"

Rabbi Ezra stressed learning the simple meaning of the *Gemara*. In keeping with Sephardi tradition, he taught his students to first master an entire *sugya* with the explanations of *Rashi* and *Tosafot*, the *Maharsha* and *Maharam Schiff*. Then, thoroughly learning the *Rif* and *Ran*, he would proceed to the *Rambam*, the *Rosh* and the *Tur*. He had a gift for *pilpul*, but avoided using it. He once started an involved *pilpul* and abruptly stopped in the middle, saying, "Sounds good? I don't like it. I like the *emmet*. Let's go the simple way." His *talmidim* absorbed his approach; and even those that later followed a different *derekh* in learning still used his explanations in their own teaching.

The *Chazon Ish* visited Porat Yosef twice: on both occasions, he asked Rabbi Ezra to say *divrei Torah*. Years later, he told his *talmidim* that Rabbi Ezra "... is not from this generation. he belongs to *dorot rishonim* (earlier generations)." The *Saba Kadisha*, Rabbi Alfandri, was said to have called him "the best rabbi we have." The *Rishon Le-Tzion*, Rabbi Ben Tzion Uziel, sought his opinion frequently, as did many Ashkenazi *gedolim* including Rabbi Shimshon Polonsky, Rabbi Tzvi Pesach Frank, and Rabbi Yaakov Yisroel Kanievsky (the Steipler).

His greatness was complemented by his unusual modesty. In spite of some very strong opinions, he never criticized other *gedolim*,

---

* Many *mussar* classics were written by Sephardim and Eastern Jews, several in Arabic, and only later translated into Hebrew, while those written in Hebrew were translated into Arabic or Ladino to make them more accessible. Throughout the Middle East, *mussar* was studied widely by all Jews.

even among his contemporaries. He never expressed his disagreements in public. He compared attempts at evaluating previous *gedolim* to weighing large rocks on a tiny gold scale. In guiding a *talmid's* learning, he would never disparage a *sefer* or its author; only his silence or recommendation of other sources would indicate his disapproval. In discussing personalities of the previous generation, he once remarked, "Who are we in comparison to those rabbis who had *ruach hakodesh?*" He was of the opinion that they had a direct line of *mesorah* from the *Anshei Knesset Hagedolah*. With them, it ended; he and his generation had preserved only the remnants.

❧ Klal uPrat — Public Affairs and Individual Needs

While strongly identified with a non-compromising attitude in Jewish affairs, he could show his support for worthy efforts in a visible public manner, without regard to political implications. After World War II, Chief Rabbi Isaac Herzog went to Rome to plead (unsuccessfully) with the Pope to return Jewish children who were hidden in monasteries during the war and were being raised as Christians. Rabbi Ezra summoned the *talmidim* of Porat Yosef to welcome Rabbi Herzog at the airport, saying, "He has been laboring for *Klal Yisroel*." Although he did not like to leave the yeshivah, Rabbi Ezra accompanied his *talmidim* to greet Rabbi Herzog on the runway when he descended from the airplane.

As devoted as Rabbi Ezra was to his *talmidim*, he would extend himself even further for a new student.

A poor boy from Iraq once requested admission to the yeshivah, but there was no money to support him. Rabbi Ezra approached Rabbi Chazan, the yeshivah's founder and secretary, and offered to reduce his own salary to admit the boy. Rabbi Chazan, torn between Rabbi Ezra's dedication and fiscal reality, reduced his own salary as well, to accept the boy, who became an accomplished *talmid chacham*.

❀ ❀ ❀

Hard times and economic pressures would have forced many *talmidim* to leave the yeshivah if Rabbi Ezra had not intervened. He confronted the father of a brilliant *talmid* who was taken from Porat Yosef to work in the family store. "We just can't afford it, Rabbi," explained the father. "If he works with me, that's one less workman I have to pay, and we need that extra money."

Rabbi Ezra nodded, put on an apron, rolled up his sleeves, and said, "Send your son back to the yeshivah. I will work for you for nothing."

Shocked, the father refused, and sent his son back. Today he is one of Israel's most prominent rabbis.

❊ ❊ ❊

Rabbi Ezra worked to build the self-image of his *talmidim*.

One *talmid* described how, after a difficult session with the rabbi, he was very depressed. Rabbi Ezra, ignoring the time of night and his own frail condition, walked the *talmid* home. This same *talmid* recalls how, when he was fourteen years old, Rabbi Ezra felt he was too insecure to withstand the pressures of Porat Yosef, so he sent him to another yeshivah for several years to build his self-confidence.

❊ ❊ ❊

Once he was walking with a young *talmid* through the streets of Jerusalem; the *talmid* was wearing a short-sleeved shirt and no jacket. For five minutes or so they walked; Rabbi Ezra, deep in thought, seemed to have a pressing problem. Suddenly he smiled; his problem was solved. He turned to his *talmid*, held up his bare arm, and said, "The hot sun will burn your arms. Don't you need protection?"

Says the *talmid*, "His problem was to tell me that it was not in keeping with my dignity to go outside without a jacket, and still not hurt my feelings."

❊ ❊ ❊

Rabbi Ezra wanted the honor the Sephardim traditionally give their rabbis extended to all *talmidei chachamim* and *b'nei yeshivah*. It was his fervent hope that as the community would feel that it had a part in the yeshivah's work, Torah study would increase among the general population. He encouraged a *talmid* learning to read the Torah in his *shul*, saying that there are people in the community who will never understand the *Gemara*, but can appreciate the contribution of the yeshivah in providing them with a *baal koreh*.

❊ ❊ ❊

Seated in a place of honor at a prestigious gathering, Rabbi Ezra noticed a young *talmid chacham* entering. There were no empty chairs, and no one offered the young man his. Rabbi Ezra called the young man over and whispered, "I suddenly feel ill and must leave. Will you take my chair?"

The young man accepted and Rabbi Ezra left the room.

❀ ❀ ❀

He would rise to greet every visitor, no matter how unlearned, and escort him *dalet ammot*, often over his visitor's protests. He set aside several hours each morning for people who had questions in *halachah* or personal matters. Although he spent *Shabbat* and *Yom Tov* away from the yeshivah, his house was always open.

❀ ❀ ❀

An American rabbi now living in Jerusalem recalls how, as a young boy learning in Haifa, he went to Rabbi Ezra's house to ask him for a *psak halachah*. "He stood up for me, shook my hand, offered me a chair, and told me how honored he was that I came to see him. I was a nineteen-year-old yeshivah *bachur*, and he treated me like a great *talmid chacham!*"

❀ ❀ ❀

Accessibility, however, did not mean automatic leniency. A businessman once asked for a *heter* to permit him to shave on *Chol Hamoed*. He could not postpone an important meeting, and he could not appear unshaven. Rabbi Ezra asked him, "If I offered you a thousand dollars to miss your meeting, would you?"

Flustered, the businessman answered yes. "For a thousand dollars you could miss this meeting, but not for your holiday which G-d gave you?"

The businessman postponed the meeting.

◆§ Reaching Out to Others

He once explained the verse in *Kohelet*, "Greater than Kohelet's wisdom was that he taught the people. The more he knew, the more he taught." Isn't this a normal progression? asked Rabbi Ezra. No, because the more one knows, the more one seeks out those of equal or greater learning to talk to. Kohelet's greatness was that as he learned more, he still kept in touch with the common man, and was able to teach the common man what he knew ... This explanation could well serve to describe Rabbi Ezra.

Rabbi Ezra avoided personal honors assiduously. When the Jerusalem *Bet Din* was in need of a *dayan* (rabbinical judge), Rabbi Uziel pleaded with Rabbi Ezra to serve. After refusing, Rabbi Ezra finally agreed on two conditions: his service was only temporary, and he would not serve as *Av Bet Din*. While serving as a *dayan*, he did not lose sight of his primary role as a teacher, and he brought along a *talmid* to serve as an investigator, meanwhile learning at first hand the fundamentals of *dayanut* in practice.

Rabbi Ezra believed the yeshivah had a responsibility to *kehillot* the world over, not just in Israel. Porat Yosef quickly became the source for rabbis and teachers for Sephardi communities in places as far flung as Egypt, South Africa, Holland, and the United States.

Counseling his fledgling rabbis, Rabbi Ezra urged them to stand fast in their adherence to *halachah*, but to understand that he could not teach them everything they would need to know. After giving a group of men *semichah*, he told them, "You have learned *Arba Turim* ('The Four Gates' of the *Shulchan Aruch*); now you must learn *Tur Chamishi* (The Fifth Gate) on your own." Asked what he meant, he replied, "Common sense."

◆§ Exile in the New City

Difficult times and political instability marked much of Rabbi Ezra's leadership of the yeshivah. The 1939 Arab riots in Jerusalem cut off access to the yeshivah building. Rabbi Ezra quickly moved the yeshivah to several synagogues in the New City of Jerusalem, delegating advanced *talmidim* to give classes, while he went from location to location supervising the functioning of the yeshivah, working incessantly from morning to night. When the riots ended, the yeshivah was able to return to its building without having suffered interruption.

The 1948 war cut off the Old City entirely, and the yeshivah building with it. Once again, Rabbi Ezra quickly reorganized the yeshivah in several synagogues, but this time, there was no return to the building; it was burned to the ground. Lost in the fire were Rabbi Ezra's unpublished writings. He refused all entreaties to rewrite them; he felt it was an omen that they were not meant for publication. His *talmidim* would be his *sefarim* — his lifetime work, and his gift to future generations.

Rabbi Ezra maintained the yeshivah in New City synagogues for several years. However, by this time, the yeshivah's endowment had lost much of its original value, and could no longer sustain the yeshivah, let alone support construction of a new building. Yosef Shalom's will provided that the yeshivah could not accept financial support from any outside source. Rabbi Ezra consulted *poskim* as to how the yeshivah could broaden its financial base without violating the will. A solution was found: the endowment could support only a limited number of *talmidim*, which would comprise the yeshivah under the will. Additional *talmidim* would be part of a "different" yeshivah, for whom contributions could be accepted. Sephardi communities the world over came to the yeshivah's aid, and a new building was built.*

◆§ Final Days

Age and weakness forced Rabbi Ezra to give up much of his demanding schedule at the yeshivah, yet he still maintained his availability to his fellow Jew. Both in the yeshivah and at home, he welcomed visitors, answered questions, and gave advice as before. To his last days, he kept a special account for the support of a poor *talmid chacham;* his own family was unaware of its existence until shortly before he died.

In those final years, he saw his labors bear fruit abundantly as the *talmidim* of Porat Yosef became the leaders of Sephardic Jewry. They sought his advice regularly. They visited him whenever possible; in the words of one: "They felt he was like the Western Wall." He, in turn, treated them with the utmost respect, believing that no matter how great his stature, no matter what his role was in their training, they were the leaders of Sephardic Jewry.

In 5729, Rabbi Ezra became seriously ill. He was confined to his bed, and drifted in and out of a coma for a full year. His *talmidim*, *talmidim* of Porat Yosef, and Sephardim the world over, all prayed for his recovery. In his final days, surrounded by his *talmidim*, he regained his consciousness. On the 19th of *Iyar*, 5730 (1970), early in the morning, Rabbi Ezra Attia passed away.

His monument is his *talmidim*, who carry on his work with

---

* Rabbi Ezra took fund-raising very seriously. When the first campaign started, he consented to pose for photographs (which he disliked doing) to be used in soliciting funds.

their own. His legacy is shared by tens of thousands of Sephardi yeshivah students, no matter where they learn. To the outsider who never experienced his greatness first hand, Rabbi Ezra's personality remains something of a mystery; unable to experience his greatness first hand, we look with little success for stories that will illuminate his life and work. An American *talmid's* recollection of his last meeting with Rabbi Ezra may tell us why.

The *talmid* visited Rabbi Ezra several months before his death. Rabbi Ezra's wife warned that he had been in a coma for three days and had spoken to no one. The *talmid* entered the room where he lay, and his wife called out, "Rabbi, Rabbi — 'Z' is here from America to see you." At that point, Rabbi Ezra stirred from his coma, and gave the *talmid* a short *drashah* on a passage from the *Shema*. He then slipped back into the coma. What was the *drashah?* The *talmid* smiled. "I'm sorry," he said, "but it was personal."

Personal. There is no better word to define Rabbi Ezra's life and teaching. The Torah was so integral to his life that his personal communications were *divrei Torah*. To his *talmidim*, his *divrei Torah* were personal communications. So much of his work was on an individual level, yet in sum, he instructed thousands. His spirit is present wherever Sephardim and Eastern Jews gather to learn Torah.

ᴇ§ The Sephardic Light

The specific greatness of Torah profiles,
as defined by the singular pristine elements
in Torah scholarship and piety,
provided by the Sephardi heritage.

Menoras Hamaor:
The Classic and its Author

"The people of our times are hungry for food and thirsty for wine; they do not hunger or thirst for the Word of G-d. They neglect to prepare for everlasting life and occupy themselves with the fleeting concerns of the moment. They spend their entire lives amassing fortunes that will end up in the hands of others — possibly even in the hands of the men who will marry the widows they leave behind. They don't even set aside a small portion of their fortunes to acquire provisions for their long journey into eternity.

"I have seen the indolence of the people who will not exert themselves to study the great volumes of the Law that are bursting with detail on all subjects. I have seen the indolence of the people who will not exert themselves to search for the Aggadah that is sprinkled throughout the Talmud and the Midrash. How it would bring sweet taste to their palates! How it would rouse their slumbering hearts and bring them to refuge under the wings of the Divine Presence! Were they even to do what is right because it would benefit themselves, in the end they would do it for its own sake.

"Therefore, I have collected selections from the laws of the basic mitzvos and the Aggadah, taking care to list every source. I have arranged these selections in an order designed to ease the task of the reader. This shall be a work that combines the Halachah and the Aggadah — a work that is equally pleasing to all."

◆§ The Need for a Sefer

This quote would appear to have been written by a contemporary *gadol* who, having made an accurate assessment of modern Jewish society, was writing a *sefer* that he hoped would inspire his people. There words were, indeed, written by a *gadol* of great stature — by a *Rishon*, in fact: Rabbeinu Yitzchok Abohav, over six hundred years ago, in the introduction to his masterwork, *Menoras Hamaor*.

Rabbeinu Yitzchok Abohav lived in Spain in the latter half of the fourteenth century. Spain, at that time, was the glittering diamond of the European continent. It enjoyed unparalleled prosperity. It was a center of enlightenment, the legacy of the Moorish occupation. Philosophy and science, poetry and art flourished as nowhere else. The Jewish population of Spain found this environment very hospitable, and it achieved its highest social station since being in exile from its homeland. Through their talent and industry, the Jewish people achieved the status of a privileged class, below the nobility but above the rest of the Spanish populace. Jews became the merchants and the financiers, the doctors and the poets, the philosophers and the ministers of the royal court; they became the "technocrats" of Spanish society.

The services they performed for the Crown were highly valued, and their rewards were lavish and conspicuous. And in the end they were corrupted. They became intoxicated by their new social freedom and mobility, and by the vistas of material opportunity that opened before them. They neglected the study of the Torah and the meticulous observance of *mitzvos*. They became more Spanish than Jewish. Jewish practice became a cultural vestige, an exercise in ethnicity rather than the intensely meaningful experience it is meant to be.

✑ An Appeal to Rediscover Their Heritage

It was to this corruption that Rabbeinu Yitzchok Abohav was addressing himself in his plaintive appeal to his contemporaries to rediscover the meaning of their heritage, to rediscover the sweet taste of the Torah and to seek provisions for their long journey into eternity. To accomplish this purpose he wrote a master work that encapsulated the basic elements of Judaism in a deceptively simple form — the *Menoras Hamaor*.

Menoras Hamaor gives but the briefest attention to legalities, concentrating instead on questions of ethics and the significance of the practical performance of the *mitzvos*. It sets forth a formula for the improvement of the individual, the conduct of his relationship with *Hashem*, and the fulfillment of his role in society. The tone is soft and gentle, almost conciliatory. The basic device is the extensive use of quotations from the homiletic portion of the *Talmud*, the *Aggadah*. Points are made with a minimum of elaboration; they serve as a mere outline to be filled in by the rich, full colors of the *Aggadah*. The author relies on the *Aggadah* itself to work its effect on the reader, because as the Talmud tells us, it "coaxes the heart of a person" (*Shabbos* 87a).

> ... One who embarks on a quest for wealth and glory
> stands to lose infinitely more than he can ever possibly gain.
> He stands to lose his share in the immortal world, for if he has
> difficulty achieving his ends he will likely turn to any means
> at his disposal, not hesitating to overstep the boundaries of
> what is permitted. Even if he does not enter the realms of the
> forbidden, he will still be squandering his life on the pursuit of
> emptiness and illusions; he will have missed the opportunity
> to fulfill his purpose and earn timeless rewards ...
>
> A person of clear vision should look about him and see
> how many truly righteous people live in grinding poverty, far
> worse than his own. His heart should go out to these people,
> and he should thank the L-rd for giving him bread to eat and
> clothing to wear, even if he only has enough to last but a day
> or two. He should not worry about what he will eat tomorrow.
> He should place his trust in his Creator. [Let him] not distress
> himself with concerns about what tomorrow will bring when
> he cannot possibly even know what the rest of today will
> bring. If his Creator has graciously bestowed upon him more
> than the minimum he needs for subsistence, then he certainly
> has cause to be grateful. He should sing the praises of his
> Creator every day and thank Him for His endless wonders
> and gracious favor in protecting him from all sorts of disasters
> to which he might fall victim. Let him not ask for embroidered
> clothing and silver vessels! Let him not ask for lavish
> banquets! Let him ask for that which he needs for his
> sustenance ...

It is impossible to assess the influence of *Menoras Hamaor* on
the Jewish community that inspired its creation. It is doubtful that it
enjoyed a very wide circulation, since almost all manuscripts at that
time were handwritten. The first formal printing of *Menoras
Hamaor* did not occur until 1514 in Constantinople. The author
himself writes that his purpose in writing this work was to improve
his own grasp of the *Aggadah* and to organize the sources he drew
upon for his speeches.

◆§ Seventy-Six Editions, Eight Translations

In the long run, however, *Menoras Hamaor* struck a responsive
chord among the Jewish people. It filled the very real need for a

concise framework of the basic tenets of Judaism. *Menoras Hamaor* can be read on many levels. It quotes the *Aggadah* without extensive comment, relying on it to be effective on an emotional level rather than an intellectual level. The Talmudic scholar, however, will find profound meaning in many of the seemingly simple statements of the author. He will also develop new insights into the passages of the Talmud from the context of their quotation and their juxtaposition to other related passages. Thus, it is a sophisticated, yet simple work, a work that is accessible without being simplistic. As such, it became one of the most beloved works of popular inspiration in Jewish religious literature, spectacularly successful in terms of dissemination. Not counting excerpts and synopses, it has appeared in seventy-six editions, originating in many cities across the European continent, North Africa, and the Near East. It has been translated into Ladino four different times, into German thrice, and once into Yiddish. It became a custom in many Jewish homes to read from *Menoras Hamaor* at the *Shabbos* table every week. Groups of men would huddle over it in the Polish *shtieblach* in the frigid winter nights. It has, perhaps as no similar work, found its way into the hearts of the people.

✑ Parallels and Differences

Today, because of the widespread lack of fluency in Hebrew, Ladino, German and Yiddish (only the first part is now available in English), *Menoras Hamaor* has lost much of its popularity. But the ingredients of its immense popularity over half a millennium are no less alive today. To be sure, there are many differences between modern Jewish society and pre-Expulsion Spanish Jewish society. Yet some parallels are striking: We, too, live in an "age of progress and enlightenment." In the western world, the political and material lot of the common man has so improved that his overriding concern is no longer how to fend off starvation but how to enjoy his work and use his leisure time to his greatest pleasure. Jews, through talent and industry, have taken advantage of the opportunities of "free" societies and have established themselves as successful merchants, professionals, and technocrats.

At the same time, unfortunately, far too many Jews who have taken advantage of the material opportunities of modern society have also fallen victim to its spiritual malaise. They have replaced Judaism as the focus of their lives with frenzied pursuit of material pleasure and prominence in non-Jewish society. Of course, democratic America bears no resemblance to royal Spain, where by royal decree alone, a haven for centuries was converted into the home of inquisition and auto-da-fe. Nevertheless, we Jews understand that we must be spiritually deserving of political asylum and tranquility.

Dovid Hamelech's warning: "Do not place your trust in princes, in man, who is incapable of deliverance (*Tehillim* 146:3)," was written for all times and only underscores the fragility of man-guaranteed social systems. The seemingly quietest of times can be the most perilous time for the Jewish people. We must always look *into ourselves* to discover what we can do to be secure. In the words of Rabbeinu Yitzchok Abohav, now too is a time to "seek refuge" under the wings of the Divine Presence. The urgency that produced *Menoras Hamaor* exists today, as well. Such works are as fresh and as relevant today as on the days they were written. People do not change; all that changes is the extent of their ability to wreak havoc and destruction.

◆§ The Sefer — Part of a Missing Whole

Menoras Hamaor is actually the first part of a trilogy designed to span the entire spectrum of practical day-to-day Judaism. The purpose of *Menoras Hamaor* was to point out the meaning of Judaism and its rewards, touching only very briefly on the practical rules of the performance of *mitzvos* and, even then, only to illustrate or underscore a homiletic theme. The second part of the trilogy, entitled *Aron Ha'edus,* was a major *halachic* work, one of the first codifications of the *halachah* tailored to the common need for an instructional guide to the conduct of a Torah life. The third part of the trilogy, *Shulchan Hapanim* — actually a subdivision of *Aron Ha'edus* — was a twelve-part work dealing with the *halachos* pertaining to *berochos* and *tefillos.* Unfortunately, the only part of this trilogy extant is the *Menoras Hamaor.*

In *Menoras Hamaor* the author uses the framework of a seven-branched *menorah* to encompass seven separate works covering seven distinct areas of Jewish thought. Each of these seven elements of the *Menorah* is written as a complete entity unto itself, with its own Prologue and Epilogue. (In the original they are identified simply as First Light, Second Light, and so forth, with a brief, descriptive subheading. In the English translation, however, the sheer verbosity of the language, as compared with the brevity of the Hebrew language, made it necessary to divide the *Menoras Hamaor* into its basic elements. Each volume is named to reflect the descriptive subheading in the original.)

The basic premise of the system of *Menoras Hamaor* is the verse, "Turn away from evil and do good, seek out peace and pursue it" (*Tehillim* 34:15). The author points out that these three steps that must be followed by "the man who desires life" (as in Verse 14, preceding this passage) must be pursued in this sequence, because each step lays the groundwork for the next. The first step must of necessity be to overcome the natural human inclination towards evil. Once the negative has been overcome, a second step replacing it with the positive must follow. One must then rise above the level of a neutral beast and condition oneself to do good. Having refined oneself as an individual, one must then go on to benefit society with that refinement, for one is meant to live as a productive member of society and to interact with other people. Only by devoting himself to the pursuit of peace can a person coexist with other people and effectively fulfill his desired role in society. Of the seven lights of the *Menorah*, the first two correspond to the first step ("Turn away from evil"), the middle three to the second step (". . . seek out peace and pursue it").

⊷§ The First Step of Leaving Evil

The First Light of the *Menorah*, *The Light of Contentment*, discusses the need to overcome the inclination to sin, to control the insatiable drives that lead a person into a frenzied pursuit of the temptations of the world, a pursuit that can bring him only harm both in this world and the next. The Second Light of the *Menorah*, *The Light of Expression*, discusses all forms of sinful speech and the ethics of responsible expression and communication. Together, these two Lights complete the first step of turning away from evil.

The Third Light of the *Menorah*, *The Light of Mitzvos*, deals with the first stage of conditioning oneself to do good. This is accomplished by the proper performance of the *mitzvos* that purify the body. The second stage is to then study the Torah, which elevates the mind and brings it to the realization of the truth. Hence, the Fourth Light of the *Menorah*, *The Light of Torah*. And since realistically a person cannot expect to be able to do only good and never falter, it is always necessary to maintain a familiarity with the ways of returning. Hence, the Fifth Light of the *Menorah*, *The Light of Teshuvah*.

The final step is accomplished by learning how to live together with others in peace and love, the theme of the Sixth Light of the

> The Kabbalists have told us that the entire Torah is comprised of various Names of the Holy One, Blessed is He. All of the words of the Torah are arranged in such a way that by different permutations they can be rearranged to form different Divine Names. Each one of the Names resulting from these permutations represents one of the multitude of Divine functions in the existence of the world. This Kabbalistic thesis provides one explanation for the concept of "Shiv'im Panim LaTorah" — The Seventy Facets of the Torah — which states that every point in the Torah can be understood in seventy different ways. In accordance with the thesis of the Kabbalists, this then would mean that the Torah is like a kaleidoscope which can be rearranged into seventy different permutations, each forming a different tapestry consisting entirely of various Divine Names. Each permutation, therefore, would have its own individual significance as a reflection of a different aspect of creation . . .
>
> We can well understand [then,] the rule that a Torah scroll which contains even the slightest mistake becomes invalid and can no longer be used for the obligatory readings from the Torah . . . even if the mistake involves a variation of a single letter that . . . does not effect the general meaning of the verse. Indeed, it may seem insignificant to us, because we are only looking at a single facet of the Torah. With a slight turn of the kaleidoscope, other permutations of the Torah emerge, complete tapestries entirely composed of various Divine Names that represent unfathomably profound secrets that hold the key to the mysteries of the existence of the world.
>
> . . . In its surface form, the Torah is arranged in such a way that ordinary people can read it and understand it . . . derive from it the rules of the mitzvos, and . . . learn moral and character lessons from the events recorded in the Torah. However, in those places where the Torah seems to be relating events which are seemingly uninstructive, realize that every word of the Torah has limitless meaning in its other forms. These hidden meanings concealed in the Torah, with only the faintest hints and allusions, reveal every detail of the material and spiritual worlds.

Menorah, The Light of Harmony. To be truly successful in this third and final step, however, a person must develop humility. This removes the final obstacle to harmonious relationships with others

— the demanding ego. Hence, the Seventh Light of the *Menorah*, *The Light of Humility*.

❧ The Light of Torah in the Center

To quote the author: '*Such are the seven Lights of the Menorah. The three Lights on each side of the Menorah shine in splendid escort to the Great Light in the Center — the Light of Torah that is as a blazing sun among seven brilliant stars ... All is of one piece, golden, pure, and sevenfold refined. Let the seven glittering Lights irradiate the Golden Menorah.*'

In his introductory ode, the author suggests a secondary purpose for *Menoras Hamaor.* Complaining that, because of the lack of an orderly arrangement of the *Aggados,* Talmudic scholars have concentrated on the *halachah,* he insists that the *Aggadah* is at least of equal importance. He contends that it is foolish to neglect the soul-elevating *Aggadah* and study only the fine points of legality; it is an '*affliction without remedy*'. With *Menoras Hamaor,* he hoped to create an orderly structure for the study of the *Aggadah.* It has even been suggested that his aim was to accomplish for the *Aggadah* what the Rambam had done for the *halachah* with his *Mishneh Torah.*

This certainly gives *Menoras Hamaor* a valuable added dimension. To the layman it is a window to an enchanting world otherwise accessible only to Talmudic scholars; it takes him by the hand and leads him on a tour of the high points of the intricate maze of the *Aggadah.* To the scholar it is a systematic arrangement that adds tremendous perspective to a deeper study of the *Aggadah.*

❧ The Man Behind the Menorah

Although Rabbeinu Yitzchok Abohav, by virtue of the authorship of *Menoras Hamaor,* is a major figure in Jewish history, little is known of his personal life — and that little must be gleaned from his introduction to the *Menoras Hamaor* and the accompanying ode. A substantial part of his life (he writes with apparent chagrin) was devoted to secular affairs and it was only in his later years that he turned to writing and the rabbinate. There is a tantalizing reference in the ode to some time spent 'in captivity,' though this might only be an allegorical allusion to the time he spent in secular pursuits. No other factual information can be elicited from his writings. What does emerge clearly is an unwitting self-portrait of a humble man and an intellectual giant, a man of soaring spirit that bursts into poetry and lyrical prose, a sensitive man with an intense love for his people.

The author's family — the Abohav family — was a very prominent Sephardic family of Spanish origin. During the Middle Ages, the Abohav family produced many illustrious *talmidei chachamim*. Among these was Rabbeinu Avraham Abohav to whom Rabbeinu Yehudah ben Asher of Toledo, the son of the *Rash*, addressed responsa in *Zichron Yehudah*. It is assumed that this Rabbeinu Avraham Abohav was the father of Rabbeinu Yitzchok Abohav, the author of *Menoras Hamaor*. After the Expulsion from Spain, in 1492, branches of the family took root in North Africa, Turkey, Italy, and the ex-Marrano communities of Northern Europe.

A descendant of the author, Rabbeinu Yitzchok Abohav II, who lived one hundred years later and died in 1493, was known as "the last *gaon* of Castille." He studied with Rabbeinu Yitzchok Canpanton and became the head of the Toledo Yeshivah. The *Chida* writes that he was a confidant of the King of Portugal. In 1491, Rabbeinu Yitzchok Abarbanel studied with him. Rabbeinu Yitzchok Abohav II wrote many works, including a commentary on *Arba'ah Turim* of Rabbeinu Yaakov ben Asher, the son of the *Rash*. Although this last work has been lost, it is quoted extensively in the *Beis Yoseif* of Rabbeinu Yoseif Caro, the author of the *Shulchan Aruch*, who refers to him as one of the greatest scholars of his generation.

The authorship of *Menoras Hamaor* is sometimes erroneously attributed to the better known Rabbeinu Yitzchok Abohav II. *Toldos Haposkim* explains that this error came about because some people had never heard of the author and therefore assumed that it was his descendant who wrote *Menoras Hamaor*, a theory disproven by a close study of certain early references (see *Chida*). It is also interesting to note that the portrait of Rabbi Yitzchok Abohav da Fonesca, a distant descendant of the author who lived in the seventeenth century and served as rabbi in the Sephardic communities of Brazil and Amsterdam,* is often mistaken for his.

The chief success of *Menoras Hamaor* throughout the ages has always been as a work of popular inspiration. In generation after generation and culture after culture, it has been an invitation to an exiled people to spurn the illusory values of their host cultures and to seek out the timeless truths of their own holy heritage. Centuries after his death, the vibrant notes of the author's clarion call still ring out:

Hark then you noble gentry
So ravenous for luxury
Turn away from the thunder
That tears mountaintops asunder
And illuminate your sight
By the seven gleaming Lights
Exalted tablets explained
By the L-rd's Finger ingrained
Come break the bread that I extend
All who truly are my friends
Drink deeply of the wines I blend
Upon the table that I've laid
Showbread beautifully arrayed
The table that stands before G-d.

---

* There is also another *Menoras Hamaor*, written by Rabbeinu Yisroel ben Yosef Alnakawa, a contemporary of the author. Except for scholarly study, however, it has remained largely unknown. There are both similarities and differences between the two works, and their relationship has always intrigued scholars.

Nehama Consuelo Nahmoud

Saddiq of the Sahara

*The story of
Ribi Ya'akov
Abu-Hasira — a
fascinating figure
from exotic times
and clime.*

Ribi Yaakov Abu-Hasira
5567/1807—5640/1880

MOROCCO IS DIVIDED lengthwise by the Atlas Mountain range. On the western, seacoast side of the mountains are Morocco's famous cities: Casablanca, Rabat, Fez, Meknes, Marakesh, Mogador.

To the east is the Sahara. This is wild country, a land of sand, camels, date palms and broiling sun. Visitors rarely came to this inhospitable territory, and not only because of the geography; the other side of the Atlas was always inhabited by tribes so renowned for their ferocity that only the most highly motivated dared to set foot there.

Jews lived on both sides of the Atlas Mountains for hundreds of years, from the time of the Second Temple until now. While most of the Jews on the coastal side of Morocco lived comfortable urban lives, those of the Sahara lived the simple life of the desert, in villages and towns, keeping a low profile so as not to draw the attention of the Berber tribesmen.

ᴥ§ The Man of the Mat

The Torah, born in the Sinai, bloomed in the Sahara like a desert flower under the care of great *saddiquim* such as those of the Abu-Hasira family, a dynasty of Kabbalists, *posquim* (deciders of Torah law) and community leaders.

Hasira is the Arabic word for *straw mat*. (The Hebrew word is *mahselet.*) *Abu*, in one sense, means *owner of*, or *man of*, as *ba'al* in Hebrew. Abu-Hasira = *ba'al hamahselet*, "the man of the straw mat."

The family's true name was Elbaz; the appellation *Abu-Hasira* was bestowed on it after an incident that occurred when Ribi (*Rav*, Rabbi) Shmuel Elbaz sailed to *Ares Israel*. When the ship was sinking, Ribi Shmuel grabbed a straw mat and sat on it. The Rabbi and the mat did not go under; instead, the current carried them to the Moroccan port of Mogador. Those who saw the *jalabiyya*-clad figure coming into port on a straw mat were astounded. The news spread quickly through the Jewish community, and as of then they spoke of Ribi Shmuel as "Abu-Hasira."

Ribi Shmuel, a contemporary of Hakham Haim Vital, lived for a time in Damascus, Syria, to study with a great master of the Kabbalah. The Hida wrote that every day of the week Ribi Shmuel meditated alone in the synagogue, and that he was known as a holy man (*Shem Hagdolim*, מע״ש).

One of Ribi Shmuel's sons, Mas'ud, became rabbi of the little Jewish community of Tafelaletch in the southern Moroccan Sahara. A son, Ya'akov, was born there in 1807.

Ya'akov's future as a *gadol* was apparent from his attitudes and behavior as a child. Even as a small boy he preferred learning and prayer to playing.

A Jerusalem scholar visiting the village stayed at the home of Ribi Mas'ud. Noticing Ya'akov poring over Tractate *Baba Qama*, he questioned him on the material he was learning. Ya'akov answered quickly and easily, and then posed his own questions; the scholar expressed his admiration for Ya'akov's expertise to Ribi Mas'ud, and then prolonged his stay in Tafelaletch to study with the boy.

As a young man, Ya'akov persisted in his lifestyle, learning and meditating alone in a special room his father prepared for him. Every question on *halakha* that Ribi Mas'ud received, he would discuss with Ya'akov, so as to train him to become a *poseq*. As the young man's reputation grew, both Jews and Arabs came to him to settle their differences, a task he accomplished with considerable success.

৯৶ Successor to Ribi Mas'ud

After Ribi Mas'ud's death, Ribi Ya'akov took his place as tender of this spiritual oasis in the Sahara. During the week he secluded himself for hours every day to study the revealed and the hidden Torah, spending only Shabat at home with the family. His son told of his father's study schedule:

> ... he would study parts of Mishna, all of which he had committed in memory, and every night he learned eight to ten chapters from *Qedashim* and *Taharos*. Then he would review *Shulhan Arukh* and the *posquim*, tracing the sources in the *Guemara*. Before midnight he would sleep a little, and then arise and say *Tiqun Hasot*, the lament for the destruction of the Temple. And until morning he would immerse himself in the Kabbalah: the *Zohar*, the *Es Haim*, and the *Mavo She'arim*. With the light of morning, he would soar like an eagle for the *misvot* of *sisit* and *tefillin* ... and he was the first of the *minyan* to arise at the synagogue and he would sit and teach ... the Rav was like a *Seraph* on the wing. (From the preface to *Ioru Mishpatekha leYa'akov*.)

৯৶ Transcendent Powers of Concentration

It goes without saying that in prayer he experienced extraordinary closeness to *Hashem*. Concentrating on *kavanot* (meanings or intentions) for nearly every word, and particularly for the Divine Names, Ribi Ya'akov was known to stand for an hour to say the *Amidah*.

His concentration was such that he was completely unaware of his surroundings.

Once when Ribi Ya'akov had gone to Fez to collect money for the poor, he prayed in a synagogue where the *minyan* was unfamiliar with his ways. Skeptical, they decided to test him, to see if his concentration during prayer was as intense as it appeared. As Ribi Ya'akov was praying, they shammed a high-decibel argument, shouting at the top of their lungs. The rabbi did not move. One of the men fired a gun — and still no reaction. When Ribi Ya'akov had ended his prayer, they asked his pardon for disturbing him. He answered: "I didn't hear you at all."

One imagines a Kabbalist ensconced in his ivory tower, spending all his days in prayer, study and contemplation of the *Pardes*, with no contact with the outside world. Perhaps this is so in some instances. Many, however, including the Ben Ish Hai, Hakham Suleiman Musafi of Jerusalem, and Ribi Ya'akov Abu-Hasira, were as known for their daily acts of *hesed* as for their erudition in the hidden Torah.

"Care for the children of the poor, for from their midst the Torah will come forth," was Ribi Ya'akov's special *misva*. He had a yeshivah in his own home for boys from poor families; all the members of the community contributed regularly towards its upkeep and operation.

⨍ The Rabbi on the Donkey

Ribi Ya'akov made frequent trips throughout Morocco and neighboring Algeria to collect money for the poor. The sight of the rabbi and his *shamash* plodding through the desert on their donkeys was familiar to the Jews of North African villages and cities. The visits of the beloved *saddiq* were always the occasion for a *fiesta* (celebration) — when the people saw him coming, they would run to get drums and tambourines and accompany him through the streets with song. During a visit, he would give sermons and be available to answer questions. The sick came to him, too, for his blessings and his prayers that they be cured.

Every Jewish community on Ribi Ya'akov's extensive travel routes had its own stories about his visits — stories of his *hesed*, of his miraculous cures, of narrow escapes from Arab wrath through his intervention:

A woman who stood to lose her child in divorce proceedings hired a carriage and overtook Ribi Ya'akov in the desert on one of his trips. When the rabbi saw her coming, he stopped and waited. The woman approached and handed him a document, relating in tears the background of the case. The *shamash* interrupted saying that the middle of the desert was not the place to discuss such problems; didn't she know that this was a dangerous no-man's land where Arabs or Berbers might gallop at any moment and kill everyone on sight?

Ribi Ya'akov reproved the *shamash* with the explanation that committing an injustice is a more serious danger. He listened to the woman, and helped her in her plight.

ᴇᴊ Disputations: To Win is to Lose

The Pact of Omar, attributed to the Caliph Omar, Muhammad's successor, formalized the second-class citizenship of non-Muslims. This *de jure* status varied in actual fact from place to place, from era to era, and from ruler to ruler. Although Ribi Ya'akov's time was one of the more oppressive periods in Moroccan history, Sheikh al-Aslam, the authority figure of Tafelaletch, held Ribi Ya'akov in high esteem and had a compassionate attitude toward the Jews, with his tribesmen in awe of him as a holy man. The local Muslim religious leaders, however, did not share these views.

One day, as Ribi Ya'akov was passing the *Paqha*, a seminary for Islamic studies, he was hailed and invited inside to participate in a religious discussion that ended in a bad-mouthing of the Jews.

Ribi Ya'akov, familiar with Koran, defended his position skillfully. But this did not sit well with his interlocutors, so they delegated three representatives to report Ribi Ya'akov's "calumny of the prophet Muhammad" to the Sultan in Fez, bypassing the sympathetic Sheikh al-Aslam. When news of the impending disaster reached the Jews of Tafelaletch they closed their shops and ran to Ribi Ya'akov as a body, lamenting: "*Wai lanu!* Woe is us! Your life is as precious to us as our own!" And they entreated him to ask the Sheikh to send men to defend them.

Ribi Ya'akov calmed his flock, telling the people to give *sedaqa* to the poor, to recite the Psalms and return to their jobs.

Soon news arrived that the three messengers had returned from Fez with the Sultan's decree of death to the perpetrator of the offense. In tears the Jews assembled before the rabbi's house.

Suddenly hoofbeats resounded. A single horseman leading two riderless mounts galloped past the knot of Jews in a cloud of dust, reining in in front of the *Paqha*.

The two absent riders were killed by falling stones as they passed under the arch in the village wall. The Muslim religious leaders believed that this had a direct connection with the holiness of Ribi Ya'akov and, as a result, they left the *saddiq* in peace.

Again the Jews gathered before the rabbi's house, this time to express their joy at the outcome of the situation.

"It was because of all of you that I was saved," he told them, urging them to increase their *hesed* and to say the Psalms often — the best protection against threats to the *Am Israel*, he explained.

৵§ Modesty as Natural as His Jalabiyya

Modesty seemed as natural to Ribi Ya'akov as his dusty white *jalabiyya*. His late grandson, the *Admor* Rav Israel Abu-Hasira of Netivot, told one of the *ma'asyot* illustrating this character quality:

On one of Ribi Ya'akov's travels he stayed overnight in a small city along the way. During the night, burglars entered and took the rabbi's saddlebags, which contained charity money he had collected en route, plus the manuscripts of some of his books.

The next morning the Jews of the city heard of the burglary and expressed their regret that they could not replace the very large sum lost; they were especially sorry about the manuscripts, since those were irreplaceable.

Ribi Ya'akov replied that he was not sorry: "If my books are acceptable in the eyes of the Almighty, they will be returned. If they are not acceptable, let them be lost."

During the conversation, four Jews walked up to the rabbi, kissed his hand and gave him the saddlebags: it was the thieves coming to ask forgiveness.

৵§ The Twelve Books of R' Ya'akov

Somehow, somewhere, Ribi Ya'akov found — or made — the time to write twelve books. They were all printed in Jerusalem posthumously, by his own wish. The first volume came out in 1884.

His writings are as multifaceted as his life was. He pursued the four basic modes of interpretation; Kabbalah, as expected; *guematria* (the numerical value of letters); as well as lessons derived from the first and the last letters of words. One of the best known of Ribi Ya'akov's works is *Ioru Mishpatekha leYa'akov*, a collection of responsa regarding everyday halachic matters, such as business transactions, inheritances, loans, power of attorney, marriage and divorce, and civil responsibility.

Another *sefer*, published in 1955 and apropos for our own days, is *Sha'are Teshuva*, a treatise on certain principles of return to the *misvot*. Still another *mussar sefer* is *Sha'are Arukha, The Gates of Healing*.

Ribi Ya'akov, like the Ben Ish Hai, Mori Shabazi of Yemen and many other Oriental Torah geniuses, also composed *piutim* (songs and hymns), which are gathered under the title *Yaguel Ya'akov — Ya'akov Rejoices.*

In addition, he left commentaries on *Humash;* an anthology of sermons; and a book with two hundred commentaries on the words *In the beginning,* the first phrase in *Tanakh.*

✌§ Three Times to the Holy Land

Ribi Ya'akov always longed to live in *Ares Israel.* Twice he started out, and both times he was stopped by the people — Jews and Arabs — who felt like children losing their father. The first time the Jews overtook him in the desert, ten miles from town, and brought him back; the second time it was the Arab mayor who told him that the presence of a *saddiq* in an area brought blessing to all its residents.

Ribi Ya'akov's third and final attempt at *aliya* came about in 1878, when he was seventy years old. His route took him through the coastal cities of Morocco, through Algeria, to Egypt. This distance took two years to travel, because everywhere he went the people kept him; and being the *ba'al hesed* that he was he could not refuse them. He learned with them, gave blessings and effected cures — as he had done on his previous visits.

In 1880 Ribi Ya'akov reached the Egyptian town of Damanhour, not far from Alexandria. There he became ill, and left this world a few days later on the twentieth of Tevet.

The head of the Jewish community of Alexandria insisted that a *saddiq* of such standing would be better honored by burial in the Alexandria cemetery. The Damanhourites disagreed. The Alexandrian delegation took the coffin and started toward Alexandria. No sooner had they stepped onto the road when a heavy downpour of rain stopped them. The Damanhourites took the coffin, and the rain disappeared as suddenly as it had come. Both communities saw this as a sign, and the rabbi was buried in humble surroundings — as he had lived all his life.

Nehama Consuelo Nahmoud

Hakham Yitzhak Hai Tayeb

5503/1743—5597/1837

TUNISIA. The word conjures up a picture of hot, white sand under a cloudless azure dome; a matching blue Mediterranean overlooked by white stucco buildings; the faint twitter of an Arab flute wafting through cobblestone alleys.

But Tunisia and her neighbors, Algeria and Morocco, have been Arab only since the heyday of Mohammad's successor Omar, in the Eighth Century; Jews were established in the region well before the Arabs ever set foot there. A well-supported belief exists that the first Jewish businessmen opened their shops in Tunisia during the reign of King Solomon.

Part of the little hyphen of land we now call Lebanon belonged to the Jewish kingdom; the rest was occupied by another Semitic people, the Phoenicians. The Phoenicians had two city-states, Tyre and Sidon (cities by those names still exist today), each with its own king. The Phoenicians were known as the world's best businessmen and shippers; indeed, there is archeological evidence that they reached North America. It goes without saying that they had branches of their export-import trade in every port of the Mediterranean, Tunis — or Carthage, as it was known in antiquity — among them.

But King Solomon was not to be outdone by the neighbors, as we know from Scripture. At one point he decided to go into a joint venture with King Hiram of Tyre: *And Hiram sent his slaves in ships, men of of ships who knew the sea; and they went to Ofir and took gold from there (Melachim I 9:27-28).* In the light of the above it is interesting to note that Tunisian Jews have always believed themselves the descendants of the Tribe of Zevulun — remember, Yaakov *Avinu* blessed his son Zevulun: *Zevulun will live by the seashore, by seaports, and his borders will extend to Sidon (Bereishis 49:13).*

Tunis-Carthage was mentioned in the Talmud, both Babylonian and Jerusalem, and we find in the Book of *Yonah* as well that Yonah was a true son of Zevulun. When he wanted to flee, he went to Tarshish (*Yonah* 1:3). Tarshish, according to *Ibn Ezra's* commentary on *Yonah,* was another name for Carthage (*Yonah* 1:1-3).

From Rome to France

The next major wave of Jewish immigration came with the Roman era, when 30,000 Jewish prisoners of war (*Jewish Wars*, *Yosifon*, 2:6,9) were shipped there to join those Jews who went to Tunisia of their own free will.

North Africa, with its important seaports along the coast, was one of those areas destined to be invaded and occupied by whoever happened to be the major power of the time. After the Romans came the Byzantines, who were replaced by the Arabs. Later Spain took its turn for a short time, and then the Ottoman Empire and finally, in the nineteenth century, France.

The Jews, meanwhile, went about their business and lived the kind of Jewish lives one might expect in such a precarious geographical position, with communities flourishing in "golden ages" only to be wiped from the map with the next invasion.

One such "golden age" occurred during the tenth century, when Torah flowered in the city of Kairouan under the tutelage of Hakham Hoshiel and Rabbenu Nissim, a correspondent of the *Gaonim* of Babel. Another bright period took place in the 1600's and 1700's with the influx of Inquisition refugees and Italian Jews.

Tunisia was visited by the *Rambam* on his way to Egypt, and later by Hakham Haim Yosef David Azulai, the *Hida*. Both these visitors wrote about their stay in Tunisia; the *Hida* was especially impressed by the three hundred rabbis in the yeshivot of Tunis.

Hakham Yitzhak Hai Tayeb

Every Sephardic community has its favorite *hakhamim*, great *poskim* and/or Kabbalists who become almost legendary figures with the passing of the generations. They are an inseparable part of the Mediterranean and Middle Eastern Jewish heritage, which never knew an irreligious, "enlightened" culture. These Torah heroes are not only part of the community; they have always been part of the individual Jew who identifies with them and takes strength and example from them.

The graves of *tzaddikim* have always been popular pilgrimage sites in the Old Country, from Tangier to Teheran; and their memorial days are still celebrated each year with a gathering, usually in the yeshivah or *beit-midrash* where, after a festive meal, the men hear sermons, sing *pizmonim* (religious poetry set to music), and study together. Stories — biographical folk tales — are handed down from parents to children. And now, transmitted in book form, they are religious "best-sellers" wherever there are Sephardic communities.

Hakham Yitzhak Hai Tayeb was one of these beloved rabbis. He was born in Tunis in 1743 into a family of *hakhamin*. True to his heritage, as a boy he loved nothing more than to study, spending hours poring over his books; and his abilities became apparent at an early age. It is told that one *erev Pesach*, when sheep were being slaughtered for the holiday, one of them was found to have water on the brain. The young Yitzhak delved into the books of law and its commentaries and said the sheep was permitted, explaining his sources with the clarity and precision of a man much older. The Chief Rabbi of Tunis, Hakham Shelomo Alfasi, was sent for. After examination he declared the sheep permitted, and he embraced the young prodigy and praised him for his astuteness and methodical approach.

Hakham Hai Tayeb studied under Hakham Yosef Zarka, who in turn was the student of the great Spanish *Gaon*, Hakham Haim Yosef David Azulai, one of the Torah geniuses of later centuries who is known for his treatises on both *Halakha* and *Kabbala*.

As a young rabbi just starting his career, Hakham Hai Tayeb lived with his mother in the austerest of material circumstances. He spent many, many hours alone in his room, learning and writing. Piles of books, and especially of papers, took up most of the available space on table and floor in the small room as the young man turned out commentary after commentary.

One day the Arab landlord came to collect the overdue rent, and Hakham Hai Tayeb told him the truth: They did not have it at the moment. The landlord went to Hakham Alfasi, the Chief Rabbi, who called the "recalcitrant" tenant to his office to try to settle the affair.

During his absence, Hakham Hai Tayeb's mother went to his room and, apparently aghast at the sight, decided to take advantage of the opportunity to tidy up. To her way of thinking, the floor was a place for debris and unwanted miscellany, not precious manuscripts; and so, armed with this logic, she proceeded to pick up the stacks of paper gracing the floor. When Hakham Hai Tayeb returned from the Chief Rabbi's office, he saw a few corners of his manuscripts, still untouched, lying among the ashes in the fireplace.

Only two of his works remain. One is חלב חיטה, "The Finest Wheat," published in 1895 in Tunisia. The other, *Arukh haShulhan*, first published in Livorno (Leghorn), Italy, 1791-1844. This six-volume commentary on the *Shulhan Arukh* has recently been reprinted in Israel, and the opinions of R' Hai Tayeb are quoted by authorities in their halakhic works.

Hakham Hai Tayeb's appointment as chief rabbi and head of the religious court was inevitable, considering his capability and his scholarship.

The story is told that after his appointment, the community leaders came to him with the recommendation that he move from his modest quarters to an apartment more befitting a man in his position. The Hakham replied no, thank you, he was happy where he was. Seeing their proposal sunk before getting out of port, the community got together, unbeknownst to the rabbi, and plotted.

Once when the Hakham had to spend the entire day away from home, community members came to his apartment with loads of building materials, and completely redid the apartment from top to bottom, outside as well as in. When he came home unusually late that evening, the Hakham's wife asked him why — and received the answer that he had had a hard time finding the apartment!

⊷§ The Convalescent

Once Hakham Hai Tayeb fell ill and was confined to bed for three weeks. Near the end of the third week, the *hakham* who was filling in for him at the yeshiva during his absence suggested to the students to take up a collection for him. The fifty students gladly contributed one coin apiece, and two young men went to take the money to him. When they arrived at the Hakham's home, they found him sitting in the sun on his patio, because he had started to recover. One student whispered to the other as they crossed the court:

"If he is sitting out here it means he is better. Maybe he doesn't need all this money. Maybe twenty-five would be enough."

So they went to the rabbi, asked him how he was getting on, and handed him twenty-five coins, saying it was from the yeshivah.

The Hakham looked at them in surprise and asked: "Does sitting on the patio mean twenty-five less?"

The two young men were taken aback — how did he know their secret? They hastened to ask the rabbi's forgiveness and gave him the rest of the money.

A certain rich merchant invited ten scholars to learn at his home every year on the holiday of Shavuot. It was his custom to honor his learned guests with a festive meal before they started studying, and he also used this opportunity to give them a contribution toward their support, to further the study of Torah.

One year, however, it happened that this businessman's affairs took a sharp and serious downward plunge; as Shavuot neared he became more and more depressed, since he knew he would not be able to afford the dinner he was accustomed to serving the study group. Seeing his downcast appearance, his wife asked what was bothering her husband, and he told her. She proposed that he take the one piece of good jewelry she had left and pawn it, certain it would bring enough to finance the Shavuot dinner.

So the merchant took the piece of jewelry to a pawn shop and received the sum they had reckoned. On his way to the *souq* (open-air bazaar) to order provisions for the dinner, he chanced upon Hakham Hai Tayeb, who immediately buttonholed him with:

"Say, you're just the man I'm looking for! I have an urgent case here, a poor bride who has no dowry."

The merchant hesitated visibly, but the Hakham insisted — and who could argue with Hakham Hai Tayeb? He handed over the money.

Although his conscience told him he had done the right thing, the man felt he was back where he started — with nothing, and no Shavuot dinner. Such were his thoughts as he turned from the alleys of the *souq* into a narrow street, where he was accosted by a non-Jew who said:

"Aren't you so-and-so, who has a wholesale house on . . . . . . Street?"

The merchant answered in the affirmative, and the non-Jew continued:

"Look, I have some merchandise here. If you can sell it for me, I'll give you a good percentage."

Again the man hesitated. The other said, "If you decide you want to do it, here is my address." The merchant started on his way again, only to be stopped a third time, this time by a courtier from the Bey's palace who knew his reputation in the business world.

"The Bey needs a certain kind of merchandise, and he wants it now, right away," he said, specifying the object in question; it was the very merchandise offered him by the man who had stopped him in the street some moments before. He told the courtier he would have it at the palace within an hour, whereupon he rushed to the address on the paper in his hand, picked up the packages and delivered them to the palace. He did receive a good percentage, double the amount he had given to the Hakham for charity.

Later on he met Hakham Hai Tayeb and recounted the fast-moving events of the day with amazement. The Hakham smiled.

◄§ Nine Days of Pesah

The general atmosphere in Tunis in Hakham Hai Tayeb's day was not unfavorable to Jews. The Bey, a tolerant man, appreciated the abilities of talented Jews, and some were employed in high positions in the country.

Under the surface, however, there was a virulently anti-Jewish element among the population. During the reigns of just rulers, this element remained relatively quiet and unseen — but every now and then it popped to the surface quite visibly and unpleasantly.

On one of these occasions, Hakham Hai Tayeb saved the entire community — by decreeing a nine-day Pesah celebration.

On the last day of Pesah, the Arab bakers readied their wares for the next day when the Jews would come by the hundreds to buy bread; the eight days of Passover made a significant dent in the revenues of these tradesmen. But that Passover some of the Jew-haters decided that now was their chance, and on that last day of the holiday they went to the bakeries and poisoned all the dough used for baking the bread for the Jews.

Hakham Hai Tayeb had received certain information, and at morning prayers on the last day, he announced that an error had been made in the calendar regarding the dates of Pesah; that the community was obliged to celebrate one more day; and that those who had run out of *matzah* were invited to eat at the homes of the community's leaders.

The next day the Arab bakers sold only one loaf of bread . . . to Hakham Hai Tayeb. Surprised and disappointed, the nefarious individuals at the bottom of the plot sent a committee to the Bey, complaining that the bakers suffered considerable loss through the refusal of the Jews to buy the bread they had prepared.

The Bey sent for Hakham Hai Tayeb and asked for an explanation. The Hakham requested that an animal be brought in, and when a servant complied with the request, he took a loaf from the folds of his *jalabiyya* (ankle-length robe), broke off a piece and fed it to the animal. After a few seconds the animal fell over, dead.

This visual explanation was not lost on the ruler. He ordered the arrest of the guilty parties, who were duly punished after confessing to the crime. (A similar story is told about the Maharal of Prague.)

A typhoid epidemic ended Hakham Hai Tayeb's career in 1837. A poem was composed and chiseled on his tombstone, ending in the words "Ribi Hai Tayeb is not dead, he lives." As far as the hearts of Tunisian Jews are concerned, this statement is not an exaggeration.

The Pilgrimage: Epilogue

In 1942, the Germans invaded Tunisia to confront the Allied armies stationed in Morocco, Algeria and western Tunisia. The occupation lasted less than a year; but that was ample time to set up an efficient, true-to-form Nazi operation, which included confiscation of property, creation of local labor camps, and regular shipments to the European gas chambers.

Toward the end of the occupation, in 1943, the Allies started bombing Tunis every day, hoping to force the Germans to surrender. The Jews, who had lived through confiscations, hunger, roundups and deportations, still had roofs over their heads, at least; but now this, too, threatened to disappear. They had only one resort, which had kept them through centuries of occupations and invasions: prayer.

The Jews of the *Hara* (ghetto) gathered and went in a group to the cemetery, to the grave of their *tzaddik*, Hakham Yitzhak Hai Tayeb. The bombers droned toward the city even as they walked. Upon arrival at their destination, they started the *Psalms* and tearful *tahanunim*.

The explosions, distant at first, became louder as the air force hit new targets. The prayers continued and so did the bombing, nearer and nearer the cemetery. Finally a plane flew over the cemetery, and the Jews froze. They threw themselves face down on the ground when a bomb began its whistling descent. The bomb landed beside the grave and then ... nothing. The Jews waited, hearts nearly still. They looked up and saw half a bomb protruding from the earth, a dud. When they grasped what had happened, they jumped up and shouted praises to *Hashem*.

Hakham Yitzhak Hai Tayeb / 129

✑§ Torah Leaders in America

The great men who met the challenge
of bringing lofty Torah standards
to the shores of a land celebrated for
materialism, pragmatism, and
defiance of tradition.

Ohr Shraga:
The Light of Reb Shraga Feivel

*A talmid's
impression
of Reb Shraga Feivel
Mendlowitz on his
thirty-fifth yahrzeit,
culled from the years
spent with him, from
the stories of older
talmidim and from
some readings.*

Reb Shraga Feivel Mendlowitz
5647-5708 / 1886-1948

WHEN RABBI ISAAC SHER, Slobodka *Rosh Yeshivah*, met Reb
Shraga Feivel during a visit to America, he greeted him by
saying, "So you are the famous Rabbi Mendlowitz I have heard
so much about!"

Taken aback, Reb Shraga Feivel replied, "I am not Rabbi
Mendlowitz, but Mister Mendlowitz."

Responded Reb Isaac Sher, "Be that as it may, but I have
heard that you have accomplished much more than any rabbi in
Israel."

❀ ❀ ❀

The Klausenberger Rav (Rabbi Yekusiel Yehuda Halber-
stam), a leading Chassidic figure, remarked at Reb Shraga
Feivel's funeral in 1948, "Until the end of generations, Jewry
will be indebted to Reb Feivel."

ᴥᔕ The Gift

What was the debt we owe Reb Shraga Feivel, so acknowledged by prominent personages of two such different schools? Perhaps it can be understood through an incident that took place in 1943 in the Eish Das Rabbis' and Teachers' Institute in Monsey, New York. Reb Shraga Feivel was seated on a lawn chair surrounded by his students on a green slope near a rock garden. He asked a *talmid* to quickly turn over one of the large stones that had been firmly embedded in the ground for many years. Once he did so, the group saw swarms of insects scurrying about. Said Reb Shraga Feivel: "See those creatures? All their lives under that rock they believed the world to be a dark, dreary place. By overturning that rock, you have revealed to them a whole new world: one of light and beauty. You have shown them the sun and the sky, giving them a new dimension in life. Your task in life as *rabbonim* and *mechanchim* is to remove the rocks from the Jewish *neshamah* and allow the light of the *Shechinah* to illuminate its life."

Reb Shraga Feivel was convinced that the stone *could* be overturned, that the *neshamah* of the American child *could* be reached by Torah, and that this was his task in America.

Because of Reb Shraga Feivel's dreams and initiatives, and the spiritual richness he transmitted to his *talmidim*, few stones have been left unturned in the effort to bring the light of Torah to every Jewish soul. He was an inspiration and moving force for virtually every genuine Torah movement in America.

I. The Years of Preparation

Reb Shraga Feivel ben Reb Moshe and Bas-Sheva Mendlowitz was born in the year 5647 (1886) in the village of Vilag on the border between Poland and Austria-Hungary. His mother died when Feivel was ten years old and his father soon moved to Rimanov.

At the age of twelve young Feivel began studying under Reb Aaron, *Dayan* of Mezo-Laboretz (home of the *Bnai Yissasschar*), who considered him to be his most gifted *talmid*. He then studied under Rabbi Moshe Greenwald, *Rav* of Chust, who was so impressed with him that he never began a *shiur* without first inquiring, "Is the boy from Mezo-Laboretz here?", while his classmates nicknamed him "the *masmid*." Rabbi Greenwald had entrusted Reb Shraga Feivel with the task of reviewing his *sefer*, *Arugas Habosem*, before it was sent to print. In fact, his *Rebbe* assigned Reb Shraga Feivel the task of editing the laws of *Mikvaos*, one of the most difficult sections of Jewish law.

At seventeen, Feivel went to Unsdorf to study under the famous Rabbi Shmuel Rosenberg, author of the *Be'er Shmuel* — a disciple of the *Ksav Sofer*. Reb Shmuel Unsdorfer made the deepest impression upon young Feivel and later served as a model for his own *derech* in teaching. By that time, Reb Shraga Feivel had learned through most *sugyos* (topics) of *Shas*. His *hasmadah* and love for learning never failed him and his extra-curricular studies were phenomenal. One year he undertook to complete *Rambam's Yad Hachazakah* with key commentaries; another year all of *Tur Shulchan Aruch* with *Beis Yosef*; and so on.

Rabbi Shmuel Kushelevitz, *Rosh Yeshivah* at Mesifta Torah Vodaath, told the family during *Shivah* that over their many years together, they had discussed Talmud numerous times. "Each time," said Rabbi Kushelevitz, "the topic was as fresh and clear to Reb Shraga Feivel as if he had just learned it."

Years later, Reb Shraga Feivel related, as he was about to cross a Scranton street, the image of Reb Shmuel appeared to him and commanded him to stop. Reb Shraga Feivel quickly halted and realized that had he not done so, he would have been struck down by an oncoming car. Again, the night before his wife gave birth, his *Rebbe* appeared to him in a dream and told him, "Tomorrow you will have a son." Reb Shraga Feivel named the boy "Shmuel" in his honor.

After receiving his *semichah* at Unsdorf at the age of eighteen, Reb Shraga Feivel continued his studies in the Pressburg Yeshivah under the guidance of Rabbi Simcha Bunim Schrieber, a grandson of the *Chasam Sofer*.

Reb Shraga Feivel's personal preparation for his role in life went beyond the formal yeshivah curriculum. He mastered *Tanach*, *Machshavah* (philosophy), *Mussar* (ethical literature), *Chassidus* and Jewish history. In fact, he invested a third of his wedding-gift proceeds in the purchase of a set of Jewish history books.

He had little patience with those who had no knowledge of history. Years later, when a student in Torah Vodaath asked him if the Prophets were written during the First *Beis Hamikdash* or the Second, he replied: "First tell me which came first, the First *Beis Hamikdash* or the Second."

At the age of twenty-two, Reb Feivel married his stepmother's younger sister, Bluma Rachel, and settled in Humenne, where his first two children were born. In 1913, at the age of twenty-seven, Reb Shraga Feivel left his family in Europe and came to America. After several attempts at establishing a business in Scranton, Pennsylvania, he became a Hebrew School teacher. Following World War I, he returned to Europe to bring his family to join him in Scranton.

As a young Talmud Torah teacher, he made his classes so vibrant that to this day, some people in Scranton still remember him. One elderly man recently told Reb Shraga Feivel's son, "I have been taught by many great teachers and inspiring professors, but never did I have a teacher as exciting as your father! *Tanach* lived for us. Whatever *Yiddishkeit* I have today, I owe to your father!"

Although Reb Shraga Feivel never envisioned himself as a trailblazing educator, many of his activities, even apparently trivial actions, served as preparation for his ultimate role — that of shaping the soul of the American yeshivah. He once remarked that when he took his children to the park, people thought he was simply babysitting. "The truth is," he said, "I would sit with them under a tree contemplating *gadlus HaBorei* (the greatness of the Creator)." There in a quiet meditative mood, he learned the *Tanya*, unwittingly preparing for the time when his classes in this work would be acclaimed as classical lessons in *Chassidus*.

II. The Move to Torah Vodaath

In 1920, Reb Shraga Feivel moved his family to Brooklyn, New York. The Yeshivah Torah Vodaath, at 206 Wilson Street, in Williamsburg, founded in 1917, was then a small struggling school. Reb Binyamin Wilhelm, one of the founders of the Yeshivah, persuaded the Board of Directors to engage Reb Shraga Feivel as principal in 1921. We must remember that Torah study was not the accepted pursuit for teenagers at that time. There were only three yeshivos in all of New York: Rabbi Yitzchak Elchanan and Rabbi Jacob Joseph, both in the Lower East Side, and Rabbi Chaim Berlin in Brooklyn. In contrast to today, when yeshivos vie with each other in attempting to raise the standards of learning and to elevate the *talmid's* dreams of greatness, in the 20's, 30's, and even the 40's, when I came to Mesivta Torah Vodaath, it was a battle simply to establish the concept of a higher yeshivah education. Reb Shraga Feivel struggled to convince parents and students of the value of Torah education beyond the elementary years.

His role could be summed up by the *Chazal* (Talmudic adage) he quoted so frequently: "Why was Avraham called G-d's beloved, *Avraham Ohavi?* Because Avraham made G-d's name beloved to all who came into his company." When Reb Shraga Feivel spoke these words, to us, his *talmidim,* he too was *Avraham Ohavi,* G-d's beloved who helped make the *Shechinah* beloved in America. From his position as principal at Torah Vodaath, Reb Shraga Feivel began to lead a Torah revolution which has resulted in the high standards we strive for today.

◄§ The Long Saturday Nights

A *talmid* from those years relates that he was once called into Reb Shraga Feivel's office and asked, "Tell me, what do you and your friends do on these long winter Saturday nights?" Sheepishly the *bachur* replied, "Well, *Rebbe,* the truth is that we go to the movies. You know, we have very little to do in the way of recreation."

Instead of scolding him, Reb Shraga Feivel said, "Why don't we all get together at my home? No learning, of course. We'll just sit and talk."

"O.K., *Rebbe,* we'll try it."

So on Saturday nights they gathered at Reb Shraga Feivel's home and talked about everything under the sun — questions young boys ask about life, death, and religion. Finally, Reb Shraga Feivel would say, "*Ober un gornist pahst nit* (No study at all just isn't right)," and he would spend a few minutes teaching the *Sefer Hachinuch* on *mitzvos,* making the lessons alive and compelling for them. (To this day, that "*bachur*" arises at five each morning to attend a *Daf Yomi* group.)

One Saturday night, Reb Shraga Feivel asked this group, "What do you think is the most important thing in life?" When no one came up with a satisfactory answer, Reb Shraga Feivel told them, "It's *cheshbon:* to account for every deed you do."

◄§ His Own Accounting System

His personal *cheshbon* included his *talmidim.* Before going to sleep every night, he reviewed a list of the students of the yeshivah, to consider how he could be of help to each one. He once remarked, "If I can no longer know where every *bachur* in my yeshivah is holding, it's a sign that the yeshivah has grown too large."

Friday nights, when even the busiest father makes time to

study with his children, Reb Shraga Feivel taught his children — the *talmidim* — *Mesechta Shabbos*. (He remarked at one of these classes, that if someone studied a *blatt Gemara* without asking the questions posed by the *Maharsha*, he did not yet "know how to learn.")

Reb Shraga Feivel had a weakness for gifted boys, and gave them much more leeway than he would ever have allowed the majority of students.

Yankel, a non-conforming teenager from the Midwest, once secretly picked the lock on a display case in the Mesifta lobby that housed a personnel directory. He rearranged the movable letters to spell out outrageous positions for the Yeshivah's administration, much to the consternation of the *hanhalah*. Reb Shraga Feivel quickly found out the culprit, and spent two hours with him in his office, probing his background, ideas, and goals, apparently each enjoying the other immensely — without a word about the crime. A spunky fellow, Yankel needed unorthodox treatment.

❦ ❦ ❦

Moshe was a brilliant fifteen-year-old who did not adhere to the Yeshivah schedule. Reb Shraga Feivel permitted him to go to Bais Medrash Elyon, where he could study independently. He tolerated his every aberration and idiosyncrasy in hope that "the light of Torah would bring him back" — until Moshe sold a set of Rashba to purchase a phonograph, which so disgusted Reb Shraga Feivel that he let him go: With no appreciation of Torah, the "light" would not penetrate.

◅§ The Time of Our Lives

Reb Shraga Feivel valued every minute. He once remarked that he learned *hasmadah* from Reb Aharon Kotler.

Leaving a meeting, he walked alongside Reb Aharon to the elevator, overhearing him mumble to himself, "Now I understand the Reb Akiva Eiger's *kushya*." Reb Shraga Feivel was overwhelmed with Reb Aharon's ability to immerse himself totally in Torah thought immediately after being involved in a pressing communal issue.

Regarding the verse, "The days of our years — *bahem* — among them are but seventy years," he said: "In a few days of our years, *bahem* — in them — you can compress whatever you've accomplished in seventy years." Only a *vort*, yet it reveals his appreciation for the value of time. His *talmidim* shall forever remember his plea, "*Bachurim, nitzt zich ois de tzeit.*" (Boys, utilize your time well.)

To him, time was the most precious gift G-d has given man, especially when its use affected others. For instance, his *Tanach* class met in the auditorium from nine to nine thirty a.m., and for a student to be late was to commit a serious crime. At five to nine, he was already sitting in his chair, ready to teach, impatient to get on with his work ... Who can forget Reb Shraga Feivel standing in the hall facing the front door, with his pocket watch in his hand, as he watched the students and the *rebbeim* file into the building? No word was needed to chastise the latecomer. One look and you knew.

◁§ The Shabbos and Yom Tov Approach

When a *Yom Tov* approached, he made certain that the boys from the poorest families were outfitted with new suits. And he also made sure that the growing needs of the *neshamah* were met. He taught us how to sing a *niggun* and how to shed a tear, how to dance and how to cry. He often remarked, "If you can't dance on Simchas Torah with what you've got, you can't cry on Yom Kippur for what you're missing."

My first exposure to Torah Vodaath was as part of a visitation organized by a group of Pirchei leaders in Baltimore (one of them now a leader of the world Agudah movement). The dancing and singing so captivated us that they gave us the impetus to leave home to learn in the "big city."

The walls of the *beis midrash* vibrated with the spirit of the season. Reb Shraga Feivel would direct the singing and the dancing — not a wild release of energy, but a leap of the spirit. "You can't jump from *niggun* to *niggun*," he would tell us. "You must wring the last drop out of a *niggun* like you squeeze juice from a lemon." I can still hear his voice ringing in my ears as he led us in the song, *Im Ani Kahn, Hakol Kahn* — If I am here, all is present (see *Succah* 53a): "*Bachurim, tantzt Rashi's p'shat*" ("I" referring to G-d). Then later: "*Bachurim, tantzt Tosfos' p'shat*" ("I" referring to *Klal Yisroel's* presence).

A Lithuanian colleague of Rabbi Shlomo Heiman from his days in the Slobodka Yeshivah asked him how he could serve as *Rosh Hayeshivah* for Torah Vodaath when it did not even have a formal *Mussar* program. Replied Reb Shlomo: "Reb Shraga Feivel's *Shalosh*

Seudos is the equivalent of *Mussar.*"

And an extraordinary experience it was! Reb Shraga Feivel graced the head table while the rest of us, with only a crusty piece of *challah* or a piece of *matzah* in hand, sat in the enveloping darkness and felt as if we were in *Gan Eden*. Young students cried from the depths of their souls while singing the *Shalosh Seudos zemiros*, "May we merit to see children and grandchildren engrossed in the study of Torah and *mitzvos* . . ." People had said that the stones of America were *treife*. But *Avraham Ohavi* — Reb Shraga Feivel — lifted the stones and bathed his *talmidim* in the light of *deveikus*, clinging to G-d.

III. Curriculum for Klal Yisroel

◆§ The Meaning of Preparation

One day he arrived late for his *Tanach* class. He sat down, opened the *sefer*, then closed it, and said, "No class today. I had set aside time to prepare for this class, but a Jew came with a tale of woe. I would not stop him, and he took away all my preparation time. Truth of the matter is that I could give a class with no preparation, and you'd probably find it more interesting, for when one is not prepared, ideas fly through one's mind; but that's not teaching. A teacher must know exactly what he wants to say to his students and what he wants to leave out. Since I am not prepared, I cannot teach today. Class is over." Can there be a better class on teaching than that episode?

He came to class prepared to teach with a wealth of Torah at his fingertips. The vast resources of *Chazal* were integrated into his personality, yet with his genius, he concealed it. Reb Shraga Feivel never tried to be *mechadesh* new thoughts, but rather to bring out the life of the old. I once had access to his *seforim* — his *Yalkut Shimoni*, *Pirkei Avos*, and his *Tur Shulchan Aruch* were filled with check marks, indicating the passages to be used in his classes.

And what classes they were! The old did become new, and was indelibly etched into the *neshamos* of all who sat spellbound as he wove his ideas with poetic phrases into a tapestry of beauty and harmony. Whether the text was *Tehillim* or *Sefer Hachinuch*, *Mesillas Yesharim* or *Derech Hashem*, *Sfas Emes* or *Samson Raphael Hirsch*, the words sprang from the pages to become part of your life.

He found the writings of Rav Samson Raphael Hirsch an invaluable source for transmitting Torah to new generations. He told his family, "It was worthwhile to learn German just to be able to understand his writings." (Hirsch's works had not yet been translated into Hebrew or English.) *Tanya* (the *Chabad* classic) according to Hirsch may sound strange or impossible, but Reb Shraga Feivel thought of both as guides to a way of life, not as philosophies of the abstract. Since both were authentic Torah thought, they overlapped, and each could — and did — shed light upon the other. He brought together the teachings of all ages and all schools of thought, and demonstrated each to be revered and relevant in his quest to spread holiness.

How he prepared! In a *Tanya* class he once remarked, "Do you think I shook that interpretation out of my armsleeves? It took me twenty years to arrive at that *p'shat*." He tried to teach us how to think and to be open to new ideas: "*Di sechel is elastish* (the mind is elastic); it can be stretched from one extreme to another if you are intellectually honest with yourself."

✤§ Unspoken Lessons

He taught with "*kol atzmosai tomarna* — All my limbs speak of G-d's glory." The veins in his forehead bulged and pressed outward, and his face would become flushed as he immersed himself into the subject matter. Reb Shraga Feivel never taught *Iyov* (Job). He was afraid that if someone were present one day when he taught Iyov's questions, making them burn with immediacy, and then would miss the next day's lesson when the answers were given, that *bachur* would always remain with the questions nagging his mind.

The auditorium was filled as the *bachurim* settled back for Mr. Mendlowitz's *Tehillim shiur*. "Kapital 84" ... He reached the third *pasuk:* נכספה וגם כלתה נפשי לחצרות ה', *My soul yearns, indeed it pines for the courtyards of G-d* ... גם צפור מצאה בית ודרור קן לה, *Even the bird found a home, the wild one a nest.* The contrast between the wild bird and the homeless Jew, between the ever-presence of the nest and absence of the *Beis Hamikdash*, was too much for him. The tears poured down his cheeks. He could not regain his composure, so he closed the *Tehillim*. "I'm sorry," he apologized. "I cannot continue." The class was over, but not forgotten.

◆§ Without a Text

Many of Reb Shraga Feivel's most compelling lessons did not come from *seforim*.

Once when *talmidim* began gathering in Reb Shraga Feivel's modest office for a class in *Tanya*, two of them found that they had no chairs. They each went to fetch one and as each entered the room with his chair, Reb Shraga Feivel chided them saying, "*Shleppers!* You brought a chair for yourself and you brought a chair for yourself, so what are you? *Shleppers!* Now if you had each brought a chair for your friend, you would each have performed an act of *chessed*. But as it is, you have only *shlepped* chairs. That's why I call you *shleppers*."

Reb Shraga Feivel once surprised a class by asking them to enumerate all 613 *mitzvos*, which of course no one could do. "If you don't know the *mitzvos* and are not aware of them, how can you expect to perform them if and when the occasion arises?"

Reb Shraga Feivel's classes started many Torah revolutions. Today, wearing kosher *tefillin* is as natural as keeping *Shabbos*. Out-of-town *talmidim* had come to Torah Vodaath with their *bar mitzvah tefillin*, usually purchased from the local Jewish bookstore or from itinerant Jewish peddlers. After Reb Shraga Feivel's classes on *tefillin*, in which he delineated the halachic requirements (such as *rebu'a* — perfect squareness) and *hidurim* (embellishments, such as *gasos*, heavier leather; *me'or echod*, one piece of leather, etc.), everyone rushed to the *sofer* (scribe) to have his checked — and, usually, replaced.

Contemporary issues were brought up from time to time in Reb Shraga Feivel's classes: "Are you expecting social justice in the great democracies? Or perhaps in the 'workers' paradise?" he'd ask, and then proceed to expose the built-in hypocrisies of man-made social systems.

In his respect for the power of the printed word, Reb Shraga Feivel joined forces with the famous *chazan*, Yossele Rosenblatt, in 1923, to produce *Dos Yiddishe Licht*, a short-lived English and Yiddish language weekly that included articles of comment and inspiration. It eventually became a daily but was forced to discontinue publication in 1927 because of financial difficulties. In fact, *Chazan* Rosenblatt went on a year-long concert tour to pay back the monies owed to creditors.

He did not hesitate to speak out on any topic, no matter how delicate or controversial. Today, a *mechitzah* is standard at a religious wedding, yet forty years ago, he had to speak out against the mingling of boys and girls at social events, decrying mixed swimming and dancing, which were accepted practices among so many in those days.

He encouraged *talmidim* who were about to get married to make the public room in their new apartments a dining room instead of the standard living room: a living room is the setting for relaxation, reading the newspaper, *batolah* — an American phenomenon, while the dining room is the place for the family to gather together for a *Shabbos* and *Yom Tov* meal, where a man can open a *sefer* and learn with a *chavrusa*.

Nor did he spare his own. A son-in-law who was in the rabbinate told me that on *Shabbos* mornings when he returned from *shul*, all swelled with pride for having delivered a stirring sermon, Reb Shraga Feivel would rise in mock reverence and say, "Nu, mine *Rabbi, vos host due heint geplapelt?* — So, my Rabbi, what have you prattled about today?" He wanted his son-in-law to understand the responsibility of preaching a sermon. Regarding rabbis who based their talks on nothing more than popular ideas or newspaper articles, he'd ask, "Is there nothing in our own literature on which to base a sermon?"

In the early years of Torah Vodaath, the Yeshivah sponsored a course in homiletics taught by Rabbi Fortman. Reb Shraga Feivel sat in on one of the classes when one of the better students, now a prominent rabbi, delivered a great address. When the *bachur* asked Reb Shraga Feivel for his opinion of the *drashah*, he said, "It was a great sermon, a good speech. You spoke about G-d, religion, faith, etc., but what was Jewish about it? A *galach* could have delivered the same talk!"

⋅§ Language of the Soul

Reb Shraga Feivel was keenly aware of the obligation of a teacher to reach the *talmid's* soul. Two of his *talmidim* became teachers in an out-of-town yeshivah where they attempted to change the language of instruction from English to Yiddish, thinking this would improve the school. When they lamented their failure to Reb Shraga Feivel, he told them, "If I knew I had ten more years to live, I would learn English."

"But why, *Rebbe?"* they protested. "All of your *talmidim* understand Yiddish."

Reb Shraga Feivel replied, "True, but English is their mother tongue, their *neshamah lashon,* and to reach *talmidim,* you must address them in their own language.

"The words from the *Shema,* 'And these words which I command you this day shall be *ahl levavecha* — on your hearts, and you shall teach them to your children.' How? They shall overflow your heart and then you'll be able to teach them to your children, from your heart to their soul!"

And how he understood the language of the *neshamah!* When Yiddel Turner would soulfully play *Keili, Keili, lama azavtani,* on his violin, Reb Shraga Feivel would close his eyes in a deep concentration that put him into a spiritual anguish, which in turn aggravated his ulcer condition, causing him acute physical pain.

◆§ Business Angles

Having been part of the business world, he understood life's realities; having tasted the bitterness of debt and failure, he was well prepared to guide his *talmidim* prudently and wisely. He considered each *bachur's* talents as well as what the Torah world needed before giving them his advice. Thus, many were encouraged to enter *chinuch,* while others were directed into business — either way, to promote Torah. His own rapport with the businessmen on the Board of Directors of Yeshivah Torah Vodaath was further indication of his ability to appreciate the various roles people play in life, and how they could be used for Torah.

Since Reb Shraga Feivel was involved with the purchase of many buildings for Torah Vodaath — school buildings and dormitories in Williamsburg, Bais Medrash Elyon in Monsey, and Camp Mesifta in the Catskill Mountains — he made sure to understand the transactions. He was one of the first to point out the *ribbis* (interest) problems with mortgages.

He had planned to build a swimming pool on the grounds of the Bais Medrash Elyon, during the time of the Eish Das program. Reb Shraga Feivel told a *talmid* that when the architect comes to survey the grounds to locate the proper site for the pool, "Don't forget to show him the rise near the main building. I think that may be the right spot." After completing his survey, the architect exclaimed, "Why of course that's the perfect site; it has the right drainage, sunlight, privacy, and protection."

∾§ The World as a Siddur

— Reb Shraga Feivel always endeavored to enlarge his awareness of G-d's omnipresence. Reb Moshe Aaron Stern recalled hiding behind Reb Shraga Feivel's home on a Friday afternoon. Reb Shraga Feivel stood on the porch, looking heavenward and repeated again and again the words from the *Zohar: "Memaleh kol almin, soveiv kol almin, v'leis asaar pahnui menai* — His glory fills the world, surrounds the world, and there is no place free of Him" ... striving for a total *deveikus* in *Hashem*.

— He saw G-d in nature and loved all things that grow. He scolded a *bachur* for ripping a leaf from a tree: "That leaf was saying *shirah* to *Hashem*; why did you have to destroy it?" When another *talmid* absentmindedly tore up a blade of grass, Reb Shraga Feivel chided him: "The *Gemara* relates that every blade of grass has a *malach* (angel) in heaven that says 'grow!' and you say 'no!' "

— He selected the site of Camp Mesifta high on a Ferndale mountaintop commanding a magnificent view with the purpose of inspiring reverence for G-d, as it is written, "Lift up your eyes and see who created all this."

— A layman once commented, "Why does he *daven* near the window and always look out?" Reb Shraga explained, "*Er meint az ich kook arois; der emes iz, az ich kook arein* — He thinks I'm looking out; in truth, I'm looking in."

Davening was sacred to him. Woe to whomever he caught talking during the *davening!* I still quake when I recall how he came running to a *bachur* sitting near me who had disturbed the sanctity of the hour. "*Arois!*" he shouted, "*Ven du vest veren baalabus vest due redden.*"

He once asked Reb Mannes Mandel (the *ba'al tefillah* on Rosh Hashanah and Yom Kippur for many years), "Out of all the long hours we spend together *davening*, how much time do we really *daven* with *kavanah*? A few minutes? So please tell me why the *davening* takes so long!"

Though he chided us for the length of our *davening*, his own *davening* was a drama of *hishtapchus hanefesh*, an outpouring of the soul. At his seat up front, on the left side of the *Beis Hamidrash* near his window (the right side was always reserved for the *Roshei Yeshivos*; he would never sit there), he stood before his beloved Creator as *Avraham Ohavi*, as a child speaking with his revered Father. No airs, no theatrics, no outward manifestations or external movements, but a silent cry, an inward yearning that made all present recall the words "*Tzamah lecha nafshi* — my soul thirsts for Thee;" words they heard him sing with so much longing at *Shalosh Seudos*, words they witnessed and could actually feel.

⋅§ ' Nistar" Mendlowitz

Reb Shraga Feivel once related that a disciple of the *Ba'al Shem Tov* asked, "Rebbe, if the '36 righteous men' are secret, hidden *tzaddikim*, does this mean then that you, the *Ba'al Shem Tov*, whose fame is renowned, cannot be one of them?" The *Ba'al Shem Tov* replied, "The world thinks it knows what a *tzaddik* is, but the righteousness of famous *tzaddikim* is far greater than what the world can imagine. Even those who are famous can be hidden *tzaddikim!*"

While it is true that the name of Reb Shraga Feivel became a byword in the Torah world, he tried to hide his greatness. Indeed, the Ponovezer Rav, Rabbi Yoseif Kahaneman, referred to Reb Shraga Feivel as "*Nistar* Mendlowitz," the secret, hidden man. He had brought his *semichah* from Europe, but he kept the document hidden away. A cleaning lady in Scranton chanced upon it and said, "Oh, so you are a Rabbi!" Reb Shraga Feivel promptly tore the document into shreds.

Nistar Mendlowitz — He dressed conservatively in the fashion of the day — suits, neckties, the normal garb of an American businessman, to remove from himself any vestige of *Rabbanus* . . . but apparently he could not part with his black velour hat. He wore his *tzitzis* over his shirt, but we rarely saw them, because he wore a vest on top of them. Long *peyos?* Yes, of course, but neatly curled and almost hidden from view. He was always immaculate, well groomed, with the outward appearance of a contemporary man, but beneath was the humble spirit of a *tzaddik* who walked with G-d.

Reb Shraga Feivel forbade his picture to be taken. The few pictures we have were snapped without his knowledge. I remember how he pursued a *bachur* who had photographed him, insisting the boy hand over the film.

Nistar Mendlowitz — Ours may be called the age of the tape recorder. Yet there is not one recorded word of Reb Shraga Feivel! What I would give just to be able to hear his voice once again say, "*Avraham Ohavi.*" But he would not permit an outsider into his classes, much less allow himself to be taped. He was even upset with those who wrote notes in class.

One night, I was in the *Beis Hamidrash* recording the day's lectures in my notebook, when I felt the desk being pushed hard into my stomach. Looking up, I was startled to see Reb Shraga Feivel leaning over me, saying, "Yitzchak, *kasveim al luach lebecha* (write them on the tablets of your heart)."

In his humility, before beginning a class in the *Beis Midrash Kattan*, on South Third Street, he would look around the room and say, "*Lomdim, arois* (scholars, leave)." Reb Yosef Levitan (recognized as one of the outstanding *lomdim* of his time) would duck behind me, so that Reb Shraga Feivel would not ask him to leave.

Nistar Mendlowitz — Opening a yeshivah high school with secular studies was a novel idea that Reb Shraga Feivel would never have undertaken without first asking a *she'eilah*, so he consulted many of the *gedolim* in Europe at that time, including Rabbi Chaim Ozer Grodzenski, Munkatcher Rav, Rabbi Elchanan Wasserman, and the Ragotchover *Gaon*. The written replies, which the family has in safekeeping, are all addressed to the late Rabbi Gedalya Schorr. Apparently Reb Shraga Feivel had asked Rabbi Schorr to send the *she'eilah* so his name would not be known to the *gedolim* in Europe.

When Yeshivah Ner Israel dedicated its building on Garrison Boulevard in Baltimore, Rabbi Yaakov Kamenetzky — as a father of two *talmidim* there — attended the ceremony. He recalled how, during the dedication, the Master of Ceremonies called out, "We will now hear a few words from Rabbi Feivel Mendlowitz." Everyone turned toward the rear and waited for him to come forward. Reb Shraga Feivel said, "There must be some mistake. They must mean someone else, for I am Mr. Mendlowitz, not Rabbi Mendlowitz," and he refused to ascend to the podium. He did give permission to announce his pledge of $800, but remained adamant in his refusal to speak. This was Reb Yaakov's first contact with Reb Shraga Feivel, and marked the beginning of a long warm relationship, culminating in Reb Yaakov serving as *Rosh Yeshivah* of Mesifta Torah Vodaath.

◄§ Above Institutional Loyalty

Rabbi Yaakov Ruderman, *Rosh Hayeshivah* of Ner Israel in Baltimore, told of the time when his yeshivah was in danger of closing. Suddenly a Jew from New York arrived, placed a handsome sum of money on his desk and left without saying a word; Reb Shraga Feivel at work! Similarly, after the Bobover Rebbe had arrived in America, Reb Shraga gave him $10,000 to help him start his *Beis Midrash*. When the Satmar Rav came to America, Reb Shraga Feivel was there with another $10,000 gift of seed money; and the Klausenberger Rav, too, received $10,000.

These sums — $30,000 in all — from a man who was burdened with the herculean task of supporting his own institution, and in fact, was forced to borrow this money! During his last days on earth, he discussed with his family ways to pay off this personal debt. As one of his *talmidim* put it, "He was an institution above all institutions." Torah was the goal, regardless of who did the task.

Even more generous than financial support of Torah was his willingness to send outstanding *talmidim* to start Lakewood's Bais Medrash Govoha — as he did for the Yeshivah Chachmei Lublin in Detroit and for Telshe in Cleveland. In addition, he refused to accept *talmidim* from the Brownsville area in Brooklyn because the Mesivta Chaim Berlin was situated there and needed *talmidim* at that time. When taken to task by the lay leaders of Torah Vodaath for giving away his best students with whom he had toiled so hard, Reb Shraga Feivel answered simply, "If that is where they will grow best and Torah will best be served, what difference does it make to me where they learn — in my yeshivah or with Reb Aharon?"

৵৵ Spreading the Light: Torah Umesorah

Reb Shraga Feivel dreamed of spreading the light of Torah study. Thus he founded Torah Umesorah to establish day schools all over America, often calling Torah Umesorah *"Mein Liebling."* A prominent educator wrote, "The best way to send information is to wrap it up in a person." Besides wrapping many packages, Reb Shraga Feivel had great plans for staffing all the new yeshivos he dreamed of establishing. He would open a special school for teachers where yeshivah graduates would develop their ability to transmit Torah: "Eish Das," an institute to service all yeshivos, where every *Rosh Yeshivah* would send his graduates for the "finishing touches." Rabbi Aharon Kotler and Rabbi Reuven Grozovsky backed the enterprise and had wanted Rabbi Yaakov Kamenetzky to head the institution. Alas, other yeshivah leaders did not fully appreciate the plan. As Reb Yaakov commented, *"Zei hobben Reb Shraga Feivel nit farshtahnen"* — others could not believe that there could be such a person not thinking of his own self-interest. Reb Shraga Feivel did open Eish Das for a short while, at the future Bais Medrash Elyon site in Monsey, in the hope that it would become a school for *rabbonim, mechanchim,* and *shochtim.* Had he been successful, who knows how much improved Torah life would be today!

◆§ Summer Growth

In spite of some frustrations, many of Reb Shraga Feivel's plans did materialize. He knew the world outside of the yeshivah, and was keenly aware that everything accomplished with his students could be dissipated in the summer months on the streets of New York. Thus Reb Shraga Feivel organized America's first yeshivah summer camp, Camp Mesifta, in Mountaindale, New York. Reb Shraga Feivel carried the financial burden of the camp and found numerous ways to keep the camp going in spite of the lack of funds. *Talmidim* would compare notes: "Did you see Reb Shraga Feivel early Friday morning helping the camp-cook clean the chickens for *Shabbos?*" — an economy measure laced with love for his *talmidim.* When Camp Mesifta moved to Ferndale, New York, it became the summer home for thousands of boys from all yeshivos during its many years of existence. *Gedolei Yisroel* also stayed there: Rabbi Elchanan Wasserman visited the camp for several weeks; Rabbi Shlomo Heiman's summers were spent there, and later Rabbi Yaakov Kamenetzky, as well as other *Roshei Yeshivos,* graced its grounds.

While Camps Torah Vodaath and Ohr Shraga are the direct heirs of Camp Mesifta, the scores of religious summer camps across North America are also carrying on its legacy.

IV. Eretz Yisroel

Much as he appreciated the American scene, Reb Shraga Feivel never really "established residence" in the United States. His home on Williamsburg's South Second Street was sparsely furnished with only bare necessities. Above the wall of his dining room, facing his chair, was a painting of the verse: "If I forget thee, O Jerusalem, may my right hand forget its cunning." Whether sitting in his dining room, or in the classroom in Torah Vodaath, this was the focus of his thoughts.

When he taught *Al Naharos Bavel* (On the Rivers of Babylon, there we sat and wept) in *Tehillim,* or *Veli'Yerushalayim* in

Shemoneh Esrei, he rarely got beyond a word or two without being so overcome with emotion that he was incapable of continuing. It was one thing for us to read about Jerusalem and its destruction; it was quite another to witness its impact on a man in our midst. Much as we have seen Jews weep for the suffering of others, share in their pain and their hope, whom else did we ever see cry for the *golus of the Shechinah?* ... After a class that pulsated with love for *Eretz Yisroel,* he remarked, "And the world says I am not a Zionist" — a fatal flaw in the eyes of American Jews of that time. Zionist he was, but without the political underpinnings; an *oheiv Eretz Yisroel* as taught by the *Rambam,* as expressed by the *shirah* of Reb Yehudah Halevi, as defined in his many Kuzari classes.

The *halachah* forbids leaving an uncovered knife on the table during *Bircas Hamazon,* for fear that the despair one feels during the paragraph dedicated to Yerushalayim may drive a person to take his life. On the Friday night in the summer of 1948, when word reached America of the fall of Jerusalem, Reb Shraga Feivel was struck down at his *Shabbos* table by a heart attack, while reciting *Uv'nei Yerushalayim* — the *berachah* regarding rebuilding Jerusalem. During that illness, I was privileged to serve him at his home and I vividly remember him under the oxygen tent, pounding his hand against the bed, murmuring over and over, "*Vos vet zein mit Eretz Yisroel?*"

He often repeated: "Each country is best suited by its very nature to bring forth certain products. Polar bears breed best near the Arctic Circle; Torah grows best in *Eretz Yisroel.*"

He was a committed member of the Agudath Israel and thus his love for *Eretz Yisroel* and the people of Israel was directed by Torah guidelines, and was beyond political considerations. He encouraged Rabbi Shlomo Heiman to become the Vice President of the Agudath Israel of America in 1938, when the movement was scorned by most Orthodox Jews, and personally raised large sums of money for the Zeirei Agudath Israel's *hatzalah* programs during the war.

When the State of Israel was declared, he said that while he does not know what will become of it in the future, at its founding it would serve as a haven for countless refugees, and that in itself is cause for rejoicing. Adding, "Only those who moan with Israel can understand her joys as well."

When asked why the State of Israel was brought into being largely by so many non-religious Jews, he answered, *"Ki lo yidach mimenu nidach! —* G-d does not want to lose any Jew and gives every Jew some thread by which he can hang on to his Jewishness. Zionism has kept otherwise assimilated Jews identified with the People of Israel, at least remaining within the Jewish fold."

Rabbi Berl Greenbaum, his late son-in-law, preserved Reb Shraga Feivel's cogent *mashal* about the birth of the State: "In a normal birth, the child emerges head first. A breech birth, when the child comes feet first, is a difficult, even hazardous birth, but the child can develop to be normal and healthy. If the State of Israel had been born head first — that is, led by *Roshei Am* (its Torah leadership) — its stability would have been ssured. But even now we can hope."

In the very early years of Torah Vodaath, a group of people had wanted to place the blue and white flag in the Yeshivah. Said Reb Shraga Feivel, "If only they would have added the *pasuk,* '*Zichru Toras Moshe avdi*' to the flag, I would have no problem putting it in the Yeshivah."

On the Saturday night following his reaction to the establishment of the State of Israel, a leading Chassidic figure of that era called for Reb Shraga Feivel and upbraided him in no uncertain terms for his "Zionistic" leanings. When he returned home, his family asked him what had happened. Reb Shraga Feivel told them, and added, "I could have answered him *Chazal* for *Chazal, Midrash* for *Midrash,* but I did not want to incur his wrath, for he is an *adam gadol,* a *tzaddik,* and besides that, he has a fiery temper."

◆§ Reaching Across Oceans

In his book *Zichronos Shel Bnei Brak,* the late mayor of the city — Yitzchok Gerstenkorn — included a chapter "In the Shadows of Torah Vodaath," in which he tells of his visit to New York in 1929. He had come to the States to raise money to found a religious *yishuv* in the Tel Aviv area — Bnei Brak. After many difficulties, he chanced upon Reb Shraga Feivel who extended a generous hand of friendship and helped him raise $6,000, a huge sum of money in those years. Gerstenkorn writes that he never met a person with such love for *Eretz Yisroel:* "Every time I mentioned *Eretz Yisroel,* tears welled up in Reb Shraga Feivel's eyes." When I visit Reb Shraga

Feivel's grave in Bnei Brak, I find solace in the knowledge that he is buried in the Torah community he helped to create.

A day before his *petirah* (passing), Reb Shraga Feivel called his son-in-law Rabbi Alexander Linchner to his bedside and instructed him: *"Tu eppes far Eretz Yisroel."* Reb Shraga Feivel added that if *Hashem* would give him life and strength, he would move one of his institutions to *Eretz Yisroel*. Rabbi Linchner kept that bequest and founded Boys Town and Merom Zion Institutes in Jerusalem, where today hundreds of underprivileged Israeli youths are given a Torah education and are prepared for a productive role in industry as well.

Even though he had packed and was ready to go to *Eretz Yisroel* several times, Reb Shraga Feivel never made the trip — why not? A member of his family suggests: "My father would never have been able to recover from the experience of standing before the *Kosel!* His soul would have fled from his body."

↭§ Fighting Illness

It should be noted that all his life's accomplishments were achieved under the pressures of ill health and pain. Even as a young man, Reb Shraga Feivel had been afflicted with a serious lung problem. His doctor in Europe had callously written him off — to his face. Legend has it that he responded, "Let the fellow say what he wants, I'll outlive him!" (*"Ich vell dem schlack überleben!"*) — and so it was. This was typical of his determination not to let anything interfere with his plans for *Avodas Hashem*.

Racked with pain due to a severe ulcer problem, he often masked his suffering with a joke or sharp saying. He once confided to a *talmid*, "The pain can be awesome at times, but so what? Life is made up of a long string of individual moments. Pain for the moment can be withstood. As for what's ahead, there's no sense in suffering what one does not yet feel."

His memorial stone carries the inscription, *"Somach b'yesurrin* (rejoiced in pain)," for good reason. Even when the pain was so severe that the doctors ordered complete rest for a full year, without any book study, he used his time to develop his philosophies of life. Among his writings from that period was a comparison between the schools of *Mussar* and *Chassidus*. (Pointing to his own bed, he once quipped, *"Chassidus* is like a hospital bed; it lifts you up.")

Typically, he said: "*Mussar* stresses: 'I have set my sins before me'; *Chassidus* — 'I have set the Lord before me.' "

◆§ ... to the Last Day

Tuesday, September 7, 1948, third day of Elul, 5708, was a black day for Torah Jewry. Reb Shraga Feivel breathed his last in his home, next door to Bais Medrash Elyon, Monsey. When we heard the shocking news — he had been improving, we had been told — a group of us traveled to Monsey to have the *zechus* of participating in the *taharah*, which was conducted in the *mikveh* of the main building of Bais Medrash Elyon. (Reb Shraga Feivel saw to it that his yeshivah always had a *mikveh* for the *bachurim*.)

From Monsey, the funeral cortege made its way to the Mesifta in Williamsburg, where thousands had gathered to pay their last respects. His *aron* was brought into the *beis midrash*, where *Tehillim* was recited. Over the years, whenever he attended a funeral with his son-in-law, Rabbi Linchner, Reb Shraga Feivel would tell him how he wanted his own funeral conducted: No eulogy, with one exception — Reb Yaakov, at the graveside ... Amongst the many buses chartered for Reb Shraga Feivel's funeral procession, the bus carrying Reb Yaakov somehow got lost and arrived at the cemetery after the interment. No eulogy was held, probably in keeping with Reb Shraga Feivel's innermost desires.

His last will to the leadership of the Mesifta is a revelation of his soul: "*Ir zolt hitten dos Hur Vahr un dos bissele Chassidus.*" Safeguard the thread of truth and the touch of *Chassidus*.

◆§ Epilogue

Two years later, a small group from the *Chevrah Kadisha* (I was privileged to be among them) gathered at his gravesite to exhume the casket, and transfer it to Israel for burial. In 1948, when he was buried, travel to Israel was almost impossible so that at the interment, a *tnai* (conditional burial) had been made to allow disinterment in the future.

His grave in the Zichron Yaakov Cemetery in Bnei Brak, not far from that of the Chazon Ish, is next to that of Reb Eliyahu Dessler (*Michtav MeEliyahu*) and Reb Isaac Sher, Slobodka *Rosh Yeshivah* — men who changed the world.

His modest monument is only one stone high and bears the following inscription:

❦   ❦   ❦

"Shraga" means light — hopefully his *talmidim* and admirers will kindle new lights so that his efforts to illuminate the darkness will continue to shine on in the future, perpetuating the work of *"The Hofchi Hatzur,"* the one who overturned the rocks to allow the light to enter.

Rabbi Yaakov Kamenetzky

*He embodied
the greatness
of Slobodka,
inspiring
generations
of Talmidim*

Rabbi Yaakov Kamenetzky
5650-5746 / 1890-1986

I. Perspective on Time

R ABBI YAAKOV KAMENETZKY is no longer with us, and now *Klal
Yisroel* has become painfully aware of its humble status. Reb
Yaakov, blessed as he was with *arichas yomim* (longevity), living a
full ninety-five years, represented a unique richness in the
Lithuanian traditions of pursuit of excellence in Torah and *midos*
(the ethical personality) associated with earlier times, a tradition that
in its fullness is so beyond the reach of our attainment that it is
almost beyond our comprehension. In his absence, that greatness of
the man and his era are now further removed from us:

Can we gauge the lifelong effect on an eight-year-old from
seeing elderly Jews back into the snowbanks to permit him — the
"illuy of Dolhinov," as Reb Yaakov was known — to pass through
the narrow path dug through the drifts, so he could keep his daily
schedule of study with their *Rav?* "The impact of their respect for
the Torah study of a mere child never left me," said Reb Yaakov.

Can we evaluate the strength of conviction of the young *Rav* of

Tzitovyan refusing to officiate at the funeral of an over-zealous congregant? The man, who had been told by his doctor to eat on Yom Kippur for health reasons, and was instructed by that *Rav* to follow this prescription, nonetheless fasted, and then died. Reb Yaakov did attend the funeral and, apparently to discourage others from following this reckless behavior, refused to officiate, since the man had in effect taken his own life.

Do we appreciate the sensitivity of a sixty-five-year-old man who stayed up all night — learning throughout, of course — to keep an early-morning appointment, rather than set his alarm for dawn since it might disturb the sleep of a non-Jewish neighbor who returned from his job at 3 a.m.? (An echo of Reb Yisroel Salanter? Of course! Rabbi Yaakov Kame etzky was a favorite of Reb Yisroel's disciple, the *Alter* of Slobodka, and was much influenced by Rabbi Naftali Amsterdam, who had been so close to Reb Yisroel.)

Do we recognize the implications when a man of eighty-five refuses to answer a highly complex *she'eila* (halachic query) "because I may at the moment forget a *Tosafos* somewhere in *Shas* (the entirety of the Talmud)" — as Rabbi Kamenetzky said just ten years before his passing? . . . And we become aware how every *psak* rendered until then was without such a liability, having *Shas*, all codes and their major commentaries at his fingertips!

Do we fathom the devotion to *klal* and *prat* (the congregation and the individual) of a man of ninety years of age who tells his loyal, protective *Rebbetzin*, as did Reb Yaakov: "Don't leave the telephone receiver off the hook — even during my lunch. Picture the frustration of the person who calls, finds the line busy, and calls again — goes on about his business, and stops his car to get out and call again, and again the line is busy . . . Besides, my feeling is that G-d granted me these extra years as a gift for me to use for others. How can I squander my time on my own comfort?"

How far removed we are from the way in which the simple facts of *halachah* absorbed by a Torah personality can graduate from *chachmah* to *binah* to *daas* — from knowledge to understanding to ingrained nature . . . the manner in which Reb Yaakov learned as a child that one holds an item requiring a *brachah* in one's right hand in honor of the *brachah*, and then, lying in a hospital bed at age ninety-four, how he strained to maneuver his right hand laden with a complement of intravenous tubes, to grasp the cup of water on which he wanted to pronounce the *Shehakol*, ignoring his free left hand.

Men such as Reb Yaakov serve as a means of viewing distant times, times of pristine purity, inhabited by men of towering greatness of scholarship and genius of character. We must quickly gather our fleeting impressions of Reb Yaakov before the light he cast upon our lives disappears into the shadows.

Reb Yaakov Kamenetzky had a keen awareness of how our generation is in desperate need of any guidance he could offer from his far-reaching perspective, rooted in the era in which he had grown. He understood this task as the responsibility of all parents to their children as part of their role as living links in the chain of *Mesorah*. In this way, he was a parent of sorts to an entire generation growing up in America. The following is just one anecdote illustrating how Reb Yaakov himself described the implications of this role:

On the plane returning from the sixth *Knessiah Gedolah* (International Conference) of Agudath Israel in Jerusalem in 1980, Reb Yaakov was seated in one of the two seats at the very front of the aircraft, next to Yerucham Meshal, treasurer of Histadrut. While the two discussed various matters ("Mainly *Tanach*, especially some questions he had on *Sefer Ruth*," reported the *Rosh Hayeshivah*), a man in his forties and a girl in her early twenties came periodically to check on Reb Yaakov's personal needs.

"*Aides de camp?*" asked Meshal.

"Oh, no," said Reb Yaakov. "My son from Brooklyn, and a granddaughter from Jerusalem who's coming to the States for a visit."

"Do you mean that you actually have contact with your children and grandchildren?" marveled Meshal. "I seldom see my children except for occasional labor conferences, and the grandchildren — never."

"That's to be expected," smiled the *Rosh Hayeshivah*. "Permit me to explain. We religious Jews have our own understanding of the passing of generations. We look back on Jewry's face-to-face encounter with G-d on Sinai at the giving of the Torah as the spiritual highpoint of world history. The generations immediately after Sinai viewed their parents with awe: 'They actually heard G-d speak!' And their children after them looked at their parents with a similar deference: 'Imagine! They actually lived with people who were present at Sinai!' And so it has been throughout the ages, to the point that my children and grandchildren believe that my familiarity with earlier generations, beyond their horizon of contact

— my relative closeness to Sinai, so to speak — endows me with a wisdom and spiritual sensitivity that they do not possess. So they respect me. And I, in turn, attempt to transmit to them whatever I may happen to have gathered from previous generations.

"But you are a Darwinist. You believe that man is in constant evolutionary ascent from the apes. Why should your children or grandchildren respect you? All your age and your generations represent to them is one step closer to the apes!"

Indeed, Reb Yaakov's familiarity with earlier generations was a blessing — one that he appreciated and delighted in sharing with others.

Before we explore the lessons he taught — by word and by example — let us first review the outline of his life, how he progressed from one stage to the next: Yeshivah *bachur*, *Kollel* fellow, teacher, *Rav*, *posek*, *Rosh Yeshivah*, leader of *Klal Yisroel*, living link to the greatness of previous generations, guide and mentor to countless individuals — leaders and humble folk alike.

II. The Stages of Man

⋈ Childhood: From Blumka's Kloiz to the Butchers' Beis Midrash

He was known as Yankel Dolhinover. He had been born in Kalushkove in January 1890, but his parents, Reb Binyomin and Itta Ettel Kamenetzky, had moved to Dolhinov — when their son, as a mere child, revealed his vast potential — in hope of finding sufficiently challenging teachers in the larger town. He was learning *Chumash* by age two, and had learned major parts of *Tanach* and committed them to memory when he was six. Understandably, the resources of Dolhinov soon also proved insufficient, and the youngster moved on to Minsk, to learn under Reb Yehoshua Tzvi Zimbalist ("Horodner") in the famed Blumka's Kloiz.*

After his *bar mitzvah*, the Dolhinover *Illuy* — as he became known — moved on to the *Katzovishe Kloiz* (the "Butchers' Beis Midrash," so called because it was built by the butchers of Minsk

---

* This was the celebrated *beis midrash* built by a lady — Bluma, by name — in gratitude for the fulfillment of the *Shaagas Arye's* blessings to her for riches and worthy children. He had blessed her in reward for her gift of *Shabbos* provisions when he was expelled from his *dayanus* of Minsk on a short Friday in 1733 for issuing a controversial *psak*. Her offspring married into the family of Rabbi Akiva Eiger, and the *kloiz* she built with her wealth became the setting for the growth of some of our people's greatest scholars.

upon the initiative of a Reb Yaakov Ochsenburg) where he studied with the slightly younger Artchele Sislovitzer (later known to us as Rabbi Aaron Kotler) and at times with Reuvain Minsker (Rabbi Reuvain Grozovsky, son of the *dayan* of Minsk, Reb Shamshon), who was three years his senior.

◆§ Slobodka Years

When he was fifteen years of age, Reb Yaakov and Reb Aaron followed their older friend to Slobodka, where Reb Yaakov became especially close to the *Alter*, Reb Nosson Tzvi Finkel. The *Alter* was known for his stress on *gadlus ha'adam* — the potential for greatness within each person — and the sensitivity one must develop toward the needs of others. For the next twenty-one years, Reb Yaakov was learning in Slobodka and associated yeshivos, and he emerged as a prototype Slobodka *talmid*.

During his years in these yeshivos and the various Torah institutions where he sought refuge during the upheavals of World War I, he encountered a number of outstanding rabbinical figures. While using the opportunity to absorb their approach to Torah study and *Mussar*, he invariably impressed one and all with his brilliance in Torah and exceptional character. The list of people he studied under, or otherwise met, includes such luminaries as: Rabbi Moshe Mordechai Epstein, *Rosh Hayeshivah* in Slobodka, who was extremely fond of Reb Yaakov (see the letter he wrote to him); Rabbi Isser Zalman Meltzer, author of *Even Ha'azel*, *Rav* and *Rosh Hayeshivah* of Slutsk, where Reb Yaakov spent several years to help strengthen the yeshivah, at the *Alter's* request; Rabbi Zalmen Sender Shapira, *talmid* of the *Beis Halevi* of Brisk and later, *Rav* of Krinik, where Reb Yaakov spent several months; Rabbi Yisroel Shulevitz and Rabbi Yechiel Michel Gordon, *Roshei Hayeshivah* of Lomza, where Reb Yaakov made a deep impression on all with his unusual *hasmadah* (diligence) during the two years he spent (1916-1917) there*; Rabbi Dov Tzvi Heller, *Mashgiach* of the Slobodka Yeshivah — who, during the yeshivah's exile in Kremenchug immediately following the war, welcomed Reb Yaakov's return and proudly accepted him as the *chasan* of his daughter Itta Ettel; Rabbi Reuvain Dov Dessler, who headed the

---

* In the words of Rabbi Aaron Zlotowitz: "Nights in the Lomza Yeshivah were not illuminated by electric lamps, but by a solitary wax candle. There was Reb Yaakov 'Minsker,' at his open *Gemara* until the last flicker of the candle — every single night."

famed Kollel, the "Talmud Torah of Kelm," where Reb Yaakov spent several years; Rabbi Chaim Ozer Grodzenski, of Vilna, who responded favorably to Reb Yaakov's petition on behalf of the *Alter* for a grant of 4,000 mark from the Vaad Hayeshivos, needed to bring the yeshivah back to Slobodka. As one of the founding members of the Kollel Beis Yisroel in Slobodka, Reb Yaakov published *chiddushei Torah* (novellae) on *Shabbos* and *Eruvin* in the institution's journal, *Kisvei Beis Yisroel*, in 1923 . . . Over ten years later, a delegation from Antwerp invited him to become their *Rav.* "How do you know of me?" he asked.

They replied that the Chazon Ish (in Bnei Brak) had recommended Reb Yaakov.

"But we've never met," he protested, "and he would never suggest a person for a position unless he knows him."

The recommendation remained a puzzle until many years later, when a visitor to the Chazon Ish saw his copy of Reb Yaakov's *Chiddushei Torah* that were published in *Kisvei Beis Yisroel*, with notes and comments on the margins. Apparently it was on that basis that he believed him to be fully qualified and most suitable for the position. (Reb Yaakov did not think so, and declined the invitation.)

◄§ From Great Rav of a Small Town to Great Rav of a Big City

During the years 1926-1937, Rav Yaakov served as *Rav* in the small town of Tzitovyan — a resort some twenty kilometers from Kelm. In spite of the extreme poverty which barely kept body and soul together, this position — typical of Lithuanian *rabbonus* — offered Reb Yaakov a golden opportunity to immerse himself in Torah and continue his growth. Summer months brought a stream of vacationing visitors, allowing him to meet a number of leading rabbinical figures.

In 1937, Reb Yaakov was asked by the Kovno *Rav* to go to America to solicit funds for a yeshivah. Reb Yaakov later recalled that the mounting anti-Semitism in Nazi Germany to the west and the incorrigible Soviet Jew-baiting to the east had made him extremely uneasy. As a result, he accepted the assignment to America with the intention of exploring the Jewish community there as a possible place of refuge. After a rude introduction to the nature of fund-raising as it was then conducted, he resigned. He was soon informed of an interim *rabbonus* in Seattle, Washington. Rabbi Solomon P. Wohlgelernter, the *Rav* of the city's Congregation Bikur Cholim, was taking a leave of absence for a half year, and confided that he was hard pressed to find someone qualified who would step in for him during his absence, and then relinquish the position upon his return — until he met Reb Yaakov.

While serving as *Rav* in Seattle, Reb Yaakov was advised that it was essential that he publish some of his *chiddushei Torah* if he expected to gain a prominent position. He wrote to his family to mail him one of his many manuscripts,* for a *sefer* devoted to resolving a number of problematic halachic decisions of the *Rambam:* The classic commentators were at loss for sources for these decisions, which Reb Yaakov, in his *sefer*, traced directly to different passages in *Tanach*. The parcel never arrived in Seattle, a loss that Reb Yaakov accepted as an expression of G-d's will that the writings not be published.

After his stay in Seattle, Reb Yaakov had planned to assume a *shamoshes* in a *shul* in San Francisco and then arrange for his family to join him. Before departing for California, he was informed that Rabbi Yehuda Leib Graubard, *Rav* of the Toras Emes *Shul* in Toronto, had passed away, and that he might apply for the position. First he sought the approval of the Kovno *Rav*, Rabbi Avraham Shapira, who had dispatched him to America.

During his interview, he was asked if he was a *chassid*. "Yes, I am," he replied. "My *Rebbe*, however, is a *Litvak*" — referring to the *Alter*. Reb Yaakov became *Rav* in Toronto, and was joined by his family, thanks to the efforts of some of the city's *baalei battim*, who recognized the treasure that had become theirs.

While in Toronto, Reb Yaakov devoted himself to raising the level of the community's religious schools, including the Eitz Chaim Elementary Day School, and the Yeshivas Maharil where boys attending public high school — because of lack of a yeshivah — learned *Gemara* for four hours every afternoon, full days on Sundays; giving regular *shiurim* to the city's *baalei battim* (which included a number of learned men of yeshivah background), and guiding as many young men as possible to pursue their studies in the senior-level yeshivos in New York and Baltimore. In his later years, he frequently referred to this or that *Rav*, *Rosh Hayeshivah* or *melamed* of Torontonian origin as "my *Olam Habba*," "my purpose

---

* When he was seventeen, he had authored another *sefer* on the *Rambam*, a study of his terminologies demonstrating how precise interpretation of the expressions can resolve a number of apparent contradictions. In 1984, his *Iyunim Bamikra*, subsequently expanded to *Emes LeYaakov*, containing some of Reb Yaakov's highly original commentaries on *Chumash*, was published.

in being in Toronto," or "the living proof that American *can* produce a Chofetz Chaim — thank G-d that I had a hand in discovering him in Toronto!"

⊷§ Rise to Prominence

The place was Baltimore, Maryland. The occasion, the *chanukas habayis* (dedication) of the new building of Yeshivah Ner Israel. Reb Shraga Feivel Mendlowitz, a product of Hungarian yeshivos, was impressed with Reb Yaakov, the prototype of Slobodka, for having traveled by train from Toronto to honor the yeshivah where his sons learned. And Rabbi Kamenetzky was fascinated by the self-effacing *Menahel* of Mesivta Torah Vodaath — the man who looked around for "Rabbi" Mendlowitz when the name was called, summoning him to the dais. ("Rabbi? Not I, I'm *Mister* Mendlowitz.") When they were introduced, Reb Shraga Feivel invited Reb Yaakov to head his Aish Dos Teachers Institute, but Reb Yaakov was not interested.

During a later visit to New York in 1945, Reb Yaakov was to meet with Reb Shraga Feivel, and he expected a repeat of the previous invitation. As part of his yearly review of the entirety of *Tanach* (Scripture), Reb Yaakov was studying the Book of Ruth. He was struck by the criticism of Elimelech for seeking refuge in Moab from the famine in *Eretz Yisroel.*

"Why fault him for ensuring his own survival?" wondered Reb Yaakov. "Except, that as a leader he had no right to forsake his people during their time of need. Nor should he have left the spirituality of the Land of Israel . . . Am I better? Do I have the right to stay in Toronto and not respond to the call of Reb Shraga Feivel to head Aish Dos? And wouldn't my children be better off with the superior Torah education available in Brooklyn? I will accept his offer!"

Reb Shraga Feivel did not mention Aish Dos but offered him the *Rosh Hayeshivah's* daily *blatt shiur* of Mesivta Torah Vodaath, to replace the then-ailing Rabbi Shlomo Heiman. Reb Yaakov felt that accepting the position could harm Reb Shlomo by making him feel discarded, and refused. The following year, in 1946, after Rabbi Heiman's *petirah*, Reb Yaakov did join Mesivta Torah Vodaath,* eventually giving the *shiur* preparatory to *semichah.*

---

* This appointment was suggested by Reb Yaakov's boyhood friend and colleague in Slobodka, Rabbi Reuvain Grozovsky, who also had refused to take over Reb Shlomo's weekly *shiur klalli* until after Reb Shlomo had passed away.

Following the will of the *Hashgachah* as he understood it, Reb Yaakov left the relative comforts of Toronto for what was to become a major chapter in his life and in the history of American Torah Jewry.

Reb Yaakov's former colleagues from Slobodka — Rabbi Reuvain Grozovsky, *Rosh Hayeshivah* of Torah Vodaath, and Rabbi Aaron Kotler, *Rosh Hayeshivah* of Bais Medrash Govoha — were quick to initiate him into the leadership ranks of the Torah community, first as a member of the Presidium of Agudath Israel of America, and then to its *Moetzes Gedolei HaTorah.* He was also initiated into the leadership of Torah Umesorah, Agudas Harabbonim, and eventually Chinuch Atzmai. His *talmidim* in the *semichah* group in the Mesivta were soon aware of his exceptional stature, as a *talmid chacham* of vast knowledge and exemplary *midos*, as were the other *talmidim* of Torah Vodaath.

With Reb Shraga Feivel's passing in 1948, Reb Yaakov, together with Rabbi Gedalya Schorr, became the heads of the yeshivah. During the years through 1968, the yeshivah opened its in-city Kollel, and eventually moved from Williamsburg to its current Flatbush location. The impact of his activities during these years cannot be measured with statistics. Rather, it is to be evaluated by the growth of each *bachur* who watched his *davening*, marked by intense concentration cloaked with minimum movement; who heard him articulate yeshivah policy regarding the criteria for selecting one *shechitah* (brand of meat) over another ("The Torah is more concerned about a *shochet's* control of his tongue than his outer appearance"), or time of *tefillah* on *Shabbos;* who was guided by him in day-to-day study in the Kollel; who posed a halachic query or asked for advice, and was treated to a deliberately paced show of quick mind, penetrating analysis, and vast knowledge; who looked into his calm, smiling face and saw a reflection of the great men who had taught him, guided him and, ultimately, entrusted him with the next generation.

◈§ Monsey Years

When Reb Yaakov stepped down from the leadership of Mesivta Torah Vodaath in 1968, shortly thereafter moving to the then-rural community of Monsey, New York, it may have been construed by some as a step toward retirement, but that was not the case. Rather, it signaled a shift in his activities, even a broadening of sorts. Under the watchful eye of his second *Rebbetzin*, the former

Mrs. Chana Urman of Toronto* (his first wife, Itta Ettel, passed away in 1954), Reb Yaakov was able to make his home and his *beis midrash* on Saddle River Road a magnet for rabbis, laymen, leaders and young people needing his *psak halachah*, his advice and his blessings. Beyond doubt, the scope of Monsey as an expanding Torah community is in great measure due to his influence.

Up until his last years, when illness curtailed his activities, Reb Yaakov traveled far and wide without hesitation for Torah causes. His *Shalosh Seudos* discourses at the annual conventions of Agudath Israel of America were always a high point of the conclave, wherein he shared brilliant insights on the *Sidrah*, woven with personal anecdotes, and presented them with their contemporary application. At the Knessiah Gedolah in 1980, Reb Yaakov declared his profound love for *Eretz Yisroel*, especially the "singular *chein* (charm) of the children of Yerushalayim." Whenever he visited yeshivos and *chadorim* in the Holy Land, Reb Yaakov was mobbed by children and *bachurim* who responded to his warmth. The love was obviously mutual.

III. The Light of His Ways

Darkness is an absence of light. Ours is not to curse the darkness but to bask in the remembered glow of the illumination that once was ours. The light of Reb Yaakov's personality, passing through the prism of his actions, gives us an opportunity to learn and to grow. For one, his life was a quest to perceive and fulfill the specific role assigned for him by Providence. (The source could be an invitation to fulfill a position or an insight from his studies — such as the passage from *Ruth.*) Throughout, he was distinguished by the Torah he learned and the *midos* that he had developed, especially during his years in Slobodka. Specifically, as he said in response to a question, as to how he had merited so long a life: "I did my best to avoid hurting others, and I never said a *sheker* (falsehood)."

The framework for this study, then, is the nature of his leadership, his dedication to protecting others from pain, and his commitment to truth.

◆§ Leadership: "Nothing in the Past Quarter of a Century"

A week after Reb Yaakov's passing, the author attended a communal function in Chicago, seated near several local rabbinical

---

* Rebbetzin Chana Kamenetzky passed away on 12 Iyar 5746 [May 21, 1986], ten weeks after Reb Yaakov.

leaders, including the head of the Chicago Kollel, the *dayan* for Agudath Israel of Chicago, the principal of a local *yeshivah ketanah*, and the head of a yeshivah geared for *baalei teshuvah*. They recalled in detail difficult halachic matters and knotty policy questions that each had brought to Reb Yaakov in recent years, how his counsel had been crucial to the running of their respective institutions, how he had traveled to Chicago in his advanced age to help this or that *mosad* ... Mention was made of similar involvement in Toronto and Los Angeles, never mind his own Monsey.

The next day (back in New York City), this encounter was described to a *Rav* from yet another community, who commented, "Do you think that anything of significance took place in the Torah community of America these past twenty-five years *without* Reb Yaakov's involvement?"

❧ ❧ ❧

Reb Yaakov was respected for his clarity of thought from the time of his youth. He was known (according to Rabbi Meir Chodosh of Slobodka, at a *hesped*) as the star of his *chabura* (company) in Slobodka, which had its share of brilliant *talmidei chachamim*, including Rabbi Aaron Kotler and Reb Yaakov's cousin, the *Rosh Yeshivah* of Ner Israel, Rabbi Yaakov Yitzchak Ruderman. At the same time, Reb Yaakov confessed to being so in awe of Reb Aaron's gifts, even while in their youth, that "his superiority was beyond my envy." The respect was mutual, for when Rabbi Moshe Sherer, president of Agudath Israel of America, would consult Reb Aaron on pressing problems facing *Klal Yisroel*, he often would say, "*Nu, ich vell zich meyashev zein mit Reb Yaakov.* (I'll discuss it with Reb Yaakov.)"

❧ Drawn From the Broader Context

Whoever approached Reb Yaakov with a *she'eilah* (halachic query) or *kushya* (question) in any area of Scripture, Talmud or Aggadah, will not forget his instant grasp of the question, his total recall of relevant texts ("I did not experience forgetting until I was seventy," he commented sadly when in his eighties, but still cited copious quotations from Talmud, Codes, and their Commentaries without error), his lucid presentation of his understanding of the matter, and his taking into account the further implications of his decisions. But during the last twenty-five years of his life, in addition to the usual halachic queries, he was deluged by people seeking counsel on communal or personal matters. Here his genius for grasping the specific situation and his insight into special needs came especially into the fore. Sometimes he quoted a *Chazal* or cited a historical precedent. Other times this was submerged, and all he would say was *"Es ducht zich mir* — it appears to me ..."

A subjective assessment of the issue? Not at all. It was more in line with the famous dictum of Reb Yisroel Salanter that he often quoted: "When the *Rosh* (Rabbeinu Asher, circa 1300) records a judgment based on a textual proof, one can find an authority with a different interpretation of the same text, and build a differing conclusion based on that other authority. But when the *Rosh* says, *'Nireh li*, It appears to me,' he is basing his judgment on the complete Talmud, which had become assimilated into his thinking process. One cannot dispute the *Rosh* on this."

Reb Yaakov's *"Es ducht zich mir"* in its way was built on the entirety of Talmud and its commentaries. Whether personal advice or responses to questions in *chinuch* submitted at "Ask the *Rosh Yeshivah"* sessions in Torah Umesorah, they consisted in their way of renderings of *psak halachah*, even when specific chapter and verse were not cited.

✎§ Agudath Israel: Communal Expression of Torah Concerns

Reb Yaakov viewed Agudath Israel as the communal expression of Torah concerns, as he articulated countless times by affiliation, by action and by the theme of numerous public addresses.

At a dinner for Agudath Israel of America, he pointed out how the *degalim* (banners) that the Tribes carried on their forty-year trek through the wilderness — each bearing the insignia of its respective *Shevet* — were not introduced until the erection of the *Mishkan*, the traveling sanctuary, one year after the Exodus. Why the delay? He explained that individuality (as represented by the *degalim*) can cause friction and destructive factionalism, unless Torah serves as a central transcending force uniting the disparate groups. The *Mishkan*, which housed the Tablets of the Law, was that central, uniting force.

Jewish life today is marked by a wide range of groups and interests, bearing a potential for heated disputes and factionalism. Ideologically, Agudath Israel serves as the spiritual core that binds these different forces together with a transcending purpose that overrides conflicts, but does not obliterate differences.

◄§ A Vehicle for Change . . .

Reb Yaakov's words in the closed-door sessions of the *Moetzes Gedolei HaTorah* are not on the public record, but several non-classified pronouncements are: Before the elections of 1979, Reb Yaakov was a committed advocate of supporting the election-campaign efforts of the Israeli Agudath Israel. "Additional votes can give us another man in the Knesset, and one man can make all the difference in coalition politics. There are so many religious interests to protect in *Eretz Yisroel* and so much more to gain. And, then, consider the opportunity to topple the *avodah zarah* (idolatry) of Socialism that has dominated *Eretz Yisroel* since 1948!"

As predicted, Agudath Israel won four seats, which provided the swing vote to give Begin a coalition based on sixty-one out of one-hundred-and-twenty seats, ending the Labor monopoly of controlling the government. Moreover, Begin's first four years in office saw an end to a number of anti-religious practices that had been plaguing the *Yishuv*, including harassment of religious girls seeking exemption from military conscription, and the abuse by pathologists of limitations on autopsies.

◄§ . . . Safeguarding Tradition . . .

A committee of rabbinical leaders met with Prime Minister Golda Meir to explain Agudath Israel's objectives — including its opposition to *Sheirut Leumi*, national service of religious girls in Israel.

"I can understand your opposition to *Giyus Banos* — military conscription of girls in the army," Mrs. Meir argued, "but what can be wrong with *Sheirut Leumi?* Is it so terrible if religious girls put in a few hours a week caring for the sick in hospitals?"

All present instinctively looked to Reb Yaakov for an explanation.

"I brought up my family in abject poverty," he said. "I owned but one shirt, which my *Rebbetzin* washed every *erev Shabbos*. Meat or chicken was a rarity on our table. My situation has improved, but I still have no savings account. Yet my children and my thirty-some grandchildren pray that they and my sixty-plus great-grandchildren grow up to be no wealthier than I, as long as they perpetuate my values. How do we succeed in preserving our value system? Because I always knew where my children were, and they know where their children are. We control and nurture our children's environment. I have a granddaughter who devotes a number of hours every week to volunteer work in Hadassah and Shaarei Tzedek Hospitals. Not because a bureaucrat in an office sends her there, but because her father and mother want her to be there. Her value system will not be influenced by others. She is her parents' daughter. That is the secret of our generational chain of loyalty, and we will not compromise on it."

⌁ ... And Source of Information

In January of 1976, en years ago, *The Jewish Observer* interviewed two religious Russian Jews. One of them expressed the opinion that public demonstrations in America are an effective tool for increasing emigration from the Soviet Union, while the other interviewee strongly disagreed. The JO editorial board was troubled: *Gedolei Yisroel* had gone on record in opposition to demonstrations. Could we publish the two interviews, simply permitting the two men to speak for themselves, or was the magazine lending dignity to an unacceptable position? Reb Yaakov was consulted, and he said, "Of course you can publish both. The first view just may be correct."

"But haven't we always condemned street demonstrations?"

"Yes, we have. In the past, they would tend to get out of hand, and could be dangerously counter-productive. So we've been against them. And even if today they possibly have succeeded in helping release more Jews, there must always be a group that tells the Russians: 'We shun such activity. You can rely on us not to seek to embarrass you!' — Then we can request special treatment for our religious needs. We — the religious community — are that group. So you may publish the one opinion, as long as you present an opposing point of view. First, however, you must determine that the American government looks favorably on demonstrations. We cannot publish anything that suggests activities that antagonize the U.S. Government."

"Kissinger has gone on record against —"

"I'm not referring to what he *says*. I'm referring to what he *wants*."

"How are we to know that?"

"And to know that," said the *Rosh Hayeshivah*, "I call Agudath Israel. I rely on the Agudah to find out what the government *really* wants."

◆§ Yiras Shomayim: A Basis for Counsel and Guidance

People seem to know instinctively where to turn for advice — to a person who cares for the individual and respects him, who is sensitive to the individual's needs, and sees beyond the problem to the solution. Our experience as Torah people has taught us to expect more: We know that a person immersed in Torah will draw from his Torah knowledge to counsel others, and — equally significant — when he is endowed with the *Yiras Shomayim* (fear of Heaven), he has the prerequisite of "G-d imparts His wisdom to those who fear Him" *(Tehillim* 25:14). So it was with Reb Yaakov.

❦ ❦ ❦

Reb Yaakov once explained his understanding of *Yiras Shomayim* in the following manner:

> After Avraham had responded to the Divine command and offered his son Yitzchak as a sacrifice to G-d at the *Akeidah,* he was told, "Now I know that you are a G-d-fearing man." In other words, Avraham's response to G-d's command demonstrated what otherwise was not apparent — his fear of G-d. Now, isn't fear an emotion that is etched on a person's features, there for all to see? What need was there for the *Akeidah* to elicit the obvious?
>
> So I thought (said the *Rosh Hayeshivah)* until I personally encountered fear. As a young man, I was warned that the Czar had dispatched officers to conscript Jewish youths into his army — a terrible fate. I was hidden in the cellar of our house. From there I heard the officer's horse gallop up to our house. Once his boots clicked on the floorboards over my head, I began to quake uncontrollably, fearing that he may find me. I later heard him leave the house and the horse hooves beat on down the road, yet I continued to tremble for the rest of the day, and the next, and the day after that . . .
>
> It then struck me that a fear that is visible paralyzes a person, and does not permit him to function. Fear of G-d is meant to be elevating and inspiring, not paralyzing. Avraham possessed that motivating kind of fear, and thus he was as warm, cordial and smiling after the *Akeidah* as he was before. His fear of G-d was internal and not manifest until he gave it expression in his ultimate act of faith, directed by *Yiras Shomayim.*
>
> Reb Yaakov could have been describing himself. While his every word reflected *Yiras Shomayim,* he always appeared relaxed, congenial.

◄§ An Awesomely Normal Approach

Walking out after a session at a National Convention of Agudath Israel, he noticed a disappointed youngster holding a camera watching him slip out of range. Reb Yaakov stepped back in front of the boy, smiled, and commanded: "Shoot!"

No, he was not publicity hungry. In fact, Reb Yaakov was so self effacing that he dispensed with many customary dignities that most people of his position took for granted. For example, when, as a lonely widower fifteen years earlier, he ordered his *Shabbos* meals at a Williamsburg restaurant on Fridays, he sat at a table with other single guests on the *Shabbos* — no special treatment necessary for the *Rosh Hayeshivah* of Mesivta Torah Vodaath ... But a photo-eager little boy mustn't be left wanting.

It was not beyond Reb Yaakov to tell the waiter in Camp Mesivta: "The *cholent* was delicious. Ask the cook if I could have doubles." Not in keeping with the dignity of his position? That didn't matter. The lesson that the waiter, and others within earshot, learned was how to express gratitude to an overworked, underappreciated cook. If he had observed closely, the waiter already knew well from the *Rosh Yeshivah's* dining habits how he carefully selected his food, following the "*Rambam's* cuisine," which involves moderation as its cornerstone.

◄§ K'vod Ha'adam: Respect for the Dignity of Man

Reb Yaakov had regard for the inherent dignity of every person — young and old, great and simple.

After a Chinuch Atzmai meeting, Reb Yaakov and Rabbi Moshe Feinstein stood outside a waiting car discussing who would sit next to the driver (the favored seat) and who would sit alone in the back. Reb Yaakov took the front seat. After Reb Moshe alighted from the car, Reb Yaakov explained, "We were clarifying who would be getting off first. That person, we decided, should sit in the back. Would he sit in the front, the longer-riding passenger would be in the back leaving you alone at the wheel, making you look like a chauffeur. But that is not the case. We appreciate your importance and did not want to compromise your dignity."

❀   ❀   ❀

There was a motion among members of the Board of Directors of Mesivta Torah Vodaath to install a time clock to monitor the amount of time the *rabbeim* spent in the yeshivah. Reb Yaakov was incensed: "How dare you install a time clock! What do you think they are — pressers? Not that there is anything wrong with being a presser. It's a decent and honest way of earning a living. But a presser works from nine to five, and then goes home and doesn't give his job a further thought until the next morning — which is fine and *ehrlich*. Not so a *rebbe*! When he goes home he thinks about his *talmidim*, and may even lose sleep over a boy's problems. Moreover, a *rebbe* may stay up late into the night preparing a superior *shiur* for his class. Should he oversleep the next day and arrive late to the yeshivah, is it out of personal indulgence? Not at all. It is out of devotion to his *talmidim*. There is no place for a time clock in a yeshivah!"

In relating the above incident about his father, Rabbi Shmuel Kamenetzky (*Rosh Hayeshivah* in Philadelphia) added that his father had been autobiographical in his description of a *rebbe's* consuming devotion to his *talmidim*. He recalled an incident when his father was staying at his home. Late at night he heard him go downstairs. He followed, to find him making an entry into his pocket diary.

"I was concerned about a certain *bachur* in the yeshivah," explained the *Rosh Hayeshivah*, "and I believe I have a way of helping him. So I rushed to jot it down in my appointment book for tomorrow to make sure that I don't forget."

❧ ❧ ❧

Rabbi Shmuel Dishon, *menahel* of Yeshivah Karlin-Stolin, recalled how the *Rosh Hayeshivah* had invited several *bachurim* to his home for *Kiddush* on Shavuos morning, shortly after his second marriage. The *Rebbetzin* had prepared a sumptuous repast, with various cheese delicacies. When Reb Yaakov saw the set table he blanched, because he had honored a custom that his grandmother had kept, to refrain from eating cheeses on Fridays. (He had said that he did not understand the basis for the *minhag*, but he would not eat foods that his parents or grandparents did not eat.) "Is something wrong?" asked the *Rebbetzin*.

"Not at all," he replied. "I just did not expect such a beautifully prepared *Kiddush*."

When she stepped out of the room, he quietly turned to the boys, explained the situation and asked them to be *mattir neder* (release him from the implied vow of not eating cheese on Friday) since he would never have accepted this custom had he known that it would cause someone pain. This was not the time to explain his practice to his new wife ... He then partook of the pastries and complimented his *Rebbetzin* on her fine baking. (According to his children, he soon resumed this *minhag*.)

❦　❦　❦

When asked of his opinion of the advisability of burial in *Eretz Yisroel*, he related a well-known incident wherein Reb Meir Simcha of Dvinsk probated a will of a wealthy woman who had expressed strong ties to the Holy Land. Rather than expend the exorbitant sums then required for transporting a body to *Eretz Yisroel* (this was in the 1920's), Reb Meir Simcha ruled that she be buried in Europe and that the remainder of the funds be used for Torah education.

Reb Yaakov then added on a personal note: "It seems to me that when *Yaakov Avinu* asked that he not be buried in Egypt, for the reasons that *Rashi* cites, he implied that under ordinary circumstances, he should have been laid to rest where his children and grandchildren were living. A father must think of his family's needs after he is gone, and must plan to be accessible for their entreaties and prayers after he has died. I imagine that after I've lived my one-hundred-and-twenty years, the expense of burying me in Israel will not be prohibitive, but I also know that my children are not men of means, and they will not be able to easily fly to my graveside to pray should I be buried in Israel."

৵§ Listening for Clues

Rabbi Abraham Kamenetzky, son of the late *Rosh Hayeshivah*, recalled how his father listened closely when a person asked him for guidance, to pick up clues as to his leanings. Once he ascertained that *halachah* would be honored, he would then take into account a person's natural inclinations and the limitations of his capacity. (Sometimes, for instance, he would help a yeshivah student devise a strategy for spiritual enhancement even when it was contrary to his parents' plans; other times he would caution a student not to violate his parents' wishes.) ... If he did not pick up a clue, he would simply shrug his shoulders and say, "*Vais ich nit* (I really don't know) ..." and wait for further indication. Or he might suggest a particular course of conduct to test for a reaction.

～§ Busy Mothers

A *Kollel* fellow discussed the various options open to his wife. She had been working fulltime, while a babysitter cared for their two infants. A third child was now on the way and the young man was now taking on some work assignments. His wife would be able to stay home with the children, the babysitter costs would be spared, and she would no longer have to work. What does the *Rosh Hayeshivah* think of a mother giving up outside work? Reb Yaakov described the ideal Jewish home with the mother caring for her children fulltime herself, and so on.

A half year later the young man returned with his wife. She now had three children, which kept her occupied all day and half the night. However, she felt limited, frustrated, and was impatient with the children.

Could she find part-time work in her field? asked the *Rosh Hayeshivah*.

When she replied in the affirmative, he suggested that she try working outside her home several hours a day.

After thanking the *Rosh Yeshivah* for his advice, and the couple had left, the husband returned for a moment and asked, "Didn't the *Rosh Yeshivah* suggest that my wife give up working, six months ago?"

"Six months ago I described the ideal situation. Today I counseled your wife in the course best suited to her needs."

☙ ☙ ☙

Another *Kollel* fellow described his wife's struggles with *davening* before leaving for work: She used to *daven Shacharis* every morning. Now that she cares for the children before she leaves, she has no time left for *Shacharis* at home. Should she perhaps *daven* on the bus on the way to work?

"She should say the prayers my *Rebbetzin* used to say when she was busy with our children: *Birkas HaTorah, Birkas HaShachar,*" said Reb Yaakov.

"And . . .?"

"*Birkas HaShachar* ends with a *Yehi Ratzon,*" said the *Rosh Hayeshivah*, and he recited the entire prayer slowly, verbatim, emphasizing a phrase here, a word there: "*. . . accustom us to Your Torah, attach us to Your commandments. Do not bring us into . . . error, nor . . . sin or transgression . . . Distance us from an evil person . . . Grant us . . . kindness and mercy in Your eyes and in the eyes of* *all who see us* ... Not a bad prayer," he commented with a twinkle in his eye.

◈ Chinuch, and Beyond

In speaking to a group of counselors in a summer camp, Reb Yaakov told them that their inevitable function as *mashpi'im* (those who have influence over others), outside a formal teaching situation, can be extremely potent, explaining that the Hebrew word for influence, *hashpa'ah*, derives from *shipua*, incline. When one stands beneath the eaves of a house during a rainstorm, the water that hits the roof drains downward and pours on the person below, drenching him far more than would the rainfall itself. Such is the effect of an incline, and such is the impact of the role of the *mashpi'a*, whose attitudes and actions set an example for those "beneath" him.

At the same gathering, he pointed out how the *Avos*, the prophets, and many other early leaders had been shepherds, a rather lowly position on the social ladder. There was a reason for this, however. Tending sheep entailed dealing with the herd as a whole while caring for the individual sheep that may stray, run ahead, or have other special needs. This exercise of responsibility on so many different levels was an excellent training ground for leadership of our people. While the occupation today is not as it was in Biblical times, it does have a contemporary counterpart of sorts: serving as counselors for the children in summer camps.

◈ Normality: Building Blocks to Greatness

Reb Yaakov always seemed to take a person's normal needs into account, even when dealing with loftier goals. We are all familiar with ambitious parents that push children beyond their endurance, or over inhibit them, provoking rebellion or producing misfits. Reb Yaakov studiously avoided such excesses.

Thus, while serving as a *melamed* in his wanderings during World War I, he puzzled the parents of his students by permitting his young charges to play freely for a spell every hour or two. Worse yet, he did not have the customary disciplinary strap hanging prominently on the wall as a warning to mischievous students. Distraught parents were only consoled by the assurances of the local *Rav* that someday the portrait of the *melamed* "Yankel Dolhinover" will grace homes alongside the ubiquitous picture of the revered *Kovno Rav*, Rabbi Yitzchak Elchanan Spektor.

His oldest son, Rabbi Binyamin Kamenetzky (*Menahel* of Yeshivah Toras Chaim), recalled how his father had called him into his study on the day after his *bar mitzvah*, climbed onto a bench to reach for a carefully wrapped package, and told him, "Now that you are *bar mitzvah*, I want to give you the most precious commodity in the world. You must promise me that you'll guard it like your very life."

He opened the package and gave him a wrist watch, adding that Reb Yisroel Salanter would often say that time *is* life, and when one wastes time, one is actually losing a portion of his life. The message lasted far longer than the wrist watch did.

❦   ❦   ❦

When the author served as supervisor of the dormitory in Mesivta Torah Vodaath, a large number of Latin American boys were enrolled in the yeshivah. Many of them would request permission to spend a *Shabbos* with relatives in the New York area, but, not knowing how observant the hosts were, the yeshivah's *hanhalah* (administration) decided to refer all such requests to Reb Yaakov for screening.

One Thursday afternoon I ushered Chaim — a sixteen-year-old boy from Mexico City — into the *Rosh Yeshivah's* office to articulate his request for him in Yiddish. After a five-minute discussion, during which Reb Yaakov learned the name of the *Rav* of Chaim's relatives, Reb Yaakov told the boy, "I'll speak to the *Rav* and then I'll let you know."

"And I'll be able to go for this *Shabbos*?"

"Oh, no. It's Thursday afternoon. I doubt if everything will be clear by tomorrow."

"What? Another week here?"

"*Bizt du nit tzufrieden daw* (aren't you pleased here)?" asked the *Rosh Yeshivah*.

"It's okay, but all I see is the same rooms and the same walls, day in and day out, week in and week out. A person needs a break once in a while, too, you know."

With that, Chaim — on the verge of tears — rushed out, fairly slamming the door behind him.

I started to apologize for Chaim, but Reb Yaakov simply shook his head, saying, "The boy is really right. For him the yeshivah, with no change in routine or scenery, is a virtual prison. *Nebach*, we have no choice. One *Shabbos* in the wrong environment can undo all the good that the yeshivah has accomplished in three months. But he is still right."

❧ ❧ ❧

A father of a diligent student in an out-of-town Mesivta high school had a problem with his son's singular devotion to his religious studies. The boy had been scoring straight A's in his secular studies until mid-term, when his mathematics grade plummeted to a C-. "I'm attentive in class and pass all my exams," explained the boy, "but I can't afford the time required for homework assignments. So, all I earn is a C-."

The father checked into the boy's study habits and found him to be a dedicated *masmid*. Shall he insist that his son do his homework at the expense of his learning, or should he overlook the low report-card grade as long as he's using his time productively? He decided to bring the question to Reb Yaakov.

The *Rosh Hayeshivah* asked the boy, "How much time would it take you to do your mathematics homework to earn a decent mark?"

"About a half hour."

The *Rosh Hayeshivah* then turned to the father. "As long as you have decided that your son should be enrolled in high school, taking the various subjects offered, he should put in the extra half hour. If it is important to do at all, then he should do it properly, not halfheartedly."

❧ ❧ ❧

A controversy ensued in a certain yeshivah — should translation and language of instruction be in Yiddish or English? What does the *Rosh Hayeshivah* think?

Reb Yaakov acknowledged that there were differences of opinion on the matter, but stressed that the key issue was: How will the children better learn Torah? Judging from his own grandchildren, who were studying in both types of yeshivos, he found those learning in English covered more ground and understood the material better than those studying in Yiddish. "But I do not want you to consider my opinion on the matter," he added. "Every generation has its own instinctive grasp of what will help it survive. Your generation seems to invest in Yiddish as an important factor; it is not for me to disagree."

◆§ Marriage and Other Problems

A young *talmid* of his in Torah Vodaath asked him how much inquiry is necessary before choosing a wife.

"When *der Alter* suggested the daughter of the *Mashgiach*, Rabbi Heller, to me, I agreed to meet the young lady. I came up to the house, and she asked me if I'd like a cup of coffee. 'Yes, thank you,' I said. 'You're welcome,' she replied. I was basically pleased with her, so we got married."

The young man was taken aback. "And that's all there was to it?" he managed to ask. "Shall I do the same?"

"Not really," smiled the *Rosh Hayeshivah*. "I knew the family well, and in those days in Europe, a girl was the product of her home. There were no other major influences on her. To be sure, I had to meet her, but no further exploration of character was necessary. Today, in America, the situation is much more unpredictable. Family is an important factor, but by no means the exclusive one."

❀ ❀ ❀

An American yeshivah *musmach*, who is very effective in his career of *Kiruv* work on college campuses, had one daughter who had graduated from an intensive teachers' seminary program, and was on the faculty of a local Bais Yaakov high school. She had been introduced to a brilliant yeshivah student whom she found interesting and attractive, but she was repelled by some of his extreme anti-secular statements, and could not see herself married to him. The parents favored the match and decided to take their daughter to Reb Yaakov to discuss the matter with him.

The *Rosh Hayeshivah* listened to the description of the young man, and the girl's complaint that "he's too 'European,' and very unworldly."

"That could be," he commented. "Some boys do insulate themselves completely from the American environment. Tell me, does he play ball?"

"Only in the summer," she replied.

"Then he's not European," he said with a smile. "But you also complain that he's not acquainted with world affairs. In truth, every man, in searching for the perfect woman for him to marry, subconsciously has an image in mind. The more similar she is to his mother — who in his experience represents perfection — the closer she is to the ideal image. Similarly, a girl searches for the ideal man, and in her frame of reference her father represents perfection. The more similar he is to her father, the more pleased she is. Your father is a *talmid chacham*, a good person, and quite worldly, and while the young man in question has the first two attributes, you find fault with him for lacking the third.

"Worldliness is surely a *ma'alah*, a positive attribute, but today's yeshivah student cannot grow fully in Torah *and* worldliness. The fact that he is less worldly is not necessarily a liability. In fact, if he were more aware of the outside world — that would be cause for hesitation. It would be a *chisaron*, a drawback, an indication that he is less of a *ben Torah*. As for your father, he needs the outside knowledge for his *Kiruv* work."

The young lady turned 180 degrees in her attitude. As the father later remarked to me, "Imagine a nineteen-year-old girl consulting a ninety-one-year-old man for affairs of the heart, and after a five-minute conversation, heeding his advice. Such is the power of a Torah personality!"

❧ ❧ ❧

In a different context, Reb Yaakov once quoted the *Alter* of Slobodka's opinion of a rabbi who had earned a secular degree: "I am not against secular knowledge as such when there is no question of *apikorsus* (heretical ideas). It is the same as material wealth — it's not a bad thing to possess. Problems only arise when one comes to believe that the riches — or the secular knowledge — make one into a superior person."

Reb Yaakov had extensive knowledge in the natural sciences. On an automobile trip to upstate New York for a *talmid's* engagement, Reb Yaakov told the driver that he was off course. "I checked a road map, and I believe we're doing fine," the driver said.

"I checked the constellations, and we're heading northeast instead of northwest," said the *Rosh Hayeshivah*.

The next gas station confirmed Reb Yaakov's assessment — fifty miles too late.

❧ Integrity

Honesty — in word, deed, and financial matters — was a hallmark of Reb Yaakov's life. It is well known that he refrained from eating *gebrochts* (matzah that had contact with any liquid) on Pesach — a custom not usually followed in his native Lithuania. One Pesach during his youth, he was visiting a family with standards in *kashrus* that were somewhat lower than his own. When invited to join them for supper, he declined, and not wanting to offend his host, he said that his *minhag* was to refrain from eating *gebrochts*. So as not to be guilty of an untruth, he then and there accepted that restriction upon himself and kept it for the rest of his life.

❈ ❈ ❈

When interviewed by a draft board in Czarist Russia, Reb Yaakov produced documents for a medical deferment. The interviewer scoffed, "Forget it! Papers like these can be bought for two *kopecks!*"

"But these are genuine," protested Reb Yaakov. "I want you to know that I've never said a false word in my life."

The officer looked into the face of the earnest young man, and accepted his papers.

❈ ❈ ❈

Reb Yaakov often told of how, as *Rav* of Tzitovyan, the postmaster consistently gave him too much change for his purchase of postage, which he always returned ... and how years later the postmaster helped Jews escape the destruction of World War II.

❈ ❈ ❈

One of Reb Yaakov's first stops on his fund-raising mission in America, in 1937, was the Manhattan office of a manufacturer. Reb Yaakov produced a copy of the receipt for the previous year's donation, and then took a seat in the waiting room. After an unusually long delay, the manufacturer returned with a check made out for a smaller amount than the receipt had recorded for the previous year.

"It's really the same as last year's contribution," explained the manufacturer.

"But the receipt is for a larger amount."

"Yes, I know. It was purposely done that way by your office in hope that I might duplicate that amount this year, but I knew that I had given less, so I checked my records. The amount on the check is correct."

Reb Yaakov was shocked. "I will not work for an institution that runs a dishonest office."

As he got up to leave, the contributor stopped him. "Here, take the check in the meantime."

"No, I am no longer the yeshivah's *meshulach*, as I resigned a minute ago. I am not authorized to accept monies on its behalf."

The manufacturer was dumbstruck. "Don't you have a family to support?" he asked.

"Yes, a wife and six children."

"Then take this," he said, whipping out two hundred dollars from his wallet.

Reb Yaakov shrank back. "I don't accept gifts."

"It's a loan. Until you get another job."

"Thank you kindly, but G-d will provide. I do not need a loan."

Reb Yaakov returned his portfolio and lists to the yeshivah office. The following day, he bumped into an old-time colleague from Slobodka, Reb Alter Poplack, who recommended him for the position of interim Rabbi for Congregation Bikur Cholim in Seattle, which Reb Yaakov accepted for the following six months.

❦ ❦ ❦

The author was once present in Reb Yaakov's office in Torah Vodaath when a parcel was delivered. The *Rosh Hayeshivah* looked at the package, checking the return address and the postage. "A new *sefer* from . . ." he said. He removed the wrapping, examined the title page, the binding, the number of pages, and said, "I imagine that he printed five hundred copies — that's about two and a half thousand dollars, or five dollars each, plus postage. Hmmm. I'll have to send him a check for seven dollars."

The family tells that each of his *seforim* has the amount paid written on the inside cover.

❦ ❦ ❦

When Reb Yaakov visited the kindergarten of his son's yeshivah in Hewlett, Long Island, he noticed that the *mezuzah* was fixed on a spot on the doorpost within reach of the children. "It's a lovely idea to let the children reach the *mezuzah*," he said, "but put the *mezuzah* where it belongs, on the upper third of the doorpost instead, and let them use a stool to reach it. Otherwise they will grow up thinking that a *mezuzah* can be put anywhere you wish. One does not raise children with untruths."

❦ ❦ ❦

Reb Yaakov's Monday afternoon *shmuessen* in the Mesivta Torah Vodaath *beis midrash* often focused on what struck some *bachurim* as trivia of life or details of the *Shulchan Aruch* — the *gazeilah* (dishonesty) of taking a place in line in front of others, using someone else's transfer to board a bus, the *bor birshus harabbim* (an obstacle in a public place) of a nailhead protruding from a *shtender* in the *beis hamidrash* (did you ever catch your jacket on one?) — like so many of the fine points of being a *Shulchan Aruch Yid* with all of its ramifications, twenty-four hours a day, that he discussed. ("There are places where one may not ever think words of Torah, yet one must be guided by them, even there, since we do have *Hilchos Beis Hakisei* — Laws of Proper Conduct in the Lavatory.") But he taught and demonstrated with his every motion that integrity is not just a matter of dramatic gestures, or avoiding grand larceny, but one of minutiae, honoring the hairsbreadth that separates Gan Eden from Gehinnom.

❈   ❈   ❈

Reb Yaakov eulogized his *rebbe*, the famed *Alter* of Slobodka, Rabbi Nosson Zvi Finkel, molder and mentor of some of the greatest men of our century, on his fiftieth *yahrzeit*. He introduced his memorial lecture with an observation on a single word used in regard to the return on the *Yoveil* (Jubilee Year) of all ancestral lands that had been sold since the previous *Yoveil*, fifty years earlier: "The sale shall be *le'olam* — forever," that is, up to fifty more years, with the advent of the following *Yoveil*. (See *Rashi* on *Shemos* 21:6.) The word *olam* also means world, informing us that as society undergoes gradual changes from year to year, with the passage of fifty years, a new world comes into existence. Thus, said Reb Yaakov, we must act swiftly at the close of the fifty years since the *Alter's* passing to recall how he thought and lived, because it was another world that he inhabited, a world remote from our experience. We must make haste to learn now whatever we can.

The applicability of Reb Yaakov's words to his own life needs no further underscoring. If we are wise we will follow his directive in regard to the world he inhabited, transported with him from Slobodka, and now taken along with him on Erev Rosh Chodesh Adar II, 5746.

⋅⊌§ Dedication to Russian Jewry

(from "An Appreciation of Rabbi Yaakov Kamenetzky"
by Rabbi Yisroel Belsky)

A chapter in the *Rosh Hayeshivah's* life which deserves special mention was his involvement with Russian Jewry. The *Rosh Hayeshivah* was deeply moved by the physical and spiritual suffering of his erstwhile compatriots and he ceaselessly searched for ways to improve their lot. One incident that sharply revealed his feelings was the visit to America by Chief Rabbi Levin of Moscow.

Rabbi Levin was an accomplished *talmid chacham* and *Yorei Shomayim*, but his visit had been orchestrated by non-religious groups and his itinerary was in their hands. Throughout the tour, misguided demonstrators clamoring for the release of Russian Jews marred his appearances. They shouted epithets at him, quoting some remark or other which indicated to them that his sympathy lay with the wrong side. To further complicate matters, the *Rav* was tailed day and night by Russian agents and, consequently, could never open his mouth. His silence was taken as a sign of complicity and a dreadful pall settled over the whole affair.

An appearance was arranged for Rabbi Levin in Boro Park and the *Rosh Hayeshivah* was asked to introduce him. Reb Yaakov began by painting a picture of Jewish life in Old Russia, depicting the *kedushah* and *temimus* that existed there. He skillfully blended anecdotes and quotations from *Chazal* to warm the crowd to the *Rav's* impending message. He made them understand that the *Rav* would say things that had veiled meanings and he encouraged the *Rav* to speak his mind. The effect was overpowering. The *Rav* spoke and the people heard. The pain of the Russian Jew found its way into the hearts of a community that had been immunized to their suffering. It set the tone for things to come.

Soon afterwards the mass immigration began. The *Rosh Hayeshivah* expanded his involvement with each passing day. It reached an apogee with the development of Yeshivah Be'er Hagolah. That institution had hardly been organized when it was beset by a struggle for its very existence. Over four hundred children had been enrolled and school was about to open when it became evident that all arrangements for classroom space had collapsed. The *Rosh Hayeshivah* then convened an emergency meeting of all yeshivah principals in New York City. He spoke to them with prophetic force.

"Know then," he began, "that our hopes and dreams for the coming of *Moshiach* are being put to the test. We cry out to *Hashem:* 'End the *Golus!* Bring back *Klal Yisroel* from the four corners of the earth!'*Hashem* asks us, 'Do you really desire it with all your heart? Let me see how you react to a miniature ingathering of just one small tribe of *Klal Yisroel.*' This has now miraculously come to pass. What have we done? Most of us just turn away from them and brutally ignore them. How can you claim that you want *Klal Yisroel* back when you spurn the first group that He sent you?"

Reb Yaakov then demanded that each yeshivah house at least one classroom of Be'er Hagolah *talmidim.* He wasn't satisfied until he received a personal commitment from each principal. Someone asked, "*Rosh Yeshivah,* what will we do if one yeshivah fails to accept a class?"

The *Rosh Hayeshivah* responded with cold fury. "What will we do? Nothing!"

Everyone was stunned by this response, but the *Rosh Hayeshivah* continued, "Yes, nothing. We will have nothing to do with such a person. He will be locked out of our camp. Barak ben Avinoam and Devorah excommunicated Mairoz for not joining the battle to save *Klal Yisroel.* Some say that Mairoz was a star. It was too holy, too high up in the heavens to join with the others. That didn't help it. It got its just deserts."

The message came across and within a few days Be'er Hagolah opened in fourteen locations. It was the *Rosh Hayeshivah* and only the *Rosh Hayeshivah* who pulled it through.

From then on, Reb Yaakov's leadership and guidance became the mainstay of Be'er Hagolah. He approached one of the chief backers of the school and asked, "What can I do to help?"

The individual hesitated.

"Perhaps I can be chairman of the *Vaad Hachinuch* (Board of Education)?"

"Yes, of course."

"Is there a meeting scheduled?"

"I don't think so."

"Then convene one for the day after tomorrow."

And so it was. The *Rosh Hayeshivah* prodded, advised, encouraged. He raised funds, visited there numerous times and spoke at all its dinners and gatherings.

One poignant scene stands out. A twelve-year-old boy from Minsk was introduced at a fund-raising dinner. The boy said a

Torah thought for the crowd in heavily accented English and there was a well-deserved round of applause. Then the *Rosh Hayeshivah* spoke. In his inimitable manner, he pieced together a beautiful mosaic portraying the Minsk that he knew in his youth. He spoke of the families that supported Torah, of the *chessed* of the masses, of the *talmidei chachamim* and *rabbonim* of a bygone era. Then he turned softly to the child at his side and said, "And now all that remains of Minsk is this one little boy." At that moment a little smattering of the *Rosh Hayeshivah's Ahavas Yisroel* rubbed off onto each one present.

The *Rosh Hayeshivah* once said: I always wondered, 'What will *Moshiach* look like?' I found the answer in a *Gemara* in *Mesechta Megillah*. The *Gemara* comments on the passage in *Megillas Esther* that "Esther charmed everyone who saw her." Rabbi Elazar explained: "This means that Esther appeared to each individual as if she were one of his own people."

To this Rabbi Yaakov commented: That's exactly how *Moshiach* will strike us. The *Satmar chassidim* say that he'll be a *Satmarer*. The *Klausenberger chassidim* think he'll be a *Klausenberger*, and the *Litvaks* are certain that he will be a *ba'al Mussar*. And then, when he comes, every *Yid* will look at *Moshiach* and say, "See, it's as I said! He's one of our very own!"

It was Reb Yaakov's love and consideration for each individual member of *Klal Yisroel* that allowed him to view *Moshiach* in such personal, yet universal, terms. His regard for the sensitivity of anyone and everyone, as much as his *kedushah* and *gadlus*, drew the masses into his orbit.

Rabbi Moshe Feinstein

*The
unassuming giant
of his
generation*

Rabbi Moshe Feinstein
5655-5746 / 1895-1986

An Appreciation

IN RABBI MOSHE FEINSTEIN, the nation recognized its living Torah scroll. From Rabbi Eliyahu Lopian, who, well into his nineties, insisted on attending a session of the *Knessiah Gedolah* (World Congress of Agudath Israel) in Jerusalem so that he could fulfill the *mitzvah* of standing up for Reb Moshe, to Rabbi Yaakov Kamenetzky, who told his eldest son that when other *gedolim* were in Reb Moshe's presence, only *he* could be referred to as *The Rosh HaYeshivah*, to the young American yeshivah students who waited in the street and pushed against police lines to see him for a moment when he attended the wedding of a grandson, to the 300,000 people who never knew him but thronged the streets of Jerusalem on Shushan Purim to escort him to his final rest on *Har Hamenuchos*, the nation of Torah knew that the short, unassuming man from Uzda, Luban, East Broadway, and FDR Drive was the giant of his generation.

Reb Moshe's effect on people was expressed aptly by a non-Yiddish-speaking man who never missed the Agudath Israel conventions. Until recent years, when simultaneous translations have become a feature of most sessions, this gentleman had not attended meetings featuring Yiddish addresses, because he could not understand the language. But whenever Reb Moshe was on the program, he would come early to get a front seat and he would listen raptly as the *Rosh Hayeshivah* spoke. When asked why, the gentleman explained, "I can't understand what Reb Moshe says, but when he speaks I feel that the *Shechinah* is communicating with us and the word of *Hashem* is coming to us from his throat." Indeed. For many people, the embodiment of *Kavod HaTorah* was the sight of Reb Moshe entering the crowded hall of an Agudath Israel convention or some other public function. He would walk — no, rush — to his seat, with concentration etched on his face and his body bent forward. Suddenly there would be total silence and people would jump up from their seats, lean, push, stand on chairs, contort their bodies to get a glimpse of him. It recalled the newspaper accounts of the Chofetz Chaim entering the Knessiah Gedolah Hall in Vienna in 1923, causing a hush to come over the auditorium as people reverently crowded to catch a glimpse of him. The Jewish soul has an instinct that enables it to recognize its *gedolim*, to sense the throat through which the voice of the *Shechinah* comes to earth.

May it be said to the credit of our people that, unlike the Babylonians whom the Talmud decries as fools because they would stand up for a *Sefer Torah*, but not for a *talmid chacham*, our generation stood up for Reb Moshe; not enough, to be sure, because we failed to honor his wishes and requests to the degree that we should have, but at least enough to show that we knew a giant strode on our earth. Now that he graces a loftier world, it is our duty to *Hashem Yisborach*, to his memory, and to ourselves, to glimpse the man so that we can stamp his legacy upon ourselves, our children and our institutions.

◄§ Origins of Greatness

There is an elderly woman on Manhattan's Lower East Side who remembers the Feinstein family from Russia. The Feinsteins were always learning, she says, all of them. Reb Moshe's father, his uncles, he; Torah was their life. It was into such a family that Reb Moshe was born on 7 Adar 5655 (1895), to Rabbi David and Rebbetzin Fayeh Gittel Feinstein, in the little town of Uzda, not far from Minsk. It is fascinating that the area in and around Minsk produced not only Reb Moshe, but several other key figures in the renaissance of Torah learning and life in America: Rabbi Reuven Grozovsky, Rabbi Aharon Kotler, Rabbi Yaakov Kamenetzky and Rabbi Yaakov Yitzchak Ruderman.

Reb Moshe was one of twelve children. His mother had suffered a number of miscarriages, until his parents received a blessing from Reb Yisroel, the Karliner-Stoliner Rebbi. Because he was born on the seventh of Adar, *Moshe Rabbeinu's* birthday, his parents named him Moshe. That was an identification that he felt keenly all his life. He considered it his duty to live up to the responsibility implied by his name. Indeed, one wonders if it was not a flash of Divine Inspiration that inspired his parents to name their child after *Moshe Rabbeinu*, for their son, too, would sit from early morning until evening answering *Klal Yisroel's* questions, and be so devoted to his people that he would always be ready to sacrifice himself for their benefit.

Reb David Feinstein was a great man in a small town. He was highly regarded as one of the outstanding *talmidei chachamim* and *poskim* in the area. Later he left Uzda to become rabbi of Starobin, a city widely known for its many scholars. In later years, Reb Moshe wrote glowingly about his father's greatness in Torah, *Yiras Shomayim*, character and selflessness, describing him as "one of the unique people of the generation." Even after gaining recognition as one of Russia's leading rabbis, Reb Moshe consulted his father often on major halachic questions and sought his opinion and approval of halachic responsa and talmudic novellae.

His uncles, the husbands of his mother's sisters, were also *talmidei chachamim* of outstanding stature. They were Rabbi Eliyahu Feinstein (known as Reb Elya Pruzhaner) and Rabbi Yaakov Kantorowitz. They and Reb David were revered men of unusual greatness, as attested by three of Reb Moshe's eulogizers in Jerusalem — the *Roshei Hayeshivah* of Ponevezh, Rabbi David Povarsky and Rabbi Elazar Shach, and Rabbi Michel Feinstein — all of whom knew the family in their youth and young manhood.

Reb Moshe credited his mother, Rebbetzin Fayeh Gittel, with teaching him the value of time and training him not to waste a moment from Torah study. All his life he spoke with respect of her piety and and love of Torah, and with pride about her descent from distinguished Torah giants of previous centuries — the *Tosafos Yom Tov, Seder HaDoros,* and the *Sh'lah HaKadosh.*

✑ Childhood Promise

Not surprisingly, he was a child prodigy. A mind like his, as he demonstrated so convincingly throughout his incredibly productive lifetime, comes along seldom in a generation. But it was not only his computer mind and flawless memory that made him outstanding. His total application to Torah study began when he was a child and continued throughout his life. He told his grandson Rabbi Mordechai Tendler that he had stopped playing chess when he was eight years old, although he enjoyed the game and was a talented player at a time and in a country where chess was a popular pastime among Talmudic scholars. He explained that successful chess playing requires great concentration and he decided that it was preferable to devote his mental exertions to the Torah. His younger sister, Rebbetzin Chana Small, recalled that when her brothers relaxed from their intensive studies, they would challenge each other with questions, "Where do you find a *Gemora* that proves such-and-such?" When he was not yet ten, he already knew the three difficult tractates *Bava Kama*, *Bava Metzia*, and *Bava Basra*, and even elderly scholars were in awe of him.

Once, when he was only eleven, he came into the room where his father was sitting with a few other rabbis, among them, his brother-in-law Reb Elya. When young Moshe entered, the rabbis rose in respect. In an almost unprecedented display of anger, Reb David Feinstein chastised the rabbis saying, "What are you doing to me? You are destroying my child — you will make him a *ba'al ga'avah* (haughty)!" Reb Moshe recalled this incident for his grandson, Rabbi Mordechai Tendler, whose impression was that the contempt with which Reb David spoke of arrogance was enough to assure that Reb Moshe would always seek to remain humble. Reb David paid careful attention to all aspects of his son's upbringing. He knew that the youngster had unlimited potential and, as Reb Moshe wrote in the introduction to the first volume of his responsa *Igros Moshe*, "... my father said of me that he hoped and was virtually positive that many would inquire of me regarding *halachah*, which is the word of *Hashem*, both orally and in writing, and that I would answer correctly, with G-d's help."

Reb Moshe told how his father not only studied with him, but also carefully supervised his education. Reb David personally paid for a private *Gemora rebbe* for his son and three other boys, to foster their maximum growth. Indeed, the *Gemora* group completed the entire tractate *Gittin* with all *Tosafos* that year. Here in the United States, Reb Moshe told that story to the president of a yeshivah who had argued that he could not afford the expense of a second *rebbe* for an oversized class.

Before his *bar mitzvah*, Reb Moshe was sent to Slutzk to study under Rabbi Isser Zalman Meltzer, the great "*Rosh Hayeshivah* of the *Roshei Hayeshivos*." Later that year, Reb Moshe was part of a group that was dispatched from Slutzk to establish a yeshivah in Shklov under Rabbi Pesach Pruskin.

Although only twelve at the time, he was selected to deliver an original *pilpul* at the yeshivah's opening dedication ceremonies (Reb Isser Zalman was the guest speaker). Seventy-five years later, Reb Moshe came across his copy of that *pilpul*, and with minor revisions found it worthy for inclusion in a volume of his published works, without explanation or qualification.

Reb Moshe always had fond memories of the four years he spent under Rabbi Pruskin in Shklov and Arntsislaw. Sixty years later, he sent a wedding gift to Reb Pesach's granddaughter, writing, "This gift is nothing compared to the gratitude I feel to my teacher and master." The admiration was mutual. Reb Pesach used to say proudly of his *talmid*, who had mastered the entire Talmud and all four sections of the *Shulchan Aruch* by the time he was seventeen, "I have a student who has surpassed me in learning and in deciding the *halachah*."

◆§ The Legend Begins

Two years before World War I broke out, Reb Moshe rejoined his father in Starobin, where they studied together and where he soon began teaching local youths. At his father's urging, he began writing halachic responsa, when he was only seventeen; his first-known written *teshuvah* [responsum] appears in *Igros Moshe*. Rabbi Tuviah Goldstein, the noted *Rosh Hayeshivah* (*Emek Halachah*) who was a longtime neighbor of Reb Moshe, recalls that he once learned through a long, complicated responsum on *ribis* (the laws of interest) in *Igros Moshe*, that was written when Reb Moshe was in his early twenties. Reb Tuviah expressed amazement to Reb Moshe that he could have had such a broad halachic scope at such a young age. Reb Tuviah recalls that it was one of two times when he heard Reb Moshe permit himself to show a bit of pride, as he recalled that he had sent the *teshuvah* to Reb Isser Zalman Meltzer, who described the *teshuvah* as *emes l'amitah*, quintessential truth.

During the second year of the war, with the Czarist Army being mauled on the western front, a conscription order went out for all young men of Reb Moshe's age. During the course of a trip, Reb Moshe stopped off to visit the Chofetz Chaim and ask for a blessing that he be spared from army service, which would have meant persecution, danger, and — worst of all for him — *bitul Torah*. The Chofetz Chaim had taken his yeshivah from far-off Radin to Russia, because much of Polish Jewry had been forced to flee from the advancing German forces. When Moshe entered the *beis midrash*, he found the Chofetz Chaim with his most famous disciple, Rabbi Elchonon Wasserman. As Reb Moshe retold the story to his students half a century later, "I went to see the Chofetz Chaim and he was sitting with Reb Elchonon. We spoke in learning and when he saw that I knew (*ven ehr hot gezehn az ich ken*), he gave me his blessing."

The Chofetz Chaim had heard much about the "Starobiner *Illuy*" and was concerned when Moshe explained the gravity of his situation. The Chofetz Chaim and Reb Elchonon both rose and escorted their young visitor out of the *beis midrash*. The Chofetz Chaim then turned to Moshe and said, "Our Sages tell us, *Whoever accepts upon himself the yoke of Torah — the yoke of government and of worldly responsibilities are removed from him* (*Avos* 3:6). It would seem that, rather than 'removed from him,' a more proper phrase would have been 'are not placed upon him.'

"There is, however, a fundamental message in this carefully worded statement of our Sages. One whose deeds are purely for the sake of *Hashem* will merit that even decrees that have already been proclaimed upon him will be removed." With these words, the Chofetz Chaim bade Moshe farewell. Not long afterward, the government proclaimed that, in view of the successful mobilization of the Russian Army, all call-ups of rabbis were suspended until further notice.

His father asked the town of Uzda, Reb Moshe's place of birth, to list him as their *Rav*, for the sake of his deferment from the army. Although Reb Moshe was only twenty at the time the people took the appointment seriously, and Reb Moshe became their *Rav*. His trials were not over, however, because he was ruled too young and able bodied for a deferment. Nevertheless he eventually succeeded in gaining an exemption. Despite the superficially natural means through which he gained his freedom, Reb Moshe attributed his success to the Chofetz Chaim's blessing.

✺§ The Rabbinate

In 1920, when Reb Moshe was twenty-five years old, he accepted a position as the *Rav* of Luban, the town with which his name has become associated. The invitation came from Rabbi Yaakov Moshe Kastenovitz who was the head of the community and its *shochet*, and who was to become Reb Moshe's father-in-law. It was a high honor indeed for such a young man, because Luban was a city of G-d-fearing Jews and the birthplace of many outstanding *geonim*, such as the Mirrer *Mashgiach*, Rabbi Yerucham Levovitz and of the *Roshei Hayeshivah* of Ponevezh, Rabbi David Povarsky. The *baalei battim* and laborers of Luban would divide the entire Talmud among themselves and make a *siyum* every Chanukah. That Reb Moshe was chosen for such a distinguished position at such a young age is eloquent testimony to his emerging stature.

A hundred years earlier this would have been the beginning of a tranquil and happy career, but when Reb Moshe came to Luban, it was already three years after the Bolshevik Revolution. Special taxes were levied against rabbis to force their resignations and it was forbidden to maintain yeshivos. Most rabbis gave in to the Soviets and left their positions. Those who did not, paid the consequences, and they were severe. The Lubavitcher Rebbe had already been imprisoned and was expelled from the country in 1927. Rabbi Yechezkel Abramsky was sentenced to hard labor in Siberia, in 1930, and served for two years before foreign interventions gained his freedom. Many other rabbis were arrested and mistreated; many were never heard from again.

The Jews of White Russia, where Luban was, had more serious problems than Communist oppression in the early 1920's. The Soviets had not yet consolidated their power and there was a civil war going on between the Red Army and the pro-Tzarist "White" army. The fact that many Jews were in the forefront of the Revolution and most other Jews embraced it — because the Revolution came out against anti-Semitism — was enough for the Whites. White Russia and the Ukraine were swept by bloody pogroms.

On Lag B'Omer in 1921, Reb Moshe seemed to have sensed an ominous atmosphere in Luban. He packed his most precious belongings — his Torah manuscripts — and fled the town. Minutes later, Luban was struck by a pogrom, and a bomb was detonated in the *Rav's* house. The assumption was that Reb Moshe had perished in the explosion.

Reb Moshe, however, continued in his flight from the area until several days later when he simply collapsed. A Russian peasant found the package of writings, and brought them to Slutsk where he turned them over to Reb Isser Zalman Meltzer who recognized them as belonging to Reb Moshe. He saw it as grounds to fear the worst, for Reb Moshe would never willfully be separated from his writings. Yet, when an inquiry came to him from Reb David Feinstein, asking if he had heard of his son's fate, Reb Isser Zalman replied, "I am confident that he is alive."

Sure enough, in a matter of days, a fatigued Reb Moshe Feinstein found his way to Slutsk, where he stayed with Reb Isser Zalman for an extended period of time. When it was safe for the refugees to return home, Reb Moshe took the lead in rebuilding the community with the generous help of the surrounding *shtet'lach*.

To commemorate the Lag B'Omer pogrom, Reb Moshe never took advantage of the break in the *Sefira* mourning period that Lag B'Omer offers. His *Sefira* bridged the entire period without interruption.

After that short separation from his precious writings, Reb Moshe resolved to buy a handsome leather carrying case for the sole purpose of taking his manuscripts with him whenever he traveled. Through a strange set of circumstances — probably due to the high quality of the case — it was stolen from him when he made use of it a year later. As a result, he accepted the day of that loss as a personal day of fast, to be kept regardless of his health.

৶ Under the Bolshevik Oppression

When the Communists put down the White rebels, they were able to turn their full "attention" to the Jews. Making the persecution even more tragic and painful was the fact that the chief inquisitors were Jews: the infamous *Yevsektzia*, or Jewish Section, whose task it was to assimilate the Jewish communities into the "Worker's Paradise." Because they were Jews, they knew the inner workings of Jewish religious life all too well and they could be fooled much less easily than could the Russians. One can imagine how heartbreaking it was for devout rabbis and laymen to receive gifts of bread at the *Pesach Seder*, to have the Yom Kippur services disturbed by the sound of raucous Jewish rallies complete with food, or to hear defiant shouts of "Down with the black rabbis! Down with the *cheder* and yeshivah! Let freedom live!"

In Luban, the Jewish community was spared the wrath of the Party and the Yevsektzia until 1930. In fact, Reb Moshe considered the five years from 1925 to 1930 as the most productive of his life. It was during this period that he wrote a famous *teshuvah* that challenged a ruling by Rabbi Yechezkel Abramsky. The two responsa were brought to the attention of Rabbi Chaim Ozer Grodzenski in Vilna, who sided with Reb Moshe. He commented: "I had heard of the two brothers (Reb Moshe and Reb Mordechai) deep in the Russian heartland, who learn Torah as it was studied a century ago!"

The educational institutions and the main synagogue were closed down. The Feinstein family was forced out of its house by an exorbitant clergy tax, and Reb Moshe was harassed with the intention of forcing him to resign as rabbi. He answered that he was ready to turn over his meager earnings to the state — an offer the Communists graciously accepted — but he could not relinquish his position as long as there were Jews who needed his services. He studied and wrote voluminously, and the people of Luban continued to revere him. Hashem was their G-d, Reb Moshe was their king, and they clung to him tenaciously.

Only once was he questioned by the police who were looking for pretexts to charge him with disloyalty. He acquitted himself so well that the inquisitor apologized, saying that he had only wanted to gain insight into Judaism. In addition, thirty Jewish political prisoners were released in Luban. Finally, however, all the *shuls* were closed and he was evicted even from his small living quarters in a *shul* building. The Feinsteins were taken in by a fellow Jewish family.

The people of Luban loved him and even many of the Jewish Communists respected him. Those two factors were undoubtedly responsible for his survival during years when most rabbis disappeared routinely, through either resignation or arrest. The quiet and respectful demeanor that became so familiar to American Jews during the last half-century of his life stood him in good stead. Though there was no doubt where he stood, he was not a public enemy of the state; to have "eliminated" him would have caused too much trouble in Luban. Even a few of the Jewish Communists tried secretly to protect him.

A particularly daring move illustrated both his courage and effectiveness. There was no possibility of maintaining the *mikveh* openly, but Reb Moshe found a way, nevertheless. When the authorities planned a public bathhouse and swimming pool, Reb Moshe prevailed upon the non-Jewish contractor to build the pool in such a way that it would be a kosher *mikveh*. He then convinced the officials that, while he shared their interest in public hygiene, the bathhouse must have a few separate times for men and women; otherwise the old-fashioned Jews who would not bathe in mixed company could not enjoy the expensive sanitary facilities generously provided by the state. Thus, Luban became the only city for miles around with a functioning *mikveh*, and the people in charge of the bathhouse must have been commended by the Party for running their facility so well that it attracted women from all the surrounding towns. The word was spread through a secret information network, with the result that some actually traveled three days in each direction to use the facility!

◄§ Total Concentration

People who observed Reb Moshe over the years were always struck by his total concentration in learning. While he put away his *tefillin* and whenever he was involved in light activity, he repeated *mishnayos* by heart. Whenever there was half-a-minute to spare he would be glancing at his *sefer*. He was always adding to his thousands upon thousands of pages of writings. Torah was the passion of his life. Only through such tenacity could he have grown so astoundingly in Torah during his sixteen years in Luban. During much of that time he was without the intellectual stimulation of students. Even when the sword of imprisonment was over his head, he was able to put every fear and distraction out of his mind and to grow uninterruptedly in Torah. One can only conclude that G-d was rewarding his utter devotion to the Torah with Divine assistance, for such greatness under such circumstances seems nothing less than supernatural.

His total concentration on Torah was legendary even when he was a young *Rav* in Luban. One of his admirers was an elderly *talmid chacham* who was well qualified to appreciate the prodigious Torah greatness of the young *Rav*. In those days, the only time Reb Moshe took an afternoon nap was on *Shabbos*, and the elderly gentleman would jokingly chide Rebbetzin Feinstein, "You are not allowed to let him sleep! Too much Torah is lost when he is not awake."

A distinguished confidant of many *gedolim* makes the following observation: At conventions or meetings, when others were speaking, Reb Moshe's face was always serious, even grave, as he listened intently — or perhaps thought about his learning. But when he spoke, his demeanor changed. There was a joy, luminescence, on his face. His love of Torah was palpable not only in his words, but in his very being.

A well-known Orthodox leader recalls that he was a young teenager the first time he saw and heard Reb Moshe. The *Rosh Hayeshivah* was the guest speaker at a *siyum* in a small out-of-town *shul*. His *hadran* was beyond the young listener's comprehension, but one part of the address made an indelible impression. "People destroyed their children by always repeating, *Es is shver tzu zein a Yid* (it is hard to be a Jew). No — it is *not* hard to be a Jew. It is beautiful and joyous to be a Jew." Reb Moshe's face glowed with pride and happiness when he said those simple words, and the young listener recalls that he too became suffused with pride in his Jewishness.

Several years ago, a distinguished rabbi asked Reb Moshe why he had not left Luban many years sooner. Reb Moshe answered simply that he was the only rabbi left in the entire region and it was his duty to stay. He left only when it became clear to him that there was no alternative. That, too, was a lifelong character trait; he had a powerful sense of responsibility and always submerged his personal inclinations and interests if he felt that they conflicted with his obligations.

Indeed, when Stalin took over, Reb Moshe sought permission to leave Russia. He did receive entry visas into the United States several times, but Russia withheld exit visas.

The Communists wanted him to resign from the rabbinate. This he would not do. Invariably, the day after a rabbi gave up his position — no matter what his reason — the local newspaper's headlines screamed: "Another Rabbi Sees the Truth / Renounces Darkness for the Light of Marxism." Reb Moshe deemed it impermissible to do anything that would provoke such damaging propaganda, even though it was so far from the obvious truth.

For seven years he tried a number of subterfuges. He even left Luban for several months, put on peasant clothing, and established residence under an assumed name in the Moscow Gubernya

(District), to apply for an exit visa under the fictitious identity. Finally, through strenuous efforts, his brothers-in-law, Rabbi Nechemiah Katz of Toledo, Ohio and Rabbi Isaac Small of Chicago, Illinois, enlisted Congressional and diplomatic intervention with the Russian Ambassador to the United States, and the Feinstein family was permitted to leave the Soviet Union.

Reb Moshe had expected to encounter difficulties in taking along his hundreds of pages of manuscripts, so he devised a method for transporting them safely out of Russia. Every day he would mail several pages of his writings to each of some thirty relatives in America, in the guise of correspondence, mailing them from a different village each day to ward off suspicion. He had hoped that, by seeing the nature of the subject matter, his relatives would understand his motives for mailing them his writings. His hopes were vindicated for almost all of the "mail" eventually was returned to him in the States. On Rosh Chodesh Elul 5696 (1936), the Feinstein family — Reb Moshe and his Rebbetzin, and three young children (Reuvain was born in America) — and the Jews of Luban bid one another their sad farewells. Many of his dear ones remained behind in and around Luban: his in-laws, who were murdered by the Nazis; his brother, Rabbi Mordechai Feinstein, the rabbi of Shklov, who died in Siberia; and many others. He went to Moscow for his exit visa, and from there to Riga, where he was invited to become rabbi of Dvinsk, as successor to the Rogatchover Gaon, who had recently passed away. But he decided to go on to the United States, where he arrived in Kislev, 5697.

Upon arriving in America, he told a close relative, "I don't care what I do here, even if I become a street cleaner. The main thing is that I am no longer under the shadow of the Bolsheviks, and my children can finally learn Torah."

◆§ The New World

It is true that Reb Moshe cared little about what sort of position he might accept in the United States, but one thing was uppermost: If at all possible, he would be involved in a life of Torah study and he would decide halachic problems for all who sought his confidence.

The leaders of the American rabbinate had heard of his Torah greatness and the phenomenal scope of his knowledge. He was invited to deliver guest *shiurim* in Mesivta Torah Vodaath and Yeshivas Rabbi Isaac Elchonon, and he accepted a position as *Rosh*

Hayeshivah in the yeshiva founded by Rabbi Yehuda Levenburg, one of the pioneer builders of Torah in America. Originally in New Haven, the yeshivah had moved to Cleveland, but Rabbi Levenburg died soon after and the yeshivah disbanded. Almost immediately came the invitation to serve as *Rosh Hayeshivah* of Mesivtha Tifereth Jerusalem, the position he held for the rest of his life, nearly fifty years.

One of his original *talmidim* in Tifereth Jerusalem recalls how Reb Moshe was introduced to them. The *menahel* of the yeshivah was Rabbi Yoseif Adler, a distinguished and popular East Side rabbi. Rabbi Adler told the students, "Whenever we needed a new *rosh hayeshivah*, I would bring a great *talmid chacham* from Europe. After a while you would grow in Torah until you needed a bigger *rosh hayeshivah*. I am not getting younger and I can't keep searching every year, so I decided to bring you a *rosh hayeshivah* who would know enough for you no matter how much you grow in learning."

Rabbi Adler could not have been more correct.

◆§ Total Torah Leader

When Reb Moshe assumed the leadership of Mesivtha Tifereth Jerusalem, the Lower East Side was still a vibrant, teeming center of Jewish life, with synagogues on virtually every block. In later years East Broadway became a boulevard of Torah institutions. In addition to the Mesivtha, there were Ezras Torah, where the eminent *tzaddik*, *gaon* and *posek* Rabbi Yosef Eliyahu Henkin directed a world-wide *chessed* apparatus; and the Agudas Horabbonim, which was considered *the* organization of European-trained rabbis who had the *Talmud* and *Shulchan Aruch* on their fingertips. Around the corner on Henry Street was the distinguished Rabbi Jacob Joseph School. Sadly, there was still an appalling shortage of yeshivos, Orthodoxy was treated condescendingly by the Jewish establishment as an irrelevant stepchild, and younger generations of Jews were slipping away from Torah and *mitzvah* observance. There were a few strong Zeirei Agudath Israel branches here and there, but the Agudath Israel of America had not yet been founded in its present form (though it would be soon, in response to Rabbi Chaim Ozer Grodzenski's urgent request to Rabbi Eliezer Silver and others). So Jewish life on the East Side was strong, but its clay foundations were crumbling, because the immigrant generations had not built yeshivos in nearly sufficient numbers.

Reb Moshe and his yeshivah quickly became a center of Torah life on the East Side. At its peak, Tifereth Jerusalem enrolled over five hundred *talmidim*, but it was more than a yeshivah, just as Reb Moshe was more than a *Rosh Hayeshivah*. MTJ (Mesivtha Tifereth Jerusalem) included a *shul* where Reb Moshe not only delivered *shiurim* to his *talmidim*, but the traditional *Shabbos Hagadol* and *Shabbos Shuvah drashos*, as well. In contrast to the four-hour-long *drashos* on *Aggada* that he had delivered for his *baalei-battim* in Luban, he usually spoke on Talmudic themes related to *Kadoshim* (sacrificial order), which attracted a large audience of yeshivah students and *lomdim* (scholars).

His primary role, however, was as decider of halachic questions, and before long, the word spread that a *posek* of the first rank was there — and available. Distinguished rabbis converged on him with knotty problems and so did local housewives with their strange-looking chicken parts — because he belonged equally to them all. Two middle-aged *talmidei chachamim*, whose fathers were butchers on the East Side, remember frequently being sent to Reb Moshe with *she'eilos*. As children they knew him as the nice, friendly man who never made them feel like unimportant intruders — as some others understandably did. As they grew older, they realized with a shock that their "friend" was one of Jewry's greatest people. It is not surprising that one woman used to call him every Friday afternoon to inquire about the time to light candles; he would answer and pleasantly wish her *a Gutten Shabbos* — as he would have done in Uzda or Luban. Did it make any difference whether he was a twenty-year-old beginner in a tiny *shtetl* or the teacher of *Klal Yisroel?* — his responsibility was to answer the queries of all Jews who needed him.

That word "responsibility" is one of the keys to understanding Reb Moshe and his career. His older son, Rabbi David Feinstein, now *Rosh Hayeshivah* of MTJ and an eminent *posek* in his own right, put it succinctly: "My father never wasted a minute, but if a poor or troubled person, or even a *nudnik*, took an hour to pour out his heart, my father could spare an hour." By nature, Reb Moshe was not a public man. He shunned the limelight, leadership, and controversy. His loves were Torah, teaching and defining the *halacha*, and committing his Torah thoughts to writing. Nevertheless, when he felt the need to assume the presidency of Mesivta Tifereth Jerusalem and the onerous burden of fundraising, he did so. When the handful of great survivors who came to America and established the *Moetzes Gedolei HaTorah* (Council of Torah Sages of Agudath Israel of America) called upon him to serve, he acceded. When, after the death of Reb Aharon Kotler, his colleagues drafted him to head the *Moetzes Gedolei HaTorah,* he accepted, as he did when called upon to head Agudas Horabbonim and Chinuch Atzmai. When the time came that he alone had the stature to decide controversies in the Torah world, he took the initiative in calling the parties to judgment. In one such instance, a party complained that it was not Reb Moshe's affair, to which he replied matter-of-factly and without any anger, "I am the father of all *yeshivos.*" This most modest of men was the last to impose his will on others; it was unpleasant for him — but when he realized the burden had fallen upon him, he felt he had no right to refuse it.

Thus he intervened countless times on behalf of yeshivah teachers or administrators who felt that their rights were not being protected. Such people used to refer to him with humorous admiration as "the *rebbes'* union." Toward the end of his life, when troubled people besieged him to pray on their behalf or to give them blessings, he once remarked to Rabbi Michel Barenbaum, the *Mashgiach* of MTJ, "They have made me into a *Chassidishe Rebbe,* but what can I do? — people are in distress and I must try to do whatever I can." He would have preferred to teach and write, and not be drafted to become the father of *yeshivos,* the *rebbes'* union or advocate for his people, but if he was needed, then he had no choice but to accept.

⊷§ Acceptance of His Role

Rabbi Aharon Kotler and Reb Moshe had enormous respect for one another, but they had different personalities and each had a role in which he was preeminent. It was as if they had divided the responsibilities for the future of Torah life. Reb Aharon was the dynamic, charismatic teacher and builder of Torah, and shaper of the revolutionary perception (for the United States) that Torah study should be the exclusive pursuit of our talented young men. Reb Moshe shunned the limelight, channeling his prodigious energies to serve as tireless leader of his own yeshivah and foremost *posek* of the nation.

After Reb Aharon passed away in 1962, Reb Moshe was chosen by his colleagues to assume the helm of *Klal Yisroel.* Leadership meant a major change in his life; indeed, it forced upon him roles that he had previously avoided. Why had he become chairman of the *Nesius* (Presidium) of Agudath Israel, so involved in day-to-day affairs of Agudath Israel? And then, why did he accept the chairmanship of the *Moetzes Gedolei HaTorah* on top of that, as well as the presidency of Chinuch Atzmai and Agudath Horabbonim, the leadership of Torah Umesorah and so forth?

The turning point can be summarized in an almost unknown incident that was witnessed by someone standing only a foot away from Reb Moshe when it took place. Reb Aharon was in the hospital during his final illness, and Reb Moshe and his students were reciting *Tehillim* in the *Beis Midrash* of MTJ. Suddenly someone entered the room and motioned that it was no longer necessary to recite *Tehillim*. Reb Moshe looked across the room at the bearer of the news and asked quietly, "Is it all over?" The head nodded yes.

Reb Moshe stood stone still with shock and disbelief on his face. He mumbled these words to himself:

"It can't be.

"But, if it is true, it is the Will of the Creator.

"This is how it must be.

"If so, then it must be good."

He repeated this monologue twice as if in a trance.

In retrospect it seems as if he could have been evaluating both the tragedy and his new responsibilities: *It can't be! But if this is G-d's will, then it must be good and we must accept it.* On the one hand, his personal struggle constituted *tzidok hadin,* an acceptance of the Divine judgment. But those who were close to Reb Moshe saw in it also that he was grappling with the Heavenly decree that would cast upon him much of the burden of leadership and responsibility that had been borne by Reb Aharon up to then. It was regarding this decree, too, that Reb Moshe could have said, "If this is G-d's will then it must be good and we must accept it."

As chairman of the *Moetzes Gedolei HaTorah*, he was constantly informed of developments in America, Israel, and elsewhere, and was called upon for decision and guidance. His presence as the primary speaker at countless functions — from Agudah Conventions and Dinners to Zeirei and Pirchei assemblies — was not a *pro forma* matter. He was there in recognition of Agudath Israel's leading role within the Torah community and of his own responsibilities within the Agudah.

◈§ The View From Total Immersion

The Rebbetzin used to plead with him, "Please join us for

supper. The *Gemora* to you is like a bottle of whiskey to an alcoholic, I can't pull you away from it!" True. He was always learning. Torah was his love, his comfort, his ambition. When the Torah was read, he would walk to the front of the *bimah* to hear better, and follow the reading from a *Chumash*. Between the readings he would always be immersed in whatever he was learning. A system was set up in MTJ whereby the young children who *davened* in the yeshivah would take turns holding a *Chumash* for him and have it ready in front of his desk. That way, the children had the honor of helping the *Rosh Hayeshivah* — and he could return to his waiting *sefer* between *aliyos* without losing a second. When there was a *bris* in the yeshivah, he would always be engrossed in his learning or writing until the baby was brought in.

A neighbor was once present in Reb Moshe's apartment when a heartbroken woman poured her woes out to him. She wept and groaned, and he shed tears and sighed with her. At the end of the conversation, he promised her, "We will do whatever we can," and then with a final sigh of pain, he went back to his *Gemora* and resumed his studies with total immersion, as if nothing had happened. When the time came, he would do what he could for her; meanwhile, the Torah had a first mortgage on his time.

Reb Moshe would begin studying and writing in his small study by 5:00 a.m. every morning. To prepare for his lengthy *pilpul shiur* every Friday, he would begin learning at 3:30 a.m. He delivered prodigious numbers of *shiurim* (lectures) and prepared for them conscientiously.

In MTJ, there was a daily *shiur* for most of his career. When MTJ opened a residential yeshivah in Staten Island under the leadership of his son Rabbi Reuvain Feinstein, Reb Moshe was there one day every week to give a *shiur* and to be available to speak to the faculty and students. And in his role as mentor to former students and leader of the Jewish community, he was called upon to speak at countless family celebrations and public functions. As his responsibilities increased with the years and he found it difficult to study uninterruptedly during the day, he would begin learning at 4:00 a.m., so that he could count on at least three hours in the morning without distractions.

Once, in an unbelievable display of thoughtlessness, someone called him before 5:00 a.m. to ask him a *she'eilah*, which he answered. The next day, the same caller asked him a question about a *Tosafos* at the same hour. Again he answered. The next morning, he posed another *she'eilah*, which the *Rosh Hayeshivah* patiently answered. Finally, on the *fourth* morning, Reb Moshe softly told his pre-dawn caller, "The reason I arise so early is so I can be prepared to answer the questions people ask when they call me later." That was the last time he heard from the caller at that hour.

On another occasion, he complained to the Rebbetzin, "If I can't find time to learn, I will remain an *am ha'aretz*." Coming from someone of such greatness, such fears sound as if they were said in jest, but Reb Moshe meant it, knowing the vastness of the Torah.

There was no minute to spare.

⋖§ Flawless Memory

He said that he did not know the meaning of the word "forget" until he was in his eighties. One of the leading senior *roshei hayeshivah* in America once called him to discuss his difficulties in *Eizehu Neshech*, one of the most complicated chapters in the Talmud. After they had gone down the list and Reb Moshe had resolved all the problems, the caller remarked that he was fortunate to have called at a time when Reb Moshe obviously had studied the chapter fairly recently. In the course of the conversation it emerged that the last time Reb Moshe had learned *Eizehu Neshech* thoroughly had been more than eight years before! There was a far more important aspect of his memory. It wasn't just that he remembered everything he had ever learned about a particular topic; that in itself would be extraordinary, but as Reb David Feinstein put it, "My father's greatness was not simply that he remembered *kol HaTorah kulah*, but that he could instantly apply any relevant thing he had ever learned all his life to any question that ever came to him."

Reb Moshe's memory was of utmost importance to him, because he could not undertake to decide complex and serious questions of *halachah* unless he could be sure that he had not overlooked any sources. Once he and several rabbis were sitting in the large communal *succah* on FDR Drive when a Talmudic passage came under discussion. Reb Moshe said that it was explained in a *Tosafos* in *Sanhedrin*, while the others all agreed that the source was not in *Sanhedrin* but in *Makkos*. He got up and rushed from the table. The others were surprised. True, he had completed his meal, but it was out of character for him to leave the table without saying *Gut Yom Tov*. Several minutes later he returned. He had crossed the courtyard and climbed the steps to his apartment to look up the

Gemora. As he had thought, it was in *Sanhedrin,* but he simply could not wait until later to verify his recollection, because truth was his most important value, his most pressing concern. If his memory was challenged, then the source must be checked — now, not later.

Once a *talmid* inquired where he could find references to a particular *halachah.* Reb Moshe told him the chapter and paragraph numbers where the *Magen Avraham* discussed it. A while later the student reported that he had found what he needed, but the paragraph number of the *Magen Avraham* was different. Reb Moshe asked him to check the number again and to report back. As it turned out, Reb Moshe had been right, but the *talmid* was curious as to why the *Rosh Hayeshivah* had been so concerned about the proper paragraph number. He explained, "I decide halachic questions from memory, and if my memory is becoming faulty, then I would not be allowed to continue doing so."

It often happened that a *talmid chacham* wished to discuss a halachic matter with Reb Moshe and prepared himself for a week or two, studying and reviewing every passage that could have some bearing on the topic. When he came to discuss the question, he would discover to his amazement and sometimes chagrin that he had nothing to add to the *Rosh Yeshivah's* knowledge. On one occasion a young *talmid chacham* came to disprove a controversial responsum of the *Rosh Yeshivah.* The visitor was clearly a scholar who had prepared himself long and well for the encounter, but the *Rosh Yeshivah* refuted every one of his arguments. While the "fray" was going on, Reb Moshe's students were angered by what they regarded as the young man's insolence, but when the discussion was over, the *Rosh Yeshivah* calmed them by smilingly remarking, "He thought he could catch me overlooking a *Pri Megadim.*" Anger turned to amusement and good feeling.

Indeed, the scope and thoroughness of his knowledge was nothing short of phenomenal. He is best known, of course, for his eight volumes of *Igros Moshe* responsa, because of their universal application, but his fifteen volumes of *Dibros Moshe* on the *Talmud* are no less remarkable. Rabbi Aharon Kotler is said to have commented after studying the *Dibros Moshe* on *Bava Kamma* that every meaningful opinion or concept on the tractate is in the *sefer.* Currently being prepared for publication are a projected ten-volume *Kisvei Maran al Hashas,* from eight thousand pages of manuscript, and *Dorosh Moshe* on *Kadoshim* as well as on the *drashos* he had delivered in Europe.

His grandson Rabbi Mordechai Tendler was almost inseparable
from Reb Moshe for twenty years, as a *talmid* and supervisor of the
publication of the *Rosh Hayeshivah's* last six works, companion,
and protector, especially during the later years when the *Rosh
Hayeshivah's* strength had to be conserved and his generous
openness to all callers had to be curbed. Rabbi Tendler noted that
after having clarified a *halachah*, Reb Moshe was absolutely free of
doubt or concern. Once he was convinced that this was the word of
Torah, it was therefore the will of G-d, and thus it was beyond
doubt. Once, he ruled that an *agunah* was permitted to remarry.
After she had married, a story began to circulate that her husband
was still alive. Her family was horrified and those who were close to
Reb Moshe were appalled that their *rebbe* would be humiliated by
an error with such tragic consequences. But, Rabbi Tendler recalls,
Reb Moshe was not even fazed by the news. He had ruled according
to the *halachah* and therefore he was certain that the rumor was
false. The *halachah* is reality; can reality be refuted by a rumor? He
was proven right. Indeed, there was no living first husband.

This writer's colleague, Rabbi Meir Zlotowitz, was present
when a similar problem was brought to Reb Moshe: Shortly after the
war, a European rabbi had permitted a Holocaust survivor to
remarry on the basis of evidence that her husband had perished in a
concentration camp. Then, after more than twenty years, when she
had grown children of marriageable age, it was discovered that her
first husband was alive in Israel! The distraught woman's rabbi had
come with her from South America to seek the *Rosh Hayeshivah's*
guidance.

He asked her to tell her story. She told how she had gone to a
well-known rabbi in one of the DP camps and, on the basis of the
available testimony and evidence, he ruled that her husband was
dead and she was permitted to remarry. The rabbi passed away not
long after and due to the chaotic post-War conditions, she had lost
the document he had given her. But she had acted on the basis of his
decision — and now this!

Reb Moshe asked her to repeat the story. She did.

He asked her to tell it a third time. The atmosphere in the room
was strained. Why was he tormenting her so? What would be added
by another repetition? She complied.

Reb Moshe's brow was furrowed in intense concentration. A heavy, tense silence froze everyone in the room. Then, abruptly he rose, leaned across the table, and said agitatedly to the woman, "It cannot be! I knew that rabbi. He was a *gaon* and a *tzaddik*. I have permitted thousands of *agunos* to remarry and I have never had such a tragedy happen, and you are telling me that such a thing could have happened to that *tzaddik?* It is impossible! It cannot be!"

The people in the room were shocked that the compassionate, mild-mannered *Rosh Hayeshivah* could speak that way to a woman in pain. But she broke down in tears and admitted that her story was indeed an untruth. She was sure her husband was dead — how could he have survived? — and when she heard that that highly respected rabbi, too, was no longer living, she made up the story, using his name.

This incident is one of many that illustrates Reb Moshe's total faith in the correctness of a *psak halachah* that was was arrived at honestly and by a qualified *posek*. As he once explained with regard to another *psak* he had rendered after a long and complex *din Torah*, "G-d assists the judgment of a qualified, sincere judge. As the Psalmist teaches: 'G-d stands in the Divine assembly of judges who seek truth and justice' (*Tehillim* 82:3)." Reb Moshe had permitted over two thousand *agunos* to remarry, without having erred. The rabbi being held responsible for the error was highly competent and devout; therefore he, too, could not have erred.

ⴵ "Temimus" — Perfect Faith

An elderly native of Radin who knew the Chofetz Chaim as a friend and neighbor explained the difference between him and the rest of us. He said, "The Chofetz Chaim believed in *Olam Habba,* and you and I believe in *Olam Habba.* But to us, *Olam Habba* is an abstract matter of faith. To the Chofetz Chaim, *Olam Habba* was as real as the room next door."

The same could have been said about Reb Moshe. To him anything stated in the Torah and the Talmud was as real as the room next door, as the noses on our faces. There could be no question, no difficulty, no caveat. If the Torah said so or the *halachah* ruled so, it was reality, and one does not doubt reality.

Reb Moshe's deep unquestioning faith found expression in his many *drashos*, some of which were published in *Kol Rom (Bastion of Faith*, in English translation). For instance, in regard to the Torah command to refrain from agricultural work on *Shmittah*, the

Sabbatical Year, Scripture says, "And if you say, 'What will we eat on the seventh year? We did not sow and did not gather our crop.' I will command My blessing upon you on the sixth year and you will produce the crop for three years" (*Vayikra* 25, 21-22).

Asks the *Rosh Hayeshivah*, "The Torah tells us that this particular blessing comes in response to a question that expresses a lack of faith in G-d's ability to provide for those who follow His counsel. How does He provide for those who follow His command *without* question?"

He answers: "People's hunger can be satisfied through having a great deal of food or by having a lower level of need so that a little food goes a long way. People of strong faith do not require open miracles, such as an over-abundant harvest. And so it was during the forty years of wandering in the wilderness — when the people lacked faith and they demanded water, bread, and meat, all three were provided in abundance by open miracles. By contrast, their clothing never frayed, it simply grew with the children as they grew, and never needed replacement . . . a silent miracle in response to unquestioning faith."

Reb Moshe could have been describing the miracle of his own unquestioning faith. A friend of the family once learned what Reb Moshe's salary was — and was appalled at how little he took. "How can he survive on so little?" the man asked. One of the *Rosh Hayeshivah's* sons explained that his parents had very simple tastes and few needs. Not only did they live in as much comfort as they sought, they were even able to give a large percentage of their income to *tzeddakah*.

This applied equally to his acceptance that whatever G-d meted out was just and merciful even though it might be terribly painful. The passing of his beloved son-in-law Rabbi Eliyahu Moshe Shisgal caused him great anguish. In his *hesped*, Reb Moshe wept as he began, but brought himself under control as he quoted the verse: הצור תמים פעלו . . . , *The Rock! — perfect is His work, for all His paths are just; a G-d of faith without iniquity, righteous and fair is He* (*Devarim* 32:4). "We do not understand," he said, "but we know that He is just. He is righteous and fair and whatever He does we accept because He is merciful."

Once someone came to ask Reb Moshe for a letter of recommendation. This was hardly an uncommon occurrence, but in this case, those around the *Rosh Hayeshivah* were incensed, because the petitioner had contemptuously and publicly attacked Reb

Moshe's halachic responsa the previous year. When Reb Moshe agreed to supply the requested letter, they were surprised and aghast. "How could the *Rosh Hayeshivah* do this for such a person?"

Reb Moshe replied incredulously that a *Yom Kippur* had passed and, as is required of every Jew, he had forgiven the malefactor. Consequently, how could anyone expect him to bear a grudge for something he had already forgiven with all his heart?

On another occasion, someone wrote a *sefer* in which he attacked Reb Moshe's responsa in disrespectful and even vulgar terms. The typesetter-printer called to ask Reb Moshe whether he should refuse to accept the job. Reb Moshe urged him to accept, explaining that both the author and the printer had to earn a livelihood. Presumably, the author felt that he had to curry favor with elements whose opinions he supported. As far as Reb Moshe personally was concerned, he had no right to stand in the way.

On the other hand, however, he was unyielding when *Kavod HaTorah* was at stake. A prominent yeshivah lay leader once came personally to Reb Moshe to beg forgiveness for having refused to accept his decision in a *din Torah* involving his institution. Instead of graciously waiving the affront, Reb Moshe admonished him sternly and only then gave his personal forgiveness. After the shamed petitioner left, Reb Moshe explained that he felt no personal resentment toward the party, but he had been required by *halachah* to defend the honor of the Torah.

◄§ Uncontested Greatness

It was clear to him that his Divinely assigned mission was to decide *halachah* for his generation and the following ones. Consequently, he had no right to decline to rule on a problem, no matter how complex or sensitive it was. Nor could he simply rule stringently to avoid the effects of possible error. He knew very well that some of his rulings were controversial, but he was secure enough to stand by his *psak* even when most authorities disagreed. At the same time he stated that other competent authorities had the right to rule differently if their research so indicated.

Concerning a responsum that raised the ire of many, he told a *talmid* that the history of halachic responsa shows that the works that gained historic acceptance did not do so until after the authors had passed from the scene. As time goes by, succeeding generations see the printed word and make dispassionate judgments of what is correct and what is not. He was not concerned that there were those who disagreed with this or that *psak*, for he was confident in the truth of his view.

Virtually every venerable sage of our time considered him the preeminent *gadol* of his time. The Ponevezher *Rosh Hayeshivah* Rabbi Shach went so far as to describe him as: "The *Gadol Hador* — without equivocation, without exaggeration, without embellishment." Leading *poskim* of *Eretz Yisroel* often referred the knottiest questions to him. The Steipler Gaon said that Reb Moshe was the leading authority of the era. Rabbi Yonasan Steif used to put on his hat and stand erect when he spoke to Reb Moshe on the telephone. Most Chassidic *gedolim* who disagreed with his traditional Lithuanian method of defining the *halachah* nevertheless deferred to him in cases of the most extreme difficulty. Indeed, even *poskim* whose understanding and tradition were in contradistinction to Reb Moshe's decisions, nevertheless acknowledged him as the greatest *posek* of his time.

Our generation was fortunate that someone of his genius lived among us to deal with the halachic problems posed by the revolutionary developments in science, medicine, economics, civil law, and assimilation. Since so many of the questions coming to him dealt with problems unimaginable in the traditional Jewish society of a century ago, it is quite natural that many of his decisions were unprecedented. And since he was forced to be the defender of congregations and rabbis under religious attack, he would often find bases for leniency under clearly defined circumstances. Some assumed that a new sort of halachic approach — outrageously dubbed "Feinsteinism" by a left fringe of Modern Orthodoxy — could be relied upon to permit whatever was needed for a Judaism of accommodation and convenience. Others simply distorted or misquoted his responsa for their own ideological purposes. One need not be a scholar to know that there is no statement in *Igros Moshe* that does not fall in the mainstream of classical *halachah*.

✺§ His Personal Credo

If one can sum up Reb Moshe's personal credo as a human being, perhaps it can be expressed best in his response to a question as to what *zechus* he attributed his eminence. His reply was given in typical understatement: מיין גאנץ לעבען האב איך קיין מאל ניט ווי געטאן א מענשן, "All my life I never hurt a human being." An understatement, because he went out of his way to bring comfort and accommodation to others.

He was as much a genius in his simplicity and normality as in scholarship. In the words of Rabbi Zelig Epstein (*Rosh Hayeshivah Shaar HaTorah*): "We recognized his greatness, yet standing before him one never felt constrained or ill at ease." And he was a model of devotion to his family. To a young man who complained that his wife was annoyed if he did not call her during the day, he responded with amazement, "But of course you should call her during the day. I always call the *Rebbetzin*." When he was in the hospital, he never failed to inquire about the *Rebbetzin's* welfare. But he was solicitous not only of those who were dearest to him. He would unfailingly exert himself to avoid inconveniencing others. Even when he was ill and weak, in the hospital or in bed at home, he would strain over toward a doctor, nurse, or attendant — doing whatever he could to ease their task, thanking them when they completed excruciatingly painful tests or treatments.

There was no more loving grandfather. He would cuddle and play with his grandchildren, and they adored him and loved to sit on his lap or roll a ball back and forth with him. Instinctively, they were calm and happy in his presence, even after long, cramped automobile trips. If his grandchildren were playing with friends when they saw him and came running, he had a hug and kiss for the playmates as well as the grandchildren. Why should a child feel slighted?

Recently, when he was in the hospital, the women in his family distributed portions of cake to the hospital personnel, doctors, nurses, orderlies, attendants — anyone who had rendered him a service in any way. It is fascinating to note that instead of eating them, many showed off their portions and treasured them, and took them home to their families. These were not ordinary pastries, but mementoes of an extraordinary man. Those hardened hospital workers had recognized that they were in the presence of holiness. They were utterly devoted to him and many wept when they heard he was gone.

Once a childless woman, a talented painter, came to him for advice and for a blessing that she would give birth. She had a child and, to show her gratitude, brought the *Rosh Hayeshivah* a painting that the *Rebbetzin* hung in the dining room. When her new baby was old enough to travel without difficulty, she brought him to visit the Feinstein family, to gratefully show the *Rosh Hayeshivah* the fruit of his blessing. After her visit, while she was waiting for the elevator, Reb Moshe himself rushed out into the hall. He remembered that her painting was no longer on the dining-room wall and she might feel slighted, so he wanted to explain that it had been transferred to a different room, because the dining room had been converted into a *shul* for the morning *minyan*.

Many complained that he was too liberal in giving letters of approval for individual or organizational charity collections or for *seforim*. He knew that the proliferation of such letters lessened the value attached to his signature, but he argued if this is the way he can help a fellow Jew open a door or gain a hearing, a bit of his own prestige was a very small price to pay.

Often, almost regularly, he would attend two or three weddings in the evening — and then travel to a *bris* in the morning. Those close to him wondered ruefully how *he* always managed to find so much time and strength to add honor to someone *else's* *simchah*, while the beneficiaries of his personal generosity seemed so busy when he needed them to attend functions for the benefit of his institutions.

Once he was suffering from a leg infection that made walking somewhat painful and he was being driven from his Yeshivah of Staten Island back to his home on FDR Drive, by Rabbi Gershon Weiss, *Menahel* of the Yeshivah. Rabbi Weiss could not escort Reb Moshe to his apartment because one of his children was in the car and crying. Instead, another passenger, a *talmid*, walked the *Rosh Hayeshivah* in and Rabbi Weiss waited in the car. Not wanting to delay Rabbi Weiss's return trip — and keep the child crying — Reb Moshe did not wait for the elevator but walked a flight of steps, despite his painful leg, so that the *talmid* could hurry back to the car, and the unhappy child could be brought home.

When people came to see him with a question or problem, he would invariably acknowledge them immediately. And when they spoke, they received his total attention. Their good news lit his face with happiness and their woes evoked sincere concern. The writer and a fellow *menahel* once visited him concerning a serious problem regarding several families. Entirely aside from his sagacious advice, he seemed as anxious and aggrieved as if his own grandchildren were the sufferers.

One of his closest and finest *talmidim* was Rabbi Nissan Alpert who passed away tragically only a few months after Reb Moshe. In Rabbi Alpert's eulogy of Reb Moshe he provided a delicate insight into Reb Moshe's method of dealing with halachic queries from troubled people. He combined *chessed* and *emes*, kindness and truth

— but first came the kindness. He would feel compassion for the questioner and that *chessed* would be the background upon which he would etch the halachic truth.

For the last twenty-five years, he had spent *Succos* in the home of his daughter and son-in-law, Rabbi and Mrs. Moshe Tendler (*Rosh Hayeshivah* in Rabbi Isaac Elchonon Theological Seminary and Rabbi of the Community Synagogue of Monsey). Reb Moshe would sleep in the *succah* and, as he did all year long, get up to learn before dawn. During the later years of his life, Rebbetzin Tendler used to arrange the chairs in a line so that Reb Moshe could support himself on them as he walked from his bed to get his morning coffee and go to the room where he learned. Every morning, the family found the chairs neatly placed around the table. Eventually they learned that it was being done by Reb Moshe himself, who wanted to spare others the extra bother of putting the chairs back where they belonged.

◦§ Source Of His Powers

Stories abound about the miraculous results of the *Rosh Hayeshivah's* blessings and prayers. True, many stories become garbled and embellished as they travel from person to person, but in their essentials they happened.

Recently, a friend of the family, who knew him well, told several stories about Reb Moshe. This friend was involved in or saw each of the incidents he related. Following are two of those anecdotes, one miraculous and the other not — perhaps.

This friend was called by an acquaintance in New York. The caller's son had spent several years in a *kollel* and had taken a course in COPE (Agudath Israel's school for vocational training), but for many months had been unable to find a job. Could he arrange for the caller to see Reb Moshe so that she could ask for a *brachah* for her son? The calls were made, the appointment was arranged and Reb Moshe assured the worried mother that her son would have *parnassah*. A few days later, the young man was called for an interview by someone who had rejected his application some months earlier — and he was hired. The *Rosh Hayeshivah's* blessing? Presumably, but the story is not over. Some time later, the narrator of the story repeated the incident to a former *rosh hayeshivah* of his and, to his surprise, the *rosh hayeshivah* exclaimed in shock, "Now I understand!" He explained that the employer had once been his *talmid* and the mother of the young man had implored him to call the employer on behalf of her son, which he promised to do. Indeed, he tried several times, but each time he was unable to get through for one reason or another, and finally forgot about it. Then, one night, he dreamt that Reb Moshe was asking him to call that same gentleman to intercede on behalf of the unemployed *kollel* fellow. He made the call and the former *talmid* promised to cooperate. They checked the dates. It was the night of Reb Moshe's blessing and shortly before the interview and hiring.

Then he told a second story.

When Reb Moshe was younger, he used to have *Shalosh Seudos* and recite *Tehillim* in the Mesivtha every *Shabbos*. One *Shabbos*, as he was reciting *Tehillim*, a mildly retarded child stood watching him. The boy went over and turned Reb Moshe's *Tehillim* on an angle to the right, and Reb Moshe continued reciting. Then the boy took the *Tehillim* and turned it completely around and Reb Moshe continued reciting. Not satisfied, the boy turned a page, but the *Rosh Hayeshivah* still was not fazed. A gentleman had watched all this and, although people went out of their way to be patient with the boy, the man had seen too much. He snapped, "Stop it, already. Let the *Rosh Hayeshivah daven!*"

Reb Moshe turned to the man and said, "He is only playing with me. I *enjoy* it when he plays with me. I love him like my own child!" With that, Reb Moshe embraced the boy and kissed him.

One of the people listening to these stories expressed it well. He explained, "Stories like the first one could happen because stories like the second one happened."

"*Shivisi* — I envision *Hashem* before me always" was etched upon his face, and found obvious expression in his *tefillah*. Indeed, to watch him at prayer was astounding and inspirational. People used to stop and stare during his recitation of the *Shema*; it was the very epitome of *Kabbolas Ol Malchus Shomayim*, the acceptance of G-d's sovereignty, as he immersed himself totally in its recitation, chanting softly with the *trop* (cantillation). Years ago when he would go to a hotel for a brief summer vacation, laymen would often gather in front of the porch to gaze at the devotion with which he recited *Tehillim* early in the morning.

Those who were privileged to take part in the *minyan* in his apartment during periods of illness could see clearly how he ignored pain and infirmity during his *tefillos*. He always *davened* every word from a *siddur* and, when his vision troubled him, his students made enlarged Xerox pages of a *siddur* for him. During periods of excruciatingly painful sciatica attacks, when standing was an agony for him and he needed assistance to rise from his chair, he insisted on standing for *Baruch She'amar* and then, a few minutes later, getting up again for *Mizmor L'Sodah* and, of course, for the *Shemoneh Esrei*. He would stand again for *Modim D'Rabbanan*. Despite the pain in his back, he maintained his constant practice of bowing very deeply during *Shemoneh Esrei*. Few of us can truly comprehend how it is possible for an ordinary mortal to feel so keenly the presence of G-d that he negates his self during prayers, but anyone who watched Reb Moshe pray *saw* it happen.

ⰷ The Most Important Legacy

There is a tendency to mythologize our *gedolim* and turn them into legends. This is understandable but wrong. It makes for reverence and marvelous narratives, but it frees us from the obligation to learn from them. *We* cannot make miracles. *We* cannot memorize the entire Torah. All we can do is tell stories and shake our heads sadly, saying, "Oh, what great people we used to have. Too bad we can't be like that."

But Reb Moshe's memory has much more to teach us than the unattainable. His faith, piety, unselfishness, responsibility to *Klal*, love of Israel, and humility were not G-d-given gifts. They were *human* achievements and as such, they are in reach of others, as well. In the words of his son, Reb Reuvain: "My father's deepest desire was to bring peace to Jewish life. If he could speak to us now, that is what he would tell us." His awesome command of Torah was not inborn. His phenomenal mind was a heavenly gift, but it was his total appreciation of this gift that made him the *gaon* and *posek* whose writings will be studied and whose decisions will be consulted for generations.

⚜   ⚜   ⚜

His last words encapsule the theme of his life. As the ambulance was speeding him to the hospital he reputedly said, *"Ich hob mehr nischt kein ko'ach."* (I have no more strength.) It was about 8:50 p.m. An hour later, he was gone.

How much strength had he had for the last several years? Very little, but whatever strength was left him was devoted to *Hashem Yisborach*, to Torah and to *Klal Yisroel*. As long as he had strength — any strength — his service continued. He would not stop working at his full capacity, as he had for ninety-one years. And then he had no more strength.

At that moment, the *Beis Midrash* of his yeshivah in Staten Island was filled with *bachurim* and young men fervently reciting *Tehillim*, imploring G-d to spare him. At 9:50 p.m., the light over his vacant *shtender* flickered and went out. A *bachur* reached over to adjust the bulb. It glowed for a moment and went out, again.

❦ ❦ ❦

He had no more strength and the light went out.

The next day, *Taanis Esther*, 150,000 people crowded the Lower East Side to bid him farewell. On Shushan Purim in Jerusalem, 300,000 people escorted him to his final rest on Har Hamenuchos, the largest *levayah* since the time of Rabban Yochanan ben Zakai.

A student of Beth Medrosh Govoha in Lakewood told his father, "Since I was old enough to go to *levayos* and hear *hespeidim* of *gedolim*, I would hear speakers say that now we are like orphans. But I never felt like an orphan because I knew Reb Moshe was here. Now I am an orphan."

They both cried.

Rabbi Yaakov Yitzchak Ruderman

The Late Rosh Hayeshivah of Ner Israel

*One of the pioneer
Roshei Yeshivah
in the U.S.,
he led his talmidim
to greatness
for over five decades.*

Rabbi Yaakov Yitzchak Ruderman
5660-5747 / 1900-1987

THE LIST CONSISTS OF hundreds of names, and all of them have two things in common — perhaps the two are really one: They are *talmidim* (disciples) of Ner Israel — married men who had studied under Rabbi Yaakov Yitzchok Ruderman. And each and every one cannot be reached by telephone for several hours every day. They are all keeping their appointed times for learning.

❦   ❦   ❦

Returning from a recent convention of Torah Umesorah, the National Organization for Hebrew Day Schools, Rabbi Ruderman remarked that he was amazed and gratified to have met so many Ner Israel alumni involved in *chinuch* (Torah education), virtually from border to border, from coast to coast as well as in other lands . . .

❦   ❦   ❦

Unyielding dedication to studying and teaching Torah is a trait that is not easily learned. Yet somehow those who were in the immediate presence of the late Rosh Yeshivah of Ner Israel, Rabbi Ruderman, were changed. They learned to love learning, and they feel compelled to educate others in that same love.

⋖§A Love so Profound

On the surface it may seem strange. Rabbi Ruderman was thought by many to be a shy man. He was obviously in love with his *seforim*, scholarly in mien, soft spoken, not readily recognized to be the type of man who could mold hosts of others in his image, especially when those others were young men who had been brought up in the permissive, fun-loving, self-centered society of mid-twentieth-century America. Yet by example — more, by contagion — having spent more than a half-century living the life of Torah, treasuring the printed word of Torah, absorbing it indelibly in his mind, imprinting it permanently onto his heart — he succeeded in transmitting his dedication through his love for the young men who came to study under him: Five *bachurim* who joined him in Baltimore in 1933 ... 600 *talmidim* of Yeshivas Ner Israel, joining thousands of alumni, who wept at his passing in 1987.

His *talmidim* observed a *Rebbe* whose encyclopedic knowledge of *Shas Bavli, Yerushalmi, Rishonim, Poskim, Acharonim* and *Teshuvos* (Talmud and its vast literature of commentaries and halachic responsa) set a lofty standard to strive for. He constantly challenged his *talmidim* to bring proof from one *Gemara* to a seemingly unrelated issue, stimulating lively discussion, deepening their interest, and broadening their horizons. He constantly focused their attention and awareness on the depth and breadth and interrelationship of all of Torah. He was always involved in a *kushya* (challenging question). He explained that he used questions as memory keys with which to remember the details of the *Gemara*. Thus no matter which *Gemara* one mentioned, he always had a penetrating query or comment at his fingertips to lend an insight to the *sugya* (topic), citing one reference after another, often from obscure responsa and forgotten commentaries. He lived with his questions, and was often observed with his lips constantly moving as he was consistently absorbed in learning. This total immersion in Talmud gave rise to many amusing incidents of apparent absent-minded behavior. Rarely was his sleep at night not disturbed by an unanswered *kushya*.

One could readily believe the story told how, as a *bachur*, Rabbi Ruderman got hold of a copy of a just-published volume of *Ohr Somayach* on *Zemanim* for one night's perusal. He had no access to a lamp, so he went through the entire *sefer* that night, by the light of the moon. His poor vision became further damaged from the experience — but he was able to quote the *sefer* copiously for the remainder of his life.

His love for Torah and for his *talmidim* went hand in hand. Whenever a *talmid* asked him a stimulating *kushya*, or offered a workable *svora* (rationale), his face would radiate with delight. More often than not, he would cite commentaries that deal with the *sugya*, and quote their opinions. And then he would point out the implications of the insight and how they affect other issues. When a *talmid* had the good fortune to say something that pleased him, he would become ecstatic. Many had the embarrassing experience of being reminded by the *Rosh Hayeshivah*, years later, of a *chiddush* that they had said and had long since forgotten, but he had treasured.

Every Ner Israel graduate knew that the first question he would face when encountering the *Rosh Hayeshivah* was, "Nu, vos *lerentstu* (what are you learning)?" He would not proceed further in the conversation until this question was properly resolved. He told each *talmid* when he left the Yeshivah that regardless of what he did to earn a living, it was absolutely essential that he study during set times every day, and he demanded it.

During the late 50's and early 60's, a Ner Israel branch was opened in Toronto (today, an independent institution). On his way to Toronto, Rabbi Ruderman would travel by train from Baltimore to Buffalo, where he "talked in learning" with the local *Rav*, Rabbi Dov Berish Zuckerman, a profound *talmid chacham*. He once advised the Toronto *bachurim* who drove him back to his train connection in Buffalo to also visit Rabbi Zuckerman. They did, and remained overnight, engrossed in Talmudic discussion until five in the morning.

In the summer of 1985, when the *Rosh Hayeshivah* was spending several weeks in Camp Agudah, he was discussing a topic in *Mesechte Kedushin* with some older boys. "The *Rashba* says it clearly," he said. To illustrate the point, he added, "I'll show you how his words underscore it."

He opened the *Rashba* and ran his fingers along the lines as he read — except, as one of the boys noticed, he had opened the *sefer* to the *Rashba's* commentary on *Mesechte Kesubos,* and he was quoting the commentary on *Kedushin* by heart. His vision was dimmed, but his memory was as sharp as ever.

The last public function that he attended was a *siyum* that the resident physician in Yeshivah Lane had made with his *chavrusa.* Although physically weak, the *Rosh Hayeshivah* — also motivated by his sense of appreciation to the doctor — found the strength to participate in the Torah *simchah.*

⌐§ Torah Pioneering Days

Rabbi Yaakov Yitzchok Ruderman was among the pioneers who came to America before World War II to strive for the impossible and achieve it: planting the seeds of Torah in the *treife* American soil. He arrived on these shores in 1931, to assume a position under his father-in-law,* Rabbi Sheftel Kramer, who was *menahel ruchani* of the Yeshivah of New Haven that had moved to Cleveland. In 1933, he struck out on his own, as the *Rav* of the Tiferes Yisroel *Shul* in Baltimore, with the understanding that he could use the facilities for a yeshivah. Five *bachurim* from Cleveland joined him in Baltimore.

There were a few staunch supporters of the Yeshivah; the general climate, however, was unreceptive at best. Only a handful of senior yeshivos existed on the American continent at that time. Coupled with the deep economic depression, the situation was precarious. The incredible *mesiras nefesh* of *Rebbetzin* Ruderman in mobilizing the women of the community for the Yeshivah overcame immense adversity. The ladies, who hosted showers where people donated food and linens for the *bachurim,* frequently had to

---

* In 1924, Rabbi Ruderman had married Feige Kramer, the oldest of five daughters born to Rabbi Sheftel and Devorah Kramer. *Rebbetzin* Devorah was one of four daughters of the renowned Rabbi Shraga Feivel and Golda Frank, in whose house *talmidim* of Rabbi Yisroel Salanter spent *Chodesh Elul.* A measure of Reb Shraga's greatness can be discerned from the fact that when he died at the age of 42, the *Gadol Hador,* Rabbi Yitzchok Elchonon Spector, participated in the *taharah.* His widow, *Rebbetzin* Golda, arranged all the *shidduchim* for her daughters. Rabbi Moshe Mordechai Epstein, *Rosh Hayeshivah* of Slobodka, Rabbi Isser Zalman Meltzer, of Slutsk, and later Yeshivah Eitz Chaim of Jerusalem, and Rabbi Boruch Yehudah Horowitz, of Alexot and Slobodka, were the other sons-in-law.

For more details, see Rabbi Chaim Shapiro's "Torah Pioneers" in *The Torah World* and Chaya Baumwolspiner's "Rebbetzin Chaya Perel Kotler," in this book.

This biographical appreciation is based primarily on material furnished by Rabbi Sheftel Neuberger, *Ram* in Yeshivah Ner Israel, and a nephew of the late *Rosh Hayeshivah.* Additional sources of information include Rabbi Dovid Cohen (Cong. Gvul Yaavetz, Brooklyn), Yeruchem Lax, Moshe Asher Reines, and several articles that appeared in *Yated Ne'eman.*

circumvent local opposition to their yeshivah activities, sometimes addressing the *Rebbetzin* by a code name when talking to her on the telephone in the presence of hostile neighbors. The *Rebbetzin* also served as a constant source of strength to the *Rosh Hayeshivah*. When a prestigious position in a New York yeshivah was offered to the *Rosh Hayeshivah*, she encouraged him to remain in Baltimore — a fortitude for which he frequently expressed his eternal gratitude.

The *Rosh Hayeshivah* and his *Rebbetzin*, Feige, left one child, *Rebbetzin* Chana Weinberg, and were blessed with six grandchildren and numerous great-grandchildren who were privileged to surround the *Rosh Hayeshivah* during his last years. Their son-in-law, Rabbi Yaakov Weinberg, is today the successor to Rabbi Ruderman as *Rosh Hayeshivah*.

The Yeshivah underwent a steady but slow growth in those early years, yet Rabbi Ruderman remained committed to the dream that a great Torah center would rise in Baltimore. Rabbi Shimon Schwab related that in the late 30's, when he was serving as *Rav* in the Shearith Israel *shul* of Baltimore, Rabbi Ruderman once pointed out a large multi-story apartment house to him as suitable for the Yeshivah. In response to Rabbi Schwab's surprised amusement, the *Rosh Hayeshivah* exclaimed, "Do you doubt that we will have a yeshivah the size of Slobodka here?"

The early growth of the Yeshivah was intensified by the recognition and support of prominent *rabbonim*. Rabbi Shraga Feivel Mendlowitz, the *Menahel* of Mesivta Torah Vodaath and unquestionably one of the most important figures in the development of Torah in America, recommended *bachurim* from New York whom he thought would especially benefit from the *Rosh Hayeshivah*. Among this group was Rabbi Moshe Sherer, today president of Agudath Israel of America. Rabbi Yaakov Kamenetzky sent his sons from Toronto, a major distance in those years, as did Rabbi Yehoshua Klavan, the *Rav* of Washington, D.C. Furthermore, when the *Rosh Hayeshivah* was ill, Rabbi Klavan traveled from Washington to say the daily *shiur* in his stead.

When the Yeshivah launched its campaign to erect the *beis midrash* building on Garrison Boulevard, the *Rosh Hayeshivah* traveled to Cincinnati to enlist the appreciable help of the legendary Rabbi Eliezer Silver, who remained a lifelong friend of the *Rosh Hayeshivah*.

The early success of the Yeshivah can be attributed to the *Rosh Hayeshivah*'s love for every *ben Torah*. The Telzer *Rosh*

Hayeshivah, Rabbi Mordechai Gifter, tells of having come to Baltimore from Europe for a visit, when the outbreak of World War II prevented him from returning to his beloved Telshe. Distraught and lonely, he found comfort in the home of the *Rosh Hayeshivah*. To provide him with encouragement, Rabbi Ruderman asked Rabbi Gifter to say *chaburos* (specialized lectures) to a select group of *talmidim*. Rabbi Gifter tells of his elation over the *Rosh Hayeshivah's* success in creating a yeshivah in America with the flavor of the yeshivos in Lithuania that he had left behind.

Each expansion of the Yeshivah took place with a leap of faith. As the *Rosh Hayeshivah* said, "If we wait until we raise the required funds, nothing will ever happen." Building a new *Beis Midrash* and dormitory in 1943 — during the height of World War II, with the shortages of men and material — was almost miraculous. In addition to serving the many refugee students that came to Baltimore to learn, Yeshivas Ner Israel eventually became the prime yeshivah for America's South and much of the West, as well as attracting a number of students from the New York metropolitan area.

In the early 60's, Rabbi Ruderman established the Ner Israel Kollel, for which he personally raised the funds. The Kollel had a profound effect on both the Yeshivah and the community. On the one hand, the *Beis Midrash* retained its best *talmidim* for many additional years, contributing greatly to the level of learning of the entire *Beis Midrash*. In addition, this established a pattern for young Torah families to settle in Baltimore, elevating all aspects of the city's Jewish community, now one of the finest in North America.

During the middle sixties, the Yeshivah's neighborhood was changing and was becoming increasingly less suitable for the Yeshivah. The relocation of this institution of over two hundred and fifty *talmidim* required over ten times as much money as the Yeshivah had ever raised in the past. Under the leadership of the *Rosh Hayeshivah* and the efforts of his brother-in-law, Rabbi Naftoli Neuberger, the Yeshivah's executive director, the Yeshivah moved, today occupying the largest yeshivah complex in the world, on its rural Pikesville campus.

๙ Background to Greatness

We are, of course, eager to learn more about the background of the man who achieved such greatness in Torah, and inspired so many others to strive for greatness of their own. Knowledge of

Rabbi Ruderman's early life is sketchy at best. He was born Shushan Purim 5660 (1900) in Dolhinov, a small *shtetl* in the vicinity of Vilna. He was the only son born after six daughters, late in life, to Reb Yehuda Leib and his wife *Rebbetzin* Sheina. A year before his birth, an elderly childless Jew known simply as Reb Yitzchok responded to *Rebbetzin* Sheina's request for a *brachah* that she would have a son; but the elderly man added that she call the child Yitzchok. When the boy was born, however, his mother wanted to name him Yaakov after her father. A *she'eilah* was posed, and it was ruled that he be given both names, Yaakov Yitzchok. (The source of this story is Rabbi Ruderman's illustrious cousin, Rabbi Yaakov Kamenetzky, who was named after the same person [his uncle]. One of Reb Yaakov's earliest recollections was saying *kriyas shema* at the bedside of his newborn cousin. Thus began a friendship that would span eight decades.)

His father, Reb Yehudah Leib, was a *melamed*, who knew *Shas* with *Tosafos* well. Rabbi Ruderman confided that although he may have eclipsed his father in Torah learning, he could not even approach his level of *avodah* and *yiras Shomayim* (service to G-d). He recalled how his father had struggled to put up his *succah* himself, only to have it collapse. He struggled again and again — refusing to enlist any help, so precious to him was the *mitzvah* of building it by himself!

Reb Yehudah Leib recognized his son's prodigious talent and made a practice of awakening young Yaakov Yitzchok early every morning to teach him *Gemara* before *davening*. He was rewarded for every *daf* he learned by heart, and as a result, mastered *Seder Nashim* and *Nezikim* (two of the Talmud's six sections) before *Bar Mitzvah*.

The reputation of the young *illuy* (genius) of Dolhinov soon spread, and the *talmidim* of Slobodka, always on the lookout for exceptional *bachurim*, heard about Yaakov Yitzchok. A *talmid* of the saintly *Alter* of Slobodka, Rabbi Nosson Tzvi Finkel, convinced the young genius to come to Slobodka — undoubtedly a major milestone in his life. He often said that without the guidance of the *Alter*, he would have never developed anywhere near his potential.

During World War One the Slobodka Yeshivah fled eastward from the approaching German army, to Minsk. It was here that Rabbi Ruderman had the *zechus* to meet the revered *Rav* of Brisk, Rabbi Chaim Soloveitchik. Unbeknown to him, Reb Chaim recognized the young *illuy's* great promise, and arranged that a wealthy acquaintance provide him with pocket money so that his learning not be adversely affected by need. Rabbi Ruderman only became aware of Reb Chaim's role in this support when it ceased upon the passing of Reb Chaim.

The *Alter* also showered the youngster with an enormous amount of attention. The future Chevron *Rosh Hayeshivah*, Rabbi Yechezkel Sarna, one of the *Alter's* closest *talmidim*, was assigned to be his "*eltere bachur.*"

Young Yaakov Yitzchok had a tremendous capacity for learning with *hasmodah* (diligence), but a total inability to adhere to the Yeshivah's *sedorim* (schedule). He used to take long walks during which he would *chazer* (review) entire tractates by heart. (He confided to a *talmid* that on his regular afternoon strolls, he would *chazer* the entire *Seder Nashim* on the way to the next village, *Seder Nezikim* on the return.) The *Alter* granted him the freedom to study his own way as long as he achieved the goals that they agreed upon. Although he had already completed the entire *Shas* by the time he was fourteen, they decided that he attempt to review the entire Talmud between Succos and Pesach that year. When the *Alter* received a telegram early that winter informing him of the death of Reb Yehudah Leib, he decided not to inform the youngster so that it would not interfere with this undertaking. Someone objected to the *Alter*, "But Yaakov Yitzchok will miss saying *Kaddish* for his father!"

"It will be a greater merit for his father's *neshamah*," replied the *Alter*, "if he finishes *Shas*. If he develops to his potential, it will be the equivalent of many *Kaddeishim.*"

Only after Pesach, when Yaakov Yitzchok had completed his goal, did the *Alter* tell his *talmid* the tragic tidings.

◆ঙ Learning from the Alter's Approach

Reb Yaakov Yitzchok was keenly aware of the special consideration that he was receiving and that it placed an enormous responsibility upon him to succeed. He also realized that the *Alter* was a master *mechanech* (pedagogue) and that he could gain much not only from how he was being treated, but from observing how the *Alter* dealt with others and how he reacted to situations.

Later in life, as *Rosh Hayeshivah*, he emulated the *Alter's* approach to *talmidim*, spending hours on end with individuals in discussions unrelated to their studies, guiding them in molding their *midos* (character) and developing their *hashkofas ha'chaim* (outlook on life).

Appearances did not impress the *Alter*. A *bachur* known not to be especially fastidious in religious matters had left Slobodka for another yeshivah and returned a year later, seeming very devout. When the *Rosh Hayeshivah* told the *Alter* of his admiration over this metamorphosis, the *Alter* commented that the improvement was only skin deep and it would not last. Unfortunately, the *Alter* was correct. The *Rosh Hayeshivah* observed and developed an uncanny ability of his own to see through externals, to the core of an individual, and was rarely taken in by those who were less than genuine.

A visiting rabbinical dignitary was called to the Torah in Slobodka, and pronounced the *brachah* slowly, with an unusual display of feeling. Young Yaakov Yitzchok shared his awe over the *brachah* with the *Alter*, who said, "Yes, very admirable — if he also says it that way every morning, during the *Birchos Hashachar* . . ."

While emotions cannot be denied, the *Alter* taught that one must control one's emotions rather than be subject to their whims. On a particular occasion, a group of his *talmidim* took advantage of an opportunity to hear Rabbi Itzel (Peterburger) Blazer deliver a *mussar schmuess* (lecture on ethical improvement). When the *Alter* later learned that some of his students wept at the lecture, he reprimanded them, "Reb Itzel should move you to think, not to cry!"

"The *Alter* guided us in weighing our choices between several good acts, evaluating them and then setting priorities," the *Rosh Hayeshivah* recalled. "He once met me in the street after I had purchased a new pair of *tzitzis* with money I had carefully saved. My face must have been aglow, because he asked me why I was so happy. When I told him, he asked me if the three dollars could not have been better spent in support of a starving family."

Rabbi Ruderman entertained plans to join a group of *illuim* that was leaving Slobodka to study under Rabbi Itzele (Ponovezer) Rabinowitz. Reb Itzele was reputed to have one of the most phenomenal minds of his generation, but was not too removed from his *talmidim* to guide them in those turbulent times. When Rabbi Ruderman told the *Alter* of his intentions, the *Alter* took him to the window and pointed to a nearby river, telling him: "You can throw yourself into the river here. Why bother traveling elsewhere to drown?" The *Alter's* harsh premonition proved true. The poverty there was extreme, and Reb Itzele was totally immersed in his studies, oblivious to the boys' needs. Before long all but two of that initial group strayed, not remaining *bnei Torah*.

The *Alter* rarely gave up on a *talmid* and was loath to expel anyone from the Yeshivah. Rabbi Ruderman's roommate exhibited a potential of exerting a negative influence on him. Rather than tell Rabbi Ruderman outright to disassociate himself from his friend, the *Alter* first invited Rabbi Ruderman to move into his own house because all the children had already married and moved out. Rabbi Ruderman recalled how, during this time, he was struck with a severe case of dysentery, but a raging winter storm prevented him from using the outdoor facilities. The *Alter* offered to keep the door to the house open as long as Yaakov Yitzchok was out, speaking to him all along "so he can find his way back" — but, in truth, simply to reassure him . . . paternal devotion to the fullest. The other *bachur* remained in the Yeshivah until the *Rosh Hayeshivah*, Rabbi Moshe Mordechai Epstein, expelled him during the *Alter's* absence.

Rabbi Ruderman often cautioned faculty members of Ner Israel that dealing with *bachurim* is *dinei nefashos* — a matter of spiritual life and death, not to be taken lightly. On occasion, other members of the *hanhalah* (administration) of the Yeshivah recommended dismissing a problem *bachur*, but the *Rosh Hayeshivah* was adamant: One never knows what the future holds. Perhaps with a little more patience, and further exposure to the Torah's corrective powers, the young man would straighten out. By and large, his position was vindicated.

Many *talmidim* had come to Ner Israel as refugees, or from troubled backgrounds, and found a home in the Yeshivah, and a father in the *Rosh Hayeshivah*. During the 30's and 40's, the *Rosh Hayeshivah's seder* table was crowded with *talmidim* who could not travel home for Pesach. Rabbi Shmuel Kamenetzky, *Rosh Hayeshivah* in Philadelphia, was among the group, and recalls how the boys valued the experience, how at home they felt with the *Rosh Hayeshivah* and the *Rebbetzin*.

Those *talmidim* who chose to devote their lives completely to Torah study, and faced strong opposition from parents, relied on the *Rosh Hayeshivah* to intercede on their behalf, and to provide the necessary encouragement and support. There are prominent *Ramim* (teachers of Talmud) who waged that battle and prevailed, thanks to the *Rosh Hayeshivah*.

Ten years ago, Rabbi Yaakov Kamenetzky was invited to address a gathering in Lakewood marking the fiftieth *yahrzeit* of the *Alter*, but could not participate. He was quoted, however, as saying that Rabbi Ruderman, who did speak, reflected the *Alter's* personality more than did any other surviving *talmidim*.

◄§ At The Feet of Gedolei Torah

Drawing on the Talmud's dictum that one can grow more from serving Torah scholars than from scholarship, Rabbi Ruderman emulated the *Alter* in seeking close contact with senior *Gedolei Yisrael*. Just as the *Alter* discussed matters or referred halachic problems to Reb Meir Simcha of Dvinsk, Reb Chaim Brisker, and Reb Chaim Ozer, Rabbi Ruderman also developed special relationships with outstanding Torah personalities. He would recall with joy, "I had the *zechus* to spend time with the Kovno *Rav*, Rabbi Avrohom Kahana Shapiro, the author of *Dvar Avrohom*! I experienced *Shabbos* with Reb Lezer Minsker, which was like spending *Shabbos* with a *malach* (angel)!"

It was the *Dvar Avrohom* who had urged the *Rosh Hayeshivah*, when he was in his early twenties, to write his masterwork *Avodas Levi*. He later joined other contemporary *gedolim* in praise of the *sefer's* contents and clarity of style. The Kovno *Rav*, in turn, had the young Yaakov Yitzchok examine each chapter of his *sefer*, *Dvar Avrohom*, before publication.

During his visits with *Gedolei Torah*, nothing escaped his scrutiny. He would relate with typical humility that as a young boy, he spent some time in the house of Rabbi Chaim Soloveitchik, "with freedom of the house as if it were my own, oblivious of the true greatness of Reb Chaim. But when Rabbi Boruch Ber Lebowitz came to visit his *Rebbe*, he would knock on the front door, trembling and perspiring before summoning enough courage to enter the house."

It was widely known that the *Rosh Hayeshivah* was considered a "favorite son" to these *gedolim*.

The *Rosh Hayeshivah* related that although he had received *semichah* (ordination) from various *gedolim*, he mostly cherished the one he received from Rabbi Meir Atlas, father-in-law of Rabbi Elchonon Wasserman, because Rabbi Meir Atlas had received *semichah* from Rav "Eizele Charif", who in turn was a *musmach* of Rav "Abbale Posvler", who had received *semichah* from the Vilna Gaon himself. The *Rosh Hayeshivah* took particular pride in being a link in this exalted chain of *mesorah*.

During his entire life, he conducted himself as if his *rabbeim* were alive, constantly asking, "What would the *Alter* do in this situation?" After many years in America, one of the leading figures of the Conservative movement, his former roommate in Slobodka, requested an audience with the *Rosh Hayeshivah*, but the *Rosh Hayeshivah* did not respond. Once they met at a hotel and he informed the *Rosh Hayeshivah* of his intention to visit him in his room. The *Rosh Hayeshivah* immediately packed his bags and left. Another time, while in Baltimore, the same leader sent a message requesting a meeting. The *Rosh Hayeshivah* sent back word that he should not come. When asked to explain this uncharacteristic lack of hospitality, the *Rosh Hayeshivah* gave his reasons. Then he added: "Besides, the *Alter* told me not to associate with him."

On the rare occasions that he visited Vilna as a young man, he spent the bulk of his time in the house of Reb Chaim Ozer, who lavished much attention on him. He spoke with special awe of the summer that he spent with Reb Chaim Ozer. The *Rosh Hayeshivah* recalled that after not having seen Reb Chaim Ozer for more than five years, he walked into his house expecting that he would have to reintroduce himself. Much to his surprise, Reb Chaim Ozer rose in his place and exclaimed: "The Dolhinover is here!" Reb Chaim Ozer then stopped in the midst of his activities to devote himself fully to his young visitor. The *Rosh Hayeshivah* would make a point of displaying similar respect to young scholars, many years later. More recently, he would apologize to young *talmidei chachamim*, explaining that due to his old age and physical condition he was unable to rise.

When in America, he maintained contact with Rabbi Chaim Ozer through correspondence, and in later years he turned to Rabbi Yechezkel Abramsky for halachic guidance. A case in point was when the Yeshivah was about to move and was selling its old building. A Baptist group offered the Yeshivah over a half-a-million-dollars more than was offered by the next highest bidder. It struck the *Rosh Hayeshivah* as beyond consideration to sell the Yeshivah building to a different religious group, yet he felt that it might be irresponsible of him to forego such a huge sum for a community purpose without consultation. He posed the question to Rabbi Abramsky who asked for time to consider the issue, before he agreed with the *Rosh Hayeshivah*.

Rabbi Abramsky, in turn, sent messages to Rabbi Ruderman to be *mispallel* for him in his illness.

◆§ Love for Seforim, and their Contents

One of the great pleasures of visiting Reb Chaim Ozer's house was the access Rabbi Ruderman enjoyed to his enormous library. He used to quote Reb Chaim Ozer to the effect that having a lot of *seforim* is a *yeitzer hora* and that one would learn more if he had fewer *seforim*. Nonetheless, the *Rosh Hayeshivah's* thirst for Torah and his indelible memory combined to form an insatiable desire to possess even more *seforim* on his bookshelf and in his mind. Apparently he chose to emulate Reb Chaim Ozer rather than heed his admonition. He constantly amazed his *talmidim* by referring to an opinion recorded in one obscure *sefer* after another, pointing to this or that volume in the marvelous collection of thousands of *seforim* that adorned his shelves.

Although he was celebrated for his total recall of all that he ever studied, he was never content with memory per se: True, as a youngster in Slobodka, the older *bachurim* would make a sport of piercing a needle through an open volume of *Gemara*, challenging him as to which word was pinpointed on a later folio. And he could answer, correctly. Or asking him how many times *Rabbeinu Tam* states a particular opinion in all *Tosafos* throughout *Shas*. And he would respond, most accurately. But this was not sufficient.

On one occasion, he was challenged with a puzzling question by one of the outstanding *Roshei Yeshivah* of Europe. Rabbi Ruderman responded by citing a passage in a *Gemara* that by implication answered the question. The challenger recognized the reference and proceeded to recite the rest of the page verbatim. "Reb ...., a *gaon adir*, remembered the *Gemara*, but not the indirect implications of its words, which by some accident I happened to recall. I then realized," said Rabbi Ruderman, "that knowing the words on the page and their meaning is insufficient. In addition, one must also carry all the implications and ramifications of each bit of knowledge in one's mind."

Whenever he traveled to New York during his youth and middle years, Rabbi Ruderman would make the rounds of the *seforim* stores. When he learned that Rabbi Chaim Brisker's novellae on the *Rambam* had been published, available for three dollars, he exclaimed, "That's all? Such a *sefer* is worth much more!" (The proprietor promptly doubled the price.)

A *talmid* once took the *Rosh Hayeshivah's Oneg Yom Tov* off the shelf to look up a reference. When the *Rosh Hayeshivah* saw the *sefer*, he recalled with pride that he had paid one hundred dollars for it in the early 40's — a major expense in those days ... further demonstrating the extent of his love of Torah and *seforim*. ("A lot of money?" he commented. "How can one live without an *Oneg Yom Tov!*") When he would receive in the mail a newly printed copy of a *sefer* that he already possessed, he would happily pay for the new edition, to encourage the publishers in their undertaking.

◄§ Many Facets, One Gem

Rabbi Ruderman described how the *Alter* treated each *talmid* differently. He would rebuke publicly one of the true *Gedolei Baalei Mussar* whenever he came to Slobodka. If he would dare speak to us in such a manner, said the *Rosh Hayeshivah*, we would have soon left. Yet there were others among his closest *talmidim* whom the *Alter* would treat with great deference, even to the point of asking permission to express mild criticism. The *Rosh Hayeshivah*, in turn, dealt with each *talmid* in the manner that he deemed best suited to that individual. He was particularly careful when saying *Mussar* to the whole Yeshivah to speak positively even while calling them to task for some shortcoming.

Just as the *Alter's* approach to his *talmidim* bespoke an appreciation for every person's individuality, so did Rabbi Ruderman's. By the same token, he was able to freely delegate authority without ever abdicating responsibility. This rare capacity allowed the introduction of other powerful personalities into the *Hanhalah* (administration) of the Yeshivah. Rabbi Dovid Kronglas, as *Mashgiach Ruchani*, left an indelible imprint on the *talmidim* that still echoes within the hearts of his *talmidim* and the walls of the *beis midrash*. In advance of engaging Reb Dovid, the *Rosh Hayeshivah* sent him a copy of *Avodas Levi*, which Reb Dovid returned with an impressive list of comments on the *chiddushim*.

Reb Dovid, who had spent his years as a *talmid* in Mir and Shanghai, favored a stern and demanding approach to the *bachurim*. He could be severe with those whose behavior fell short of the standards he set, and indeed it was perceived by many that the *Rosh Hayeshivah* was not always in agreement with Reb Dovid's methods. Yet, when he was questioned as to why he had granted the *Mashgiach* such latitude, he replied that each person functions best within the context of his own personality and convictions. Reb Dovid was engaged as *Mashgiach* and *Ram* because of his unique personality and talents. If he were coerced to act differently, he would no longer be Reb Dovid. He succeeded in infusing the *talmidim* with great devotion to Torah and *yiras Shomayim* because of the freedom that was given to him to function as *he* understood.

Beyond doubt, Ner Israel succeeded in reaching a broad range of young men because Rabbi Ruderman had the breadth to engage brilliant *talmidei chachomim* and gifted teachers who had their individual approaches to Torah and *chinuch* — such as Reb Dovid or, his own son-in-law and successor as *Rosh Hayeshivah*, Rabbi Yaakov Weinberg: Many independent-minded young men who did not respond to more rigid types of guidance blossomed under the tutelage of Rabbi Weinberg's probing intellect, and today occupy leading positions in *rabbonus* and *chinuch*.

Similarly, the *Rosh Hayeshivah* entrusted a young German refugee with the responsibility of the executive directorship of the Yeshivah — his brother-in-law to-be, Rabbi Naftoli Neuberger, who contributed vastly to the raising of Ner Israel to its present-day status.

✑ Through the Keyhole of an Anecdote

Rabbi Ruderman frequently told anecdotes of *Gedolei Yisroel*, which provided his *talmidim* with insight into his own behavior:

One of the highlights of the national convention of Agudath Israel of America was the address that Rabbi Yaakov Kamenetzky customarily delivered at the close of *seudah shlishis*. The audience would sit in rapt attention until long after *Shabbos* was over. Invariably, Rabbi Ruderman would leave in the middle, to telephone his *Rebbetzin* in Baltimore. He would always apologize to Reb Yaakov afterwards, and they would remind one another of Reb Nochum: The *Chofetz Chaim* had told Rabbi Ruderman how he frequently visited Rabbi Nochum Horodno to observe his conduct so as to learn from him. The *Chofetz Chaim* happened to be with this *tzaddik* one Chanukah evening. It was several hours into the night and Reb Nochum had not yet lit the *menorah*. Finally, very late that night, long after the streets had emptied of people (after the preferred time), Reb Nochum's wife came home, and only then did he light the *menorah*. The *Chofetz Chaim* could not contain himself and asked Reb Nochum for an explanation, since his *Rebbetzin* could have fulfilled her obligation through her husband lighting earlier, in her absence.

Reb Nochum answered, "*Halachah* decrees that if one has

enough money for either *ner Shabbos* or *ner Chanukah*, but not for both, *ner Shabbos* takes precedence, because it promotes *sholom bayis*. My wife is *moser nefesh* — she works extremely hard — to enable me to devote my life to Torah study and *avodas Hashem*. She enjoys being present for the lighting. This *sholom bayis* factor makes it incumbent upon me to wait for her and forego lighting at the proper time."

The *talmidim* witnessed many occasions when the *Rosh Hayeshivah* acted according to the message of this story.

A group of women, wives of *talmidim* of the *Rosh Hayeshivah* who live in *Eretz Yisroel*, asked for an audience with him when he was attending the most recent *Knessiah Gedolah* (International Conference of the World Agudah Movement in 1980). After asking each of the group about her family, the *Rosh Hayeshivah* inquired as to why they had asked for this meeting. They replied that they wished to express their gratitude to him. They felt as a group that their husbands treated them with greater respect and deference because they had observed how their *Rebbe* had treated his *Rebbetzin*.

✒ A Peer Amongst Gedolei Yisroel

The incredible scope of his knowledge gave him the facility to communicate with *Gedolei Yisroel* of diverse backgrounds. Thus he was as comfortable with contemporaries of the Lithuanian circle as he was with those of Polish, Chassidic and Sefardi segments of Jewry.

There were several occasions when the Satmar Rebbe met privately with a group of senior *Roshei Yeshivah* to discuss his differences with them. Rabbi Ruderman returned from those meetings with enormous respect for the greatness and piety of the *Rebbe*. He told us that essentially the *Rebbe* is correct in his basic views; the specific situation of our times, however, calls for a different approach.

He treasured his friendships with his own contemporaries. Rabbi Yitzchok Hutner, whom Rabbi Ruderman had known from their years in Slobodka, once came to Baltimore for a *simchah*, and stayed overnight so he could visit with the *Rosh Hayeshivah* the next morning. After arriving in the Yeshivah at 9:30, he and the *Rosh Hayeshivah* embraced each other, and adjourned to a room where they remained until 5:00 P.M. Rabbi Hutner later commented that he considered it a *Yom Tov* for having had the *oneg ruchni* (spiritual elation) of spending the day with the *Rosh Hayeshivah*.

Rabbi Ruderman recalled that when Rabbi Hutner came to America in the late 30's, the *Rosh Hayeshivah* invited him to join him in Baltimore, which Rabbi Hutner politely refused, explaining that he wished to remain his close friend and couldn't envision that possibility if he were to come to Baltimore. He further elaborated on a grand design he had for a yeshivah of his own where he would be able to implement his own unique ideas of *chinuch* and *avodah*. The *Rosh Hayeshivah* then remarked that that projection accurately describes Mesivta Rabbi Chaim Berlin as it is currently flourishing.

In 1936, Rabbi Aharon Kotler visited America for the first time to raise money for his yeshivah in Kletsk. He stayed with Rabbi Ruderman for over a month (their *Rebbetzins* were first cousins), and the *Rosh Hayeshivah* spared no effort in helping him raise funds in Baltimore. While Rabbi Aharon was there, a dinner was held for the benefit of a Conservative institution, and $25,000 — a vast sum in those days — was raised in one evening. Reb Aharon was very perturbed by this *chillul Hashem*. He must spend weeks going from person to person with all its attendant difficulties and disappointments to raise paltry sums for the yeshivah in Kletsk, while a deviant group raises such enormous sums in one night!

The *Rosh Hayeshivah* consoled Reb Aharon by pointing out that the Torah requires signs to be posted pointing the way to *orei miklat* — the cities of refuge where unintentional murderers found refuge — while no signs show the way to Yerushalayim. A murderer running for his life, explained Rabbi Ruderman, represents a terrible act, a *chillul Hashem*; and if he does not have to ask for directions, he passed quickly and anonymously, minimizing the *chillul Hashem* of his act. A person traveling to Yerushalayim, however, represents a *Kiddush Hashem* that is enlarged every time he asks someone for directions. Similarly, every person approached by Reb Aharon on behalf of Kletsk represents a new opportunity for *Kiddush Hashem*. By contrast, the other institution represents the opposite, and the quicker its moment in the spotlight is over the better.

Whenever Rabbi Ruderman visited *Eretz Yisroel*, he invariably returned with personal impressions of the great men he had met. Following the Fifth Knessiah Gedolah in 1965, for instance, he spoke glowingly of his meeting with the *Chebiner Rav*: his *atzilus* (nobility) had reminded him of Rabbi Chaim Ozer ... During the sixth Knessiah Gedolah, he and the Ponovezer *Rosh Hayeshivah*, Rabbi Eliezer Schach, exchanged visits, each going out of his way to repay the other his earlier visit ... During this same trip to *Eretz Yisroel*, Rabbi Ruderman paid a visit to *Dayan* Weiss of the Eida Hachareidis. The *Dayan* reciprocated with a visit in which the two engaged in an animated, joyful Torah discussion, for over four hours.

∽§ Responsibility for Klal Yisroel

Rabbi Ruderman taught a sense of responsibility for *Klal* by example. To be sure, the Torah commands every Jew to carry responsibility for his fellow. In his case, it seemed that his love for Torah spilled over and permeated his love and sense of *achrayus* (responsibility) for others.

Moreover, he saw Torah as the prime tool for exercising one's *achrayus*. He directed his *talmidim* to incorporate Torah lessons in their *kiruv* (outreach) activities, because Torah possesses powers that are even superior to "rap sessions" in opening up the hearts of Jews estranged from their heritage. In fact, at a lecture at a Torah Umesorah Convention, he devoted more than half of his presentation to a *Dvar Torah*, later explaining that Torah study in itself is a source of *chizuk* and encouragement.

During the war years, the Yeshivah saved as many people as it could by providing a maximum number of affidavits. The *Rosh Hayeshivah* served for many years as the chairman of the *Vaad Roshei Yeshivah* of Torah Umesorah, and was an active member of the Board of Governors of Chinuch Atzmai-Torah Schools for Israel ... Upon the invitation of Rabbi Aharon Kotler, he became involved in Agudath Israel of America, and served as a deeply involved member of the *Moetzes Gedolei HaTorah*, the movement's highest policy-making body. Indeed, he attended the national conventions of Agudath Israel regularly where he honored the gatherings with his addresses. For decades he also maintained regular contact with the organization and was involved in all of its important issues. He urged his *talmidim* in turn to become involved with *Klal* work and assume responsibilities within whatever community they find themselves. Whether in *rabbonus, chinuch,* lay leadership or professional *Klal* work, *talmidim* of the *Rosh Hayeshivah* are well represented and occupy key positions of influence and importance.

His Legacy: Kavod HaTorah

The stature and demeanor of the *Rosh Hayeshivah* was in itself an expression of the magnitude of Torah greatness. When he entered the *beis midrash*, the entire Yeshivah rose, of course, in his honor — and stood in awe for the image of a living *Sefer Torah* that he projected.

Even in the informal setting of Camp Agudah, where he spent the last five summers of his life, he inspired youngsters with his words of encouragement and his interest in their accomplishments — whether memorization of *Mishnayos*, which they had expected him to appreciate, or the excitement of Color War activities: "What does the *Rosh Hayeshivah* think of our frantic behavior?" they wondered. Indeed, he confided in Rabbi Yaakov Kamenetzky during a visit that the latter paid him one summer, "A pity we did not have a camp like this for the children of Litta. So many *neshomos* would have been saved for Torah!" The numerous *Roshei Yeshivah* that came to visit with him every summer, the respect they demonstrated toward him, but most of all, his mere presence, stirred the hearts of all who were privileged to see him . . . his lips moving, reviewing volumes of *Shas*.

❈ ❈ ❈

Our generation was blessed with a living link to the great *Mesorah* of Torah and *Mussar* of the *Alter,* and ultimately of Rabbi Yisroel Salanter. He would often conjecture how Reb Yisroel would have reacted in a given situation. The *Rosh Hayeshivah* told of the time the *shammos* in Dolhinov forgot to bring the *kitul* (white garment that the *chazzan* wore) to *shul* for *Shmini Atzeres*. The people were very upset and publicly rebuked the *shammos.* Drawing on what Reb Yisroel might have said, he pointed out that wearing a *kitul* is merely a *minhag*, a custom, whereas embarrassing a fellow Jew publicly and disturbing *Simchas Yom Tov* are *d'Orayso*, prohibited in the Torah.

During the Yeshivah's early difficult years, the *Rosh Hayeshivah* refused a donation of $1,000, an enormous sum in those days, believing that the donor was giving away all his money and would be left penniless as a result. Weeks later the donor's daughter confirmed the *Rosh Hayeshivah's* suspicions and thanked him for his thoughtfulness.

As Reb Yisroel often pointed out, how important it is to keep one's priorities in perspective!

❧ ❧ ❧

Every *Yom Tov*, the *bachurim* danced the *Rosh Hayeshivah* home from the Yeshivah. When the Yeshivah was still located on Garrison Boulevard, traffic was stopped for the joyous procession, creating a stirring demonstration of *Kavod HaTorah*. One *Shemini Atzeres*, as he was entering his home, he turned and told the *bachurim* at his side, "Look up *Sanhedrin* 7a." The *Gemara* there describes how one can avoid letting *kavod* go to one's head.

When thousands of *talmidim* and admirers, *rabbonim* and laymen, *mechanchim* and *Roshei Yeshivah* converted on the Yeshivah Ner Israel campus to bid farewell to Rabbi Yaakov Yitzchok Ruderman, on Sunday, 14 Tammuz, July 12, the *Kavod HaTorah* was overwhelming. And the *Rosh Hayeshivah* could not object.

Yaakov Yosef Reinman

Remembering Reb Shneur Kotler

*In his
illustrious father's
footsteps . . .
Torah knowledge
coupled with
unusual humility
and compassion*

Rabbi Shneur Kotler
5678-5742 / 1918-1982

That *Horav Hagaon* Reb Shneur Kotler was a man of unusual humility, compassion, and consideration . . . in possession of vast Torah knowledge . . . a person who felt the weight of *Klal Yisroel's* problems on his shoulders — this was universally recognized. Perhaps when the passage of time has dulled some of the pain of his untimely passing and affords us a historical perspective of his achievements, a fuller assessment of his greatness will be possible. The essay published here presents the impressions of the late *Rosh Hayeshivah* of Bais Medrash Govoha as recorded by a *talmid.*

I. The Rosh Hayeshivah

THE ROOTS OF REB SHNEUR'S greatness and his role as a leader in *Klal Yisroel* reach back to the earlier generations of his illustrious family. He was born in 1918, to Reb Aharon Kotler in Slutzk, Poland, where his maternal grandfather, Reb Isser Zalman Meltzer, was *Rosh Hayeshivah* and *Rav.* He spent his early childhood in

Kletzk where Reb Aharon had become *Rosh Hayeshivah* in 1921, and he later studied under Reb Baruch Ber Leibovitz in Kamenitz. In 1940, Reb Shneur joined his grandfather in Yerushalayim. It was there, as head of the Yeshivah Eitz Chaim, that Reb Isser Zalman had introduced the Lithuanian system of analytic Talmud study to the Holy Land. Reb Shneur spent many years learning under his tutelage, becoming a leading disciple, and developed a very close personal relationship with him. People who knew them remarked on the striking similarity between their personalities and characters. While in *Eretz Yisroel*, Reb Shneur also attended the *shiurim* of the Brisker Rav, Rabbi Yitzchok Zev (Reb Velvel) Soloveitchik, the *shmuessen* of Reb Izak Sher and Rabbi Yechezkel Sarna in the Chevron Yeshivah, and had close contact with many other leading Torah figures, including the old Gerer Rebbe, who is said to have remarked about him, "This *bachur* is worth his weight in gold!"

Incidentally, his years in *Eretz Yisroel* gave him a strong sensitivity to the problems and attitudes of the people of the land, which in turn contributed to his success in his later role as a leader of international scope.

In 1947, Reb Shneur came to America to be with his father, Reb Aharon, who had founded Bais Medrash Govoha in Lakewood in 1943.

The awesome greatness of Reb Aharon is well known to all. He was a fiery presence in the mid-20th century, and left an indelible mark on the international Jewish community that may well affect the lives of our people for generations to come. He was a *gadol hador* in *tzidkus* as well as in Torah (as the Satmar Rav said at his funeral).

When Reb Aharon came to America, he found a Jewish society drifting away from the mainstream that had marked Jewish life in Europe. Devotion to Torah and *mitzvos*, the hallmark of Jewish continuity throughout history, was waning. The concept of universal study of Torah as the fundamental activity of Jewish people was more a memory than a thriving reality.

Undaunted, Reb Aharon set out to build a yeshivah in the original European form. He had escaped the destruction of European Jewry and brought with him the seeds of Torah study at the highest level — the ambition to strive for greatness in Torah, the concept of *Kavod HaTorah* (the glory of Torah), the all-encompassing nature of Torah — and replanted them in America. He did not lower his standards to adapt to the American *bachur*: He demanded that the American *bachur* measure up to his high standards. His *shiurim* were the same as he had said for his *talmidim* in Kletzk. And they responded. To the amazement of skeptics, he produced *talmidei chachomim* of excellence who were later to form the vanguard of a rejuvenating force for American Jewish society.

Reb Aharon battled for the acceptance of the idea of Kollel. He felt that the focus of the life of every Jew should be the study of Torah; earning a living was but a necessity. Only by learning in Kollel could a young man develop this perspective. When necessity would force him out of the yeshivah into the world at large, he would be well armed.

◆§ Passing the Torch

When Reb Aharon passed away in 1962, the heavy mantle of leadership fell on the shoulders of his only son, Reb Shneur, who was but forty-four at the time.

Only a small group of people were present when — during the week of *shivah* — the lay leadership of Bais Medrash Govoha entered the room where the late *Rosh Yeshivah's* family was sitting, and proclaimed, "*Yechi Hamelech!* (Long live the King!) *Mazel Tov!*"

Reb Shneur broke into incontrollable sobbing — surely for the freshly felt grief that he was experiencing; in addition, no doubt, for the terrible sense of inadequacy anyone might feel in being expected to fill the awesome gap left by so great a spiritual giant as Reb Aharon — anyone, but especially a person so self effacing as Reb Shneur.

When Reb Shneur took over the yeshivah, he found a world that was ripe for Torah expansion. The Torah World needed someone willing and able to devote tremendous energy and talent to accomplish that goal, someone with broad vision and relentless drive. Above all, it needed a leader who would himself be a symbol of the elevating power of the Torah, a man to whom people could relate on a personal level. With time, Reb Shneur proved himself eminently suited to the task.

In his convictions and aspirations, Reb Shneur was the same as his great father. He, too, was steeped in the long chain of *mesorah* and struggled to preserve it in its original form. He, too, believed that all people possessed a measure of greatness, and he too urged them to live up to it. And in matters of principle, he was like Reb Aharon — outspoken and unyielding. But in style and personality they were very different. Reb Aharon was a challenger; Reb Shneur, a conciliator. Reb Aharon was fire; Reb Shneur was velvet.

⊷§ Eclipsed Greatness

The genius of Talmudic analysis, Rabbi Chaim Soloveitchik of Brisk, once commented that the *Chofetz Chaim's* greatness as a *tzaddik* was so dazzling that it blinded people to his greatness as a *talmid chacham*. The same could be said of Reb Shneur as a man whose seemingly limitless *Ahavas Yisroel* inspired so great an outpouring of love from others that at times it seemed to overshadow his awesome standing as a *talmid chacham*. Those who spoke to him, however, could not but be overwhelmed by the encyclopedic scope of his knowledge. Indeed, there was practically no *sugya* (topic) in *Shas* with which he was not intimately familiar, on which he could not quote *Rishonim* and *Acharonim* from memory on the spot. His *shiurim* were wide ranging and finely conceptual. His command of *Tanach*, Aggada, Midrash, and *maamorei Chazal* was breathtaking: quoting obscure Midrashim verbatim, citing the precise *pasuk* or *Chazal* for every occasion, even serving as a resource for his father, Reb Aharon, when he was searching for the elusive passage or quote. While he delivered his *shmuessen* in the yeshivah, one could almost see his mind at work as he developed his basic theme, supporting it with new proofs and applications as he spoke. He drew on his vast knowledge and, with his originality, translated it into a panoramic vision of recognition of the Creator's design for the world and the role of the individual in it.

⊷§ Growth of Bais Medrash Govoha

At the time he became the *Rosh Hayeshivah*, Bais Medrash Govoha was relatively small by today's standards. There were barely one hundred *bachurim* in the yeshivah, and some thirty-five young men in the Kollel. Under his direction, the yeshivah went through a period of spectacular expansion. Approximately twenty years later, when he passed away, the yeshivah had close to one thousand *talmidim* — about half of them in the Kollel, and virtually all of them mature *bnei Torah* over the age of twenty.

Under Reb Shneur, Bais Medrash Govoha developed into more than just a yeshivah. It became a center of learning such as the world perhaps has not known since the days of the yeshivah in Pumbadissa in Bavel; true to its name, it became an "exalted house of study." Besides the main *Mesechta* that the yeshivah studies, the yeshivah encompassed many *chaburos* (study groups) concentrating on other areas across the entire spectrum of *Shas* (the entire Talmud) and *Shulchan Aruch* (Codes) — some of these *chaburos* containing as many as one hundred members, yeshivos within the yeshivah . . . each of these *chaburos* usually having at least several exceptional *talmidei chachamim* in its ranks. Lakewood became a world of opportunity for the industrious *talmid* . . . a place where he could find literally hundreds of *talmidei chachamim, baalei havanah* (men of depth), and *baalei halachah* (applied Torah law), with whom he could discuss any subject, and who might possibly even take him as a *chavrusa* (study partner) . . . where he could move from yeshivah to yeshivah, within the same walls, to develop himself in every *seder* of *Shas* and in *halachah lema'aseh* . . . where he could find *bnei Torah* who came together from every continent . . . where he could feel the very heartbeat of the Torah as it pumps vitality to the centers of the world . . .

Reb Shneur accomplished this incredible feat by running the yeshivah with an extremely delicate touch in dealing with others, using his gifts of mind and heart.

Reb Shneur treated every *talmid* as an adult and expected him to perform as such. Reb Shneur spoke to each young *bachur* with the same *derech eretz* and deference that he would show to a venerable *gadol*. He never called anyone by his first name without prefixing it with "*Reb.*" He never made any personal demands on a *talmid*, for he was there for the sole purpose of giving to the *talmid*.

Entering the *bais midrash* with 400 people present to deliver a *shiur* or *shmuess*, Reb Shneur would quickly scan the entire assemblage, and then begin. Later, he would buttonhole a *talmid* to discuss a point in the *shiur*, or call over another *talmid* who he felt should have been present but wasn't. In that momentary glance upon entry, he could "roll-call" the entire assemblage and file away the data for subsequent use. He faced a vast crowd and saw individuals.

◄§ The Burden

The yeshivah's growth brought with it a tremendous increase in Reb Shneur's burden. Besides saying *shiurim*, speaking in learning with an increasing number of *talmidim*, and dealing with them on a one-to-one basis, the financial load became staggering. Reb Shneur worked tirelessly with the administration and lay leadership to raise money for the ever-growing operating budget of the ever-expanding yeshivah, while completing the building of a beautiful *bais midrash*, dormitories, and dining-room building.

During these past ten years of Reb Shneur's life, Lakewood experienced a new phenomenon: *Talmidim* leaving the yeshivah for business or the professions had developed so strong a bond with the yeshivah that they purchased homes and settled near the yeshivah, forming a satellite community in Lakewood of over one hundred families. Because of these families and the older members of the Kollel, the Lakewood Cheder — a boys' school and a girls' school — emerged, with a combined enrollment of over seven hundred children. Reb Shneur devoted a great deal of attention to guiding this community, and to overseeing the *Cheder*, its curriculum, its policies, and its internal problems, spending many a sleepless night struggling with its problems.

II. Man of Klal Yisroel

Rabbi Yechezkiel Abramsky, known for his *Chazon Yechezkiel* commentary on *Tosefta*, had been a *Rav* in Russia, and later in London, and was described by many as the prototype *Rav*, whose imposing presence was such that he inspired awe in all who came in contact with him.

In his later years, when living in the Bayit Vegan section of Yerushalayim — and, incidentally, no less imposing — he told a visitor, "Don't compare me to Reb Aharon Kotler. I'm busy with my writings on *Tosefta*, my *shiurim*, and an occasional meeting for Chinuch Atzmai and the like — but that's it. Reb Aharon carries all of *Klal Yisroel* on his shoulders."

At Reb Shneur's *leviah*, Rabbi Yaakov Kaminetzky cited Elisha's lament for his mentor, Eliyahu Hanavi: "My father, my father, chariot of Israel!"

"How awkward for me to use these words about Reb Shneur," said Reb Yaakov, "when I was at the *Bar Mitzvah* of his father, Reb Aharon, who was my junior in years. Yet the expression is most appropriate. Reb Shneur was father and mother not only to the Yeshivah in Lakewood, he also carried on his shoulders the burdens of *Klal Yisroel*! ... He left worthy successors to fill his role in Bais Medrash Govoha, but who can replace him in regard to *Klal Yisroel*?'

Indeed, Reb Shneur did follow in the footsteps of his father with time and assumed a leading role in major Torah-disseminating organizations all over the world. Reb Aharon did not concentrate exclusively on his own yeshivah, but felt personally responsible for all of *Klal Yisroel* and the proliferation of Torah all over the world. He was a life-force in Vaad Hatzalah, a world leader of Agudath Israel, at the helm of Torah Umesorah, a founder of Chinuch Atzmai, and he was deeply involved in many other projects and organizations.

Like his father before him, Reb Shneur was driven by a boundless sense of responsibility for the furtherance of Torah everywhere. Using the yeshivah as a base, he spread Torah in countless communities: He was instrumental in establishing yeshivos and *kollelim* in cities across the continent, and beyond — even as far away as Melbourne, Australia — with Bais Medrash Govoha providing *Roshei Yeshivah*, *magiddei shiur*, and even a nucleus of *talmidim* for struggling new institutions. He helped set up the organizations, develop community backing, and inspire support by personally meeting with key people — all over the world.

If any yeshivah anywhere, from Argentina to Israel, was in trouble or needed help, he was ready to contribute with the same dedication and energy that he devoted to the welfare of his own yeshivah, thinking nothing of flying across the country for a day or two to iron out difficulties or to raise funds.

Reb Shneur's *Klal* activity carried a unique imprint all his own. Everything he did seemed to reverberate with a profound love — a special love for every individual Jew, which combined to form an intense love for all of *Klal Yisroel* — a love that expressed itself in terms of a deep-felt feeling of *achrayus* (responsibility). Indeed, he always kept his sights raised beyond his own yeshivah. In one of his last letters, he writes that whenever he spoke at a fund-raising affair for the yeshivah he never mentioned Bais Medrash Govoha; he spoke only of the greatness and importance of Torah as a concept.

Like his grandfather and his father before him, Reb Shneur was a leading figure in the international Agudath Israel movement; he served on both the presidium of Agudath Israel of America and, later, on the *Moetzes Gedolei HaTorah* (Council of Torah Sages) in America — involved in both the practical, day-to-day concerns of the movement as well as in its broader policy-making board. In addition, he was active in the leadership of Torah Umesorah and Chinuch Atzmai.

Reb Shneur saw Agudath Israel as the primary vehicle for carrying out his responsibilities for *Klal Yisroel* as a whole:

— In 1971, when reports reached America that Soviet Jews were being permitted to emigrate to *Eretz Yisroel*, Reb Shneur called the national offices of Agudath Israel of America, urging that the topic of helping them be put on the agenda of the annual convention. A short time later, Reb Shneur called again: "A meeting should also be convened in New York." As usual, Reb Shneur begged, urged and demanded action — stressing the historical dimensions of what was happening — and volunteered his own time and effort . . .

He did the same again when Soviet Jews began to come to these shores, carrying a major part of the burden of the Be'er Hagolah Institute for Russian children.

— When Iranian students began to come to America in large numbers, to escape the hazards of Khomeini's government, a group of *Roshei Yeshivah* and community leaders met at the Agudath Israel national offices to plan to meet their needs. Recalls one of the participants: "We spent hours trying to determine how each individual school or community could deal with respective aspects of the problem. Then Reb Shneur spoke up, painting in broad brush strokes the need for large-scale action: 'We must plan on a community-wide basis, engage rabbis and teachers familiar with the halachic traditions and *minhagim* of this group . . .'

"It all sounded so abstract and quixotic, but as we look around and see what has happened since, Reb Shneur's words were truly visionary."

Rosh Hashanah, 5743: The incredibly crowded study hall of Bais Medrash Govoha is silent. Everyone is on his feet waiting for the *tekios* to begin . . . hearing the silence, a silence deepened by the absence of Reb Shneur's annual pre-*tekios* address — truly a fever-pitched plea to be concerned over the needs of *Klal Yisroel* and to beseech G-d to answer these needs: Torah education in Eretz Yisroel . . . military security of the beleaguered country . . . Soviet Jewry . . . Iranian Jewry . . . alienated Jewish youth joining cults . . . South American Jewry . . . the well-being of the diminishing number of Torah scholars . . . These problems were a tangible presence in the *Bais Hamidrash*, which fairly throbbed with the *Rosh Yeshivah's* urgent concern. His words reverberated as words emanated from a man with a burning mission in life who felt compelled to enlist others in his undertakings. That's how it had been for some fifteen Rosh Hashanos. But this year, his voice is stilled and silence fills the crowded *Bais Hamidrash*.

III. Gifts of the Heart

Friday night in the yeshivah: Hundreds of *talmidim* and visitors line up to wish the *Rosh Yeshivah* a "Good *Shabbos*." As they file quickly by, Reb Shneur responds with a nod to each "Good *Shabbos*" greeting, seeming to make a mental note of each greeter as he passes, projecting a warm smile, a *mazel tov* to a new father, quickly inquiring after everyone's welfare. Suddenly he pulls someone out of the line for a lengthy exchange and carries on a conversation with him, while continuing to acknowledge each greeting . . . dealing with hundreds, as a mass and as distinct individuals.

Reb Shneur had an uncanny knack for pinpointing a person's interests, needs, level of scholarship, and attention span. In a friendly conversation, he would zero in on the best subject for a discussion and maintain the dialogue — for quite a while, at times, but never for too long. A halachic problem, a passage in *Navi*, historical insights, communal problems in a Midwest community, Israeli politics, progress in a *shidduch* — he knew the topic and often offered valuable insights, workable remedies and solutions, and words of comfort and encouragement. Of course, this ability reflected a keen intelligence; but more, it reflected gifts of the heart, a feeling of genuine love that the other person could feel. Reb Shneur seemed to identify with every Jew he met, putting himself in their place.

After a yeshivah function in a New York City hotel, Reb Shneur stepped out to a waiting car. Opening the front door to enter he noticed five young people crowded on the back seat to make room for him in the front. He stepped back and closed the door, refusing to enter: "There's no room."

"Don't worry," he was assured, "they are managing very well."

But the *Rosh Hayeshivah* was adamant. "They are not lap-children," he insisted, "and we can't expect them to ride back to Lakewood in such discomfort. I'll get another ride."

At Reb Shneur's urgent request, a real-estate broker met with him — to arrange a second mortgage on his home. It seems that

Reb Shneur became aware of two parties undergoing extreme difficulties with their business, and he wanted to lend them $30,000 to tide them over their crisis.

Even as a child of five, he would often forego supper, claiming that he wasn't hungry, if he felt that it would involve too much bother for his mother.

◆§ Only the Other Person's Burden

Several *talmidim* were accompanying Reb Shneur on a stroll in the warm spring sunshine. He had just returned from the hospital after undergoing surgery, and they were full of hope that he would recover. He grimaced in obvious pain with every step, but he spoke not a word about himself. He only inquired after their affairs.

Passing the neighborhood *shul*, they came upon an elderly man sitting on a bench, who had also just come out of the hospital. Reb Shneur sat next to him and — gently refusing to discuss his own condition — encouraged the old man to speak about himself. The man sensed Reb Shneur's genuine concern and he opened up. As he spoke of his pains, his fears and anxieties, Reb Shneur hung on his every word, both men apparently deeply satisfied with the discussion.

On the way back, Reb Shneur remarked to one of the *talmidim*, "*Baruch Hashem* I was able to finish the letter you asked of me a few weeks ago. In my present condition, I could never write it properly." This was the only mention he made of his extreme discomfort.

His dedication and sheer hard work were of unbelievable intensity. On a typical day he would arise early to learn before *Shacharis*. After *Shacharis* he would schedule personal meetings with *talmidim* which were often interrupted by a barrage of telephone calls from all over the world. The weekly *shiur* and periodic *shmuessen* took time and effort, but he was forced to spend much of his time away from Lakewood. His involvement in the yeshivah's affairs had him travel to New York almost daily for conferences, parlor meetings, and other fundraising functions, as did his other *Klal* obligations. Flying to other cities was almost a weekly necessity. In addition to these activities, however, he participated in countless *simchos* of *talmidim* and friends; he simply could not bring himself to refuse. He felt impelled to share their joy. Regardless of when he returned home — even in the middle of the night — he would sit down and learn until three o'clock in the morning — unbelievably, with interruptions for *Klal* and yeshivah affairs, even at that hour.

To most of us, such a schedule is beyond conception: such energy, such stamina seem superhuman. The difficulties of such a routine are much more than physical; the mental and emotional strain are even more taxing. An ordinary person would not have managed to maintain such a schedule, but Reb Shneur was no ordinary person. He was completely given over to *Klal Yisroel*; he had no personal life nor family life in the conventional sense. He elevated his family and imbued them with the same sense of mission that possessed him. His *Rebbetzin* stood by his side with valor and dedication to match his own. He left behind him a home of *kedushah*, unaffected by material values.

At the wedding of a *talmid* where Reb Shneur was the *mesader kiddushin* (officiated), the *chassan's* family had a custom of paying the *mesader kiddushin* under the *chupah*, and then and there, the *chassan's* mother handed Reb Shneur a check for $100. When the canceled check was later returned, endorsed by the yeshivah, she called Reb Shneur and told him, "The check was not for the yeshivah. It was for you personally."

Reb Shneur replied, "Ach! If only I had known, I would have given it to Chinuch Atzmai. It's in such desperate need now!"

◄§ Man of Peace

Reb Shneur's ability to identify closely with others undoubtedly contributed to making him a "man of peace." It is to his credit that the yeshivah and the community never experienced the type of dissension and squabbling that have affected other rapidly growing yeshivos and communities. When issues inevitably arose that provoked polarization, inflamed tempers, and seemed to call for decisive action, Reb Shneur did not assert his authority, even when it was indisputably his. Rather, his first concern was, always, to defuse the situation and restore calm, then to discuss the problem in a rational atmosphere and to find a solution that provided both justice and harmony.

Many times this process would frustrate the combatants because Reb Shneur seemed to be delaying a decision needlessly.

Often, this tactic was out of an awareness that he might cause someone pain that was avoidable. His motives were only guessed at later, at best.

At the end of Yom Kippur, Reb Shneur made a practice of *davening Maariv* before the *amud*. Somehow it seemed appropriate to hear his sweet, warm voice raised in song to the *Borei Olam* at the start of the new slate. It made the *kedushah* of Ne'ilah linger in the air even after the *Aron Hakodesh* had been closed. Reb Shneur, however, had reasons of his own: One year, he had told the *shaliach tzibbur* not to wait for him to finish *Maariv Shemoneh Esrei* because everyone was hungry and weak from the fast. The *shaliach tzibbur*, however, did wait. Reb Shneur then decided to be the *shaliach tzibbur* himself for *Maariv*, for whenever he *davened* before the *amud* he automatically finished more quickly.

• Typical of his distaste for dissension, at the last Knessiah Gedolah of Agudath Israel in Yerushalayim, he spoke of the importance of avoiding *lashon hora* (slander), and the destructive forces it unleashes. He proposed that Jewish people all over the world learn a portion of the *Sefer Chofetz Chaim* every single day — a *daf hayomi* of sorts of self-improvement.

• In the same vein, Reb Shneur used public platforms to plead for harmony among Jews. At the last National Convention of Agudath Israel of America that he attended, in November, 1981, he marked the occasion of his father's nineteenth *Yahrzeit* to call the people to a sense of responsibility for *Klal*, and to work together with harmony.

• He sounded a similar note with unusual poignancy at his last public appearance — at the Agudath Israel Annual Dinner in May, 1982 — where, in great pain from his terminal illness, he cited a Midrash that calls for Jewry to emulate *malachim* by being united in voice and mind in declaring Heavenly authority.

• Again, at the last meeting of the *Moetzes Gedolei HaTorah*, which he attended weeks before his passing, he encouraged measures for preserving harmony within the organization at large.

The Steel Frame

Three years before his own passing, Reb Shneur and his family were struck a crushing blow: his twenty-six-year-old son, Meir, who had recently been married and had a small child, died an agonizing death. Reb Meir was a *ben Torah* to his very last fiber, a source of joy to all who knew him. He loved everyone and was beloved by everyone. Reb Shneur was as close to him as a father can be to his son. When he died, Reb Shneur was devastated. And it was in his overwhelming grief that he showed the steel that buttressed his soft exterior.

In the chapel, before the *leviah*, he turned to one of his *talmidim* who was working with Iranian youth that had fled Khomeini's Islamic revolution. He said, "Don't think that during the *shivah* you won't be able to consult with me and enlist my help. I want you to continue coming to me with every problem as if nothing had happened."

During the *shivah*, every *Rosh Yeshivah* that came to be *menacheim avel* left persuaded to take some of these young men into his yeshivah. Personal grief did not interfere even slightly with the faithful execution of his responsibilities.

When he himself fell ill during his last winter, this steel showed through once again. He drew on his last ounce of strength to contribute to *Klal Yisroel*. He was literally carried to the yeshivah to deliver *shiurim* and *shmuessen*. He spoke to the yeshivah from his hospital bed by radio hookup and, his voice breaking, said that he felt as if everyone in the yeshivah was his *ben yachid* (cherished only child).

The last meeting of the *Moetzes Gedolei HaTorah* during Reb Shneur's lifetime was originally scheduled to be held in his home, but he refused the honor. He would not hear of making the senior members travel to Lakewood. Instead, perilously ill, he traveled to New York. He had to rest every half hour or so, but he participated constructively and creatively until the conclusion of the meeting.

When the doctor told him that he had but a few months to live, he told the *Rebbetzin* on the way out, "I have so much locked inside my head, *seforim* to be written, things to accomplish." He remarked that it was not the pain of his illness that concerned him but how his condition would affect his ability to help others. Among the various responsibilities he mentioned, he divulged that he had been secretly supporting eleven poor families. While others will step in to support the yeshivah in his absence, who would take care of these families?

When waiting to enter surgery, he spent two hours making a *cheshbon hanefesh* (personal accounting). He said to the *Rebbetzin*, "There is a person who insulted *bnei Torah* and I think I may have answered him a little too harshly. Please call him up and ask for his forgiveness."

During his last days, he was lying in the hospital and groaning. Asked if he was in pain, he replied that he was thinking of the casualties in Lebanon.

◂§ The Source of His Strength

Reb Shneur's rare inner strength brings to mind one of his own Torah commentaries:

The *pasuk* tells us that *Hashem* "appeared" to Avraham in Elonei Mamrei. The *Ohr Hachayim Hakadosh* asks why this prophecy is expressed as "appeared," while all other prophecies to Avrohom — to leave the land of his fathers, to take his son Isaac to the *Akeidah*, and so on — are expressed as *Hashem said to Avraham*.

Reb Shneur referred to a *pasuk* in *Iyov* (42:5): After Iyov's friends had come to argue with him and reconcile him to his afflicted state, the *pasuk* tells us that G-d spoke directly to Iyov from a storm-wind. And Iyov answered, *"L'shaima ozen shmaticha v'atah eini ra'asicha* . . . I had heard of You by ear, but now my eyes have seen You. Therefore, I am remorseful and I have become consoled for the dust and ashes." Yet G-d's words to Iyov were essentially the same as what his friends previously had told him, which he had rejected.

Reb Shneur explained that when a person's understanding is based on logic, he can never be totally satisfied; there is always a lingering doubt. But when he sees the same thing in actuality, empirically, all doubts are dispelled. No unanswered question can affect his perception of what he has seen as the truth. This is implicit in Iyov's confession: As long as I knew all of this only by ear, I was not fully satisfied. But now that my eyes have seen the *Shechinah*, all questions become meaningless, and I have become reconciled to my condition.

When *Hashem* commanded Avraham to leave the land of his fathers, or to take his only son, Yitzchak, and sacrifice him at the *Akeidah*, this was a *nisayon* — a test. Had G-d appeared to Avraham to issue these commands, the imperative to listen would have been so obvious that there would have been no *nisayon*. Therefore, He only spoke to him.

G-d's *bikur cholim* visit to Avraham, however, was not meant to be a *nisayon*. This type of divine encounter, comforting him in his sickness, could be conveyed through "appearance," without compromising its purpose.

To a certain extent, Reb Shneur had aspects of this rare quality of *"eini ra'asicha* — my eyes have seen You." He lived on a different plane. His real world — the world that he occupied — was the world of *ruchnius*, spirituality, and it transcended the barriers of time; the past, the present, and the future were all immediate realities: The past was alive in his mind. When he spoke of what his father or other *gedolim* said or did, it was more than just a memory. They were in the room with him, vibrant and gloriously alive . . . He had a total awareness of the present, and what had to be accomplished . . . And he had a vision of the future, of a reinstated *Malchus Shamayim* — the Heavenly Kingdom on earth. It was a goal that sustained him and drove him throughout his life. His *shmuessen* rang with vision.

When he *davened,* it was obvious that he saw himself standing before G-d, which inspired a keen awareness of his life goal. And so he had the strength to rise above his afflictions and continue with his holy work.

◆§ Symphony of Life

On 3 Tammuz, 5742, Reb Shneur went up to the *yeshivah shel ma'alah.* Although the gravity of his condition was known, the world was stunned. All over the world people had been saying *Tehillim* and fasted for his recovery. Somehow it was unthinkable that he should not recover. *If only one percent of the people in his condition recovered, who else was more worthy of being included in that one percent? If those that recovered did so only through a miracle, who was more worthy of the miracle?* But it was not to be.

Tens of thousands of people gathered, unconsolable, at his *leviah,* here and in *Eretz Yisroel.* The outpouring of genuine grief from every diverse segment of the international Jewish community was a tribute to how universally respected and loved he had been.

Reb Shneur was a poet; everything he wrote or spoke had a lyric, poignant quality. He loved music and song, but the most beautiful poem and the most magnificent music he composed was his own life. Every day of his life was an elegant verse, every deed an exquisite turn of phrase. Every smile was a lilting melody, every word an enchanting note. His accomplishments have left us a better world. His image will linger in our minds, as an inspiration and a challenge.

✒️ Chassidic Leaders

The inspiring greatness of men who
— by stirring example —
taught their followers to love G-d,
His Torah, and His children
with boundless devotion.

The Last Days of a Tzaddik

*His
parting words
to his
talmidim . . .
"Nor mit
simchah —
only
with joy!"*

Rabbi Meir Shapiro
5647-5694 / 1887-1934

Athough Rabbi Meir Shapiro *was only in his thirties at the time he presented the idea of Daf Yomi to the Knessiah Gedolah in Vienna, it became widely accepted, and he in turn became an object of affection and admiration.*

Years later when Rabbi Meir Shapiro visited the revered Chofetz Chaim, the latter told him: "I am especially fond of you — and why? — because of the Daf Yomi. You have to your credit a tremendous achievement, and in Heaven they are pleased with your efforts. You should know that there — in the 'World of Truth' — man is not honored for his good deeds nearly as much as he is honored for his study of Torah. In the World to Come, each Jew is honored for the measure of Torah he has studied. They call out: 'WELCOME TO THE MAN WHO STUDIED MESECHES BERACHOS! WELCOME TO THE MAN WHO STUDIED MESECHES SHABBOS!' Each one sits on a seat engraved with the name of the Mesechta which he learned.

"Until now, many of the seats were empty; people studied only certain Mesechtos, neglecting others. But now, thanks to you, all the seats are being filled, and what a joy there is in Heaven!"

The young, inspiring rabbi who authored this plan became celebrated for his achievements in many other endeavors — he was president of the Agudath Israel of Poland, and Agudath Israel's delegate to the Siem (the Polish parliament), became Rav of the great Jewish community of Lublin, and founded the pace-setting yeshivah in that community, Chachmei Lublin. Admired for his leadership qualities, his ready wit, and his Torah scholarship, Reb Meir Shapiro became a legendary figure in Poland, beloved by Jews in all walks of life — at his passing, even the cynical Socialist and Yiddishist sectors mourned his death with special editions of the newspapers in his honor. It was for his personal warmth, however, that he was most beloved. The following reminiscences, based on material recorded in "Meir B' Ahavah," by RABBI BENJAMIN MINTZ, translated by RABBI CHAIM URI LIPSCHITZ, capture that special warmth in his last days, and convey how it formed a deep bond that tied talmid to rebbe, disciple to mentor.

⋖§ Monday, Tuesday and Wednesday

On Monday, the fourth of Cheshvan, 5694 (1933), Rabbi Meir Shapiro entered the immense library of his yeshivah, Chachmei Lublin, and remarked to someone standing near him that he felt very cold one minute and extremely hot the next. He entered his private room and lay on the bed, remaining there the entire day.

The next day, Tuesday, he did not deliver his regular *shiur* (lecture), but rested instead. Later in the day, he asked for two of his disciples, whom he requested to sing *"Ye'ancha Hashem B' Yom Tzarah* (G-d will answer you on your day of crisis)." He hummed along with them, as if he were saying, "I am with you, I am with you, I too am beseeching the Almighty in my behalf."

The yeshivah continued in its daily routine, no one aware that its leader was gravely ill. He seemed calm but as the evening approached, his pain became noticeable, and a doctor was summoned. He diagnosed the ailment as an inflamed throat, but did not seem overly concerned.

On Wednesday morning it was very difficult for him to utter a word. Yet he moved his lips continuously, repeating prayers and some Talmud, his agonizing pain clearly visible on his face.

After midnight, he called for the students who had been

studying in the *beis hamidrash*. When they assembled around his bed, he asked them to sing a *piyut* (liturgical composition) that he would lead every Yom Kippur after midnight. As they sang, he listened attentively, humming along.

Suddenly, his face seemed like a burning fire, his eyes like two bright stars. With all of his strength he raised his hands high and shook his head, as if he had had a confrontation with some hidden entity, which sees but cannot be seen. He did not sleep the entire night and it was apparent that his pain had intensified further, but he did not register any complaint, accepting his agony with love.

⋽ Thursday, The Heavens Were Clouded

Thursday arrived and the heavens were clouded. Strong winds shook the yeshivah walls, as if the world were returning to chaos. The doctor examined him again but still failed to detect any emergency.

Reb Meir whispered in a very low voice, audible only to those able to crowd close to him: "Our sages say that pain removes sin from a man. They also say that no one is appointed to lead a community until his sins are forgiven. In my case, both factors are present, the pain and the appointment to leadership." (Several days before, he had been chosen to become *rosh beis din* of Lodz, the greatest Jewish metropolis in Poland.) He then turned his glowing face aside, saying," I do not have time to be ill."

In spite of his mounting pain, he greeted each visiting disciple with a joyful expression. One of his students put his *tallis* and *tefillin* on for him, and he nearly fainted while the student was completing his task. Speaking had become almost impossible for him, yet he *davened* for a full two hours.

He was forced to write a note for every request, which terribly distressed those with him. They begged his permission to visit the old cemetery in Lublin to beseech the *tzaddikim* buried there to supplicate to the Almighty for him. He shook his head and lifted his hand to say there was no need, but faced with their unrelenting pleas, he finally yielded and permitted a *minyan* to go. He wrote a note asking his students to pray that all who were sick might be healed, without singling himself out. His students related that at that moment, his eyes lit up and his face brightened, his fatherly expression moving them deeply.

Thursday night several doctors examined him and still did not find him to be in great danger. The students were dumbfounded.

Why was G-d limiting the doctors' perception of what seemed so obvious to them?

◆§ Included in Their Maariv Prayers

Reb Meir wrote a note requesting ten of his disciples to enter to *daven Maariv* and include him in their prayers. Not only ten, but everyone who was able to entered and *davened*. Tears rolled down the cheeks of each and every person assembled. They probably never in their life prayed with such feeling and devotion, seeing their *rebbe* lying there with eyes closed and face aglow. Even the youngest person present could testify that the *Shechinah* was resting on their mentor. They concluded *Maariv* and Reb Meir opened his eyes, gazing at each and everyone in the room with love and devotion. It was not easy to look into his eyes, burning as they were like two fiery coals.

After midnight he gestured to his students that he wished to be cleansed. They were reluctant at first, but he frowned as if urging them to hurry before it was too late. They changed him completely, washed and wiped his hands well, and placed his head on his cushion. A sign of contentment was then seen on his face.

He signaled to his students to move him from his room to the adjacent reception room. As they carefully carried him on his bed into the room they noticed that its two doors were inscribed, one with: "Donated by the Bikur Cholim of Chicago," the other: "Donated by the Benevolent Society of St. Louis." These now took on special meaning during these last minutes of his life.

◆§ "Now Will Be the Real Joy"

No sooner did they switch his room than his *Rebbetzin* entered, crying audibly. He motioned her to come closer. He took a pencil and with shaking hands wrote on a sheet of paper, "Why are you crying? Now will be the real joy."

He gestured that his *talmidim* dress him in a new white shirt, which they did with the utmost awe. He adjusted his *peyos* (side curls) and passed his hands over his face. Signaling again for a pencil, he grasped it with trembling hands and in unconnected letters wrote the last words he recorded before his soul departed: "All of you drink 'l' chaim'."

As a result, a most moving episode took place: Whiskey and cake were brought in and portions were handed out to each person in the room. Each made the necessary blessings, partook of the refreshments, and proceeded in line to offer his hand to the *tzaddik* and wish him *"l' chaim."* Reb Meir took each hand, held it for a few moments while he looked into the person's face, who without exception was so moved that his entire body trembled.

An unlearned fellow who earned his living by supplying the students with cakes and cookies stood in the corner, not daring to enter the inner circle of *bnei Torah* and close associates. But Reb Meir moved his head in his direction and winked at him to come closer. Reb Meir took hold of his hand and held it for five minutes. Who knows what this sage was thinking during the last minutes of his life!

After everyone completed his turn, offering his hand in *"l' chaim,"* Reb Meir struggled to say something. With his last ounce of strength he moved his lips to form the words, *"Becho bit'chu avoseinu* (Our fathers trusted in You).*"* They understood that he wanted them to sing the song he had composed to accompany these words.

◄§ A Dance as Never Before

They began to dance as they never had before nor ever would again. With tears rolling down each and everyone's cheeks, they clapped their hands in rhythm, formed a circle and began to dance. The higher they lifted their feet, the more the tears ran. They did their best to make sure that their *rebbe* did not notice their crying, and whenever they were unable to hide their tears, they slipped into the next room, where hundreds were saying *Tehillim* with an outpouring of emotion that must have penetrated the very heavens, yet trying to keep the sounds of the *Tehillim* from reaching their *rebbe's* ears.

With every passing minute their *rebbe's* condition worsened, and they realized that these were the last minutes of his sacred life.

The entire yeshivah was crowded into these two rooms — in one room, dancing feverishly, in the next room sobbing with heart-rending cries and prayers. Their *rebbe* followed the song, swaying his hand with the rhythm while his face seemed to burn. They then began to dance in circles around his bed. He detected their sobs and motioned to some students to come closer. He was then able to whisper his last words, *"Nor mit simchah* — only with joy!*"*

They tried to hide their feelings, but it was impossible. When one student called out in an emotional voice, "Who will offer part of his life to our *rebbe?"*, everyone in the room shouted, "I will! We will! We all will!" Reb Meir beckoned to the young man who triggered this outpouring of devotion to come close. He took hold of his hand, pressed it with love and looked to everyone. The *talmid* felt the *rebbe's* hand close. The student emitted a loud scream. Everyone rushed over to the bed, and saw that their *rebbe's* *neshamah* had departed. *Zecher tzaddik livrachah.*

Ozrov: A Dynasty of Kedushah

*A tribute
to the
fifth Rebbe
of Ozrov*

Rabbi Moshe Yechiel Epstein
5597-5650 / 1837-1890

WHILE JUDAISM KNOWS of all types of dynasties, some tell special tales of holiness perpetuated and reinforced with the passing of time. Dynasties of *kedushah* — of true Torah holiness — reflect the paradox of continuity and originality, of conformity and individualism, proclaiming that the new has merged with the old, adding but not displacing, bringing honor to the new without reducing the esteem of the old.

Thus, Rabbi Yitzchak Ze'ev Soloveitchik shines in his own right as the Brisker Rav, while clearly the successor of his great father, Reb Chaim, and grandfather, Reb Yoseif Dov (author of the *Beis Halevi*). The *Sfas Emes* speaks to us with a unique voice, even as he is manifestly — indeed, appropriately — the natural heir of the *Chidushei HaRim* to the leadership of Gur.

Rabbi Moshe Yechiel HaLevi Epstein, fifth in the chain of Torah leaders of Ozrov, was a unique *gadol* of his generation, imprinting his personal stamp on the thousands who were privileged to have had contact with him and upon the multitudes who study his monumental works, *Aish Das* and *Be'er Moshe*. Yet, in his own mind, he was merely an unworthy successor to the truly great heritage of Ozrov.

As he himself once related of his feelings during his youth:

> When I contemplate the greatness of my ancestors, who were also my teachers — as I consider their incredible holiness in the most trying of times, their absolute devotion to G-d, and the literally miraculous events of their lives — I am reminded of the *Gemara* in *Sanhedrin* (93a): "When Chananya, Mishael and Azarya emerged unscathed from the fiery furnace, all the nations of the world came and smote those Jews who had, in fact, worshiped the image set up by the king: 'You have such a G-d, yet you worship an image!' they declared." I, too, thought: How can people go about their everyday lives and not cleave unto G-d when the miracles of such great lives were displayed before our eyes?

⊷§ Links in the Chain of Modesty

The first rabbi of Ozrov, later known as *Reb Leibush Hagadol* (the Great), was a quiet and modest man, who preferred anonymity and the solitude of spiritual contemplation to the turbulent life of a chassidic *rebbe*. His teachers — the *Chozeh* of Lublin, the *Yid Hakadosh* of Parshysche, and Rabbi Avrohom Yehoshua Heshel of Opt — prevailed upon him in 5572 (1812) to accept the position of rabbi of the city of Ozrov, near Apt, Poland. Only when his own *rebbe*, Rabbi Meir of Opt, passed away (5585/1825), did Reb Leibush reluctantly begin accepting *chassidim*. His following grew steadily, and at his death in 5597 (1837), the name Ozrov had been embedded into the hearts of European Jewry as a mother-city of Torah in the tradition of Belz, Gur, and Lublin.

The second link in the Ozrover chain was Reb Leibush's son, Rabbi Yechiel Chaim Epstein. After serving as *rav* in a number of neighboring cities, Rabbi Yechiel Chaim eventually returned to Ozrov as both the rabbi and chassidic leader. While his family's ingrained modesty helped obscure many of the details of Rabbi Yechiel Chaim's life, the people had a way of recognizing his greatness in piety and character, and by the time of his death in 5648 (1888), he was revered throughout Poland and beyond.

Reb Yechiel Moshe's son, Reb Leibush, personified the quality that later became a trademark of his own grandson, the late Ozrover

Rebbe: greatness concealed by surface simplicity. Indeed, a short interpretation of Reb Leibush on the daily prayers epitomizes his approach to character development:

> At the end of the *Yishtabach* prayer in *Shacharis* — the morning service — we say *Habocher b'shirei zimrah* (He who chooses the songs [of Israel]). *"Shirei,"* Reb Leibush said, *"*comes from the word *shiraim* — that which remains behind. Every prayer, every contact with G-dliness, must leave an indelible impression upon the soul. G-d's delight in man's prayer depends upon the imprint of the prayer itself upon that soul. Each prayer can provide an opportunity of scaling new heights and achieving new understanding — all unapproachable before prayer. This must take place within the person. The surface — the outside man — must remain unobtrusive and simple, unaffected as before."

This depicts the mode of life of Reb Leibush (grandfather of the late *Rebbe*), who passed away more than seven decades ago.

⋲§ The Father

Rabbi Avrohom Shlomo Epstein succeeded his father as *Admur* in 5674/1914 when the "guns of August" signaled the outbreak of the First World War, ushering in a time that proved difficult for the world and devastating for the Jewish communities of Europe. It was a time when *Klal Yisroel* needed Torah leaders of vision and hope, whose personal courage could overflow to those who looked to them for solace. Forty-nine years old at the time of his ascendancy to the position of rabbi, Rabbi Avrohom Shlomo brought a lifetime of Torah study and virtual immersion in G-dliness to the task of leadership.

Typical of those years was the sudden search and ransacking of Jewish homes with the ostensible purpose of finding concealed weapons. On one of these occasions, it was Rabbi Avrohom Shlomo's modest home that was chosen for the "honor." The burly Russian soldiers went from the rabbi's house to the adjacent synagogue and continued their assault. Suddenly one of the intruders flung open the *Aron Hakodesh* (Holy Ark) and was about to rip through the Torah scrolls with his bayonet. In what seemed like a flash, Reb Avrohom Shlomo placed his frail body between the menacing weapon and the precious scrolls. As the blade was raised to his own throat, the *Rebbe* declared, "I will not allow you to touch the holy Torah scrolls," and, eyes gleaming and defiant, he glared at the astonished officer until the troops left, impressed with the rabbi's courage.

Ever since childhood, Reb Avrohom Shlomo considered each moment of life to be a unique, precious opportunity for *avodas Hashem*. Each night, before allowing himself the luxury of a few hours of sleep, he would examine every minute of the day to determine if it could have been better spent. If any amount of time were found wanting, he would cry bitterly and profusely until, his pillow drenched with tears of *teshuvah* (repentance), he drifted off to sleep.

Very often, the indifference to danger and disregard for personal comfort were simply due to Reb Avrohom Shlomo's total and absolute involvement in the *mitzvah* he was performing or the Torah he was studying.

One Succos his family watched anxiously as Reb Avrohom Shlomo slept in the *succah* each night. Not unusual? But Reb Avrohom Shlomo had broken both legs just before *Yom Tov* while placing the *s'chach* on the roof of the *succah*.

❊ ❊ ❊

On one of those Succos days during the war, Reb Avrohom Shlomo entered the *succah* as mortar shells exploded from all directions. Punctuated by the staccato of rifles and the jarring crash of fearsome new sounds of destruction, the *Rebbe* raised his voice above the din, and with utter abandon and joy pronounced the blessing over the *lulav* and *esrog*. At that moment, as his son Rabbi Moshe Yechiel recalls, the outer trappings of the world were irrelevant besides the ultimate joy of performing one of G-d's *mitzvos*.

❊ ❊ ❊

Early one *Shabbos* morning during the war, the door to their house flew open and a phalanx of Russian soldiers stalked into the house demanding "the contraband wine." The *Rebbe* patiently explained that he had no illegal wine, but to no avail. The house was overturned, and when still nothing was found, the head of the platoon threatened to kill the *Rebbe*.

Assigning an armed guard to watch over the "dangerous

prisor.er," the sergeant announced that he would return shortly and transport the intransigent *Rebbe* to headquarters in Zabichust for execution.

The entire family was panic stricken, but Reb Avrohom Shlomo remained serene. "Today is Shabbos," he reminded his household, and the tranquility on his face radiated to all around him, as he made his *Kiddush* in the majestic tones so familiar to his intimates and *chassidim*.

In the meantime, his son Reb Moshe Yechiel slipped into a nearby room, signaled to a passerby to come to the window, and instructed him to inform a certain Jew who had the ear of the military governor of the city ... Within a short time, the military governor, who had had occasion to be impressed with the rabbi's integrity, arrived and dismissed the guard. When the sergeant returned, the governor castigated him for his unauthorized action and asked the rabbi if he should be punished. Concerned that the ruffian not take out his revenge on some unsuspecting fellow Jew, Reb Avrohom Shlomo requested mercy for the culprit.

⋖§ A Genius Cloaked in Modesty

On the sixth day of Teves, 5650 (1890), a son was born to Reb Avrohom Shlomo, and was named Moshe Yechiel. In his message of congratulations, the Shinaver *Rebbe* — the *Divrei Yechezkel* — indicated that the boy would be a luminary to future generations.

In his youth, Reb Moshe Yechiel often studied Torah for twenty consecutive hours in a standing position, reflecting the age-old tradition (*Sotah* 49a and *Megillah* 21a) that Torah be studied with awe and reverence. This diligence was to continue unabated for close to seventy years of uninterrupted Torah study. By the age of seventeen he knew the entire *Zohar* by heart, although in his humility, he hid this fact from his father.

At the age of twenty-six, while his father was still alive, Reb Moshe Yechiel was appointed rabbi and chief *dayan* (judge) of the city of his ancestors, Ozrov. Reb Avrohom Shlomo had settled in Apt after the expulsion of 1915 and could not bring himself to return to Ozrov even after the Russian armies had left. When he passed away in 1918, Reb Moshe Yechiel reluctantly accepted the mantle of chassidic leadership as well.

In 5681 (1922), although only thirty-one years of age, Reb

Moshe Yechiel was appointed to an Agudath Israel delegation visiting America. His colleagues on the committee were the *Gaon*, Rabbi Meir Dan Plotzki, as well as the renowned Dr. Nathan Birnbaum and other venerable members of the Agudath Israel World leadership; nonetheless, the Gerrer *Rebbe* cautioned them "not to make any decision without consulting the *Rebbe* of Ozrov."

Although he was developing creative thoughts in virtually every aspect of Torah, Reb Moshe Yechiel made the decision not to commit any of his thoughts to writing until the age of forty. Upon reaching that milestone, he convened a festive *siyum* meal for completing *Shas* — the entire Talmud — for the tenth time. Soon thereafter, the *Rebbe* completed a major halachic work on the *Rambam* and sent it for comment and criticism to one of the Torah giants of Lithuania. The work was somehow lost in transit and the Ozrover *Rebbe* saw in the loss a heavenly sign that he not publish in the field of *halachah*. From then on, he devoted his creative energies exclusively to works on *Chumash*, Torah philosophy, and *Aggadah*. He was nevertheless known among the *gaonim* of his time as a towering giant in *halachah*, as well.

◀§ To Publish in Purity

The *Rebbe* did not begin writing any of his monumental works until the age forty, the traditional age of understanding (*Avos* 5:21). Even then, he did not publish until he was sixty years old. In explanation of his reticence, he once remarked, "In these times of moral pollution, the very atmosphere is contaminated and makes it difficult to compose works in holiness. The preparation must therefore take longer, and so must the safeguards."

Imagine the safeguards the *Rebbe* infused into his works, patiently withholding them for over *twenty years* until the time he deemed right!

Typical of the incredible care the *Rebbe* took in preparing his works for publication is the story behind the financing of the first volume of his magnum opus — the *Aish Das:*

> One of the *Rebbe's* admirers and supporters from Toronto came to visit the *Rebbe* one day, but was not admitted. Upon further entreaties that he had an urgent matter to discuss, he entered and found the *Rebbe* self-absorbed, preoccupied, and soaked in perspiration. He inquired what was wrong, and the *Rebbe* told his visitor that he was ready to publish his first work

An Ozrover Sampler

● If one studies carefully the passages concerning the creation of the world, one finds the word *emes* — truth — hidden in the last letters of certain words. The word *emes* appears in this way six times to teach us that *Hashem* implanted truth into each of the Six Days of Creation. Why is there no seventh *emes* corresponding to the day of *Shabbos*? This teaches us that *Shabbos* itself is truth and needs no implantation from outside (*Be'er Moshe* 1:238).

● And Avrohom said, "My L-rd, if I have found favor in Your eyes, do not pass from upon Your servant" (*Bereishis* 18:3). The *Gemara* (*Shabbos* 127a) derives from here that taking care of guests is even greater than greeting the *Shechinah* (G-d's presence). Surely, it is difficult to understand how any activity whatsoever could be greater than receiving the Divine Presence. The answer may be found in the *Shalah's* explanation of the *mitzvah* of *Hachnosas Orchim* — receiving guests:

The essence of this *mitzvah*, says the *Shalah*, is that of following in G-d's ways. For are we not all guests in G-d's world? Were He for a moment to forsake His guests, there would be no world (G-d forbid). For this reason, welcoming mortal guests leads to humility, for we instantly realize that all are equally guests before the L-rd. Personally welcoming the *Shechinah* could lead to arrogance and must therefore yield to *Hachnosas Orchim* (*Be'er Moshe*, 1:484).

and could obtain the funds, but could not bring himself to utilize money from questionable sources. The financing, too, would have to be pure, else what worth was all the holiness infused into the *sefer* itself?

The visitor, greatly moved, asked the *Rebbe* if he would accept his own contribution, and the *Rebbe* acquiesced. And so, the first volume of *Aish Das* saw light.

◆§ The Prolific Pen

In view of the extraordinary care that went into each word that flowed from the Ozrover *Rebbe's* pen, his productivity is staggering: eleven published volumes of *Aish Das* totaling over seven thousand pages, and *Be'er Moshe* on all of *Chumash* containing almost five thousand pages.

And what pages they are!

The eye unaccustomed to the *Rebbe's* writings is overwhelmed by the myriad references on each page. Well over one-hundred-thousand quotations from Talmud, Midrash, *Zohar* and classical *mussar* works make each volume a veritable encyclopedia of Torah thought.

The late *Mashgiach* of the Mirrer Yeshivah, Rabbi Hirsh Feldman, commented that even if the *Rebbe's* poor eyesight would have allowed it, the simple time factor would have made it impossible for the *Rebbe* to look up each reference before committing it to paper. This testified to a phenomenal memory, backed by a lifetime of Torah study, which allowed him to plunge effortless through the fathomless depths and broad expanses of Torah literature to retrieve the pearls he needed for each subject and discourse.

And yet, as we study the works, we sense a profound reason behind this torrent of citations. In a letter to a follower, the *Rebbe* himself explains this special quality of all his works:

"Each statement of *Chazal* (our sages) is unique. No two parables are exactly alike, no sentence or even word is ever superfluous. To the unattuned ear, the allusions may seem identical; to the sensitive educated listener, however, they complement but do not duplicate each other."

The Ozrover *Rebbe*, like a master composer, orchestrated the myriad tones, themes and compositions of *Chazal* into a harmonious symphonic whole. The more we study his works, the more finely attuned becomes our appreciation of the majesty and mystical beauty of our sages' expression ... As Rabbi Yechezkel Sarna, the late *Rosh Yeshivah* of Chevron, commented, "I cannot imagine but that the angels themselves are writing these *seforim*."

The *Rebbe* provided a road map through the ages, charting the source and development of each sagely statement: "Each *gadol* shed fresh light upon ancient themes, each of them adding themselves and *of* themselves to the great Torah chain. Their originality, however, is steeped in tradition, the uniqueness tempered by the matrix of *Chazal*. And it was in demonstrating the poetic beauty of this paradox that the Ozrover *Rebbe* excelled. Upon studying a section of *Aish Das* intensively, the reader retains the breathtakingly panoramic view of the landscape of *Chazal*, while gaining a new and intimate appreciation of each element of the scene.

● And she said, "This time I shall thank the L-rd and she [Leah] ceased to give birth" (Bereishis 30:35). The Rebbe of Lublin explained that Leah's declaration of "this time I shall thank the L-rd" was the cause for her to stop having children after naming Yehudah. The Matriarchs — Sarah, Rivkah, Rachel and Leah — were on such a high level of holiness that they were expected to give thanks to G-d not only for favors past but even for those they trusted would occur in the future. Their attitude is reflected in the Birkas Hamazon — the blessing after a meal: "He has been good to us, He is good to us, He will be good to us." We therefore see that we must thank G-d, on faith, for the future. Leah had limited her gratitude to favors past.

This faith in the future is indicated in the Mishnah (Berachos 54a): "One should give thanks for the past and cry to G-d concerning the future." The true believer in G-d already sees the salvation of the future in the prayer of today and so his cry for the future goes hand in hand with the gratitude for the past. Indeed, on Pesach at the seder we proclaim this aloud: "Who had redeemed us and redeemed our ancestors in Egypt ... so should G-d help us to arrive at other such joyous days ... and we will sing to you a new song for our deliverance" — a deliverance yet to be realized! In our state of spiritual elevation of Pesach night, we already sing in appreciation of future benevolence.

⮬ The Three Loves

While virtually no area of Torah is left untouched in the Ozrover seforim, one theme runs throughout the Aish Das. As the Rebbe himself indicates on the opening page of every volume, the works are designed to foster the three loves a Jew is enjoined to embrace: Ahavas Hashem, Ahavas Torah and Ahavas Yisroel (love of G-d, love of Torah, and love of Israel).

One example of the Torah's expression of these three loves is seen by the Rebbe in the Keruvim, the childlike figures atop the Holy Ark in the Mishkan — the Tabernacle:

And the Keruvim are to spread their wings upwards, forming a cover to the kapores over the Ark, and their faces shall be one to the other (*Shemos* 25:20). *The wings spreading upwards,* symbolizing love of G-d; they *form a cover over the Ark* containing the Tablets, in love of Torah; *and they face each other,* representing love of Israel.

Simple words. Yet just as when Reb Chaim Brisker explained a passage in the *Rambam* we could not imagine how we had failed to see it so clearly before, so does the Ozrover's simplicity hide the profound beauty of his interpretations.

✌§ The Gaon in Tzedakah

The Ozrover did not merely expound on "the three loves" in his written works. His entire life expressed that ideal. Although he rarely explored the world beyond "the four ells of *halachah*," his heart went out to every Jew, no matter how simple or far from Torah. He sat as an honored member of the *Moetzes Gedolei Hatorah* (Council of Torah Sages), the rabbinical policy-making body of Agudath Israel (he had been asked to be its president) at ease with his colleagues. At the same time, his fatherly love overflowed to any Jew who came to his home and sought his help, to the degree that — for example — he used to reserve an hour every day over a long period of time to chat with a *baalas teshuvah* who was experiencing difficulties in her personal life.

Those who came to his humble home for help left not only with their spirits rejuvenated, but with material assistance as well. Often, the *Rebbe* would dole out the last penny in the house to the needy.

Before the *Rebbe* was about to remarry, he warned his wife-to-be, "You should know that it is my custom to give away much — what might be considered beyond my means — to charity."

One *Erev Pesach* during the Depression years, when the *Rebbe* resided in the Bronx, there was virtually no food or money in the house. With his customary serenity, the *Rebbe* reassured his *Rebbetzin* and their household that Hashem would provide. Later an old woman knocked on the door and told the *Rebbe* her tale of woe, seeking a blessing. As the *Rebbe* gave her his blessing and words of encouragement, the woman put a few dollars on the table. The *Rebbe* refused the donation: "Keep it for yourself and have a *kosher* and happy Pesach."

After she left he explained to his astonished family, "Surely this woman's need is as great as ours, so how can we

● The most important element in *tzedakah* — charity — is the attitude with which it is given. As the *Sefer Yeraim* teaches, it is essential not to make the poor feel downtrodden when they accept the charity, but to encourage and uplift them. In this way, we can understand the words of the *Gemara*, "As you have vowed unto the L-rd your G-d, which you promised *with your mouth*" (*Devarim* 23:34). "With your mouth" refers to *tzedakah* (*Rosh Hashanah* 6a). *Tosfos* explains that *with your mouth* refers to *tzedakah* in line with the words of the Prophet: "The word is gone forth from my mouth in *tzedakah* — righteousness."

How does the *Gemara* prove from there that "your mouth" refers to charity? Furthermore, what is *Tosfos'* proof? Surely, the passage in Yeshayahu cited by *Tosfos* is spoken by G-d, and charity is given by man!

The answer is that true charity depends upon the mouth as much as the pocketbook. This is demonstrated in the passage from Yeshayahu. In addition, it indicates that charity given properly elicits a like response from Above, and brings the blessings of Divine charity to the donor.

take her few dollars?"

G-d did come to the *Rebbe's* aid in the form of an unexpected check from a wealthy follower, but (*chassidim* say) this incident could not add to the *Rebbe's* trust in *Hashem*, for his *bitachon* was already complete, even when there seemed no prospect for hope.

When a day had passed without an opportunity to help the needy, the *Rebbe* would sigh softly, "My soul yearns to give charity — would that I were worthy to perform the *mitzvah!*"

◄§ Source of Wisdom and Solace

Wherever the *Rebbe* lived, his home became a haven for Jews of all types. Aged scholars who had come to discuss abstruse mystical passages waited with the needy who knew they would receive fatherly words of encouragement along with the means to get through the week, or even to get their businesses started.

From 5687 (1927) until 5713 (1953), the *Rebbe's* residence was in the Bronx. He later moved to Tel Aviv, where he became the focal point of many Torah endeavors. Although the *Chazon Ish* personally implored him to join him in Bnei Brak, the Ozrover felt that he could do more for Torah and *Klal Yisroel* in Tel Aviv, and there he remained for the rest of his life.

Even in the New York years when the *Rebbe* would often spend the summer in the Catskills, his bungalow became a Torah center. The hill upon which he paced, beloved *sefer* in hand, was soon called "Mount Sinai" by all who resided in the area. Those privileged to be the *Rebbe's* neighbors in the Bronx recall catching sight of the *Rebbe's* gaunt figure appearing and disappearing from view through the curtained windows of his apartment, as he studied Torah.

Many of those former neighbors recall that they returned to their own sleep more peacefully, reassured in the knowledge that the *Rebbe* was vigilantly continuing his holy labors for *Klal Yisroel*.

Many Jews who knew of the *Rebbe's* wisdom and practical knowledge would, before going to court, consult the *Rebbe* at least to receive a blessing:

> After detailing the case he was about to plead in court, a businessman asked the *Rebbe* for a *berachah* that his day in court would go well.
>
> Instead of giving him the requested blessing, the *Rebbe* said, "Please ask your lawyer to come see me before going to court."
>
> When the lawyer arrived, the *Rebbe* gave him point by point instructions on how to conduct his client's case. After the man won his case, he went to pay his lawyer. The barrister replied, "Pay me only for the time I spent in court. I had no necessity for research. The *Rebbe* did it all."

◈§ "Even if He Takes Your Soul"

The greatest tragedy of the *Rebbe's* own life was the drowning of his only son at the age of twenty-one in the year 5709 (1949). From the beginning, it was clear that the *Rebbe* was worried about his son's achieving a normal lifespan. At his *bris* the *Rebbe* named him *Alter* (literally, "old man" — a name often given to someone gravely ill), and added the name "Avrohom Shlomo" after his *bar mitzvah*. At this festive Torah affair, when receiving blessings of *mazel tov*, the *Rebbe* was heard to whisper softly, "הלואי זאל ער בלייבען מיינער — May it only be G-d's will that he remain mine!"

In the year of his son's death, the *Rebbe* had left for a short visit to the Holy Land, expressing concern for his son's safety to his friends. The tragedy happened while the *Rebbe* was in Israel, and it was decided not to notify him until he returned. At the airport, he was met by his friends, the venerable *Rabbeim* of Boyan and Kapishnitz, who gently told him the crushing news.

Those who were there will never forget the extraordinary self-control and ultimate love of G-d the *Rebbe* exhibited in those grievous moments. The *Rebbe's* only visible reaction was the moving statement: "ואהבת את ה' אלוקיך ... בכל נפשך — *And you shall love the L-rd your G-d . . . with all your soul — even if He takes your soul. My son was an integral part of my own soul.*"

✑§ Glimpses into Greatness

Only rarely did those around the *Rebbe* gain a glimpse into the almost heroic efforts that went into his quiet but world-shaking *avodah*. One such occasion each year was the *Rebbe's na'anuim* — the waving of the *lulav* during *Hallel*. For over thirty minutes, the *Rebbe* would labor — gracefully, mystically swaying — with profound and abstruse *kavanos* in mind.

On Yom Kippur, as he "fell *korim*," the traditional prostrations signifying total obeisance to G-d, there was no outer hint at internal turmoil. Yet, he was soaked with perspiration from the internal exertions, exhausted from storming heaven for his brethren around the world.

His labors for *Klal Yisroel* on Yom Kippur may be seen as the leitmotif of the Ozrover *Rebbe's* life. As one of his admirers put it, "The *Chofetz Chaim* compiled a *mesechta* (tractate) on *Lashon Hara* — the laws of gossip and slander — and the Ozrover made a *mesechta* of *Ahavas Yisroel* — the love of Israel."

✑§ The Holy Passing

On *Rosh Chodesh Shevat*, 5731 (1971), the *Rebbe* was in his room, absorbed as usual in holy and sublime matters. He requested a glass of tea, made the blessing, and was once again alone in his room. The glass shattered and the *Rebbe's* dedicated *gabbai*, Reb Yechiel Friedman, realized that something was wrong. He rushed into the *Rebbe's* room, followed by the worried *Rebbetzin*. The *Rebbe* was standing, but apparently had had a stroke: he was totally motionless and could not speak. Some time later, in the hospital, the ostensibly paralyzed *Rebbe* was seen to calmly straighten his *peyos*, stroke them into his beard and close his eyes. He then passed away, as if — in the Talmud's expression — by a Heavenly kiss.

The drink of tea follows the tale told of many *gedolim*, especially among *chassidim*, who pronounce the *Shehakol* blessing — *All is in existence by His word* — immediately before their passing. The smoothing of the *peyos* and beard, too, has been seen in the last moments of the lives of great sages.

◆§ The Legacy

The Ozrover *Rebbe* left a dual legacy, unfortunately rare in recent times. His dynasty lives on, in the person of his dedicated grandson, Rabbi Tanchum Becker, who heads the Kollel Aish Das in Tel Aviv, which is dedicated to the perpetuation of the *Rebbe's* works. And the *Rebbe* himself lives on in the thousands of pages of *Aish Das* and *Be'er Moshe*, continuing to illuminate to new generations of Jews every corner of rabbinic literature, and perpetuating the three loves he deemed so important. In increasing *our* love of G-d, *our* love of Torah, and *our* love of our fellows, we too keep the *Rebbe* of Ozrov alive.

Nisson Wolpin

The Skullener Rebbe

*A Rebbe
passes away,
and the
world
weeps*

Rabbi Eliezer Zisya Portugal
5656-5742 / 1896-1982

IT IS RARE THAT the passing of an elderly saintly chassidic *Rebbe* should attract attention beyond his circle, and stir the hearts of the widest possible spectrum of world Jewry. Such was the case on 29 *Av* 5743 / August 18, 1982, with the *petirah* (death) of the Skullener Rebbe, Rabbi Eliezer Zisya Portugal, at the age of eighty-six.

The *Rebbe* was a *tzaddik* of unusual stature who had become a legend in his own time. While his rare purity of character, his *tzidkus* and his boundless *Ahavas Yisroel* (love for his fellow Jews) would have won him admiration in any era, they were especially awe-inspiring in his particular time and place.

• In this era marked by narcissism and selfishness, he devoted his life completely to helping others, saving countless lives! Immediately after World War II, he adopted close to four-hundred orphaned children and, incredibly, took care of their needs as though they were his own children. His *Rebbetzin* cooked for them, and he led many of them to the *chupah*. He remained in Rumania after the Communists took control of the country and ministered to the personal and spiritual needs of countless others — persuading a girl not to marry out of the faith, bribing a prison guard to permit food to reach an inmate, "convincing" a state official to permit a fellow Jew to immigrate, while he stayed on, eventually serving several prison sentences under the most brutal conditions for his activities.

On one occasion he actually gave his hard-won exit visa to a head of a family of eleven. When the official whom he had "paid" for a visa, in a fit of anger and confusion, accused him of reneging on their agreement, the *Rebbe* replied, "Eleven souls are more important than one."

Up until his final years — even when blind and frail — he personally administered his *Chesed L'Abraham* network of *hatzalah* (rescue) and educational institutions, totally unconcerned about himself.

● In a land of brutality and oppression, he was the epitome of love, sensitivity, and forgiveness. After his arrival in America in 1960, he continued to work feverishly, tirelessly, for the release of hundreds and hundreds of Jews, sending them packages, helping them travel to America or Israel, paying for the education of their children.

An aide once pointed out that a woman whom he had brought over from Europe had actually informed the Rumanian government of his religious activities, resulting in his arrest and imprisonment. Why go to such effort and expense to save a person of her ilk?

"You have no idea how much she suffered beforehand, and how tempting the authorities make it to inform," the *Rebbe* said with tears in his eyes. "*Zie's doch a Yiddishe tochter* — you'll see how she'll change!" Then he added, "What do you think Lot looked like when Avraham *Avinu* pleaded with G-d that he be spared destruction from Sodom?"

Numerous religious Jews, many in chassidic garb, confess to having been *mechallel Shabbos befarhesya* (public *Shabbos* desecrators) in Rumania, before the *Rebbe* had gained their release; and only now — through the *Rebbe's* love and selflessness — did they come to realize the value of leading a Torah life.

● In a time of egocentricity, the *Rebbe* was the spirit of

simplicity and humility, both when he was under a system that thrived on duplicity, and when in our own land of unabashed overstatement.

In an interview (to which the *Rebbe* consented so as to publicize his *Chesed L'Abraham* Fund) the *Rebbe* was asked how he and his *Rebbetzin* managed to care for the personal needs of so many children after the war. Replied the *Rebbe*, "*Der Heiliger Bashefer hott rachmones gehatt oif zeine kinder* — The Holy Creator had mercy on His children." The *Rebbe*? His role didn't count!

In his *tzava'ah* (ethical will), read at his funeral, he requested all assembled to forgive him if they ever gave him contributions for his holy work because they thought him a *tzaddik* — which (he protested) he was not. "So let all gathered say, '*Machul lach! Machul lach! Machul lach!*'" (We forgive you! We forgive you! We forgive you!)

● In an age of shedding inhibitions and brazenness, this singular saint dealt with the moral dregs of society — high political officials and lowly prison wardens in Rumania — and became involved in the personal problems of many a Jew who had lost or seemed never to have had the basics of *Kedushas Yisroel*. Yet his own life was a model of spirituality and sanctity: "Why don't we (in America) teach our children of the importance of *shmiras einayim* (guarding our vision from moral contamination)?" he pleaded with an educator — only demanding of others what he himself did.

● When doubt and agnosticism became fashionable, the *Rebbe* became a symbol of unyielding belief. "Help your children with the basics of *emunah*," he instructed a conference of youth leaders of Pirchei Agudath Israel — themselves senior yeshivah students. "Teach the children *Rambam's* Thirteen Principles of Faith. Inspire them with tales of spiritual heroism from the Midrash and the Talmud," he pleaded ... while he, in turn, represented a fresh chapter in the on-going saga of Jewry's eternal heroism.

● In our "do-it-yourself era" when every man pulls for himself, his *avodah* in *tefillah* — the hours upon hours of all-encompassing concentration when he poured out his heart to G-d in his prayers, day after day — was staggering. *Shacharis* was a four-hour effort. Saying the *Shema* on an ordinary evening *Maariv* took twenty-five minutes ... It should be no surprise that when he said his customary *Shema* in the intensive-care unit of a hospital during an illness, the doctors were alarmed when the cardiogram readings fluctuated wildly with every carefully articulated word.

• In the darkest of conditions, the *Rebbe* never failed to see the light of G-d's intervention.

"*Baruch gozeir umekayeim* — We bless G-d for decreeing and sustaining," said the *Rebbe*. "He passes terrible decrees, but He grants us the strength to endure the worst: When the Communists imprisoned me, they tried to break my spirit. After days of starving me, only allowing me a bit of water, they gave me a bowl of steaming, tempting vegetable soup — with a piece of *treifah* meat floating in it ... and they gleefully watched as I hungrily picked up the spoon. But then I spotted the meat, and I would not give in. *Baruch gozeir umekayim.* G-d gave me the strength to refuse!"

His joyful melodies, celebrating hope and confidence in G-d's love for His people, have become classics.

• In this time of alleged mutual exclusivity of heart and mind, thought and action, love and discipline, the Skullener *Rebbe* had mastery of both aspects of every paradox — immersed in the spiritual and Kabbalistic phases of each *mitzvah* as well as the demands of *halachah*, down to its most minute detail ... devoted to the *Klal* and the individual — his body and his soul.

In this age of pinpoint specialization and general dilettantism, the Skullener *Rebbe* was a broad-spectrum specialist: He devoted all his energies toward being a *gutte Yid*, and he succeeded in a manner that embraced his entire being, as he in turn embraced all Jewry.

Who will ever fill the void he leaves behind!

~§ Great Women

Attitudes, values, and achievements
of women whose very lives
were shaped by the words of Torah,
to change the lives of thousands —
some, who had known them,
and others,
who may have never
heard their names.

Schwester Selma

*A heroine
of the building of
Shaare Zedek
Hospital
in Jerusalem*

Nurse Selma Mayer
5644-5744 / 1884-1984

◆§ Typhoid Welcome

L ATE ONE EVENING in December, 1916, a lone donkey cart lurched
toward Jaffa Gate in the Old City. Its passenger was a slight
young lady, dressed in prim German style and clutching an
old-fashioned suitcase. When she arrived at the Hotel Amdursky, a
Mr. Porush came to greet her on behalf of the Shaare Zedek
Hospital.

"Would you rather spend your first night at the hotel, or come
directly to the hospital?" Mr. Porush asked.

Nurse Selma Mayer, who had come to work for Shaare Zedek,
chose to go straight to the hospital. What she found when she again
got off the donkey cart may have been rather more than she had
bargained for.

She was shown to a small, stark room in the hospital, with a
"brand-new" bed, a tiny table, and only a bit of hanging space for
clothing — nothing for linens. Refined, German-born Selma was

amazed at the enormous difficulties caused by her simple request for
a bath. Later that evening, she met Dr. Moshe Wallach, the director
of the hospital. She recalls that he was very kind, but she soon had
her first encounter with the special spirit Dr. Wallach maintained in
his hospital. As she tells it:

> I first asked for a cup of coffee since I was very tired from the
> trip. He asked me at once when I had last eaten meat, because of
> the milk in the coffee.

Schwester (nurse) Selma spent a memorable night in that
"brand-new" bed, getting acquainted with the bedbugs. She opened
her window the next morning to an exotic Middle Eastern
donkey-and-camel scene, and prepared for her first day on the job.
But the real surprise was waiting for her when she reported for duty
— a typhoid epidemic!

∽§ Meet Dr. Wallach

Shaare Zedek had opened its doors in 1902 with forty beds as
the only modern Jewish hospital in the New City of Jerusalem.
Misgav Ladach and Bikur Cholim in the Old City were inadequate
to meet the needs of the growing population, and the threat of
missionary influence from professionally staffed and well-equipped
Christian hospitals was a real danger. Dr. Wallach, an intimate of
Rabbi Yosef Chaim Sonnenfeld and Rabbi Yosef Tzvi Dushinsky,
joined this hospital which was founded in answer to this problem.
"Wallach Hospital" was meticulous in its observance of *Shabbos* and
Kashrus. Dr. Wallach even posted a sign in the clinic waiting-room
insisting on separate seating, a rule that he personally enforced.

Dr. Moshe Wallach (1866-1957) was the son of an Orthodox
German-Jewish family from Cologne. He completed his medical
training in 1889. From the time of his arrival in *Eretz Yisroel* two
years later, this *tzaddik* devoted his life, day and night, weekday
and *Shabbos*, to the well-being of his fellow Jews. In the terrible
sanitary conditions of old Jerusalem, Dr. Wallach sought out people
who needed his help, regardless of their ability to pay. Many times,
rather than take a fee, he pressed money on very poor patients.

Yet Dr. Wallach, the hospital's only physician, was not an easy
man to work for. He was known for his strict religious standards,
and a vehement displeasure for anything short of perfection —
which was balanced by a lively sense of humor. The combination of
the first two qualities was enough to scare away prospective

personnel. Before a nurse was hired in Shaare Zedek, she was first thoroughly tested on the laws of *Kashrus*. Then came what Schwester Selma called "general questions." For example:

"What would you do if you saw some cotton lying on the floor?" Dr. Wallach would ask.

"I would pick it up," the girls answered.

"Oh no, you would walk by quickly and think: Let the next one pick it up."

Next question:

"Do you know that you have to be home (at the hospital) by eight o'clock in the evening? Will you keep this rule?"

"Yes, of course," the candidate would reply.

"No, you will come in late and climb over the wall!"

(No nurse could leave the premises without written permission from Dr. Wallach, and then only until 8:00. He made a practice of standing at the hospital's small gate with the gatekeeper to be sure they really all were back on time.)

And woe to the staff member who fell asleep on the job! In her memoirs, Schwester Selma recalls:

"When Dr. Wallach was tired, he went to sleep at four o'clock in the afternoon and slept until about ten o'clock at night. Then he came ... and supervised the night help ... He used to shout so much that first of all the patients awoke, but also the tired nurses and warders ... Once he found a warder sleeping on a stretcher. He took off the man's slippers and took them to his room." Confused and barefoot, the warder searched the entire building for the missing slippers.

Then there was "an elderly woman helper who did night duty. She was sitting on a chair and had fallen asleep. He took off her earrings without her noticing it."

When she awoke the next morning, the poor lady was shocked at the idea of an earring thief in Shaare Zedek!

If a baby cried at night, Dr. Wallach "came running. 'Nurse! Have a look at what's going on! Maybe the baby is sore, or thirsty, or has a stomach-ache!' "

Another evening, Dr. Wallach found a strange woman lingering at the gate.

"Please," she begged. "Let me in for just five minutes to see my husband. He had an operation yesterday. But let me in quick, before that crazy Wallach comes by."

"I'll take you up," said Dr. Wallach. "But really only for five minutes. I'll wait for you at the door."

He called the woman out when her five minutes were up, and she thanked him again and again.

"What is your name? You're such a kind person."

"I'm that crazy Wallach," he replied.

The Nightingale Inspiration

Dr. Wallach threw all his soul into his work, and he expected the hospital staff to do the same. There had been a Dutch-trained head nurse — briefly — but she found the primitive conditions unbearable and left. Then, in 1916, during the First World War, Dr. Wallach traveled to Europe to search for urgently needed personnel. When he discovered thirty-two-year-old Schwester Selma Mayer of the Salomon Heine Hospital in Hamburg, Germany, he finally met his professional match. It took her four long weeks by train via Central Europe, Turkey, and Damascus to reach *Eretz Yisroel*, and when she finally arrived, the welcome was not inviting. But Schwester Selma was not one to be scared away.

Selma Mayer was born in the small town of Hanau, Germany, on February 3, 1884, one of five children. Selma's mother passed away when she was five. When she read about Florence Nightingale's work in the Crimean War as the first nurse, Selma found the answer to her wish to "give to others that which I had missed so much: mother-love and the love of human beings." She began her nursing career in the Heine Hospital in 1906. In 1913, she was one of the first two Jewish nurses to be certified in Germany. In later years she would be known as the "Jewish Florence Nightingale" for her many years of selfless work at Shaare Zedek. Opportunities for dedication presented themselves at once.

"Normal": Only Relative

When Schwester Selma reported for work, she found only fifty hospital beds, but thousands of patients streaming to the hospital in desperate need of treatment. With little food and water available, Jerusalemites were easy prey not only to the typhoid epidemic, but also to typhus and meningitis. Another hundred beds were crammed in. After that, the practical nurses were moved from their quarters down to the basement to make room for still more patients. Schwester Selma dressed her untrained helpers in overalls and hoods in an effort to protect them from infection, and they went to work.

"With their lice-infested clothes, the people were stuck into the bathtub," she recalled. "Then the clothes were cut open, the patients undressed and shaved all over."

The epidemic lasted over a year. To further complicate matters, the Turks frequently checked the building for illegal (and useful) items. The hospital had many bandages, sent from Germany, but they had to be buried to keep them safe from the Turks.

Dr. Wallach and Schwester Selma visited every patient morning and night. For the first four weeks, she took along a notebook and marked down whatever needed improvement. Gradually, in spite of the lack of skilled workers, she introduced European-style order to the wards. She showed the girls how to make a hospital bed, and taught some of the more capable ones to bandage and give injections.

There was a nightmarish day of heavy bombing in 1918 — a *Shabbos* — when the staff and patients had to be moved to the basement which had no toilet. Then peace was declared, and "slowly work became more normal."

The term "normal" was only relative. There was no electricity, no running water, and certainly no ambulances. In that pre-automobile era, the only way to get a patient to the hospital was by hand-borne stretcher. With no staff available to carry the stretcher, it was up to the patient's family to either carry it themselves or hire porters. Dr. Wallach went on foot to all parts of the Old City and the New, both to decide if hospitalization was needed, and to treat patients in case immediate treatment was called for. For severe hemorrhage cases, Schwester Selma came along, carrying the sterile equipment and bandages.

She never forgot one very hot *Shabbos* when Dr. Wallach was called to the Old City. From the family's description, he suspected that patient might need immediate surgery.

"He accompanied the people to the Old City and took along the necessary instruments. He returned walking next to the stretcher with an injection in case the patient collapsed on the way. He had, however, sent a young man ahead so that everything could be prepared for an operation. A young Arab then did this [sterilized the equipment] on a Primus [kerosene heater]."

❧ Special Service

Dr. Wallach was often summoned for happier occasions as well. A very popular *mohel*, he performed countless circumcisions, keeping an exact record of the names and dates. Schwester Selma personally designed and always prepared a sterile tray of equipment, including small rolls of gauze and dermatol powder, for every circumcision. One *bris* was scheduled for a day struck by a devastating snowstorm. Never one to be deterred by circumstances — after all, a *bris* must be held on time — Dr. Wallach was brought to Mea Shearim by four men. This was more complicated than it sounds, since the men had to tie ropes around the doctor to lead him through the snowdrifts!

In addition to its regular wards, Shaare Zedek had a tiny laboratory, a clinic and, for a time, the only isolation ward in Jerusalem. In the clinic, Dr. Wallach and an assistant painted everyone's throats as the cure for all ills; but the isolation ward, which was even cruder than the main building, was meticulously run. It was not easy.

There was neither heating nor plumbing. A tin bathtub was rolled into the room, filled with water heated on the ubiquitous kerosene heater. When food was brought in from the hospital kitchen, it was immediately reheated in the isolation ward's own pots. Laundry was soaked in lysol for twenty-four hours before being sent to the main laundry shed. Every nurse had to serve a full month in the isolation ward; during this period they were not allowed to go out or have visitors and, except during the polio epidemic, slept in the ward. But Schwester Selma writes that while it demanded great efforts, it was "well worth it in every respect."

❧ Of Duty, Joy and Courage

Schwester Selma served as head nurse, operating-room nurse, and pinch-hitter nurse; she still did deliveries and taught the sketchily trained midwives basic skills. Until 1930, "every spiderweb on the ceiling, every drop of water, every piece of cotton on the floor ... and the *kashrus* in the tea kitchen" were her exclusive responsibility. During Dr. Wallach's absences to attend Agudath Israel meetings, Schwester Selma was left in full command of the entire hospital.

When Schwester Selma came to Jerusalem, she brought along a copy of an Indian poem by Tagore, which she hung in her room as her motto:

I slept and dreamt
that life was joy.
I awoke and saw
that life was duty.
I acted and behold,
duty was joy.

Yet duty was not always joy; sometimes it was stark courage. In 1929, the Arabs attacked the Jews of Hebron in the infamous Hebron Massacre. The victims, among them many students of the *Chevron Yeshivah*, were literally cut to pieces with knives. Hebron was barricaded, but a rescue crew managed to get through and pull out many of the wounded, who were rushed to Shaare Zedek and Hadassah Hospitals. Specialists from all over the city assembled in the operating room, but there was no team of surgical nurses to assist them. There was only Schwester Selma. Alone, she prepared the operating room and all the necessary instruments. For twenty-three hours without a break she stood, handing instruments to the surgeons as patient after patient was wheeled in. She could not wipe away her tears for fear of contaminating her sterile gloves.

◆§ School for Nurses

After twenty years in *Eretz Yisroel*, Schwester Selma took on a new challenge. Why shouldn't Jewish nurses receive training of the same calibre as the non-Jewish nurses? In 1936 the Shaare Zedek Nursing School was opened with pediatrician Dr. Karl Mayer as its first teacher. Schwester Selma guided the school for over twenty years, and was its inspiration for decades more — at eighty, she still picked up litter in the wards to show the girls "that there is nothing humiliating in our work." Today, the Schwester Selma Award is given yearly to the school's outstanding graduate.

For years, Schwester Selma had taught midwives how to diaper newborns. Now she taught her students everything she learned in nursing school, plus the countless practical techniques she had developed in her many years of work in Jerusalem. Perhaps the most important things she taught were her own attitudes toward nursing, those attitudes that made her so very special:

"Again and again I told them: Those who come to us need help."

"When dealing with the patient, try everything to cause him as little pain as possible."

"Spare no effort."

"The patient quickly recognizes a good nurse."

During the British Mandate, examinations for registered nurses were given by British authorities. The doctors of the British Government Hospital were so impressed with the results that they sought after Shaare Zedek-trained nurses for their own hospital.

The Polio Epidemic

With the passage of years, Shaare Zedek developed and expanded. Electricity, running water, central heating, gas cooking stoves, and eventually an elevator were installed. New departments were opened, new doctors and nurses were added to the staff. Yet Schwester Selma's greatest challenge came long after the demise of the paraffin lamp which had illuminated the operating room.

In the early 1950's Israel was stricken by an epidemic: infantile paralysis (polio). Shaare Zedek's isolation ward, the only one in Jerusalem, was full of victims, mostly little children, who needed round-the-clock care. At first, young nurses were forbidden by the Ministry of Health to work in polio wards. Schwester Selma and Dr. Adolf Fraenkel had to search for people to operate the old-fashioned iron lungs, since the on-duty nurse could not leave the machine until her replacement stood at her side, ready to take over. The untrained people they were able to recruit needed constant supervision, but when the assistants saw how hard Schwester Selma herself worked, they too did their best. After the epidemic, in 1958, Dr. Jonas Salk, inventor of the polio vaccine, visited Shaare Zedek. "He looked at our polio ward and was astounded how so much could be done under such primitive conditions."

Forgotten? Never!

From the time she arrived in *Eretz Yisroel*, Shaare Zedek Hospital was Selma Mayer's only home. So absorbed was she in the "duty that took up all my time" that she never married. Her contract entitled her to a three months' vacation in Germany every three years, but she went only twice, in 1922 and 1925. Both times she was tempted to stay; she was even offered the directorship of the

Eidingen Stift Institution in Leipzig. But by 1922, Schwester Selma had adopted the first of three 'daughters',* babies who had been abandoned in the hospital. She returned to Jerusalem for, as she wrote, "How could I desert the child Zamura!" It is certainly possible that this *mesiras nefesh* paid its own dividends. Had Schwester Selma stayed on in Germany, what would have been her fate in the Holocaust?

A student recalls Schwester Selma: "She was up every morning at five-thirty, and never went to bed without touring the entire hospital to make sure everything and everyone was all right." In spite of her professionalism, she never forgot to make a special cup of tea for a patient who refused the hospital brew, or to offer a cup of wine to a sleepless patient. Her unique abilities of dedication and selflessness attracted a very wide circle of admirers. In 1974, she was named a "Worthy of Jerusalem" and "Schwester Selma Day" was announced. In 1975, she was included in a Time Magazine cover story on Living Saints. She was honored by statesmen and rabbis, and once, by the sister of a Holocaust victim.

A woman who was about to be deported left her large, valuable diamond ring with her sister, whose chances of survival were better than her own.

"Here," the woman said, "take my diamond ring, and if I do not return, give it to a human being who has never married and has devoted her life to helping other people."

The sister survived. When she read about Schwester Selma in foreign newspapers, even as far away as Vienna, she chose her as the recipient of the ring.

Schwester Selma passed away on 2 Adar 5744 (February 5, 1984), two days after her one hundredth birthday. In her last years, she said, "I am afraid *Hashem* has forgotten me (i.e., to take my soul)."

We hardly think so.

---

* One daughter was killed by a bomb on Ben Yehuda Street in 1948. The other two were trained as a nurse and a dental technician. One, even as a grandmother, saw Schwester Selma as the head of her family. The nurse was one of the three who sat with Schwester Selma in day-and-night shifts after her stroke.

Chaya Baumwolspiner

Rebbetzin Chana Perel Kotler

"The golden chain should continue."
Rebbetzin Chana Perel Kotler recognized herself in
that chain — which values Torah more than gold.

5654?/1894?—5746/1986

"MEN MEINT ICH BIN A MENTSCH," the *Rebbetzin* was wont to say ("They think that I'm a *mentsch"*). "They think that the daughter of Reb Isser Zalman should be a *mentsch!"* She would then continue, *"Vos bin ich? Ich bin a poshuteh shifchah.* (What am I? I'm a simple maidservant.")

Chazal tell us that even the maidservant at the *Yam Suf* saw more of the Divine Glory than did the Prophet Ezekiel (*Shemos* 15-2). On her own admission, *Rebbetzin* Chana Perel Kotler spent her entire life by the "sea"; the daughter of Rabbi Isser Zalman Meltzer and the wife of Rabbi Aharon Kotler, she personally witnessed a realm of spirituality, intense as it was profound. As a child, the *Rebbetzin* was taken by her father to see Rabbi Itzele Petersburger and, as she recalled, the impression remained with her an entire lifetime. She belonged to — and was a prime member of — the Torah aristocracy of yesteryear.

If, in her humility, the *Rebbetzin* saw herself as a *poshuteh shifchah* against the stature of the spiritual giants with whom she lived, we may recognize that, at the same time, this proximity enabled her to formulate her life's role as the *poshuteh shifchah* in the service of *Hashem*.

◄§ Her Spiritual Heritage

"What became of the rich men of Kovno?" the *Rebbetzin* would frequently ask ... "There were many men in Kovno wealthier than my *Zeide*. Where are they today? And my *Zeide?*... He's represented in Slobodka, Slutzk, Kletzk, Chevron, Eitz Chaim,

---

* No one in the *Ezras Nashim* who heard the fervor of the *Rebbetzin's* "Omein Yehei Shemei Rabba" could ever doubt her special awareness of the *Shechinah*. Nevertheless, the *Rebbetzin* considered it necessary to constantly "work" on herself. She would carry in her pockets small *tzetelach* (notes) on which were written *pessukim* and *Ma'amorei Chazal*, which inculcate *bitachon.*

Baltimore, Lakewood. He knew how to live!"

Rebbetzin Chana Perel Kotler had good reason to be conscious of her spiritual heritage. Her maternal grandfather was Reb Shraga Feivel Frank, a wealthy Lithuanian manufacturer, whose main "business" was Torah. The archetype "*Rambam's balabos*," he learned for at least eight hours a day, and gave both moral and financial support to the *Mussar Kloiz* which congregated in the attic of his Kovno home. There, the Torah and *mussar* giants of the day would meet — Rabbi Yisroel Salanter, and his *talmidim*. Rabbi Itzele Blazer (Petersburger), Rabbi Naftoli Amsterdam, and Rabbi Avrohom Shenker all used the Frank home as their regular place of *mussar* study, as did the *Alter* of Kelm who frequently came. In the realm of commerce, Reb Shraga Feivel was unconventional. Where do we hear of a landlord who anonymously sent money to his own tenants, so that they could pay their rent on time? ... an entrepreneur who repeatedly loaned money to a debtor who never repaid the loan? ... a businessman who once turned down an investment opportunity offering great wealth from a German commercial concern for fear that, if he had too much money, his daughters would not marry *talmidei chachomim*.

Here was a man to be reckoned with! So much so, that when he passed away at an early age in 5647 (1887), Rabbi Yitzchok Elchonon Spektor, the *Rav* of Kovno, personally participated in his *taharah*, and out of respect for Reb Shraga Feivel's request, allowed no eulogies at his funeral. "Normally," said the Kovno *Rav*, "I would ignore such a request; but I am afraid to disregard Reb Shraga Feivel's word."

What is the legacy of such a man? Before his passing, Reb Shraga Feivel charged his wife, Golda, to marry his four daughters to Torah scholars of the first order.* No expense was to be spared on their support! In this manner, the Franks became the spiritual mentors of some of the greatest yeshivos in Europe, in *Eretz Yisroel*,

---

* The four selected sons-in-law were: Rabbi Moshe Mordechai Epstein (*Rosh Yeshivah* of Slobodka and Chevron); Rabbi Isser Zalman Meltzer (*Rosh Yeshivah* of Slutzk and Yeshivas Eitz Chaim, Yerushalayim); Rabbi Boruch Horowitz (*Rosh Yeshivah* of Slobodka and *Rav* of Aliksot, Lithuania); and Rabbi Sheftel Kramer (*Rosh Yeshivah* in Slutzk, and later in New Haven Connecticut).

The Frank's legacy of Yeshivos continued into the next generation, with the establishment of Bais Medrash Govoha, Lakewood (where Rabbi Aharon Kotler, Rabbi Isser Zalman's son-in-law, became *Rosh Yeshivah*), and Ner Yisroel, Baltimore (headed by the older son-in-law of Rabbi Sheftel Kramer, Rabbi Yaakov Yitzchok Ruderman). For more details see "Torah Pioneers" by Chaim Shapiro, in JO May '75.

and in the U.S.A. In 5652 (1892) the Frank's second daughter, *Rebbetzin* Baila Hinda, married Rabbi Isser Zalman Meltzer — one of the finest *talmidim* of Rabbi Chaim Soloveitchik of Brisk. In her we find the role-model that her daughter, *Rebbetzin* Chana Perel Kotler, most likely sought to follow.

◆§ Her Role Model

"The golden chain should continue," the *Rebbetzin* would insist.

Rebbetzin Chana Perel recognized her place in that chain — which values Torah more than gold — and saw it as her responsibility to ensure its continuation. The *Rebbetzin* would relate that her mother, *Rebbetzin* Baila Hinda, would have rather cut her own flesh than cause Reb Isser Zalman a moment of "wasted Torah."* It was with this acknowledgment of the pre-eminence of Torah that the young Chana Perel grew up.

> *The entire stock was stolen from her little Kovno store.** Yet, Rebbetzin Baila Hinda remained silent; nothing should distract Reb Isser Zalman from his Torah in Slutzk. Without a word of their perilous financial situation, she continued, single-handedly, to support her family, since the Rosh Yeshivah would accept no salary — not even food — from the yeshivah. Only when he was additionally offered the Rabbonus of Slutzk did she explain their financial plight, so that this could be taken into consideration when he made his decision.****

One can safely assume that *Rebbetzin* Chana Perel chose to follow the path set by her mother. Yet she lived amongst a weaker

---

* *Rebbetzin* Baila Hinda's own Torah knowledge was outstanding. As the Ponevezer *Rav* once said, in three hundred years there had not been such a woman. She knew *Tanach* "*Ba'al Peh*," and would often quote extensive passages, explaining them according to the *Malbim* ... At eighty-six when lying sick in bed, she recited from memory chapters from *Iyov*, with the *Malbim's* commentary!

** When the Frank fortune was ultimately lost, the *Rebbetzin* had opened a small store from which she provided for her family. At the same time (5654/1894), Reb Isser Zalman and his brother-in-law, Rabbi Moshe Mordechai Epstein, were offered positions in the Slobodka Yeshivah by "*Der Alter*," Rav Nosson Tzvi Finkel.

*** From Slobodka, Reb Isser Zalman went on to head the Yeshivah in Slutzk in 5657 (1897). Founded by *Der Alter*, at the request of the Slutzker *Rav*, the *Ridvaz*, the yeshivah began with a nucleus of fourteen top *talmidim* from Slobodka, under Reb Isser Zalman's guidance. After the departure of the *Ridvaz* for Chicago in 5662 (1902) — and later to Tzfas — Slutzk chose its *Rosh Yeshivah* as its *Rav*.

generation, and came to settle on untrodden soil.* That *Rebbetzin* Chana Perel was nevertheless able to emulate her mother so effectively, to transfer her outlook onto alien shores, attests to a personal triumph of her own.

⋅§ Her Outlook

"Oy, die narishe veltele," the *Rebbetzin* would chide, *"Die narishe ziebetzig yohren!"* ("The foolish seventy years!")

Rebbetzin Chana Perel viewed the world through the perspective of *Chazal,* as but an anteroom to the World-to-Come (*Pirkei Avos* 4:21), and paid little regard — if any — to material things.

> *A talmid accompanied the Rebbetzin to the bank, where she was depositing Reb Aharon's Chiddushei Torah in a vault. The talmid noticed how she kept edging herself into a corner behind the heavy door of the bank, as though reluctant to be seen . . .*
>
> *Finally, she confided: "I am afraid that anyone might think that I have precious stones. Not that those things have any value. They say that one can accomplish important things with money. Be that as it may! . . . I daven that my children should have no more than they need."*

The *Rebbetzin* inwardly abhorred the quest for possessions. When a child insisted, "It's mine," she would ask: *"Vos meint dos,* 'mine'?" emphasizing her conviction that everything belongs to *Hashem.* The family member who would tell her, "I'm going home now," would be gently reminded that it wasn't actually her home.

Once, for a period of twelve years she did not buy herself a new dress. (Yet her appearance was always neat.) And, when she did need to buy new clothing, she did not *reject* the notion of window-shopping; for her the idea simply did not exist.

> *A young friend of the family paid a compliment to the Rebbetzin. How nice she looked! How becoming her dress was!*

---

* In 5681 (1921), the Yeshivah of Slutzk was forced to flee from Bolshevik rule. Reb Aharon re-established the Yeshivah in Kletzk (Poland), while Reb Isser Zalman continued on to Yerushalayim to establish the Yeshivah Eitz Chaim. The Kotlers remained in Kletzk, where the Yeshivah flourished, until the outbreak of World War II. With the over-riding intention of finding a safer base from which to save *neshamos* from certain death, the *Rosh Yeshivah* and the *Rebbetzin* managed to escape to the U.S.A., arriving in 5701 (1941). Totally immersed in *Hatzalah* work in the first years, Reb Aharon became *Rosh Yeshivah* of Bais Medrash Govoha, Lakewood, in 5703 (1943), while continuing his crucial work on behalf of European refugees.

The *Rebbetzin* was puzzled, almost hurt. Why should people place a value on a person's externals?

Rebbetzin Chana Perel decried luxury and indulgence. To the grandchild who commented on a tasty dish, she would say, "*Essen iz gut? Torah iz gut!*" She would then explain: "You have to eat to be healthy, and to have strength to serve *Hashem.*"

The *Rebbetzin's* own diet was sparing. Her breakfast invariably consisted of a glass of warm water with a drop of milk, and a slice of dry bread. She would take only small amounts of food, for fear of not being able to finish her portion, and whenever her grandchildren ate with her, she made her meal from their leftovers. The *Rebbetzin* ate "luxury" foods only if they would otherwise be wasted, and from the time of the Holocaust, she never had a sweet thing in her mouth — "So many *tzores* for *Klal Yisroel!*" she would say, "Such a *Churban!* How can I indulge in sweets?"

While the *Rebbetzin's* lifestyle was simple, it was never bare. She would satisfy her own needs on very little, yet she would happily treat a grandchild with candies ... She would buy yesterday's fruits and vegetables at reduced prices, yet she would serve them to her family as attractive platters, compotes and jams ... she ruled out indulgence for herself, yet would never impose these standards on others. The *Rebbetzin* was, without question, a *porushah* (ascetic), but there was nothing spartan about her, and there was no shortage of warmth, caring or charm in her make-up.

◆§ The Disregard of the "Zich" / Ego

"You don't do anyone a favor by giving him *kavod* (honor)," the *Rebbetzin* would comment. *Rebbetzin* Chana Perel shunned *kavod*, both as Reb Aharon's *Rebbetzin* and as a private individual. She sought no recognition of her own personal worth. It was her task, she considered, to give *chashivus* (importance) to others, and she did so with alacrity. Even in her later years she would hasten to open doors for neighbors in her apartment building, and insist upon sharing the burden of their parcels.

The *Rebbetzin* was an ever-listening ear, advising, empathising. In the words of an old lady who shed tears at the *Rebbetzin's* passing, "It was not only what she said that helped ... she cried with me, and that made all the difference!"

But regarding herself, she would always ask, "*Vos iz a mentsch?*" Indeed, in all the many years she knew her, a close family member cannot recall ever having heard her say, "I said," or "I did."

The Rebbetzin was standing far back in line in a busy New York bakery, patiently waiting for her turn. The raised voice of a saleslady suddenly called out, "Rebbetzin Kotler, can I help you?"

The *Rebbetzin*, with embarrassment, made her purchase in haste, and with a look of apology to the other shoppers, hurried from the store.

❊ ❊ ❊

The Rebbetzin was attending a wedding, and the baal hasimchah reserved a seat for her at the head table.

Yet, the *Rebbetzin's* place remained empty. She had slipped into the hall unnoticed, and seated herself at the table nearest the door — the children's table!

❊ ❊ ❊

The Rebbetzin bought a raffle ticket for the yeshivah. The drawing was held at one of the monthly sessions of the Ladies' Auxiliary. Those present were the Rebbetzin's friends and associates over a period of twenty-five years. She knew them well.

The winning number was called ... the Rebbetzin secretively tore up her ticket. She had won! — but, as she later told her family, how could she stand up in front of all the other ladies to claim her prize?

❧ For the Sake of Torah

"What is life about without the spreading of Torah and the sanctification of the Name of *Hashem?*" the *Rebbetzin* would ask, often adding, with firm resolution, her own maxim: "*Ayn chayim ello Torah* (Without Torah one cannot live)." *Rebbetzin* Chana Perel Kotler lived in the fullest sense. Her world was visibly created for the sake of Torah *(Bereishis* 1:1, *Rashi)* — Torah was her reality! Even her daily conversation was spiced with *divrei Torah*. Her grandchildren recollect how, whilst performing the most mundane household chores, she would quote a *passuk* from *Tanach*, tell a story of a *gadol*, or cite a *mussar* thought or a *Ma'amar Chazal*. "This was spread on the bread we ate," a grandson recalls.

The *Rebbetzin's* own Torah knowledge was impressive. Her cousin, the late *Rebbetzin* Ruderman, remembered how the young

Chana Perel, as a girl, was devoted to her *seforim;* until the last years of her life, she never made a trip without a *mussar sefer* in her hand. It is not surprising that the *bachurim* loved to speak with her ... she had a comprehensive knowledge of *Tanach* and an inspirational knowledge of *Ma'amorei Chazal.* Indeed, her father, Reb Isser Zalman, often mused that with her *guten kop* she could have been a brilliant *talmid chacham.*

And yet, the *Gemara (Sotah* 21a) asks, how does a woman earn merit for *limud Torah* (Torah study), considering that she is not commanded to learn?

The *Gemara* explains that for bringing her children to their *rebbe,* and for waiting for her husband to return from the yeshivah, a woman is rewarded. From her support, and not from her study, a woman receives her portion in Torah. *Rebbetzin* Chana Perel Kotler knew well how to draw her share ...

◆§ For the Ben Torah

"What am I in comparison to a *ben Torah?*" the *Rebbetzin* would question. In a world created for the sake of Torah, the place of the *ben Torah* was pre-eminent.

> *Rosh Hashanah morning, the Lakewood Yeshivah was immersed in tefillah ... And the kitchen help had failed to show up!*
>
> *Who was able, at such a moment of spiritual elevation, to face the practical reality that the yeshivah bachurim must eat? ... In the kitchen, Rebbetzin Chana Perel was busily washing dishes so that the bachurim could be served their meal on time!*

Through day-to-day behavior, the *Rebbetzin* taught *Kavod HaTorah.* She would stand up for every yeshivah *bachur,* even for a young boy, if he was already studying Torah ... she was bothered by the *ben Torah* who took time to meticulously hang up his coat ... she discouraged the young *ben Torah* in her own family from clearing off the table or doing other housework. She was saddened, above all, to see the *ben Torah* waste time, and it gave her most pleasure to see him learn.

> *After the petirah of Reb Aharon in 5723 (1962), a close talmid would visit the Rebbetzin in New York.*
>
> *She would serve him a refreshment, and he would talk a little about the Rosh Yeshivah, and about the progress that the*

Yeshivah was making. The Rebbetzin clearly enjoyed the conversation; but, when the young man took out his own Gemara to learn, her face would light up with obvious nachas.

✑ For the Yeshivah

"Who are the nobility? The *Rabbonim!*" the *Rebbetzin* would quote the words of *Chazal* (*Gittin* 62a). The handmaiden of the *ben Torah*, she was the faithful servant of the Yeshivah.

A *talmid* from the Kletzk days remembers the *Rebbetzin* as a "mother" to the *bachurim* . . . especially the Russian boys, who were never able to return to their families under Bolshevik rule. If Kletzk had been their place of refuge, the *Rebbetzin* made it their home.

Rebbetzin Chana Perel saw herself primarily as Reb Aharon's *Rebbetzin*, yet from her tireless efforts for the Yeshivah, to her sensitive concern for the individual *bachur*, she earned her own share in the Yeshivah. She was constantly *mispallel* — and even fasted — for the existence of the Yeshivah and the *shtieging* of the *bachurim*. She shared the aspirations, and she shared the joys.

> *Not long after the Rosh Yeshivah's petirah, a close talmid went abroad to get married and, as a result, missed the last part of the zman. On his return, he took his young kallah to visit the Rebbetzin. On seeing him, the Rebbetzin could not contain herself with excitement: "Such a Yevamos zman we haven't had in a long time!"*

After the *petirah*, a *minyan* was maintained in the *Rebbetzin's* New York apartment for the *Kaddish* year, and continued for a number of years.* The *Rebbetzin* personally arranged the chairs herself, doing all she could to ensure the smooth running of the *minyan*. A *talmid*, who is today an eminent *Rosh Yeshivah*, would often send his two sons to the *Minyan* so that they should take a peek at the way the *Rebbetzin davened* in the kitchen. Witnessing her concentration, and hearing the intensity of her, *"Bechol levovcho, b'chol nafshecho, uv'chol me'odecho,"* would surely inspire their *tefillos*.

Wherein lies the success of a yeshivah? The *Rebbetzin* recognized success not in terms of numbers, but in the quality of the learning. When under the guidance of the *Rebbetzin's* son, Reb Shneur, the strength of its learning precipitated the Yeshivah to

---

* The *minyan* later moved to its own premises on Sixteenth Avenue in the Boro Park section of Brooklyn, where it is known as "The Lakewood Minyan."

swell in number — to become one of the world's foremost Torah *mosdos* — the *Rebbetzin's* gratitude to *Hashem* knew no bounds.

As she looked down at the spread of white *taleisim* at a *Shabbos davening*, as she looked out at the droves of black hats leaving the Yeshivah after a weekday *Minchah*, the *Rebbetzin* would turn her head away ... she could not look! "Even I should watch myself from giving an *ayn hora*," she would say, afraid that her overwhelming pride in the yeshivah should be damaging to it in any way.

As the faithful servant of the Yeshivah, the *Rebbetzin* was, by necessity, on its payroll. Yet she viewed the Yeshivah's funds as *hekdesh* (sacred) ... As often as she could, the *Rebbetzin* did not take anything from the Yeshivah. When she did, she did so with trepidation. First, she would make quite sure that her last check had been completely used up ... and this normally required the bank clerk to remind her that her meager funds were nearly depleted. Even then the *Rebbetzin* would make every effort to economize, in order to stretch her resources as far as she could ... Why take a check on Monday, when one could do until Thursday?

The *Rebbetzin* treasured Yeshivah money. She was never tempted to use it on anything that wasn't strictly necessary. There were times when she would deny herself the obvious pleasure of spending *Shabbos* in Lakewood — where Reb Aharon stayed from Thursday to Monday, remaining in New York during the rest of the week on Yeshivah business — for fear of not being able to justify the bus fare.* Indeed, from the time she came to America, the *Rebbetzin* kept notebooks, in which she wrote down how the stipend she received from the Yeshivah was spent; even the few cents that she would give to a child to buy candy were recorded in her accounts!

◄§ For the Rosh Yeshivah

"How can a person live without the *Rosh Yeshivah?*" the *Rebbetzin* would sigh ... If "without Torah one cannot live," what was life without the *Rosh Yeshivah*, who was the embodiment of Torah?

The *Rebbetzin* described Reb Aharon's *petirah* as, "My personal *Churban*." Once asked what she *davened* for, she replied:

---

* Whenever the *Rebbetzin* came to Lakewood, Reb Aharon would instruct the *Rebbetzin*, on her departure, to take along a sandwich from the Yeshivah for the trip. If the sandwich was not eaten en route, she would make sure to pay for it.

"For two things I pleaded my whole life. I asked the *Ribbono Shel Olam* that if an evil fate was decreed on the *Rosh Yeshivah*, it should happen to me instead. And He did not accept my *tefillah*..." (Her second request was for Torah *nachas* from the grandchildren — the golden chain should continue...) While the *Rosh Yeshivah* was alive, it can be literally said, as in the words of a grandchild, "Everything was for the *Rosh Yeshivah*."

It was a typical busy morning. The phone rang. The Rebbetzin ran to answer it, and brought the receiver to the Rosh Yeshivah, who was immersed in a sefer. When the Rosh Yeshivah had finished speaking, she returned to replace the receiver. This was repeated several times throughout the morning.

Lunchtime, the Rebbetzin carefully removed all the bones from the Rosh Yeshivah's portion of fish. The Rosh Yeshivah was able to complete his meal quickly, and to return to his Gemara. Later, the Rosh Yeshivah had to leave for a meeting; the Rebbetzin squatted to polish his shoes, whilst he was putting on his coat. Not a second of the Rosh Yeshivah's precious time was to be wasted!

The *Rebbetzin* lived, as it were, for the *Rosh Yeshivah's* sake, never making demands upon him, which would take him away from his *avodah*. In the early days of the Yeshivah she actually took on much of its administrative functions herself, meeting with the butcher, paying the bills and so on. The *Rebbetzin* even learned to imitate the *Rosh Yeshivah's* handwriting, to pen letters that he would later read and sign. She could not recall — in all her married life — ever knowingly distracting the *Rosh Yeshivah* from his studies. Reb Aharon was able to devote day and night to Torah; this, in no small measure, must be attributed to the *Rebbetzin*. And he repeatedly made it clear how deeply he appreciated her devotion.

She asked for nothing in return. When the Rosh Yeshivah arranged for her to make her first visit to *Eretz Yisroel* in 5709 (1949) — where she would see her aged parents, whom she had not seen for many years — the *Rebbetzin* was delighted that the *Rosh Yeshivah* considered that "after thirty years of '*avodas perach*' (hard labor)," as he put it, she fully deserved to. The *Rosh Yeshivah's* approbation of her efforts seemed to please her as much as the prospects of the trip itself.

Yet the *Rebbetzin* took her own efforts for granted. The *Rosh*

Yeshivah belonged to his Torah, to his Yeshivah, and to his *talmidim* . . . she had no claim of her own! *Talmidim* remember that the *Rebbetzin* would never sit at the *Shabbos* or *Yom Tov* table in Lakewood, so that the *Rosh Yeshivah* could share the *seudah* with the *bachurim.*

> *In the final moments of Reb Aharon's life, a few close talmidim huddled around their Rebbe's hospital bed. One might assume that the Rebbetzin would wish them to leave, to treasure those last minutes alone.*
>
> *It was the Rebbetzin who withdrew from the room, and stood quietly in the doorway . . . Their claim to the Rosh Yeshivah was greater than hers.*

And yet, when it came to Torah, the *Rebbetzin* was exacting, demanding. She was inwardly pained when she saw the *Rosh Yeshivah's* time needlessly wasted; she once begged him to put the phone down on a persistent and disrespectful caller. "I can't understand your patience," she sighed, when the *Rosh Yeshivah* desisted. She refused to allow a prestigious new high school to be named after Reb Aharon, since it included a secular studies program of which the *Rosh Yeshivah* did not approve. And when, after the *petirah*, a group of *talmidim* brought up the idea that the *Rosh Yeshivah* be buried in Lakewood (rather than in *Eretz Yisroel*), so that they would always feel his influence, the *Rebbetzin* did not agree, commenting, "If you want the *Rosh Yeshivah* with you, learn the way he would want you to learn, act the way he would want you to act. Then the *Rosh Yeshivah* will always be with you."

◄§ Servant of Hashem

"He has told you, Man, what is good; and what does the L-rd require of thee?" the *Rebbetzin* would quote, "To do justly, and love kindness, and to walk humbly with your G-d" (*Michah* 6:8). The *Rebbetzin* would teach as she lived, her example providing the best lesson.

Rebbetzin Chana Perel lived with the constant desire "To do justly, and love kindness, and to walk humbly with your G-d." She embodies the *emunah p'shutah* (pure faith) of the *shifchah al hayam*; with this clarity of vision she could only see the will of Hashem . . . nothing else existed.

Reb Aharon and his Rebbetzin spoke in subdued tones in the

Rosh Yeshivah's hospital room. The Rebbetzin shed a few tears . . .
Reb Aharon seemed alarmed by her anguish . . . The Rebbetzin
quickly wiped her eyes, "Es vet zein gut (It will be good)," she
comforted him.

"Es iz shoin gut (It is already good)," he comforted her.

At the airport a few days later, waiting for the aron (coffin) to
be transported to Eretz Yisroel, the Rebbetzin related this story,
repeating the words, again and again, "Es iz shoin gut . . . Es iz shoin
gut."

For the Rebbetzin, it was already good, for it was the will of
Hashem, and she was all accepting. Her emunah p'shutah never
wavered, never compromised. As a servant of Hashem she sought
only to serve her Maker.

The hospital authorities had recognized the exceptional
circumstances of their illustrious patient. The "No Visitors" rule
was dropped. Talmidim stood trembling in the corridors, their lips
quivering with Tehillim. In the Rosh Yeshivah's own room, a
minyan was beseeching the Ribbono Shel Olam by day and by
night.

And then the worst happened! Who could contain the wail of
grief, the howl of pain, the crying of bereft children? Who but the
solitary figure, the Rosh Yeshivah's wife for over fifty years, who
silently closed the doors of the other patients' rooms, so that they
would not be disturbed and frightened by the outcry?

Mrs. Shoshana (Nekritz) Perr

And Sarah Was Listening ...

Rebbetzin Sarah Yaffen

5647-5744 / 1887-1984

W HEN WE WRITE *about great men who succeeded in elevating themselves through living a Torah existence, and at the same time changed the world around them, we should also focus on the women who were part of their lives and shared in their achievements. One such person was* REBBETZIN SARAH YAFFEN, *the late daughter of the famed Alter of Novarodok, Rabbi Yoseif Yoizel Horowitz, founded a network of Yeshivos in pre World War I Eastern Europe. The Alter was succeeded by his son-in-law, the late Rabbi Avrohom Yaffen — who headed the Novarodok Yeshivos in the 1920's and 30's and then, after World War II, brought the Novarodok tradition to America in the form of Yeshiva Bais Yoseif, in Brooklyn. Rabbi Yaffen was succeeded by his son, Rabbi Yaakov Yaffen, and his late son-in-law, Rabbi Yehuda Leib Nekritz.*

In these pages we offer a sketch of an unusual woman whose lifetime spanned a full century and was deeply involved in the development of the Mussar Movement from Novarodok to Bialystok, from Siberia to Boro Park, to Jerusalem: in many respects, the Jewish woman par excellence. The following appreciation of Rebbetzin Yaffen was penned by her granddaughter, MRS. SHOSHANA (NEKRITZ) PERR.

◆§ And Sarah Was Listening ...

"You'll come back for Shalosh Seudos," my hostess said. This was her son's Bar Mitzvah weekend, and I quickly agreed. "It's for women only and you'll speak," she added, half-jokingly.

I wasn't sure of her seriousness or of my ability to prepare something relevant. I did think of an intriguing vort from one of the speeches delivered at the Bar Mitzvah ... Fine. I knew my topic, but something was upsetting me. *How could I tell over that which had been spoken publicly? Wasn't it demeaning to assume that no one listened? Why is it a given that women rarely listen to a speech delivered at a simchah, actively enjoying conversation of their own? Is it because they never have to tell over a vort? Is it because they're seldom asked to speak? Because they are unburdened by the expectation of having to listen? Is it a habit learned from having to strain to hear behind a separating mechitzah?*

Yet the Torah's presentation of woman is quite different: ושרה שמעת פתח האהל, *"and Sarah was listening at the opening ...," says the pasuk (Bereishis 18, 10) — whenever she could, wherever there was an opportunity, an opening.*

The mystery and power of flowing thought is such that one idea follows another in a system of its own, not always easy to connect. And so the searching for a topic, my disturbance, the pasuk bearing Sarah's name suddenly conjured up the image of my grandmother and gave me a topic I could use without misgivings.

⇐§ Bobba at the Opening

I always saw her listening at the doorway, at the table, in a crowd, or one-to-one. And she was never asked to speak or to "say over," so there my theory evaporates into thin air.

It's true my Bobba always peeked behind the curtains, always managing to hear, to listen. Nothing ever stood in Bobba's way.

She listened with avid interest, with a thirst, though never formally schooled — as she herself would often tell me. "I know nothing on my own. That which I know is only what I heard from my father, the *Rosh Yeshiva* (as she called her husband), *talmidei chachomim,*" [איך ווייס גארניט נאר וואס איך האב געהערט פון מיין טאטן, פון דעם ראש ישיבה אין פון בני תורה.] the many who frequented her home, and the *bachurim* she loved as much as her own children.

She gave the credit of all she was to the *Mussar* she had heard. [גיב א קוק וואס די שיחת חולין פון מוסר איז.] The effect of *Mussar*, even the casual conversation, the small talk, had made an uneducated woman into what she had become. [איך בין אן עם הארציטע און איך בין אט אזוי.]

But the key word was שומעת — listening. She always listened, expecting to understand, questioning if she didn't, criticizing that which she didn't like, adding her own, enjoying fully the good *vort*, the *bon mot*, the cleverness, the depth, the originality and the message. My Bobba Yaffen, how I suddenly missed her!

Story after story, memory after memory, continued with the slower speed of memory which lingers, pains, when one is gone. Memory excites in its sharpness, sketching the person in indelible strokes.

✥ The Rebbe's "Smicha"

My grandmother and the Gerrer Rebbe ... a story I had not witnessed, but heard first hand. My grandparents moved to *Eretz Yisroel* in their later years, to 11 Slonim, in Me'ah She'arim.

Varied visitors passed through that *Pesach*, that opening, each with a history and relationship of his own. Many came from the same world of Torah and *Mussar*, others from a different world with a history and tradition of their own.

The Gerrer Rebbe came to visit my grandfather, Reb Avrohom Yaffen. Bobba asked the Zaide to speak to the Rebbe on the behalf of someone needy — asking a favor. They spoke of many things. But the Zaide had his own reason for not asking the Rebbe for the favor. The Bobba, listening in the kitchen, realized that the request would not be made and came in to ask herself. The *gabbai* tried to stop her, saying, "The Rebbe doesn't speak to women." She gently, but no less firmly, quieted the *gabbai* and then made her request ... "Things were different with my father," she commented. [ביי מיין טאטען האב איך נישט אזוי געזעהן.]

My husband had the *zechus* of visiting privately with the *Beis Yisroel* (The Gerrer Rebbe) sometime later. The most animated part of the conversation, he told me, was when the Rebbe raised the subject of the Bobba.

"I hold her to be a real *Rosh Yeshivta*," he said with a twinkle.

The *Rosh Yeshivta* — Don't be mistaken. You had to hear my Bobba speak about *di menner* (the men). Her face lit up as she would say, "They're home" — from *shul*, from learning, from important meetings. Her face lit up with love and awe and expectation of their being what they ought to be, bringing home the words, the information she would love to listen to, think about, internalize, transform into her own.

"Never let your husband carry out the garbage," she taught me as a girl. "Let him help you in other ways, you'll be greater when he is greater," she said, stretching my girlish imagination.

✑ To Receive in Order to Give

Someone asked if a *Baal Mussar* gives *Mussar* or receives it. The Bobba was adept at both.

> *The Zaide once referred to the long hot trips he had made between Williamsburg and the Yeshiva in Boro Park during the summer months. Bobba sighed, "For the amount of work that was invested, there could have been more success."*
>
> *"Sha," said the Zaide. "Against whom are you complaining?"*

She was later to repeat to great-grandchildren the Zaide's critique, the Zaide's *Mussar* — the challenge of purity in *middos* (character), the challenge of *emuna* (faith).

When she gave *Mussar*, she gave it with a flourish. From our end, it was called receiving a *cheilek*, a portion.

> *A cousin related that, when he was a teenager learning in Eretz Yisrael, the Alter's Yahrzeit was commemorated with fifteen shmuessen (talks) held in various Mussar institutions. He and a cousin, a grandchild of a different branch of the family tree, slipped out during the tenth shmuess. Nothing escaped the Bobba's eyes. The next day she called him in and gave him a cheilek:*
>
> *"The Alter's aynikul (grandchild) missing a shmuess?" she chastised sharply, demanding absolute devotion.*
>
> *"But Bobba," he insisted, "the cousin also left."*
>
> *"He's not an aynikul."*

✑ The Legacy

She made us into *aynik'lach* by passing on to us the legacy, by constantly demanding. Whenever questioned about the Alter, she would share her recollections in minute detail, but then add: "What's the good of telling stories if you don't learn from them?" [אבער וואס איז די פעולה אז מען לערענט זיך נישט אפ?]

To be an *aynikul* was to inherit an obligation, a responsibility. It was never to be used as an object of pride.

The Bobba always spoke of growth, of *shteiging*; moving, reaching, growing was the challenge. [נישטא בלייבען אויפין זעלבען ארט.] ... Before his wedding, it was the *brocha* of *shteigen* that she bestowed upon her great-grandson.

But Bobba would explain, "One must grow — but when you grow make sure it's upwards, never in breadth, never crowd someone else's space." [– וואקסען אין דער הייך נישט אין דעם ברייט – נישט שטופין יענעם.]

Someone explained at *Shiva* — using a metaphor from that week's *Perek* — that in the process of *Mesora*, all that one has received is given over. The Bobba was transmitter of the *Mesora* of the Alter . . . the Alter's in spirit, if not in form.

> *A noted Rosh Yeshiva used to say in his shmuessen that bitachon (faith) was difficult to achieve. Upon hearing this from him, Bobba said to him, "My father said that bitachon can be easily acquired."*
>
> *Those who heard the Rosh Yeshiva's later shmuessen noticed the change: He said bitachon can be easily acquired.*
>
> *My favorite story, which she told over about her father, the Alter of Novarodok, was of a night they spent together when she was a child. Sitting in the dark because there was no money to buy the necessary kerosene, he comforted the family by saying, "Think how fortunate we are, how rich. If we had money we would use it to buy kerosene, but we could never buy the precious experience of not having, for all the money in the world."*
>
> *With these words he captured her spirit and fired her imagination for a lifetime. Sarah listened and was to give over.*

She taught me the ins and outs of the *Machzor* as I sat next to her during *Yomim Noraim* on the radiator; chairs were needed for the women in the *Ezras Noshim* of Bais Yoseif. She was proud of keeping up with the *tzibbur*, adroitly turning pages in the *Machzor*. She knew which *pesukim* were repeated, which *piyutim* were deleted, when the *shatz* precedes the *tzibbur*, when the *tzibbur* precedes the *shatz*.

Shavuos night, a highlight of the year, she first prepared the food at home for those who would return to find it early in the morning. She took me along, at twelve or one in the morning, to watch *di menner* at their best, learning in the *Beis Midrash* — totally involved in the *Milchamto shel Torah* — the forays of Talmudic battle. She gazed at them with love and pride and helped me see them through her eyes.

Yet she was down to earth and practical. I'd often hear her say,

"A normal person is a precious commodity." [איז מענטש נארמאלער א
א יקר המציאות.]

✒ A Matter of Will

"Nothing can stand in the way of determination," [אין דבר עומד
בפני הרצון.] she would always say . . . and we would see it in her will
power, her own determination. It was the Bobba who published my
grandfather's five *seforim* after his *petirah* (passing), insisting: "The
man is the book and the book is the man." [דער ספר איז דער טאטע,
דער טאטע איז דער ספר.]

She demonstrated will power even as it applied to life itself. "I
cannot" didn't exist in her vocabulary. [ניטא איך קען נישט – ס'איז
דא איך וויל ניט.] She recognized the failure to do as a failure of will.

You had to see the Bobba cross a busy intersection. "Wait for
the light," I would shout after her, glued to the corner, holding my
breath. Bobba forged ahead, sure of her purpose. "They'll wait for
me," she would retort. They always did.

✒ Gilding the Mitzva

She took pride in a well-set table, not to impress, but to invite,
to say, "We cared that you came, we value your presence."

She was a lady that always dressed with care and taste. To
Bobba it was more than just the innate feminine desire to look
presentable. It was a part of *Kiddush Shem Shomayim* of *Kavod
haTorah.*

"I always sought *di shenste un di beste* — the best *shidduchim*
for the *talmidim* of the yeshiva," she told us with pride, "so that
everyone would recognize their value, the esteem and honor they
deserve."

My *cheilek* came in young adulthood. I complained to the
Bobba about the arduous and draining ordeal of *shidduchim.*

"You don't appreciate the singular opportunity of speaking
with a *talmid chacham*, one immersed in Torah study?" [עס פאסט
דיר נישט צו פארברענגען מיט א תלמיד חכם?] she demanded. She was
telling me to listen once again. She changed my attitude to dating
completely. The next young *talmid chacham* who called encountered a most receptive audience, someone who listened with rapt
attention to the words of a potential *gadol.*

She groomed me for the hardships that are part of public life.
"To be a leader," her father had taught her, "one must be capable of

swallowing nails" — swallowing injustice, insults and jealousies. She would repeat his words: "A person must be able to get along even with the Devil or risk the possibility of becoming a devil himself."

When Rabbi Yechezkel Sarna, the late Rosh Yeshiva of Chevron, would visit my grandfather, he would say, "I came to see Reb Yoizel," referring to my Bobba. My grandfather would smile with pleasure — and Bobba would protest. "The Mumme (aunt) was Bobba's title in the Mir Yeshiva family — she was the Mumme of the Rosh Yeshiva, Rabbi Chaim Shmulevitz. Her sister was Rabbi Chaim Shmulevitz's mother.

◆§ Matzah Without Tears

My grandfather was *niftar* (passed away) Erev Pesach 1970. My brother, who was learning in *Eretz Yisrael* at the time, told me that when lighting the candles, Bobba cried, but then she pulled herself together and with a strength reminiscent of her father, the Alter of Novarodok, she bid the grandchildren to proceed with the *seder*, to sing all the songs without deletions. She never left the table till the very end. From upstairs, where other relatives lived, my brother heard weeping, but downstairs where the Bobba sat, a *seder* was celebrated, as every year.

After her husband's *petirah*, it was her *kollel* behind her house that gave her *chiyus*. She listened to the sounds of Torah, *tefilla*, *Tehillim*, and *Mussar* around the clock.

She had helped her father. She had helped her husband. But now she felt that she alone bore the primary obligation to continue the heritage of Novarodok. She assumed the responsibility of supporting the *Kollel* of Torah and *Mussar* with all her ingenuity and all her strength.

"Listen to the sound of *Mussar* being learned!" she'd say with pride to visiting guests. She served a *Kiddush*, she made the *cholent*, taking pleasure in giving out little sweets to the children of the *bnei Torah* in the *Kollel*.

"She never missed a *tefilla*, three times a day," wrote a grandchild in a letter. "Even in the end, when she could no longer see and we *davened* with her, if it chanced that we missed a word, she would correct us."

My father spoke of her as his mother, remembering how she gave him money for a tailored suit when he was a *chassan*, though there was no money to make a dress for her to wear at the occasion.

In the hospital they called her the *chachoma*, the *pikchit* — she charmed the nurses. Yet we were moved by her *emunah peshutah*, her simple faith.

A group of seminary girls, who kept the Bobba company during their free time and had become attached to her, came in to during their free time and had become attached to her, came in to wish Bobba a good year on Erev Rosh Hashana. They wished her nachas from her children, grandchildren and great-grandchildren.

"Wish me *nachas* as well from all *bnei Torah*," she corrected them. "All *bnei Torah* are my children."

◆§ She Taught Us . . .

My sister thought that Bobba would surely live to greet *Moshiach*, taking us along with her.

"What can we learn from Bobba?" my sister asked the children gathered round about her in a circle. "What can't we learn from Bobba?" said one great-grandchild in a comeback reminiscent of the Bobba.

Someone seeking to comfort the mourning family said soothingly, "The Bobba will be a *meilitz yosher* for her children, for *Klal Yisroel*. She'll beseech, she'll beg to *Hashem Yisborach* to grant them what they need."

"Not the Bobba," said another grandchild. "She won't beseech, she won't beg — she'll demand, as she did on earth."

"She didn't demand returning to yesterday — to live in the past," said a great-grandchild. "She lived in the present, and was interested in every detail of the current yeshiva world: growth, problems, successes, rising stars. The world of today was her world."

" '*Bas kuf k'bas kof* — at one hundred years like at twenty,' " a grandson eulogized. "She lived such a meaningful life. '*Bas kof k'bas zayin* — at twenty like a seven-year-old' — combining a maturing strength of will with the freshness of youth that always seeks to know . . ."

Indeed, her mind stayed clear up to the end, as is written about *talmidei chachomim*: Their minds stay clear, their thoughts unconfused, their convictions strengthened through life's experiences, even when advancing in age.

❧ ❧ ❧

Overflowing with subject matter, charged with emotion, I arrived late for the Shalosh Seudos Celebration of the Bar Mitzva.

"The guest speaker has arrived," I said with a smile.

"I would never do that to you, Shonnie," my friend said with a smile.

Late that night I felt grateful to my friend because it was the energy and power of the unspoken words that produced this memoir.

Devora Kitevits

An Appreciation of
Rebbetzin Kaplan

*She rewrote
the book
on Torah education
for girls.*

Rebbetzin Vichna Kaplan
5673-5746 / 1913-1986

Introduction

THROUGHOUT THE AGES, certain *gedolim* have stood out as the *rabban shel kol bnei hagolah* —- the master teachers of their generation. These past four generations had two women who served as great leaders. Sarah Schenirer, who passed away on 26 Adar, 5695 (1935), stemmed the tide of assimilation of young girls enrolled in Polish "Gymnasiums" (high schools) by founding Bais Yaakov schools, thus preserving *Yiddishkeit* as it had been in the past.

Rebbetzin Vichna Kaplan, a disciple of Sarah Schenirer, toiled for forty-nine years, carrying Sarah Schenirer's message to America. She founded the first Bais Yaakov High School and Teachers Seminary in America. Not only did she keep Jewish daughters loyal to their faith, she guided them in creating Jewish homes and founding a tradition, the likes of which America had never seen. She imbued her students with a philosophy of life, and through them and their households, through their children and their students, her impact was far-reaching — fomenting a virtual revolution in American Jewish life.

Whereas the influence of *gedolim* generally filters down to women through the medium of the man's world — the yeshiva, the *psak*, the *tisch* — Rebbetzin Kaplan's influence was directed towards the women and girls themselves. We felt that she belonged to us — the girls and women — someone whom we could embrace and confide in, who not only understood our problems, but had experienced them ... someone through whom we could become great by listening to her speak, by walking with her, by sharing in her work, by doing some humble task for her.

We lost our personal *gedolah*. Now, when we aspire to greatness in our daily life, we must look for the path she paved for us. We have no choice but to live with the memories she gave us and learn from them.

I. European Years

◄§ Her Heart Was on Cracow

Rebbetzin Vichna Kaplan was born in Slonim, Russia, about 1913. Her father, Reb Ephraim Yehoshua Eisen, was famous for his *tzidkus*. Her mother, Mereh Gitel, was the daughter of Rabbi Chaim Leib Lubchansky, *Rav* of Baranovich.

By the time she was eleven both her parents had passed away. She and her brother, Dovid, went to live with their mother's brother and sister-in-law who had no children of their own — Rabbi Yisroel Lubchansky, the famed *mashgiach* in Reb Elchonon Wasserman's yeshiva in Baranovich, and his wife, daughter of the *gaon*, Reb Yoisel Horowitz, "The Alter of Novarodok." Vichna Eisen, her cousins, and friends attended "Meselevsky's," a private religious school for girls.

When sixteen, Vichna read about the Bais Yaakov Seminary in Cracow and set her heart on going there. But the Seminary refused her application because she lacked a diploma from preparatory school. Not content with the refusal, Rebbetzin Kaplan wrote directly to Sarah Schenirer: "Should my whole future be changed because of such a small matter?" Still she did manage to earn that diploma by taking private lessons. However, she had no funds to pay the Seminary tuition and was only able to attend because of Reb Shmuel (Dr. Leo) Deutschlander, who obtained a scholarship for her.

✺§ Seminary Rules and Regulations

Upon arriving in Cracow as part of a group of some one hundred fifty young girls, she was presented with the conditions that Seminary students were required to sign before beginning their two-year course of study:

Upon completion of Seminary every girl would have to teach for two years. This could not be in the graduate's hometown, where presumably she would be too busy with her own family to devote herself fully to her teaching career. After the initial three months in Seminary, the administration would evaluate each student's performance. Girls judged to lack the potential for teaching would be asked to leave.

The girls were deeply upset by the rules. They feared that their opportunities for marriages would be seriously limited if they were forced to live away from their hometown. Others worried about the blot on their reputations if they would be sent home from the Seminary.

Her former classmates,[1] who had met Rebbetzin Kaplan in Warsaw on the way to Cracow, recall how she had encouraged the other girls not to despair, but simply to get started.

They also remember her as the top student in her class. Besides knowing much more than the average girl, she had a superior intelligence, and made memorable presentations at assemblies. In time, young Vichna began to assist Sarah Schenirer in various ways, such as collecting *tzeddaka* from house to house for her fund to support poor families.

The Seminary program was quite intensive. The entire day was dedicated to formal classes and study, with no distractions whatsoever. The only breaks in the schedule were the Pesach and Succos intersessions. Even one additional visit home required special permission.

The only other allowance for travel was to help start a new Bais Yaakov in one of the small *shtetlach* of Poland. This was usually launched by a team of a teacher and a Seminary student. Rebbetzin Kaplan was once dispatched to Baranovich with a teacher, Miss Hamburger, to lobby for opening a Bais Yaakov school there. Her speech had unusual impact,[2] and Baranovich opened its Bais Yaakov school.

Dr. Judith Rosenbaum[3] would teach *Shir Hashirim* Friday nights. After *Shabbos* the girls would approach Rebbetzin Kaplan:

"Vichna, please tell us over the *shiur* so we can write down notes. You know it the best." With her characteristic humility, she would say, "I don't know it the best, but I'll tell it to you anyway." And then she repeated the *shiur* verbatim — not using her own language, but the teacher's words.

Rebbetzin Kaplan told her children that when she left for her first intersession trip home, Sarah Schenirer confided in her, "From the first letter you sent me, I saw that you are going to help me in the movement." Others who were present remember Frau Schenirer saying. "You will succeed me, but you will be greater." Rebbetzin Kaplan, of course, never repeated this.

Indeed, all her classmates knew that she was the closest *talmidah* to Sarah Schenirer but no one was jealous, because they all recognized that she had earned the special relationship.

⋘ The Years in Brisk

The two years in Cracow came to a glorious end on her graduation night — an event that Rebbetzin Kaplan often recalled for her *talmidos:* "Sarah Schenirer danced and sang 'Vetaheir Libeinu (Purify Our Hearts)' with us the entire night."

Rebbetzin Kaplan was sent to Brisk where, for some five years, she served as the only teacher for *limudei kodesh* in the school, besides studying with girls in their older teens before school hours. She frequently consulted the Brisker *Rav*, Rabbi Yitzchok Zev Soloveitchik, who was responsible for the school.

Rabbi Dovid Soloveitchik of Yerushalayim, writes: "I remember how ... my sainted father and teacher would be extremely lavish in his praise of the love for Torah and *yiras Shomayim* that [Rebbetzin Kaplan] implanted [in her charges]. He would add that she had great advantage in that she was raised and educated in the home of her uncle, the *gaon* and *tzaddik* Rabbi Yisroel Yaakov Lubchansky and that she had absorbed much Torah, *yiras Shomayim* and exemplary *midos* from him, which she drew on to be *mechanech* (educate) her students."

Twenty-some years later, an American girl — undecided about which seminary to attend in *Eretz Yisroel* — consulted the Brisker *Rav* in Yerushalayim. He advised her: "Return to Vichna Kaplan's Seminary. There you will learn how to educate the next generation."

When she was in Brisk, the Jewish community was threatened with a pogrom. In response to her query, the Brisker *Rav* advised her to leave, since she could not help in the situation. On the last day of school before the feared pogrom, Rebbetzin Kaplan was preparing to flee to Kamenitz, but first she hired a taxi to take home several girls who were stranded at the school. Only then did she leave.

Once, before returning home for vacation, Rebbetzin Kaplan decided not to return to Brisk. The city lacked funds for her salary and she could not afford to work without pay. She later received a telegram signed by the Brisker *Rav* telling her to come back, so she returned — only to discover that the telegram had been forged! She stayed on anyway. Perhaps she had reasoned if the people in town had to lie to keep her, they must be in desperate straits.

In view of her financial situation, the following incident becomes more poignant. Rebbetzin Kaplan and the writer were once discussing a specific book for use in our Child Guidance classes in the Brooklyn Seminary. Because of a questionable anecdote in the book, Rebbetzin Kaplan decided that we not use it. Sensing my disappointment, she told me that when she was teaching in Brisk she had purchased history books with her hard-earned money. As she was preparing a lesson, deciding on which information was acceptable and which she could not use, she suddenly asked herself: "What am I doing? Trying to get kosher information from non-kosher sources!" So she discarded the entire set of books.

Vichna Eisen was remembered fondly by all the people she met: The Brisker *Rav's* daughters, whom she taught, and became best friends with ... her landlady, who told others how her concern for all creatures great and small even extended to their house cat, which she brought in from the cold every night ... the *talmidah* who married an ordinary fellow during wartime, and on her own volition honored the rules of *tznius:* "Weren't we brought up in a certain way of life? It stays with us."

Rebbetzin Sora (Kaplan) Zeilberger, who had been her student in the earlier grades in Brisk, recalls "When I was older, I studied privately, but 'the girls' and I still visited her in her room after *licht bentschen* Friday nights. She would tell us stories until our fathers picked us up after *Maariv* ... She was always with us. On *Shabbos* afternoons she supervised the Basya (Bnos Agudath Israel) groups, where she told stories and played games with us. Whatever she did impressed us ... such as the grand play she produced for Purim, which attracted the whole town."

⤐ A Suitable Match

On 28 Elul, 5695 (Sept. 1935), Mrs. Laya Schwartz wrote a letter to the famed *mashgiach* of the Mir Yeshiva, Rabbi Yeruchem Levovitz, asking him to find a suitable *shidduch* for a young lady she knew in Brisk, Vichna Eisen. Her words describe her aptly:

"She is perfect, straight, good of heart, and all her aspirations are lofty. She strives constantly for self-perfection, constantly rising in her attainment; her soul is beautiful and she has an indomitable spirit ... Primarily, she impresses one with the high goals she's set for herself — an excellent person, she was created for greatness."

The actual *shadchan* was Rebbetzin Kaplan's landlady, who had seen Reb Boruch learning in the Brisker *Rav's shul*. She delegated a yeshiva fellow to approach him, but the *bachur* added on his own that since neither he nor the Eisen girl had any money, it made no sense to even suggest the match. Reb Boruch, however, accepted the suggestion, while ignoring the advice. "She was a *shem davar* (widely admired)," he later told his children.

After the two had met, Rabbi Kaplan had to leave for America on Chanuka 5696. They corresponded and became engaged by mail! Rabbi Kaplan still cherishes his *chassan* gift from his *kallah* — *Koveitz He'aros* on *Yevomos*, by the illustrious Baranovich *Rosh Hayeshiva*, Rabbi Elchonon Wasserman.

Reb Yisroel Yaakov was unhappy that his niece should move to America. He advised her to consult the Brisker *Rav* who replied — "To join him, you can go anywhere!" It was the only time the *Rav* had consented to someone to go to America, according to his son, Reb Berel (Yosef Dov) Soloveitchik.

Before leaving, Rebbetzin Kaplan petitioned the Bais Yaakov headquarters in Cracow (which administered not only the Seminary but all the elementary Bais Yaakov schools in Poland, and all related publications) for permission to start a Bais Yaakov school in America. Reb Yehuda Leib Orlean, successor to Sarah Schenirer as head of the organization, granted her permisson.

Rebbetzin Kaplan left friends and family in Brisk and Baranovich for America, arriving almost forty-nine years to the day before her passing. The wedding took place eleven days later, on *Rosh Chodesh Elul* (September 1937) in the lunchroom of Yeshiva Torah Vodaath, on Wilson Street in Williamsburg, with the *Rosh Hayeshiva*, Rabbi Shlomo Heiman as *mesader kiddushin*.

II. The Bais Yaakov Comes to America

✒§ Early Attempts[4]

In the 1920's the only Hebrew schools for girls were afternoon Talmud Torahs and Sunday schools with co-ed classes, and boys' *Bar Mitzva* classes, which some girls joined. These schools were basically culture oriented and not religious in content. Some more religious girls studied privately at home.

Inspired by Sarah Schenirer in Europe, Reb Binyomin Wilhelm together with his brother-in-law, Reb Ben-Tzion Weberman, and Rabbi Shraga Feivel Mendlowitz (*menahel* of Torah Vodaath), and other community leaders founded the Beth Jacob Hebrew School for Girls in 1925 — the first all-girls afternoon school.

Two Bais Yaakov-type elementary day schools later opened in Williamsburg — Bais Sarah and Bais Rochel, through the initiative of Mr. and Mrs. Avrohom Spinner — but these attempts did not last more than two or three years. Then, through the herculean efforts of this enlarged group of *askonim*, the Beth Moses Hospital building was purchased, and the Bais Yaakov elementary (day) school in Williamsburg was opened in the winter of 1937 with a kindergarten and several grades. The founding principal was Rabbi Kreiser, followed by his successor, the late Rabbi Avrohom Newhouse.[5] This Bais Yaakov grew and blossomed for many years.

Mrs. Fruma Laya Mandel, mother of Rabbi Manis Mandel,[6] started *frum* girls' groups on *Shabbos* in East New York and then in Williamsburg. These Bnos Yisroel groups became part of Bnos Agudath Israel. Rebbetzin Mandel also held night classes for girls in Williamsburg for a year or two . . .

When Rebbetzin Kaplan arrived, there was as yet no religious school for teenage girls. Rebbetzin Kaplan began with a class of seven eager girls[7] of high school age, who gathered around the dining-room table in the Kaplans' small apartment at 134 South 9th Street in Williamsburg. Here the beginnings of the Bais Yaakov High School and Teachers Seminary took place.

Rebbetzin Genauer recalls: "Rebbetzin Kaplan was an answer to my parents' prayers. The only other Jewish high schools were far to the left in religious orientation, and many parents later did not eat in their children's homes. We had heard about Sarah Schenirer and the Bais Yaakov in Cracow from Rebbetzin Pincus[8] when she had come back and called a meeting to organize us. We fell in love with her. She had so inspired us that we were prepared for Rebbetzin

Kaplan and her plans.

"As a fifteen year old, I went to public high school, then traveled to the Bronx to teach a Talmud Torah class, and then returned to Williamsburg. From 7 to 10 P.M. *every night* we learned around the dining-room table in Rebbetzin Kaplan's house.

"Rebbetzin Kaplan's devotion was always apparent. She knew what each one of us needed and lacked. She had an all-encompassing memory about each of us. I was ambitious at eighteen and could not decide whether to marry then or not. Through her influence I married my late husband, an American who had learned in Kelm.

"I visited her in the hospital after she had given birth. She was preparing her *shiurim* in the hospital bed! ... She took our notebooks home to mark — even the spelling — making notations, i.e., 'This thought is not written out clearly.'

"From Rebbetzin Kaplan's house we moved to Keap Street, then to the 'old Mesifta building' [at Bedford corner Taylor]. By then we were already two classes. Then, to 143 South 8th Street, the address that thousands of Bais Yaakov students will always remember. We thought it a beautiful building! [Rabbi Boruch Kaplan then left his position as a *maggid shiur* in Mesivta Torah Vodaath to help his wife carry the financial administration of Bais Yaakov.] My father, Reb Nisson Pilchick, used to go out nights soliciting money for the school."

☙ The Ruach Dimension

The Kaplans borrowed money to open a summer 'learning' camp at Engel's farm in Connecticut. For many of the girls, it was their first adventure in the country. As in the city, Rebbetzin Kaplan was the only teacher in camp, and taught the girls all morning, despite her obligations to her young, growing family. She even tried to bring *Yiddishkeit* to the people in the area, and invited people from New Haven to special events, such as the campfire.

Rebbetzin Kaplan strove to bring the *ruach* of her Cracow years to Williamsburg. She met with the girls on Friday nights, at Bnos Agudath Israel groups on *Shabbos* afternoons, even had *Seudah Shlishis* and *Melave Malka* with them. This *Shabbos* spirit drew many girls to join her school.

Rebbetzin Esther Weissman (who joined Bais Yaakov a few months after it opened) recalls one stormy Friday night when Rebbetzin Kaplan came to the Bais Sarah Talmud Torah building where the *Shabbos* group met. When they entered the building they found the lights off. Someone called in the janitor to put them on — and Rebbetzin Kaplan left into the rainy night for a few minutes. She had gone to inquire if it was permissible to use the room now that the lights had been opened especially for them ... There were so many *halachos* that the girls had never even heard about — which she taught them by example.

After five years, the first group of girls graduated. The school was growing. Yet the love and attention for each student was not diminished. Rebbetzin Chana (Fishbein) Lubart[9] came from Chicago straight to the Kaplans' home. They had found her a room with the Pilchicks, walked her over to her new quarters, and gave her seven dollars to pay for the room-and-board for the first week — as they continued to do for several weeks, until her older sisters, who were working, could support her.

This *ad hoc* approach changed in 1944, when a dormitory was opened in the South 8th Street building.

⮞ The All-Day High School

Rabbi and Rebbetzin Kaplan opened the full-day high school in January, 1944. It was the seventh year of the school's existence, but attending a Bais Yaakov high school was not matter of course as yet.

Rebbetzin Chana Adler Wessel[10] was to graduate public elementary school in January 1945, and saw nothing wrong with continuing on in public high school. Most of the girls in her class were religious, the mode of dress was proper — boys were permitted to wear only white shirts, ties and slacks, and girls were required to wear dresses with some sort of sleeve. There were separate entrances and separate seating for boys and girls, and a chapter of Psalms was recited at the opening of each assembly! The public school building's physical plant and the honors given to a bright student were attractions. She acceded to her father's wishes and went to Bais Yaakov in the fall of 1944, with the understanding that if she chose she could return to public school after several months.

"I feel that Rebbetzin Kaplan saved my life," says Rebbetzin Wessel. "If not for her, I dread to think what would have happened to me and my sisters, who followed in my footsteps. She gave me a feeling of worth, importance. Rebbetzin Kaplan taught this class *all* the subjects (sometimes with a child on her lap when her babysitter didn't show up) with infinite patience, despite the class knowing so pathetically little. She built our confidence by keeping her beautiful lessons simple and not beyond our grasp ... She broadened our horizons. She gave us a dream, a purpose: We were pioneers, building Yiddishkeit in America. We learned that there's a Jewish future for the Jewish woman.

"There was another facet to Rebbetzin Kaplan. She was approachable, she listened and took things to heart. A girl could share her teenage dreams and problems with Rebbetzin Kaplan, and even forty years later tell her things that she could not tell anyone else. She never failed to ask later how this one or that one was doing."

During the war years, the Kaplans applied for thousands of student visas to enable many refugees to enter this country. The Bais Yaakov Seminary was far above all other educational institutions in the number of girls that it saved from Europe, despite harassment from the Immigration Department, which had difficulty accepting that one institution could guarantee support for such a large amount of girls.

❧ Growth and Expansion

As the Orthodox community grew, so did the Bais Yaakov School. In September 1958 a branch was opened in the Boro Park section of Brooklyn, soon to equal — and then surpass — the main Williamsburg school, which eventually closed, in 1977. The one-year Intensive Seminary program began in September 1968 — a new concept in its time — in which girls immerse themselves fully in limudei kodesh from 8:15 A.M. to 3:30. The observation and student-teaching programs have become fine-honed and demanding.

Rebbetzin Kaplan's students are today teachers and principals all over the world — from the largest Bais Yaakov High School and Seminary in the world (Yerushalayim) to the largest Bais Yaakov elementary school (in Boro Park) — from Tifrach to Flatbush. Chassidic schools sprang up, and again Rebbetzin Kaplan's students helped establish them, teach in them, and head them — in Puppa, Ger, Bobov, Lubavitch and Satmar.

Despite the fact that Bais Yaakov schools in America are not affiliated in any formal way, Rebbetzin Kaplan's advice and suggestions were sought after. "What does the Rebbetzin say?" was a constant consideration. When Bais Yaakov-type schools organized a mass tznius rally at the Brooklyn Academy of Music some fifteen years ago, of course Rebbetzin Kaplan addressed the audience. And when five thousand women and girls gathered to commemorate the fiftieth *Yahrzeit* of Sarah Schenirer in Adar 5745, Rebbetzin Kaplan was a leading force in the assembly.

She felt that her responsibilities extended beyond the school walls. In the past few years, Rebbetzin Kaplan called directors together to discuss the *ruach* in their camps: It should be a continuation of what the schools strive so hard for during the year, to be reflected in the camp activities as well as in conduct on days off.

Whether it was a man from Toronto crusading against the evils of television or a teacher from Flatbush concerned about the erosion of *tznius*, an educator doing *kiruv* work in New Jersey or a former *talmidah* begging her and Rabbi Kaplan to say *Tehillim* for a sick family member — each one found his way to Rebbetzin Kaplan's office.

III. Leader of the Revolution

In the past fifty years, women have changed the face of Jewish orthodoxy in America, with Rebbetzin Kaplan at the helm of the revolution. And now, just study the contrast: In 1937, the *frum* Jewish girl wore pants and sleeveless garments. Now the discussion is whether knee socks are "good enough" ... Married women covering their hair was an unheard-of rarity; now they are grappling with what style *sheitl* is suitable for a young Rebbetzin ... No one was called by his/her Jewish name; today it's almost an oddity to hear a yeshiva boy or Bais Yaakov girl called by an English name ... When a match was proposed, the first question the young lady asked was: "What does he do for a living?" Today, it's: "How long will he learn?" When the highest level of *frumkeit* was identified as a home where the father *davened* and attended a *shiur*, Rebbetzin Kaplan taught the girls to dream of being worthy of marrying a *talmid chacham*.

Rabbi Aharon Kotler is quoted as having said, "If not for Bais Yaakov, all the yeshivos would be forced to close!"

His late Rebbetzin, Rivka Chana Perel Kotler, said that Reb Aharon held that Rebbetzin Kaplan did more for Torah *Yiddishkeit* than all the *roshei yeshivos*. Rabbi Elya Lopian concurred: "The yeshivos are very important, but the Bais Yaakov is more important. Without the Bais Yaakov the yeshivos could not exist." ... The

Satmar Rebbe once dispatched his *hoiz bachur* to say "*yeyasher koach*" to Rabbi Boruch Kaplan, thanking him for making it easier for his boys to find suitable *shidduchim*.

She demonstrated to the girls and the women how to elevate oneself to the highest level. The prevalence of *chesed* and *tzeddaka* organizations, *shiurim* for women, *shmiras halashon* classes and telephone *chavrusos* — and the joy that her students find in being devoted mothers and teachers of *Yiddishkeit* — these are the embodiment of her teachings. The fervor in contemporary women's *avoda*, the integrity of their *emuna*, their aspiration to true *shleimus* — and the will to perpetuate these ideals to future generations — these are the fruits of her labor.

◆§ The Power of Personal Sacrifice

How could one person inspire so many followers, and evoke such a strong response in them that they pattern their very lives after hers? Perhaps it was the personal sacrifice that was invested in her work.

Rebbetzin Kaplan's greatest dream for her students and for her own children was that the girls marry *talmidei chachamim* and the boys should be *talmidei chachamim*, never to leave the *koslei beis midrash*. When someone brought her regards from one of her sons saying that he is known to be a great *talmid chacham*, Rebbetzin Kaplan commented, "You know just what to say to gladden a mother's heart!" She avoided disturbing her sons during their *seder* (learning period), and when forced to do so, she would ask him to please pay back the time of their conversation during free time, and to ask his *chavrusa* to do the same.

And despite her profound love and respect for learning, and despite Rabbi Boruch Kaplan's success as a *rosh yeshiva* in Mesivta Torah Vodaath — he was ready to make the almost unbearable move of leaving the *Beis Midrash* to help the school; that was the first sacrifice.

Rebbetzin Kaplan's second sacrifice was the time not spent with her own children. In an interview for a magazine article about the working mother, Rebbetzin Kaplan was asked what type of work is suitable for the woman who seeks something to do with her time once her children are in school. "Do you mean dealing with the empty-nest syndrome?" asked Rebbetzin Kaplan. "I thought that only set in after all the children married. While her children are in school, doesn't a mother have enough to do in the home? Why should a woman feel useless simply because her children are away from home for several hours?"

She then went on to describe the anguish and inner conflict that she had experienced every day that she left her children when they were younger. "Why must I leave my children with someone who will tell them the story of the 'The Three Bears' while feeding them, when I could impart so much *yiras Shomayim* to them with every spoonful of cereal? And, even in the best of cases, when I would have the most wonderful babysitter, I agonized over why I must leave my children's *chinuch* to someone else while I leave them behind so I should tend to someone else's children!" She added that for years she had wished she could meet *Eliyahu Hanavi* and he would tell her what to do. If he would tell her to go home, she would do so joyfully. If he would tell her to continue on to school, then she would at least know she is doing the right thing.

When her first graduate married a *Kollel* man, put on a *sheitl*, and taught in a Bais Yaakov School, then she knew she had made the right choice! The conflict was resolved, but the anguish of leaving her children at home never left her.

IV. Master Teacher

Rebbetzin Kaplan taught by example — not only by what she did, but what *she was*. "I feel as if I grew up under her. I received my education in *Eretz Yisroel*, but my *l'maaseh* (practical application) came from Rebbetzin Kaplan" — in the words of Rebbetzin Dvora Zoberman.[11]

◄§ Anivus

Rebbetzin Kaplan was an ordinary housewife at home. So much so, that her own daughter-in-law said that it took years for her to realize that she was a public figure. Even in school, despite being the dean — head of all the departments and principal of the Seminary — Rebbetzin Kaplan did not put on airs.

Those close to her saw how nervous she was before delivering a speech, despite a career of over fifty-five years of speaking! "The world is made up of two halves," she told a close worker, "the fortunate and the unfortunate. And the unfortunate have to speak."

She refused to allow a car to be sent to pick her up for a N'shei Ahavas Chessed speech. "The bus stops right there." And yet, she would worry about the same extracurricular trip being too strenuous for other senior-staff members and insisted that the school provide car service.

Rebbetzin Kaplan's youngest daughter, Blumie (Rosengarten), was making a sign "W. KAPLAN" for her mother's office door. "That's all you're going to write? Won't you write 'Dean' on the sign?" a student demanded. Her daughter explained that she was bound by *kibud av vo' eim*; that is what her mother told her to write. "Well," said the girl, "someone else can add a word or two. "So she put "REBBETZIN" before the "W. KAPLAN" and added "DEAN" at the end. Rebbetzin Kaplan looked at the completed sign, and — not wanting to insult anyone — just never used it.

When entering a classroom to take over for a master teacher, she told her: "It will be hard to teach this class after they had an expert like you on the subject."

Rebbetzin Kaplan always convened meetings to weigh any decisions or changes in school. Good ideas were always given consideration no matter who presented them. A radical change was once seriously considered, and a protest was voiced: "But you've been doing it the other way for fifty years!" Rebbetzin Kaplan answered in her firm way: "I will listen even to a child if it's the right thing." She was not embarrassed to admit that we may have overlooked something for fifty years.

Rebbetzin Kaplan's yardstick till her death in guiding her own school was, "What would Sarah Schenirer say to this?" The same self-effacement that made her see herself as a messenger from the last generation made her the living example for our generation.

◆§ Kavod Habriyos

Rebbetzin Kaplan dealt diplomatically and graciously with every situation. With two phones ringing, third line buzzing, someone knocking on her office door, and someone already seated in her office, Rebbetzin Kaplan took care of each one without slighting the others. Always careful to offer a visitor a seat, to offer teachers lunch when it was lunch time, she realized her visitors' needs before they themselves were aware of them.

At staff meetings, she always took the time to explain the situation and to give every person a chance to express his or her opinion. She only interrupted — "We have to be careful to say only what is *noge'a* (relevant)" — when she sensed that a remark was leading to *lashon hora, avak lashon hora* or *rechilus* (slander or gossip). When she had to reprimand someone, she did not wait for the situation to become embarrassing, but nipped it in the bud — in advance. Rabbi Uri Hellman, principal of the Bais Yaakov High School, describes how Rebbetzin Kaplan would remind the staff at the opening of class meetings that only what is relevant may be said, and nothing may be said about any party who is not involved. Indeed, Rabbi Boruch Kaplan remarked that in all the years he knew her, he never heard his wife express a *ta'anah* (complaint) about anyone, nor ever say a word of *lashon hora*.

She was meticulous in avoiding hurting others: Rabbi Hellman says that in the forty years that he worked for Rebbetzin Kaplan he could not recall a single incident in which she issued a command ... The writer's mother, who worked for the Ladies Auxiliary of Bais Yaakov, told her children: "Rebbetzin Kaplan never hangs up the phone first. She waits to hear you hang up."

When announcing a *simcha* to her children, she called them in order of age to avoid making an older child wonder why he was called *after* a younger one ... Rebbetzin Kaplan always asked the director of the school plays to make sure that the script contain no line that might prove insulting to a public-school janitor who might watch the play ... When a new private nurse walked in during Rebbetzin Kaplan's confinement in the hospital, she complimented her with, "I heard so much about you! When my daughter-in-law called the agency, they recommended you so highly." A bright smile lit up the nurse's face.

To an alumna of twenty years, Rebbetzin Kaplan said, "I was waiting many years to meet you. I've been wanting to ask your forgiveness."

The *talmidah* expressed astonishment, to which the Rebbetzin explained, smilingly, "You remember how you often came late to class. I once commented, 'Late again!' Please forgive me for the remark."

◂§ Her Responsibility and Love to each Student

Every school has to make crucial decisions about accepting students into the school, about expelling students when necessary. One administrator postulated that if Bais Yaakov would accept a below-average student in the freshman class, it would reflect badly on the school. Rebbetzin Kaplan answered, "I couldn't care less for our reputation as long as we do the right thing. Is she basically a good girl , or will she ח״ו have a bad influence on others? Each and every girl is entitled to a Bais Yaakov *chinuch*."

Rebbetzin Kaplan could spend hours deciding an individual girl's placement. There were times that she spent sleepless nights out of concern that each girl should be in the right place and develop properly. If a girl wasn't accepted into the group, she would call in key students and discuss with them ways to make the student feel accepted.

Rebbetzin Kaplan would convene a faculty meeting before demoting a student from a full-day Seminary to the half-day program.

Rebbetzin Renee (Adler) Hershberg[12] recalls a meeting weighing expulsion of a girl from the school. When it seemed as if her fate were sealed, Rebbetzin Hershberg said, "Yes, but ... "

Rebbetzin Kaplan interrupted her — "We're keeping her." A mere "but" about expelling her was sufficient reservation to warrant keeping the girl in the school.

One of the students in question later commented: "She did not expel me. I sensed that she had some kind of trust in me. She saw something that no one else could see, an expectation that I had to fulfill. I remember the first time she called me by my first name — I was shocked that she knew me as a person. I remember feeling loved when she said it ... She never reprimanded me. Once or twice she questioned me very softly, very quietly. She made the decision to keep me. I owe a lot to that." Imagine Rebbetzin Kaplan's *nachas* when she learned of the marvelous work for *Yiddishkeit* this student does in her town!

Rebbetzin Miriam (Weiss) Dissin[13] writes in *Hamodia:* "Rebbetzin Kaplan would call in a girl and talk about various subjects, and then say, 'I was told you did this and this, and I said it's impossible. A girl like you couldn't have done that. There might be a mistake. Or maybe you fell in this one time.' The girl couldn't disappoint Rebbetzin Kaplan."

Adds Rebbetzin Engelsrath,[14] "I never saw a girl come out of Rebbetzin Kaplan's office crying. She always had something positive to add with the *mussar.*"

She arranged private meetings with small groups of Seminary girls, and would even sit in at conferences on high-school students, to get to know them all. "One of our main goals," said Rebbetzin Kaplan, "is to discover every Seminary girl's talent and develop it."

A broad range of extracurricular activities were scheduled to encourage each girl to find her particular niche. Among the many activities, however, never did she permit Broadway productions to be used as school plays for the public.

Rebbetzin Kaplan sent many a student to summer camp, paying from the school's meager funds, or somehow getting the money together. If the school decided a student would be better off in Seminary away from home (such as Gateshead), RebbetzinKaplan would even foot the expense.

Rebbetzin Kaplan added ר״ל on a girl's record if it were noted that she was orphaned or otherwise marked by misfortune, needing special treatment.

At school plays, she checked that each performer had transportation home.

During a visit to *Eretz Yisroel*, Rebbetzin Kaplan met a *talmidah* who had been active in drama and dance. Not seeing the heavy grandmother standing before her, Rebbetzin Kaplan asked, "Do you still dance?"

Years ago, a group of former students decided to travel to *Eretz Yisroel* by Zim Lines, leaving on *Erev Shabbos*, which is contrary to *halacha*. In addition, Rebbetzin Kaplan feared a harmful precedent, so she personally visited the most influential girl of the group to convince her to change her reservation. While she was talking to the girl, a call came from the Kaplan house that one of the children was hurt, to which Rebbetzin Kaplan said, "I don't care what the *sotton* will do, I'm not leaving till she agrees." The girl changed her reservation, as did the rest of the group.

An applicant to the Seminary lived in the Southwest. Rebbetzin Kaplan arranged for some seniors to correspond with the girl, and even meet her at the airport. On Orientation Day Rebbetzin Kaplan opened with: "Usually, I speak *Yiddish*, but I'm sure there are many girls here who don't understand *Yiddish*, so I'll speak in English." Staff members were certain the switch was made in deference to that one student, who needed special *kiruv*, because the following year the orientation speech was in *Yiddish* again. This student was very unhappy, despite all the effort of the *hanhala* and her fellow students. Rebbetzin Kaplan gave her carfare to visit her parents — roundtrip, of course. The girl never did come back, but she left feeling Rebbetzin Kaplan's boundless love.

At times, Rebbetzin Kaplan would direct an entire speech to an individual. A former *talmidah* wrote her that she feels as though she failed Rebbetzin Kaplan because she's not a teacher. Soon afterward, Rebbetzin Kaplan spoke about the beauty of motherhood, and fulfillment achieved in the home ... When she heard that some girls felt like second-rate citizens because their *chassanim* were not going to sit and learn, at that Seminary graduation (5745) she spoke about the *talmid chacham* who has to go to work. In essence he's a *talmid chacham* even though necessity forces him into business. Just like the *Schneider* (tailor) in Mir who repaired shoes, but was still called the town *Schneider* not the *Schuster* (a cobbler — his temporary occupation, but not his true profession) ...

A graduate teaching in *Eretz Yisroel* wrote her that she felt shunned by students and staff alike, without knowing why. Some time later, the principal of her school walked into her classroom and announced to the class, "We don't know what a treasure we have amongst us. This teacher is one of the *choshuv'steh talmidos* (outstanding students) of Rebbetzin Kaplan, and she is married to a great *talmid chacham.*" This was the turning point in her career. It seems that Rebbetzin Kaplan understood the source of the problem from a distance and had written a letter to this principal, explaining that the students should not disrespect this teacher simply because she wore cosmetics. It is the American fashion. "I, too, wear lipstick at times," wrote Rebbetzin Kaplan.[15]

❧ Ne'emonus V'Emes/Trust and Integrity

Her secretary of twenty-five years ago noticed her marking down every time she ate a school lunch, and paying for it at the end of the week — even though she offered lunch to her staff and considered it part of their salary.

* Clips or rubber bands in her house that may have come from school were excluded from personal use.

* Even though complimentary tickets to the annual school play were given to staff members, Rebbetzin Kaplan always paid for hers.

* Whenever her children called her in school she marked down how many minutes she spoke to them and deducted the time from her salary base. (She was paid on a per-hour rate.) She kept a small notebook to record these and similar notations.

* She was allotted fifteen minutes to address the audience at the Sarah Schenirer 50th *Yahrzeit* gathering. She practiced her speech with a timepiece again and again, to make certain that she would not be using time that was not hers.

* Her co-workers never heard her discussing her own personal matters on school time. When asked about a family member, she answered briefly and went on with her work. "Sometimes we worked together for hours at a stretch. I do not recall her *once* mentioning family in the middle of work," reports Rebbetzin Engelsrath.

* In the 1940's, Rabbi and Rebbetzin Kaplan faced a crucial decision. They had to part ways with Mr. X, the school benefactor, who felt peeved when his offer to sponsor a "charm course" for the girls was summarily overruled by the Kaplans. The financial burden was awesome; no other laymen had been cultivated during the time that Mr. X underwrote all the bills. Rebbetzin Kaplan called an assembly and explained the situation carefully to the students. She would not compromise, even when the school's very existence was at stake.

* Many years ago, Rebbetzin Wessel applied to Rebbetzin Kaplan for a teaching job and was turned down. She had six years of teaching experience, was highly successful — and could not understand the rejection. She pressed Rebbetzin Kaplan for an explanation, who said, "Your school is about to establish a high school. I don't want to take good teachers away from them." Only after assuring Rebbetzin Kaplan that she was leaving the previous school regardless of whether she was accepted in Bais Yaakov, did Rebbetzin Kaplan accept her.

✥ Seeds of Chessed

In his *hesped*, Rabbi Avrohom Kaplan related how his parents spent hours trying to gain the release of two old women from a mental hospital where they had been coerced to commit themselves. It was close to sundown on Friday when the Kaplans finally found an old-age home to which the ladies could be transferred. The Kaplans left their belongings behind and walked home. The Kaplan children visited these women with *Shabbos* food every Friday, and Bais Yaakov girls visited them during the week ... Very likely, this was the beginning of the expansive *chessed* and *bikur cholim* activities in this school, as well as schools all over the globe.

Rebbetzin Kaplan had her own agenda of private *chassodim*. For instance, she used to visit a *giyoress* on *Shabbos* and study with her. Later, she traveled by bus to have her *sheitl* done by this woman, to keep up the contact.

She never lost control of herself, even in the most trying situations. She once told Rebbetzin Bender that arriving home from work she would sometimes find all the children crying. To whom should she give her attention first — to the baby who's most helpless, or perhaps to another child whose need is more urgent? She would listen to each child's story, and then decide who earned priority.

Rebbetzin Kaplan *never* raised her voice, not at home — even when the nine boys and four girls בע"ה were very lively youngsters — and not at school. Rabbi Avrohom Kaplan does not remember his mother ever ordering her children to do something. She always said, "If it's not too hard, maybe you could do this or that . . .", adding, "If you don't do it, you won't be *oveir kibbud eim*" — derelict in honoring your mother.

Shir HaShirim

"כל השירים קודש ושה"ש קודש קדשים"

*"All the scriptures are holy,
but Shir HaShirim is the holiest of the holies."*

As growing administrational responsibilities forced Rebbetzin Kaplan to curtail her time in the classroom, she still taught the graduating classes one subject: *Shir HaShirim.* She taught it simply and beautifully, explaining the most complex *Rashis* in a lucid manner..

"When she mentioned 'The *Shechina* says' in her *Shir HaShirim* class, we felt as if she were the author," recalls a 5744 graduate, "with tears flowing . . ." She had not changed. Early graduates (5720) remember the same scene — "She would teach *Shir HaShirim* with a tissue in her hand, the tears rolling down her cheeks, wiping them as she taught."

Her office: Lunchtime, and hundreds of girls are milling about, there's laughter and music, and you're standing next to Rebbetzin Kaplan's door — knocking. You strain your ears to hear the melodious "Come in," lest you cause her to run and open her door for you. You take a deep breath to gain composure, turn the knob slowly, and prepare yourself — to face the *Shechina* that rested upon her.

Others may question this, but this is how we *talmidos* felt. Maybe that explains her *hatzlacha.* She said "*Tzeis'chem l'shalom*" to a busload of students leaving to a Bais Yaakov convention and told them they should make a great *Kiddush Hashem*. That group ended up in eight newspapers and on many radio stations — because, caught up in a blizzard, they refused to violate the *Shabbos* and elected to stop in a village midway to their destination ... When a student requested permission to work in a camp where there were not many Bais Yaakov girls — but she felt she could influence others — Rebbetzin Kaplan wished her *hatzlacha*, and the following year many girls from that camp joined the Seminary.

Her own children were also amazed: If Rebbetzin Kaplan said, "I don't see what you'll have from this job," the job didn't work out. If she said, "Yes, this could be," then it did work out. No wonder we'd be eager to discuss our plans with her; we felt that her *bracha* would make things go well ...

V. Changing of the Guard

Erev Shabbos Nachamu, Rebbetzin Kaplan jumped out of bed two hours before *lichtbentshen*; she had dreamed that she missed candle-lighting. She *bentched* right then because she knew her family would not awaken her again to light the candles. She refused to come to the *Shabbos* table. She was too weak to dress for *Shabbos*, and said it would not be a *kavod* for the *Shabbos* table.

As she was leaving for the hospital on Sunday, the phone rang. Rebbetzin Engelsrath was calling about certain decisions. Rebbetzin Kaplan told her that she (Rebbetzin Engelsrath), together with Rabbi Kaplan's son Reb Yisroel Yaakov, and Rebbetzin Bender should make the decisions.[16] "*Hashem* should give you the *da'as* to make the right decisions."

"*Amen*," answered Rebbetzin Engelsrath.

At that moment Rebbetzin Kaplan transferred her life work to others.

The doctors did not give up. "You're a diamond and we have to polish you up," they told her. They recognized the shining brilliance of this patient who, when requesting something, cautioned her children, "Maybe there isn't enough for the other patients."

Her condition deteriorated rapidly. Nothing could be done, and our diamond was taken away from us. In the midst of the frenzied calls to all camps and yeshivos to say *Tehillim*, the message was changed: *We can't daven for refuah anymore.*

Again calls were made, and we gathered to perform the final act of charity that we could perform for our great leader.

◄§ PostScript

"Mommy, are you in *aveilus* for Rebbetzin Kaplan?" asks the writer's five-year-old when she sees the tears streaming down my cheeks. Yes, the tears were hot under my lids when I wanted to say *Modeh Ani*, because Rebbetzin Kaplan is my conscience. "What would she think?" is always in mind when making a *bracha*, because her *brachos* were always loud and clear ... when taking a *bentcher* in hand to say *Bircas Hamazon*, because Rebbetzin Kaplan always reached for her *Siddur* after lunch ... What would she think of my *davening* — she, who put on her *sheitl* and slipped on her shoes and when asked by her children, "Ma, where are you going?" answered, "I'm not going away; I'm going to *daven Mincha*" ... Would she approve of my aspirations, she who ended her *brachos* with אז דער עיקר איז דער רבש״ע זאל האבן נחת "The main thing is that *Hashem* should have *nachas*" ... When I want to answer my children, impatiently — what would she think? ... There is so much I still wanted to tell her, so much more time that I wanted to spend with her, so much more to learn ...

When Sarah Schenirer passed away, the little girls in Bais Yaakov of Brisk cried. They saw all the adults crying. Rebbetzin Zeilberger remembers someone telling Rebbetzin Kaplan to calm down the little children. Rebbetzin Kaplan answered through her tears, זאלן זיי וויינען. זאלן זיי וויינען *"Let them cry. They should cry."*
And so should we.

Notes

1. Rebbetzin Basya (Epstein) Bender and Rebbetzin Chava (Shlomovitz) Wachtfogel, who joined the high school and Seminary in 1939 and 1944, respectively, greatly assisted Rebbetzin Kaplan in many matters. Many of Rebbetzin's colleagues from her own seminary days taught in her Bais Yaakov, despite lucrative offers to teach elsewhere. Together with her, they forged a strong unique link to the original Bais Yaakov in Cracow.

2. According to her Baranovich friend, Sora Baila Gutman (Rebbetzin Mendel Kaplan).

3. Rebbetzin Dr. Judith (Rosenbaum) Grunfeld, the Seminary girls' favorite teacher, lives in London now.

4. The historical background was furnished by Mrs. Leah (Wilhelm) Herskowitz.

5. Rabbi Newhouse led the elementary Bais Yaakov school for many years. He also pioneered the concept of *frum* girls' camps, as we know them today, when he opened his famed Machane Bais Yaakov in Ferndale.

6. Dean of Yeshiva of Brooklyn, which includes separate schools for girls and boys.

7. Sylvia (Pilchick) Tehillim, Faigy (Pilchick) Genauer, Sora Wolfson, Rochel Rose (Wolf) Gitelis, Faigy (Rubin) Horowitz, Chanie (Mendlowitz) Greenbaum, and the late Rivky (Mendlowitz) Karp.

8. Rebbetzin Chava (Weinberg) Pincus, born in America, studied in Bais Yaakov Seminary in Cracow. She taught for Rebbetzin Kaplan until she and Rabbi Avrohom Chaim Pincus moved to *Eretz Yisroel* in 1964. They are currently in Santiago de